T0183853

Lecture Notes in Computer Science   11542

Commenced Publication in 1973
Founding and Former Series Editors:
Gerhard Goos, Juris Hartmanis, and Jan van Leeuwen

More information about this series at http://www.springer.com/series/7412

Marina Gavrilova · Jian Chang ·
Nadia Magnenat Thalmann ·
Eckhard Hitzer · Hiroshi Ishikawa (Eds.)

Advances in Computer Graphics

36th Computer Graphics International Conference, CGI 2019
Calgary, AB, Canada, June 17–20, 2019
Proceedings

 Springer

Editors
Marina Gavrilova
University of Calgary
Calgary, AB, Canada

Nadia Magnenat Thalmann
University of Geneva, MIRALab
Carouge, Switzerland

Nanyang Technological University
Singapore, Singapore

Hiroshi Ishikawa
Waseda University
Tokyo, Japan

Jian Chang (iD)
Bournemouth University
Poole, UK

Eckhard Hitzer
International Christian University
Tokyo, Japan

ISSN 0302-9743   ISSN 1611-3349   (electronic)
Lecture Notes in Computer Science
ISBN 978-3-030-22513-1   ISBN 978-3-030-22514-8   (eBook)
https://doi.org/10.1007/978-3-030-22514-8

LNCS Sublibrary: SL6 – Image Processing, Computer Vision, Pattern Recognition, and Graphics

This Springer imprint is published by the registered company Springer Nature Switzerland AG
The registered company address is: Gewerbestrasse 11, 6330 Cham, Switzerland

Preface

Welcome to the proceedings of the 36th Computer Graphics International Conference (CGI 2019)!

CGI is one of the oldest international conferences in computer graphics in the world. It is the official conference of the Computer Graphics Society (CGS), a long-standing international computer graphics organization. CGI and CGS were initiated by Professor Tosiyasu L. Kunii, from the University of Tokyo, in 1983. Since then, the CGI conference has been held annually in many different countries around the world and gained a reputation as one of the key conferences for researchers and practitioners to share their achievements and discover the latest advances in computer graphics and related fields. This year, CGI 2019 was organized by the CGS and the University of Calgary, Biometric Technologies Laboratory, Computer Science Department, with support from Alberta Ingenuity, Faculty of Sciences and VPR Office at the University of Calgary. The conference was held in Calgary, Alberta, Canada, during June 17–20, 2019. CGI 2019 was organized in cooperation with ACM/SIGGRAPH and EUROGRAPHICS.

This book of proceedings contains CGI full papers, CGI short papers, and ENGAE workshop papers. CGI 2019 received 221 submissions from over 30 countries, in addition to ENGAGE workshop submissions. From the CGI 2019 submissions, 26 were selected as full LNCS papers (around 12%) and 23 as short LNCS papers (approximately 11%), in addition to 35 papers accepted directly for *The Visual Computer*. To ensure the highest quality of publications, each paper was reviewed by at least three experts in the field, while many papers were reviewed by five to six experts. The papers were reviewed by 225 international domain experts, including 132 IPC members and 93 invited sub-reviewers.

The selected papers cover both the theoretical as well as the most advanced research topics in computer graphics. The topics include 3D reconstruction and rendering, virtual reality and augmented reality, computer animation, geometric modelling, geometric computing, shape and surface modelling, visual analytics, image processing, pattern recognition, motion planning, gait and activity biometric recognition, machine learning for graphics, and applications in security, smart electronics, autonomous navigation systems, robotics, geographical information systems, medicine, and art.

In addition to CGI conference papers, this book of proceedings features papers from the ENGAGE 2019 Workshop (four full and five short papers), focused specifically on all aspects of geometric algebra and surface reconstruction. The workshop has been part of CGI conference since 2014.

We would like to express our deepest gratitude to all the IPC members and external reviewers, who provided high-quality reviews. We would also like to thank all the authors for contributing to the conference by submitting their work. Our special appreciation goes to the Organizing Committee, who contributed to the success of CGI 2019 and to the team at Springer. We also would like to acknowledge the contribution and support of the CGI 2019 sponsors, including the Biometric Technologies laboratory, the Computer Science Department, Faculty of Sciences, VPR office at the University of Calgary, Alberta Ingenuity, and CGS.

June 2019   Marina L. Gavrilova
                                                         Nadia Magnenat Thalmann
                                                                      Jian Chang
                                                                   Echkard Hitzer
                                                                 Hiroshi Ishikawa

Organization

International Program Committee

Usman Alim	University of Calgary, Canada
Ryoichi Ando	Kyushu University, Japan
Marco Attene	CNR IMATI, Italy
Melinos Averkiou	University of Cyprus, Cyprus
Selim Balcisoy	Sabanci University, Turkey
Loic Barthe	IRIT, Université de Toulouse, France
Jan Bender	RWTH Aachen, Germany
Bedrich Benes	Purdue University, USA
Silvia Biasotti	CNR IMATI, Italy
Nicolas Bonneel	CNRS, Université de Lyon, France
Stefan Bruckner	University of Bergen, Norway
Yiyu Cai	Nanyang Technological University, Singapore
Tolga Capin	TED University, Turkey
Jian Chang	Bournemouth University, UK
Parag Chaudhuri	Indian Institute of Tech Bombay, India
Li Chen	School of Software, Tsinghua Unversity, China
Falai Chen	University of Science and Technology, China
Jie Chen	University of Oulu, Finland
Marc Christie	University of Rennes 1, France
David Coeurjolly	CNRS, Université de Lyon, France
Frederic Cordier	Université de Haute Alsace, France
Remi Cozot	IRISA, University of Rennes 1, France
Zhigang Deng	University of Houston, USA
Julie Digne	CNRS, Université de Lyon, France
Jean-Michel Dischler	University of Strasbourg, France
Yoshinori Dobashi	Hokkaido University, Japan
Yuki Endo	Toyohashi University of Technology, Japan
Parris Egbert	Brigham Young University, USA
Petros Faloutsos	York University, EECS, Canada
Jieqing Feng	Zhejiang University, China
Ioannis Fudos	University of Ioannina, Greece
Issei Fujishiro	Keio University, Japan
Xifeng Gao	Florida State University, USA
Marina Gavrilova	University of Calgary, Canada
Enrico Gobbetti	CRS4 Visual Computing, Italy
Laurent Grisoni	University of Lille 1, France
Roberto Grosso	Friedrich-Alexander-Universität Erlangen-Nürnberg, Germany

Shihui Guo	Xiamen University, China
Stefan Guthe	TU Darmstadt, Germany
Atsushi Hashimoto	Kyoto University, Japan
Hua Huang	Beijing Institute of Technology, China
Hui Huang	Shenzhen University, China, China
Yuki Igarashi	Meiji University, Japan
Satoshi Iizuka	Waseda University, Japan
Hiroshi Ishikawa	Waseda University, Japan
Kei Iwasaki	Wakayama University, Japan
Xiaogang Jin	Zhejiang University, China
Prem Kalra	IIT Delhi, India
Takashi Kanai	University of Tokyo, Japan
Yoshihiro Kanamori	University of Tsukuba, Japan
Hyungseok Kim	Konkuk University, South Korea
Jinman Kim	University of Sydney, Australia
Stefanos Kollias	National Technical University of Athens, Greece
Yuki Koyama	National Institute of Advanced Industrial Science and Technology (AIST), Japan
Barbora Kozlikova	Masaryk University, Czech Republic
Arjan Kuijper	Fraunhofer IGD & TU Darmstadt, Germany
Tsz Ho Kwok	Concordia University, Canada
Yu-Kun Lai	Cardiff University, UK
Guillaume Lavoue	INSA, CNRS, Lyon, France
Ligang Liu	University of Science and Technology of China, China
Nadia Magnenat Thalmann	NTU, Singapore and MIRALab-University of Geneva, Switzerland
Xiaoyang Mao	University of Yamanashi, Japan
Kresimir Matkovic	VRVis Research Center, Austria
Jianyuan Min	Google, USA
Bochang Moon	Gwangju Institute of Science and Technology, South Korea
Shigeo Morishima	Waseda University, Japan
Michela Mortara	CNR IMATI, Italy
Sudhir Mudur	Concordia University, Canada
Heinrich Mueller	University of Dortmund, Germany
Tomohiko Mukai	Tokyo Metropolitan University, Japan
Soraia Musse	Pontificia Universidade Catolica do Rio Grande do Sul, Brazil
Yukie Nagai	The University of Tokyo, Japan
Masayuki Nakajima	Uppsala University, Sweden
Luciana P. Nedel	Universidade Federal do Rio Grande do Sul, Brazil
Junyong Noh	KAIST, South Korea
Makoto Okabe	Shizuoka University, Japan
Masaki Oshita	Kyushu Institute of Technology, Japan
Zhigeng Pan	Hangzhou Normal University, China
Daniele Panozzo	NYU, USA

Lihua You	Bournemouth University, UK
Yonghao Yue	The University of Tokyo, Japan
Zerrin Yumak	Utrecht University, The Netherlands
Xenophon Zabulis	FORTH, Greece
Jian J. Zhang	Bournemouth University, UK
Kang Zhang	University of Texas at Dallas, USA
Jianmin Zheng	Nanyang Technological University, Singapore
Youyi Zheng	Zhejiang University, China
Kun Zhou	Zhejiang University, China
Changqing Zou	University of Maryland, USA

Contents

ENGAGE'19 Workshop Full Papers

ENGAGE'19 Workshop Short Papers

CGI'19 Full Papers

Polarization-Based Illumination Detection for Coherent Augmented Reality Scene Rendering in Dynamic Environments

A'aeshah Alhakamy[1,2]([⊠]) and Mihran Tuceryan[1]([⊠])

[1] Indiana University - Purdue University Indianapolis (IUPUI), Indianapolis, USA
aalhakam@iupui.edu, {aalhakam,tuceryan}@iu.edu, aalhakam@purdue.edu
[2] University of Tabuk in Tabuk, Tabuk, Saudi Arabia
https://www.cs.iupui.edu/tuceryan/,
https://www.ut.edu.sa/en/web/u12562

Abstract. A virtual object that is integrated into the real world in a perceptually coherent manner using the physical illumination information in the current environment is still under development. Several researchers investigated the problem producing a high-quality result; however, pre-computation and offline availability of resources were the essential assumption upon which the system relied. In this paper, we propose a novel and robust approach to identifying the incident light in the scene using the polarization properties of the light wave and using this information to produce a visually coherent augmented reality within a dynamic environment. This approach is part of a complete system which has three simultaneous components that run in real-time: (i) the detection of the incident light angle, (ii) the estimation of the reflected light, and (iii) the creation of the shading properties which are required to provide any virtual object with the detected lighting, reflected shadows, and adequate materials. Finally, the system performance is analyzed where our approach has reduced the overall computational cost.

Keywords: Augmented and mixed environments · Interaction design · Scene perception · Texture perception

1 Introduction

A realistic and immersive experience in augmented reality is one of the problems in computer graphics that still has major limitations and challenges. The main approach is to extract the illumination data in the physical environment and use it to render the virtual objects inserted into the final scene. An illumination model that renders the scene to be perceived as realistic can be challenging if some assumptions are not made. Several innovative techniques are required to render a realistically dynamic scene in augmented reality. In this paper, we propose a new system that (1) uses the properties of polarized light to detect the incident lighting (direct illumination) in the scene, (2) estimates the reflected

M. Gavrilova et al. (Eds.): CGI 2019, LNCS 11542, pp. 3–14, 2019.
https://doi.org/10.1007/978-3-030-22514-8_1

lighting (indirect illumination), and (3) creates the shading properties to apply the previous characteristics on each virtual object material. The system composites seamlessly the three major components of the 3D virtual object into the live main camera of the AR device. The live-feed of the panoramic 360° camera captures omnidirectional views as an input from the surrounding mediums. Any AR device (e.g., head mounted display, projection display, handheld mobile, or webcam camera) can be instrumented with such a camera.

The first component to tackle in this problem is the **detection of incident light** where the light falls directly from the light source onto the objects. An improvement to the method of detecting the direct illumination source was made through the use of polarization filters. Such filtering reduced the unwanted reflections and glares on the radiance maps [8]. The live-feed from the 360° camera was used for detection after being subjected to polarized filtering. The second component focuses on the **estimation of the reflected light** where the reflected lights bounce off the surfaces

Fig. 1. An example showing the difference between the direct incident light (direct illumination) and the indirect reflected light (indirect illumination).

between the objects whether real or virtual (see Fig. 1). A 2D texture of the local area surrounding each 3D object is extracted from the main view of the AR to be uploaded in the Image-Based Lighting (IBL) property of each object as needed. The third component applies the detected direct illumination angle along with the corresponding shadow, and the indirect illumination while **creating the shading properties** required for each object based on the material features. The lighting conditions, camera position, and object location can be changed in real-time effortlessly. Finally, the differential rendering [5] is used to composite the computer-generated objects with the physical lighting in AR. The resources and algorithms for IBL have been optimized to provide a 360° live-feed as a direct light source.

2   Related Work

2.1   Use of Polarized Light in Computer Vision

The art of photography influenced the idea of polarization to be used in this research (see Fig. 2). Physics-based computer vision was advanced when Horn introduced the optical models of reflection and imaging in (1975) [1]. Polarized light is more than a human perception of intensity and color; the information about polarization-based vision go beyond vision based on intensity or shading. Chen and Wolff [6] presented a theoretical development and application for material classification using polarization phase-based method according to intrinsic electrical conductivity. Also, Ngo Thanh et al. [15] presented a shape reconstruction technique which used shading and polarization with one constraint for both:

a pair of light directions for shading, and a pair of polarizer angles for polarization. Shen et al. [19] developed a scheme for dehazing and denoising unclear images where polarizing images on different days were collected to verify the noise reduction algorithm and details optimization.

Fig. 2. Illustration how the Circular Polarizer/Linear (CPL) camera filter used to reduce reflections and glare.

2.2   Incident Light Sampling and Detection

The physical environment map is captured in order to illuminate the virtual object, known as Image-Based Lighting (IBL) [5]. Due to the low performance of sampling the environment map for a realistic IBL with correct shadows, the procedure is mainly used in offline rendering. Nevertheless, some studies have shown significant optimization for methods which can render in real-time. Ramamoorthi et al. [7] presented an analytical expression for irradiance environment maps under the Spherical Harmonic (SH) coefficients of lighting. Debevec [5] used a technique introduced in his previous work [3] to acquire the correct calculation of scene incident light using multiple radiance maps through a variance cut algorithm. Then, he used this calculation to illuminate the synthetic objects with arbitrary material properties.

2.3   Reflected Light and Global Illumination

A photo-realistic rendering must address the indirect illumination between the objects which was contributed by the inter-reflections of light between surfaces in the final scene. Since Keller [4] introduced Instant Radiosity in 1997, it was developed to replace the Virtual Point Lights (VPLs) in order to approximate the reflected lights. The current hardware would be suitable for this method which does not require excessive pre-computations. Knecht et al. [10] combined the instant radiosity with differential rendering which renders the scene once for plausible realistic mixed reality systems while maintaining a frame rate of 30 fps interactively. Kán et al. [11] estimated the indirect illumination from a photon map by performing a density estimation on every hit diffuse surface at the ray-tracing rendering. Gruber et al. [16] reconstructed a scene geometry using an RGB-D sensor that supports fast updating and static scene geometry that in turn enables user interaction with reflected lights.

2.4   Panoramic 360° Live-Feed

The deployment of a 360° panoramic video has appeared in Virtual and Mixed Reality (VR/MR) applications. In some game engines, a pre-recorded video was provided for immersive experience and realistic lighting in the dynamic environments. Rhee et al. [17] developed an immersive system for interactive mixed reality which used a Low Dynamic Range (LDR) 360° video on Head-Mounted Displays (HMDs) where IBL was optimized to provide a fast and correct lighting source information. Fan et al. [18] studied the prediction of Field-of-Views (FoVs) when the viewer was watching 360° video using HMDs. However, it is rare to find studies that deploy a 360° panoramic video in augmented reality.

3   Method and Implementation

A quick overview of the system components are described in this section where a coherent final scene is produced in dynamic environments. For a more organized flow, the system components are examined in four subsections although they work simultaneously in real-time. A visualized version of the overview is shown in Fig. 3.

Polarization of 360° *Live-Feed.* The white surfaces, unwanted reflections, and glare that was confusing our light detection algorithm in our previous work are reduced or absorbed completely after polarizing the incident light from the physical environments.

Detection of Incident Lights. The polarized lights reaching the 360° camera view are investigated through computer vision sampling methods to calculate the angle and direction of multiple physical lights.

Estimation of Reflected Lights. The lights bouncing between the virtual and real objects are extracted from the local regions surrounding each object of concern and then applied through the image-based lighting mode.

Creation of Shading Properties. The virtual object materials and features are defined in this section where specific shaders are created in order to meet the requirements of reading from a live-feed cameras.

Rendering. Differential rendering is used and enhanced to perform with lower computational cost in real-time. The direct and indirect illumination are addressed separately for differential rendering shown in Fig. 3. The rendering paths include normal maps and specular maps per-pixel lighting where any additional passes would not be necessary for reflection depth and normal buffers.

Tracking. The positional device tracker supported by Vuforia AR engine was used for a robust 6 degree-of-freedom (DOF) target tracking. Yet, an additional modifications were added through separate scripts to support the lighting conditions in our system when the objects, camera, and marker are changing locations.

Hardware Description. The main device used to test the system has Intel®Core™ i7-3930k CPU @ 3.20 GHz 3201 MHz, six core(s), 64.0 GB RAM, and NVIDIA GeForce GTX 970 GPU. For data input devices a DSLR Nikon D7200 was used as the main AR camera and a live-feed RICOH THETA S 360° is dedicated to read the environment maps. Three Polarizing films (filters) were used to reduce reflections and glare.

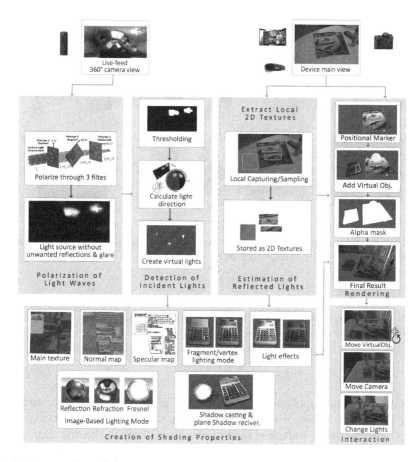

Fig. 3. An overview of the entire system components: Polarization of 360° Live-feed, detection of incident light, simulation of reflected light, and creation shading property followed by rendering and interaction.

3.1 Polarization of 360° Live-Feed

Natural and artificial illumination yield light waves with electric field vectors that lie in planes oriented in every direction that is perpendicular to the propagation direction. The polarization of light is based on the quantum state of a photon described in [2,9,13]. In this section, the polarized filters are investigated in order to focus only on the genuine light sources while reducing unwanted reflections and glares which could be mistaken as light sources. Three polarizing film sheets are used as an initial component of the system. The light transmitted through the first filter is vertically polarized, while a second polarizer perpendicular to the first one is added to absorb the polarized light passing through the first film. However, the interesting part is that when a third filter is placed between the previous two perpendicular polarizers at a 45° angle, it allows some of the light to get through the last filter (see illustration in Fig. 4).

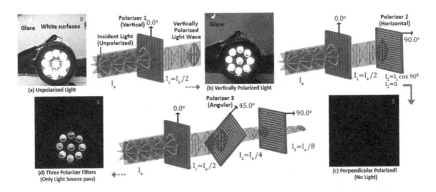

Fig. 4. Polarization of light waves through three filters: Vertical, Horizontal, and angular in order to capture the light source only.

The matrix representations can model the different types of polarizers as vectors. The vertical $|\uparrow\rangle\langle\uparrow|$, horizontal $|\rightarrow\rangle\langle\rightarrow|$, and angular $|\nearrow\rangle\langle\nearrow|$ directions can be represented as the following vectors:

$$|v\rangle = \begin{pmatrix} 1 \\ 0 \end{pmatrix}, |h\rangle = \begin{pmatrix} 0 \\ 1 \end{pmatrix}, |\Theta\rangle = \begin{pmatrix} \cos(\theta) \\ \sin(\theta) \end{pmatrix}$$

Let the intensity of unpolarized light be noted as I_o. Then the polarized light passing though the three filters can be illustrated using Dirac notation for the photons. The vertically polarized light transmitted through the first film is $I_1 = \frac{I_o}{2}, |\uparrow\rangle = \frac{1}{\sqrt{2}}[|\nwarrow\rangle + \langle\nearrow|]$. This is followed by the photons passing through the second polarizer: $I_2 = \frac{I_o}{4}, |\nearrow\rangle = \frac{1}{\sqrt{2}}[|\uparrow\rangle + \langle\rightarrow|]$, thus, producing the final notation as: $I_3 = \frac{I_o}{8}, |\rightarrow\rangle$.

The basic principle of matrix mechanics is used to examine the three polarizers' mathematical apparatus. The unpolarized light vibrating from the light source is a combination of every polarization angle from 0 to π radians. The absolute magnitude square to the probability amplitude represents the final probability. Thus, the amount of light passing through the vertical polarizer is 0.5 which results from integrating every angle, and with $\frac{1}{\pi}$ as the normalization constant, the value can be calculated as:

$$\frac{1}{\pi}\int_0^\pi \left| (1\ 0) \begin{pmatrix} 0 & 0 \\ 0 & 1 \end{pmatrix} \begin{pmatrix} \cos(\theta) \\ \sin(\theta) \end{pmatrix} \right|^2 d\theta = 0.5 \tag{1}$$

As mentioned above, for the vertical polarized light, passing through the horizontal filter, both perpendicular to each other, the probability is shown as:

$$\frac{1}{\pi}\int_0^\pi \left| (0\ 1) \begin{pmatrix} 0 & 0 \\ 0 & 1 \end{pmatrix} \begin{pmatrix} 1 & 0 \\ 0 & 0 \end{pmatrix} \begin{pmatrix} \cos(\theta) \\ \sin(\theta) \end{pmatrix} \right|^2 d\theta = 0 \qquad (2)$$

Yet, when a third 45° angled filter is sandwiched between the vertical and horizontal filters, the final probability shows the final unpolarized light

$$\frac{1}{\pi}\int_0^\pi \left| (0\ 1) \begin{pmatrix} 0 & 0 \\ 0 & 1 \end{pmatrix} \begin{pmatrix} 0.5 & 0.5 \\ 0.5 & 0.5 \end{pmatrix} \begin{pmatrix} 1 & 0 \\ 0 & 0 \end{pmatrix} \begin{pmatrix} \cos(\theta) \\ \sin(\theta) \end{pmatrix} \right|^2 d\theta = 0.125 \qquad (3)$$

This probability represents the whole polarized physical scene where most of the information is lost but the incident lights in the real world can be detected in a practical approach as shown in the next section. This concept can be utilized in designing and making the necessary hardware to help in detecting direct illumination sources in scenes. The major advantage of using polarization is that it is a fast and practical method for the determination of the automatic statistical thresholds. This is in addition to producing better color fidelity of the real light source. On the other hand, polarizing filters are additional physical resources required for the system, and the environment maps after polarization filtering cannot be used for indirect illumination simulation.

3.2   Detection of Incident Lights

The live-feed from the panoramic 360° camera produces a continuous radiance map that can be sampled efficiently. For a dynamic environment map that runs in real-time, the luminance pixels are captured using a thresholding approach. An automatic threshold value is given, and a pixel is considered as part of a light source if its intensity is above the threshold. A mask is produced that only depicts the area of light sources. The radiance map image is converted to gray-scale to ensure connectivity in white color-space. In order to determine the threshold automatically, two approaches are considered: (1) Calculate the median of the radiance map histogram because the temporal and spatial variations of the real-time environment change drastically which will affect the overall threshold value. (2) The polarized light allows only a small amount of incident light to pass through. Thus, the range of threshold is expanded significantly to a static binary value which performs faster in real-time.

In order to reduce the noise among the sampled points, Gaussian Blur is applied before thresholding. An erosion morphological transformation was applied with a rectangular kernel in small size to discard the pixels near boundaries of the mask. This is followed by a dilation transformation with a kernel triple in size to that used in the erosion. The pixel's luminance indicates the incident light in the radiance map which was extracted as a series of regions based on their area size to define the main light first, then the second light and so on. Identifying the color of the light provides more realistic illumination information which is computed based on the mean color for collective pixels in each region area. The resulting color is more accurate when the polarizing filters are used where the incident lights are the main objects. The error metric for the pixel of basic color Pb and the polarized one Pp is: $\sum_{Pixels}|(R_b, G_b, B_b) - (R_p, G_p, B_p)|$.

The intensity of the pixels also is calculated relative to the entire radiance map which is used to determine the soft and hard shadow strength based on the light type. The centroid of the sampled regions is converted from the screen coordinates (x, y) to the spherical coordinates (θ, ϕ) using the inverse spherical projection after normalization as shown in Fig. 3 in the second step of detecting the incident light. The spherical coordinates are represented as: $(\theta, \phi) = \int_1^{lights}(\tan^{-1}\frac{y}{x}, \cos^{-1}\frac{z}{r})$. Where $r = \sqrt{x^2 + y^2}$ and $lights$ is the number of lights detected in the panoramic 360° view which influences the inverse spherical projection. Eventually, the virtual light that represent the location of the detected incident light is represented as follows:

$$(x, y, z) = \int_1^{lights}(\frac{\sin\phi\cos\theta}{\pi \times dh}, \frac{\cos\phi}{\pi \times dw}, \frac{\sin\phi\cos\theta}{\pi \times 90}) \qquad (4)$$

However, these coordinates have a negative direction in the reverse direction of the view as shown:

$$(x, y, z) = \int_1^{lights}(\frac{\sin\phi\cos\theta}{\pi \times (dh - 90)}, -\frac{\cos\phi}{\pi \times (dw - 180)}, \frac{\sin\phi\cos\theta}{\pi \times 90}) \qquad (5)$$

These created virtual lights are normalized for the 3D engine where quaternions are used to represent the orientation or rotation of the lights. Also, when the light is turned off it can easily be deactivated.

3.3   Estimation of Reflected Lights

This section describes how the extraction of the reflected lights is performed. These type of light is also known as indirect illumination or reflected light which simply simulates any reflective interactions among the real and virtual object surfaces. The area surrounding the virtual objects from the 360° live-feed view is captured to depict any lighting variations and instantly reflected on the virtual objects' shading properties in the IBL mode. The virtual object is attached with a 3D plane to capture the local area as a 2D texture. The mesh vertices of the 3D plane use a filter to keep updating the value at 100 fps rate. In order for the object layer to only read the texture in the area of interest, a culling mask is used where the other parts of the main view are ignored. The mesh of the background plane dispatches every 10 fps to obtain the main texture and assign it to the video texture. The resulting mesh has transformed vertices from the 3D world to the view port of each point. The orientation of the AR device is modified with the screen orientation. A renderer on a virtual camera captures the targeted texture and uploads it to IBL defined texture property. The quality of the local texture is normalized based on the current standards of the entire AR view. This simulation is perfect for diffuse and glass materials as shown in Fig. 1.

3.4   Creation of Shading Properties

Most current 3D engines provide predefined shaders through the CG language and OpenGl. However, due to the specific purposes of the current system that deals with a live-feed 360° camera, multiple unique shaders are created to meet the system's needs. Each virtual object is a collection of vertices that consist of UV data, normals, and more. Some of the object material features can be pre-computed such as: main texture, normal map, specular map, while other can be computed at run-time; even the predefined properties can be influenced by the real-time properties. There are two main type of shaders used in this system:

Surface Shader. The virtual objects that reflect the light and have material features are assigned to this shader. Three passes are used but not necessarily in every rendering frame: (i) fast forward base for the main incident light, (ii) forward add for any additional lights, and (iii) shadow caster. The created shader allows the vertex of fragment rendering options for the lighting mode. It provides local additional reflected lights and other properties such as Lambert Diffuse, Blinn Phong Specular, IBL Reflection, IBL Refraction, IBL Fresnel.

Unlit Shader. The virtual objects that cast shadow only without having any materialistic lights have this shader. For instance, the background on each placed virtual object must reflect shadows on the surfaces under them or they will look like floating objects in the air. Thus, to cut through the plane surfaces, an alpha mask is used to make the background planes have a transparent material but receive shadows from the other objects.

4   Results and Evaluation

Several environments, lighting conditions, and locations are tested through the evaluation process in order to ensure that our system, as promised, has a visually Coherent Augmented Reality scene. Some example of the results are presented in Fig. 5.

4.1   Direct Illumination Evaluation

The shadow cast from the virtual objects is an indication of the incident light location when it is compared with the shadow cast from the real object. Therefore, the basic approach of calculating the direction of the sunlight is used in this step of the evaluation process. The real object's shadow s and height h provides the required inputs to calculate the angle θ that indicates the location of the light source as $\theta = \tan^{-1} \frac{h}{s}$. The angle of incident light is calculated manually in the physical scene. The measured angle then listed aligns with the corresponding detected angle ϕ that is obtained through the methods explained in Sects. 3.1 and 3.2. Table 1 shows the small amount of error as calculated in degrees between both angles. The error statistics is averaged using the root-mean-square-error (RMSE) given by the formula: $RMSE = \sqrt{\frac{\sum_{i=1}^{6} Error_i^2}{6}} = 1.567$. This resulting average is slightly improved compared to the older version of our system which did not include polarization [20,21].

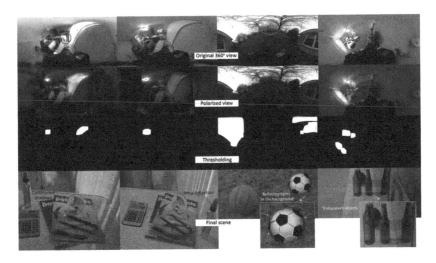

Fig. 5. System results with different lighting conditions and locations where each case has: (1) Original 360° view "the red circles indicate the locations of unwanted reflections and glares mistaken with light sources", (2) the view after polarization, (3) Threshold with minimal requirements, (4) the final image of the scene. (Color figure online)

Table 1. The measured angle θ compared with detected angle ϕ in degrees and the corresponding errors.

Scene no.	Shadow length $(s")$	Measured $(\theta°)$	Detected $(\phi°)$	Error
1	26	-169.13	-168.05	-1.08
2	4.3	229.15	230.06	-0.91
3	14	19.61	18.55	1.06
4	3	-120.97	-120.04	-0.93
5	16	17.32	15.2	2.12
6	7	35.52	36.45	-0.93

4.2 Performance Evaluation

Global illumination has a major influence on the performance cost of a AR/MR system. Our previous work investigated several methods that can calculate the reflected lights with minimal cost. These methods include cube map (CM) [21], 2D Textures Sub-Sampling (2D) [20], and polarization (PZ) that is also compared with the methods presented in [12,14,16] (GR12, GR14, and GR15, respectively; see Table 2). The categories of interest include: (FPS) number of frame per second where our system has achieved the required range of (30fps/60fps) for real-time execution, (Update) describes the process of the entire pipeline in [ms], (Input) is about the data captured through the main camera and the 360° view. (Tracking) is involved with geometry reconstruction and 6-DOF camera tracking, the (Surfaces) involves the surfaces extracted by the renderer

Table 2. Performance evaluation compared to our previous methods: Cube Map (CM), 2D Textures Sub-Sampling (2D), with the current method polarization (PZ), also compared against methods from other research (GR12, GR14, GR15).

Operation	Related work			Ours		
	GR12	GR14	GR15	CM	2D	PZ
FPS[1/s]	5.8	12.29	22.46	6	45	50
Update[ms]	172.4	81.36	44.53	173.4	35.9	32.4
Input[ms]	7.3	7.44	7.02	0.04	0.05	0.06
Tracking[ms]	11.1	10.24	10.64	2.31	1.9	1.10
Surfaces[ms]	6.69	6.69	12.6	4.21	4.42	4.56
Rendering[ms]	0.92	0.98	0.87	0.51	0.43	0.32

including occlusion computation. (Rendering) the time used for the virtual objects rasterization, differential rendering and the composition of AR scenes.

5 Conclusion and Future Work

In depth, the study of light and the physics of light are the keys aspect to rendering a realistic looking scene in computer graphics in general. In this work, we combined the idea of light wave polarization in physics and photography with a new platform represented in AR. The confusion of reflections and glare where they were mistaken with the light sources was eliminated after passing the light through the three polarizing filters (vertical, diagonal, and horizontal), which allowed the direct illumination to pass through and get detected instantly. The indirect illumination and object materials were addressed to ensure a visually coherent scene for the perception study. Although the augmented scenes do not operate without tracking, further investigation into the depth map and localization would benefit our future work of mimicking the reflected lights to result in more realistic rendering that uses the depth of every real object available in relation with the virtual objects. Furthermore, we would like to explore more shading and physics-based material effects which can improve the overall realism of the scene.

References

1. Horn, B.K.: Obtaining shape from shading information. Psychol. Comput. Vis. 115–55 (1975)
2. Zerner, M.C.: Semiempirical Molecular Orbital Methods. Reviews in Computational Chemistry, pp. 313–365. Wiley, Hoboken (1991)
3. Debevec, P.E., Andmalik, J.: Recovering high dynamic range radiance maps from photographs. In: SIGGRAPH97, pp. 369–378 (1997)
4. Keller A.: Instant radiosity. In: Proceedings of the 24th Annual Conference on Computer Graphics and Interactive Techniques. ACM Press/Addison-Wesley Publishing Co., pp. 49–56 (1997)

5. Debevec, P.: Rendering synthetic objects into real scenes: bridging traditional and image-based graphics with global illumination and high dynamic range photography. In: Proceedings of the 25th Annual Conference on Computer Graphics and Interactive Techniques, SIGGRAPH 1998, pp. 189–198. ACM, New York (1998). ISBN 0-89791-999-8

6. Chen, H., Wolff, L.B.: Polarization phase-based method for material classification in computer vision. Int. J. Comput. Vision **28**(1), 73–83 (1998)

7. Ramamoorthi, R., Hanrahan, P.: An efficient representation for irradiance environment maps. In: Proceedings of the 28th Annual Conference on Computer Graphics and Interactive Techniques, pp. 497–500 (2001)

8. Debevec, P.: Image-based lighting. IEEE Comput. Graphics Appl. **22**(2), 26–34 (2002)

9. Brom, J.M., Rioux, F.: Polarized light and quantum mechanics: an optical analog of the Stern-Gerlach experiment. Chem. Educ. **7**(4), 200–204 (2002)

10. Knecht, M., Traxler, C., Mattausch, O., Purgathofer, W., Wimmer, M.: Differential instant radiosity for mixed reality. In: 9th IEEE International Symposium Mixed and Augmented Reality (ISMAR), pp. 99–107 (2010)

11. Kán, P., Kaufmann, H.: High-quality reflections, refractions, and caustics in augmented reality and their contribution to visual coherence. In: 2012 IEEE International Symposium on Mixed and Augmented Reality (ISMAR), pp. 99–108 (2012)

12. Gruber, L., Richter-Trummer, T., Schmalstieg, D.: Real-time photometric registration from arbitrary geometry. In: IEEE International Symposium Mixed and Augmented Reality (ISMAR), pp. 119–128 (2012)

13. Jie, B.K.: Physics of Quantum Key Distribution, CS2107-Semester IV, 107 (2014–2015)

14. Gruber, L., Langlotz, T., Sen, P., Hoherer, T., Schmalstieg, D.: Efficient and robust radiance transfer for probeless photorealistic augmented reality. In: IEEE Virtual Reality (VR), pp. 15–20 (2014)

15. Ngo Thanh, T., Nagahara, H., Taniguchi, R.I.: Shape and light directions from shading and polarization. In: Proceedings of the IEEE Conference on Computer Vision and Pattern Recognition, pp. 2310–2318 (2015)

16. Gruber, L., Ventura, J., Schmalstieg, D.: Image-space illumination for augmented reality in dynamic environments. In: Virtual Reality (VR), pp. 127–134 (2015)

17. Rhee, T., Petikam, L., Allen, B., Chalmers, A.: Mr360: mixed reality rendering for 360 panoramic videos. IEEE Trans. Visual. Comput. Graphics **4**, 1379–1388 (2017)

18. Fan, C.L., Lee, J., Lo, W.C., Huang, C.Y., Chen, K.T., Hsu, C.H.: Fixation prediction for 360 video streaming in head-mounted virtual reality. In: Proceedings of the 27th Workshop on Network and Operating Systems Support for Digital Audio and Video, pp. 67–72 (2017)

19. Shen, L., Zhao, Y., Peng, Q., Chan, J.C., Kong, S.G.: An iterative image dehazing method with polarization. IEEE Trans. Multimedia (2018)

20. Alhakamy, A., Tuceryan, M.: AR360: dynamic illumination for augmented reality with real-time interaction. In: 2019 IEEE 2nd International Conference on Information and Computer Technologies ICICT, pp. 170–175 (2019)

21. Alhakamy, A., Tuceryan, M.: CubeMap360: interactive global illumination for augmented reality in dynamic environment. In: IEEE SoutheastCon (2019). Accepted and Presented

BioClouds: A Multi-level Model to Simulate and Visualize Large Crowds

Andre Da Silva Antonitsch, Diogo Hartmann Muller Schaffer,
Gabriel Wetzel Rockenbach, Paulo Knob, and Soraia Raupp Musse$^{(\boxtimes)}$ (iD)

School of Technology, Pontifical Catholic University of Rio Grande do Sul,
Porto Alegre, Brazil
andre.antonitsch@acad.pucrs.br, soraia.musse@pucrs.br

Abstract. This paper presents a multi-level approach to simulate large crowds [18] called BioClouds. The goal of this work is to model larger groups of agents by simulating aggregation of agents as singular units. This approach combines microscopic and macroscopic simulation strategies, where each group of agents (called cloud) keeps the global characteristics of the crowd unity without simulating individuals. In addition to macroscopic strategy, BioClouds allows to alter from global to local behavior (individuals), providing more accurate simulation in terms of agents velocities and densities. We also propose a new model of visualization focused on larger simulated crowds but keeping the possibility of "zooming" individuals and see their behaviors. Results indicate that Bio-Clouds presents coherent behaviors when compared to what is expected in global and individual levels. In addition, BioClouds provides an important speed up in processing time when compared to microcospic crowd simulators present in literature, being able to achieve until one million agents, organized in 2000 clouds and simulated at 86.85 ms per frame.

Keywords: Crowd simulation · BioCrowds · Collision avoidance ·
Macroscopic simulation · Microscopic simulation · Crowd visualization

1 Introduction

Imagine that you are inside an airplane and there is a huge crowd on the ground. If the height is enough to see the crowd, you are probably not able to perceive the individuals or their respective behaviors. Now, let us say that you can zoom in and out the level of detail of the crowd in such situation, allowing to perceive some issue or even dangerous situations that can arise. This is the main idea we want to explore in this paper: the relationship between macro and microscopic simulation and visualization in crowds, speeding up the performance while loosing accuracy, but keeping a way to zoom in the crowd and perceiving the individual behaviors. The field of crowd simulation has been studied for a long time and its applications range from the optimization of evacuation plans, simulation of behaviors influenced by cultures and computer animation applied to

© Springer Nature Switzerland AG 2019
M. Gavrilova et al. (Eds.): CGI 2019, LNCS 11542, pp. 15–27, 2019.
https://doi.org/10.1007/978-3-030-22514-8_2

entertainment, e.g. games and movies. As such, understanding and modeling the behavior of the crowd remains an important field of study [10, 13]. In this work we focus on the relationship between agent behavior, crowds and big crowds. Also, we aim to propose a way to change between micro and macroscopic approaches, which impacts the visualization in a continuous way. We call this relationship a multilevel model of crowds and it implies the study of simulation aspects itself as well as the visualization.

Although micro and macroscopic models already exist in the literature (we mention many methods in next section), we miss a model where we can play interactively with advantages of each model in order to accomplish a certain goal. For example, let us say that in a certain moment it is adequate to visualize big crowds as unities. However, in a certain time/space, it could be useful to visualize agents moving and avoiding collisions, in order to visually perceive the real density imposed by the space restrictions and the huge amount of agents into the crowds. This is the specific area we want to contribute with this paper. This work proposes a model capable of simulate a huge amount of agents, visualizing them as unities and, at the same time, providing an interactive way to change the simulation and visualization from macro to microscopic level.

2   Related Work

Most notable macroscopic models for crowd simulation include Treuille [14], Hughes [4] and Helbing [3]. The work proposed by Treuille et al. [14] define four hypothesis which control the crowd dynamics and are based on: (1) goal, (2) speed, (3) discomfort field and (4) optimization of path length, time to achieve the goal and discomfort. Hughes [4] presents a theory where individuals in a given crowd are guided by reason and behavioral rules and, therefore, the crowd itself is also governed by such rules. Helbing [3] proposes a model of crowd simulation based on the field of fluid dynamics. His work describes the relation between crowds of pedestrian and adaption of Boltzmann gas kinetic equations for crowds, deriving fluid dynamic equations for crowds. So, the adapted equations apply the concepts of pressure, friction and temperature to the domain of pedestrians. The author also proposes that the model can be used for computing the optimal flow speed of crowds, maximizing the diversity of perceptions on it and avoiding panic and critical situations. Regarding microscopic models, Reynolds [11] proposes a simulation model for flocks of birds, schools of fishes and herds of various animals. Bicho et al. [6] proposes BioCrowds, a collision avoidance model based on space discretization. In BioCrowds, agents are particle shaped and do not interact directly with each other, but with the space around them. The space is discretized into a set of dispersed markers. During each simulation step, each agent captures markers around it (inside a given radius) and use them to calculate its movement vector, where each marker can belong to zero or one agent (i.e. closest agent). The method assures the collision avoidance for each step by ensuring that each agent takes possession of a Voronoi portion of the environment. Any position inside the space an agent owns is a position that no other agent can assume at the same step of simulation, thus avoiding collision. Pelechano et al. [9] propose HiDAC, a model for simulating local agent motion and global agent path finding for high-density autonomous crowds. Each agent in HiDAC computes its own behavior based on perceptions of local crowd density, social forces and physical forces. Best et al. [2] propose an extension of the ORCA model [15] which computes the effect of local density on the behaviour of a crowd of agents. The model aims to replicate a more accurate representation of the Fundamental Diagram measured with humans in the ORCA model. Xiong et al. [16] use of the accepted concept that a hybrid simulation model should combine both microscopic and macroscopic simulations to leverage computational efficiency and simulation accuracy. Their hybrid model divides the simulation into two pre-defined regions: a region of macroscopic simulation and a region of microscopic simulation. The authors use the work of Van der Berg et al. [15] as the microscopic model, and the work of Hughes [4] as the macroscopic model for a continuous crowd. Sewall et al. [12] presents a hybrid simulation model which simulates regions of two types, continuum and agent-based. The method utilizes agent-based techniques inside regions-of-interest and continuum techniques on all the remaining regions of the simulation. The difference between our model and the region based proposal by Xiong et al. [16] and Sewall et al. [12] is that we achieve the multi-level (or hybrid methodology) in any space or time of the crowd simulation in an interactive way.

3   Proposed Model

Overview: As mentioned before, BioClouds model is an extension of BioCrowds model [6]. The main BioCrowds concepts are kept, such as the agent perception radius, the BioCrowds space competition behavior and the collision avoidance characteristics. BioClouds model presents aspects from both macroscopic and microscopic models. One significant difference between BioCrowds and BioClouds is that entities in BioClouds, named clouds, represent a crowd as a unity. Clouds can have different amount of agents so their perception radius is adjusted as a function of preferred density of agents. For instance, a certain cloud i that represents a unity of 5000 agents with a preferred density of 2 agents/sqm should occupy a space of 2500 sqm, for instance a region of 50×50 m. This cloud must behave in a coherent way in space and time with the crowd it represents. If the simulation level is changing from macro to microscopic, clouds should allow agents generation and should keep coherence in aspects as densities and velocities. The environment in BioCrowds is discretized into markers, which are attributed to only one agent in order to provide a completely free-of-collision algorithm. Both markers and agents are infinitesimal shapes. Similarly, the BioClouds model is a space discretization based model. However, instead to use infinitesimal markers in the space, matrix cells of 2 m $\times 2$ m (4 sqm) are used to represent the simulated environment.

As stated before, space markers are used to discretize the space and are defined as an uniform grid of square cells. In this work, it is used cells of area $= 4$ sqm for cells of side $= 2$ m. The cells can be owned by, at most, a single cloud of agents at a time, in order to provide collision avoidance. Obstacles can be simulated as an absence of cells in a given region of space, so *clouds* will not be able to mark such regions as owned by them and, therefore, are not going to move into that region. The area that cells represent is a parameter of the model and can be adjusted as intended.

Clouds are aggregations of agents which have common characteristics and goals. The number of agents a certain cloud C_i contains is one of the C parameters. Indeed, the cloud is a structure that contains a set of parameters, defined as follows: $C_i = \{A_i, dD_i, dS_i, dA_i, R_{i,t}, sR_i, g_i, jD_{i,t}, jA_{i,t}\}$, where A_i states for the number of agents inside cloud i, dD_i is the desired density the cloud should achieve, dS_i is the desired speed and dA_i is the desired area such cloud wants to occupy in order to keep the desired density. In addition, $R_{i,t}$ is the cloud radius at instant t, estimating that its shape is a circle[1]. Indeed, this parameter states for the radius of the perception area where cloud i is going to search for space markers (i.e. cells in BioClouds) in the environment. Clouds can update their $R_{i,t}$ radius parameter if instantaneous density is different from desired one. Such update is defined by a radius change speed sR_i parameter, which determines how much the perception radius can change in a single simulation step, the maximum change is defined by dS_i, as later described in Eq. 2. In addition, g_i states for cloud i goal. Finally, the instantaneous values $jD_{i,t}$ and $jA_{i,t}$ are the instantaneous density and area, respectively, at instant t.

The main behavior of the cloud is to move towards its goal while trying to keep its desired structure (density and velocity) and avoid collision with obstacles and other clouds. It implies that the cloud tries to keep its preferred density parameter dD_i which, in its turn, is related to the cloud area dA_i. Once the number of agents A_i and the desired density dD_i are defined for a cloud C_i, the desired cloud area is computed such as: $dA_i = \frac{A_i}{dD_i}$, as well the initial radius of the circular shape to contain the cloud: $R_{i,0} = \sqrt{\frac{A_i}{dD_i \Pi}}$. Therefore, C_i will try to keep its desired density during the motion to achieve the goal g_i. However, due to space constraints (for example, crowded situations), clouds can lose space (i.e. cells) to other clouds. Such behavior diminishes the instantaneous area $(jA_{i,t})$ occupied by C_i at instant t, which can increase the instantaneous density $(jD_{i,t} = \frac{A_i}{jA_{i,t}})$. In fact, $jA_{i,t}$ and $jD_{i,t}$ are computed at each frame and depends on the area (in cells) that the cloud is occupying at the moment. The collision avoidance algorithm is based on the fact that markers in BioCrowds (or cells in BioClouds) are attributed to only one agent/cloud, respectively. In BioCrowds, the Euclidean distance is used to decide if a certain marker should be attributed to a determined agent, since markers are attributed to the closest agent. However in BioClouds, clouds can have different radius (due to different number of agents) so we propose to use another distance function in order to provide

---

[1] In order to provide a collision free algorithm, we consider that our clouds should be represented by convex polygons, so in order to avoid extra computation, it is considered as a circle only local density purposes.

a correct way to attribute the markers to the clouds, allowing free-of-collision clouds movement. To do so, the Power of a Point distance [1] method was chosen, because it partitions the space into an emergent Voronoi-like diagram, so it keeps the method collision-free. To clarify, the power of a point distance function is defined in Eq. 1:

$$Pd_{i,k,t} = d(\boldsymbol{X}_{i,t}, \boldsymbol{a}_k)^2 - R_{i,t}^2, \tag{1}$$

where $\boldsymbol{X}_{i,t}$ is the center position of cloud C_i at frame t, $\boldsymbol{a}_k$ states for the position of a given marker/cell k that the cloud C_i is computing the distance, function $d(,)$ denotes the inner product and $R_{i,t}$ is the estimated C_i radius at frame t. Considering the relation between the power of a point distance weight and the radius of a circle, the area a cloud occupies is approximated to that of a circle. Considering that clouds can lose space, increasing instantaneous density, when competing for space, R_i must be updated in a next frame to reflect how the cloud shape can change to accommodate agents, and at the same time limit how compressed a cloud can possibly be. $R_{i,t+1}$ is then computed according to the ratio between its instantaneous density $jD_{i,t}$ and the preferred density dD_i, as seen in Eqs. 2 and 3:

$$R_{i,t+1} = R_{i,t} + min(dS_i, max(-dS_i, sR_i\ \beta_t\ R_{i,t})), \tag{2}$$

where β_t can be defined as shown in Eq. 3:

$$\beta_t = min\left(\frac{jD_{i,t}^2}{dD_i^2}, 2\right) - 1. \tag{3}$$

Having $Pd_{i,k,t}$ for each agent i and each cell k at frame t, the less distance obtained value indicates the closest cloud to attribute the referred cell. Afterwards, the same motion vector computed in BioCrowds, as a function of closest markers and goal position, is applied to compute next cloud position.

In order to propose BioClouds Visualization, we use two approaches. Once a *macroscopic visualization* of crowds generally focuses more on visualized simulation data than individual accuracy of the visualized agents, this work uses a macroscopic visualization based on a simple heatmap, describing the instantaneous agents density at each occupied cell. Each cloud represents a region of space populated by a particular group of agents, determined by the cells the cloud captured which are colored according to the instantaneous density (agents/sqm). Figure 1 shows examples of BioClouds heatmap visualization with densities varying from 1 agent/sqm in the blue regions, to 5 agent/sqm, in the green regions and a maximum of 10 agent/sqm in the red regions. In this figure we simulated 62500 agents organized in 250 clouds, each on with 250 agents. The environment is 1000 × 1000 m.   It is expected that a *microscopic visualization* provides accurate representation of each particular agent, like its position, speed, interactions with others and etc. To that effect, this work allows a microscopic visualization method for macroscopic crowd simulations. The trade-off of having increased visualization accuracy and individual details is the increased computational time. Our proposed solution is the creation of a microscopic visualization

Fig. 1. A macroscopic heatmap visualization of a crowd. This image shows a crowd of 62500 agents. Blue regions show low densities. Red regions show high densities. (Color figure online)

window (MVW). This window works as a *magnifying glass* for the macroscopic simulation, allowing for increased simulation details and interactions inside the defined visualization region. MVW uses the BioCrowds model to simulate the agents contained in the cloud and it is a rectangular region defined by a position (x, y) in BioClouds space width w and height h, where x, y, w and h are user defined values. If a certain cloud i capture cells inside MVW, it will have the appropriate quantity of agents spawned in the window (relative to the cloud space inside MVW). These agents are endowed with same characteristics as their cloud (i.e. velocities, goals, desired densities) and evolve moving and avoiding collisions with others using BioCrowds. The number of agents to be created is defined by the number of captured cells (N_i) from C_i which are inside MVW. Each cell in the environment has *cellArea* area, cloud i has the instantaneous density $jD_{i,t}$ and the total number of agents A_i represented by C_i. Then $nA_{i,t}$ agents should be created in order to keep the cloud desired density. Equation 4 describe such concepts:

$$dA_{i,t} = N_i \times cellArea \times jD_{i,t}, \tag{4}$$

where $dA_{i,t}$ states for the wished number of agents to be created in MVW at frame t. In fact, the only requirement is to avoid to create more agents than the total number of agents represented in the cloud, so $nA_{i,t}$ describes the instantaneous number of agents to be effectively created at frame t: $nA_{i,t} = max(dA_{i,t} - A_i, 0f)$. In order to maintain the cohesion of agents belonging to the same crowd, the BioCrowds cohesion model proposed by Knob et al. [5] was utilized. Such cohesion represents the willingness of agents of a given group to stay close and together with each other. Thus, a group with a high cohesion should have agents closer to each other, when compared with another group with a low cohesion value. The cohesion equations presented in their work maintain groups of agents together around their group center. In the BioClouds microscopic visualizations, we used the cloud position as a group center to attract cohesive agents. Figure 2 shows an example of our microscopic visualization containing 200 agents inside a MVW of 2500 sqm.

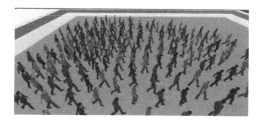

Fig. 2. A microscopic visualization of a crowd. This image shows agents being simulated individually inside the MVW.

4   Experimental Results

This section presents some experimental results obtained by our model. Section 4.1 shows that the proposed clouds are accurate representation of the agents they are trying to personify, while Sect. 4.2 shows some performance comparison among BioClouds, BioCrowds and other works in literature.

4.1   BioClouds Accuracy

The goal of this section is to show that the clouds, in our method, accurately represent the agents inserted on them. We designed three experiments (A, B, and C) in order to compare the average densities and speeds between BioCrowds and BioClouds methods. Experiment A simulates a single crowd of agents, while experiments B and C simulate crowds of various sizes in a bidirectional flow. The BioCrowds agents density measurement was performed by dividing the number of agents in a certain cloud by the convex-hull area the cloud occupies. For all three experiments, the MVW is positioned at the center of the environment, with $w = 80$ and $h = 50$. Biocrowds agents are spawned when the cloud 1 enters the MVW and are removed when the agents leave the MVW. The environment in these experiments is a flat square of terrain with no obstacles, measuring 150 by 150 m. Experiment A simulates one only crowd (1) of agents walking unobstructed. The cloud 1 starts the experiment at a position $(0, 74)$ in a 2D coordinates and moves towards its goal at position $(150, 74)$, at a max preferred speed of 1.3 m/s. Cloud 1 represents 200 agents at a preferred density of 0.5 agent/sqm. Figures 3(a) and (b) show the obtained density and speed results for experiment A, respectively. The graphs compare how closely the cloud density and speed (in blue), relate to the density and speed of agents which are spawned (in red). In an unobstructed scenario, agents follow closely the behaviour of the cloud which created them, as shown by the low deviation between the red and blue lines. The small variations are due to the microscopic simulation where agents avoid collisions and interact with others, what does not happen in BioClouds. In fact, in the same time we show that both behaviors are coherent, we show the main advantage of our method when allowing to perceive (and quantitatively measure) the impact of individuals in the simulation.

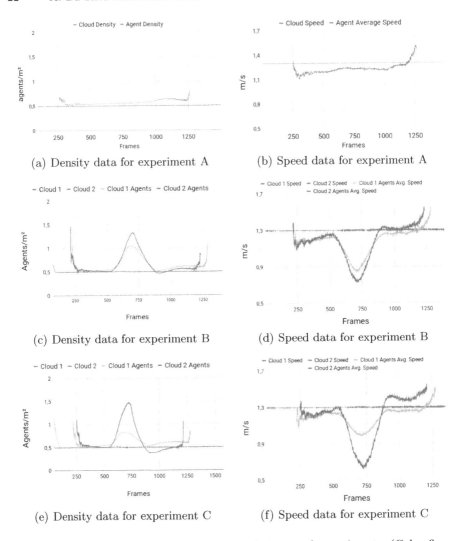

(a) Density data for experiment A

(b) Speed data for experiment A

(c) Density data for experiment B

(d) Speed data for experiment B

(e) Density data for experiment C

(f) Speed data for experiment C

Fig. 3. Comparison between clouds and crowds in tested experiments. (Color figure online)

Experiment B simulates two equal sized crowds (names 1 and 2) of agents walking towards each other in a bidirectional flow. Cloud 1 starts the experiment at position $(0, 74)$ and moves towards its goal at position $(150, 74)$, at a max preferred speed of 1.3 m/s. Cloud 2 starts the experiment at position $(150, 74)$ and moves towards its goal at position $(0, 74)$, at a max preferred speed of 1.3 m/s. Both clouds 1 and 2 represent 500 agents each at a preferred density of 0.5 agent/sqm each. Figures 3(c) and (d) show the obtained density and speed results for experiment B, respectively. In this experiment it is easy to see the impact of the two crowds when being simulated in a microscopic way while crossing each other. As we can perceive such disturbance caused by the crowds is not visible in the clouds. Experiment C simulates two different sized crowds of agents (500 and 250 agents) walking towards each other. Cloud 1 starts the experiment at position $(0, 74)$ and moves towards its goal at position $(150, 74)$, at a max preferred speed of $1.3\,\mathrm{m/s}$. Cloud 1 represents 500 agents and has a preferred density of $0.5\,\mathrm{agent/sqm}$. Cloud 2 starts the experiment at position $(150, 74)$ and moves towards its goal at position $(0, 74)$, at a max preferred speed of $1.3\,\mathrm{m/s}$. Cloud 2 represents 250 agents and a preferred density of $0.5\,\mathrm{agent/sqm}$ each. Figures 3(e) and (f) show the obtained density and speed results for experiment C, respectively. Comparing with experiment B it is easy to see that as there are more agents, higher is a variation due to the number of individuals and their interactions in the simulation. In fact, one can say that our method succeeds to simulate crowds as unities and also to show the impact of individuals in the simulation in the same time.

Figures illustrated in 3 show the graphs of distinct crowds interacting. In red and blue the graphs show the values for the clouds. In green and yellow the graphs show the values for the average of the agents the clouds spawned. It is easy to see that when simulating clouds there is no variation in densities and speeds. On the other hand, the interaction among agents crossing others increases densities above the estimated density by the cloud. As well as reducing speed below the estimated velocity of the cloud. These data indicates that when simulating and seeing clouds there is a expected loss of accuracy what can be observed when simulating our microscopic method. The aspect we want to highlight here is that Clouds or Crowds can be simulated and visualized in specific points in order to obtain the accuracy and also take benefit from the optimized computational time (discussed in Sect. 4.2). Also, a qualitatively analysis was performed. Figure 4 presents some snapshots of the Experiment B. Two clouds are walking towards their respective goals, placed in opposite directions (Fig. 4(a)). When the clouds enter inside the MVW area, agents begin to be spawned (Fig. 4(b)). It is possible to see that such agents are distributed along the area of the cloud which is already inside the MVW. Local interactions between agents can be seen in Fig. 4(c), where agents of both clouds are forming lanes while crossing each other. In Fig. 4(d), it is possible to see the variation the crowd shape adopts in relation to the expected cloud shape. It happens due to local interactions that are simulated in microscopic level. Even so, agents were able to stay nearby their respective cloud center, so, when they start to leave the MVW area, the clouds begin to resurface (Fig. 4(e)). Therefore, when agents already left the MVW area, only the clouds continue to be simulated (d). Figure 4(g) shows a zoomed in instance of Fig. 4(c).

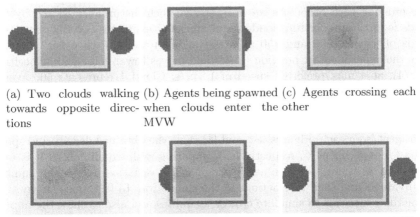

(a) Two clouds walking towards opposite directions

(b) Agents being spawned when clouds enter the MVW

(c) Agents crossing each other

(d) Agents crossed each other

(e) Agents leaving the MVW and clouds resurfacing

(f) Agents left the MVW, just clouds remaining

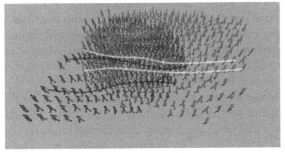

(g) A zoomed image of Figure 4(c) shows the formation of lanes in the MVW.

Fig. 4. Snapshots from Experiment B.

4.2 Performance

The goal of this section is to show that BioClouds achieves better performance when compared with other works in literature, in this case BioCrowds and the method proposed by Narain et al. [7]. BioClouds performance is dependant on the current radius size of each cloud, since each cloud attempts to capture each cell inside its radius what is used to compute the cloud motion. Considering that the perception radius of a cloud increases in situations of space competition, the performance is affected by the densities of each cloud. To test BioClouds performance we designed 4 experiments (D, E, F and G), with varying sizes of crowds, with different configurations of number of clouds and cloud sizes. These experiments are simulated using BioClouds without a MVW, to test the performance of the macroscopic simulation module. The experiments were run with a i7-3770 CPU 3.40 GHz, 16 GB of RAM and a GeForce GTX 660 GPU.

For the experiments D, E, F and G, the environment is a flat square of terrain with no obstacles, measuring 1000 by 1000 m. Experiments D and E consider a crowd of 200 thousands agents. Experiments F and G analyses a crowd of 1 million agents. The preferred density of agents in these experiments is of 3.0 agent/sqm, as to represent a densely packed crowd [8]. Experiments D and E simulate each one two crowds of 100 thousands agents moving towards each other. Experiment D has *400* clouds of 500 agents each, while experiment E has *200* clouds of 1000 agents each. The clouds are spawned in the rectangles delimited by the diagonals $\{(0,50),(100,450)\}$ and $\{(400,50),(500,450)\}$. Experiments F and G simulate two crowds of 1 million agents moving towards each other. Experiment F has *2000* clouds of 500 agents each. Experiment G has *1000* clouds of 1000 agents each. The clouds are spawned in the rectangles delimited by the diagonals $\{(0,150),(200,850)\}$ and $\{(800,150),(1000,850)\}$. Since there is variation in time per frame during the simulation (due to radius variation), we computed the median time per frame for each simulation. Table 1 shows the obtained time per frames for BioClouds, and a comparison with the results obtained by Narain et al. [7]. BioClouds is capable of simulating a greater number of agents than the competitive work, with shorter times per frame. In addition, our work shows simulations with a larger number of agents. To assess the impact of the MVM during large crowd simulations experiments D, E, F and G were simulated with a 25 by 25 m MVW positioned in the center of the simulated environment. We measured the maximum amount of agents inside the MVW and the median time per frame, for each scenario (see two last columns in Table 1).

Table 1. Obtained results per experiment and comparison with other studies.

Experiments	Agents	Clouds	Cloud size	Time/frame	Agents in MVW	Time/frame
BioClouds - Case D	100k	400	500	20.80 ms	4037	190.94 ms
BioClouds - Case E	100k	200	1000	25.60 ms	2905	166.36 ms
BioClouds - Case F	1 m	2000	500	86.85 ms	4866	317.41 ms
BioClouds - Case G	1 m	1000	1000	105.22 ms	5235	562.96 ms
Narain et al. [7]	100k	-	-	447 ms	-	-
Narain et al. [7]	80k	-	-	806 ms	-	-

5   Final Considerations

This paper described BioClouds, a new model to simulate crowds as units but in the same time allowing to simulate and visualize individual and group details as lanes, interactions, collisions avoided and the disturbance people can cause in each other regarding speeds and densities. The proposed BioClouds model is a multi-level approach to simulate huge crowds that allows to alter from microscopic to macroscopic levels. It achieves the goal of improving the computational performance when simulating really huge crowds (with a million of agents), while the method is appropriate for simulations where individualized visualization is required in a certain space-time. The selective and user defined MVW approach allows for individual-accurate simulation in zones of interest allowing a better understanding of emergent crowd behaviours. BioClouds extension is sufficiently accurate to represent global crowd behavior of BioCrowds as we showed in our results. In addition, we provide a way to simulate and visualize individuals that represent the clouds. That is why our multi-level method can be interesting in certain applications where we want to simulate really huge crowds but having the control to zoom in the crowd to analyse some individual behavior. As future work, there are still problems to solve. The aggregation and disaggregation of entities, as proposed by Xiong et al. [17], would improve BioClouds by allowing to split clouds into other clouds and then in singular BioCrowds agents to finally then aggregating agents back into the clouds. Also, a real world validation would more accurately relate BioClouds to real life situations.

References

1. Aurenhammer, F.: Power diagrams: properties, algorithms and applications. SIAM J. Comput. **16**(1), 78–96 (1987). https://doi.org/10.1137/0216006
2. Best, A., Narang, S., Curtis, S., Manocha, D.: Densesense: interactive crowd simulation using density-dependent filters. In: Proceedings of the ACM SIGGRAPH/Eurographics Symposium on Computer Animation, pp. 97–102. Eurographics Association (2014)
3. Helbing, D.: A fluid dynamic model for the movement of pedestrians, vol. 6, June 1998
4. Hughes, R.L.: A continuum theory for the flow of pedestrians. Transp. Res. Part B: Methodol. **36**(6), 507–535 (2002)
5. Knob, P., Balotin, M., Musse, S.R.: Simulating crowds with ocean personality traits. In: Proceedings of the 18th International Conference on Intelligent Virtual Agents, pp. 233–238. ACM (2018)
6. de Lima Bicho, A., Rodrigues, R.A., Musse, S.R., Jung, C.R., Paravisi, M., Magalhes, L.P.: Simulating crowds based on a space colonization algorithm. Comput. Graph. **36**(2), 70–79 (2012)
7. Narain, R., Golas, A., Curtis, S., Lin, M.C.: Aggregate dynamics for dense crowd simulation. In: ACM Transactions on Graphics (TOG), vol. 28, p. 122. ACM (2009)
8. Narang, S., Best, A., Manocha, D.: Interactive simulation of local interactions in dense crowds using elliptical agents. J. Stat. Mech.: Theory Exp. **2017**(3), 033403 (2017)
9. Pelechano, N., Allbeck, J.M., Badler, N.I.: Controlling individual agents in high-density crowd simulation. In: Proceedings of the 2007 ACM SIGGRAPH/Eurographics Symposium on Computer Animation, SCA 2007, pp. 99–108, Aire-la-Ville, Switzerland. Eurographics Association (2007). http://dl.acm.org/citation.cfm?id=1272690.1272705
10. Pelechano, N., Allbeck, J.M., Kapadia, M., Badler, N.I.: Simulating Heterogeneous Crowds with Interactive Behaviors. CRC Press, Boca Raton (2016)
11. Reynolds, C.W.: Flocks, herds and schools: a distributed behavioral model. SIGGRAPH Comput. Graph. **21**(4), 25–34 (1987). https://doi.org/10.1145/37402.37406

12. Sewall, J., Wilkie, D., Lin, M.C.: Interactive hybrid simulation of large-scale traffic. ACM Trans. Graph. (TOG) **30**(6), 135 (2011)
13. Thalmann, D., Musse, S.R.: Crowd Simulation. Springer, London (2013). https://doi.org/10.1007/978-1-4471-4450-2
14. Treuille, A., Cooper, S., Popović, Z.: Continuum crowds. ACM Trans. Graph. (TOG) **25**, 1160–1168 (2006)
15. Van Den Berg, J., Guy, S.J., Lin, M., Manocha, D.: Reciprocal n-body collision avoidance. In: Pradalier, C., Siegwart, R., Hirzinger, G. (eds.) Robotics Research. Springer Tracts in Advanced Robotics, vol. 70, pp. 3–19. Springer, Heidelberg (2011). https://doi.org/10.1007/978-3-642-19457-3_1
16. Xiong, M., Lees, M., Cai, W., Zhou, S., Low, M.Y.H.: Hybrid modelling of crowd simulation. Procedia Comput. Sci. **1**(1), 57–65 (2010)
17. Xiong, M., Tang, S., Zhao, D.: A hybrid model for simulating crowd evacuation. New Gener. Comput. **31**(3), 211–235 (2013)
18. Xu, M.L., Jiang, H., Jin, X.G., Deng, Z.: Crowd simulation and its applications: recent advances. J. Comput. Sci. Technol. **29**(5), 799–811 (2014)

Am I Better in VR with a Real Audience?

Romain Terrier[1,2(✉)], Nicolas Martin[1], Jérémy Lacoche[1,3], Valérie Gouranton[2], and Bruno Arnaldi[2]

[1] IRT b<>com, Rennes, France
`romain.terrier@b-com.com`
[2] Univ Rennes, INSA Rennes, Inria, CNRS, IRISA, Rennes, France
[3] Orange Labs, Rennes, France

Abstract. We present an experimental study using virtual reality (VR) to investigate the effects of a real audience on social inhibition. The study compares a multi-user application, locally or remotely shared. The application engages one user and a real audience (i.e., local or remote conditions) and a control condition where the user is alone (i.e., alone condition). The differences have been explored by analyzing the objective performance (i.e., type and answering time) of users when performing a categorization of numbers task in VR. Moreover, the subjective feelings and perceptions (i.e., perceptions of others, stress, cognitive workload, presence) of each user have been compared in relation to the location of the real audience. The results showed that in the presence of a real audience (in the local and remote conditions), user performance is affected by social inhibitions. Furthermore, users are even more influenced when the audience does not share the same room, despite others are less perceived.

Keywords: Virtual Reality · Social influence · Audience

1 Introduction

The new trend is toward multi-users in Virtual Reality (VR) [30]. People are able to share, in real time, the same Virtual Environment (VE) and their experience causing social mechanisms [1] (e.g., social anxiety, social inhibition, empathy, group effects, leadership). Moreover, social VR applications allow people to share the same VE in different ways. On the one hand, they can be colocated when each user is in the same location. On the other hand, when each user is in a different, remote location, they are distant. This differentiation increases the possible social inhibition; indeed, the effects and the appearance of social inhibition are not well known in VR. Therefore, one question remains: does our behaviour change in VR depending on whether our audience is real or remote? Using previous experimental studies in psychology, we designed an experiment in which one user must perform a new and unknown task in front of distant or colocated others. In each condition, others are sharing the same VE as the user. The goal of this study is to analyze the differences in social inhibition depending on the location of the audience.

M. Gavrilova et al. (Eds.): CGI 2019, LNCS 11542, pp. 28–39, 2019.
https://doi.org/10.1007/978-3-030-22514-8_3

2   Related Work

2.1   Social Influence and Audience Effects in the Real World

In the real world, everyday tasks are often done in presence of other people or with them. The perception one has of the other people affects his/her actions and behaviours [8] by imitation effects [5] or by a priming effect [25]. Firstly, the mere presence of other people (*audience*) is enough to influence individual behaviours [34] and to cause social facilitation [7]. The audience acts like an amplifier: it increases the dominant response - task complexity dependent - of the user. Thereby, the realization of an easy or well-known task will be facilitated by the mere presence of an audience, a concept known as facilitation [11]. In contrast, the realization of a complex or new task requiring a learning phase will be impaired [33], this is known as social inhibition. However, social inhibition or facilitation are not only generated by the mere presence of an audience [12]. How the audience is perceived or interpreted also affects the user, whose performance varies depending on the audience's status (i.e., evaluative or non-evaluative audience) [14]. Indeed, the user performs worse when facing an evaluative audience [16] than when alone because of the "evaluation apprehension" effect. A user must perceived an experimenter as an expert, and so evaluative, even if the experimenter is just an observer [27]. Also, knowing the identity of the audience (i.e., a friend) reduces accuracy and answering time given by users [32]. Social norm effects can also influence other behaviors: in a risky situation and in the presence of an audience users tend to diminish their 'risk-taking' actions (e.g., poker gambling) [20]. Thus, many studies have been published on the social effects of an audience on a user (i.e., the mere presence, the evaluation apprehension, social norms, distraction, perception of the audience, predictability of the audience) and all refers to social facilitation or inhibition. Moreover, the social influence of a virtual audience on a user could be different when compared to the influence of a real audience due to the particularities of VR.

2.2   Social Inhibition in VR

Researchers have used Shared Virtual Environments (SVEs)-inducing co-presence (i.e., *"being there together"* [22]) - to study users' behaviour in VR (e.g., paranoia, phobia, stress, anxiety) [21]. Participants are either physically in the same room (i.e., colocated) or in a remote place (i.e., distant). Several studies [9,31] on social influence focus their scope on analysing social inhibition in VR. Social inhibition occurs when one performs a new or unknown task in front of an audience, resulting in a decrease in performance (e.g., less qualitative, less quantitative, slower) [3]. Many VR studies specialize their research in the type of the audience (e.g., real versus virtual in 2D or 3D, close versus far). The first studies of the Social Inhibition of Return (e.g., increase in answering time in front of a co-actor) found that an agent in the VE caused a longer response time (e.g., $\sim 20\,\mathrm{ms}$) [31]. In a previous study, only the presence of a real co-actor caused this effect compared to a 2D-agent displayed on TV [23]. Moreover, a user study [15] focused on the difference of impact between three types of audiences: alone, with avatars, and with agents. The study is based on previous works of Blascovich et al. [2] who found that users had fewer correct answers when executing the unlearned task in presence of an audience. In the Hoyt et al. study [15], social inhibition occurred in VR but not social facilitation, and only in the presence of avatars. Indeed, if agents are judged and perceived as non-evaluative, the emergence of the inhibition can be prevented [7]. Moreover, agents exert less social influence than avatars on user feelings or behaviours [28] resulting in non-existant or low social inhibition. In the Hoyt et al. study [15], lower performance (e.g., lower number of correct answers during a novel task) was caused by social inhibition. However, the assistant stayed in the room even if the condition was without an audience, and that could have had an impact on results. There is still uncertainty regarding the effect of the audience type on users. Some results showed social inhibition in the presence of an agent while others showed social inhibition only in the presence of an avatar in a VE. One limitation of these previous studies is that the co-presence is not often measured, reducing data on the perception of others in a VE. As an audience in a VE can induce evaluation apprehension and self-evaluation effects on users, it can influence the perceived stress [19] and workload [6] of users during the accomplishment of a task. In summary, studies demonstrated the impact of a virtual audience on a user depending on its type (i.e., avatar, agent) and the user's perception of it (i.e., evaluative, non-evaluative). Nevertheless, there is a lack of studies that consider the location of the audience, although the issue of physical distance has always been confronted [18]. Today, applications can be shared and users can be located remotely (i.e., distant) or in the same room (i.e., colocated). Therefore, our study proposes to address this topic through analysing how different audience locations affect the impact of social inhibition.

3   Social Inhibition Experiment

The aim of this experiment is to evaluate the impact of audience's location (i.e., colocated, distant) on users in a VE. The audience takes the form of two examiners in the VE to establish the social inhibition of the participant. This paper does not focus on social facilitation because past studies only found results on inhibition [15]. The study is a between-subjects design with one independent variable: the presence of examiners. The participant performs the task according to three conditions: (1) alone (ALONE), (2) with examiners sharing the VE and the same real room than the participant - colocated audience - (IN), (3) with examiners sharing the VE but not the same real room - distant audience - (OUT) (see Fig. 1). The evaluation is about performance (objective measures: completion time, and type of answer), stress, cognitive workload and perception of others (subjective measures based on questionnaires). Our hypothesis is that the distant audience has less impact on users than colocated because avatars of the distant audience can be perceived as agents. Co-presence is lower with agents [15], reducing evaluation apprehension and self-awareness. Consistent with the experimental design and limitations of previous studies, our hypotheses are:

H1 In the presence of an audience (i.e., IN, OUT), the performance (i.e., types and time of answers) of users will be diminished in comparison to without audience (i.e., ALONE).

H2 In the presence of an audience (i.e., IN, OUT), stress and cognitive workload of users will be higher in comparison to without audience (i.e., ALONE).

H3 Participants will feel the presence of others and their influence more when examiners are physically in a same room (IN) than in a remote room (OUT).

H4 When examiners and users are physically in the same room (IN) than physically in a remote room (OUT) the effects of the audience will be stronger (i.e., poorer performance, higher stress and cognitive workload).

Fig. 1. Setup. User: (left) alone, (middle) audience colocated or (right) distant.

3.1 Technical Details and Material

Technical Details. Participants were equipped with an HTC Vive and its two controllers. The VE was a virtual office with a table, a blackboard and chairs (see Fig. 1). Only three people shared the same VE. The application was built in Unity3D with the SteamVR plugin. The VE and interactions were synchronized using a software layer based on Photon Engine 4. Users and examiners were represented by human-like avatars of the same gender (see Fig. 1). We used a T-pose based calibration to adjust the proportion of the avatar for each different user. The avatar animation was based on the rotation and the positions of the two controllers and the HMD using the plugin FinalIK (VRIK)[1]. The skeleton positions were inferred using inverse kinematics.

---

[1] http://root-motion.com.

Material. Four questionnaires were used. First, the Short Stress State Questionnaire (SSSQ) [13] measured task engagement, distress and worry using a Likert scale (1-not at all; 5-extremely; 34 questions). Then, the Raw Task Load Index (RTLX) [4] evaluated mental demand, physical demand, temporal demand, effort, performance, and frustration (6 questions). Then, the Slater, Usoh, Steel questionnaire (SUS) [29] measured the feeling of presence using a Likert scale (1-related to low presence; 7-related to high presence; 6 questions). Finally, the questionnaire regarding the perception of others (QPO) (only for IN and OUT) was based on multiple co-presence questionnaires [24,26]. It measured two dimensions: perception of the presence of others and their perceived influence (I was in the presence of others; I forget the others and I was focused on the task as if I was alone; I felt observed; My performance was influenced by the presence of others in the VE), and the negative or positive impact of this influence (I was embarrassed by the presence of others in the VE; The presence of others in the VE helped me perform the task; I felt embarrassed by what others might think of me). The QPO uses a Likert scale (1-not at all; 7-extremely; 7 questions).

3.2 Participants

The experimentation was carried out with 57 unpaid users: 16 females and 41 males, from 19 to 59 years old ($M_{age} = 35$, $sd_{age} = 10$), and with various backgrounds (i.e., students, human resources, engineers, managers, and assistants). Users were split into three groups: 18 participants in the ALONE condition, 20 in the IN condition, and 19 in the OUT condition. 15 users had never experienced VR, 21 users had used VR less than 5 times, 14 users less than 20 times, and 7 users more than 20 times. Demographic characteristics of participants were well distributed among groups.

3.3 Experimental Design

The experiment involved two exercises: (1) a short tutorial, (2) the main task (see Fig. 2).

Tutorial. A description of the controller was written on the blackboard: the touchpad was divided in two colored sides, left (orange) and right (blue). Then, users performed a short training during which they were asked to click on the right or left side of the touchpad eight times.

Main Task. It consisted of a categorization of numbers and came from the works of Blascovich et al. [2], and Hoyt et al. [15]. Participants had ten blocks to discover the rules of categorization. Each block included twenty-five trials. For each trial, the participant had 3 s to give an answer. Specifically, in each trial, two numbers were displayed on a board in the VE and the user was allowed 3 s to say whether the two numbers belonged together in category A or category B. The answer was either correct, categorization found (OK), or incorrect, mistake on the given categorization (NOK), or finally out of time, no answer given before 3 s

(OT). Audio and visual feedback were given: a soft beep and a green check mark for OK answers or a buzzer and a red-cross for NOK and OT answers. Category A numbers followed one normal distribution ($\mu = 46.5$, $\sigma = 8$, lower limit = 25, upper limit = 68), and category B numbers followed another one ($\mu = 90.7$, $\sigma = 8$, lower limit = 69, upper limit = 112). The numbers were the same for each participant. After each block, the score (as a percentage) was displayed on the blackboard. To complete the task, users needed to obtain eighty percent of correct answers on two consecutive blocks to successfully pass the task. If the user did not find the rule after ten blocks, the task was stopped.

3.4 Experimental Protocol

Step 1. All participants read and signed a consent form in which the experiment, its purpose, data recorded, data anonymity, and the possibility to stop the experiment whenever they wanted, were briefly described. Furthermore, each participant filled out a demographic questionnaire.

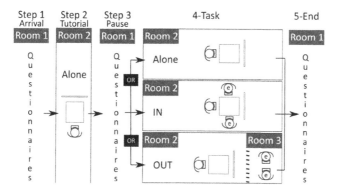

Fig. 2. Design and steps of the experiment

Step 2. Users were brought into a new room for the tutorial. The instructor gave information for the use of controllers and for the calibration, then equipped the user, left the room and told the user to continue alone. All instructions were given on the blackboard and by a synthesized voice. The instructor came back to notify the user that the tutorial was over.

Step 3. Users were directed to another room to fill out three questionnaires to establish their initial perceived state: the SSSQ, the RTLX, and the SUS. Then participants were redirected to the experiment room.

Step 4. Depending on the condition, participants received different information before performing the main categorization of numbers task. The way to answer was the same as in the tutorial. To elicit more social inhibition, the two examiners (i.e., one female, one male being also the experimenter) were introduced as evaluative. During the task, examiners could only cough or move their arms, hands and head. All noises were caught and played through headphones for the three conditions. Examiners were neither allowed to speak nor to answer the user. In the IN condition, participants saw and greeted the examiners before doing the task. In the OUT condition, participants never physically met the examiners. They only knew that they shared the same VE as the examiners, and that avatars embodied real people. Then, examiners equipped themselves and invited the user to continue the experiment. Participants were also informed that their performance could not be observed by any distant person (except the audience) and that the instructor would leave the room in the OUT condition. Instructions and mechanism of the task were displayed on the blackboard before beginning. Quantitative data of performance (dependent variable) were recorded: type of answers - number of correct (OK), incorrect (NOK), and out of time (OT) answers - and answering time (AT; between $0.00\,s$ and $3.00\,s$).

Step 5. Participants completed three or four questionnaires (depending on the condition) in order to give their final perceived state: the SSSQ, the RTLX, the SUS, and the QPO.

3.5   Results

As all of the trials were performed by each participant (i.e., repeated measures), linear mixed models were used [10]. To evaluate the effect of one variable using linear mixed models, two nested models were compared based on their deviance (chi-square): one without this variable (i.e., the null model), and one with this variable. We compared the effects between the three conditions (i.e., ALONE, IN, and OUT) on levels of stress, cognitive workload, and presence using Kruskal-Wallis (data not normally distributed). Then, we performed an unpaired two-samples t-test (normally distributed data) to analyze differences in the perception levels of others. Only significant results of main or interaction effects ($p < .05$) are discussed.

Objective Performance. To better evaluate variations, differences were measured between the first block performed by users and the last one (1 block = 25 trials, and 1 trial = 3 s. to categorize 2 displayed numbers). Here are the descriptive results of performance: AT ($M_{alone} = 1.29$, $sd_{alone} = .71$; $M_{in} = 1.37$, $sd_{in} = .71$; $M_{out} = 1.54$, $sd_{out} = .81$), OK ($M_{alone} = .70$, $sd_{alone} = .46$; $M_{in} = .68$, $sd_{in} = .47$; $M_{out} = .61$, $sd_{out} = .49$), NOK ($M_{alone} = .25$, $sd_{alone} = .43$; $M_{in} = .27$, $sd_{in} = .44$; $M_{out} = .30$, $sd_{out} = .46$), and OT ($M_{alone} = .05$, $sd_{alone} = .22$; $M_{in} = .05$, $sd_{in} = .22$; $M_{out} = .08$, $sd_{out} = .28$).

Answering Time. The analysis showed an effect of the condition over the AT ($\chi^2 = 7.88, p = .019$) and an additive effect of the condition and trial ($\chi^2 = 1053.47, p < .001$). The answering time varied from one trial to an other (see Fig. 3). Comparisons between conditions (post-hoc tests) showed a significant difference between ALONE and OUT ($z = -2.76, p = .015$), partially supporting

H1. There was no significant interaction effect ($\chi^2 = 3.23, p = .198$). In other words, the AT was diminished when the audience was distant as opposed to no audience. The comparisons between OUT and IN, and between IN and ALONE were not significant; **H1** and **H4** are not supported. The AT was not significantly diminished when the audience was colocated as opposed to no audience, similarly for the distant audience compared to colocated audience.

Type of Answers. We conducted the analyses on the number of OK, NOK, and OT given by participants between models. The value registered was: for OK 0 (i.e., not correct) or 1 (i.e., correct), for NOK 1 (i.e., incorrect) or 0 (i.e., not incorrect), and for OT 1 (i.e., out of time) or 0 (i.e., in time). We used Mixed-Effects Logistic Regression with random effects. The effect of the trial was significant over the number of OK, NOK, OT ($\chi^2_{ok} = 351.45, p_{ok} < .001$; $\chi^2_{nok} = 146.81, p_{nok} < .001$; $\chi^2_{ot} = 183.49, p_{ot} < .001$). The interaction effects between the condition and the trial (see Fig. 3) were also significant ($\chi^2_{ok} = 15.25, p_{ok} < .001$; $\chi^2_{nok} = 11.09, p_{nok} = .004$; $\chi^2_{ot} = 18.33, p_{ot} < .001$). The number of OK grew quicker in the ALONE condition, than in the IN and also in the OUT. The number of NOK and OT decreased quicker in the ALONE condition, then in the IN and finally in the OUT. This interaction between conditions and trials (CONDI*TRIAL) in these three variables support **H1**, but not **H4**. In other words, the evolution of the type of answers over trials was significantly different in relation to the location of the audience. Specifically, the number of OK increased more slowly over the trials in the presence of the audience (i.e., IN or OUT) as opposed to without audience (i.e., ALONE) but the evolution was quicker in the presence of the colocated audience compared to the distant audience. Furthermore, the number of NOK and OT decreased more slowly over trials in the presence of the audience (i.e., IN or OUT) as opposed

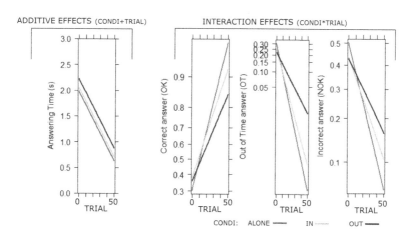

Fig. 3. Additive and interaction effects of Trial and Condition on answering time and on type of answers

to without the audience (i.e., ALONE) but the evolution was quicker in the presence of the colocated audience compared to the distant audience.

Subjective Feelings and Perceptions. *Perception of Others.* Using the QPO, the t-test showed a main effect on the Perception of Others and their Influence ($t(31.33) = 2.43, p = .021$). Users perceived the examiners more significantly and felt more influenced by them when they were physically colocated ($M_{in} = 4.99$, $sd_{in} = 0.83$) than distant ($M_{out} = 4.09$, $sd_{out} = 1.40$). No other significant difference was found. **H3** is supported by these results.

Stress. Kruskal-Wallis tests did not show significant differences regarding all dimensions of the SSSQ: Engagement ($M_{alone} = 3.75$, $sd_{alone} = 1.13$; $M_{in} = 3.46$, $sd_{in} = 1.11$; $M_{out} = 3.54$, $sd_{out} = 1.30$), Worry ($M_{alone} = 1.78$, $sd_{alone} = 1.02$; $M_{in} = 1.99$, $sd_{in} = 1.17$; $M_{out} = 2.12$, $sd_{out} = 1.22$), and Distress ($M_{alone} = 1.83$, $sd_{alone} = 1.07$; $M_{in} = 1.69$, $sd_{in} = 1.03$; $M_{out} = 1.86$, $sd_{out} = 1.10$). **H2** and **H4** are not supported by these results. In other words, participants' stress levels were not significantly affected by audience location.

Cognitive Workload. The Kruskal-Wallis tests did not find significant differences regarding all dimensions of the RTLX ($M\epsilon[15.00; 62.00]$). **H2** and **H4** are not supported by these results. In other words, participants' workload was not significantly affected by audience location.

Presence. The one-way ANOVA test did not find significant differences: $M_{alone} = 3.5$, $sd_{alone} = 2.05$, $M_{in} = 4.10$, $sd_{in} = 1.88$, $M_{out} = 4.17$, $sd_{out} = 1.79$.

4   Discussion

The results show that the presence of examiners influenced the participant's natural performance improvement (i.e., answering time, and type of answers) when doing a repeated task. Firstly, objective measures show a significant improvement of correct answers within the time frame as well as a reduction of false and out of time answers. This can be explained by a natural improvement due to repetitions during the task. But the improvement is not the same between conditions. The interaction effects between the audience and the trials showed that the evolution within the time frame, positive or negative (depending of the objective measure) was slower when an audience was present compared to absent. The manifestation of social inhibition among users due to the presence of an audience seemed to result in a decrease of the natural performance evolution during this specific task. Our results are consistent with previous social inhibition studies [15]. Thus, **H1** is partially supported because results on answering time show no clear distinction between with or without audience. The only significant difference is between the distant and the colocated audience.

Secondly, social inhibition is not perceivable in cognitive workload and stress. The results of questionnaires did not demonstrate any differences despite the anxiety of the evaluation that could be induced by the examiners. Thus, **H2** is not supported. This result could be due to the variability of mathematical skill of participants [17]. Indeed, perception and resources used to perform the task may vary between participants. Unfortunately, mathematical aptitude was not evaluated in the current study.

Thirdly, results comparing the subjective perception of others between colocated (i.e., IN) and distant (i.e., OUT) audiences show significant differences. Participants seemed to perceive the examiners more significantly and seemed to feel more influenced by them when they were physically colocated than when they were distant. Thus, **H3** is supported. However, participants did not find significant differences between conditions that resulted in a negative influence. Moreover, the overall score of the negative influence of examiners was not high probably because examiners were passive during the experiment and did not cause any additional stress.

Finally, users' performance refutes **H4**. Statistical analysis present significant differences between conditions (i.e., IN, and OUT). Indeed, previous interaction effects (i.e., audience over trial) also show that the positive or negative evolution of the performance was even slower when users and audience were distant. Therefore, a stronger social inhibition seems to occur in distant users compared to users who were next to one another. This is most likely the explanation for the slower natural performance improvement (i.e., type of answers) of participants. The results seem to indicate that the reason users negatively experience their performance (when everyone is in the same real room) is not related to the extent to which they perceive or feel the presence of others. To sum up, the performance of participants seems to be affected by the presence of an audience and the type of the audience (i.e., IN, OUT). Furthermore, the significance of the perception of others seems to also depend on the type of the audience.

5   Conclusion

In this paper, we explored the effects of social inhibition induced by the presence of examiners on a user in a VE. In VR, the user had to perform a unknown and challenging task.

Analyses focused on performance, stress, users' cognitive workload and their perception of others. Three types of audience were evaluated: no-audience, physically colocated examiners embodied by avatars in the application, and physically distant examiners also embodied by avatars.

Firstly, the results show a difference between users' reactions when they are in the presence of others compared to no-audience in the VE. Indeed, the natural performance improvement occurred more slowly when the audience was colocated than with no audience, and even more slowly with a distant audience than a colocated audience. A slower improvement with a distant audience could be due to a weaker perception of others compared to a colocated audience.

More generally, users in VR seem to be affected by social inhibition in the presence of an audience, and they seem to be even more affected when the audience is physically distant, in a remote room. In this way a learning or training process using repetition could be influenced by an audience. Designers of such applications should pay attention to the setup before building the application. It could be interesting to explore the variation of the social inhibition through the same audience types but with a different task (e.g., fire drills, training for maintenance, evaluation of a service) or with an audience not present in the VE but physically present in the same room as the participant (e.g., a demonstration in an exhibition).

References

1. Blascovich, J., Loomis, J., Beall, A.C., Swinth, K.R., Hoyt, C.L., Bailenson, J.N.: Target article: immersive virtual environment technology as a methodological tool for social psychology. Psychol. Inq. **13**(2), 103–124 (2002)
2. Blascovich, J., Mendes, W.B., Hunter, S.B., Salomon, K.: Social "facilitation" as challenge and threat. J. Pers. Soc. Psychol. **77**(1), 68 (1999)
3. Bond, C.F., Titus, L.J.: Social facilitation: a meta-analysis of 241 studies. Psychol. Bull. **94**(2), 265 (1983)
4. Byers, J.C.: Traditional and raw task load index (TLX) correlations: are paired comparisons necessary? In: Advances in Industrial Ergonomics and Safety l. Taylor and Francis (1989)
5. Chartrand, T.L., Bargh, J.A.: The chameleon effect: the perception-behavior link and social interaction. J. Pers. Soc. Psychol. **76**(6), 893 (1999)
6. Claypoole, V.L., Dewar, A.R., Fraulini, N.W., Szalma, J.L.: Effects of social facilitation on perceived workload, subjective stress, and vigilance-related anxiety. In: Proceedings of the Human Factors and Ergonomics Society Annual Meeting, vol. 60, no. 1, pp. 1169–1173 (2016)
7. Cottrell, N.B., Wack, D.L., Sekerak, G.J., Rittle, R.H.: Social facilitation of dominant responses by the presence of an audience and the mere presence of others. J. Pers. Soc. Psychol. **9**(3), 245 (1968)
8. Dijksterhuis, A., Bargh, J.A.: The perception-behavior expressway: automatic effects of social perception on social behavior. In: Advances in Experimental Social Psychology, vol. 33, pp. 1–40. Academic Press (2001)
9. Emmerich, K., Masuch, M.: Watch me play: does social facilitation apply to digital games? In: Proceedings of the 2018 CHI Conference on Human Factors in Computing Systems, CHI 2018, pp. 100:1–100:12 (2018)
10. Gueorguieva, R., Krystal, J.H.: Move over anova: progress in analyzing repeated-measures data and its reflection in papers published in the archives of general psychiatry. Arch. Gen. Psychiatry **61**(3), 310–317 (2004)
11. Guerin, B., Innes, J.M.: Social facilitation and social monitoring: a new look at Zajonc's mere presence hypothesis. Br. J. Soc. Psychol. **21**(1), 7–18 (1982)
12. Guerin, B.: Mere presence effects in humans: a review. J. Exp. Soc. Psychol. **22**(1), 38–77 (1986)
13. Helton, W.S., Näswall, K.: Short stress state questionnaire. Eur. J. Psychol. Assess. **31**(1), 20–30 (2015)
14. Henchy, T., Glass, D.C.: Evaluation apprehension and the social facilitation of dominant and subordinate responses. J. Pers. Soc. Psychol. **10**(4), 446 (1968)
15. Hoyt, C.L., Blascovich, J., Swinth, K.R.: Social inhibition in immersive virtual environments. Presence: Teleoperators Virtual Environ. **12**(2), 183–195 (2003)

16. Innes, J.M., Young, R.F.: The effect of presence of an audience, evaluation apprehension and objective self-awareness on learning. J. Exp. Soc. Psychol. **11**(1), 35–42 (1975)
17. Jamieson, J.P., Peters, B.J., Greenwood, E.J., Altose, A.J.: Reappraising stress arousal improves performance and reduces evaluation anxiety in classroom exam situations. Soc. Psychol. Pers. Sci. **7**(6), 579–587 (2016)
18. Knowles, E.S.: Social physics and the effects of others: tests of the effects of audience size and distance on social judgments and behavior. J. Pers. Soc. Psychol. **45**(6), 1263 (1983)
19. Kushnir, T.: Stress and social facilitation: the effects of the presence of an instructor on student nurses' behaviour. J. Adv. Nurs. **11**(1), 13–19 (1986)
20. Lemoine, J.E., Roland-Lévy, C.: The effect of the presence of an audience on risk-taking while gambling: the social shield. Soc. Influence **12**(2–3), 101–114 (2017)
21. Sanchez-Vives, M.V., Slater, M.: From presence to consciousness through virtual reality. Nat. Rev. Neurosci. **6**(4), 332 (2005)
22. Schroeder, R.: Being there together and the future of connected presence. Presence: Teleoperators Virtual Environ. **15**(4), 438–454 (2006)
23. Skarratt, P.A., Cole, G.G., Kingstone, A.: Social inhibition of return. Acta Psychol. **134**(1), 48–54 (2010)
24. Slater, M., Sadagic, A., Usoh, M., Schroeder, R.: Small-group behavior in a virtual and real environment: a comparative study. Presence: Teleoperators Virtual Environ. **9**(1), 37–51 (2000)
25. Smeesters, D., Wheeler, S.C., Kay, A.C.: Indirect prime-to-behavior effects: the role of perceptions of the self, others, and situations in connecting primed constructs to social behavior. In: Advances in Experimental Social Psychology, vol. 42, pp. 259–317. Academic Press (2010)
26. Steed, A., Slater, M., Sadagic, A., Bullock, A., Tromp, J.: Leadership and collaboration in shared virtual environments. In: Proceedings IEEE Virtual Reality (Cat. No. 99CB36316), pp. 112–115, March 1999
27. Stotland, E., Zander, A.: Effects of public and private failure on self-evaluation. J. Abnorm. Soc. Psychol. **56**(2), 223–229 (1958)
28. Swinth, K.R., Blascovich, J.: Perceiving and responding to others: human-human and human-computer social interaction in collaborative virtual environments. In: Proceedings of the 5th Annual International Workshop on PRESENCE, vol. 392 (2002)
29. Usoh, M., Catena, E., Arman, S., Slater, M.: Using presence questionnaires in reality. Presence: Teleoperators Virtual Environ. **9**(5), 497–503 (2000)
30. Velho, L., Lucio, D., Carvalho, L.: Situated participatory virtual reality. In: Proceedings of XVI Simposio Brasileiro de Jogos e Entretenimento Digital (2017)
31. Wienrich, C., Gross, R., Kretschmer, F., Müller-Plath, G.: Developing and proving a framework for reaction time experiments in VR to objectively measure social interaction with virtual agents. In: 2018 IEEE Conference on Virtual Reality and 3D User Interfaces (VR), pp. 191–198, March 2018
32. Wolf, L.K., Bazargani, N., Kilford, E.J., Dumontheil, I., Blakemore, S.J.: The audience effect in adolescence depends on who's looking over your shoulder. J. Adolesc. **43**, 5–14 (2015)
33. Yu, R.F., Wu, X.: Working alone or in the presence of others: exploring social facilitation in baggage x-ray security screening tasks. Ergonomics **58**(6), 857–865 (2015)
34. Zajonc, R.B.: Social facilitation. Science **149**(3681), 269–274 (1965)

Video Sequence Boundary Labeling
with Temporal Coherence

Petr Bobák[1(✉)] , Ladislav Čmolík[2] , and Martin Čadík[1,2]

[1] Faculty of Information Technology, Brno University of Technology, Brno, Czechia
{ibobak,cadik}@fit.vutbr.cz
[2] Faculty of Electrical Engineering, Czech Technical University in Prague,
Prague, Czechia
{cmolikl,cadikm}@fel.cvut.cz

Abstract. We propose a method for video sequence boundary labeling which maintains the temporal coherence. The method is based on two ideas. We limit the movement of the label boxes only to the horizontal direction, and reserve free space for the movement of the label boxes in the label layout. The proposed method is able to position label boxes in video sequence on a lower number of rows than existing methods, while at the same time, it minimizes the movement of label boxes. We conducted an extensive user experiment where the proposed method was ranked the best for panorama video sequences labeling compared to three existing methods.

Keywords: Labeling · Boundary labeling · Temporal coherence

1 Introduction

Labels and short textual annotations, are used to communicate the position of objects together with additional information about them (e.g., names of the objects) in a single image. The position of the labels in relation to the labeled objects (i.e., the label layout) is crucial for functional labeling. In this work, we focus on boundary labeling, where the labeled objects are approximated with points denoted as anchors. The labels are enclosed in label boxes positioned on the top side of the scene so that no pair of label boxes overlaps. The labels are associated with the labeled objects by vertical leader lines that interconnect the label boxes with the anchors.

We specifically focus on boundary labeling of panorama video sequences. Imagine a footage from a drone flying through the mountain terrain (or a city full of skyscrapers). The labels and corresponding positions of mountain summits can be obtained from geo-referred terrain models using camera pose estimation techniques [2]. For various panorama boundary labeling examples see Fig. 2. Creating label layouts for such video sequences introduce the problem of *temporal coherence* of the resulting label layouts. In other words, the labels should not

© Springer Nature Switzerland AG 2019
M. Gavrilova et al. (Eds.): CGI 2019, LNCS 11542, pp. 40–52, 2019.
https://doi.org/10.1007/978-3-030-22514-8_4

jump abruptly from one position to another, but should keep their positions or move in a predictable manner.

In this work, we present three main contributions: (1) A novel algorithm designed both for video sequences and images. The algorithm is capable of positioning the labels on a lower number of rows than existing algorithms, making the label layout more compact in vertical direction. (2) For video sequences the algorithm minimizes movement of the labels during playback of the sequences. If the labels move during the playback, they move in a predictable manner. (3) We present the results of a user study designed to evaluate label layouts of panorama video sequences. In the study we have evaluated our algorithm against three existing boundary labeling methods. The results of the study show that the proposed method is preferred over the other three methods with statistical significance.

2   Related Work

In this section, we divide the boundary labeling methods into two groups based on the flexibility of the label boxes. Finally, we discuss methods that provide temporally coherent movement of the label boxes.

The methods working with *fixed labels* take as the input a set of anchors and a set of label boxes positioned on top of the scene. The task is to assign one label box to each label and connect each label box with the corresponding anchor with a leader line. Bekos et al. [3] introduced a method for boundary labeling where a set of anchor points is connected with a set of predefined label boxes positioned in one or up to three rows with rectilinear leader lines. The method finds the leader lines whose combined length is minimal. Benkert et al. [5] later showed that better label layouts can be produced if we consider criteria such as the number of bends of the leader lines and distance between the leader lines, in addition to the length of the leader lines criterion.

The methods that work with *flexible labels* take as the input a set of anchor points only. The task is to determine positions of the label boxes and connect each label box with the corresponding anchor with a leader line. Maass and Döllner [15] presented two methods that produce panorama label layouts. In both methods the labels are processed according to the distance of the labeled objects from the camera and the label box is centered with respect to the vertical leader line. Gemsa et al. [10] presented an optimization method that for a set of anchor points positions the label boxes on the lowest possible number of rows using dynamic programming. Each label box is connected with a corresponding anchor point with vertical leader line and no leader line intersects any label box.

The methods that are addressing the temporally coherent movement of label boxes strive to determine such label boxes that do not change their positions abruptly and move in a predictable manner. Götzelmann et al. [11] focus on the labeling of animated 3D objects such as engines with moving pistons. Čmolík and Bittner [7] proposed real-time external labeling technique for 3D objects where the label boxes are moving coherently during slow interaction (e.g., rotation) with the scene. Vaaraniemi et al. [22] first determine positions of label boxes in a 3D space and during interaction with the scene use a force based approach to resolve overlaps of the labels. Maass and Döllner [15] and Tatzgern et al. [20] proposed similar hysteresis approaches to make the movement of label boxes temporally coherent. Kouřil et al. [13] proposed another hysteresis approach adapted for internal label boxes.

Unfortunately, none of the approaches is applicable to the panorama video sequence labeling problem, where a small movement of one label box can decrease the free space available for another label box which in turn can lead to an abrupt change in the position of the label box. Consequently, the change in position can again limit free space available for another label box.

3   Problem Definition

In this section we define the video sequence boundary labeling problem. The input is a video sequence S with $|S|$ frames and a set of label boxes $\mathcal{L}$. Each frame $f_i, i \in 1 \ldots |S|$ has the same width w_S and height h_S. Each label box $l_k \in \mathcal{L}$ is visible at least in one frame in the video sequence and has defined width w_{l_k}, height h_{l_k}, and text t_{l_k}. The height h_{l_k} is constant for all label boxes in $\mathcal{L}$.

Each frame f_i has a set of anchors A where each anchor a_j has its position $(x_{a_j}, y_{a_j}), j \in 1 \ldots |A|$ and a set of label boxes $L \subseteq \mathcal{L}$ where each label box l_j is associated with the anchor a_j. The task is to find a position of each label box $l \in L$ associated with each anchor $a \in A$ of each frame $f \in S$ so that the label boxes fulfill the following requirements for the video sequence boundary labeling problem:

1. The label boxes are aligned to rows starting from the defined line hl_S, e.g., the horizon.
2. The label boxes do not overlap with each other.
3. [Optional] The positions of label boxes should correspond to distances of the labeled objects from the camera. The closest label boxes should be in the lowest row.
4. The label boxes should be positioned on the lowest number of rows possible.

5. The label boxes are connected with the corresponding anchors with vertical leader lines.
6. The leader line is connected to the label box as close to the center of the label box as possible.
7. The movement of the label boxes through the video sequence is temporally coherent. In other words, vertical and horizontal movement of the label boxes is minimized across all the frames in the sequence S.

4   Temporally Coherent Labeling Method

Our approach is based on two fundamental ideas: (1) we restrict the movement of the label boxes only in a horizontal direction and (2) we reserve space for the horizontal movement of the label boxes in the label layout. This way the movement of one label box cannot influence the movement of any other label box, thus requirement 7 is fulfilled. To reserve the space for movement of the label boxes in the label layout, we propose to:

- Create an anchor interval $\alpha_i = [min_{\alpha_i}, max_{\alpha_i}]$ and calculate an average camera-to-anchor distance d_{α_i} for each label box $l_i \in \mathcal{L}$ where min_{α_i} and max_{α_i} are the minimal and maximal x-coordinates of anchors that are associated with the label box l_i through all the frames of the sequence S (see Fig. 1(a)). Similarly, the distance d_{α_i} is the average distance of the anchors that are associated with the label box l_i through all the frames of sequence S.
- Create a label box interval $\lambda_i = [min_{\lambda_i}, max_{\lambda_i}]$ for each label box $l_i \in \mathcal{L}$ where the width of the label box interval $w_{\lambda_i} = \max(max_{\alpha_i} - min_{\alpha_i}, w_{l_i})$. The label box interval λ_i is associated with the anchor interval α_i, thus $d_{\lambda_i} = d_{\alpha_i}$ (see Fig. 1(a)).

In order to determine a temporally coherent labeling of the given sequence S, we need to solve the following two subproblems.

1. *Label box interval to row assignment:* Determine the row r and left bound min_{λ_i} of the label box interval λ_i (then $max_{\lambda_i} = min_{\lambda_i} + w_{\lambda_i}$) for each label box $l_i \in \mathcal{L}$ so that the label box intervals fulfill the requirements 1–5 from Sect. 3. Please note that this subproblem is solved only once for the given sequence S. See Fig. 1(a) for an example of a label box to row assignment.
2. *Within row label box placement:* Determine the offset o_i between the x-coordinate of anchor x_{a_i} and the x-origin min_{l_i} of the label box l_i (origin refers to lower left corner) for any given frame $f \in S$. This reflects the requirements 2 and 5–6 from Sect. 3. Please note that this subproblem is solved for each frame of the given sequence S. See Fig. 1(a) for an example of label box placement in each row.

4.1   Label Box Interval to Row Assignment

We formulate the problem as a mixed-integer nonlinear programming (MINLP), which combines combinatorial optimization over binary variables with nonlinear optimization over continuous variables [4].

The instance of MINLP is formulated as the minimization of the objective function F_1 with respect to decision variables $I^r_{\lambda_i}$ and min_{λ_i} (the latter is considered in constraints). The objective function is defined as

$$F_1 = \sum_{i=1}^{|\mathcal{L}|} \sum_{r=1}^{R} I^r_{\lambda_i} \hat{r} + I^r_{\lambda_i} \delta(\hat{d}_{\lambda_i}, \hat{r}), \tag{1}$$

where $I^r_{\lambda_i} \in \{0,1\}$ is a binary variable that indicates if the label box interval λ_i is placed in row r and enforces the requirement 1. We consider at the most

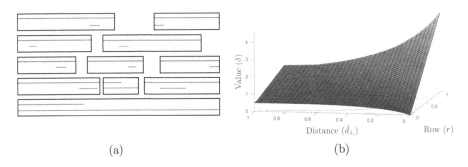

Fig. 1. (a) Graphical visualization of the label box intervals λ_i (boxes) in an example of video sequence. The red solid line inside the box shows the corresponding anchors interval α_i, the blue solid line represents the label width w_{l_i}. (b) Function δ with $c_1 = 0.1$, $c_2 = 0.8$ and $c_3 = 0.5$. (Color figure online)

$R = |\mathcal{L}|$ rows. The hat modifier in the above given variable (e.g., $\hat{d}_{\lambda_i}$) denotes the unity-based normalized value of that variable. The product in the first term of F_1 supports the requirement 4. The function $\delta(\hat{d}_{\lambda_i}, \hat{r})$ in the second term of F_1 is defined as

$$\delta(\hat{d}_{\lambda_i}, \hat{r}) = \frac{|\hat{r} - c_1\hat{d}_{\lambda_i}| + |c_2\hat{r} - \hat{d}_{\lambda_i}| + c_3|\hat{r} - \hat{d}_{\lambda_i}|}{(\hat{d}_{\lambda_i} + c_2)^2} \tag{2}$$

and supports the requirement 3. The purpose of the δ function is to a establish relation between normalized distance $\hat{d}_{\lambda_i}$ and the row r where the label box interval λ_i and the corresponding label box interval α_i is placed.

The constants c_1, c_2 and c_3 were selected experimentally with the requirement 3 in mind. We have achieved the best results with $c_1 = 0.1$, $c_2 = 0.8$ and $c_3 = 0.5$, see Fig. 1(b). Note that the function $\delta(\hat{d}_{\lambda_i}, \hat{r})$ is the reason why F_1 is a nonlinear objective function. If the second term is omitted (requirement 3 is optional), then the problem formulation is reduced to MILP.

In order to fulfill the requirement 2, we define the following four objective constraints. First, we define the constraint for an overlap restriction as

$$min_{\lambda_i} + w_{\lambda_i} \leq min_{\lambda_j} + M \cdot (1 - I^r_{\lambda_i}) + M \cdot (1 - I^r_{\lambda_j}), \tag{3}$$

where we define the order so that $min_{\alpha_i} \leq min_{\alpha_j} \wedge l_i \neq l_j$ and $l_i, l_j \in \mathcal{L}$. This constraint only needs to be applied in the case that both label box intervals are in the same row r which is indicated by the binary decision variables $I^r_{\lambda_i}$ and $I^r_{\lambda_j}$. The use of a binary variable to activate and deactivate the constraint is a well-known trick in MILP [6,10]. The constant M needs to be sufficiently large in order to deactivate the constraint (i.e., the constraint is always true for any combination of λ_i and λ_j that are not in the same row). We set M equal to the frame width w_S, which works well in our experiments.

From the definition of the label box interval λ_i and from the requirement 5 it follows that the interval must completely overlap its associated anchor interval

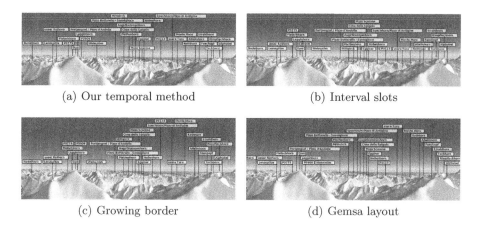

(a) Our temporal method   (b) Interval slots

(c) Growing border   (d) Gemsa layout

Fig. 2. Four different panorama label layouts calculated for the mountain tops.

α_i. Therefore, we introduce constraints to enforce that α_i is the sub-interval of λ_i as $min_{\lambda_i} \leq min_{\alpha_i}$ and $min_{\lambda_i} + w_{\lambda_i} \geq max_{\alpha_i}$.

Finally, only one variable $I^r_{\lambda_i}$ for the label box interval λ_i is allowed to be 1. This reflects that λ_i is allowed to occupy only one row. We define this restriction as $\sum_{r=1}^{R} I^r_{\lambda_i} = 1$.

4.2   Within Row Label Box Placement

We formulate the subproblem as a convex quadratic programming (QP). When each label box interval is assigned to a row and its left bound min_{λ_i} is set, it remains for us to determine the positions of each label box for a given frame f so that the requirements 2 and 5–6 are fulfilled. The instance of QP is formulated as the minimization of the objective function F_2 with respect to the offset decision variable o_i. The objective function for the given frame f is defined as

$$F_2 = \sum_{a_i \in A} \left(o_i - \frac{w_{l_i}}{2} \right)^2. \tag{4}$$

The function F_2 enforces requirement 6 only. In order to enforce requirements 2 and 5, we need to define objective constraints.

To enforce requirement 2, we define a constraint for each pair of label boxes l_i and l_j associated with anchors a_i and a_j in the given frame f as $x_{a_i} - o_i + w_{l_i} \leq x_{a_j} - o_j$, where we suppose an order so that $x_{a_i} < x_{a_j} \wedge l_i \neq l_j$. Furthermore, in order to fulfill requirement 5 we define the constraints $o_i \geq 0$ and $o_i \leq w_{l_i}$. Finally, we want to restrict a label box overflow with vertical bounds defined by width w_S of the given frame. This is accomplished by a pair of constraints $x_{a_i} - o_i \geq 0$ and $x_{a_i} - o_i + w_{l_i} \leq w_S$.

5   Results

We used GUROBI 8.0 with a MATLAB interface as optimization solver. The running time needed to solve the subproblem 1 (*label box interval to row assignment*) is approximately 1.5 s (for 40 labels), and the optimal solution for smaller instances (20 labels and less) is found in less than 200 ms. The measurement was performed for one video sequence on Intel® Core i5-3570 @ 3.40 GHz with 24 GB RAM (for more details please see the supplementary material[1]). However, since even the MILP is NP-hard, the computational time for MILP (and consequently MINLP) can vary from sequence to sequence and can grow significantly an increasing number of binary variables (i.e., with the number of labels) [4,9]. The solution is accepted as optimal when optimality gap (relative distance between the best known solution and bound) is less than 0.01%. The solver applies several primal heuristics and a branch-and-cut algorithm with different types of cutting planes (e.g., Gomory, MIR, StrongCG) to solve the MINLP problem [12].

The optimization in the subproblem 2 (*within row label box placement*) is defined as convex QP, thus it can be solved in polynomial time [23]. Furthermore, the label box placement can be solved independently for each row, hence the optimization is prompt and highly parallelizable.

We have implemented three existing methods (*gemsa* [10], *growing border* [15], and *interval slots* [15] methods) to compare them with the proposed method. The label layouts produced with these methods are in Fig. 2(b)–(d).

We have calculated the maximum number of rows in the layout for all implemented methods for three video sequences with a minimum length of 100 frames. The results show that the *temporal method* achieves the best results (see Fig. 3(a)). For the temporally coherent movement of the label boxes, it is crucial that the label boxes do not jump abruptly. Therefore, we have calculated the *displacement metric* for all implemented methods (see Fig. 3(b) and (c)). We calculate the displacement as the difference in the position of the given label between two subsequent frames. We calculate the displacement in x and y direction separately. The results suggest that labels in our proposed methods are more temporally coherent than in the other reviewed methods. The greatest discrepancy is visible for the y-displacement, where the labels placed using our methods are fixed in a single row.

6   User Experiments

We have conducted an evaluation with users to assess if our *temporal method* (1) improves the ability of the user to follow the label boxes in time, (2) how it influences the ability of the label layout to mediate the interconnection between the labels and the labeled objects, and (3) if the users prefer such a label layout to the other layouts.

---

[1] Supplementary material: http://cphoto.fit.vutbr.cz/panorama-labeling/.

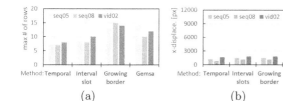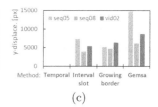

(a)   (b)   (c)

Fig. 3. The maximum number of rows per video sequence determines the vertical compactness of the labeling (a). Total label displacement per video sequence in x-axis (b) and y-axis (c). The y-displacement for the *temporal* method is zero.

For the evaluation, we have created a web application which the participants accessed through a web browser. First, each participant was instructed about the testing procedure; then, the participant provided their age and gender. The evaluation was divided into two experiments.

6.1 Experiment 1 – Accuracy

In the first experiment, we assessed the impact of the label layout on the users accuracy in the object-label and label-object assignment tasks. The experiment was one factor with four levels. The independent variable was the labeling method. In the evaluation, we used four methods to calculate the label layouts: *gemsa*, *growing border*, *interval slots*, and our *temporal* methods. We calculated the label layouts for three video sequences.

The experiment was designed as a between-subject. In other words, one participant was tested with only one labeling method to eliminate the learning effect and fatigue. For each participant, the order of video sequences was counterbalanced with a 3 × 3 balanced Latin square [16, Section 5.11] to eliminate the carry-over effect.

The first experiment consisted of a sequence of three tasks defined as follows. Task 1: Find the label associated to a highlighted anchor. Task 2: Find the anchor associated to a highlighted label. Task 3: Follow a certain moving label for 2 seconds and then select the label. For a detailed description of the tasks, please see the supplementary material of this paper.

Each participant repeated each task 10 times for each video sequence. We measured the *error rate* (the number of wrongly selected labels/anchors relative to all selected labels/anchors). After each video sequence we have conducted a subjective evaluation of the easiness of the visual search (task 1–3), the confidence (task 1–2) and the need to focus (task 3). The participants provided their subjective evaluation on Likert scales from 1 to 5.

Task 1 and its subjective evaluation was completed by 60 participants (12 females) with the age ranging from 19 to 54 years ($\bar{x} = 25.31$; $\sigma = 6.49$). Task 2 and its subjective evaluation was completed by 49 participants (11 females) with the age ranging from 19 to 54 years ($\bar{x} = 25.86$; $\sigma = 7.04$). Finally, task

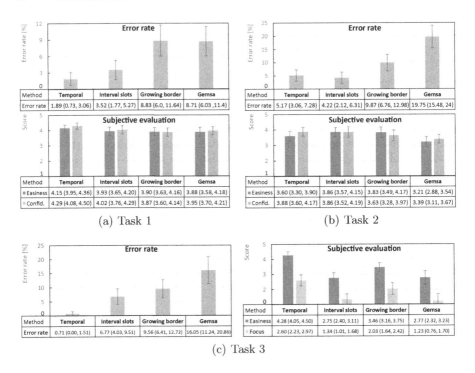

(a) Task 1   (b) Task 2

(c) Task 3

Fig. 4. Results of the Experiment 1 – Accuracy: Error rate and subjective evaluation for the task 1 (a), task 2 (b), and task 3 (c).

3 and its subjective evaluation was completed by 44 participants (10 females) with the age ranging from 19 to 54 years ($\bar{x} = 26.32$; $\sigma = 7.29$).

We evaluated the collected data for all video sequences together. We performed a statistical evaluation of the measured data using confidence intervals. We transformed the measured number of errors onto error rates with the LaPlace method [14] and calculated the confidence intervals of the error rates as adjusted Wald intervals, a method recommended for completion rates [1,18]. We calculated the confidence intervals for Likert scales as confidence intervals for rating scales [19, Chapter 3]. We use 95% confidence intervals for error rates, completion times and Likert scales. When the confidence intervals are disjointed, we can report that the means of the measured data are significantly different.

For tasks 1 and 2, the average error rates and average score from subjective evaluation together with their 95% confidence intervals are shown in Fig. 4(a) and (b). For task 3, the average error rates, and average scores from the subjective evaluation, together with their 95% confidence intervals, are shown in Fig. 4(c).

For task 1, the results show that the *temporal* and *interval slots* methods achieve a significantly lower error rate than the *growing border* and *gemsa* methods. For task 2, the results show that the *temporal* and *interval slots* methods achieve a significantly lower error than the *gemsa* method. Furthermore, the *interval slots* method achieves a significantly lower error than the *growing bor-*

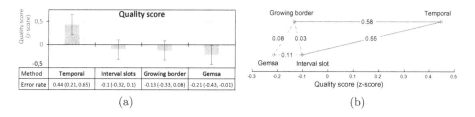

Fig. 5. (a) Overall quality scores. (b) Statistical significance and quality scores.

der method. The participant stated that the task 2 was significantly easier with the *interval slots* method than with the *gemsa* method. For task 3, the results show that the *temporal* method achieved significantly lower error rate than the other methods. In the subjective evaluation, the participants reported that the task 3 was significantly easier to complete with the *temporal* method than with the other methods. Furthermore, the participants reported that they had to focus significantly less with the *temporal* method than with the *interval slot* and *gemsa* methods. We have not detected any other significant differences between the methods.

In general, the results show that due to temporally coherent movement of the label boxes, our *temporal* method allows us to follow label boxes moving in time significantly accurately than the other methods. At the same time, our *temporal* method mediates the interconnection between the labels and the labeled objects, the same as or better than the other methods.

6.2 Experiment 2 – Preference

To assess the users preferences among different label layouts, we have conducted the subjective experiment using a psychophysical technique of paired comparisons [8,21]. We have used specifically the two-interval forced choice (2IFC) experiment paradigm to verify the overall quality of labeling methods (*gemsa, growing border, interval slot, temporal*) where the number of methods is denoted as $m = 4$. We chose set of $s = 3$ video sequences. For single given video sequence each participant had to compare $\binom{m}{2} = 6$ pairs – all possible combinations of m methods. A total of 40 participants (10 females) with the age ranging from 19 to 54 years ($\bar{x} = 26.61$; $\sigma = 7.46$) completed in total 240 parwise-comparisons. For each participant, the order of the pairs of methods to compare was counterbalanced with a 6×6 balanced Latin square [16, Section 5.11] to eliminate learning and carry-over effects.

The data were stored in count matrix $\mathbf{C}$ with a $m \times m$ shape for each participant. The element c_{ij} represents the number of times that method i was selected better than method j. We converted the participant matrices $\mathbf{C}$ into interval quality score (z-score) scale and computed a statistical significance using customized MATLAB framework [17].

In order to convert the count matrix $\mathbf{C}$ to the interval quality score scale the Thurstone's Law of Comparative Judgment model is used with respect to Case V [17,21]. In order to reject the null hypothesis H_0, where the difference in perceived quality scores is zero, we applied the Two-tailed test at a significance level $\alpha = 0.05$.

The overall quality score is depicted in Fig. 5(a). The results for panorama video sequence labeling, using our proposed *temporal* method, exhibit the best quality score, followed by *interval slot* and *growing border*. The worst perceived method is considered the *gemsa* method.

The statistical significance for surveyed methods is presented in Fig. 5(b). The results show that difference between our *temporal* method and the rest of the surveyed methods is statistically significant. Thus, we can reject the null hypothesis H_0 in the *temporal*-other pairs. However, H_0 can not be rejected for the other-other pairs. This means that we have not detected significant difference in perceived quality among the *interval slot, growing border* and *gemsa* methods.

7 Conclusions

We proposed a novel method for video sequence boundary labeling using optimization. We compared the method with three other methods in an extensive user study. The results of the study show that with our method, the users are able to follow moving label boxes significantly more accurately than with the concurrent methods. At the same time, our method mediates the interconnection between the labels and the labeled objects the same as or better than the other methods. The proposed method was ranked the best for the boundary labeling of panorama video sequences by participants of the study. In other words, the proposed method should be preferred for the labeling of the panorama video sequences to the other methods.

Acknowledgements. This work was supported by Research Center for Informatics No. CZ.02.1.01/0.0/0.0/16_019/0000765; by V3C – "Visual Computing Competence Center" by Technology Agency of the Czech Republic, project no. TE01020415; by the Ministry of Education, Youth and Sports of the Czech Republic within the activity MOBILITY (MSMT-539/2017-1) ID: 7AMB17AT021, and from the "National Programme of Sustainability (NPU II) project IT4Innovations excellence in science - LQ1602"; and by the IT4Innovations infrastructure which is supported from the Large Infrastructures for Research, Experimental Development and Innovations project "IT4Innovations National Supercomputing Center - LM2015070". Access to computing and storage facilities owned by parties and projects contributing to the National Grid Infrastructure MetaCentrum provided under the programme "Projects of Large Research, Development, and Innovations Infrastructures" (CESNET LM2015042).

References

1. Agresti, A., Coull, B.A.: Approximate is better than 'exact' for interval estimation of binomial proportions. Am. Stat. **52**(2), 119–126 (1998)
2. Baboud, L., Čadík, M., Eisemann, E., Seidel, H.P.: Automatic photo-to-terrain alignment for the annotation of mountain pictures. In: CVPR 2011, pp. 41–48. IEEE Computer Society, Washington, DC (2011)
3. Bekos, M.A., Kaufmann, M., Potika, K., Symvonis, A.: Multi-stack boundary labeling problems. WSEAS Trans. Comput. **5**(11), 2602–2607 (2006)
4. Belotti, P., Kirches, C., Leyffer, S., Linderoth, J., Luedtke, J., Mahajan, A.: Mixed Integer Nonlinear Programming. Cambridge University Press, Cambridge (2012)
5. Benkert, M., Haverkort, H., Kroll, M., Nöllenburg, M.: Algorithms for multi-criteria one-sided boundary labeling. In: Hong, S.-H., Nishizeki, T., Quan, W. (eds.) GD 2007. LNCS, vol. 4875, pp. 243–254. Springer, Heidelberg (2008). https://doi.org/10.1007/978-3-540-77537-9_25
6. Chen, D.S., Batson, R.G., Dang, Y.: Applied Integer Programming: Modeling and Solution. Wiley, Hoboken (2011)
7. Čmolík, L., Bittner, J.: Layout-aware optimization for interactive labeling of 3D models. Comput. Graph. **34**(4), 378–387 (2010)
8. David, H.: The Method of Paired Comparisons. Griffin's Statistical Monographs & Courses, C. Griffin (1988)
9. Garey, M.R., Johnson, D.S.: Computers and Intractability; A Guide to the Theory of NP-Completeness. W. H. Freeman & Co., New York (1990)
10. Gemsa, A., Haunertand, J.H., Nöllenburg, M.: Multi-row boundary-labeling algorithms for panorama images. ACM TSAS **1**(1), 289–298 (2014)
11. Götzelmann, T., Hartmann, K., Strothotte, T.: Annotation of animated 3D objects. In: SimVis. SCS, pp. 209–222. Publishing House (2007)
12. Gurobi Optimization, LLC: Advanced Gurobi Algorithms (2016). http://www.gurobi.com/pdfs/user-events/2016-frankfurt/Die-Algorithmen.pdf
13. Kouřil, D., et al.: Labels on levels: labeling of multi-scale multi-instance and crowded 3D biological environments. IEEE TVCG **25**(1), 977–986 (2019)
14. Lewis, J.R., Sauro, J.: When 100% really isn't 100%: improving the accuracy of small-sample estimates of completion rates. J. Usability Stud. **1**(3), 136–150 (2006)
15. Maass, S., Döllner, J.: Efficient view management for dynamic annotation placement in virtual landscapes. In: Butz, A., Fisher, B., Krüger, A., Olivier, P. (eds.) SG 2006. LNCS, vol. 4073, pp. 1–12. Springer, Heidelberg (2006). https://doi.org/10.1007/11795018_1
16. MacKenzie, I.S.: Human-Computer Interaction: An Empirical Research Perspective. Newnes, Oxford (2012)
17. Perez-Ortiz, M., Mantiuk, R.K.: A practical guide and software for analysing pairwise comparison experiments (2017). http://arxiv.org/abs/1712.03686
18. Sauro, J., Lewis, J.R.: Estimating completion rates from small samples using binomial confidence intervals: comparisons and recommendations. In: Proceedings of the Human Factors and Ergonomics Society Annual Meeting, vol. 49, no. 24, pp. 2100–2103. SAGE Publications, Thousand Oaks (2005)
19. Sauro, J., Lewis, J.R.: Quantifying the User Experience: Practical Statistics for User Research. Elsevier, Amsterdam (2012)
20. Tatzgern, M., Kalkofen, D., Grasset, R., Schmalstieg, D.: Hedgehog labeling: view management techniques for external labels in 3D space. In: 2014 IEEE Virtual Reality, pp. 27–32 (2014)

21. Tsukida, K., Gupta, M.R.: How to analyze paired comparison data. UWEE Technical report 206 (2011)
22. Vaaraniemi, M., Treib, M., Westermann, R.: Temporally coherent real-time labeling of dynamic scenes. In: Proceedings of the 3rd International Conference on Computing for Geospatial Research and Applications, COM.Geo 2012, pp. 17:1–17:10. ACM, New York (2012)
23. Ye, Y., Tse, E.: An extension of Karmarkar's projective algorithm for convex quadratic programming. Math. Program. **44**(1), 157–179 (1989)

Two-Layer Feature Selection Algorithm for Recognizing Human Emotions from 3D Motion Analysis

Ferdous Ahmed[(✉)] and Marina L. Gavrilova

University of Calgary, Calgary, AB, Canada
{ferdous.ahmed1,mgavrilo}@ucalgary.ca

Abstract. Research on automatic recognition of human emotion from motion is gaining momentum, especially in the areas of virtual reality, robotics, behavior modeling, and biometric identity recognition. One of the challenges is to identify emotion-specific features from a vast number of expressive descriptors of human motion. In this paper, we have developed a novel framework for emotion classification using motion features. We combined a filter-based feature selection algorithm and a genetic algorithm to recognize four basic emotions: happiness, sadness, fear, and anger. The validity of the proposed framework was confirmed on a dataset containing 30 subjects performing expressive walking sequences. Our proposed framework achieved a very high recognition rate outperforming existing state-of-the-art methods in the literature.

Keywords: Emotion recognition · Kinect sensor · Gait analysis · Human motion · Genetic algorithm · Feature selection

1 Introduction

Emotion recognition based on human body movement is an emerging area of research. Recent studies have linked specific body movements and postures to emotion [28]. Currently, more research efforts are focused on improving the system's ability to distinguish nonverbal cues expressed through body movements. A computer system capable of predicting emotion through observation can drastically enhance the quality of social interaction with humans [19,25]. Recently, Tahir et al. in [26] used a robot as a social mediator to increase the quality of human-robot interaction. Application of emotion recognition in biometric security domain includes body movement and facial expression analysis for video surveillance [1,30]. Application of emotion recognition in medical domain includes identification of signature behavior of patients having specific psychological conditions [10].

Over the years, researchers attempted to recognize emotions from various modalities such as the face, head, body and hand [24,27]. However, as described in paper [7], very few studies (less than 5%) have focused on whole-body expressions for emotion analysis. Several reasons exist for using body movement as a

M. Gavrilova et al. (Eds.): CGI 2019, LNCS 11542, pp. 53–67, 2019.
https://doi.org/10.1007/978-3-030-22514-8_5

viable modality for emotion recognition. De Gelder stated in paper [7] that the performance of body expression is on par with static and dynamic face stimuli among human observers. A computer model may even exceed the performance of a human observer since it can detect subtle motion changes not readily apparent to the human. Moreover, data acquisition of the body expression is noninvasive compared to other modalities and more immune to the problem of occlusion. Over the years, researchers have successfully developed a large number of motion descriptors. The goal of this research is to identify human motion features which will predict the intention and the emotional state of an individual. The basic concept is to create a comprehensive list of motion features, that encompasses all nuanced movements relevant to the emotional state of the individual [17]. However, it is not a trivial task. One of the significant challenges is to compute the relevance of the motion features to a specific emotion. The computational model can be trained focusing only on relevant features.

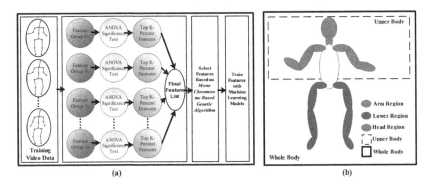

Fig. 1. (a) An overview of the proposed framework for emotion recognition from body motion features. (b) An overview of the body segmentation for feature extraction.

In this paper, a filter-based feature selection algorithm ANOVA (analysis of variance) [11] was used to select some of the features based on the measure of relevance. Several popular feature ranking algorithms were investigated, including mutual information (MI) [22], Chi-squared score [21], ReliefF [21] and ensemble of tree-based algorithm. Based on two criteria: monotonicity and reliability, ANOVA was chosen to be the best feature selection algorithm. Based on the significance test of ANOVA, only some of the relevant features were selected from each group describing a quality of human motion. Finally, a mono-chromosome based genetic algorithm was utilized to extract a feature subset maximizing emotion recognition rate. Then supervised machine learning algorithms previously proved to be effective in the biometric domain, was used to recognize human emotions. Based on the proposed framework, we achieved 83.33% emotion recognition rate using Linear Discriminant Analysis (LDA), which outperforms other state-of-the-art approaches experimented on this dataset. The overall contributions of the presented research are summarized as follows:

- Introduction of a novel framework for emotion recognition that employs a two-step process for feature selection.
- Development of a two-layer feature selection algorithm that combines the power of a traditional filter-based feature selection algorithm and a genetic algorithm.
- Identification of the most relevant motion features for emotion recognition from a comprehensive list of motion features.
- Introduction of several new temporal features that exhibited improvements over existing temporal features.
- Organization of motion features into disparate groups and computation of relevance for each feature groups.

The strength of the proposed framework was validated on a proprietary dataset containing 30 subjects.

2 Previous Work

Emotion can be expressed through eye gaze direction, iris extension, postural features or movement of the human body [19]. Pollick et al. in [20] showed that arm movements are significantly correlated with the pleasantness dimension of the emotion model. Bianchi-Berthouze et al. in [5], introduced an incremental learning model through gestural cues and a contextual feedback system to self-organize postural features into discrete emotion categories. Several researchers attempted to recognize emotion from dance movement. Camurri et al. in [6] extracted the quantity of motion and contraction index from 2D video images depicting dance movements of the subjects to recognize discrete emotion categories. Very recently, Durupinar et al. in [8] conducted a perceptual study to establish a relationship between the LMA features and the five personality traits of a human. Recently, researchers have also focused on recognizing emotion in arbitrary recording scenarios using deep learning architectures [16].

One of the biggest challenges of emotion recognition is the high dimensionality representation of the motion features. Also, the literature provides very little guidance as to what type of motion features are suitable for emotion classification. Therefore, most of the methods are biased towards a particular set of motion features. For instance, Glowinski et al. in [12] extracted energy, spatial extent, symmetry and smoothness related features and then used Principal Component Analysis (PCA) to create a minimal representation of affective gestures. In paper [9], authors used a similar approach to reduce the dimension. Senecal et al. in [24], analyzed body motion expression in theater performance based on LMA features. The researchers also used a multilayer perceptron to visualize the emotion on Russell's Circumplex model. Saha et al. in [23], manually picked nine features related to velocity, acceleration and angular features to identify six emotions. In order to eliminate irrelevant features before applying any model, two general categories of feature selection algorithms are used: filter-based and wrapper-based approaches [29]. Typical filter-based technique includes

ReliefF based approaches [21], information theoretic approaches [22], statistical approaches [21] and ensemble of decision tree-based approaches. Feature subset from the relevant list of features can be selected using recently proposed genetic algorithm based framework [3].

3   Proposed Methodology

3.1   Overview

The main component of the proposed framework involved a two-layer feature selection process as shown in Fig. 1. In the first layer, irrelevant features calculated using ANOVA were discarded. The first layer cannot ensure optimum model performance based on all the relevant features. Therefore, the objective of the second layer is to find the best subset of features from the output of the first layer. The first step of the methodology involved the extraction of various low-level and high-level geometric and kinematic features previously developed for 3D motion synthesis, classification, and indexing [14]. As researchers have yet to establish a consensus on the right combination of various motion features specific to emotion, this paper extracted a comprehensive list of motion features. The low-level features were computed either on a single frame or over a sequence of frames spanned over a short period, characterizing various aspects of human motion [17]. The high-level features are derived from low-level spatial, geometric and kinematic features that are semantically meaningful to movement experts and suitable for perceptual evaluations. These features were grouped into eleven disparate groups described in Sect. 3.2. Spatial discretization (specific joint or a set of joints) and temporal discretization (single frame versus a group of consecutive frames) was applied to some motion features. A temporal profile consisting of twelve different statistical values were also obtained for a subset of these motion features. A one-way variance analysis was conducted on the set of features belonging to each of the motion feature group. The features that failed to pass the significance test (p-value < 0.005) were discarded immediately. Then, based on a threshold (a model parameter to control the number of extracted features), a predefined percentage of top relevant features were extracted for the second step of the process. The second step involved using a genetic algorithm to identify the optimal feature subset, that maximizes the emotion recognition rate. The number of generations was kept to 1000 to restrict the overall computation.

3.2   Feature Extraction

Based on a thorough analysis of the existing literature, a comprehensive list of 3D motion features was extracted. These features were grouped into eleven unique categories minimizing the number of overlapping features as much as possible.

- **Group of Features 1.** This group of features consists of low-level feature descriptors, that measure the speed of the motion such as velocity, acceleration, and jerk. If X defines a motion that is described as n consecutive poses, where $X = x(t_1), x(t_2), x(t_3), ..., x(t_n)$. Then velocity is defined as [17]:

$$v(t_i) = \frac{X(t_{i+1}) - X(t_i)}{2\delta t} \tag{1}$$

and the magnitude of the velocity is defined as follows:

$$v(t_i) = \sqrt{v_x(t_i)^2 + v_y(t_i)^2 + v_z(t_i)^2} \tag{2}$$

The acceleration and the jerk were computed based on the second and third order derivatives of the position vector using similar equations.

- **Group of Features 2.** This feature group is related to the trajectory of the movement. It is expected to have a higher curvature of the hands that follows a contour of a circle compared to the hands that follow a straight line [12]. The curvature was calculated using the following equation:

$$\kappa(t_i) = \frac{||v(t_i) \times v'(t_i)||}{(\sqrt{v_x(t_i)^2 + v_y(t_i)^2 + v_z(t_i)^2})^3} \tag{3}$$

where, $v(t_i)$ corresponds to velocity of a joint at time t_i.

- **Group of Features 3.** This feature group represent an aggregated speed over a set of joints and defined as the "quantity of motion" in the literature [17]. The quantity of motion (QoM) is calculated as a weighted sum of velocities of groups of joints. QoM for K number of joints is defined as:

$$QoM(t_i) = \frac{\sum_{k \in K} w_k v_k(t_i)}{\sum_{k \in K} w_k} \tag{4}$$

For simplicity, the weights were set to 1. The joints of the body were segmented into five groups: arm region, head region, upper body, lower body and finally the whole body encompassing all major joints (see Fig. 1). Features were extracted separately for each of the body segments.

- **Group of Features 4.** This feature group represents the bounding volume of various segments of the body defined over the temporal domain. To increase the accuracy of the estimation, a convex hull was calculated instead of just a rectangular box enclosing the region of the body joints.

- **Group of Features 5.** This feature group captures the displacement of the major joints of human body using following equation:

$$D(t_i) = ||X^l(t_i) - X^k(t_i)|| \tag{5}$$

where k is the reference joint and l is any other joint of the body. The base of the spine was chosen as the reference joint.

- **Group of Features 6.** In this category we computed verticality (maximum distance of the y components for all the joints), extension (maximum distance from the center of mass to all other joints), elbow flexion (joint relative angle formed by shoulder, elbow and hand where elbow was used as the reference joint) [2], arm shape (magnitude of the vector from hand to base of the spine), hand relationship (distance between left and right hands) and feet relationship (distance between left and right feet), similar to motion features described in [17].
- **Group of Features 7.** This feature group resembles the effort component of the LMA descriptor. The analysis was applied to four sub-categories of effort. These sub-categories are weight, time, space and flow of the effort. The weight sub-category explains the strength of the movement, and it was computed as follows:

$$E(t_i) = \sum_{k \in K} E_k(t_t) = \sum_{k \in K} \alpha_k v^k(t_i)^2 = Weight(T) = maxE(t_i), i \in [1, T]$$

(6)

Movement can be described as strong versus weak/light [17]. The time sub-category of effort explains whether the movement was sudden (quick/urgent) or sustained (steady). It was computed based on the following equation:

$$Time(t_i) = \frac{1}{T} \sum_{i=1}^{T} a^k(t_i) \tag{7}$$

where $a^k(t_i)$ is the acceleration of the kth joint. The space effort explains whether motion effort was focused towards a particular spot (direct) or several spots (multi-focused and flexible) and is computed as [17]:

$$Space(t_i) = \frac{\sum_{i=1}^{T-1} ||x^k(t_{i+1}) - x^k(t_i)||}{||x^k(t_T) - x^k(t_i)||} \tag{8}$$

The flow sub-category of effort computes the fluidity of the movement:

$$Flow(t_i) = \frac{1}{T} \sum_{i=1}^{T} j^k(t_i) \tag{9}$$

where $j^k(t_i)$ is the jerk of the kth joint. T, in all the equations as mentioned earlier, is the size of frames under consideration. The above-mentioned features were extracted for the body segments illustrated using Fig. 1.
- **Group of Features 8.** This feature group provides an estimate of the spatial extent of the bounding triangle formed by the hands and the head, similar to features described in [12]. This group of features explains the coverage by the hands and the head over time.
- **Group of Features 9.** This feature group represents the symmetry of the movement. Asymmetry is correlated with the relaxed attitude and high social status of a person [18]. Therefore, spatial asymmetry was computed using a

geometric entropy-based method to measure the expressivity of the body movement. The geometric entropy of each hand's trajectory was measured using a method described in paper [12]. The geometric entropy explains how dispersed or spread of the movement compared to the available space and defined as follows:

$$H = \frac{2 * LP}{c} \tag{10}$$

where LP is the path length of the center of mass of the left or right arm region and c is the perimeter of the convex hull of the selected region. The measure was taken for both left and right arm region separately. Then the overall spread was calculated using the following equation:

$$SI(t_i) = \frac{H_{lefthand}}{H_{righthand}} \tag{11}$$

- **Group of Features 10.** This feature group measures the displacement associated with the center of mass (CoM) and the balance of the body during expressive movement. The displacement was calculated for each of the body segments shown in Fig. 1. The balance of the body was calculated using the displacement of the center of mass of the upper and the lower body.
- **Group of Features 11.** This feature group measures the overall area that is covered by the convex hull of projection of parts of the body during movement. This feature explains the overall space occupied during movement.

3.3   Temporal Profile

Some of the features introduced in the previous section were defined over the time domain. In order to reduce the noise without eliminating the high-frequency components, Savitzky-Golay filter (window length = 11, polynomial order = 3) [12] was applied. We introduced twelve statistical measures to characterize feature over time domain. These measures capture how motion features evolve. These time features computed explained as follows:

Feature 1–5: The following features were calculated to capture the overall behavior over some time: min, max, mean, standard deviation, and min versus max ratio.

Feature 6: This feature measures the amount of white noise present in the time series. The spectral flatness was computed by taking the ratio of the geometric and the arithmetic mean of the power spectrum of the time series.

Feature 7–8: The mean of the extreme values (local minimum and maximum values) were calculated and then added to the temporal profile.

Feature 9–10: To characterize the transition from one extreme value to the next, the slope of their movement over time was computed. "Onset" and "offset" slope was computed based the direction of the slope between two consecutive local minimum and local maximum value. Then the mean value was added to the temporal profile.

Feature 11: Average time between two consecutive extreme values were computed.

Feature 12: This feature characterizes whether the local minimum and local maximum value were reached using similar speed. This feature is defined as the ratio of the onset and the offset slopes previously calculated.

3.4   Filter-Based Feature Selection

First of all, we used a standard normalizer (z-score normalization) to normalize all the motion features. The problem working with a large number of features is that some of these features might not exhibit any variation among the target classes. These features may prevent the classification model from selecting features that can generalize. For this purpose, several standard filter-based techniques were investigated to discard irrelevant features. These filter-based techniques include ReliefF [15] and one of it's variant to detect feature interactions, Spatially Uniform ReliefF (SURF) [13], entropy-based method like Chi-squared score, statistical measure like analysis of variance (ANOVA), ensemble of decision tree based approach (with 200 estimators) and mutual information (MI) [4]. Based on two criteria investigated: monotonicity and stability/consistency, ANOVA was chosen as the filter-based feature selection algorithm.

3.5   Feature Subset Selection Using Genetic Algorithm

Even though ANOVA provides the most relevant features, it can only ensure significant variation between at least one pair of target classes. Therefore, a mono-chromosome based genetic algorithm similar to the method defined in paper [3] was utilized to extract a combination of relevant features to improve the emotion recognition rate.

4   Experimental Analysis

4.1   Dataset

The experiment was conducted on 30 subjects of a proprietary dataset. Each subject performed five different emotionally expressive walking sequences including a separate neutral walking sequence. Laban movement analysis (LMA) framework was used as a guideline to synthesize human motion styles similar to paper [24]. We focused on subjects' structural and physical properties of their body shape, dynamic quality of movement, and surrounding space utilization during movement expressions. None of the subjects had any prior acting experience. Each emotional walking sequence was recorded for 20 seconds using Microsoft Kinect v2. A total of 3000 seconds of recorded video data containing approximately 90,000 frames were recorded. Subjects walked in front of Kinect in a circular fashion showing both sides of the body.

4.2   Selection of the Filter-Based Technique

There are many filter-based techniques developed over the years. We considered six different techniques for this research. Out of the six techniques analyzed, one technique was chosen based on two criteria. These criteria are discussed as follows:

Consistency. We examined whether the feature ranking algorithms provide consistent rank over various subsets of the dataset. The dataset was split randomly into two folds 100 times, each time computing the rank generated by the filter-based technique from each fold. The expected outcome is to have a minimum difference between the computed ranks. The result is shown in Table 1 indicates ANOVA as the most consistent ranking algorithm outperforming ReliefF (with neighbor size 30) by a small margin.

Monotonicity. We examined the level of monotonicity by various feature ranking algorithms. The term "monotonicity" indicates the gradual performance decline along the ranked order of features generated by the algorithm. We utilized LDA and SVM to measure the "monotonicity" within an interval of 30 consecutive frames. Then Pearson correlation (to measure the linear relationship) and Spearman rank-order correlation, that measures the non-parametric measure of the monotonicity were computed for each of the filter-based algorithms. We chose ANOVA since it exhibited the highest level of average monotonicity among the feature ranking algorithms as shown in Table 2.

Table 1. Level of inconsistency by various feature ranking algorithms

Feature selection algorithm	Level of inconsistency (0: Lowest, 1:Highest)
ReliefF (number of neighbors = 30)	0.5339 ± 0.0188
Spatial uniform reliefF (SURF)	0.8844 ± 0.0275
CHI squared score	0.6472 ± 0.0209
Mutual information (MI)	0.7021 ± 0.0286
Ensemble tree based algorithm	0.9605 ± 0.0247
ANOVA (analysis of variance)	*0.5149 ± 0.0149*

Table 2. Measured monotonicity for various filter-based feature selection algorithms. (PCC = Pearson Correlation Co-efficient, SCC = Spearman Correlation Co-efficient)

Feature selection algorithm	PCC		SCC		Average
	LDA	SVM	LDA	SVM	
ReliefF (number of neighbors = 30)	−0.88	−0.89	−0.87	−0.91	−0.89
SURF (spatial uniform reliefF)	−0.82	−0.1	−0.83	−0.89	−0.48
CHI-squared score	−0.89	−0.88	−0.89	0.89	−0.89
MI (mutual information)	−0.85	−0.86	−0.85	−0.86	−0.86
Ensemble of decision trees	−0.83	−0.69	−0.83	−0.65	−0.75
ANOVA (analysis of variance)	*−0.94*	*0.85*	*−0.94*	*−0.85*	*−0.90*

4.3   Feature Analysis

From the analysis presented in the previous section, ANOVA was used to select relevant features. For each of the motion feature groups, ANOVA provides F-score that signifies how the mean differs between various emotion categories compared to the amount of variation observed within each group. Higher value signifies higher relevance. ANOVA also provides P-score that describes the statistical significance of the result. For this research, P-value was chosen as 0.005. Based on the P-value measured, any feature failing to pass the significance test was automatically discarded from consideration. The remaining features were sorted based on their relevance and the top 30% features from each motion feature groups were chosen and passed to the genetic algorithm.

From an initial selection of 1297 motion features, 557 features passed the significance test, and 167 features were retained for feature subset selection process. Careful observation of the distribution of the selected features shown in Table 3 suggest that features related to the speed such as acceleration, velocity, and quantity of motion was mostly retained. Surprisingly, the trajectory related features (group 2) were mostly discarded using this process.

Table 3. The number of features passed the ANOVA significance test.

	G1	G2	G3	G4	G5	G6	G7	G8	G9	G10	G11
Total extracted features	396	132	48	48	144	108	240	12	37	72	60
Features selected	175	5	25	24	51	61	122	9	8	29	29

In order to analyze how the feature relevance differs among the motion feature groups, the top two features from each group were extracted, as shown in Fig. 2. The most crucial motion feature computed was the time sub-category of the effort component (average acceleration for a small period) of the arm region. This experiment indicates that the speed of an arm movement was significantly different across various emotion categories. Acceleration of the arm and the knee was given very high relevance in the first group. One key aspect to notice here is that, the mean acceleration of the knee was not chosen. Instead, the mean of local minimum values was given higher relevance which indicates it is more important to observe acceleration changes during a transition, rather than the overall acceleration that is maintained. Figure 2 also shows that the time taken to change the motion trajectory of the hands reveal the type of emotion observed in the gait sequence. Group 6 also reveals an interesting result. The overall elbow flexion angle maintained (mean) is not as important as the transition speed between the elbow flexion angle's extreme values over time. Note that the speed of movement was more important and indicative of specific emotional response for the upper region, especially the arm region. On the other hand, area and volume covered, rather than the speed of motion were more relevant for the lower part of the body.

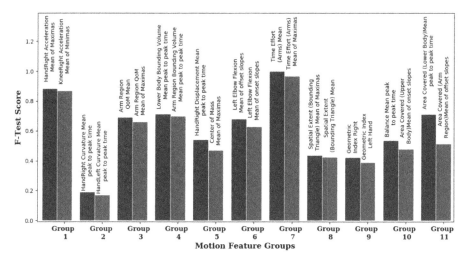

Fig. 2. Comparison of feature relevance of the top two features selected from each motion feature group using ANOVA. (blue bar = best feature, green bar = second best feature) (Color figure online)

The time sub-category of the effort component needs further inspection as it is the most relevant feature computed. From Fig. 3, it is safe to conclude that the subjects exhibited more effort when they were happy or angry compared to when they were sad or fearful. The time sub-category of effort alone cannot distinguish all five emotional states of the subjects and therefore, it is also safe to conclude that, only the features selected using ANOVA algorithm alone is not enough to distinguish all emotional states. However, a combination of motion features can be used. The result obtained using ANOVA only guarantees significant variation of mean between at least one pair of emotion category.

4.4   Feature Subset Selection

From the previous section, it was concluded that the filter-based feature selection algorithm alone could not reliably distinguish among various emotion categories. Therefore, a genetic algorithm discussed in Sect. 3.5 was utilized. In order to test the performance of a feature subset, machine learning models such as Support Vector Machine (SVM), Linear Discriminant Analysis (LDA), Naive Bayes classifier, K-Nearest Neighbor and Decision Tree was used. The parameters for the SVM classifier such as C (margin maximization of the decision function), γ (influence of the training samples), decision type (one-versus-all or one-versus-rest), and kernel type (radial basis or linear function) were chosen based on an exhaustive grid search. We used the singular value decomposition as the solver for the LDA. The number of neighbors for the KNN classifier was chosen as eleven based on the result obtained in paper [3]. We used five-fold cross-validation during the

experiment. We avoided biased learning by not taking samples from the same
subjects during both the testing and the training sets.

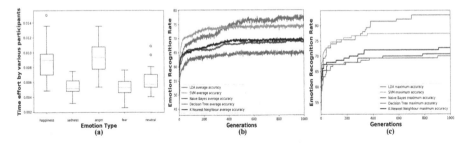

Fig. 3. (a) Boxplot showing the time sub-category of effort feature of the arm region
computed for various subjects. Improvement of emotion recognition rate of different
classifiers over various generations (number of chromosomes = 30). (b) Average emotion
recognition rate. (c) Maximum emotion recognition rate.

4.5 Performance of the Best Feature Subset

We measured the effectiveness of the feature subset by computing the sample
Pearson correlation coefficient for each pair of emotions categories as shown in
Fig. 4. It is evident from this figure that the between-group correlation among
samples of different emotion categories was significantly reduced using the proposed method. The within-group correlation of the neutral and the sadness emotion group was increased. The correlation of angry emotional state remained
fixed at 1 which indicates detection of anger during expressive movement was
easy compared to other emotion groups.

4.6 Comparison with Other Methods

To compare the proposed framework with prior research in emotion recognition
domain, features defined in two recent state-of-the-art papers: paper 1 [24] and
paper 2 [23], were implemented and tested on our proprietary dataset. For both
papers, experiments were conducted using original features introduced in those
works with both LDA and SVM classifiers. As seen from Fig. 4, emotion recognition accuracy for those methods was in the range of 44% to 62%. Next, feature
selection was enhanced through applying ANOVA filter and discarding all the
features failing to pass the significance test. This modification did not affect the
performance of the method based on paper 2, however led to an increase of accuracy for paper 1 based method to 58% with LDA and to 64% with SVM classifier.
Our original framework achieved 56% to 59.3% accuracy of emotion recognition
when all the features were selected. However, enhanced with the ANOVA filter,
the performances reached 61% to 67%. Best performance was achieved when the
genetic algorithm was applied after the initial ANOVA relevant feature selection:

83.33% emotion recognition rate using LDA classifier and 77.33% using SVM classifier. This result is 13–27% higher than accuracy obtained for paper 1 with ANOVA filter and 27–39% higher than emotion recognition accuracy reported for paper 2 with ANOVA filter. This experiment demonstrates the superiority of the proposed framework for identifying emotions from human motion.

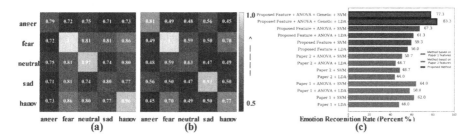

Fig. 4. Sample Pearson correlation co-efficient visualized (a) before and (b) after selection of features using ANOVA feature selection algorithm. (c) Recognition performance of the proposed method and its variants vs. feature selection methods presented in Paper 1 [24] and Paper 2 [23].

5   Conclusion and Future Work

In this study, we proposed a novel framework for emotion recognition from body movement. We utilized a combination of filter-based feature selection technique followed by a mono-chromosome based genetic algorithm to determine a combination of motion features to identify the emotion from body movement accurately. The ANOVA technique helped to identify the unnecessary features. Hence, this technique reduced the search space for the genetic algorithm. Both layers of the feature selection algorithm complemented each other in improving the emotion recognition rate. The technique was useful in measuring the significance of each motion features for the task of recognition. The developed framework achieved a high emotion recognition rate of 83.33% outperforming other recent methods.

Acknowledgements. Authors would like to acknowledge partial support from NSERC DG "Machine Intelligence for Biometric Security", NSERC ENGAGE on Gait Recognition and NSERC SPG on Smart Cities funding.

References

1. Adey, P.: Facing airport security: affect, biopolitics, and the preemptive securitisation of the mobile body. Environ. Plann. D: Soc. Space **27**(2), 274–295 (2009)
2. Ahmed, F., Paul, P.P., Gavrilova, M.L.: DTW-based kernel and rank-level fusion for 3D gait recognition using kinect. Vis. Comput. **31**(6–8), 915–924 (2015)

3. Ahmed, F., Sieu, B., Gavrilova, M.L.: Score and rank-level fusion for emotion recognition using genetic algorithm. In: ICCI*CC 2018, pp. 46–53. IEEE (2018)
4. Battiti, R.: Using mutual information for selecting features in supervised neural net learning. IEEE Trans. Neural Netw. 5(4), 537–550 (1994)
5. Bianchi-Berthouze, N., Kleinsmith, A.: A categorical approach to affective gesture recognition. Connect. Sci. 15(4), 259–269 (2003)
6. Camurri, A., Lagerlöf, I., Volpe, G.: Recognizing emotion from dance movement: comparison of spectator recognition and automated techniques. Int. J. Hum.-Comput. Stud. 59(1–2), 213–225 (2003)
7. De Gelder, B.: Why bodies? Twelve reasons for including bodily expressions in affective neuroscience. Biol. Sci. 364(1535), 3475–3484 (2009)
8. Durupinar, F., Kapadia, M., Deutsch, S., Neff, M., Badler, N.I.: Perform: perceptual approach for adding ocean personality to human motion using laban movement analysis. ACM Trans. Graph. (TOG) 36(1), 6 (2017)
9. Fourati, N., Pelachaud, C.: Toward new expressive movement characterizations. In: Proceedings of Motion in Games (2012)
10. Fragopanagos, N., Taylor, J.G.: Emotion recognition in human-computer interaction. Neural Netw. 18(4), 389–405 (2005)
11. Gelman, A., et al.: Analysis of variance-why it is more important than ever. Ann. Stat. 33(1), 1–53 (2005)
12. Glowinski, D., Dael, N., Camurri, A., Volpe, G., Mortillaro, M., Scherer, K.: Toward a minimal representation of affective gestures. IEEE Trans. Affect. Comput. 2(2), 106–118 (2011)
13. Greene, C.S., Penrod, N.M., Kiralis, J., Moore, J.H.: Spatially uniform reliefF (SURF) for computationally-efficient filtering of gene-gene interactions. BioData Min. 2(1), 5 (2009)
14. Kapadia, M., et al.: Efficient motion retrieval in large motion databases. In: Proceedings of the ACM SIGGRAPH Symposium on Interactive 3D Graphics and Games, pp. 19–28. ACM (2013)
15. Kira, K., Rendell, L.A.: The feature selection problem: traditional methods and a new algorithm. In: Aaai, vol. 2, pp. 129–134 (1992)
16. Kollias, D., et al.: Deep affect prediction in-the-wild: Aff-wild database and challenge, deep architectures, and beyond. arXiv preprint arXiv:1804.10938 (2018)
17. Larboulette, C., Gibet, S.: A review of computable expressive descriptors of human motion. In: Proceedings of the 2nd International Workshop on Movement and Computing, pp. 21–28. ACM (2015)
18. Mehrabian, A.: Nonverbal Communication. Routledge, Abingdon (2017)
19. Noroozi, F., Corneanu, C.A., Kamińska, D., Sapiński, T., Escalera, S., Anbarjafari, G.: Survey on emotional body gesture recognition. arXiv preprint arXiv:1801.07481 (2018)
20. Pollick, F.E., Paterson, H.M., Bruderlin, A., Sanford, A.J.: Perceiving affect from arm movement. Cognition 82(2), B51–B61 (2001)
21. Robnik-Šikonja, M., Kononenko, I.: Theoretical and empirical analysis of reliefF and RReliefF. Mach. Learn. 53(1–2), 23–69 (2003)
22. Ross, B.C.: Mutual information between discrete and continuous data sets. PloS One 9(2), e87357 (2014)
23. Saha, S., Datta, S., Konar, A., Janarthanan, R.: A study on emotion recognition from body gestures using kinect sensor. In: 2014 International Conference on Communication and Signal Processing, pp. 056–060. IEEE (2014)

24. Senecal, S., Cuel, L., Aristidou, A., Magnenat-Thalmann, N.: Continuous body emotion recognition system during theater performances. Comput. Animat. Virtual Worlds **27**(3–4), 311–320 (2016)
25. Sultana, M., Paul, P.P., Gavrilova, M.: Social behavioral biometrics: an emerging trend. Int. J. Pattern Recognit. Artif. Intell. **29**(08), 1556013 (2015)
26. Tahir, Y., Dauwels, J., Thalmann, D., Magnenat Thalmann, N.: A user study of a humanoid robot as a social mediator for two-person conversations. Int. J. Soc. Robot. **14**(4), 1–14 (2018)
27. Tarnowski, P., Kołodziej, M., Majkowski, A., Rak, R.J.: Emotion recognition using facial expressions. Procedia Comput. Sci. **108**, 1175–1184 (2017)
28. Wallbott, H.G.: Bodily expression of emotion. Eur. J. Soc. Psychol. **28**(6), 879–896 (1998)
29. Wang, H., Khoshgoftaar, T.M., Van Hulse, J.: A comparative study of threshold-based feature selection techniques. In: 2010 IEEE International Conference on Granular Computing (GRC), pp. 499–504. IEEE (2010)
30. Yanushkevich, S.N., Stoica, A., Srihari, S.N., Shmerko, V.P., Gavrilova, M.: Simulation of biometric information: the new generation of biometric systems. In: Proceedings of International Workshop Modeling and Simulation in Biometric Technology, pp. 87–98 (2004)

Improved Volume Scattering

Haysn Hornbeck$^{(\boxtimes)}$ (ID) and Usman Alim

University of Calgary, Calgary, AB, Canada
{hhornbec,ualim}@ucalgary.ca

Abstract. This paper examines two approaches to improve the realism of volume scattering functions. The first uses a convex combination of multiple Henyey-Greenstein distributions to approximate a more complicated scattering distribution, while the second allows negative coefficients. The former is already supported in some renderers, the latter is not and carries a significant performance penalty. Chromatic scattering is also explored, and found to be beneficial in some circumstances. Source code is publicly available under an open-source license.

Keywords: Volume scattering · Volume rendering ·
Computer graphics · Path tracing

1 Introduction

The commercial graphics industry has shifted towards more computationally-intensive algorithms, particularly ray- and path-tracing [7]. Scientific visualization has followed the same trend, such as the addition of Osprey to VTK [28]. Progress has been made on architectural speed-ups [5], noise reduction [23], and surface scattering [16].

Surprisingly, little attention has been paid to volume scattering. The Hyperion renderer is quite efficient at casting volumetric rays through clouds, yet the scattering function uses a simplistic statistical model [5]. More sophisticated models exist, however they are either tuned to cloud scattering or difficult to incorporate into a path tracer [4]. Owing to its convenient mathematical properties, the Henyey-Greenstein (HG) distribution – introduced by Louis Henyey and Jesse Greenstein in 1941 [17] – is the de-facto standard for modelling volumetric scattering. However, it cannot represent scattering with both strong forward and backward peaks.

This paper tries to fill the gap, by exploring two techniques to improve the realism of HG distributions (Fig. 1). In Sect. 3, we approximate a complicated volume scattering function (VSF) via a convex combination of HG VSFs. This improves realism (see Sect. 6), is widely supported in existing path tracers, and has minimal performance impact. In Sect. 4, we introduce the idea of "negative probability" and remove the constraint that the combination be convex. We allow affine combinations and show that they lead to much better fits. However, commonly employed convex sampling strategies for sampling multiple VSFs cannot

M. Gavrilova et al. (Eds.): CGI 2019, LNCS 11542, pp. 68–80, 2019.
https://doi.org/10.1007/978-3-030-22514-8_6

Fig. 1. Four scattering functions applied to the Walt Disney Animation Studios cloud dataset (CC-BY-SA 3.0). From left: isotropic scattering; a Henyey-Greenstein with $g = 0.927$; a convex linear combination of eight Henyey-Greensteins, fitted to dirty terrestrial clouds with 50% humidity [18]; a non-convex linear combination of eight Henyey-Greensteins fitted to the same model. Clouds have been brightened to bring out fine details.

be used with affine combinations. We explore alternative sampling techniques that further improve realism but come with a heftier performance penalty. We also analyse chromatic scattering (Sect. 5) and show that subtle chromatic effects can be easily approximated via a single VSF.

The remainder of this paper is organized as follows. Section 6 showcases our results and also analyses the performance of all techniques. Section 7 discusses the limitations of HG fits. While these techniques apply to a wide variety of substances, our focus in this paper is on cloud VSFs as they have been heavily studied. Sample code is publicly available under an open-source license to encourage implementation [20].

2 Background and Related Work

In general, solids and liquids demonstrate quantum mechanical effects on macroscopic scales. For instance, a photon passing by atoms induces them to generate magnetic fields, which in turn interfere with the photon and generate distinct phase and group velocities [9]; put another way, light is refracted by matter. This is most easily modelled by imposing a surface normal that represents material boundaries.

Gasses also exhibit these effects, for instance the "flattening" of the Sun or Moon near the horizon is also due to refraction, but their diffuse nature means there is no clear boundary. Instead, we can model gasses as composites of randomly-dispersed particles. Photon-particle interactions occur with a certain probability [3], and the orientation of the particle is also probabilistic. We can model the latter with a scattering phase function, or the probability density function (PDF) of a particle scattering in any given direction; these are also known as volume scattering functions, or VSFs, in the literature. They correspond to $p(x, \omega, \omega')$ within the volume rendering equation:

$$(\omega \cdot \nabla)L(x, \omega) = -\sigma_t(x)L(x, \omega) + \varepsilon(x, \omega) + \\ \sigma_s(x) \int_{4\pi} p(x, \omega, \omega')L(x, \omega')d\sigma(\omega'), \tag{1}$$

which accounts for the change in radiance $L(x, \omega)$ in the direction ω due to out-scattering, emission and in-scattering respectively. Rotational symmetry allows

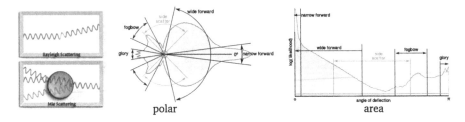

polar   area

Fig. 2. A summary of volume scattering. From left to right: the two most common forms of scattering, a polar chart of a VSF labelled with commonly-discussed portions, and the corresponding area chart. Though the former are more intuitive to understand, area charts are better at revealing subtle details. Both use log-space, as most VSFs are highly anisotropic.

us to simplify the function to the scattering angle θ relative to the vector of travel. Further information can be found in a review paper from Hege *et al.* [15].

Most gaseous scattering in real life can be accounted for by two models [25]. Rayleigh scattering occurs when the particles are much smaller than the photon's wavelength, and depends only on the relative cross-section of the particle. Mie scattering occurs when the particles are as large or larger than the wavelength, and also depends on the index of refraction of the particle. The latter scattering is much more complicated than the former, exhibiting narrow forward and backward scattering with periodic peaks that complicate the fogbow portion (see Fig. 2). Mie scattering has seen decades of study [8], yet it is still too computationally intensive for use in path tracing. Unfortunately, it is common in real life. Clouds are the most famous example, but Mie scattering also occurs with aerosols such as the bacteria, dust, water vapour and air bubbles that are pervasive in the atmosphere and ocean [30].

In order to handle complicated VSFs, one fix proposed by Adolf Witt was to linearly combine two HG functions [29]. This paper focuses on a generic fit instead of a constrained one. We investigate both convex and affine combinations of multiple HG functions. The use of multiple scattering distributions has been explored by other authors. Bouthors *et al.* [4] converted a five-dimensional table into a custom function and seven two-dimensional tables, via an empirical fitting process. The result achieved impressive performance, but required a lot of ad-hoc exploration and atypical functions like a skewed Gaussian distribution. Gkioulekas *et al.* explored the use of tent functions to represent arbitrary scattering, though these too are non-trivial to implement [12]. The techniques presented in this paper use functions that already exist in most path tracers, and in some cases no code modification is necessary.

3   Convex Linear Henyey-Greenstein Combinations

There has been little study of treating the Henyey-Greenstein distribution as a fitting function. A VSF can be expressed as a convex combination of HG functions; in mathematical terms,

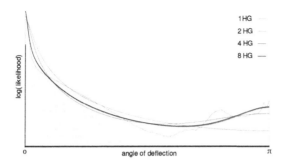

Fig. 3. Fitting a linear combination of Henyey-Greenstein distributions to Material 33, polluted terrestrial clouds with 50% relative humidity, as generated by OPAC [18].

$$VSF(\theta) \approx \sum_{k=1}^{n} w_k \cdot HG(\theta, g_k), \qquad (2)$$

where $w_k > 0$ and $\sum_k w_k = 1$. Nearly all path tracers allow this, for instance Blender's Cycles [1] and Mitsuba [22]. This is also true of Open Shading Language [14], so Appleseed, prman, Arnold, and other OSL renderers should be no different [21].

The authors used a Bayesian fit for the linear combinations of Henyey-Greenstein functions, with the likelihood function defined as

$$\mathscr{L}(\sigma, W, G \mid VSF) = \prod_{c=1}^{m} \mathscr{N}(\sum_{k=1}^{n} w_k \cdot HG(\theta_c, g_k)|VSF(\theta_c), \ \sigma), \qquad (3)$$

$$\mathscr{N}(x|\mu, \sigma) = \frac{1}{\sigma} e^{-\frac{(x-\mu)^2}{2\sigma^2}}, \qquad (4)$$

$$\Theta = \{\theta_1, \theta_2, \ldots \theta_m\}, W = \{w_1, w_2, \ldots w_n\}, G = \{g_1, g_2, \ldots g_n\}, \qquad (5)$$

where Θ is the set of m angular deflections the VSF was sampled at, W the set of n weights for the linear combination of HGs and G the matching anisotropy factors, while $\mathscr{N}(x, \sigma^2)$ is a Gaussian penalty function with variance σ^2. The prior was flat for valid inputs. While other fitting methods are faster, Bayesian fitting allows the relative importance of each parameter to be assessed. The posterior distribution was generated with emcee [10], and the maximal likelihood used as the "best" fit. All results were stored in the material database [20].

Figure 3 is typical of scattering functions encountered in reality, with strong narrow forward scatter plus a weaker wide component, a complex fogbow and weak backscatter. Adding more components to the linear combination improves the fit, but only to a point.

Figure 4 presents scatterplots of the posterior, with maximal likelihoods marked by boxes. When using one or two Henyey-Greensteins to match this scattering function, the posterior clusters around the expected number of peaks. With four or eight HGs, however, only three clusters appear in the posterior. This strongly implies that three HG functions provide the most efficient fit to the scattering function.

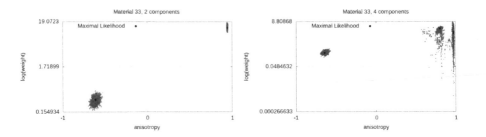

Fig. 4. Scatterplots of the posterior for Material 33. Only combinations of two and four Henyey-Greensteins are shown.

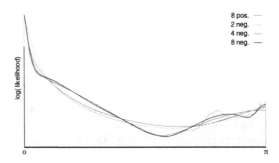

Fig. 5. Fitting various linear combinations of Henyey-Greenstein distributions to Material 33, with negative weights allowed. The convex combination of eight distributions is included for comparison.

4   Affine Linear Combinations

We have only considered convex linear combinations because negative weights violate the axioms of probability. Nevertheless, the concept of "negative probability" has been invaluable for modelling quantum interference, such as that found in the double-slit experiment [26]. The linear combination is still positive everywhere, so negative values are not output directly, but they nonetheless influence the shape of the distribution. By allowing $w_k < 0$ in the linear combination, we obtain an affine combination which might achieve a better fit compared to a convex combination. Figure 5 shows that allowing negative probability does indeed improve the fit, when given more than two components. The forward- and side-scattering portions are better captured, with only the subtle details of the fogbow lost. The fit continues to show improvement with eight components.

The scatterplots in Fig. 6 show a much richer posterior. The four-component version now has four peaks, although they no longer have the Gaussian appearance of Fig. 4. The eight-component version has few clear peaks, suggesting that more components would improve the fit, that the MCMC algorithm is having difficulty exploring the fitness landscape, or both.

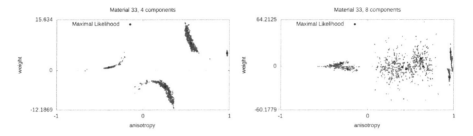

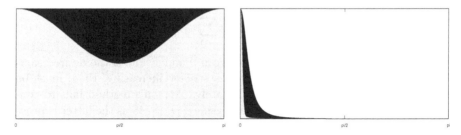

Fig. 6. Scatterplots of the posterior for Material 33, with negative probability allowed. Only combinations of four and eight Henyey-Greensteins are shown.

Fig. 7. Two separate scattering functions, in purple, with two reasonable choices of envelopes, in black. (Color figure online)

Unfortunately, no path tracer appears capable of handling negative probability. Cycles' nodes prevent the use of negative weights. Mitsuba's scene description could accommodate negative weights, but the parser rejects them. Open Shading Language permits negative weights, but only due to poor input checking.

All of the referenced path tracers use convex sampling to handle linear VSF combinations. Each weight is normalized by the sum of all weights, then used as the probability of selecting the matching component. That specific VSF is then sampled. The use of probability means this algorithm only returns a representative sample of convex VSF combinations.

4.1 Sampling from Distributions with Negative Probability

To permit negative probability, we must find an alternative to convex sampling. Markov Chain Monte Carlo is an obvious choice, as it only depends on a PDF.

Frisvad *et al.* acheived good results via rejection sampling [11]. Figure 7 helps illustrate the theory behind this. On the left is the Rayleigh scattering function. Using a uniform distribution to pick a random angle, then a random height between 0 and the peak of the Rayleigh distribution, is the equivalent of throwing a dart within the bounding rectangle. Three-quarters of the time, it will land on the part of the graph representing the Rayleigh distribution and we will accept the sample. If it does not, we continue sampling until it does. The result is a random sample of the target distribution.

On the right of Fig. 7 is Material 33, which is more typical of scattering distributions. If we were to again use a rectangular box for an envelope, we would reject about 98.95% of our samples. It would be more efficient to use a Henyey-Greenstein function as an envelope, as it drops the rejection rate to approximately 79.4%. We would need to determine an appropriate anisotropy parameter for the envelope, as well as a scalar value to ensure it is always greater or equal to the target.

Alternatively, we can use the convex sub-portion of the combination, as by definition it envelopes the full function. This is better tuned than using a single distribution, at the cost of more computation. See the source code for the full implementation [20].

A third alternative relies on root-finding. Integration is a linear operation, so it is trivial to find the zero of

$$-\xi + \int_0^x VSF_c(\theta) \ d\theta = -\xi + \sum_{i=1}^n w_i \int_0^x HG(\theta, g_i) \ d\theta \qquad (6)$$

where ξ is a uniform random variable between 0 and 1, and x the desired sample. As the Henyey-Greenstein's integral is strictly increasing, there must be exactly one zero for arbitrary x. Unfortunately, Newton's method fails to converge. Instead, bisection will be tested alongside TOMS748 as the latter is provably optimal in some cases [2].

5   Chromatic Scattering

The scattering of light depends on its wavelength. Even clouds exhibit this chromatic scattering, when they partly occlude the sun. Unfortunately, most renderers assume volumetric scattering is achromatic. Some permit the colour channels to pass through different VSFs, but this triples computation and introduces artefacts.

Listing 1.1. An Open Shading Language implementation of Material 33, which implements approximate chromic scattering.

```
shader material0033VSF   ( color Color = color (1.0 ,  1.0 ,  1.0) , float Density = 0 ,
    output closure color BSDF = 0 ) {

    BSDF = Density * Color * (
        0.0319 *  color (1.0 ,  0.8333 ,  0.7430)  *  henyey_greenstein (−0.6418) +
        0.3610 *  color (0.6348 ,  1.0 ,  0.7989)  *  henyey_greenstein ( 0.8016) +
        0.2402 *  color (1.0 ,  0.2116 ,  0.2758)  *  henyey_greenstein ( 0.8154) +
        0.6216 *  color (0.8023 ,  0.9034 ,  1.0)  *  henyey_greenstein ( 0.9740) );
    }
```

Subtle chromatic scattering may still be approximated, however. If all colour channels have roughly the same scattering function, they could all pass through one VSF combination but make per-channel adjustments via colour tinting. This fails gracefully when the spectral channels are wildly different. Listing 1.1 demonstrates an implementation, and Fig. 8 shows a chromic fit.

6   Results

For testing, the cloud dataset released by Walt Disney Animation Studios was imported into Blender 2.79b, and rendered with Cycles. The VSF was Material 33, polluted terrestrial clouds with 50% relative humidity [18]. Chromatic scattering was used.

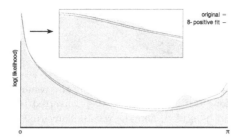

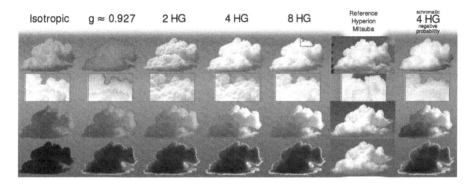

Fig. 8. Chromatic scattering for material 33, comparing a convex 8-component Henyey-Greenstein to the original scattering function. To reduce clutter, only the red and blue wavelengths are shown. (Color figure online)

Fig. 9. A comparison of the three techniques, using the Walt Disney Animation Studios cloud dataset, under varying lighting conditions. Slight tone-mapping has been applied to better match the reference image. The reference cloud photo is copyright Kevin Udy, CC-BY-SA 3.0.

Figure 9 and the accompanying video show a surprising amount of variation between VSFs. The single Henyey-Greenstein version has a blurred quality, while the two-component variant looks high-contrast. The four- and eight-component variants are somewhere in-between.

The changes in each combination's brightness can be explained by the scattering function. The single Henyey-Greenstein version is heavily biased towards forward scatter, so when the illumination is from behind the viewer little of it bounces back. Adding more HG functions reduces that bias.

Cycles does not have support for negative probability. Instead, a new node was added to the 2.8 development branch that simulated negative probability via look-up tables. Negative probability has a softer look, similar to the single Henyey-Greenstein, however it adds dark "tufts" at regions parallel to the viewing plane. These are present in the original photo, and can be explained by a relative lack of side-scattering (see Fig. 5).

Chromatic scattering has an effect, as Fig. 10 shows. For this material, it gives a bluish cast to the area of the cloud opposite the light source when convex

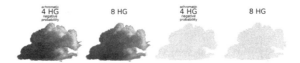

Fig. 10. Chromatic differences due to the "tinting" of the volume scattering functions. To reveal the subtle colour shift, the original was converted to L*a*b*, L* replaced with a flat colour, a* and b* scaled, and the results converted back to sRGB. (Color figure online)

Henyey-Greenstein combinations are used. If one spectral component has more narrow forward scattering, it will penetrate further into the material but be less likely to scatter towards the camera, while more side- and back-scatter will behave oppositely. The result is a colour gradient that varies with depth and the relative strength of the two effects. Here, the convex HG combination has less blue forward-scatter and more red side/back scatter than the original VSF. Bluish light may be less likely to bounce towards the camera, but if the reddish light has already been scattered away it will nonetheless dominate.

6.1   Benchmarks

Figure 11 shows the datasets used for benchmarking, all of which invoke negative probability. Material 6 is a simple four-component Henyey-Greenstein with two negative weights, corresponding to Gkioulekas *et al.*'s milk soap [12]. Material 33 is an eight-component combination with four negative weights, more typical of real-world scattering functions. "Difficult," a four-component with one negative weight, does not correspond to any specific material but has unusually high anisotropy.

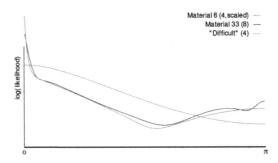

Fig. 11. The three VSFs used for benchmarking. Material 6, milk soap, has been artificially scaled to better reveal its shape.

Table 1. The performance of each algorithm on Material 6. Each algorithm generated 8,388,608 samples 26 times, then an average and 16/84 confidence interval were estimated. They were run on an Intel Core i3-6100 in a single thread, and compiled with the CUDA 10.0 toolkit and GCC 7.3.0, with O3 optimizations. Average nanoseconds per sample are shown.

Algorithm	Material 6	Material 33	"Difficult"
Convex sampling	26.75 ± 0.057	32.26 ± 0.11	31.71 ± 0.072
Näive MCMC	17356 ± 5.6	32150 ± 12	16962 ± 6.0
Rejection, 1HG	344.2 ± 0.44	7299.3 ± 2.4	5105 ± 3.0
Rejection, multi-HG	438.5 ± 0.50	5613.5 ± 2.3	675.7 ± 0.44
Bisection	568.5 ± 0.34	880.9 ± 0.48	568.9 ± 0.52
TOMS748	331.4 ± 0.27	775.1 ± 0.54	614.7 ± 0.54

Table 1 presents the performance of each algorithm, plus a convex sampling baseline. Näive MCMC sampling performs poorly, and also returns poor samples of the VSF. Rejection sampling performs best with Material 6, and worst with non-trivial scattering functions. An envelope of multiple Henyey-Greenstein functions does well with difficult cases. The root-finding algorithms perform quite well, with TOMS748 generally outperforming bisection. All of the above algorithms are at least an order of magnitude slower than convex sampling, however. Table 2 has timing information for the GPU. With memory transfers factored out, the GPU implementations behave similarly to their CPU counterparts. The rejection methods perform worse than expected on the more difficult datasets, however, which may be due to overhead from random-number generation.

Table 2. The average nanoseconds per sample of each algorithm on a GeForce GTX 970 with 1,664 CUDA cores. All data transfer across the PCIe bus is excluded. The other benchmarking parameters are unchanged.

Algorithm	Material 6	Material 33	"Difficult"
Convex sampling	0.9044 ± 0.005692	0.9109 ± 0.005690	0.9082 ± 0.005538
Rejection, 1HG	10.31 ± 0.06882	642.3 ± 0.3828	436.7 ± 0.3036
Rejection, multi-HG	16.94 ± 0.1808	478.6 ± 0.2599	40.52 ± 0.2582
Bisection	17.61 ± 0.2074	34.13 ± 0.3099	17.39 ± 0.1599

7   Discussion

The authors' extensive practice fitting linear combinations suggests there are limitations to Henyey-Greenstein fitting.

$$HG_{\cos}(x, g) = \frac{1 - g^2}{(1 + g^2 - 2gx)^{\frac{3}{2}}}, \quad x = \cos(\theta) \tag{7}$$

$$HG_{\cos}(x, g)' = \frac{3g(1 - g^2)}{(1 + g^2 - 2gx)^{\frac{5}{2}}} \tag{8}$$

$$HG_{\cos}(x, g)' = a(b - cx)^{-\frac{5}{2}},$$
$$a = 3g(1 - g^2), \ b = 1 + g^2, \ c = 2g \tag{9}$$

$$HG_{\cos}(x, g)' = au^{-5}, u = \sqrt{b - cx} \tag{10}$$

For a function, the number of local extrema is determined by the roots of its derivative. Equation 10 demonstrates the cosine-weighted derivative of Henyey-Greenstein is a Laurent polynomial. Such a polynomial with minimal degree $-n$ can have no more than n roots [13]. The fractional exponent can be handled by substitution, which may introduce extra roots but here does not because u has exactly one root. No linear combination of those derivatives can change the degree. Thus the derivative of arbitrary combinations of $HG(\theta, g)$ can only have five roots, and thus no more than five local extrema. As Fig. 3 suggests, however, Mie scattering can generate more than five.

8   Conclusion

Of all the exact sampling methods tested, bisection is the most reliable. Other algorithms gave faster performance in certain circumstances, but even TOMS748 was unable to consistently outperform bisection. The major exception was MCMC, which was always the slowest technique, but it should be stressed that this implementation of MCMC is extremely naïve. Hamiltonian Monte Carlo can be orders of magnitude faster than the implemented algorithm [19]. An approach which benchmarks multiple algorithms on a per-function basis, then uses the fastest of them to sample, should give the best performance. Warped sampling as per Clarberg et al. [6] may also prove useful.

There are also volume scattering functions which cannot be captured by any of these algorithms. Sun dogs are formed when ice crystals in high-elevation cirrus clouds align in a particular manner [24], which violate the assumption of rotational symmetry. The scattering in the human eye has a diffraction component that violates that symmetetry plus the movement of particles causes temporal variance [27]. The current state-of-the-art for those phenomenon are image-based approximations or ray tracing, even though volume functions could describe them.

There is much more research to be done in volume rendering, and the reward is a much richer variety of physical phenomenon that can be simulated.

References

1. Blender Foundation. https://www.blender.org/foundation/
2. Alefeld, G.E., Potra, F.A., Shi, Y.: Algorithm 748: enclosing zeros of continuous functions. ACM Trans. Math. Softw. **21**(3), 327–344 (1995)
3. Bitterli, B., et al.: A radiative transfer framework for non-exponential media. In: SIGGRAPH Asia 2018 Technical Papers on - SIGGRAPH Asia 2018, pp. 1–17. ACM Press, Tokyo (2018)
4. Bouthors, A., Neyret, F., Max, N., Bruneton, E., Crassin, C.: Interactive multiple anisotropic scattering in clouds, p. 173. ACM Press (2008)
5. Burley, B., et al.: The design and evolution of disney's hyperion renderer. ACM Trans. Graph. **37**(3), 1–22 (2018)
6. Clarberg, P., Jarosz, W., Akenine-Möller, T., Jensen, H.W.: Wavelet importance sampling: efficiently evaluating products of complex functions, vol. 24, pp. 1166–1175. ACM (2005). http://dx.doi.org/10.1145/1073204.1073328
7. Deng, Y., Ni, Y., Li, Z., Mu, S., Zhang, W.: Toward real-time ray tracing: a survey on hardware acceleration and microarchitecture techniques. ACM Comput. Surv. **50**(4), 1–41 (2017)
8. Du, H.: Mie-scattering calculation. Appl. Opt. **43**(9), 1951–1956 (2004)
9. Feynman, R.P., Leighton, R.B., Sands, M.: The Feynman Lectures, vol. 1. Addison-Wesley, Reading (1963)
10. Foreman-Mackey, D., Hogg, D.W., Lang, D., Goodman, J.: emcee: the MCMC hammer. Publ. Astron. Soc. Pacific **125**(925), 306–312 (2013). arXiv: 1202.3665
11. Frisvad, J.R.: Importance sampling the Rayleigh phase function. J. Opt. Soc. Am. A **28**(12), 2436 (2011)
12. Gkioulekas, I., Zhao, S., Bala, K., Zickler, T., Levin, A.: Inverse volume rendering with material dictionaries. ACM Trans. Graph. **32**(6), 162:1–162:13 (2013)
13. Goodman, T.N., Micchelli, C.A., Rodriguez, G., Seatzu, S.: Spectral factorization of Laurent polynomials. Adv. Comput. Math. **7**(4), 429–454 (1997)
14. Gritz, L., Stein, C., Kulla, C., Conty, A.: Open shading language. In: ACM SIGGRAPH 2010 Talks, p. 33. ACM (2010)
15. Hege, H.C., Höllerer, T., Stalling, D.: Volume Rendering - Mathematicals Models and Algorithmic Aspects, June 1993. https://opus4.kobv.de/opus4-zib/frontdoor/index/index/docId/499
16. Heitz, E., Hanika, J., d'Eon, E., Dachsbacher, C.: Multiple-scattering microfacet BSDFs with the Smith model. ACM Trans. Graph. (TOG) **35**(4), 58 (2016)
17. Henyey, L.G., Greenstein, J.L.: Diffuse radiation in the galaxy. Astrophys. J. **93**, 70–83 (1941)
18. Hess, M., Koepke, P., Schult, I.: Optical properties of aerosols and clouds: the software package OPAC. Bull. Am. Meteorol. Soc. **79**(5), 831–844 (1998)
19. Hoffman, M.D., Gelman, A.: The No-U-turn sampler: adaptively setting path lengths in Hamiltonian Monte Carlo. J. Mach. Learn. Res. **15**(1), 1593–1623 (2014)
20. Hornbeck, H., Alim, U.: VSF Database (2019). https://gitlab.com/hjhornbeck/vsf-database, https://doi.org/10.5281/zenodo.2629410
21. Imageworks, S.P.: Open shading language readme (2018). https://github.com/imageworks/OpenShadingLanguage
22. Jakob, W.: Mitsuba renderer (2010)
23. Kalantari, N.K., Bako, S., Sen, P.: A machine learning approach for filtering Monte Carlo noise. ACM Trans. Graph. **34**(4), 122:1–122:12 (2015)

24. Mishchenko, M.I., Macke, A.: How big should hexagonal ice crystals be to produce halos? Appl. Opt. **38**(9), 1626–1629 (1999)
25. Newton, R.G.: Scattering Theory of Waves and Particles. Texts and Monographs in Physics, 2nd edn. Springer, New York (1982). https://doi.org/10.1007/978-3-642-88128-2
26. Scully, M.O., Walther, H., Schleich, W.: Feynman's approach to negative probability in quantum mechanics. Phys. Rev. A **49**(3), 1562–1566 (1994). https://doi.org/10.1103/PhysRevA.49.1562
27. Spencer, G., Shirley, P., Zimmerman, K., Greenberg, D.P.: Physically-based glare effects for digital images. In: Proceedings of the 22nd Annual Conference on Computer Graphics and Interactive Techniques - SIGGRAPH 1995, pp. 325–334. ACM Press (1995)
28. Wald, I., et al.: OSPRay - a CPU ray tracing framework for scientific visualization. IEEE Trans. Vis. Comput. Graph. **23**(1), 931–940 (2017)
29. Witt, A.N.: Multiple scattering in reflection nebulae. i - a Monte Carlo approach. Astrophys. J. Suppl. Ser. **35**, 6 (1977)
30. Zhang, X., Lewis, M., Lee, M., Johnson, B., Korotaev, G.: The volume scattering function of natural bubble populations. Limnol. Oceanogr. **47**(5), 1273–1282 (2002)

An Interactive Virtual Training System for Assembly and Disassembly Based on Precedence Constraints

Zhuoran Li[ID], Jing Wang[(✉)], Zhaoyu Yan, Xinyao Wang, and Muhammad Shahid Anwar[ID]

Beijing Institute of Technology, Beijing 100081, China
lzrideapad@outlook.com, {wangjing,3120180824}@bit.edu.cn,
zhaoyu.yan@outlook.com, shahidanwar786@gmail.com

Abstract. Compared with traditional training modes of assembly/disassembly, the virtual environment has advantages for enhancing the training quality, saving training resources, and breaking restrictions on training equipment and place. In order to balance the training quality, experience quality, and especially training costs, an interactive virtual training system for assembly and disassembly is discussed in this paper. The training is based on assembly precedence constraints among assembly paths. Also, the developer interface and the user interface are both provided for facilitation of the management, development, and modification of training contents. Two important modes of user interfaces are provided and based on immersive virtual reality (VR) devices and conventional desktop devices (the computer screen, keyboard, and mouse) for different economic conditions. Meanwhile, to improve the development efficiency of the training contents, the system is programmed as a software development kit providing the developer interface with parameter-input fields for Unity3d the virtual simulation engine. Finally, two subjective evaluation experiments are conducted to evaluate the usability in the training experience of interaction and precedence constraints via the desktop interface, and explore the difference of usability in the training experience between immersive VR environment and desktop environment provided by the training system.

Keywords: Virtual environment · Training system · Assembly and disassembly · Precedence constraint

1 Introduction

The society being advanced rapidly, the traditional training mode cannot meet the increasing social requirements any more due to restrictions on the training equipment, training time, training place and training costs. Researchers are constantly exploring its combination with the field of training, especially assembly/disassembly training [16]. Compared with the traditional assembly/disassembly training mode, the virtual training system can enhance the

M. Gavrilova et al. (Eds.): CGI 2019, LNCS 11542, pp. 81–93, 2019.
https://doi.org/10.1007/978-3-030-22514-8_7

efficiency of student teaching and worker training [19,25], and also contribute to reducing the waste of training resources.

However, for the existing computer-aided design (CAD) software, such as SolidWorks® and Inventor®, it needs to consider assembly constraints, hierarchical relationships, assembly relations and so forth, but not strict assembly/disassembly sequences. For developing and applying suitable customized training systems according to different application scenarios, professional programming skills are further required. Additionally, due to the constraint of the development period and development costs, customized training software are usually developed based on conventional desktop devices (generally the computer screen, keyboard, and mouse), and there are generally fewer interactive functions but more animation demonstrations in training contents, which make less contribution to the user experience.

In order to balance the training quality, experience quality and especially training costs, an interactive virtual training system for assembly/disassembly based on precedence constraints is discussed in this paper. Generally, for the virtual training on assembly/disassembly, researchers tend to develop based on the assembly/disassembly sequence of assembly units [3,8,27]. We focus on the precedence constraints among assembly paths which are defined to direct to positions on the same assembly reference. Ko et al. [14] propose that the assembly can be naturally represented as a hierarchical tree structure, as shown in Fig. 1. In the tree structure, each branch node and its child nodes can form the structure of "reference unit- assembly unit". Therefore, the entire assembly and disassembly process of an assembly model can be exactly covered by our development method of "reference unit-assembly path". For the sake of clarity, the main contributions/innovations of our work are summarized as follows:

- The introduced training system based on assembly precedence constraints among paths has following advantages: Tedious settings of assembly units can be avoided (e. g. reduce the shape accuracy requirement of the model collider). The challenge of "exponential explosion" in the development of complex precedence relations for assembly models with large numbers of assembly units can be prevented (e. g. many same units can be assembled to different locations). Modular programming and functionalities development can be facilitated.
- Both the developer interface and the user interface (UI) are provided, which is beneficial to management, quickly development, and modification of the training content.

Discussing our training system, the word of "assembly unit" is used rather than the designated "part", "component" or "sub-assembly". An assembly unit is a unit can be independently assembled, and a product can be divided into a number of assembly units.

2   Related Work

In the 1990s, the Fraunhofer Institute for Industrial Engineering (Germany) issued the first virtual assembly system. People could experience an interactive assembly process in the virtual environment provided by this system, which can also be used to analyze and evaluate the reliability of the assembly process [7]. In 1995, Washington State University and the National Institute of Standards and Technology (America) collaboratively conducted the exploration on manufacturing design in the VR environment. As a result, the Virtual Assembly Design Environment (VADE) was developed [11,12]. Since then, a wave of research on virtual assembly (VA) was set off. To study the potential advantages of assembly planning in virtual reality (VR) environments, Ye et al. [29] showed an experiment with three different operating environments (traditional engineering, desktop VR, and immersive VR). The results revealed that the two VR environments have advantages in improving the overall assembly planning performance of the subject, and also in dealing with the handling difficulty. Wan et al. [26] reported some optimization techniques used in a Multi-modal Immersive Virtual Assembly System (MIVAS), which enables assembly planners to perform assembly tasks on complex assemblies in a large-scale virtual environment. Sreng et al. [23] found that visual symbols and the associated visual effects seem beneficial to understanding the distance and contact force among parts, while the light source seems to help focus the attention of the user on main contact areas. Seth et al. [22] introduced the System for Haptic Assembly & Realistic Prototyping (SHARP) which is a platform independent application, and proposed a two - hand haptic interface using the PHANToM® haptic devices. Brough et al. [6] discussed the development of a virtual environment-based training system named Virtual Training Studio (VTS). It provides three training modes including the interactive simulation, the 3D animation, and the video.

These researches and discoveries promoted the application of virtual simulation technology in training and manufacturing industry, led to the gradually maturation of relevant theories and technologies, and clarified the application prospect of virtual training step by step. Nevertheless, the use of VR platforms for assembly tasks should be further evaluated [9].

In addition, it still needs time to achieve the large scale use of VR training system to the entire manufactory industry due to the comparatively high price of immersive devices and software. Li et al. [17] introduced a low-cost VR technology used in maintenance training, and use an object-oriented approach to combine a new disassembly sequence planning technique and the evolutionary algorithm with VR. Jiang et al. [13] introduced a virtual assembly platform considering lower cost, they used the MAYA and CATIA to build virtual scenes, Kinect V2 to capture the user position, and Unity3d to achieve the interaction. Concerning the balance of experience quality and application costs, our training system provides both the VR interface and desktop interface in Sect. 4.

Acquisition of training contents is also a problem currently. Liu et al. [18] proposed an original data decomposition and information translation method (DDITM), which can be used to divide the information of the assembly body

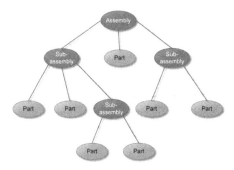

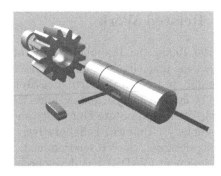

Fig. 1. An assembly is divided into several hierarchies in the assembly structure tree

Fig. 2. The blue lines are the instances of assembly path objects in a virtual scene (Color figure online)

in the CAD system into geometric information, topology information, assembly information, etc., and transmits them into the VA application separately. Hu et al. [10] introduced a script-driven virtual assembly simulation system based on assembly sequence concurrent planning. It can automatically generate assembly sequences for training. Stork et al. [24] proposed a data-import mechanism that can capture knowledge from diverse, heterogeneous enterprise resources, and integrates it into a model for virtual assembly training. However, there always exist the restrictions of the development period and requirement of programming skills. To increase the development efficiency. Section 3 introduces a distributed management solution for assembly paths and assembly references in the virtual environment. Also, our system is programmed as a software development kit (SDK) for Unity3d the simulation platform for facilitating development of training contents without programming.

In summary, constant reviews of existing systems and frequent studies of new opportunities from the academic literature will lead to greater competitiveness by improving product quality and reducing time to market [15].

3   Methods

3.1   Precedence Constraints Based on Assembly Paths

In the proposed system, an assembly path is essentially an object in the random access memory, and it is added with functionalities of detection and operation guidance, as depicted in Fig. 2. When the trainee moves a model to a path in the virtual scene and triggers the assembly function via the input device, the system calculates whether there are paths intersect a mesh model (assembly unit). If the designated model is detected, its position and posture data are changed to preset data stored on the detecting path, Then the assembly unit model can be guided along the path to the correct position on the reference unit. For the same reason, the assembly unit model can be guided away from the reference unit along the path under the correct disassembly operation.

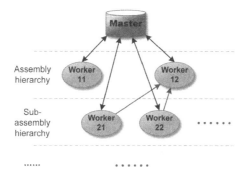

Fig. 3. Distributed management of assembly paths. The worker node represents the assembly reference node, and the black two-way arrow represents the two-way flow of messages. For the blue one-way arrows, they represent that the components assembled based on Worker 21 and Worker 22 are assembly units of Worker 12, and the Worker 21 and Worker 22 are required to send the result of integrality check to Worker 12 for assembly (Integrality check of the component) (Color figure online)

3.2 Distributed Management of Assembly Paths

A distributed management solution is proposed here to make the development of training content clear and convenient, as shown in Fig. 3. Each assembly reference model serves as a worker node to store and process precedence constraint data of paths belonging to it, and the worker nodes are managed by a master node. Nevertheless, since the training system is running on a separate computer, the worker nodes and the master node are pseudo nodes actually.

Management Process in Training Process. For the assembly operation, after the trainee moves a model to an assembly path and sends an assembly command via the input devices, the entire paths detect the model under the management of assembly reference nodes. If a model is detected by a certain path and it matches that path, the corresponding assembly reference node then sends a message of correct operation to the master node. Otherwise an error message will be sent. After the master node receives a message, an object reference in the master node will point to the detected model object and acquire the preset training information of the current assembly operation. Then the operation guiding function (Sect. 4.2, operation determination module) of the master node is activated for guiding the selected model to the correct assembly position along the matched path. After an assembly operation is successfully performed, the precedence constraint data managed by the assembly reference node is transferred to the next state for determining subsequent assembly/disassembly operations. For the disassembly operation, when the trainee selects an assembly unit model from the reference unit and sends the disassembly command, the assembly reference node will directly send the relevant message to the master node, and then the master node and the reference node will work in the same way as that of the assembly operation.

Integrality Check of Component. When the trainee assembles a component in a lower hierarchy to the reference unit in a higher hierarchy, the former is required to send the result of integrality check to the latter. The mechanism of integrality check is that only after the specified positions directed by assembly paths of a reference unit have been assembled overall, which means integrality in this paper, can the component assembled based on that reference unit be assembled to a higher hierarchy as an assembly unit. Otherwise, the disassembly operation will be determined as an error, and the relevant message will be sent to the master node. This mechanism is also described in Fig. 3.

4   Framework and Development

The introduced system is implemented as an SDK for Unity3d, and mainly consists of three parts, including the developer interface, function group, and user interface. The output of the developer interface connects the function group, and there is a two-way data interaction between the function group and user interface, as demonstrated in Fig. 4.

4.1   Developer Interface

The developer interface is designed to quickly develop, modify, and manage the training content. The model input unit is used to import the assembly model. The attribute data and name of the model can be modified or reset in the developer interface. A model can be original made in Solidworks as the ".stl" format file and then be converted in Blender to the mesh presentation (the format of ".fbx") required by Unity3d. The assembly path setting unit is used to set the positional data of the start point and end point of the path corresponding to each assembly position on the reference unit model. The training information input unit is used to add training tips for assembly unit models, and assembly/disassembly events activated on different assembly positions. The parameter input unit is used to set the value of the precedence relationship for assembly paths. Characteristic parameters are programmed as public variables and exposed on the developer interface as object reference and data input fields, so that developers even lacking programming skills are enabled to quickly develop an interactive virtual training application for assembly/disassembly.

4.2   Function Group

The function group consists of the timing module, model detection module, operation determination module, data processing module, and information composition module.

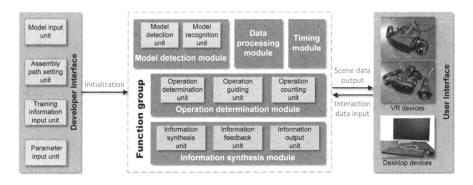

Fig. 4. The framework of the virtual training system for assembly/disassembly

Timing Module. The timing module is designed for timing the training process, which can be beneficial to analysis of the training effect.

Model Detection Module. This module will automatically generate a model detection unit on each path. In order to save the computational resources, only after the trainee sends the command of assembly, will each model detection unit works to detect whether there exists a model on the corresponding path for once, instead of real-time detection. If the selected model is detected on a path, the model recognition unit will automatically acquire its name, attribute data, and preset training information. And then the obtained data will be sent to the operation determination module and the information synthesis module.

Operation Determination Module. The operation determination unit determines whether the selected assembly path can currently guide the selected assembly unit model to perform assembly/disassembly actions based on the precedence constraints. The assembly guide unit guides the selected assembly unit model to assemble/disassemble along the selected path. The operation counting unit records the assembly/disassembly operations and sends operation messages to the information synthesis module.

Data Processing Module. After receiving the work instruction from the operation determination module, the data of precedence relationship managed by the assembly reference node being conducted the assembly/disassembly operation on are processed and calculated in the data processing module to transfer to the next record state, so that assembly paths can guide the subsequent assembly/disassembly operations.

Information Synthesis Module. The information synthesis unit combines the messages received from different function modules (such as the training information, operation result, error type and so forth) into the prompt text. The information feedback unit displays the prompt text to different locations on the UI canvas to remind the trainee. The information output unit saves each operation information of the trainee in the textual form and outputs it to an external file for evaluation by the trainer.

4.3   User Interface

Taking into account both training effects and training costs, the user interface is programmed as two main modes respectively based on immersive VR devices and conventional desktop devices. For the former, the purpose is to provide the trainee with a better immersive experience. The Steam VR plugin [2] and VRTK plugin [1] for Unity3d are applied here to exchange the data between VR devices and the training system. Also, using the VR controller to select and move the assembly unit model is more in line with natural behavior characteristics. For the latter, it is designed to reduce the economic cost on training compared with that of the former, which leads to that the trainee needs to use a keyboard and a mouse to interact with the system.

5   Case Study

To explore the usability of the training system in user experience and developer experience, the CB-B gear pump is taken as a study case, as demonstrated in Fig. 5. Two subjective evaluation experiments are conducted to assess the system usability.

5.1   Usability Evaluation on Interaction and Precedence Constraints in Disassembly Training

Experimental Setup. To test the usability of the interaction based on precedence constraints provided by the training system in user experience, a heuristic evaluation method [28] is applied and three experience modes (Exp1, Exp2, and Exp3) based on the desktop interface are designed. Exp1 is watching a 3D animation of disassembling the gear pump model in the correct sequence. Exp2 is disassembling the ordinary gear pump model without precedence constraints (no restriction on disassembly sequence). And Exp3 is disassembling the gear pump model under precedence constraints. Four evaluation factors are concerned in this experiment, including: (1) Cognition of assembly hierarchy (Item 1–1): Measure how much clearly the user can understand the assembly hierarchy and disassembly sequence. (2) Reasonability of disassembly process (Item 1–2): Measure how much reasonability of the virtual disassembly process the user can feel in the experience. (3) Immersion of the experience (Item 1–3): Measure how much feeling of presence and control the user can get in the experience. (4) Guiding ability of the experience (Item 1–4): Measure if the experience can guide the user to complete the virtual disassembly process. The three experience modes are with the same UI as depicted in Fig. 5. According to the research of Nielsen et al. [20] that the number of usability results found by aggregates of evaluators reaches the point of diminishing returns around the point of 10 evaluators, 10 graduate students having professional knowledge of mechanical assembly and virtual simulation are invited as experts in this test. The participants consist of 5 males and 5 females, and their ages are from 24 to 26. Each participant is

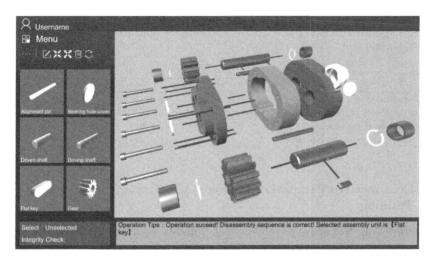

Fig. 5. The part models of the CB-B gear pump. The UI canvas in this picture is actually developed for desktop devices

trained about half an hour, and each experience mode is evaluated after being experienced once, The four evaluation factors need to be rated within the score range 1–10 (the higher, the better).

Results and Discussion. Since there are three conditions(Exp1, Exp2, and Exp3), and the survey results are discrete, the Friedman test (non-parametric test) is applied to analyze the scores in Table 1. The level of significance here is selected as $\alpha = 0.05$. With the data analysis, for Item 1–1, $p = 0.000 < 0.05$, for Item 1–2, $p = 0.001 < 0.05$, for Item 1–3, $p = 0.006 < 0.05$. The results indicate that there is a statistically significant difference among the different conditions in each Item. Then the Wilcoxon signed-rank test with Bonferroni correction is adopted as the post hoc test method. The significance level with Bonferroni correction is selected as $\alpha' = 0.017$. According to the average scores shown in Table 1, it can be concluded that: (1) Comparing Exp1 with Exp3, the existence of interaction can enhance the immersion quality for trainees under the desktop devices ($p = 0.008 < 0.017$), but it may not make an obvious contribution to the cognition process in training (for Item 1–1, $p = 1.000 > 0.017$, for Item 1–2, $p = 0.196 > 0.017$). (2) Comparing Exp2 with Exp3, the precedence constraint can significantly improve the cognition, reasonability, immersion, and guiding ability of the training process in the virtual environment (for Item 1–3, $p = 0.016 < 0.017$, for Item 1–4, $p = 0.008 < 0.017$). Meanwhile, the test results also indicate that if the desktop environment is chosen for virtual assembly/disassembly training due to the restriction of economic costs, the training content (precedence constraints in this experiment) should be taken as a priority in the development of training software, which can even affect the training quality, and then considers interaction to improve the experience quality of training process.

Table 1. The minimum, maximum and average scores of the four evaluation factors for three experience modes. Since Exp1 is watching the animation, the scores for Exp1 on Item 1–4 are null

Item	Evaluation factor	Exp1			Exp2			Exp3		
		Min	Max	Average	Min	Max	Average	Min	Max	Average
1–1	Cognition of assembly hierarchy	6	10	8.2	1	7	4.4	5	10	8
1–2	Reasonability of the disassembly process	6	10	7.6	1	7	4.1	7	9	8.2
1–3	Immersion of the experience	4	8	5.6	3	10	6.8	7	10	8.2
1–4	Guiding ability of the experience	/	/	/	1	10	4.5	6	10	8

5.2 Comparative Evaluation Between VR Training and Desktop Training

Experimental Setup. To explore the difference of the usability between immersive VR environment and desktop environment provided by the training system, the latter is set as a benchmark. The Participant needs to firstly experience the disassembly process via the immersive VR devices, then the desktop devices, and the process is under precedence constraints. Five evaluation factors are applied for comparison rating and analysis, including: (1) Immersion of the experience (Item 2–1). (2) Cognition of assembly hierarchy (Item 2–3). (3) Guiding ability of the experience (Item 2–4). These three are the same as in Sect. 5.1. The other two factors are: (4) Comfort of interaction (Item 2–2): Measure how much feeling of comfort the user can get in interaction. (5) Degree of precedence constraints (Item 2–5): Measure how much precedence constraints the user can feel in the experience. Other 10 graduate students are invited in this experiment. And the user characteristics keep the same as in the first experiment. The comparison score ranges from -5 to 5, and the positive number represents the evaluation factor of the VR experience is better than that of the desktop experience while the negative number represents worse. The larger the absolute value of the score, the larger the difference is, and 0 means no difference. Furthermore, the system usability scale (SUS) [5] is applied in this experiment. The SUS is a quick and common method to evaluate the usability of a product or a user interface, and Bangor et al. [4] found it is more advantageous for small samples $(n < 14)$.

Results and Discussion. The score distributions are statistically processed by their quartiles, as shown in Fig. 6. It is evident that the score boxes of Item 2–1 and Item 2–2 are comparatively short, at a high level, and without whisker structure. And it means all participants agree that the disassembly training in the VR environment has significant advantages in immersion and interaction referring to that in the desktop environment. For Item 2–3, $Q1 = 0$, $Q2 = Q3 = 3$, for Item 2–4, $Q1 = 1$, $Q3 = 3$, which means that most participants think it is more beneficial to the cognition of assembly hierarchy and disassembly process to train in the immersive VR environment, and feel a comparatively stronger guidance effect. Meanwhile, it can be intuitively found that the score boxes of Item 2–3

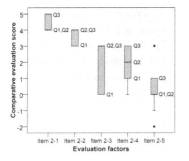

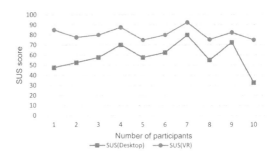

Fig. 6. The box-plot of comparative evaluation scores for the five
evaluation factors

Fig. 7. SUS scores for Desktop interface and VR
interface provided by the training system

and Item 2–4 are obviously lower than those of Item 2–1 and Item 2–2. For Item
2–5, two abnormal values appear, and the score box is between 0 and 1, it seems
that the subjective feeling of precedence constraints degree are more likely to
be unaffected by the training environment. The SUS scores of 10 participants
are depicted in Fig. 7. It can be clearly seen that the SUS score of the desktop
interface and that of the VR interface are in curves revealing the same trend,
and it is verified the former is higher than the latter by Wilcoxon test ($\alpha = 0.05$,
$p = 0.005 < 0.05$). When the SUS score of a product reaches 69 or so, the usability
of the product reaches an average level [4,21]. The average SUS score of the
desktop interface is 58.75, below the average level around 10 points. The average
SUS score of the VR interface is 81.05, above the average level around 10 points.
The results intuitively demonstrate that there is a comparatively big gap in the
overall usability between the VR interface and desktop interface. Nevertheless,
the latter is still meaningful and acceptable, taking into account the advantage
of the desktop interface on saving economic costs, and the main advantage of
the VR environment is enhancing the experience quality of user immersion and
interaction in the training process.

6   Conclusion

An interactive virtual training system for assembly/disassembly based on precedence constraints is proposed in this paper, providing both the developer interface and the user interface. The usability of the training system is evaluated by
two subjective experiments. However, there are some limitations in the research.
For the first experiment, participants need to disassemble the same object (CB-
B gear pump) in all three conditions in for controlling experimental variables.
Therefore, there could be a learning effect, where the disassembly becomes easier
overtime. We chose to remove it by the randomization of the condition order.
However, It could need to be studied in the future how much effectively the
randomization removes this. For the second experiment, the experimental time
is not set as a basis for analysis considering the order effect. Moreover, the

experiment is focused on the performance of the VR interface compared to the desktop interface, so the experimental results are not enough to point out the precise advantages of the VR interface. It might be due to inherent advantages of VR, or it might be just that the desktop interface is not designed perfectly. Further experiments should be designed to collect more data, and more usability tests should be designed to find out whether there are flaws in the user interface and interactions in the future.

References

1. VRTK - Virtual Reality Toolkit (2017). https://vrtoolkit.readme.io/
2. SteamVR Plugin (2018). https://store.steampowered.com/steamvr
3. Banerjee, A., Banerjee, P.: A behavioral scene graph for rule enforcement in inter-active virtual assembly sequence planning. Comput. Ind. **42**(2–3), 147–157 (2000)
4. Bangor, A., Kortum, P., Miller, J.: Determining what individual sus scores mean: adding an adjective rating scale. J. Usability Stud. **4**(3), 114–123 (2009)
5. Brooke, J.: SUS-a quick and dirty usability scale. Usability Eval. Ind. **189**(194), 4–7 (1996)
6. Brough, J.E., Schwartz, M., Gupta, S.K., Anand, D.K., Kavetsky, R., Pettersen, R.: Towards the development of a virtual environment-based training system for mechanical assembly operations. Vir. Real. **11**(4), 189–206 (2007)
7. Bullinger, H., Richter, M., Seidel, K.A.: Virtual assembly planning. Hum. Factors Ergon. Manuf. Serv. Ind. **10**(3), 331–341 (2000)
8. Christiand, C., Yoon, J.: Assembly simulations in virtual environments with optimized haptic path and sequence. Robot. Comput. Integr. Manuf. **27**(2), 306–317 (2011). https://doi.org/10.1016/j.rcim.2010.07.015
9. Gavish, N., et al.: Evaluating virtual reality and augmented reality training for industrial maintenance and assembly tasks. Interact. Learn. Environ. **23**(6), 778–798 (2015)
10. Hu, X., Zhu, W., Yu, T., Xiong, Z.: A script-driven virtual assembly simulation system based on assembly sequence concurrent planning. In: International Conference on Mechatronics and Automation, ICMA 2009, pp. 2478–2483. IEEE (2009)
11. Jayaram, S., Connacher, H.I., Lyons, K.W.: Virtual assembly using virtual reality techniques. Comput.-Aided Des. **29**(8), 575–584 (1997)
12. Jayaram, S., Jayaram, U., Wang, Y., Tirumali, H., Lyons, K., Hart, P.: VADE: a virtual assembly design environment. IEEE Comput. Graph. Appl. **19**(6), 44–50 (1999)
13. Jiang, S., et al.: Research on low cost virtual assembly training platform based on somatosensory technology. In: 2017 IEEE International Conference on Industrial Engineering and Engineering Management (IEEM), pp. 250–254. IEEE (2017)
14. Ko, H., Lee, K.: Automatic assembling procedure generation from mating conditions. Comput.-Aided Des. **19**(1), 3–10 (1987)
15. Lawson, G., Salanitri, D., Waterfield, B.: Future directions for the development of virtual reality within an automotive manufacturer. Appl. Ergon. **53**, 323–330 (2016)
16. Leu, M.C., et al.: CAD model based virtual assembly simulation, planning and training. CIRP Ann. **62**(2), 799–822 (2013)

17. Li, J.R., Khoo, L.P., Tor, S.B.: Desktop virtual reality for maintenance training: an object oriented prototype system (V-REALISM). Comput. Ind. **52**(2), 109–125 (2003)
18. Liu, J.S., Yao, Y.X., Pahlovy, S.A., Li, J.G.: A novel data decomposition and information translation method from CAD system to virtual assembly application. Int. J. Adv. Manuf. Tech. **28**, 395–402 (2006)
19. Murcia-Lopez, M., Steed, A.: A comparison of virtual and physical training transfer of bimanual assembly tasks. IEEE Trans. Vis. Comput. Graph. **24**(4), 1574–1583 (2018)
20. Nielsen, J., Molich, R.: Heuristic evaluation of user interfaces. In: Proceedings of the SIGCHI Conference on Human Factors in Computing Systems, pp. 249–256. ACM (1990)
21. Sauro, J., Lewis, J.R.: Quantifying the User Experience: Practical Statistics for User Research. Morgan Kaufmann, San Francisco (2016)
22. Seth, A., Su, H.J., Vance, J.M.: Sharp: a system for haptic assembly and realistic prototyping. In: ASME 2006 International Design Engineering Technical Conferences and Computers and Information in Engineering Conference, pp. 905–912. American Society of Mechanical Engineers (2006)
23. Sreng, J., Lécuyer, A., Mégard, C., Andriot, C.: Using visual cues of contact to improve interactive manipulation of virtual objects in industrial assembly/maintenance simulations. IEEE Trans. Vis. Comput. Graph. **12**(5), 1013–1020 (2006)
24. Stork, A., et al.: Enabling virtual assembly training in and beyond the automotive industry. In: 2012 18th International Conference on Virtual Systems and Multimedia (VSMM), pp. 347–352. IEEE (2012)
25. Stratos, A., Loukas, R., Dimitris, M., Konstantinos, G., Dimitris, M., George, C.: A virtual reality application to attract young talents to manufacturing. Procedia CIRP **57**, 134–139 (2016)
26. Wan, H., Gao, S., Peng, Q., Cai, Y.: Optimization techniques for assembly planning of complex models in large-scale virtual environments. Int. J. Image Graph. **3**(02), 379–398 (2003)
27. Wang, Y., Tian, D.: A weighted assembly precedence graph for assembly sequence planning. Int. J. Adv. Manuf. Technol. **83**(1–4), 99–115 (2016)
28. Xia, P., Lopes, A.M., Restivo, M.T., Yao, Y.: A new type haptics-based virtual environment system for assembly training of complex products. Int. J. Adv. Manuf. Technol. **58**(1–4), 379–396 (2012)
29. Ye, N., Banerjee, P., Banerjee, A., Dech, F.: A comparative study of assembly planning in traditional and virtual environments. IEEE Trans. Syst. Man Cybern. Part C (Appl. Rev.) **29**(4), 546–555 (1999)

Multi-character Motion Retargeting for Large-Scale Transformations

Maryam Naghizadeh$^{(\boxtimes)}$ and Darren Cosker

University of Bath, Bath, UK
{M.Naghizadeh,D.P.Cosker}@bath.ac.uk

Abstract. Unlike single-character motion retargeting, multi-character motion retargeting (MCMR) algorithms should be able to retarget each character's motion correcly while maintaining the interaction between them. Existing MCMR solutions mainly focus on small scale changes between interacting characters. However, many retargeting applications require large-scale transformations. In this paper, we propose a new algorithm for large-scale MCMR. We build on the idea of interaction meshes, which are structures representing the spatial relationship among characters. We introduce a new distance-based interaction mesh that embodies the relationship between characters more accurately by prioritizing local connections over global ones. We also introduce a stiffness weight for each skeletal joint in our mesh deformation term, which defines how undesirable it is for the interaction mesh to deform around that joint. This parameter increases the adaptability of our algorithm for large-scale transformations and reduces optimization time considerably. We compare the performance of our algorithm with current state-of-the-art MCMR solution for several motion sequences under four different scenarios. Our results show that our method not only improves the quality of retargeting, but also significantly reduces computation time.

Keywords: Motion retargeting · Computer animation ·
Character interaction · Mesh deformation · Joint stiffness ·
Space-time optimization

1 Introduction

Single-character motion retargeting (SCMR) is "the problem of adapting an animated motion from one character to another" [4]. SCMR is a widely studied field and has many applications ranging from animation to robotics. However, many of these applications require more than one character to be retargeted together, e.g. fighting characters in an animation or collaborative robot tasks.

This research is co-funded by the European Union's Horizon 2020 research and innovation programme under the Marie Skłodowska-Curie grant agreement No. 665992, and the UK's EPSRC Centre for Doctoral Training in Digital Entertainment (CDE), EP/L016540/1.

M. Gavrilova et al. (Eds.): CGI 2019, LNCS 11542, pp. 94–106, 2019.
https://doi.org/10.1007/978-3-030-22514-8_8

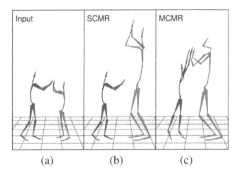

Fig. 1. The green character from the input (a) is retargeted to 2.0x its original size via SCMR (b) and MCMR (c). The interaction between blue and green characters is lost in SCMR while MCMR successfully preserves the high-five. (Color figure online)

SCMR is lacking when it comes to solving such problems since retargeting each character independently results in interaction loss among the characters. We will refer to these problems as multi-character motion retargeting (MCMR), which aims at generating motion for multiple target characters given the motion data for their corresponding source subjects. MCMR is different from individually retargeting multiple characters at the same time, which is illustrated in Fig. 1. When the green character from the input is individually retargeted to 2.0x its original size via SCMR, the high-five interaction between the blue and green characters is lost. However, this interaction is successfully maintained when an MCMR solution is used to perform the retargeting. MCMR is even more difficult when the scale change for one character is very different from the other one. Such cases are common in games and movies. For example, movies like *Avatar* and *Lord of the Rings* use motion retargeting to drive characters that are much taller or shorter than the human actors controlling them. Current solutions include using physical props to direct actor eye-lines towards the correct target above the other actors body, or having actors stand on boxes or stilts. Even so, a significant amount of clean-up is required, increasing post-processing time considerably. Moreover, acting under such circumstances is quite inconvenient for the actors.

In this paper, we propose an algorithm for large-scale MCMR that uses distance-based interaction meshes with anatomically-based stiffness weights. Existing MCMR solutions fail under large-scale character changes because they are tailored to cases where the height relationship is similar between source and target characters. These algorithms cannot adapt to increasing scale changes mostly because they do not consider human anatomy in their work and assume equal freedom of movement for all joints along the human skeleton. In order to attribute different levels of motion freedom for skeletal joints, we use stiffness weights, which have been successfully employed in large mesh deformations [13]. We use stiffness weights to define how costly it is for the interaction mesh to deform around each joint. The intuition behind stiffness weights is that they act like joint angle constraints; when a mesh does not deform around a joint after retargeting, the angles between its neighbors and itself do not change either. Our proposed method can successfully retarget motion for characters under large-scale transformations with greatly reduced computational time in comparison to existing MCMR approaches. To summarize, our contributions include:

1. Proposing the first MCMR algorithm tailored for large-scale character transformations.
2. Introducing an interaction mesh structure suitable for small and large-scale character transformations.
3. Introducing anatomically-based joint stiffness weights that improve retargeting quality while significantly reducing retargeting time.

2   Related Work

Single-Character Motion Retargeting. Motion retargeting is defined as "the problem of adapting an animated motion from one character to another" [4]. Early retargeting solutions focused on retargeting motion between characters with identical skeletal structure [3,4,17], mainly using inverse kinematics and space-time optimization. More recent approaches include formulating motion retargeting as a distance-based optimization problem [2] and using recurrent neural networks [18].

Context-Aware Motion Adaptation. Many retargeting studies do not consider the interaction of characters with the rest of the scene. However, retargeting characters independently often causes interaction artifacts in the scene and requires further manual work to fix them. Some studies define interaction descriptors between two objects, which are used to group objects according to their functionality or calculate the similarity between two scenes [8,9,14]. Zhao et al. introduce the *interaction bisector surface* (IBS) for capturing the spatial relationships among the objects in a scene [20]. IBS is mainly useful for applications with geometrically well-defined rigid objects and cannot be used to model interaction between deformable structures. These methods cannot readily be used for modelling the interaction space around a character due to its dynamic nature. Early solutions include defining constraints to achieve the desired relationship among the character and its surroundings [4,12]. One recent solution is provided by Zhao et al., which extends the application of IBS [20] to character-object interaction [19].

Multi-character Motion Retargeting. Not much research has been conducted on maintaining intercharacter relationship in motion retargeting. Ho et al. propose a method to maintain character interaction by introducing the concept of *interaction meshes* [7]. An interaction mesh is a structure that represents the spatial relationship among subjects and is obtained by performing *Delaunay tetrahedralization* [15] on the joint cloud of the subjects in the scene. The objective of their method is to solve the retargeting problem while preserving the structure of the interaction mesh. To do so, they formulate motion retargeting as a space-time optimization problem. The main limitation of this algorithm is that it does not always succeed in producing realistic postures especially when source and target characters have very different scales.

Ho et al. introduce a multi-resolution version of [7] by cutting the motion sequence into smaller pieces and solving each one separately, which makes the algorithm parallelizable and improves its computation time to some extent [6]. Another study uses the interaction mesh for interactive partner control [5]. In this study, the algorithm compares motion capture input to frames from a motion database that contains motion sequences of a duo (one labelled as active and the other as passive). The best match is decided via a metric that considers Euclidean distance from the input pose as well as temporal coherence to previous frames. The final motion is synthesized by using the method in [7] to retarget the active partner's pose to match the scale of the user.

Jin et al. propose the *Aura Mesh*, a volumetric mesh structure that encapsulates the spatial relationship between two skinned characters [10]. During the pre-processing stage, aura meshes are constructed for the source and target characters. At run-time stage, collision points of the aura meshes are used to embody the semantics of the interaction between characters. Inverse kinematics is used to generate the final motion by respecting the desired collision positions and minimizing a few other energy terms pertaining to motion naturalness such as pose preservation and foot contact. While very useful for retargeting close interaction between characters, this method suffers from a few disadvantages; retargeting is performed frame-by-frame and the output is interpolated to achieve smoothness, which can violate the original constraints. Furthermore, their method relies on having equal mesh topology for all characters in order to establish correspondence among aura meshes. This means that it cannot retarget characters with different mesh topologies. Finally, the method fails under large scale differences between source and target characters.

3   Methodology

First, we will formally define the inputs of the algorithm as depicted in Fig. 2.

Motion Sequence ($\mathcal{V}$). Input motion contains 3D joint position data for source subjects over time. Let n be the number of frames in the motion sequence: $\mathcal{V} = (V_1, V_2, ...V_n)$. For each frame i, V_i is a vector composed of joint position vectors for all source subjects.

Joint Stiffness Matrix (S). Joint stiffness matrix is a new parameter that we introduce in this paper. It is a square diagonal matrix that contains stiffness weights for the joints:

$$S = \begin{pmatrix} s_1^1 & 0 & 0 & 0 & \cdots & 0 \\ 0 & s_1^2 & 0 & 0 & \cdots & 0 \\ 0 & 0 & s_1^3 & 0 & \cdots & 0 \\ 0 & 0 & 0 & s_2^1 & \cdots & 0 \\ \vdots & \vdots & \vdots & \vdots & \ddots & \vdots \\ 0 & 0 & 0 & 0 & \cdots & s_a^3 \end{pmatrix} \tag{1}$$

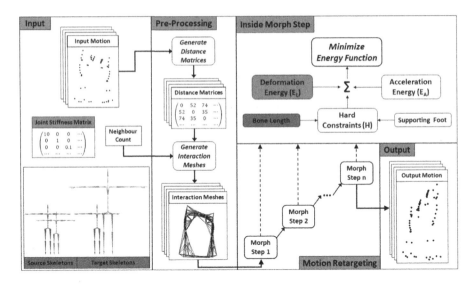

Fig. 2. An overview of our approach

where a is the number of joints in the skeleton, and s_j^1, s_j^2 and s_j^3 hold the stiffness weight for the j-th joint along X, Y and Z axes, respectively. These weights define how undesirable it is for the interaction mesh to deform around the j-th joint along each axis.

Bone Lengths (L). L is comprised of two vectors: L_S and L_T, which contain bone length values for source subjects and target characters.

Neighbor Count (N). N is the number of connections per joint in the interaction mesh.

3.1 Pre-processing

The pre-processing stage has two steps: calculating distance matrices and building interaction meshes.

Calculating Distance Matrices. The first step in pre-processing phase is calculating a distance matrix for each frame in the motion sequence, which contains the Euclidean distance between all joint pairs in the scene.

Distance-Based Interaction Mesh. First introduced in [7], interaction mesh is a mesh structure that represents the spatial relationship between subjects for all frames along the motion sequence. The interaction mesh in [7] is obtained via Delaunay tetrahedralization of the 3D points that represent skeletal joints of the subjects in the frame. These joints constitute the vertices of the interaction mesh and a connection between a pair of vertices represents a spatial relationship between their corresponding joints. A sample interaction mesh generated via this method is depicted in Fig. 3(a).

We propose a new distance-based method to create interaction meshes. Given a neighbor count N, the algorithm builds an interaction mesh for each frame

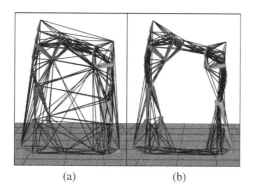

(a)   (b)

Fig. 3. Delaunay tetrahedralization produces interaction meshes with global connectivity (a), while our distance-based mesh prioritize local interactions (b). (Color figure online)

using its corresponding distance matrix to find the N closest joints in the space around each joint. By connecting each joint to its N closest joints, a distance-based interaction mesh is obtained that prioritizes local connectivity; unlike the interaction mesh constructed via Delaunay tetrahedralization. Figure 3(b) shows a sample interaction mesh created using our distance-based approach where each joint has 12 connections. The intuition behind our distance-based approach comes from the fact that if interactions are preserved locally, they would be maintained globally as well. Moreover, global connections can affect large-scale retargeting adversely because distant connections are often not meaningful or necessary for the spatial relationship between the characters. For instance, the connections between the elbow of the green character and the leg joints of the blue character in Fig. 3(a) force the green character to bend unnaturally when it is retargeted to a taller character.

3.2   Motion Retargeting with Joint Stiffness

Similar to [7], our algorithm takes on a step-wise approach to solve the retargeting problem. Instead of going directly from original scale to target scale, the algorithm divides the scale difference between source and target to k equal *morph steps* and solves them separately. First, step 1 is solved, then step 2 and so on; until the final result is produced in the last step. The output of each step provides the input for the next step. The following equation describes the objective function that each morph step is trying to minimize in our method:

$$\arg\min_{V_i',\lambda_i} \sum_{i=1}^{n} E_L + w_\Delta E_A + \lambda_i^T (H_i V_i' - h_i) \tag{2}$$

which is the sum of deformation (E_L) and acceleration (E_A) energies subject to the satisfaction of hard constraints $(\lambda_i^T (H_i V_i' - h_i))$. In this equation, V_i' is the vector containing the updated joint positions for frame i, λ_i represents the Lagrange multipliers for frame i, n is the number of frames, w_Δ is a constant weight assigned for acceleration energy, H_i is the hard constraint Jacobian matrix for frame i and h_i is a vector that contains the hard constraint values for frame i. Note that unlike [7], we do not consider the soft constraints (collision and positional constraints) in our energy function.

Deformation energy (E_L) is the term that preserves the spatial relationship between the subjects by minimizing the deformation of the interaction meshes during retargeting. Equation (3) is used in [7] to minimize the Laplacian deformation energy [1] of the interaction meshes:

$$E_L(V_i') = \frac{1}{2}V_i'^\mathsf{T}M_i^\mathsf{T}M_iV_i' - b_i^\mathsf{T}M_iV_i' + \frac{1}{2}b_i^\mathsf{T}b_i \tag{3}$$

where V_i' contains the updated joint positions for frame i, b_i holds the original Laplacian coordinates for frame i and M_i is the Laplacian matrix.

The deformation energy term defined by Eq. (3) assumes that deformation cost is equal for all joints. An unintended side effect of this is that the optimization tries to preserve the relative height relationship among the subjects. This results in a squashing effect when one of the subjects is being retargeted to a taller character and stretching effect when it is being retargeted to a shorter one. This issue becomes bolder for large-scale character transformations since the height relationship among the subjects is required to change after retargeting. This issue happens because Eq. (3) is oblivious to the fact that not all joints in the human body have the same freedom of movement. For example, elbow and knee joints can move more freely compared to the spine joints. In order to resolve this problem, we introduce a weight for each joint in the deformation energy that defines how *undesirable* it is for this joint to violate its position in the interaction mesh. We do this by adding the stiffness weight matrix (**S**) to Eq. (3) and obtaining the following new deformation term:

$$E_L(V_i') = \frac{1}{2}V_i'^\mathsf{T}M_i^\mathsf{T}\mathbf{S}M_iV_i' - b_i^\mathsf{T}\mathbf{S}M_iV_i' + \frac{1}{2}b_i^\mathsf{T}\mathbf{S}b_i \tag{4}$$

Joint stiffness matrix defines a stiffness weight for each joint in the skeleton. The matrix instructs the objective function to tolerate deformation around joints with low stiffness value and protect the mesh structure around joints with high stiffness value. It should be noted that the stiffness value for a joint is meaningless on its own, and that our joint stiffness weights operate in a relative way (for example, weights of 2 and 20 for a pair of joints act the same as weights of 4 and 40). Therefore, the relationship among the values defines how costly it is for the objective function when the mesh deforms around the joints with respect to each other. With that in mind, we divide the joints in the skeleton to three levels of priority: *stiff*, *normal* and *loose*. A good analogy is to think of stiff, normal and loose stiffness levels as hard, medium and soft joint angle constraints. We make the assumption that the joints along the spine (including the hip joint) are the least free in their movement in human skeleton and should be in the stiff category. We also make the assumption that the elbow and knee joints are the most freely-moving joints in the human skeleton and include them in the loose category. Finally, we label the rest of the joints in the skeleton as normal.

Note that we calculate Laplacian coordinates in a similar fashion to [7] and that Laplacian weights are inversely proportional to the Euclidean distance between the vertices in the interaction mesh. Also, hard constraints and acceleration energy are included in our energy function in a similar manner to [7].

4   Results and Discussion

We tested our algorithm on the following motion sequences: high-five, handshake, kicking, dance and Ogoshi[1]. Our selection includes both simple and complex types of interaction to cover a wide range of motions. We refer to simple interactions as motion instances where the spatial relationship among the subjects is partial, such as shaking hands. On the other hand, the spatial relationship in complex interactions (e.g. dancing) span the whole body.

Setting Parameter Values. Unlike Delaunay tetrahedralization, our method receives the number of connections per joint as input. We tested our method's retargeting quality for various neighbor counts. For most interactions, 12 connections per joint provides satisfactory results. However, complex interactions may require up to 16 connections per joint. We set the stiffness weight for normal joints to 1. Therefore, for loose joints, the stiffness weight should be between 0 and 1, and for stiff joints, it can range from 1 to infinity. After experimenting with various weights, we observed that a too small stiffness value for loose joints creates unrealistic poses, and a very large stiffness weight for stiff joints increases the convergence time of the algorithm without producing any better results. We suggest that a good stiffness weight for loose joints is between 0.05 and 0.2, and a good stiffness weight for stiff joints lies between 5 and 50. For all our experiments, we used 0.1 and 10 for loose and stiff joints, respectively. Finally, as suggested by [7], w_Δ and the number of morph steps were set to 0.2 and 10 in all our experiments.

4.1   Retargeting Results

In order to analyze the effect of distance-based interaction meshes and joint stiffness on the final output separately, we conducted our experiments in four different scenarios: (1) Interaction mesh is generated via Delaunay tetrahedralization and the energy function does not include joint stiffness (SRP-WOS)[2]; (2) Interaction mesh is generated via Delaunay tetrahedralization and the energy function includes joint stiffness (SRP-WS); (3) Interaction mesh is generated via our distance-based method and the energy function does not include joint stiffness (DB-WOS); and 4) Interaction mesh is generated via our distance-based

---

[1] Video results are provided in the supplemental material.

[2] This is the same [7] with the exclusion of collision and positional constraints.

(a)   (b)   (c)

Fig. 4. The first row depicts three sample frames from high-five, dance and Ogoshi motion sequences. The second, third, fourth and fifth rows show the result of retargeting the green subject to 2.0x its original size using spatial relationship preserving method without (SRP-WOS) and with (SRP-WS) stiffness, and distance-based method without (DB-WOS) and with (DB-WS) stiffness, respectively. DB-WS produces realistic results by bending the knees and arms when needed to preserve the interaction between the characters without squashing the spine joints. (Color figure online)

method and the energy function includes joint stiffness (DB-WS). We will use the terms "DB-WS" and "our method" interchangeably.

Figure 4 shows our results for three sample frames from high-five (Fig. 4(a)), dance (Fig. 4(b)) and Ogoshi (Fig. 4(c)) sequences. The second, third, fourth and fifth rows show the result of retargeting the green subject to 2.0x its original size using SRP-WOS. SRP-WS, DB-WOS and DB-WS, respectively. The height relationship between the subjects changes after doubling the green subject's scale. SRP-WOS fails at adapting to the new height relationship between the characters and tries to maintain the original relationship by squashing the green character along the spine. SRP-WS performs slightly better as the stiffness weights preserve the natural alignment of the spine joints. However, the global nature of the Delaunay mesh forces the green character to bend backwards unrealistically in the high-five sequence. DB-WOS manages to adapt to the new height relationship among the characters but the spine looks crooked. DB-WS successfully adapts to the new scale of the green character by bending the knee joints when required and keeping the spine joints intact. One can notice the difference between the effect of using distance-based meshes versus adding joint stiffness by comparing SRP-WS and DB-WOS. This example highlights how adding stiffness improves posture while using distance-based meshes improves the adaptability of the algorithm to changes in the height relationship among characters.

Another noticeable observation is that head orientation cannot be retargeted properly with any of the four methods. This is because the head orientation depends on the subject's gaze target. Since the gaze target can be anywhere in the space, retargeting the head orientation correctly is not possible solely using the interaction mesh. To resolve this issue, the gaze target must be detected during the pre-processing phase (e.g. using an eye tracker) and the direction of the head must be adjusted after retargeting to face the gaze target.

4.2   Computation Time

The algorithm is implemented in MATLAB 2017b and all the computation times are recorded on an Intel Xeon 2.90 GHz CPU with 32 GB RAM.

Table 1(a) compares pre-processing times for when Delaunay tetrahedralization is used for mesh generation versus when our distance-based method is used. The pre-processing times for the distance-based method is slightly longer than the Delaunay method, which is due to the time spent building distance matrices. Notice how pre-processing time increases for both scenarios with the number of joints per subject. This is expected as the time required for generating interaction meshes grows with the number of joints.

Table 1(b) compares retargeting time results for when joint stiffness is not included in the objective function versus when it is. We see that adding stiffness massively improves the retargeting time. This improvement happens because the joint stiffness matrix guides the optimizer towards the answer by inciting it to prioritize preserving the structure of the mesh around the joints with relatively higher stiffness values and not restrain the mesh around the joints with

Table 1. Time analysis

			a. Pre-processing time results[1]			
			Delaunay tetrahedralization		Distance-based	
Name	No. of frames	No. of joints[2]	No. of connections	Pre-processing time[3]	No. of connections	Pre-processing time[3]
High-five	110	34	12.06	0.065	12	0.111
Handshake	110	34	12.28	0.066	12	0.112
Kicking	85	25	11.44	0.046	16	0.079
Dance	250	32	11.87	0.065	16	0.115
Ogoshi	255	25	11.59	0.054	12	0.082

			b. Retargeting time results[1]		
				Retargeting time[3]	
Name	No. of frames	No. of joints[2]	No. of connections	Without stiffness	With stiffness
High-five	110	34	12	7.95	0.30
Handshake	110	34	12	8.05	0.36
Kicking	85	25	16	2.39	0.24
Dance	250	32	16	31.27	0.78
Ogoshi	255	25	12	15.92	0.26

			c. Total run-time results[1]			
			Total run-time[3]			
Name	No. of frames	No. of joints[2]	SRP-WOS	DB-WOS	SRP-WS	DB-WS
High-five	110	34	7.90	8.06	0.37	0.41
Handshake	110	34	8.05	8.15	0.42	0.47
Kicking	85	25	2.40	2.46	0.30	0.32
Dance	250	32	31.32	31.38	0.84	0.89
Ogoshi	255	25	15.93	16.03	0.32	0.36

[1] The times in this table are obtained by averaging over 10 runs of the algorithm for high-five, handshake and kicking sequences and 5 runs for the dance and Ogoshi sequences. The standard deviation values are negligible in all cases.   [2] per subject   [3] sec/frame

relatively lower values. Having different stiffness values for the joints makes the energy function an easier problem to solve since the deformation cost is not evenly distributed among the joints. This helps the optimizer to narrow down its search space much faster and find the solution in considerably less time. Another interesting observation is that without stiffness, the retargeting time for each frame increases with the number of frames, whereas this increase is more marginal with stiffness.

Table 1(c) compares the total run-time of our method versus the other three. While SRP-WS edges out DB-WS for best run-time, both methods have significant time advantage over the other two.

5   Conclusion and Future Work

In this paper, we introduced a new algorithm for large-scale multi-character motion retargeting (MCMR). We compared our method with the state-of-the-art MCMR solution. We demonstrated that our method not only outperforms existing skeletal MCMR approaches in terms of retargeting quality but it also improves run-time, is more scalable and can deal with larger sequences more efficiently. Our method produces animations that can be used to considerably reduce the amount of post-processing, by providing a much better starting point for further editing. One of the limitations of our work is that it does not include physics constraints such as balance. This can be resolved by adding a balance term to our energy function similar to [6]. Another direction for future work would be to include priors over the ranges of acceptable joint angles to avoid unlikely postures. Finally, it would be interesting to explore the effect of different forms of deformation energy such as Bi-Laplacian [11] and As-Rigid-As-Possible [16] on the quality of retargeting.

References

1. Alexa, M.: Differential coordinates for local mesh morphing and deformation. Vis. Comput. **19**(2), 105–114 (2003)
2. Bernardin, A., Hoyet, L., Mucherino, A., Gonçalves, D., Multon, F.: Normalized Euclidean distance matrices for human motion retargeting. In: Proceedings of the Tenth International Conference on Motion in Games, MIG 2017, pp. 15:1–15:6. ACM, New York (2017)
3. Choi, K.J., Ko, H.S.: Online motion retargetting. J. Vis. Comput. Animation **11**(5), 223–235 (2000)
4. Gleicher, M.: Retargetting motion to new characters. In: Proceedings of the 25th Annual Conference on Computer Graphics and Interactive Techniques, SIG-GRAPH 1998, pp. 33–42. ACM, New York (1998)
5. Ho, E.S.L., Chan, J.C.P., Komura, T., Leung, H.: Interactive partner control in close interactions for real-time applications. ACM Trans. Multimedia Comput. Commun. Appl. **9**(3), 21:1–21:19 (2013)
6. Ho, E.S.L., Wang, H., Komura, T.: A multi-resolution approach for adapting close character interaction. In: Proceedings of the 20th ACM Symposium on Virtual Reality Software and Technology, VRST 2014, pp. 97–106. ACM, New York (2014)
7. Ho, E.S., Komura, T., Tai, C.L.: Spatial relationship preserving character motion adaptation. ACM Trans. Graph. (TOG) **29**(4), 33 (2010)
8. Hu, R., van Kaick, O., Wu, B., Huang, H., Shamir, A., Zhang, H.: Learning how objects function via co-analysis of interactions. ACM TOG **35**(4), 47:1–47:13 (2016)
9. Hu, R., Zhu, C., van Kaick, O., Liu, L., Shamir, A., Zhang, H.: Interaction context (icon): towards a geometric functionality descriptor. ACM TOG **34**(4), 83:1–83:12 (2015)
10. Jin, T., Kim, M., Lee, S.H.: Aura mesh: motion retargeting to preserve the spatial relationships between skinned characters. Comp. Graph. Forum **37**(2), 311–320 (2018)
11. Kobbelt, L., Campagna, S., Vorsatz, J., Seidel, H.P.: Interactive multi-resolution modeling on arbitrary meshes. In: Proceedings of the 25th Annual Conference on Computer Graphics and Interactive Techniques, SIGGRAPH 1998, pp. 105–114. ACM (1998)

12. Lee, J., Shin, S.Y.: A hierarchical approach to interactive motion editing for human-like figures. In: Proceedings of the 26th Annual Conference on Computer Graphics and Interactive Techniques, SIGGRAPH 1999, pp. 39–48 (1999)
13. Müller, M., Gross, M.: Interactive virtual materials. In: Proceedings of Graphics Interface, GI 2004, pp. 239–246. Canadian Human-Computer Communication Society (2004)
14. Pirk, S., et al.: Understanding and exploiting object interaction landscapes. ACM Trans. Graph. **36**(3), 31 (2017)
15. Si, H., Gärtner, K.: Meshing piecewise linear complexes by constrained delaunay tetrahedralizations. In: Hanks, B.W. (ed.) Proceedings of the 14th International Meshing Roundtable, pp. 147–163. Springer, Heidelberg (2005). https://doi.org/10.1007/3-540-29090-7_9
16. Sorkine, O., Alexa, M.: As-rigid-as-possible surface modeling. In: Proceedings of the 5th EG Symposium on Geometry Processing, SGP 2007, pp. 109–116. EG Association (2007)
17. Tak, S., Ko, H.S.: A physically-based motion retargeting filter. ACM Trans. Graph. **24**(1), 98–117 (2005)
18. Villegas, R., Yang, J., Ceylan, D., Lee, H.: Neural kinematic networks for unsupervised motion retargetting. In: The IEEE Conference on Computer Vision and Pattern Recognition (CVPR), June 2018
19. Zhao, X., Choi, M., Komura, T.: Character-object interaction retrieval using the interaction bisector surface. Comput. Graph. Forum **36**(2), 119–129 (2017)
20. Zhao, X., Wang, H., Komura, T.: Indexing 3D scenes using the interaction bisector surface. ACM Trans. Graph. **33**(3), 22:1–22:14 (2014)

Video Tamper Detection Based on Convolutional Neural Network and Perceptual Hashing Learning

Huisi Wu, Yawen Zhou[✉], and Zhenkun Wen

Shenzhen University, Shenzhen 518000, China
zhou_yw@163.com

Abstract. Perceptual hashing has been widely used in the field of multimedia security. The difficulty of the traditional perceptual hashing algorithm is to find suitable perceptual features. In this paper, we propose a perceptual hashing learning method for tamper detection based on convolutional neural network, where a hashing layer in the convolutional neural network is introduced to learn the features and hash functions. Specifically, the video is decomposed to obtain temporal representative frame (TRF) sequences containing temporal and spatial domain information. Convolutional neural network is then used to learn visual features of each TRF. We further put each feature into the hashing layer to learn independent hash functions and fuse these features to generate the video hash. Finally, the hash functions and the corresponding video hash are obtained by minimizing the classification loss and quantization error loss. Experimental results and comparisons with state-of-the-art methods show that the algorithm has better classification performance and can effectively perform tamper detection.

Keywords: Video tamper detection · Perceptual hashing ·
Convolutional neural network · Temporal representative frame

1 Introduction

Perceptual hashing is a perceptual content of one-way mapping from multimedia presentations to perceptual hash values [1]. Using visual perceptual hashing theory in analyzing and processing massive media, the perceptual features can be obtained. Then, the video tampering can be detected and located by using a short summary hash comparison matching [2]. Perceptual hashing has become one of the effective ways to verify the authenticity of multimedia data, which has led developers to be particularly interested in monitoring multimedia videos

Supported in part by grants from the Natural Science Foundation of Guangdong Province, China (Nos. 2018A030313381), the Shenzhen Research Foundation for Basic Research, China (Nos. JCYJ20170302153551588).

M. Gavrilova et al. (Eds.): CGI 2019, LNCS 11542, pp. 107–118, 2019.
https://doi.org/10.1007/978-3-030-22514-8_9

and detecting duplicate or pirated videos over the Internet [3]. Perceptual hashing has gradually become the mainstream technology for multimedia security certifications such as audio, image and video. In addition to security related applications, perceptual hashing can also be applied to image registration and retrieval [4]. Digital video undergoes regular digital processing during transmission and storage, such as JPEG compression, without changing the content of the video. Traditional cryptographic hash functions such as SHA-1 and MD5 convert input information into fixed-length strings, making them very sensitive to bit-level changes, so they are not suitable for video hashing. Video hashing should have perceptual robustness and discriminative capacity. Perceptual robustness: Hash functions should be robust enough for content-preserving operations such as contrast changes, geometric transformations, and JPEG compression. The hash does not change unless the video is maliciously tampered by an attacker, such as object deletion and object insertion. Discriminative capacity: Videos of different content should have different hash.

In the past few years, deep learning has performed well in solving various problems such as image target recognition, speech recognition, and natural language processing. Among various types of neural networks, convolutional neural networks are the most intensively studied. The emergence of large-scale tag data such as ImageNet [5] and the rapid improvement of GPU computing performance has led to rapid research on convolutional neural networks. Although CNN has achieved considerable results in image and video hashing, few studies have applied CNN for content authenticated of image and video hashing technology, which is necessary to improve security and recognition. Currently, there is very little research on the video hashing of CNN applied to digital forensics. Inspired by the research [6], this paper proposes a DCNN-based video hashing learning method. The method first decomposes the video into continuous temporal representative frame (TRF) sequences, which are used as the input to train visual features through convolutional network. The hashing layer is used to learn the independent hash function and generate a binarized video hash. The hash is stored as information independent of the video.

2   Related Work

In recent years, many video hashing methods have been proposed. These methods fall into two main categories: video frame based hashing and entire video sequence based hashing. Video frame based hashing is processing the video as a set of image frames, and uses the image hashing technique to extract the image hash from each frame and finally combine it into a video hash. Lee et al. [7] obtained a video hashing method by studying the gradient direction centroid (CGO). This method is very robust to JPEG compression and noise effects, but is too sensitive to geometric transformations such as rotation. To study the rotation invariance of video hash, Roover et al. [8] proposed a radial hashing (RASH) based video hashing method. Entire video sequence based hashing is to treat the video as a whole rather than a collection of video sequence frames. Coskun et

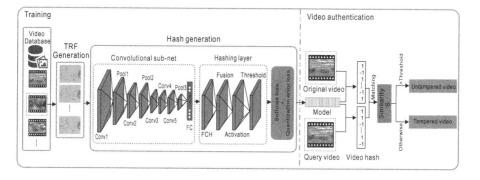

Fig. 1. The framework of our video authentication algorithm.

al. [9] performed a three-dimensional discrete cosine transform on the overall video sequence, and then extracted the perceptual features from three dimensions by discrete cosine transform (DCT), and introduced a random scrambling DCT basis to ensure the security of the algorithm. This algorithm is efficient, but contains fewer human perception factors.

With rapid development of deep learning technology, many digital forensics methods have also begun to adopt deep learning tools, the most commonly used of which is the convolutional neural network (CNN). Chen et al. [10] attempted to extract the median filtering residual (MFR) feature from the falsified image to train the CNN. The classification accuracy of CNN after training is higher than 90%. Yao et al. [11] added three pre-processing layers in front of the traditional CNN model to reduce temporal redundancy between video frames, reduce the computational complexity of image convolution and enhance the residual signal left by video forgery. Experiments show that the CNN model with pre-processing layer has good classification performance.

3   Method

The framework of our video authentication algorithm in this paper is shown in Fig. 1. It mainly includes two parts (training and video authentication). During the training phase, we decompose the video into continuous temporal representative frame (TRF) sequences for training our network model. In the authentication phase, we use the trained model to get the video hash of the original video and the query video. By calculating the similarity values of the two hashes, we determine whether the query video is a tampering video.

3.1   Temporal Representative Frame Generation

The traditional video frame processing method mainly uses a convolutional neural network to extract features for each video frame without considering the correlation between consecutive frames of the video. In order to better characterize

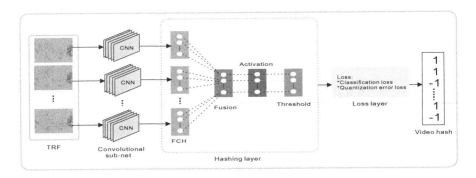

Fig. 2. The process of video hash generation.

a video, We use the temporal representative frame (TRF) proposed by Liu [12] to decompose the video into a continuous temporal representative frame sequence. Because the TRF contains the information of the video spatial-temporal domain, the hash generated by the TRF also contains the characteristics of the spatial-temporal domain. The video is decomposed into fixed length continuous video segments, and then each video segment is cumulatively weighted according to visual weights to generate a temporal representative frame containing spatial-temporal domain information. The temporal representative frame is generated as follows

$$F(m,n) = \sum_{t=1}^{j} w_i F(m,n,i) \tag{1}$$

where, $F(m,n,i)$ is the pixel intensity of the (m,n) position of the i-th frame in each video segment after decomposition, and $F(m,n)$ is the pixel intensity of the TRF. j is the length of the video segment being decomposed, and w_i is the temporal domain visual weight. The change accepted by the human eye is 12 to 16 frames, so the attacker needs to tamper with at least 12 to 16 frames. Therefore, each video is divided into segments, each segment containing $j = 30$ frames, each segment having 50% overlap with adjacent segments.

3.2 Hash Generation

The framework for generating a video hash is shown in Fig. 2 and consists of three parts: Convolutional sub-net, hashing layer and optimization. Given a video $\chi = \{x^{(1)}, x^{(2)}, ..., x^{(n)}\}$, where $x^{(t)}$ represents the t-th TRF. The goal of video hashing is to generate the binary video hash $b \in \{-1,1\}^k$ for video χ, the generated k-bit hash is used for video authentication.

We chose the AlexNet structure in [5] as the first part of the proposed framework for learning visual features. Because AlexNet is simple and able to extract good features, we use it to verify the validity of our model. Although GoogleNet and VGGNet can also learn visual features, different network structures are not our focus. The specific parameter settings of convolution sub-net is shown in

Table 1. Parameter settings of convolutional sub-net.

Layer	Parameter settings
Conv1+Pool1	Filter: $96 \times 11 \times 11$, S: 4, Pad: 0; Pool: 3×3, S: 2; LRN
Conv2+Pool2	Filter: $256 \times 5 \times 5$, S: 1, Pad: 2; Pool: 3×3, S: 2; LRN
Conv3	Filter: $384 \times 3 \times 3$, S: 1, Pad:1
Conv4	Filter: $384 \times 3 \times 3$, S: 1, Pad:1
Conv5+Pool3	Filter: $56 \times 3 \times 3$, S: 1, Pad: 1; Pool: 3×3, S: 2; LRN
FC	Output: 4096

Table 1. "Filter" indicates the number and size of the convolution kernel, "S" indicates the step size, "Pad" indicates the size of the zero padding, "Pool" indicates the size of the pool kernel, the step size of each pooling layer is 2, and "LRN" indicates that the Local Response Normalization (LRN) is used. The Rectification Linear Unit (ReLU) is adopted for all weight layers. Convolutional sub-net can be viewed as a nonlinear function $f_{CSN}(*)$. The corresponding visual feature $z^{(t)}$ of frame $x^{(t)}$ is expressed as follow

$$z^{(t)} = f_{CSN}(x^{(t)}) \tag{2}$$

In this paper, the hashing layer includes fully-connected hash layer (FCH) layer, fusion layer, activation layer and threshold layer. We construct an independent hash function for each TRF through the FCH layer to obtain a frame-level feature, then fuse all frame-level features through the fusion layer to obtain video-level feature. The output of the video-level feature is limited in the range $[-1, 1]$ by the activation layer. The threshold layer is used to generate a binarized video hash. The FCH layer is used to construct an independent hash function for each TRF, and the corresponding formula is expressed as follows

$$v^{(t)} = W_t z^{(t)} \tag{3}$$

where, matrix W_t represents the weight matrix of the t-th FCH layer, and the dimension of $v^{(t)}$ is q. The fusion layer uses time series pooling strategy [13] to combine the TRF-level features of the video into a video-level feature. Time series pooling strategy can reduce the length of video hash and improve the efficiency of training. Then the feature sequence $\{v^{(1)}, v^{(2)}, ..., v^{(n)}\}$ of the video χ is obtained, and the spatial-temporal domain feature of the video-level are calculated by the pooling layer. Here we use the average pooling as follows

$$V = \frac{1}{n} \sum_{t=1}^{n} v^{(t)} \tag{4}$$

Hyperbolic tangent function is adopted for the activation layer to limit the outputs in the range $[-1, 1]$, the corresponding formula is as follows

$$R = \frac{1 - e^{\beta V}}{1 + e^{\beta V}} \tag{5}$$

where, β is the hyperparameter used to control the smoothness. The threshold layer will get the spatial-temporal domain feature to convert the binary number $\{-1, 1\}$, and its output is defined as follows:

$$H = \begin{cases} -1, & R \le 0 \\ 1, & R > 0 \end{cases} \tag{6}$$

The output of the threshold layer is a binarized video hash.

3.3 Optimization

Since the finally obtained hash is a discrete value, it is necessary to consider both the classification loss L_s and the quantization error loss L_q into the overall loss function. The corresponding formula is as follows:

$$L_{overall} = L_s + \lambda L_q \tag{7}$$

where, λ is the weight factor of the quantization error loss as a whole loss. When the network structure performs a classification task, a softmax classification loss L_s is generated. The discrete error loss L_q is generated by the fusion layer output continuous value R and the discrete value H of the threshold layer output [14]. The formula is as follows

$$L_q = f(H - R) \tag{8}$$

where, $f(*)$ indicates the 2-norm distance.

After the deep network architecture is trained, given a video, we can get the corresponding video hash H.

3.4 Video Authentication

Video content authentication is used to determine whether the detected video is a tampering video or not. We use the correlation coefficient as a metric to calculate the similarity between the two video hashes. Suppose that the hashes of two videos are given $H = [h_1, h_2, ..., h_q]$ and $H' = [h'_1, h'_2, ..., h'_q]$. Therefore, the correlation coefficient is defined as

$$S = \frac{\sum\limits_{i=1}^{n}(h_i - \mu_1)(h_i' - \mu_2)}{\sqrt{\sum\limits_{i=1}^{n}(h_i - \mu_1)^2}\sqrt{\sum\limits_{i=1}^{n}(h_i' - \mu_2)^2} + \varepsilon} \tag{9}$$

where, ε is a small constant to avoid singularity when $\sum\limits_{i=1}^{n}(h_i - \mu_1)^2 = 0$ or $\sum\limits_{i=1}^{n}(h_i' - \mu_2)^2 = 0$, μ_1 and μ_2 are the means of H and H' respectively. If S is bigger than the predetermined threshold T, then the two videos are determined to be visually similar videos. Otherwise, they are different versions of the video or one of the videos is another tampering version.

Table 2. The used content-preserving operations and their parameter values.

Operation	Parameters setting	Number
Frame rate change	Subsampling factor: 2, 3, 4	3
Contrast adjustment	Strength: ±10, ±20	4
Salt and Pepper noise	Density: 0.02, 0.04, 0.06, 0.08	4
JPEG compression	Quality factor: 30, 40, 50, 60, 70, 80, 90, 100	8
Scaling	Ratio: 0.5, 0.75, 0.9, 1.1, 1.5, 2.0	6
Rotation	Degree: ±0.25, ±0.5, ±0.75, ±1.0	8

Table 3. Robustness results of similar videos.

Operation	Minimum	Maximum	Mean	Standard deviation
Frame rate change	0.9738	0.9995	0.9834	0.0073
Contrast adjustment	0.8538	0.9996	0.9558	0.0591
Salt and Pepper noise	0.9170	0.9999	0.9758	0.0151
JPEG compression	0.9977	1	0.9998	0.0004
Scaling	0.9931	1	0.9987	0.0018
Rotation	0.9897	0.9996	0.9901	0.0047

4   Experimental Results

This section describes the experimental results and demonstrates the effectiveness of the method.

4.1   Dataset and Parameter Settings

We use two video datasets to demonstrate the effectiveness of the proposed method, UCF-101 activity recognition dataset [15] and SYSU-OBJFORG video dataset [16]. In this experiment, we randomly selected 3,000 videos from UCF-101 dataset to train and validate our network structure, of which 2500 videos were used for training and 500 videos were used for verification. SYSU-OBJFORG dataset was used to verify the validity of our method, including 100 original videos and 100 tampered videos. The tampered video is obtained by adding and deleting the regional target from the corresponding original video, and there is no obvious tampering trace in the tampered frame. All experiments were implemented on the open source Tensorflow framework. Each video is adjusted to $256 \times 256 \times 150$, which is 150 frames per video, and each frame is 256×256. The temporal domain visual weight w_i is 0.65, the length of the hash q is 100, and the weight of the quantization error loss λ is set to 0.3.

4.2   Perceptual Robustness

Robustness evaluation is an analysis for the content-preserving operations. A video hash should be approximately same after any non-malicious digital

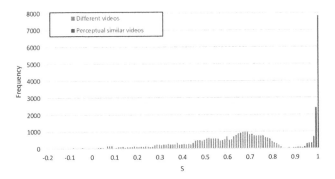

Fig. 3. The histogram of the S for perceptual similar and different videos.

operation. These activities consist of rotation, JPEG compression, frame rate change, noise, contrast adjustment, and scaling. To verify the robustness of the algorithm, 100 original videos are processed by content-preserving operations as shown in Table 2 to generate the similar video dataset. The experimental result of robustness are shown in Table 3. In addition to the effect of contrast changes, the minimum value S of similarity values obtained by other operations is greater than 0.9. The mean value S of the similarity values obtained by all operations is greater than 0.95, and the corresponding standard deviation is small. Hence, the proposed method is robust to content-preserving operations.

4.3 Discriminative Capacity

In order to analyze the classification performance of the algorithm, 200 videos from UCF-101 dataset are compared with 100 original videos in SYSU-OBJFROG dataset for cross-comparison, and the similarity distribution map is shown in Fig. 3. As can be seen from Fig. 3, S of similar videos is concentrated at 1, and S of different videos is concentrated at 0.69. It can be seen that the method conforms to the definition of the correlation coefficient, that is, it indicates a positive correlation when it is close to 1, and it is irrelevant when it is close to 0, and a negative correlation when it is close to −1. The minimum and maximum S are −0.1632 and 0.8863, respectively. When the threshold is set as 0.89, the method can accurately distinguish different videos, and the resolution of similar videos will be slightly misjudged (0.35%). If the strong contrast adjustment is not considered, the method has good classification performance.

4.4 Performance Analysis

In order to evaluate the robustness of the algorithm and the tamper detection capability, the experimental results are displayed using a receiver operating characteristic (ROC) curve. The ROC is a characteristic curve plotted using false positive rate (FPR) P_{FPR} along the abscissa and true positive rate (TPR) P_{TPR} along the ordinate. The P_{FPR} and P_{TPR} are defined as follows

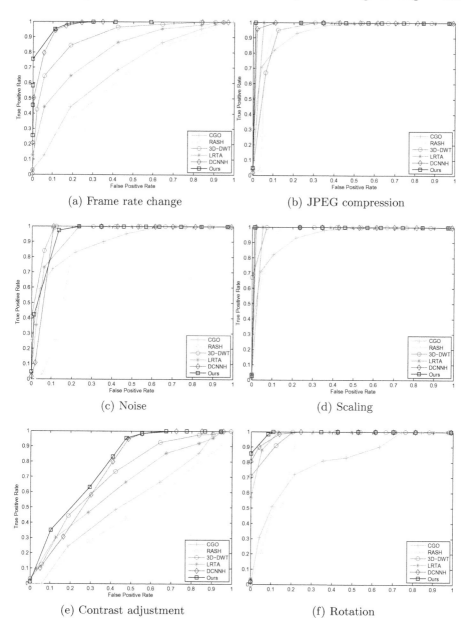

(a) Frame rate change

(b) JPEG compression

(c) Noise

(d) Scaling

(e) Contrast adjustment

(f) Rotation

Fig. 4. Perceptual robustness and discriminative capacity of the different algorithms.

$$P_{FPR} = \frac{N_F}{N_D} \qquad (10)$$

$$P_{TPR} = \frac{N_T}{N_S} \qquad (11)$$

where N_F indicates the number of visually different videos or tamper videos judged as similar videos and N_T indicates the number of perceptually identical videos judged as similar videos. The N_D and N_S denote the total number of visually dissimilar videos or tamper videos and the total number of perceptually similar videos, respectively. Our method is compared to the following methods: CGO [17], RASH [8], 3D-DWT [18], LRTA [19] and DCNNH [20]. The same parameter settings suggested in the corresponding paper are used here.

The CGO and RASH algorithms extract video hash based on video frames, averaging 2 dimensions per frame, and for a video containing 150 frames, the corresponding hash dimension is 300. The spatial-temporal domain based hash algorithms such as LRTA and 3D-DWT uses 128 dimensions. The DCNNH algorithm for extracting video hash based on deep neural networks uses 256 dimensions. The hash length of our method is 100, it is the smallest.

Figure 4 shows the ROC curves of the six algorithms under different content-preserving operations. It can be seen from Figure A that the CGO and RASH algorithms are not good enough for the ROC performance when the frame rate changes, and the hash is not robust enough. Because both algorithms extract the hash based on the frame, the correlation between video frames and frames is not considered. LRTA, 3D-DWT, DCNNH and the proposed algorithm are based on spatial-temporal domain extraction hash, which are more robust than frame-based methods in terms of frame rate change operations. The algorithm proposed in this paper is the most robust in this operation. As shown in Fig. 4b, the performance of different algorithms under contrast conversion is very different. This is because the operation has a large change to the video content, so all algorithms perform not good. However, the algorithm proposed in this paper is better than other algorithms. In Fig. 4c, the 3D-DWT algorithm is the most robust to noise interference because the algorithm has filtered most of the high frequency noise in the process of extracting features. For scaling and JPEG compression, all algorithms perform well. Therefore, the proposed algorithm is robust to content-preserving operations and superior to other algorithms.

A reliable authentication algorithm should tolerate different content-preserving operations while detecting tampering with the video. The tampered video is obtained from SYSU-OBFORG dataset. Figure 5 shows the ROC curves of content tampering and content-preserving operations for six algorithms at different thresholds. The criteria for better perceptual hashing algorithm is that it should have high P_{TPR} with low P_{FPR}. It can be observed from Fig. 5 that the proposed method P_{TPR} (i.e. 0.9413 with zero P_{FPR}) and P_{FPR} (i.e. 0.1081 with P_{TPR} one) is higher and lower respectively as compared to other methods. It can be seen that the algorithm can accept most content retention operations and implement detection of video content tampering.

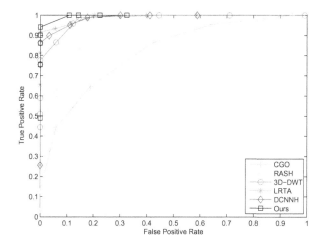

Fig. 5. Tamper detection performance of the different algorithms.

5   Conclusions

In this paper, we have proposed a robust video hashing learning method based on convolutional neural network which is against the content-preserving operations and has a better discrimination ability for tampering. The main contribution of the algorithm is to use TRF as the input of the convolutional neural network to learn the temporal-spatial domain visual features. The hashing layer is designed to learn an independent hash function for each TRF and generate the final video hash. Considering the influence of quantization error in the whole framework model, it is also added into the optimization objective functions, so that a more expressive hash is obtained.

References

1. Niu, X., Jiao, Y.: An overview of perceptual hashing. Acta Electronica Sinica **36**(7), 1405–1411 (2008)
2. Schneider, M., Chang, S.-F.: A robust content based digital signature for image authentication. In: 1996 Proceedings of International Conference on Image Processing, vol. 3, pp. 227–230. IEEE (1996)
3. Lu, J.: Video fingerprinting for copy identification: from research to industry applications. In: Media Forensics and Security, vol. 7254, p. 725402. International Society for Optics and Photonics (2009)
4. Wolfson, H.J., Rigoutsos, I.: Geometric hashing: an overview. IEEE Comput. Sci. Eng. **4**(4), 10–21 (1997)
5. Krizhevsky, A., Sutskever, I., Hinton, G.E.: Imagenet classification with deep convolutional neural networks. In: Advances in Neural Information Processing Systems, pp. 1097–1105 (2012)
6. Han, D., Liu, Q., Fan, W.: A new image classification method using CNN transfer learning and web data augmentation. Expert Syst. Appl. **95**, 43–56 (2018)

7. Lee, S., Yoo, C.D.: Video fingerprinting based on centroids of gradient orientations. In: Proceedings of 2006 IEEE International Conference on Acoustics, Speech and Signal Processing, ICASSP 2006, vol. 2, p. II. IEEE (2006)
8. De Roover, C., De Vleeschouwer, C., Lefebvre, F., Macq, B.: Robust video hashing based on radial projections of key frames. IEEE Trans. Sig. Process. **53**(10), 4020–4037 (2005)
9. Coskun, B., Sankur, B., Memon, N.: Spatio-temporal transform based video hashing. IEEE Trans. Multimedia **8**(6), 1190–1208 (2006)
10. Chen, J., Kang, X., Liu, Y., Wang, Z.J.: Median filtering forensics based on convolutional neural networks. IEEE Sig. Process. Lett. **22**(11), 1849–1853 (2015)
11. Yao, Y., Shi, Y., Weng, S., Guan, B.: Deep learning for detection of object-based forgery in advanced video. Symmetry **10**(1), 3 (2017)
12. Liu, X., Sun, J., Liu, J.: Shot-based temporally respective frame generation algorithm for video hashing. In: IEEE International Workshop on Information Forensics and Security (WIFS), pp. 109–114. IEEE (2013)
13. Wang, X., Gao, L., Song, J., Shen, H.: Beyond frame-level CNN: saliency-aware 3-D CNN with LSTM for video action recognition. IEEE Sig. Process. Lett. **24**(4), 510–514 (2017)
14. Peng, T., Li, F.: Image retrieval based on deep convolutional neural networks and binary hashing learning. In: 2017 IEEE International Conference on Acoustics, Speech and Signal Processing (ICASSP), pp. 1742–1746. IEEE (2017)
15. Soomro, K., Zamir, A.R., Shah, M.: Ucf101: a dataset of 101 human actions classes from videos in the wild. arXiv preprint arXiv:1212.0402 (2012)
16. Chen, S., Tan, S., Li, B., Huang, J.: Automatic detection of object-based forgery in advanced video. IEEE Trans. Circ. Syst. Video Technol. **26**(11), 2138–2151 (2016)
17. Lee, S., Yoo, C.D.: Robust video fingerprinting for content-based video identification. IEEE Trans. Circ. Syst. Video Technol. **18**(7), 983–988 (2008)
18. Saikia, N.: Perceptual hashing in the 3D-DWT domain. In: 2015 International Conference on Green Computing and Internet of Things (ICGCIoT), pp. 694–698. IEEE (2015)
19. Nie, X., Liu, J., Sun, J., Zhao, H.: Key-frame based robust video hashing using isometric feature mapping. J. Comput. Inf. Syst. **7**(6), 2112–2119 (2011)
20. Ma, C., Gu, Y., Liu, W., Yang, J., He, X.: Unsupervised video hashing by exploiting spatio-temporal feature. In: Hirose, A., Ozawa, S., Doya, K., Ikeda, K., Lee, M., Liu, D. (eds.) ICONIP 2016. LNCS, vol. 9949, pp. 511–518. Springer, Cham (2016). https://doi.org/10.1007/978-3-319-46675-0_56

Phys-Sketch: Sketching 3D Dynamic Objects in Immersive Virtual Reality

Jose Abel Ticona[1]([✉])[iD], Steeven Villa[1][iD], Rafael Torchelsen[2][iD],
Anderson Maciel[1][iD], and Luciana Nedel[1][iD]

[1] Institute of Informatics, Federal University of Rio Grande do Sul (UFRGS),
Porto Alegre, Brazil
{jatlarico,dsvsalazar,amaciel,nedel}@inf.ufrgs.br
[2] Universidade Federal de Pelotas (UFPel), Pelotas, Brazil
rafael.torchelsen@inf.ufpel.edu.br
http://inf.ufrgs.br/~jatlarico, http://inf.ufrgs.br/~dsvsalazar,
http://rafaeltorchelsen.wordpress.com, http://inf.ufrgs.br/~amaciel,
http://inf.ufrgs.br/~nedel

Abstract. Sketching was traditionally a 2D task. Even when the new generation of VR devices allowed to sketch in 3D, the drawn models remained essentially static representations. In this paper, we introduce a new physics-inspired sketching technique built on the top of Position-based Dynamics to enrich the 3D drawings with dynamic behaviors. A particle-based method allows interacting in real time with a wide range of materials including fluids, rigid bodies, soft bodies and clothes. Users can interact with the dynamic sketches and sculpt them while they move, deform and fall. We analyze the expressiveness of the system from the regard of two experienced artists. Thus, this paper also gives a starting point to move towards an improved generation of physics-enabled sketching applications.

Keywords: 3D sketching · Real-time physics-based simulation ·
Human-computer interaction · Immersive-environments

1 Introduction

Virtual and Augmented Realities (VR and AR) are in part tricking our senses to improve the feeling of presence. Several factors directly influence how successful the user experience is, such as the quality of the graphics and 3D models. However, this static part by itself does not produce a full VR or AR experience. Elements' behavior, as well as the way they move and how the user interacts with them, also play a fundamental role. Usually, looking for minimizing

This study was partly funded by the Coordenacao de Aperfeicoamento de Pessoal de Nivel Superior - Brasil (CAPES) - Finance Code 001, and partly by CNPq. We also acknowledge FAPERGS (project 17/2551-0001192-9) and CNPq-Brazil (project 311353/2017-7) for their financial support.

© Springer Nature Switzerland AG 2019
M. Gavrilova et al. (Eds.): CGI 2019, LNCS 11542, pp. 119–130, 2019.
https://doi.org/10.1007/978-3-030-22514-8_10

the computation-time, designers choose to not use physically-accurate objects. Therefore, adopting kinematic behaviors is quite popular. Having said that, for a true VR experience, one has to consider physical behaviors of objects made of diverse materials, not to mention the ways people interact with them.

Virtual modeling is a growing area due to the development of new VR, interaction, and visualization techniques. This area is promising in the sense that it can improve creativity and reduce the development time of virtual models, environments, and animations.

Some popular applications were recently proposed to allow 3D creations employing immersive interaction, such as the TiltBrush [3] released in 2016 by Google. This application addresses several immersive interaction issues when painting in 3D. In the same way, Quill [2], from Facebook, lets the user create and animate virtual models. These approaches were successful in allowing users on materializing ideas, since both introduced tools to sculpt, draw, and paint.

In spite of that, the more noticeable weakness on the mentioned tools lies in their kinematic nature, this being reflected on the impossibility of choosing a particular material for a given object. Some of the applications let the user associate materials to their models. Then again, this is limited to rendering properties. A lack of physics-based behavior is thus noticeable: drawings or objects created are static along all the experience. The interaction between bodies is entirely kinematic and awkwardly real. However, the literature offers well developed, stable and interactive methods to deal with objects dynamics. Position-based dynamics, for instance, significantly reduces the computation time of physically plausible simulations. Recent developments in this area let us simulate significant natural phenomena [13].

Considering the issues mentioned above, we propose a novel immersive sketching application to create elements with different materials. Our solution allows for physics-based interactions between objects in real-time using position-based dynamics (PBD). This model is stable and permits to create expressive dynamic-sketches involving several types of physical behaviors such as rigid solid bodies, liquids, gases, soft solids, and clothes. As an example, it is possible to change the flow of a river by adding or digging into the ground while the river is flowing, or even to create beautiful waterfalls using the same methods. Moreover, this approach also allows the user to see in real time the behavior of recently created soft bodies or even clothes, in a rich direct manipulation environment.

2   Related Works

Recently, some works have proposed the use of immersive methods to let artist sketch, draw and even sculpt. GravitySketch [1], is a recent application which gives an immersive experience and additionally let the user interact without controllers by using leap motion. Works as Canvox by Kim et al. [6] proposes the division of the whole canvas in smaller volumes of interest to give more details using octrees. Although This work notably improves the sketching stage, they neglect the after-sketching interaction. Likewise, Multiplanes by Barrera et al. [4] aid the user to sketch by automatically generating planes as the user draws a line. This strategy is a 3D immersive analogous of the conventional CAD sketching pipeline but, once again, the authors focused on the sketching omitting further physical interactions with the already drawn objects.

Recently, Seo et al. [15] presented Aura Garden in 2018, a collaborative sculpting environment for light. This environment lets users draw and animate in mid-air with different materials, but all those materials are non-physical (excluding wood), so it is not possible to simulate interactions neither among them or the user. Eroglu et al. [5] presented a successful physic-based model to sketch in VR. This work focused on fluid modeling, letting the user change the fluid properties and freely draw in space. Although they did an outstanding work, their method is limited to fluids, and do not take into account solids or soft bodies. Lately, in 2018, Claybook [14] was released for most of the video-game consoles, this game let users generate dynamic content made of clay. Objects phases are liquid or solid, but it doesn't allow users to create rigid bodies. Besides, it is not immersive at the date of publication of this manuscript. To sum up, a common failure of the above-commented studies is the few or even nonexistent physics-based animation on the process, limiting the dynamism of the creations. Thus, the interactivity of the objects decreases. To solve that, we put our efforts in developing a possible real-time physics-enabled environment to both, sketch and animate bodies.

3   System Overview

The proposed system is divided into two main modules: First of all, the *Sketching* module which is the creation stage, where the user draws objects. Users are allowed to select materials and sketch in any possible position using the available brush shapes. However, for the sake of controllability, objects are unprovided of physical properties during the sketching step. Additionally, for performance reasons bodies being sketched, are represented as a set of spheres (see Fig. 1 left)

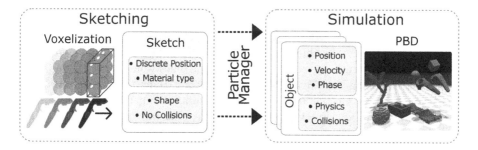

Fig. 1. The interaction technique in our design switches between two states: sketching and simulation. The first state is used to create new particle-elements into the scene, and the dynamic behavior is given to the bodies on the second stage depending on the properties of the material.

through a process called *Voxelization*. Section 4 explain in detail the processes involved in the sketching stage; Afterwards, in the *Simulation* stage, physics is assigned to the bodies (see Fig. 1 left). In this step, the animated bodies interact with both; user and environment. Moreover, users can touch, stretch or move any of them as desired. The system is built over the standard position-based dynamics (PBD) framework: We update both velocities and positions of the virtual tool using the external tracking system once the main PBD calculations were finished.

4 Sketching

Primarily, to create an object within our framework, the user must follow two steps: first sketch the body (*Sketching*); and next provide it with physical behavior (*Simulation*). Although both stages are well demarcated for the user all along the creative process, the simulation continues running on background for the existing bodies.

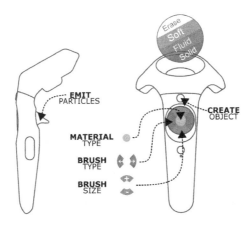

Fig. 2. Functionalities of the tool for interactions while sketching

Separation of stages is, thus, important to improve the sketching experience; without this discrimination, newly introduced particles would start falling after its creation, reducing usability to the system and making the creation of consistent sketches difficult. Therefore, in the beginning, the generated particles do not have any animation. Furthermore, the primary interaction tool is the brush, which has three functions: create, remove and move objects. Whats more, the user can easily select the object properties through the controller buttons as shown in Fig. 2(a). Additionally, the amount of particles introduced in the environment is given by the size and shape of the brush; new particles are evenly generated through voxelization (See Sect. 4.1).

Algorithm 1. Voxelization

1: **procedure** VOXELIZATION(P)
2:     $p = discretization(P)$ (Using Eq. 4)
3:     **if** $p \in M$ & $M[p] < 0$ **then**
4:         $P' = interpolation(p)$ (Using Eq. 5)
5:         $M[p] = index$
6:         $Particles[index] = P'$
7:         $index + +$

Therefore, to emit particles the user must press and hold the trigger. Similarly, the circular trackpad is used to navigate through brush shape and size options. Finally, pressing the center of the trackpad changes the material type (2). Furthermore, movement through the scene is allowed during all the simulation. However, there are physical (Room size) and computational (Simulation Size) constraints to the movement through the scene, even though the virtual space is not limited.

4.1   Voxelization

The manner as the particles are created plays a fundamental role in the simulation: placing more than one particle at the same position could generate overshoots at the first timesteps. In order to solve this issue, we use voxelization in the sketching stage; where each particle represents a voxel. The environment divided into a 3D grid $M \in R3$. Subsequently, M is initialized with -1 values. When a body is placed into the scene, the values of M are changed to 0 for the position of occupied by the thew body. This proceeding is shown in Algorithm 1 Finally, to remove particles, the Algorithm 2 is applied. We sync the coordinates of the space and the coordinates of our binary 3D grid using the following relations:

$$p' = p - c \tag{1}$$
$$Q' = Q - C \tag{2}$$
$$\frac{p'}{Q'} = \frac{|w|}{|W|} \tag{3}$$

Algorithm 2. Remove Particles

1: **procedure** PARTICLEREMOTION(P)
2:     $p = discretization(P)$ (Using Eq. 4)
3:     **if** $p \in M$ & $M[p] \geq 0$ **then**
4:         $indexRemove = M[p]$
5:         $M[p] = -1$
6:         $removeParticle(indexRemove)$

Where p is a positive integer of the 3D grid, p' the virtual coordinate system (VCS), translated by the center grid (c), and Q is the (Physic) World Coordinate System (WCS). Similarly, (C) is the center of the tracking system. $|w|$ and $|W|$ are the width of the 3D virtual grid and the physical workspace respectively. Consequently, this gives us the Correlation 3. Moreover, in order to translate world positions to the discrete space (VCS), we use the Eq. 4, while for bringing back the particles to the world space (WC), we use the Eq. 5.

$$p = (Q - C)\frac{|w|}{|W|} + c \tag{4}$$

$$Q = (p - c)\frac{|W|}{|w|} + C \tag{5}$$

4.2 Particle Interpolation

Brush movement tend to be fast during the simulation, it creates non-connected curves in the space. To avoid holes in the sketch, the brush shape is used as extrusion plane in each timestep. To do this, we calculate the velocity vector opposed to the controller movement. Secondly we find the traveled distance $(||V||\Delta t)$, and next we calculate how many particles (i_{max}) fit in that distance (see Eq. 6).

$$i_{max} = Round(\frac{||V||\Delta t}{d_{particle}}) \tag{6}$$

Moreover, we divide this distance $(||V||\Delta t)$ by the diameter of a particle $(d_{particle})$ to get the maximum number of particles (i_{max}) to project along the opposite velocity direction. Finally, in Eq. 7 we proceed to calculate the exact positions of the new particles.

$$P'(i) = P - i\frac{V}{||V||}d_{particle} \qquad \forall i \in [0, i_{max}] \tag{7}$$

At the end of this stage, we have position information, but particles are not dynamic so far. However, in the next section when we discuss particle dynamics through our particle management.

5   Simulation

Lagrangian models are widely used to perform real-time simulations. Methodologies as Position-based dynamics (PBD) [10] or Smoothed-particle hydrodynamics became more and more popular lately. Likewise, recent publication model physical behaviors as solids, fluids [8], gases [12] and even complex phenomena as phase transitions [13] PBD as starting point. Lagrangian models in contrast with Eulerian approaches, treat the bodies as the origin of its calculations. Consequently, it is unnecessary to calculate properties along a grid. This is useful especially when the domain of the simulation is unknown. There are several meshless methods used to model continuum mechanics; we chose Position-Based Dynamics [10] by reason of its unconditional stability and its low computational cost.

PBD is a particle-based animation technique that uses a set of constraints to calculate the positions of the particles in each timestep. Namely, it tries to fit the position of each particle based on a set of constraints. A given particle can admit an arbitrary number of constraints, but a constraint must comprise at least two particles. Furthermore, the solver must iterate to set the positions of the particles based on the constraints, reducing the value of each constraint. Thus, we can look at this process as an optimization problem. This is a successful way to simulate a wide variety of bodies such as clothes, deformable, rods, and elastics. However, it is not adequate for a rigid body or fluid simulations. Hence, techniques as Smoothed-particle hydrodynamic (SPH) are used to resolve such weakness. Indeed in 2013 the SPH-PBD integration was named Position-based fluids (PBF) [8] and made it possible to simulate fluids in the same frameworks as PBD. Finally, to simulate rigid bodies, we used shape matching technique [9].

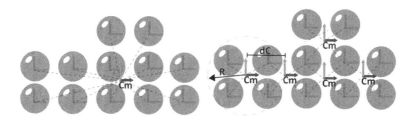

Fig. 3. (Left) Solid body: the coordinates of the particles are computed based on the mass center (Cm) of the body. (Right) Soft bodies: several coordinate systems are created based on two properties: the radius r and the distance dC between clusters, each cluster has a Mass center Cm, allowing articulated behavior.

5.1 Particle Management

We simulate a contrasting set of materials in this work; as a consequence, the procedure to simulate each material differs. In the following lines, we describe in detail the management of the particles/bodies, based on their materials.

Solids. Solid bodies are generated, firstly, calculating the center of mass of the entire body by summing up all the particle positions and later dividing by the total number of particles in the body. The transformations to a rigid body are directly applied to its mass center, and finally, applied to each particle using the relative positions (Fig. 3 left). This is know as Shape Matching [11]

Soft Bodies. In contrast, Soft bodies contain more mass centers. In this case, several CMs are calculated from a cluster of particles given a radius R and a minimum distance between clusters dC. This results in a structure of articulated bodies contained inside a total body. Similarly, as in solid bodies, every particle belonging to a cluster has a relative position to the CM of the cluster [9]. Figure 3(Right) shows how the coordinate system is created. A brief look to Fig. 3(left) and (right) shows the main differences between structures.

Liquids. We simulate fluids using Smoothed-particle hydrodynamics technique (SPH). Further information could be found in Macklin and Müller [8].

Collision Handling. We based the collision detection on the *Flex* Model (by Nvidia). Consequently, our system detects only particle-particle but not particle-mesh collision. Such limitation forces us to model everything in the scene with particles, including the tools (controllers). Hence, we modify the radius of solid particles constrained to $R_{Solid} < R_{Fluid}$ in order to handle solid-fluid collisions, this prevent possible leaks of fluid particles through spaces between solid particles. Controller-objects collisions are managed common particle interactions. However, the dynamic of those particles is given by the external tracking and not by the simulation dynamics. The collision system remains stable under normal conditions, but there is a maximum velocity where the particles would pass through an object because of the simulation timestep, due to this value is considerably high, it is not an issue.

6 Rendering

The rendering is divided into two parts: Fluids and Rigid-Soft bodies. Fluid rendering was done using Anisotropic Kernels because this is the standard system used by Flex. This approach render the objects based on the neighboring particles, namely performing Principal Component Analysis (PCA) over the neighbors. More information about this method could be found in the Yu & Turk paper published in 2013 [16]. For solid and soft rendering applied marching cubes (MC) algorithm [7] to the model voxelization to arrange particles through space, is a straightforward way to get a conceptual visualization of the objects. During the simulation, we know from the neighborhood search, which particles are on the surface of the object, so we apply MC only on outer particles, reducing computational cost.

7 Results

The sketching system was implemented and tested in a Dell workstation with an i7 3.2 Ghz Processor, 16 Gb Ram, and NVIDIA GeForce GTX 1070 Graphic Card, running Windows 10 and CUDA 9.2. All images and videos used in this paper were generated using HTC Vive headset and controllers for visualization and interaction (see Fig. 4). However, the sketching system is also compatible (and indeed was tested) with Oculus Rift headset and touch controllers. We also successfully tested Leap Motion for interaction.

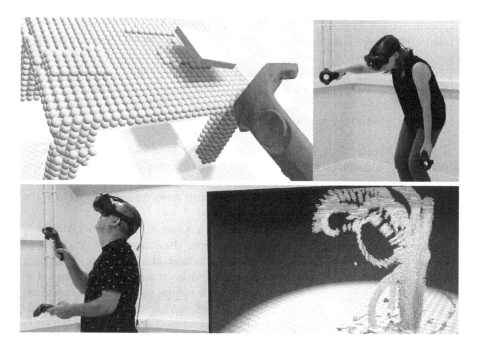

Fig. 4. Top: one of the invited artists is refining her sketch by removing particles. Bottom: sketching process of a three

Regarding performance, we got average timesteps between 15 ms and 33 ms; the late was reached when the amount of particles raises over 100k. In this case, the rendering is not fluid anymore. The system represents the workspace in a grid of $151 \times 151 \times 151$, where each cell potentially corresponds to one particle. As occupied cells are saved in memory and performance is mandatory, we restricted the max number of particles to 20% of the grid, or 688,590 particles. To run the scene of the Fig. 5, a total of 80k particles with a 28 ms for frame was used. There were 8 iterations for the run simulation and with a timestep of 16.6 ms.

7.1 Expressiveness

We invited two artists to informally test the immersive sketching application to create some sketches using the tools presented in Sect. 4. Both had no previous experience with VR. The test was divided into three stages and artists were free to spend as many time as they wanted in each stage:

1. Training stage: The system was introduced to the participants, letting them become familiar with the controls, and the virtual tool for 3D sketching in virtual environments. So, they first need to choose a material and a shape; Here the brush was introduced to them. We showed them how to change between shapes, sizes, and materials, to conclude we requested them to do it themselves drawing a free sketch.

2. Drawing stage: The artists were asked to draw a table and a container to be filled with water. Then, users were requested to interact with the objects they previously created.
3. Expression stage: The rtists were asked to sketch something original. For this stage, the gravity was set to zero. The sketched objects still reacts according to the materials they are made, but can freely float in the air, what can be seen as an interesting feature for artistics expression.

The experiments took approximately 40 min, where 15 min were spend for training and 25 min for executing the given tasks. Precisely, the first artist spent 40 min on the application while the second one spent 35 min. None of them reported any symphon of cyberseekness, and both were very comfortable in the virtual environment.

The artists executed a lot of gestures with their arms, also walking and jumping in the real world. During all the process, they changed their positions – walking and crouching – looking for a better point of view to continue their sketches. An interesting behavior we perceived in both was that they moved in such a way to avoid to collide or even to cross the virtual objects. From observing this behavior and as the result of an informal post-test interview, we can conclude they experienced a high sense of presence in the virtual environment.

Subjects also highlighted the comfort of working with physical objects referring to the soft bodies and water behavior. A drawback reported by one artist was the lack of a strong haptic feedback. Currently, our model only conveys vibrotactile feedback by means of the VIVE controllers when the controller strikes an object in the scene. In the expression stage, the subjects reported an improvement in the experience due to zero gravity. Even though this behavior is non-physical it let them draw objects without building supports.

Another comment of the users is that the best strategy to sketch is using the dominant hand to create particles and the other hand to do different actions, like erasing, for instance. As a suggestion, they highlighted the potential of mixing different materials into a single object, for example, to allows the creation of a solid object with a soft part. They also mentioned that the behavior of the objects is credible, but the rendering of solid and soft objects must be improved. Finally, they also stated that the choice of the color and texture is relevant in the artistic process. However, despite these suggestions for future improvements, they were very excited to keep using the sketching system to create new scenarios and artistic installations.

8   Conclusions and Future Work

In this paper we proposed and prototyped a particle-based system to sketch and simulate virtual objects with physical behavior in a VR environment. Results shown the performance achieved is sufficient to support 3D interaction and fluid animation of the objects. An example is shown step by step in the sequence of Fig. 5.

Fig. 5. In these sequence, we show how our tool allows us to use physics during simulation. This figure shows a pail, a bucket and a rope that joins the pail and the bucket, during the simulation we see how the bucket that has more weight lifts the pail, then we create a container of water that will fill the pail and then match the weights.

The first informal experiments with target users has shown promising results. The users, even if they did not have any previous experience with VR, felt comfortable to move and interact in the virtual environment proposed. They also did not report any cybersickness symptom during the 40 min each one spent fully immersed. Regarding the scenes sketched until now, they are interesting and sufficient to demonstrate the expressive power of the sketching system proposed. However, even if the main concepts about immersive sketching of dynamic objects have been verified, we are aware that the system needs to be improved to be regularly used for artists.

Notice that the rendering of the objects has a "legolized" appearance. An improvement of the render by smoothing the shapes would, we suppose, significantly improve the user experience. The marching cubes method generates smoother forms when the voxels are smaller. However, smaller voxels will demand more precision from the artists to sketch, as well as more computer power to simulate the objects behavior.

Path-constrained sketches are highly limited in terms of accuracy since the straight lines and geometries, in general, depend on the user ability to draw. Next works must move ahead introducing other tools, including the possibility of defining primitive bodies as cubes, spheres, rectangles, stars, etc. Additionally, the possibility of creating bodies using extrusions and revolutions would expand the range of applications of our tool. Further sketching tools as resizing or mixing up materials must be explored and evaluated. However, this work illustrates how physics-based interactions reinforce the sketching experience and provides tools to create *living sketches*.

A fully immersive experience should include tactile and force feedback. Besides, this could improve the performance of digital artists when sculpting or modeling their artwork, as drawing in the air lacks a support for accuracy. This is a possible future work.

References

1. Gravity Sketch - Bringing Virtual Reality Into Your Design Workflow. https://www.gravitysketch.com/
2. Quill VR illustration and animation tool built to empower artists and creators. https://quill.fb.com/
3. Tilt Brush by Google. https://www.tiltbrush.com/
4. Barrera Machuca, M.D., Asente, P., Lu, J., Kim, B., Stuerzlinger, W.: Multiplanes: assisted freehand VR drawing. In: Adjunct Publication of the Annual ACM Symposium on User Interface Software and Technology (UIST 2017 Adjunct), pp. 1–3 (2017). https://doi.org/10.1039/b924500f
5. Eroglu, S., Gebhardt, S., Schmitz, P., Hausch, D., Kuhlen, T.W.: Fluid sketching immersive sketching based on fluid flow. In: 2018 IEEE Conference on Virtual Reality and 3D User Interfaces (VR), pp. 475–482. IEEE (2018)
6. Kim, Y., Kim, B., Kim, J., Kim, Y.J.: CanvoX: High-resolution VR Painting in Large Volumetric Canvas (2017)
7. Lorensen, W.E., Cline, H.E.: Marching cubes: a high resolution 3D surface construction algorithm. In: ACM Siggraph Computer Graphics, vol. 21, pp. 163–169. ACM (1987)
8. Macklin, M., Müller, M.: Position based fluids. ACM Trans. Graph. **32**(4), 1 (2013). https://doi.org/10.1145/2461912.2461984
9. Macklin, M., Müller, M., Chentanez, N., Kim, T.Y.: Unified particle physics for real-time applications. ACM Trans. Graph. **33**(4), 1–12 (2014). https://doi.org/10.1145/2601097.2601152
10. Muller, M., Heidelberger, B., Hennix, M., Ratcliff, J.: Position based dynamics. J. Vis. Commun. Image Representation **18**(2), 109–118 (2007). https://doi.org/10.1016/j.jvcir.2007.01.005
11. Müller, M., Heidelberger, B., Teschner, M., Gross, M.: Meshless deformations based on shape matching. In: ACM Transactions on Graphics (TOG), vol. 24, pp. 471–478. ACM (2005)
12. Ren, B., Yan, X., Yang, T., Li, C.F., Lin, M.C., Hu, S.M.: Fast SPH simulation for gaseous fluids. Vis. Comput. **32**(4), 523–534 (2016). https://doi.org/10.1007/s00371-015-1086-y
13. Salazar, S.V., Ticona, J.A., Torchelsen, R., Nedel, L., Maciel, A.: Heat-based bidirectional phase shifting simulation using position-based dynamics. Comput. Graph. **76**, 107–116 (2018). https://doi.org/10.1016/j.cag.2018.09.004
14. Sebastian, A., Sami, S.: GPU-based clay simulation and ray-tracing tech in Claybook. https://www.claybookgame.com/, www.secondorder.com/
15. Seo, J.H., Bruner, M., Ayres, N.: Aura garden: collective and collaborative aesthetics of light sculpting in virtual reality. In: Extended Abstracts of the 2018 CHI Conference on Human Factors in Computing Systems, pp. Art 12:1–Art12:6 (2018). https://doi.org/10.1145/3170427.3177761
16. Yu, J., Turk, G.: Reconstructing surfaces of particle-based fluids using anisotropic kernels. ACM Trans. Graph. (TOG) **32**(1), 5 (2013)

Field-Aware Parameterization for 3D Painting

Songgang Xu[1], Hang Li[2], and John Keyser[2(✉)]

[1] Intel Corporation, Folsom, CA 95630, USA
`songgang.xu@gmail.com`
[2] Texas A&M University, College Station, TX 77843, USA
`hangli@tamu.edu`, `keyser@cse.tamu.edu`

Abstract. We present a two-phase method that generates a near-isometric parameterization using a local chart of the surface while still being aware of the geodesic metric. During the first phase, we utilize a novel method that approximates polar coordinates to obtain a preliminary parameterization as well as the gradient of the geodesic field. For the second phase, we present a new optimization that generates a near isometric parameterization while considering the gradient field, allowing us to generate high quality parameterizations while keeping the geodesic information. This local parameterization is applied in a view-dependent 3D painting system, providing a local adaptive map computed at interactive rates.

Keywords: Parameterization · Painting system · Geodesic

1 Introduction

The ability for a designer to model not only the geometry but also the color and appearance of a model (which we will refer to as "painting") is a critical aspect of many 3D modeling systems. Although interfaces have long provided the ability to paint directly on a 3D model, the colors are usually stored in a 2D domain, such as in a texture map. Despite its widespread use and several advantages, texture mapping has several shortcomings. 3D painting usually requires only a local surface parameterization, while many parameterization methods are global, not real-time, or generate texture distortions. In particular, the need to determine a map (including the unfolding process, seams, and dealing with multiple charts), and then for the texture artist to consider the orientation of this mapping while painting something nominally 2D, can be problematic.

In recent years, methods have emerged that address these shortcomings. One of the key works is by Schmidt et al. [13], who provided an efficient local parameterization for 3D painting, later extended to stroke parameterization [14]. They tried to minimize the distortion of textures by approximating the exponential map. Though many methods have been used to approximate the exponential map or locally "unwrap" a triangle mesh, most still encounter problems with

© Springer Nature Switzerland AG 2019
M. Gavrilova et al. (Eds.): CGI 2019, LNCS 11542, pp. 131–142, 2019.
https://doi.org/10.1007/978-3-030-22514-8_11

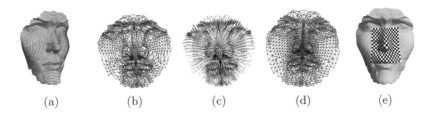

Fig. 1. Field-aware parameterization pipeline. (a) Geodesic field. (b) Unwrapping. (c) Gradient field. (d) Folding removal. (e) Result.

low-quality parameterizations (spreading distortion poorly for painting applications), triangle foldings, or failures for surfaces with sharp or complicated local features.

In our work, we present a two-phase method that not only provides awareness of the geodesic metric but also is insensitive to the local surface connectivity so that triangle foldings are avoided in most cases while providing good texture space distortion distribution from the geodesic information. Preliminary versions of this work have appeared in [19]. We demonstrate the pipeline of our parameterization method in Fig. 1. The first phase obtains the approximated polar coordinates for the local charts. In phase two, we augment the isometric framework by incorporating information from the geodesic field. Though geodesic distance can be constrained in existing parameterization optimization methods, those types of constraints are usually nonlinear, which implies the solution is not globally optimal and the computing complexity is increased. In our method, we represent the geodesic field using a set of affine transformations, which are blended into an isometric framework. We also represent the geodesic field using its intrinsic gradients, upon which we build two methods aligned with those gradients. Those formulations allow us to build linear systems, which are efficient for computation. The isometric setting of the optimization allows us to avoid triangle foldings for most general cases. In the rare cases where folding still happens, we can use a post processing method to resolve it. Utilizing this novel two-phase parameterization technique, we build our 3D painting system that provides a local adaptive and interactive painting environment.

The features of our system fall into three major areas:

1. We provide an efficient incremental unwrapping method that provides approximate geodesic polar coordinates for each vertex. The distortion is lower at the center, and higher near the boundary, which is more natural for strokes in 3D painting.
2. We incorporate the geodesic field's gradient into an isometric parameterization framework and derive two methods for parameterization using the gradient field. This allows us to remove the sensitivity to the surface connectivity and helps us avoid triangle foldings in most cases, but also helps maintain awareness of the geodesic metric.
3. We incorporate our local parameterization technique into a novel 3D painting system, which allows users to paint on the surface directly with our parameterization supporting smooth, continuous, oriented strokes.

2   Related Work

A very wide range of techniques have been applied in recent years to address the problems of distortion and performance in surface parameterization. We refer to the work presented by Floater [3] for a literature survey on methods of authalic (area-preserving), conformal (angle-preserving), and isometric (length-preserving) mapping, as well as some hybrid methods. Most methods can be applied to a whole surface or its local chart if they are homomorphic to a disc. Strictly speaking, though the methods may be applicable to painting applications, they usually do not provide good local parameterization, which usually has a center point. Those methods distribute the distortion as evenly as possible so that high distortions can happen anywhere on the mapped texture. To overcome those problems, Schmidt et al. [13] proposed the decal map, a true local method that approximates the exponential map on the surface chart. Melvaer and Reimers [11] approximated the exponential map using the geodesic metric. The center information is considered naturally by the exponential map in both methods. However, some high texture distortions as well as frequent triangle foldings cannot be overcome, and discontinuities of color will appear across the texture atlas. Schmidt's later work [14], though extending the decal map, still lacks explicit avoidance of sensitivity to mesh connectivity and frequent triangle foldings. Besides those methods, the method presented by Liu et al. [10], built on the isometric approach, is related to our work. The as-rigid-as-possible (ARAP) energy is formulated for optimization so as to parameterize texture coordinates, which is a nonlinear parameterization that is solved by a local/global technique. The local/global framework provides the possibility to add constraints that make the system aware of the geodesic metric without breaking the isometric setting.

3   Local Chart Parameterization

In this section, we explain our parameterization techniques in two phases: incremental unwrapping and field-aware parameterization.

3.1   Incremental Unwrapping

Most local parameterization methods utilizing incremental unwrapping are based on the approximation of the local chart by the exponential map and geodesic metric, which builds correspondences between points on the continuous surface and the tangent plane at a given initial center point. In exact algorithms for computing geodesic distance, roots for different vertices are maintained during the computation, which is ignored in fast marching. For a convex manifold model, we know all the geodesic paths share the same root, the initial point [7]. This allows us to build an exponential map using geodesic paths starting from the same initial point on the model. We follow the traditional incremental unwrapping technique to build our unwrapping paradigm.

Table 1. Comparison of our method with fast marching methods.

Model	Faces	Our method			Fast marching			Exact
		Time (s)	Max abs	Ave rel	Time (s)	Max abs	Ave rel	Time (s)
Plane	2,048	0.029	0.00%	0.00%	0.029	1.01%	1.10%	0.042
Sphere	3,840	0.062	0.00%	0.00%	0.058	0.21%	0.10%	0.12
Cat	24,192	0.41	1.23%	0.33%	0.38	2.31%	1.65%	1.78
Face	35,568	0.57	1.75%	0.25%	0.53	2.23%	1.04%	1.51
Armadillo	69,184	1.18	1.11%	0.72%	1.12	1.36%	1.18%	2.78
Bunny	69,451	1.12	0.49%	0.18%	1.05	0.91%	0.89%	3.24

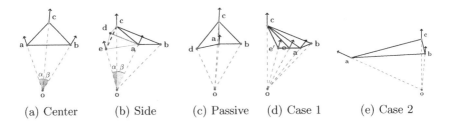

(a) Center   (b) Side   (c) Passive   (d) Case 1   (e) Case 2

Fig. 2. Three local solvers and two special cases.

Initialization. If the center point **o** is a vertex, we unwrap the 1-ring of the initial point to its discrete tangent plane. Otherwise, the tangent plane is the triangle that contains the point. All vertices adjacent to the initial point are marked *Alive*.

Propagation. We compute geodesic distance for vertices beyond the 1-ring using the *Alive* vertices. In detail, for one vertex, we try to find two *Alive* vertices in the same triangle by traversing its neighbors. For the center solver in Fig. 2a and side solver in Fig. 2b, assume we are updating vertex **c**. We find two *Alive* vertices **a** and **b** to compute the geodesic distance and the polar angle of **c**. If the vertex has only one *Alive* neighbor, then we use the passive solver in Fig. 2c to update it.

The center solver in Fig. 2a deals with the case where the geodesic path of **c** goes through the edge **ab**. With 2D geometric computation, **c**'s geodesic distance $\delta(\mathbf{c})$ and polar angle $\tau(\mathbf{c})$ can be obtained with **a**'s and **b**'s geodesic distance $\delta(\mathbf{a})$, $\delta(\mathbf{b})$ and polar angles $\tau(\mathbf{a})$, $\tau(\mathbf{b})$.

c might be on the left (Fig. 2b) of vertex **a** or on the right of vertex **b**, in which case we use the "side solver" technique. We unfold triangles sharing vertex **a**, until we find one *Alive* vertex that neighbors **a** where the geodesic path goes across the edge connecting them both. In Fig. 2b, we first unfold $\triangle$ **cad** and $\triangle$ **dae**. **e** is *Alive* and **co** crosses **ea**. We stop unfolding and solve for $\delta(\mathbf{c})$ and $\tau(\mathbf{c})$ with vertices **a**, **b** and **e**. A symmetric approach will unfold triangles around vertex **b**.

If we cannot find two adjacent *Alive* neighbors around **c**, we use the passive solver in Fig. 2c, which updates a new vertex using just one *Alive* neighbor. The distance value for **c**, $\delta(\mathbf{c})$, is set to the minimum value of $\delta(\mathbf{a}) + |\mathbf{ac}|$ among all Alive vertices, **a**, adjacent to **c**. **c** also inherits the polar angle $\tau(\mathbf{a})$ from **a**.

There are two cases that our method may not work perfectly. In Fig. 2d, **a**, **b**, **e** and **e'** are *Alive* vertices. The side solver cannot be used in this situation as **co** does not cross **ea**. We need to find another edge at the left side of **ae**, such as **ee'**, so that **co** crosses **ee'**. But there's still a possibility that **co** doesn't cross **ee'**. In Fig. 2e, **b** is an *Alive* vertex, and $\tilde{\delta}(\mathbf{a}) > \tilde{\delta}(\mathbf{b}) + |\mathbf{bc}| > \tilde{\delta}(\mathbf{c})$ where $\tilde{\delta}(\cdot)$ means the actual geodesic distance. So we update **c** *Alive* first with passive solver which $\delta(\mathbf{c}) = \tilde{\delta}(\mathbf{b}) + |\mathbf{bc}|$. And then **a** is labeled as *Alive*. So updating **a** after **c** introduces an error because the geodesic from **c** to **o** crosses **ab**. Fortunately, these two cases rarely happen in practice and the distortion which is caused by the error is acceptable even if it happens.

Polar Coordinates Construction. After finishing propagation, each vertex **v** has been associated with its geodesic distance $\delta(\mathbf{v})$ and its polar angle $\tau(\mathbf{v})$, i.e, the polar coordinates, which are easily transformed to the texture coordinates. Figure 3 shows comparisons between our incremental unwrapping method, the method (least squares conformal map) in the conformal setting, and the method (as-rigid-as-possible map) in the isometric setting. Since global parameterization methods are not sensitive to the center point, our method can generate lower distortion around the center.

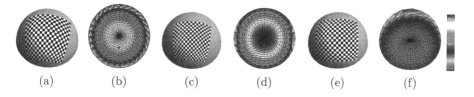

| (a) | (b) | (c) | (d) | (e) | (f) |

Fig. 3. Incremental unwrapping results (e, f) compared with isometric (a, b) and conformal (c, d) settings. a, c and e show the texture mapping result. b, d, and f show the area distortion distribution.

As an approximated method for computing geodesics, we compare our results with the original fast marching method numerically in both accuracy and performance. We use the accurate method proposed in [7] and the code from [18] to obtain the precise geodesic distance $\tilde{\delta}(v)$ for each vertex. Table 1 reports the maximal absolute difference $|\tilde{\delta}(v) - \delta(v)|$ as the percentage of the object diameter and the average relative difference $|\tilde{\delta}(v) - \delta(v)|/\tilde{\delta}(v)$. As shown in Table 1, our method has better accuracy than fast marching while achieving very similar performance.

Similar to many other incremental unwrapping methods, our parameterization results may still have triangle foldings. The field-aware optimization in the next part overcomes this problem while still keeping the geodesic metric information. We note that Crane et al. [2] and Sharp et al. [15] presented a method computing geodesic distance via heat flow. This method can be used in our scheme. But the computation speed is slower than ours.

3.2 Field-Aware Parameterization

In this part, we modify an isometric parameterization (ARAP) to be aware of the geodesic metric. ARAP makes a strong assumption that only rotational transformations are allowed for triangle faces during the parameterization. Therefore, ARAP measures the difference between the real affine transformation matrix and the rotational matrix of each triangle. The energy for optimization is the summation of individual differences,

$$E_{\text{ARAP}} = \sum_{t=1}^{|T|} A_t ||J_t - R_t||_F^2, \tag{1}$$

where A_t is the area of triangle t, J_t is the affine transformation from the original triangle t to its image, R_t is the rigid transformation matrix, and $|T|$ is the number of triangles. Since we have the geodesic field which also acts as a parameterization, we can use the corresponding affine transformation matrix to represent the parameterization information naturally. We present a method augmenting ARAP.

Augmentation Method. We use Jacobian G_t to indicate the transformation from the original triangle t to its image in the geodesic field. The energy function of our new field-aware system can be formulated by a blending parameter $\lambda_1 > 0$ as below,

$$E_{\text{AUG}} = \sum_{t=1}^{|T|} A_t ||J_t - R_t||_F^2 + \lambda_1 A_t ||J_t - G_t||_F^2. \tag{2}$$

For clarity, we call this parameterization method the *augmentation* method. The local-global method, which solves the nonlinear problem in ARAP, can be used again to solve the new field-aware system. In detail, we can compute R_t and G_t in the local phase. In the global phase, the field-aware Poisson equation is formulated by considering G_t and the blending parameter λ_1 for all triangles as,

$$(1 + \lambda_1) \sum_{j \in N(i)} [\cot \theta_{i,j} + \cot \theta_{j,i}](\mathbf{u}_i - \mathbf{u}_j)$$

$$= \sum_{j \in N(i)} [(R_{t(i,j)} + \lambda_1 G_{t(i,j)}) \cot \theta_{i,j} + (R_{t(j,i)} + \lambda_1 G_{t(j,i)}) \cot \theta_{j,i}](\mathbf{x}_i - \mathbf{x}_j). \tag{3}$$

where $i = 1, \ldots, |T|$, $N(i)$ indicates vertex neighbors around vertex i, $\mathbf{x}_i$ is the coordinates of vertex i, and $\mathbf{u}_i$ is the parameterization coordinates of vertex i.

Here pair (i, j) indicates the halfedge from vertex i to j, and $\theta_{i,j}$ is the angle opposite to the halfedge (i, j).

Hard Field Alignment. The field-awareness in system (2) is achieved by blending the affine transformation matrices, which encapsulate information of the geodesic field. Instead of using this full-fledged information, we can instead align with just the gradient field over the geodesic distance during the global optimization phase, which produces comparable results. In detail, the Poisson equation can be represented by submatrices as $\begin{bmatrix} L & 0 \\ 0 & L \end{bmatrix} \cdot \begin{bmatrix} U \\ V \end{bmatrix} = \begin{bmatrix} \mathbf{b}_u \\ \mathbf{b}_v \end{bmatrix}$, where L is the discrete Laplace-Beltrami operator matrix, U and V are vectors formed by the u-components and v-components of texture coordinates respectively, and $\mathbf{b}_u$ and $\mathbf{b}_v$ are corresponding right sides of the linear system.

For one triangle t, assume vertex indices are i, j and k. The gradient on this face is $\mathbf{d}_t = [g_k \cdot (\mathbf{u}_j - \mathbf{u}_i) + g_i \cdot (\mathbf{u}_k - \mathbf{u}_j) + g_j \cdot (\mathbf{u}_i - \mathbf{u}_k)]^\perp$, where g_i is the geodesic distance we obtained during the incremental unwrapping phase. Assume the matrix on the left side of this system is K, formed by g_i, and the right side is $[\mathbf{g}_u, \mathbf{g}_v]^T$, formed by uv-components. Then we obtain a field-aware system as $\begin{bmatrix} K & 0 \\ 0 & K \end{bmatrix} \cdot \begin{bmatrix} U \\ V \end{bmatrix} = \begin{bmatrix} \mathbf{g}_u \\ \mathbf{g}_v \end{bmatrix}$. We combine the field-aware system with the original ARAP system by parameter $\lambda_2 > 0$,

$$\begin{bmatrix} L + \lambda_2 K^T K & 0 \\ 0 & L + \lambda_2 K^T K \end{bmatrix} \cdot \begin{bmatrix} U \\ V \end{bmatrix} = \begin{bmatrix} \mathbf{b}_u + \lambda_2 K^T \mathbf{g}_u \\ \mathbf{b}_v + \lambda_2 K^T \mathbf{g}_v \end{bmatrix}. \tag{4}$$

Relaxed Field Alignment. Under some conditions, artists might prefer more regular grids at the cost of somewhat less direction from the geodesic metric. We can allow alignment with directions only (and not magnitudes) by adding relaxing variables into face gradients, which allows the system to be field-aware in a milder way. Within the isometric setting, we add s_t for triangle t and align with $s_t \mathbf{d}_t$ instead of $\mathbf{d}_t$. Therefore, s_t provides the relaxation for the direction alignment. Assume Λ is a set of diagonal matrices composed by s_t, and $\mathbf{g}_u^D$ and $\mathbf{g}_v^D$ are diagonalized $\mathbf{g}_u$ and $\mathbf{g}_v$ respectively. System (4) can be relaxed as

$$\begin{bmatrix} L + \lambda_2 K^T K & 0 & \lambda_2 K^T \mathbf{g}_u^D \\ 0 & L + \lambda_2 K^T K & \lambda_2 K^T \mathbf{g}_v^D \\ \lambda_2 (K^T \mathbf{g}_u^D)^T & \lambda_2 (K^T \mathbf{g}_v^D)^T & \lambda_2 (\mathbf{g}_u^D)^T \mathbf{g}_u^D + \lambda_2 (\mathbf{g}_v^D)^T \mathbf{g}_v^D \end{bmatrix} \begin{bmatrix} U \\ V \\ \Lambda \end{bmatrix} = \begin{bmatrix} \mathbf{b}_u \\ \mathbf{b}_v \\ 0 \end{bmatrix}. \tag{5}$$

Figure 4 shows results of ARAP, the augmented field-aware system by blending the affine transformation, the hard alignment system and the relaxed alignment system. Since the relaxed system isn't aware of the magnitude of the field gradients, it is not as sensitive to the geodesic metric as the hard alignment system. However, the awareness of directions of gradients provides a reasonable compromise between ARAP and the incremental unwrapping. In our experiments, we found it usually converged within twenty iterations with the original ARAP and five to ten iterations after augmenting the original method with the new geodesic information. And the triangle foldings were removed meanwhile in most cases.

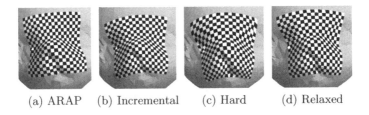

(a) ARAP   (b) Incremental   (c) Hard   (d) Relaxed

Fig. 4. Relaxed alignment is a good compromise between ARAP and hard alignment

Finally, for most cases where the incremental unwrapping produces triangle foldings, our optimization process removes those foldings. However, if any folding happens, a folding-free result can be guaranteed by a post processing by the method proposed in [8].

There are lots of bijection methods that guarantee solving the folding problem ([4,5,9,12,16]). But speed is essential to a painting system. None of them are as fast as the incremental unwrapping method. And our system is not sensitive to the folding areas, because local geometry is usually flat and folding always happens when faces are far away from the center.

4   Painting System Implementation

We developed our field-aware parameterization method in order to improve the quality of real-time 3D painting. We have implemented it as a core part of our 3D painting system. The key features of our system are a view-dependent local parameterization and view-dependent oriented painting.

Our system stores colors using Mesh Colors [20], but would be easily adapted to other surface-based color storage schemes [1,21]. Our method, by interactively generating local 2D maps, makes it possible to apply all the standard 2D image manipulation tools even to such 3D surfaces, without having to worry about issues such as seams and chart boundaries.

4.1   View Dependent Local Parameterization

Painting is a local behavior. So we want to separate the local surface region being painted and unfold it for mapping the brush strokes without global parameterization. We need to create a local chart from *relevant* triangles falling under the brush in the 3D screen space view. Locally, the surface might be convex, concave or saddle. We use our two-phase method to parameterize the local surface on the fly. Our parameterization adapts to the screen position of the painting tool and the perspective view of the model. In detail, we have three steps to build the local chart by our method.

Center Triangle Picking. Given the brush center, we pick the center triangle as the one containing the brush center. Note that an AABB or BSP tree for the model can help to accelerate this operation.

(a) Model   (b) Parameterization Views

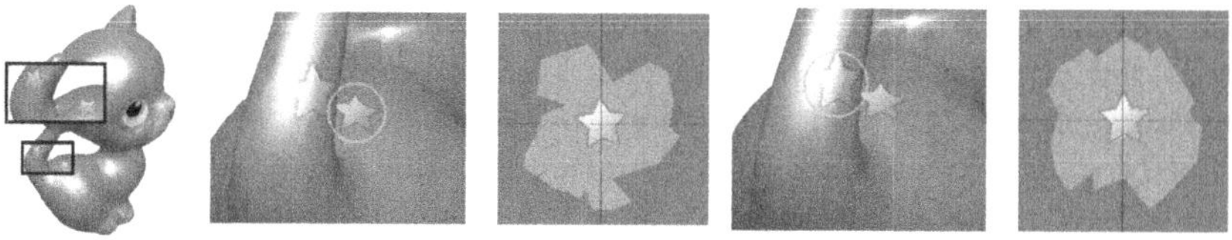

Fig. 5. View dependent local parameterization. Our system can distinguish close placements in screen space (the tail and the back).

Boundary Triangles Picking. The second step aims to find the visible triangles whose image on the screen intersects with the brush region. Instead of focusing on all triangles covered by the brush, we only identify those intersecting the brush's screen-space boundary. We call these *boundary triangles*, which can be obtained using ray intersection or screen-space picking.

Local Chart Construction. Given the center triangle and a set of boundary triangles, we construct a local chart that will encompass the region surrounding the center point including both nearby triangles falling under the brush in screen space and hidden triangles that nevertheless need to be painted on by the stroke. The local chart, which is a continuous triangular 3D surface, is homeomorphic to a disc. We can apply our parameterization on it directly.

Figure 5 gives two parameterization examples from our system that highlight the benefits of our local parameterization. In Fig. 5b, even though the brushes overlap the silhouette of the model, the brush strokes are painted correctly on the model itself, wrapping around the model locally. Compared to [6] these results justify that our parameterization method is not sensitive to the local geometry, and compared to pure projection methods this demonstrates that we can have true 2D operations over the surface.

4.2   View Dependent Oriented Painting

Artists can zoom in or out, translate or rotate the model. These operations change the perspective view of the model surfaces, i.e. the canvas. Many current painting systems require the user to adjust the orientation or the scaling size of textures (strokes). In our system, they are decided by the current view perspective of the model. Our painting implementation adapts to those changes of views and paints the model in a correct way.

Orientation. While some strokes are radially symmetric (e.g. solid, Gaussian blur), others have orientation (e.g. stamp). We thus want our local parameterization to have a "good" orientation. We compute the directions of principal curvatures at each vertex. The texture orientation is decided by the vertex frame nearest to the texture center. We also allow the artist to rotate the mapping view manually so that the stroke can be mapped in an arbitrary angle if desired.

Brush Strokes Construction. To illustrate painting operations, we implemented a few different brush operations modeled on typical 2D brushes available in systems such as GIMP and Photoshop. The properties we observed in typical brush strokes include *size* and *pattern*, and we implemented several examples of each in different brushes and stamps. Since we do not have a 2D raster canvas, and parameterizations change rapidly, we do not have the notion of a pixel size for determining scaling, as is typical in 2D paint systems. We can define the size in terms of the 3D view (typical), or the 2D parametric space based on geodesic distance.

Coloring Samples. With the local chart parameterized and oriented, we can map the texture to the surface by projecting the region of strokes onto the (u, v) domain, where the local chart is unfolded. The mesh color sample points of the triangles within the local chart are also mapped into the (u, v) domain, and are assigned the appropriate color based on the stroke and brush parameters.

Stroke Parameterization. Stroke parameterization is a fundamental tool to parameterize the region around a 3D curve on the surface [14,17]. We do this by sampling a series of points on the curve, unwrapping the surface around each point separately. This gives us a local parameterization around the curve. In this case, the orientation is defined by the tangent line of the curve instead of principal directions.

If the stroke self-intersects, ARAP cannot solve the stroke parameterization problem by treating them as a series of local charts. The shape may be bent a lot by ARAP and inconsistent around the intersection.

4.3   Painting Results

Our painting system is implemented on a PC with an Intel Core(TM) i7 3.4 GHz processor and 16 GB RAM, where the parameterization occurs in real-time with the mouse movement. We show some example results here.

(a) Editing view   (b) Editing view   (c) Result

Fig. 6. Painting a genus 2 model.

We first test our system on different geometric shapes. Figure 6 shows our painting results on a high genus model.

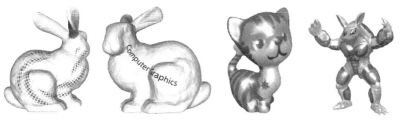

(a) Stroke parameterization.   (b) Objects painted with our system.

Fig. 7. Painting results.

We demonstrate stroke parameterization and how we maintain both orientation and accurate distance computation from a series of points making up a stroke. Figure 7a shows results from both a pattern brush and a text brush.

Finally, we invited art students to try our paint system, and they generated the complete painting results, with examples shown in Fig. 7b.

5   Conclusion

Our two-phase local parameterization is an efficient method for mapping texture on the local surface. The incremental unwrapping flattens the surface by approximating the exponential map, which has a comparable performance to the fast marching method. The optimization obtains texture coordinates with a few iterations. All this makes our method very efficient for constructing real time parameterizations in 3D painting systems. We provide a novel way to make the gradient in the texture field align with any given field during optimization. We use this to make our parameterization aware of the geodesic metric so that the distortion is redistributed away from the center point. Two methods with different gradient alignments are proposed, which allow corresponding numeric systems to have a linear form so that the computing complexity is reduced.

Our method has two limitations that would be avenues for future work. First, the method does not handle holes in a surface ideally, since the geodesic path cannot go over holes using current solvers. Second but related, our method assumes the region being mapped is relatively local, such that it is reasonable for the triangles within to be homeomorphic to a disc.

References

1. Burley, B., Lacewell, D.: Ptex: per-face texture mapping for production rendering. Comput. Graph. Forum **27**(4), 1155–1164 (2008)
2. Crane, K., Weischedel, C., Wardetzky, M.: Geodesics in heat: a new approach to computing distance based on heat flow. ACM Trans. Graph. (TOG) **32**(5), 152 (2013)

3. Floater, M.S., Hormann, K.: Surface parameterization: a tutorial and survey. In: Dodgson, N.A., Floater, M.S., Sabin, M.A. (eds.) Advances in Multiresolution for Geometric Modelling, pp. 157–186. Springer, Heidelberg (2005). https://doi.org/10.1007/3-540-26808-1_9

4. Fu, X.M., Liu, Y.: Computing inversion-free mappings by simplex assembly. ACM Trans. Graph. (TOG) **35**(6), 216 (2016)

5. Fu, X.M., Liu, Y., Guo, B.: Computing locally injective mappings by advanced MIPS. ACM Trans. Graph. (TOG) **34**(4), 71 (2015)

6. Igarashi, T., Cosgrove, D.: Adaptive unwrapping for interactive texture painting. In: Proceedings of the 2001 symposium on Interactive 3D graphics, pp. 209–216 (2001)

7. Joseph, S., Mount, D., Papadimitriou, C.: The discrete geodesic problem. SIAM J. Comput. **16**(4), 647–668 (1987)

8. Kami, Z., Gotsman, C., Gortler, S.J.: Free-boundary linear parameterization of 3D meshes in the presence of constraints. In: 2005 International Conference on Shape Modeling and Applications, pp. 266–275. IEEE (2005)

9. Kovalsky, S.Z., Galun, M., Lipman, Y.: Accelerated quadratic proxy for geometric optimization. ACM Trans. Graph. (TOG) **35**(4), 134 (2016)

10. Liu, L., Zhang, L., Xu, Y., Gotsman, C., Gortler, S.J.: A local/global approach to mesh parameterization. In: Computer Graphics Forum, vol. 27, pp. 1495–1504. Wiley, Hoboken (2008)

11. Melvær, E.L., Reimers, M.: Geodesic polar coordinates on polygonal meshes. In: Computer Graphics Forum, vol. 31, pp. 2423–2435. Wiley, Hoboken (2012)

12. Rabinovich, M., Poranne, R., Panozzo, D., Sorkine-Hornung, O.: Scalable locally injective mappings. ACM Trans. Graph. (TOG) **36**(2), 16 (2017)

13. Schmidt, R., Grimm, C., Wyvill, B.: Interactive decal compositing with discrete exponential maps. ACM Trans. Graph. (TOG) **25**, 605–613 (2006)

14. Schmidt, R.: Stroke parameterization. In: Computer Graphics Forum, vol. 32, pp. 255–263. Wiley, Hoboken (2013)

15. Sharp, N., Soliman, Y., Crane, K.: The vector heat method. arXiv preprint arXiv:1805.09170 (2018)

16. Smith, J., Schaefer, S.: Bijective parameterization with free boundaries. ACM Trans. Graph. (TOG) **34**(4), 70 (2015)

17. Sun, Q., et al.: Texture brush: an interactive surface texturing interface. In: Proceedings of the ACM SIGGRAPH Symposium on Interactive 3D Graphics and Games, pp. 153–160. ACM (2013)

18. Surazhsky, V., Surazhsky, T., Kirsanov, D., Gortler, S.J., Hoppe, H.: Fast exact and approximate geodesics on meshes. ACM Trans. Graph. (TOG) **24**, 553–560 (2005)

19. Xu, S.: Numerical and geometric optimizations for surface and tolerance modeling. Ph.D. thesis, Texas A&M University, December 2015

20. Yuksel, C., Keyser, J., House, D.H.: Mesh colors. ACM Trans. Graph. **29**(2), 1–11 (2010)

21. Zhang, X., Kim, Y.J., Ye, X.: Versatile 3D texture painting using imaging geometry. In: Korea-China Joint Conference on Geometric and Visual Computing (2005)

A Novel Method of Multi-user Redirected Walking for Large-Scale Virtual Environments

Tianyang Dong, Yifan Song, Yuqi Shen, and Jing Fan$^{(\boxtimes)}$

Zhejiang University of Technology, Hangzhou 310023, China
fanjing@zjut.edu.cn

Abstract. The wireless virtual reality (VR) solution for Head-Mounted Display (HMD) expands the support to multi-user VR system, so multiple users or participants can collaborate in the same physical space for a large-scale virtual environment. The foremost technical obstacle of multi-user VR system is how to accommodate multiple users within the same physical space. It needs address the problem of potential collisions among these users who are moving both virtually and physically. By analyzing the challenges of multiple users, this paper presents a novel method of multi-user redirected walking for large-scale virtual environments. In this method, an improved approach is presented to calculate the rotation gains, and a user clustering algorithm is adopted to divide the users into groups that are automatically adjusted based on the distance between the boundaries or the size of remaining space. Then a heuristic algorithm for three-user or two-user redirected walking is designed to solve the problem of multi-user roaming in a faster and more efficient way than traditional methods. To verify the validity of our method, we used a computer simulation framework to statistically analyze the influence of different factors, such as the physical space size and the number of users. The results show that our multi-user redirected walking algorithm for large-scale virtual environments is effective and practical.

Keywords: Redirected walking · Virtual reality · Head-mounted display · Multiple users · Virtual roaming

1 Introduction

In fact, real-world physical workspaces and technological limitations may restrict the free exploration of a large-scale virtual environment, but VR technology is pushing the limits of human experience. In a large-scale virtual environment, the participants try to freely explore immersive virtual environments by some locomotion techniques, e.g., joystick and trackball. However, the existing researches have shown that walking as the most natural way of behavior has many advantages of improving their sensory experience [1]. Redirected Walking (RDW) is a collection of VR locomotion techniques to allow user roaming in the virtual environment. It can enable the users of VR system to walk on paths in the real world, which may vary from the paths they perceive in the virtual environment. What's more, the virtual environments may be larger than the physical space through natural walking [2].

© Springer Nature Switzerland AG 2019
M. Gavrilova et al. (Eds.): CGI 2019, LNCS 11542, pp. 143–154, 2019.
https://doi.org/10.1007/978-3-030-22514-8_12

Multi-user VR systems for a large-scale virtual environment open up opportunities to use VR in many fields, such as playing a multi-user game, holding a meeting or designing a new building. Therefore, it is a new trend for multiple users to roam a large-scale virtual environment in the same physical space. In order to meet the needs of multiple users sharing the same physical space, the VR system must monitor all possible collision of users immersed in the virtual environment and adopt an appropriate strategy of collision avoidance. Because of the increasing of users and the limitation of physical space, the process of collision avoidance is very complicated. So far, there is no effective way to solve the multi-user redirected walking problem. Bachmann [3] and Azmandian et al. [4] have proposed some solutions for two users sharing the same physical space. However, when there are more users to roam in the virtual environment, these methods are unable to achieve this goal of collision avoidance.

In order to solve the problem of multi-user roaming, this paper presents a novel redirected walking method for multiple users who share the same physical space to avoid collisions among users. In this paper, we presented an improved approach to calculate the rotation gains, and adopted a user clustering algorithm to divide the users into groups that are automatically adjusted based on the distance between the boundaries or the size of remaining space. Then different heuristic algorithms of three-user or two-user redirected walking are adopted for each group to deal with the evolving challenges of multiple users. In addition, this paper provides a systematic evaluation of the impact of physical space size and users' steering target setting strategies for this redirected walking method. Therefore, the best strategies of redirected walking can be obtained efficiently to deal with various application scenarios.

2 Related Works

The redirected walking algorithm is a common method for users to explore large-scale virtual environments in a small physical space. The traditional redirected walking algorithm focused on single users and the limitations of physical space size. Steinicke et al. reviewed and summarized the steering strategies in redirected walking [5], which are referred to as gains. To ensure that the introduced gains are not noticeable, the threshold of the gains can be experimentally determined [6]. The threshold of gains and the limited size of a physical space prevent the steering strategy from completely avoiding collisions. Therefore, the fail-safe redirected mechanism (reset) is also required to complete the entire redirected walking [7]. The reset mechanism will affect a user's experience to a certain extent. So Nescher et al. attempted to reduce the probability of boundary collision [8]. Their prediction algorithm predicts a user's behaviors to select the optimal redirected walking strategy. For the problem that the prediction algorithm needs to manually annotate the virtual environment, Azmandian et al. proposed a method to automatically generate an environmental annotation map and adopt the navigation grid to predict a user's trajectory [9]. As redirected walking changes the mapping and may cause distortion of the virtual scene, Dong et al. [10] proposed a novel divide-and-conquer method that is referred to as Smooth Assembled Mappings (SAM) to solve this problem. Since the majority of research is based on the physical space conditions with relatively regular shapes, Chen et al. [11] proposed the idea of applying redirected walking to an irregular physical space. For the problem that there may be obstacles in the physical space, Sun et al. [12] proposed a method which detects saccadic suppression and redirects the users during the temporary blindness.

In general, these redirected walking algorithms are based on one user. When multiple users are present in the same physical space, collisions among users will occur. The VR system must predict an impending collision and develop a collision avoidance strategy. Multi-user and boundary constraints render the collision avoidance particularly complex, and few attempts have been made to solve the multi-user redirected walking problem. Podkosova et al. [13] present two experiments to study people's preference of obvious interference in virtual environments when they will collide with others. They suggest that people prefer the signal to contain a "stop" command when they are in dangerous situation and the type of scenario influences users' preference of a notification avatar. Bachmann et al. [3] proposed forecasting and collision avoidance strategies to solve the problem of sharing tracking areas between two users. Azmandian et al. [4] proposed a new relative velocity collision prediction method and developed a computer simulation framework to evaluate the influence of physical space size and space sharing strategies for the two-user redirected walking algorithms.

By now, there is still no effective redirected walking method for multiple users who collaborate in large-scale virtual environment. Bachmann's method is based on two users, and their collision avoidance is performed by classifying collisions between two users. This kind of collision avoidance strategy is inapplicable to more users.

3   Multi-user Redirected Walking

As the number of user increases, if it still considers the interaction between one user and other users, the complexity of the problem will substantially increase. To solve this problem, this paper presents a novel method of multi-user redirected walking for large-scale virtual environments in shared physical spaces. In this method, an improved approach is adopted to calculate the rotation gains. When there are more than three participants, the users are divided into groups, which are automatically adjusted based on the distance between the boundaries or the size of remaining space. At last, different heuristic algorithm of three-user or two-use redirected walking is applied to each group to address the challenges of multi-user redirected walking.

3.1   Gains of Multi-user Redirected Walking

To reduce collision between two users, this paper attempt to establish a separate offset center target for each user. To better solve the collision problem, our method uses redirected walking forecasting prediction to predict the future walking path and then summarize the collisions among users into three kinds and apply different collision avoidance strategies to them. After the collision avoidance is completed, the user is again steered to the original target. To enable users to explore large virtual scenes in a small-scale physical space, the thresholds of three gains are evaluated and applied in the redirected walking algorithm [6], as shown in Fig. 1. The first two gains are applied during a user's walking process, and the rotation gains are applied during a user's rotation process.

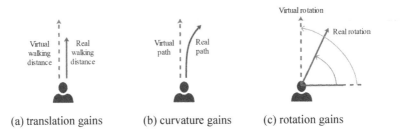

Fig. 1. Three gains of redirected walking.

Translation gains, as shown in Fig. 1(a), are used to scale a user's forward walking distance. Usually, the actual walking distance can be reduced by 14% or increased by 26% compared with the virtual scene [6].

Curvature gains, as shown in Fig. 1(b), are applied during a user's forward walking. User will walk on a curved actual path whose radius is r. The straight path will be mapped on a circle with a minimum radius of 7.5 m [14].

Rotation gains, as shown in Fig. 1(c), can be used to effectively scale a user's perceived rotation angle when the user is stationary, and the actual rotation angle can be downscaled by 20% or up-scaled by 49% compared with the virtual rotation angle [8]. Usually the target is in the central region of physical space. If a user is facing the target, he will walk on a straight path. In order to steer the users to the target as much as possible and let the user walk on a curved path to make better use of physical space, we present an improved method to calculate the rotation gains. In this method, we consider the user's angle of rotation in the virtual environment and the distance $D_{uTotarget}$ between the user and the target as influence factor. We first calculate the possible orientation of the user after applying the maximum and minimum rotation gain. If $D_{uTotarget}$ is greater than 1.25 m, we attempt to steer the user to turn to the state that the orientation vector $Vector_u$ is at an angle α to the vector $Vector_{uTotarget}$, where α is set to 60° and $Vector_{uTotarget}$ represents the vector of the user facing the target. When $D_{uTotarget}$ is less than 1.25 m, a smaller α is better. Therefore, the desired angle of rotation is obtained, then the rotation gains are calculated for the redirected walking.

3.2   Clustering of Roaming Users

When there are more than three users in a physical space, this method of multi-user redirected walking uses a user clustering algorithm to divide the users into groups. First, it gets four groups of users that are closest to the corresponding boundaries from the top, bottom, left and right sides, and there are up to three users in each group. Second, it identifies the group that has minimum sum of distance between any two users in each group and gets the user in this candidate group who is farthest from its corresponding boundary and the user who is not in this candidate group but is closest to the corresponding boundary. Then, according to these two users, it can get a middle line as virtual boundary that is parallel to the corresponding boundary. In addition, the position of virtual boundary is adjusted according to the distance between the boundaries or the size of remaining space. Finally, it repeats these steps until there are no more than three users in remaining space. Specially, for the case that four users in remaining space, it will divide them into two groups and each group has two users.

As shown in Fig. 2, the large points represent users, the dotted lines represent users' history paths, and the arrows represent users' movement directions. There are four groups from the top, bottom, left and right sides in Fig. 2(a), and group (User4, User5, User6) has the shortest distance between the users. Thus, this group is identified as Group1 and its corresponding boundary is right side. Then a blue virtual boundary parallel to the right side is drawn based on User6 and User1, which is in the middle of User6 and User1, as shown in Fig. 2(b).

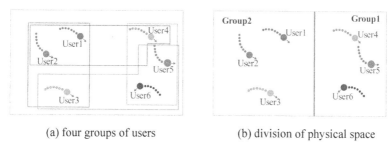

(a) four groups of users   (b) division of physical space

Fig. 2. The clustering of six users. (Color figure online)

3.3 Heuristic Redirected Walking Algorithm

In this paper, a heuristic algorithm is designed to solve the problem of virtual roaming in a faster and more efficient way than traditional methods. The purpose of heuristic redirected walking algorithm is to enable all users in the same physical space to avoid collisions of each other while exploring the large-scale virtual environments. Thus, this heuristic algorithm will simultaneously take into account the states of users and choose different strategies according to different situations. The parameters in our method are based on experience and previous researches [5] [6]. For three users, three situations will occur, including two-user collision, one user collides with other two users, and three users collide at the same time. As shown in Figs. 3, 4, 5 and 6, the grey area represents the area where collision will occur; the red, green and blue points represent three different users; the red, green and blue crosses represent the steering targets of the corresponding users, and the dotted lines represent the future paths of the user.

(1) *Two-user Collision.*

In this case, collision detection only detects that two users will collide in the future. For the user who is farther away from the boundary (User1), our algorithm will establish a temporary steering target on the other side for User1, now new steering target is on User1's right side rather than left side. If the non-collision user (User3) and User1's temporary target are on the opposite side of User1, as shown in Fig. 3, the temporary target is 90° to User1's orientation, and 4 metres from the user; If the non-collision user (User3) and User1's temporary target are on the same side of the User1, as shown in the Fig. 4, the temporary target is 3 metres from User1 and the angle for User1 to turn to the temporary target is α, where α = 180°-β and β is the angle required for User1 to turn to User3. If β is less than 30° or greater than 150°, α is directly set to 90°. In the collision avoidance process, if the non-collision user collides with other users due to the temporary target, it uses 2:1-Turn [11] to the non-collision user.

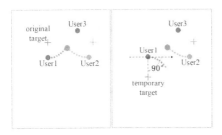

(a) collision prediction (b) collision avoidance

Fig. 3. Collision avoidance for User3 and temporary target are on the opposite side of User1 (Color figure online)

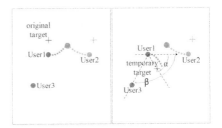

(a) collision prediction (b) collision avoidance

Fig. 4. Collision avoidance for User3 and temporary target are on the same side of User1. (Color figure online)

(2) *One user collides with other two users.*

In this case, the collision detection detects that two users simultaneously collide with a third user but detects that no collision occurs between the two users, as shown in Fig. 5(a), User1 and User2 collide with User3 but no collision occurs between User1 and User2. Our algorithm will establish a new temporary steering target on the other side for these two users (User1, User2). Temporary targets are located 90° to their orientation and 4 m from these users. The third user is not steered to the corresponding target and the translation gain is applied to reduce the advancement distance in the actual environment, as shown in Fig. 5(b).

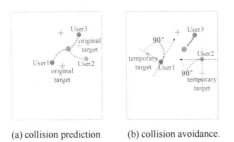

(a) collision prediction   (b) collision avoidance.

Fig. 5. Illustration of one-two collision prediction and avoidance. (Color figure online)

(3) *Three users collide at the same time.*

In this case, the collision detection detects that three users collide at the same time, as shown in Fig. 6(a). Our algorithm calculates the orientation angle between two users. Then we select two users with the smallest angle and establish new temporary targets on the other side for them (User1, User2). The temporary targets are located 90° to their orientation and 4 m from the users. The third user (User3) maintains the status quo, as shown in Fig. 6(b).

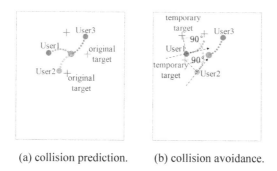

(a) collision prediction.   (b) collision avoidance.

Fig. 6. Illustration of three-user collision prediction and avoidance. (Color figure online)

4 Experiment and Evaluation

4.1 Computer Simulation Framework

A computer simulation framework is used to simulate the experiment. The virtual path consists of a series of navigation points, and the simulated user continuously moves towards the next navigation point at a linear velocity of 1 m/s. In the process, a user is kept facing the navigation point, that is, attempting to walk in a straight line in the virtual world. When the navigation point is reached, the simulated user stops and rotates with an angular velocity of 90°/s to face the next navigation point. No noise was added in this experiment to ensure that the simulated user would walk along the virtual path that was calibrated using a series of navigation points.

The virtual path is randomly generated by the computer simulation software. The distance between two virtual world navigation points is randomly set from 2 to 8 m. The virtual paths have randomized 90° turns, and their total length is approximately 500 m.

The warning distance of 0.5 m is used to avoid a boundary collision, that is, we trigger the reset mechanism when the distance between a user and the boundary is less than 0.5 m. In this experiment, the reset mechanism uses a 2:1-Turn reset, which enables the user to complete 180° turning.

The experimental results were analyzed based on the physical space size and target setting strategies. In the simulation framework, we counted the number of user collisions. For the statistics of the number of collisions of users, any two users with a distance of less than 0.5 m are recorded as a collision. When the collision occurs, the users of the collision will cross each other and continue to complete the simulation walk.

4.2 Experiment 1: Study the Performance of Multi-user Redirected Walking

Experimental Process

To study the effectiveness of the proposed algorithm, we conducted a comparative experiment analysis of three users and six users based on the multi-user redirected walking algorithm and calculated the number of collisions among users. In the experiments, the result without using the redirected walking algorithm is regarded as a baseline.

The experiments were performed using the eight physical sizes of 12×6, 16×8, 20×10, 24×12, 28×14, 32×16, 36×18, and 40×20 m.

For three users, their offset center targets are located at $(0, Y/4)$, $(-X/4, -Y/4)$, and $(X/4, -Y/4)$ respectively. For six users, their offset center targets are located at $(-X/4, Y/4)$, $(0, Y/4)$, $(X/4, Y/4)$, $(-X/4, -Y/4)$, $(0, -Y/4)$, $(X/4, -Y/4)$, and $(X/4, -Y/4)$ respectively, where X represents the width of the physical space along the x axis, and Y represents the length of the physical space along the y axis.

The simulated user's starting points are located at their respective offset center targets, and all users are oriented in the positive direction of the y axis. For each case, 40 experiments are repeated. The results are shown in Fig. 7, "+RDW" meaning the use of multi-user redirected walking and "−RDW" meaning not use. The eight physical spaces include a small room environment and a large playground environment, and the first few spaces are more prone to user collision. Obviously, the number of users and the size of physical space have a great influence on collision events.

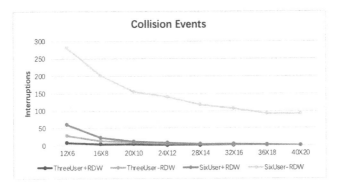

Fig. 7. User collision event statistics.

Result Analysis

The experimental results show that the number of collisions decreases by 70.36%, 67.19%, 64.27%, 80%, 72.50%, 74.58%, 71.43% and 70.83% in the case of three users from a smaller space to a larger space. When the physical space is large, such as 24×12, 28×14, 32×16, 36×18, 40×20 m, our algorithm can almost reduce the number of collisions to zero. When the physical spaces are small (12×6, 16×8, 20×10 m), our algorithm achieves excellent results but it cannot completely avoid collisions.

In the case of six users, the number of collisions decreased by 78.66%, 88.34%, 92.64%, 94.81%, 95.81%, 96.52%, 98.36%, and 99.32% for different physical space sizes. When the physical space is large (36X18 and 40X20 m), our algorithm can almost reduce the number of collisions to 0. When the physical space is not so large (20×10, 24×12, 28×14, and 32×16 m), our algorithm also has a significant effect, but it cannot completely avoid collisions. When the physical space is small (12×6, 16×8 m), more collisions may occur.

The experimental results show that the application of our multi-user redirected walking method can reduce the probability of user-to-user collisions to a certain extent. The expansion of the physical space and the number of users is also conducive to the reduction of user-to-user collisions to a certain extent.

4.3   Experiment 2: Comparing the Effect of Target Settings and Space Size on Redirected Walking

For redirected walking technology, all users are steered to their targets when a collision is not predicted. The preset offset center targets will inevitably affect the performance of the algorithm; thus, the use of a shared single center or multiple offset center targets to apply the Steer-To-Center algorithm must be decided.

Experiment Process

In this experiment, two target setting strategies were tested: a strategy with a single shared center and a strategy with multiple offset center targets with the same number of users. For a more complete comparison, both the situation with three users and the situation with six users were tested. In the test, we counted the number of user events (internal collisions or 2:1-Turn due to collisions among users).

For the physical space shared by three users, if it is a single shared center target, the center target is located in the physical space center $(0, 0)$, and the simulated user starting points are located in the physical space at the three positions $(0, Y/4)$, $(-X/4, -Y/4)$, $(X/4, -Y/4)$. If multiple offset center targets exist, the three offset center targets are located in the physical space at the three positions $(0, Y/4)$, $(-X/4, -Y/4)$, $(X/4, -Y/4)$. The simulated user's starting points are located at these three positions. All users are oriented in the positive direction of the y axis, X represents the width of the physical space along the x axis, and Y represents the height of the physical space along the y axis.

For the physical space shared by six users, if the space has a single shared center, the center is located in the physical space center $(0, 0)$, and the simulated user starting points are located in the physical space at six positions $(-X/4, Y/4)$, $(0, Y/4)$, $(X/4,$

Y/4), (−X/4, −Y/4), (0, −Y/4), (X/4, −Y/4). If multiple offset centers exist, the six offset center targets are located in the physical space at the six positions (−X/4, Y/4), (0, Y/4), (X/4, Y/4), (−X/4, −Y/4), (0, −Y/4), and (X/4, −Y/4). The simulated user starting points are located at these six positions. All users are oriented in the positive direction of the Y axis, X represents the width of the physical space along the x axis, and Y represents the length of the physical space along the y axis.

The sizes of the physical space include 12×6, 16×8, 20×10, 24×12, 28×14, 32×16, 36×18, and 40×20 m in eight categories, which have 16 cases. For each case, 40 experiments were repeated.

Result Analysis

The impacts of the target setting strategy and the physical space size on the number of user events is investigated, as shown in Fig. 8.

For three users, multiple offset center targets are always better than a single shared space but these two-target setting strategies have a small impact on user events in different size of physical space.

For six users, multiple offset center targets are always better than a single shared space. However, when the size of physical space is large (32×16, 36×18 and 40×20 m), these two-target setting strategies have less impact on user events. When the size of physical space is not large (12×6, 16×8, 20×10, 24×12 and 28×14 m), the advantage of the multiple offset centers strategy is more distinct.

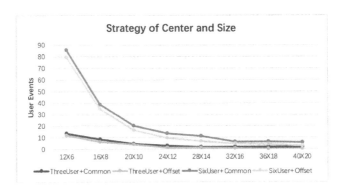

Fig. 8. User events statistics about strategy of center and size.

4.4   Discussion

The experimental results show that our multi-user redirected walking algorithm has an excellent effect on avoiding collisions among users. In the case of three users, in all of eight physical spaces, the collision avoidance rate exceeds 60%, especially when the space is larger than 36X18 m, in which the number of collisions is almost zero. In the case of more than three users, the redirected walking algorithm can adapt to the actual physical spaces of different sizes, and the improvement is distinct. For the case of six users, with the exception of smaller spaces of (12×6 m) and (16×8 m), the collision avoidance rate of other scenes can reach 90%. When the space is larger than 36×18 m, the number of collisions of six users is almost zero.

In the experiments, we also found that the size of physical space and target setting strategy will affect the collisions among users.

In the case of three-user redirected walking, regardless of which target setting strategy is adopted, the physical space is larger and fewer collisions occur among users. When the physical space is greater than 16×8 m, the user events can be reduced to less than 10 for both target setting strategies. In general, the target setting strategy has less impact on user event.

In the case of redirected walking for six users, the larger is the space, the smaller is the number of collisions. When the space is small, the number of user event decreases more significantly as the space size increases. When the space size is greater than 32×16 m, the user event can be reduced to less than 10 for both target setting strategies. As the physical space expands, the impact of the targets setting strategies on user events becomes increasingly smaller.

No matter how many users there are in the physical space, this paper provides a common way to divide the physical space into two subspaces recursively. Ultimately, there are only two or three users in each subspace. Therefore, as the number of users increases, there will be more subspaces. For instance, if ten users collaborate to roam in a large virtual environment, the physical space will be divided into four subspaces. Obviously, the physical space must be large enough to reduce the number of collisions for so many users.

5 Conclusion

In this paper, we investigated the redirected walking strategy for large-scale virtual environments in which multiple users share the same physical space. First, we proposed the improved methods to calculate rotation gains and group users. In this way, multiple users are clustered into groups that are automatically adjusted based on the distance between the boundaries or the size of remaining space, and each group contains a maximum of three users. Then, we divided the physical space into multiple subspaces based on these user groups and used three-user or two-user heuristic redirected walking algorithms in these subspaces. By adding temporary targets and applying different gains, we can effectively avoid the collisions among users. A series of experiments were conducted using a computer simulation framework and the experimental results show that our multi-user redirected walking strategy can work well. In case of three users to explore large-scale virtual environments, our method can avoid collisions about 64% to 80%. In case of six users, our method can avoid collisions about 78% to 99%.

We also explored the advantages and disadvantages of different target setting strategies and physical space sizes in the algorithm. When the space is larger, our algorithm can reduce the number of interruptions among users. In small- or medium-sized spaces, the reduction of interruptions is more distinct. For the target setting strategy, multiple offset center targets are beneficial for reducing the occurrence of collisions among users.

In future work, we will explore the effects of different shapes of physical space and more users on the performance of our redirected walking algorithm. More importantly, we will apply our redirected walking algorithm to head-mounted display to support multi-user VR solutions.

Acknowledgements. This work was supported by National Natural Science Foundation of China (No. 61672464, No. 61572437).

References

1. Usoh, M., et al.: Walking > walking-in-place > flying, in virtual environments. In: Proceedings of SIGGRAPH 1999, pp. 359–364 (1999)
2. Razzaque, S.: Redirected walking. Ph.D. thesis, Chapel Hill, NC, USA (2005)
3. Bachmann, E.R., Holm, J., Zmuda, M.A., et al.: Collision prediction and prevention in a simultaneous two-user immersive virtual environment. In: Virtual Reality. IEEE (2013)
4. Azmandian, M., Grechkin, T., Rosenberg, E.S.: An evaluation of strategies for two-user redirected walking in shared physical spaces. In: 2017 IEEE Virtual Reality (VR). IEEE (2017)
5. Steinicke, F., et al.: Real walking through virtual environments by redirection techniques. J. Virtual Reality Broadcast. **6**(2) (2009). https://doi.org/10.20385/1860-2037/6.2009.2
6. Steinicke, F., et al.: Estimation of detection thresholds for redirected walking techniques. IEEE Trans. Visual. Comput. Graph. **16**(1), 17–27 (2010)
7. Williams, B., et al.: Exploring large virtual environments with an HMD when physical space is limited. In: Proceedings of the 4th Symposium on Applied Perception in Graphics and Visualization, pp. 41–48. ACM, July 2007
8. Nescher, T., Huang, Y.Y., Kunz, A.: Planning redirection techniques for optimal free walking experience using model predictive control. In: 2014 IEEE Symposium on 3D User Interfaces (3DUI), pp. 111–118. IEEE, March 2014
9. Azmandian, M., Grechkin, T., Bolas, M., Suma, E.: Automated path prediction for redirected walking using navigation meshes. In: 2016 IEEE Symposium on 3D User Interfaces (3DUI), pp. 63–66. IEEE, March 2016
10. Dong, Z.C., Fu, X.M., Zhang, C., Wu, K., Liu, L.: Smooth assembled mappings for large-scale real walking. ACM Trans. Graph. (TOG) **36**(6), 211 (2017)
11. Chen, H., Chen, S., Rosenberg, E.S.: Redirected walking strategies in irregularly shaped and dynamic physical environments. In: 25th IEEE Conference on Virtual Reality and 3D User Interfaces (VR 2018). Workshop on Everyday Virtual Reality (2018)
12. Sun, Q., et al.: Towards virtual reality infinite walking: dynamic saccadic redirection. ACM Trans. Graph. **37**(4), 1–13 (2018). Article 67
13. Podkosova, I., Kaufmann, H.: Preventing imminent collisions between co-located users in HMD-based VR in non-shared scenarios. In: Proceedings of the 30th International Conference on Computer Animation and Social Agents, CASA 2017 (2017)
14. Hodgson, E., Bachmann, E.: Comparing four approaches to generalized redirected walking: Simulation and live user data. IEEE Trans. Visual. Comput. Graph. **19**(4), 634–643 (2013)

Broker-Insights: An Interactive and Visual Recommendation System for Insurance Brokerage

Paul Dany Atauchi[(✉)] [iD], Luciana Nedel[iD], and Renata Galante[iD]

Institute of Informatics – Federal University of Rio Grande do Sul (UFRGS), Porto Alegre, Brazil
{paul.dfatauchi,nedel,galante}@inf.ufrgs.br,
http://www.inf.ufrgs.br/~paul.dfatauchi,
http://www.inf.ufrgs.br/~nedel,
http://www.inf.ufrgs.br/~galante

Abstract. The black box nature of the recommendation systems limits the understanding and acceptance of the recommendation received by the user. In contrast, user interaction and information visualization play a key role in addressing these drawbacks. In the brokerage domain, insurance brokers offer, negotiate and sell insurance products for their customers. Support brokers into the recommendation process can improve the loyalty, profit, and marketing campaign in their client portfolio. This work presents Broker-Insights, an interactive and visualisation-based insurance products recommender system to support brokers into the decision-making (recommendation) at two levels: recommendations for a specific potential customer; and recommendations for a group of customers. Looking for offering personalized recommendations, Broker-Insights provides a tool to manage customers information in the recommendation task and a module to perform customers segmentation based on specific characteristics. With the help of an eye-tracker, we evaluated Broker-Insigths usability with ten naive users on the offline fashion and also performed an evaluation in the wild with three insurance brokers. Results achieved show that data mining methods, while combined with interactive data visualization improved the user experience and decision-making process into the recommendation task, and increased the products recommendation acceptance.

Keywords: Recommender system · Visual analytics · Data mining · Insurance brokerage

This study was partly funded by the Coordenação de Aperfeiçoamento de Pessoal de Nível Superior – Brasil (CAPES) – Finance Code 001, and by the Conselho Nacional de Desenvolvimento Científico e Tecnológico (CNPq).

M. Gavrilova et al. (Eds.): CGI 2019, LNCS 11542, pp. 155–166, 2019.
https://doi.org/10.1007/978-3-030-22514-8_13

1   Introduction

Recommendation systems are becoming very popular and widely used in many traditional and emerging domains such as commerce, news and tourism [12,16]. Such systems help the users into the decision making to choose the most relevant and accurate items (products or services) that meet their needs, preferences, and tastes [1]. Recommender systems use different resources such as rating of items, transaction data, and items description. The most common methods used are collaborative-based filtering, content-based filtering, knowledge-based filtering and hybrid filtering [1,4].

There are several drawbacks in recommendation systems, such as the cold-start problem where there is no-prior information about the new user preference (user-items sparsity) or about the items purchased or rated (new items), user experience where the controllability (manipulation of parameters in the recommendation process) and justification (explanation why the recommendation is performed) are not taken into account. Thus, the black box nature of the recommender systems limits the understanding and acceptance of the recommendation suggested for the users.

Segmentation in combination with a popularity and predict ratings based strategy result in a good choice to deal the cold-start problem [7,15,19,23]. Recent works reported that the user interaction and data visualization improve the user experience into the recommendation process; increasing the understanding and recommendation acceptance [5,10,11].

Our study case is centered on the insurance brokerage domain in Brazil. An insurance broker is an intermediate between the insurer and the policyholder. The broker offers, negotiates and finally sells products for their customers. For retain existing policyholders, insurance brokers activities required to be carried out consists of exploring and identifying of potential customers for recommend insurance products (e.g., Gretel a young girl that live in the south of Brazil have a car insurance product purchased, she needs more products) as well as identify interesting recommendations to offer (e.g., recommend life insurance for Gretel with 80% of probability of acceptance based on her purchasing behavior considering similar people to her).

This paper proposes an interactive and visual recommender system to support brokers into the decision-making (recommendation) considering two levels: recommendations for a specific potential customer and recommendations for a group of customers. So, our work provides to the brokers a tool to manage customers information in the recommendation task. Furthermore, it provides a module to perform customers segmentation based on specific characteristics to offer the most personalized recommendations. The recommender system was evaluated with users based on user-centered tasks involved in the recommendation process and based on the System Usability Scale (SUS) questionnaire. Results showed that our system improves the user experience into the insurance product recommendation process.

The main contributions of Broker-Insights are four-folds:

- Controllability: Group customers based on specific attributes bring a diverse variety of recommendations. We look for that the broker can answer situations such as, *what insurance products can you recommend for Gretel that have 26 years old, live in the south of Brazil and have a car insurance purchased?*
- User Interaction and Interactive Data Visualization: The user interaction and interactive data visualization help into the cognitive process and human visual interpretation. The broker can able to answer questions such as *identify potential customers that that have 30–50 years old, males and that live in the west of Brazil for offer insurance products).*
- Justification: The justification of the recommendation is a crucial factor that has a strong relationship to the recommendation acceptance, e.g., *for what reason the recommendation is offered to the customer?* To address that problem, each recommendation is explained based on their measures.
- Cold-start Problem: To address the no-prior sales information and as a complement to the recommendation based on purchasing behavior, the most popular products in the customer group are taken into consideration for recommending. The broker will able to answer questions such as *what are the most popular products to offers for the customer identified?*

This remainder of this paper is structured as follows: a brief theoretical backgrounds is detailed in Sect. 2, Sect. 3 reviews related work, our proposed Broker-Insights recommender system is described in Sect. 4, Sect. 5 discusses the experimental results, while Sect. 6 concludes the paper.

2   Theoretical Background

The association rules mining is one of the most used methods of data mining with several applications such as products recommendation, medical diagnostics, customer market analysis, etc. This method aims to find related items in the transaction data [2, 24].

Given a set of items $I = \{I_i\}$ where $i \in \{1, .., n\}$ and n denotes the number of items and a set of transactions $T = \{T_j\}$ where $j \in \{1, .., m\}$ and m denote the number of transactions, each transaction contains a subset of items $T_j = \{I_s\}$ where $s \in K$ and $K \subset \{1, .., n\}$ that indicates the active items in the transaction T_j. The rules are generated in the form $X \Rightarrow Y$ where X and Y are itemsets in the transaction T, called antecedent and consequent respectively. The transaction T_j is composed by X_j and Y_j where $X_j \cup Y_j = T_j$ and $X_j \cap Y_j = \Phi$. The importance of the rule $X \Rightarrow Y$ can be measured by the *support* (see Eq. 1) and *confidence* (see Eq. 2), that means, the probability of appearance together of the itemsets X and Y in the transaction data and the probability of the itemsets X and Y appearance together given the appearance of the itemset X respectively.

$$support\,(X \Rightarrow Y) = P\,(X \cup Y) \tag{1}$$
$$confidence\,(X \Rightarrow Y) = P\,(Y \mid X) \tag{2}$$

The apriori algorithm [3] is widely used and a fast algorithm for mining transaction data. This method uses the prior knowledge of frequent itemset properties that consists in that all subset of a frequent itemset must be frequent, and all subset of an infrequent itemset must be infrequent. For prune itemsets, the apriori algorithm uses minimum support and confidence. This property improves efficiency in time and reduces the search space in the rule mining process.

3   Related Work

In the insurance domain several recommender systems were proposed. Rahman et al. [21] developed a web insurance policies recommender system via a case-based reasoning algorithm where the recommendation is performed based on the similarity of user characteristics and past recommendation solutions. Gupta and Jain [7] proposed a life insurance recommendation system based on association rules and addressed the cold-start problem for new clients based on a dual clustering method. Rokach et al. [22] introduced an insurance rider recommendation system based on an item-item collaborative filtering approach. Mitra et al. [17] proposed a recommendation pilot within the insurance domain. They developed an insurance policy and rider recommendation system based on an user-user collaborative filtering approach. Xu et al. [25] proposed a vehicle insurance recommender system based on the association rule mining and customer segmentation. Qazi et al. [20] presented an insurance products recommender system based on the Bayesian Networks approach using customer information and portfolio data.

The black box nature of the recommender systems limits the understanding and acceptance of the recommendations suggested for the users. The interactive recommender systems address the natural questions of the users such as *why reason some recommendation is offered?*, *how the recommendation system obtained the recommendations?* or *is it possible to intervene in the recommendation process?* He et al. [10] proposed a framework that involves recommendation and visualization methods to solve several drawbacks such as transparency, justification, controllability, cold-start problem and diversity. Valdez et al. [5] analyzed several works that take into consideration human factors and visualization methods that improve the user experience as well as the acceptance level. Another critical factor is the interaction with the recommender systems. Jugovac et al. [11] presented an overview of the interaction aspects involved in the recommender systems taking into consideration the result presentation and interaction in the recommendation process.

The association rule algorithm suffers the overload of rule generation that difficults the rule exploration. In past years, several works were proposed to turn easy the exploration of association rules. These works proposed several visualizations of rules such as scatter plots, matrix visualizations, graphs, mosaic plots, parallel coordinates, grouped matrix-based visualization and glyphs [8,9,18].

Since most insurance products recommender systems are focused on the algorithm approach, our proposed recommender system focuses on the user experience in the recommendation process to improve the understanding and recommendation acceptance.

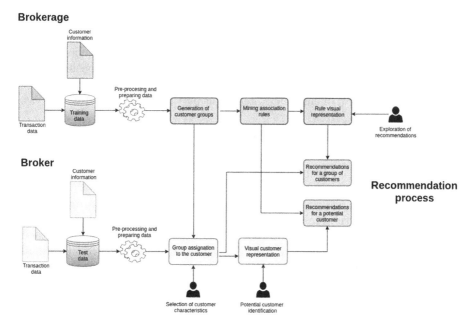

Fig. 1. The framework of the proposed interactive and visual insurance products recommender system.

4 Broker-Insights Recommender System

In this section we present the proposed interactive and visual insurance recommender system. Figure 1 shows the framework of the Broker-Insights.

4.1 System Overview

Our proposed recommendation system consists of three parts: brokerage, broker, and recommendation process detailed below.

– **Brokerage part:** Takes as input the portfolio of brokers belong to the brokerage (training data). These data are prepared and preprocessed. Finally, the data are segmented by considering the customer information to create the recommendation models that will be used in the recommendation process. The top part of Fig. 1 shows these steps.

- **Broker part:** Receives the portfolio of a specific broker (testing data) to prepare and pre-process. The customers are segmented and each customer is assigned with one segment according to the characteristics selected by the broker and the clusters generated in the brokerage part. In addition, the customer data are visually represented to allow exploration and identification of potential customers. The bottom part of Fig. 1 shows this stage.
- **Recommendation process:** Once the recommendation models are built and the testing data are preprocessed and visually represented, the insurance products recommendation in the broker portfolio occurs. Recommendations acts at two levels: recommendations of insurance products for a specific potential customer, and identification of interesting recommendations of insurance products for a group of customers. The right part of Fig. 1 shows this process.

4.2 Broker-Insights Running Example

Given a customer portfolio, the broker can offer recommendations to their customers at two levels: recommendations of insurance products for a specific customer and identification of recommendations of insurance products to offers for a group of customers.

In the first level, the broker can segment their customers based on interesting characteristics, e.g., gender and region. After this, the broker can filter their customers based on their characteristics (e.g., gender-male, region-São Paulo) as well as to explore them visually to identify potential customers to offer recommendations. To identify a potential customer, the broker looks for the color alert level of the customer (node) in the scatterplot visualization. After identifying the potential customer, the recommender system provides two types of recommendations for the identified customer: one based on the purchasing behavior and the other based on the most popular products (see Fig. 2).

In the second level, the broker can find interesting recommendations to offer for a group of their customers. The broker visually explores the customer groups. After the broker identified one target group, he can explore the recommendations that can be offered inside the customer group selected. The broker can visualize and explore the recommendations using the Table and Scatterplot visualization (see Fig. 3).

4.3 Generation of Customers Groups

Customer segmentation matters. Customer segmentation groups customers into homogeneous sets based on their similar characteristics and allows the extraction of useful information. For satisfying the control requirement by the brokers of a segment based on specific characteristics to offer a more personalized recommendations, we consider groups of customers (training data) based on all combinations of the customer characteristics. Thus, each customer characteristics combination will allow mining the data inside that group to generate recommendations (model). For customer segmentation, we employed the mean-shift algorithm [6] due to its capacity to determine clusters through exploiting the density in the data distribution.

4.4   Mining Association Rules and Rules Visualization

In the previous section, we got the customer groups based on the customer characteristics combination. For each customer group, the transaction data is mining using the apriori algorithm [3]. The association rules generated are used as the core of our recommender system.

As a natural characteristic of the association rule algorithm is the overhead of rule generation, this increases the effort into the rule exploration and identification process. We visually represent the rules using the Table view and Scatterplot visualization to address this problem in order to turn easy the process of exploration and identification of rules. Additionaly to the support and confidence, we introduce a new measure called customer-affected that denote how many customers in the broker portfolio are affected by the recommendation.

4.5   Cold-Start Problem

In order to solve the cold-start problem for customers that do not have products purchased (new users), we use the popularity strategy where the customer receives the most popular products as recommendations. The popular products are obtained based on the products purchased by customers in the group that the customer is in. Thus, the popular recommendations are most personalized at the same time that address the cold-start problem.

4.6   Groups Assignment and Visual Representation of Customers

For each customer in the testing data (customer portfolio), a label is assigned based on the segments generated in the training phase. The customer portfolio are visually represented to facilitate the exploration and identification of potential customers to offer insurance products in the customer level recommendation. We use the scatterplot visualization to allow this. Each node in the scatterplot represents one customer. The node color is encoded with the color gradient between green, yellow and red; colors are inspired in the semaphor colors to denote the alert level of the customer.

5   User Experiments

To evaluate Brocker-Insights, we conducted two user studies. The first one was conceived to evaluate the interface usefulness and the visualizations proposed based on the user-centered tasks (see Table 1) using an eye-tracker tool. The user-centered task was obtained across an iterative process involving a broker (final user), a data scientist and a requirements engineering specialist. The second user study evaluates the real use of the recommender system by the target users (brokers) based on the user-centered questionnaire (see Table 3) as well as the system usability evaluation based on the SUS - a questionnaire level satisfaction. In this qualitative evaluations, we addressed the acceptability of this system in the workflow of insurance products recommendation process performed by the brokers.

5.1   Experimental Setup

- **Dataset:** The data is composed by customers information (age, gener and postal code) and past sales (8 products). After the data was prepared and pre-processed, the data training is composed of 850 customers and 1054 transactions.
- **Association rules parameters:** For mining the transaction data using the apriori algorithm [3], we set the minimum support and confidence threshold as $support - min = 0.1\%$ and $confidence - min = 0.1\%$ respectively.
- **Customer segmentation:** The bandwidth in the mean-shift algorithm [6] was obtained as the mean of the maximum pairwise distances for each data point in the data distribution with their neighbors (30% of the data points).

5.2   Interface Usefulness and Visualization Study

We designed the recommender system interface based on the task-centered user approach [13]. For the evaluation of the interface usefulness and visualization, we prepared a set of very simple and fundamental tasks (see Table 1) to be accomplished by naive users in a specific and pre-defined order to perform the recommendation of insurance products. We tested the system with naive users based on the assumption that with an overview about the data, the tool and its functionalities provided, the user can perform tasks for the recommendation of insurance products. This guarantee that the tool will be easier to learn and use.

The experiment took approximately 10 min and 10 users (8 males and 2 females) between 20 and 35 years old took part in it.

We used a Tobii Pro X2 Eye Tracker system to verify if the users were easily finding the answers for each given task. Table 2 shows the number of correct answers for each task, as well as the mean time spent with each task. Despite Task 8, all other tasks were correctly achieved for most of the users in an acceptable time, on average never higher than 30 s.

Figures 2, 3(1) and 3(2) present the fixations and duration of the users' gaze for Tasks 4, 7, and 11 respectively. Analyzing the heatmaps on these three example tasks, we can observe that users' fixation and gaze converge quite well to the image regions where the answers are. In this way, we can conclude our interface is quite clear and easily understandable.

Table 1. User tasks performed in the interface usefulness and visualization study of the recommender system.

User tasks - Recommendation of insurance products both potential customers as well as recommendations to group of customers
Task 1 – Identify the attributes by which customers are grouped
Task 2 – Identify the values of the attributes by which customers are filtered
Task 3 – Look at customers and say how many customers have 2 products
Task 4 – Which purchased products the customer selected?
Task 5 – What are the 2 most popular products for recommending to the selected customer?
Task 6 – How many recommendations with conditional purchase probability greater than 21% are recommended for the customer selected?
Task 7 – How many customers are affected by the selected recommendation?
Task 8 – Look at the summarization of customer group information and say which group was selected and describe which characteristics this group have
Task 9 – Which is the conditional purchase probability of the selected customer to purchase travel insurance if the customer has bought automobile and business insurance?
Task 10 – Look at the nodes (recommendations) and say what is the color of the node that affect the largest quantity of customers
Task 11 – Which is the conditional probability of purchase to recommend of travel insurance for customers who purchased the green card insurance?

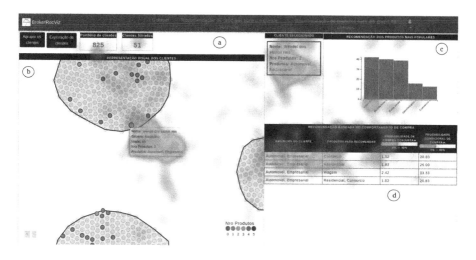

Fig. 2. Recommendation for a potential customer. (a) Options to segment and filters the customers. (b) Visual customer representation. (c) Most popular products for recommend. (d) Recommendations based on the purchasing behavior. Heatmap, fixations and duration of the users' gaze for Task 4 (Which purchased products the customer selected?).

Table 2. Number of correct answers and average time spent for each of the tasks performed by the 10 users in the interface usefulness and visualization study.

Task	1	2	3	4	5	6	7	8	9	10	11
Correct answers	10	10	9	10	5	10	10	9	10	8	9
Average time (sec)	17.8	24.3	20	20.9	27.2	13	10	33.1	21.9	20.4	22.3

5.3   In the Wild Evaluation

In order to evaluate the acceptability and usability of the system by the target users during their daily work, we asked for three experts on insurance brokerage to use our system. The system was deployed into the internet and put available online. After following a brief tour in the recommender system, users were invited to explore Broker-Insights for some time and, after that, the brokers answered a centered-user questionnaire (see Table 3) to evaluate the level of satisfaction and understanding of the recommender system in the recommendation process. The System Usability Scale (SUS) questionnaire [14] was used to evaluate the usability of the system. The average SUS score obtained 75, that corresponds to an acceptable usability value.

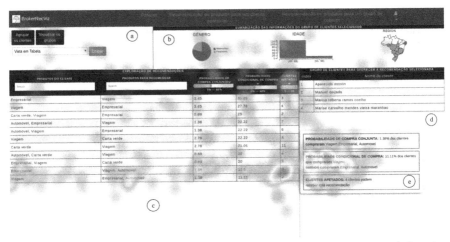

(1) Recommendations for a group of customers - Table view. Fixations and duration of the users' gaze for Task 7 (How many customers are affected by the selected recommendation?)

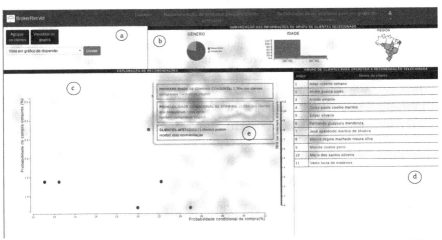

(2) Recommendations for a group of customers - Scatterplot view. Fixations and duration of the users' gaze for Task 11 (Which is the conditional probability of purchase to recommend of travel insurance for customers who purchased the green card insurance?).

Fig. 3. (a) Options to segment the customers and to visualize the customer groups, (b) visualization of the customer group selected, (c) visual representation of recommendations to offer for the customer group selected, (d) list of customers affected by the recommendation selected, (e) explanation of the recommendation.

Table 3. Questions to evaluate the level satisfaction and understanding of the recommendation system.

User questions - Recommendation of insurance products both potential customers as well as recommendations for a group of customers
Question 1 – Were you able to pick interesting characteristics to target your customers?
Question 2 – Were you able to gain a general understanding of your customers by visualize the information from your customers?
Question 3 – Were you able to identify potential customers to offer insurance products based on the color of the circles?
Question 4 – Was it helpful for you to get the most popular recommendations to offer your selected customer?
Question 5 – Was it useful for you to get recommendations based on buying behavior to offer to your selected customer?
Question 6 – Were you able to gain a general understanding of your customers by viewing your customers' group information?
Question 7 – Did you find the measure "PROBABILITY OF JOINT PURCHASE" relevant?
Question 8 – Did you find the measure "CONDITIONAL PROBABILITY" relevant?
Question 9 – Did you find the measure "CUSTOMERS AFFECTED" relevant?
Question 10 – Were you identify interesting recommendations to offer to a group of your customers with the "table" view?
Question 11 –Were you identify interesting recommendations to offer to a group of your customers with the "scatter plot" visualization?

6   Conclusion

In this paper we introduced Broker-Insights, an interactive recommender system for insurance brokerage based on data mining methods and data visualization. The insurance recommender system provides recommendations for a specific potential customer as well as recommendations for a group of customers.

With the advantages of the user interaction, data visualization, and data mining methods, our recommender system turns possible to solve several drawbacks existing in the insurance products recommendation systems such as controllability, justification and the cold-start problem.

In the experiments, we found that the involvement of the user into the recommendation process generates consciousness about what happens in this process and consequently, increases the acceptance of the recommendations suggested by the recommender system.

As a future work, we plan to run new user tests with a larger number of specialists to better evaluate the system usability, the acceptability and effectivity of the system. In this direction, we wonder to answer questions as: *how helpful are the recommendations made? how many recommendations were converted on sales?*

References

1. Adomavicius, G., Tuzhilin, A.: Toward the next generation of recommender systems: a survey of the state-of-the-art and possible extensions. IEEE Trans. Knowl. Data Eng. **6**, 734–749 (2005)
2. Agrawal, R., Imieliński, T., Swami, A.: Mining association rules between sets of items in large databases. ACM SIGMOD Rec. **22**, 207–216 (1993)
3. Agrawal, R., Srikant, R., et al.: Fast algorithms for mining association rules. In: Proceedings of 20th International Conference on Very Large Data Bases, VLDB, vol. 1215, pp. 487–499 (1994)
4. Bobadilla, J., Ortega, F., Hernando, A., Gutiérrez, A.: Recommender systems survey. Knowl.-Based Syst. **46**, 109–132 (2013)
5. Valdez, A.C., Ziefle, M., Verbert, K.: HCI for recommender systems: the past, the present and the future. In: Proceedings of the 10th ACM Conference on Recommender Systems, pp. 123–126. ACM (2016)

6. Comaniciu, D., Meer, P.: Mean shift: a robust approach toward feature space analysis. IEEE Trans. Pattern Anal. Mach. Intell. **5**, 603–619 (2002)
7. Gupta, A., Jain, A.: Life insurance recommender system based on association rule mining and dual clustering method for solving cold-start problem. Int. J. Adv. Res. Comput. Sci. Softw. Eng. **3**(7), 1356–1360 (2013)
8. Hahsler, M., Chelluboina, S.: Visualizing association rules: introduction to the r-extension package arulesViz. R Project Module, pp. 223–238 (2011)
9. Hahsler, M., Karpienko, R.: Visualizing association rules in hierarchical groups. J. Bus. Econ. **87**(3), 317–335 (2017)
10. He, C., Parra, D., Verbert, K.: Interactive recommender systems: a survey of the state of the art and future research challenges and opportunities. Expert Syst. Appl. **56**, 9–27 (2016)
11. Jugovac, M., Jannach, D.: Interacting with recommenders-overview and research directions. ACM Trans. Interact. Intell. Syst. (TiiS) **7**(3), 10 (2017)
12. Karimi, M., Jannach, D., Jugovac, M.: News recommender systems-survey and roads ahead. Inf. Process. Manag. **54**(6), 1203–1227 (2018)
13. Lewis, C., Rieman, J.: Task-centered user interface design. A practical introduction (1993)
14. Lewis, J.R.: The system usability scale: past, present, and future. Int. J. Hum.-Comput. Interact. **34**(7), 577–590 (2018). Taylor & Francis
15. Lika, B., Kolomvatsos, K., Hadjiefthymiades, S.: Facing the cold start problem in recommender systems. Expert Syst. Appl. **41**(4), 2065–2073 (2014)
16. Lu, J., Wu, D., Mao, M., Wang, W., Zhang, G.: Recommender system application developments: a survey. Decis. Support Syst. **74**, 12–32 (2015)
17. Mitra, B.P.S., Chaudhari, N., Patwardhan, B.: Leveraging hybrid recommendation system in insurance domain. Int. J. Eng. Comput. Sci. **3**(10), 8988–8992 (2014)
18. Mukherji, A., et al.: FIRE: a two-level interactive visualization for deep exploration of association rules. Int. J. Data Sci. Anal. **7**(3), 201–226 (2019)
19. Pandey, A.K., Rajpoot, D.S.: Resolving cold start problem in recommendation system using demographic approach. In: 2016 International Conference on Signal Processing and Communication (ICSC), pp. 213–218. IEEE (2016)
20. Qazi, M., Fung, G.M., Meissner, K.J., Fontes, E.R.: An insurance recommendation system using Bayesian networks. In: Proceedings of the Eleventh ACM Conference on Recommender Systems, pp. 274–278. ACM (2017)
21. Rahman, S.S.A., Norman, A.A., Soon, K.: MyINS: a CBR e-commerce application for insurance policies. Electron. Commer. Res. **5**(1), 373–380 (2006)
22. Rokach, L., Shani, G., Shapira, B., Chapnik, E., Siboni, G.: Recommending insurance riders. In: Proceedings of the 28th Annual ACM Symposium on Applied Computing, pp. 253–260. ACM (2013)
23. Sobhanam, H., Mariappan, A.: Addressing cold start problem in recommender systems using association rules and clustering technique. In: 2013 International Conference on Computer Communication and Informatics (ICCCI), pp. 1–5. IEEE (2013)
24. Solanki, S.K., Patel, J.T.: A survey on association rule mining. In: 2015 Fifth International Conference on Advanced Computing & Communication Technologies (ACCT), pp. 212–216. IEEE (2015)
25. Xu, W., Wang, J., Zhao, Z., Sun, C., Ma, J.: A novel intelligence recommendation model for insurance products with consumer segmentation. J. Syst. Sci. Inf. **2**(1), 16–28 (2014)

Auto-labelling of Markers in Optical Motion Capture by Permutation Learning

Saeed Ghorbani[1]([✉]) [ID], Ali Etemad[2][ID], and Nikolaus F. Troje[1][ID]

[1] York University, Toronto, ON, Canada
saeed@eecs.yorku.ca, troje@yorku.ca
[2] Queen's University, Kingston, ON, Canada
ali.etemad@queensu.ca

Abstract. Optical marker-based motion capture is a vital tool in applications such as motion and behavioural analysis, animation, and biomechanics. Labelling, that is, assigning optical markers to the pre-defined positions on the body, is a time consuming and labour intensive post-processing part of current motion capture pipelines. The problem can be considered as a ranking process in which markers shuffled by an unknown permutation matrix are sorted to recover the correct order. In this paper, we present a framework for automatic marker labelling which first estimates a permutation matrix for each individual frame using a differentiable permutation learning model and then utilizes temporal consistency to identify and correct remaining labelling errors. Experiments conducted on the test data show the effectiveness of our framework.

Keywords: Labelling · Motion capture · Computer animation · Deep learning

1 Introduction

Optical motion capture is an important technology for obtaining high accuracy human body and motion information. Motion capture has been widely used in applications such as human motion analysis [4,20], producing realistic character animation [11,14], and validation of computer vision and robotic tasks [10,18] During the recording step, the motion of passively reflecting markers, which are attached to the body according to a predefined marker layout, are tracked by multiple high-resolution (spatial and temporal) infrared cameras. Then, the 3D positions of markers are computed from 2D data recorded by each of the calibrated cameras by means of triangulation. The result of this process is a set of 3D trajectories listed in random order. Each trajectory represents the motion of a single marker in terms of its 3D position over time. The first step after recording phase is to label each trajectory, therefore assigning it to a specific body location. This process can be very time-consuming and therefore a friction point for many motion capture systems. Furthermore, this process is susceptible to user errors. Labelling is more challenging when one or multiple markers are

© Springer Nature Switzerland AG 2019
M. Gavrilova et al. (Eds.): CGI 2019, LNCS 11542, pp. 167–178, 2019.
https://doi.org/10.1007/978-3-030-22514-8_14

occluded (for simplicity we use term *occlusion* for any type of missing marker in the data) over time, hence splitting the motion of these markers into multiple trajectories. Commercial motion capture softwares have designed frameworks to reduce the amount of manual work in this step. In these frameworks, a model can learn the geometry of that participant's body and applies it to label subsequent measurements. However, they typically require manual initialization where one or more motion capture sequences have to be labelled manually for each participant. Here, we are proposing an end-to-end, data-driven approach for automatic labelling which does not require a manual initialization. We formulated the labelling at each frame as a permutation estimation where shuffled markers are ranked based on a pre-defined order. Then, in a trajectory labelling step, temporal consistency is used to correct mislabelled markers. Our framework can be reliably run in real time that potentially results in a faster, cheaper, and more consistent data processing in motion capture pipelines.

2   Related Works

Typically, motion capture labelling comprises of two main steps: the initialization step, where the initial correspondences are established for the first frame, and the tracking step which can be defined as keeping track of labelled markers in the presence of occlusion, ghost markers, and noise. A number of approaches have been introduced to address the tracking of manually initialized motion capture data. Holden [8] proposed a deep de-noising feed-forward network that outputs the joint locations directly from corrupted markers. Herda et al. [7] proposed an approach to increase the robustness of optical markers specifically during visibility constraints and occlusions by using the kinematics information provided by a generic human skeletal model. Yu et al. [21] proposed an online motion capture approach for multiple subjects which also recovers missing markers. They used the standard deviation of the distance between each pair of markers to cluster the markers into a number of rigid bodies. Having fitted rigid bodies, they labelled the markers using a structural model for each rigid body and a motion model for each marker. Loper [11] proposed a marker placement refinement by optimizing the parameters of a statistical body model in a generative inference process. Another group of approaches attempt to minimize user intervention by automating the initialization step as well. Holzreiter [9] trained a neural network to estimate the positions of sorted markers from a shuffled set. Labelling of the markers was carried out by pairing up the estimated marker locations with the shuffled set using the nearest neighbour search. Meyer et al. [13] estimated the skeletal configuration by least-squares optimization and exploited the skeletal model to automatically label the markers. They applied the Hungarian method for optimal assignment of observation to markers while requiring each subject to go into a T-pose to initialize the skeletal tracker. Schubert et al. [17] improved their approach by designing a pose-free initialization step, searching over a large database of poses. Finally, Han et al. [5] and Maycock et al. [12] proposed auto-labelling approaches specifically designed for hands. Han et al. [5] proposed a technique to label the hand markers by formulating the task as a keypoint regression problem. They rendered the marker locations as a depth image and fed it into a convolutional neural network which outputs the labelled estimated 3D locations of the markers. Then, they used a bipartite matching method to map the labels onto the actual 3D markers. Maycock et al. [12] used inverse kinematics to filter out unrealistic postures and computed the assignment between model nodes and 3D points using an adapted version of the Hungarian method. Although their approach was focused on hands, it can be applied to human body motion.

3   System Overview

The first stage of our framework is a preprocessing step which is applied on individual frames, making the array of markers invariant to spatial transformations. For the next stage, we propose a data-driven approach that avoids the need for manual initialization by formulating automatic labelling as a permutation learning problem for each individual frame. Towards this end, we present a permutation learning model which can be trained end-to-end using a gradient-based optimizer. We exploited the idea of relaxing our objective function by using doubly-stochastic matrices as a continuous approximation of permutation matrices [1]. During the running phase, each individual frame is automatically labelled using the proposed permutation learning model. The result is a sequence of individually labelled frames where each trajectory might be assigned to multiple labels over time. We then evaluate temporal consistency in the resulting trajectories and use it to identify and correct the labelling errors that occurred during the previous stage. To correct the inconsistencies in each marker trajectory, a score is computed for each candidate label using a confidence-based score function. Then, the label with the highest score will be assigned to the marker trajectory in a winner-takes-all scheme. Figure 1 shows the block diagram of our main framework.

3.1   Data Preprocessing

Prior to applying our permutation learning model, we ensure that the input data are invariant to translation, orientation, and the size of the subjects. We first calculated the centroid of the array of markers for each frame and then subtracted from the marker locations to make each frame invariant to translation. To make the data invariant to the orientation of the subject, we applied principal component analysis (PCA) to the cloud of the markers. We first aligned the direction with the largest principal component with the z-axis. Then, the second principal component was aligned to the x-axis to make the poses invariant to the rotations around z-axis. Finally, the size of the subject was normalized by scaling the values between 0 and 1 independently for each of the three spatial dimensions.

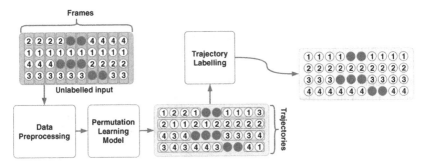

Fig. 1. An overview of our proposed framework: the input to our system is a sequence of unlabelled (shuffled) 3D trajectories. After the preprocessing stage, the label for each marker is estimated by applying permutation learning to each individual frame. The resulting labelled frames are then concatenated to form trajectories again. These trajectories are then used as input to the trajectory labelling stage where a temporal consistency constraint is used to correct mislabelled markers

3.2   Permutation Learning Model

The motion capture data at each frame can be represented by the 3D positions of N markers utilized in the recording process. *Labelling* is defined as assigning the 3D positions of these markers to specific, fixed body locations. This process can be described as permuting a set of shuffled 3D elements to match a predefined order. Let us define a labelled frame as $X = [m_1, m_2, \ldots, m_N]^\top$, to be an ordered array of N markers, where m_i represents the 3D position of the i_{th} marker. Then, a shuffled frame $\tilde{X} = PX$ can be considered as a permuted version of X where the markers are permuted by a permutation matrix $P \in \{0, 1\}^{N \times N}$. Hence, given a shuffled frame, the original frame can be recovered by multiplying the shuffled version with the inverse of the respective permutation matrix. It should be noted that for a permutation matrix P, $P^\top = P^{-1}$. Our goal in this step is to design a trainable parameterized model $f_\theta : \mathcal{X}^N \to \mathcal{S}_N$ which takes a shuffled frame $\tilde{X}$ as input and estimates the permutation matrix P that was originally applied to the frame. Then, having the permutation matrix P we can recover the sorted frame X, $X = P^\top \tilde{X}$.

The main difficulty in training a permutation learning model using backpropagation is that the space of permutations is not continuous which prohibits computation of the gradient of the objective function with respect to the learning parameters since it is not differentiable in terms of the permutation matrix elements. To address this problem, Adams et al. [1] proposed the idea of utilizing a continuous distribution over assignments by using doubly-stochastic matrices as differentiable relaxations of permutation matrices. This approach has been successfully exploited in other applications [15,16]. A DSM is a square matrix populated with non-negative real numbers where each of the rows and columns sums to 1. All $N \times N$ DSM matrices form a convex polytope known as the Birkhoff polytope $\mathcal{B}_N$ lying on a $(N-1)^2$ dimensional space where the set of all $N \times N$ permutation matrices are located exactly on the vertices of this polytope [3]. Therefore, DSMs can be considered as continuous relaxations of corresponding permutation matrices. We can interpret each column i of a DSM as a probability distribution over labels to be assigned to the i_{th} marker. Also, all rows summing to 1 ensures the inherent structure of permutation matrices. Accordingly, instead of mapping directly from 3D positions to the permutation matrices, we propose to learn a model $g_\theta : \mathcal{X}^N \to \mathcal{W}_N$, where $\mathcal{W}_N$ is the set of all $N \times N$ DSMs. That way, computing the permutation matrix from the DSM simply becomes a bipartite matching problem.

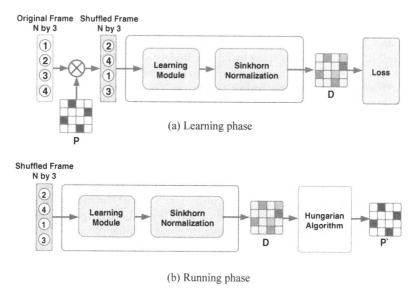

(a) Learning phase

(b) Running phase

Fig. 2. An overview of our permutation learning model: In (a), the learning phase is depicted, where the parameters of the learning module are optimized to minimize the cross-entropy loss. In (b), the running phase is illustrated, where the Hungarian algorithm is applied to the outputted DSM to estimate the optimal permutation matrix.

Our permutation learning model is composed of two main modules: the learning module and the Sinkhorn normalization (see Fig. 2). The learning module $h_\theta : \mathcal{X}^N \to \mathbb{R}_+^{N \times N}$ is the parameterized component of our model, which learns the feature representation of the data structure from the available poses, taking the 3D positions in each frame and outputting an unconstrained square matrix. We implement this module as a feed-forward deep residual neural network [6]. The last dense layer consists of $N \times N$ nodes with a sigmoid activation outputting a $N \times N$ non-negative matrix. The learning module is illustrated in Fig. 2. One naïve approach would be to treat the problem as a multi-class, multi-label classification task with N^2 classes. However, this approach would ignore the inherent structure of permutation matrices with the possibility of resulting in impossible solutions. To enforce the optimizer to avoid these erroneous solutions we need our model to output a DSM which replicates the inherent structure of permutation matrices. An effective way to convert any unconstrained non-negative matrix to a DSM is using an iterative operator known as Sinkhorn normalization [1,19]. This method normalizes the rows and columns iteratively where each pair of iteration is defined as:

$$S^i(M) = \begin{cases} M & \text{if } i = 0 \\ \mathcal{T}_R(\mathcal{T}_C(S^{i-1}(M))) & \text{otherwise,} \end{cases} \tag{1}$$

where $\mathcal{T}_R^{i,j}(M) = \frac{M_{i,j}}{\Sigma_k M_{i,k}}$ and $\mathcal{T}_C^{i,j}(M) = \frac{M_{i,j}}{\Sigma_k M_{k,j}}$ are the row and column-wise normalization operators, respectively. The Sinkhorn normalization operator is defined as $S^\infty : \mathbb{R}_+^{N \times N} \to \mathcal{W}_N$ where the output converges to a DSM. We approximate the Sinkhorn normalization by an incomplete version of it with $i < \infty$ pairs of iteration. The defined Sinkhorn normalization function is differentiable and the gradients of the learning objective can be computed by backpropagating through the unfolded sequence of row and column-wise normalizations, unconstrained matrix, and finally learning module parameters.

During the running phase, a single permutation matrix P' must be predicted by finding the closest polytope vertex to the doubly-stochastic matrix D produced by the model. This can be formulated as a bipartite matching problem where the cost matrix is $C = 1 - D$. As a result, we use the Hungarian algorithm over the cost matrix to find the optimal solution of the matching problem. Finally, each individual frame is sorted (labelled) by the transpose of the corresponding estimated permutation. The learning and running phases are illustrated in Fig. 2.

3.3 Trajectory Labelling

After applying our permutation learning model to all the frames in the entire sequence, we have a sequence of individually labelled frames ordered in time. However, the integration of sequences of individual marker locations into trajectories that extend over time, which is already conducted by the motion capture system during data collection, and the expectation that labels should remain constant during the motion trajectory, can be used to enforce temporal consistency. Each trajectory can be defined as the sequence of tracked marker locations which ends with a gap or when recording stops. Therefore, in each motion sample, the movement of each marker might be presented in multiple trajectories over time. We can exploit the temporal consistency of each trajectory to correct the wrong predictions for each marker during the trajectory. One naïve idea is to assign each trajectory to the label with the highest number of votes in the assignment predictions for the corresponding marker. However, there are situations where a label has been assigned to a marker with the highest number of times but with low confidence. Thus, we propose a winner-takes-all approach where a score is computed for each label which has been assigned at least once to the marker in the trajectory. Then the winner with the highest score will be assigned to the corresponding trajectory. The score for label i assigned to the query marker j is computed as follows:

$$S_i = |T_i|^q \left(\Sigma_{t \in T_i} |c_{i,j}^{(t)}|^p \right)^{\frac{1}{p}} \tag{2}$$

where T_i is the set of frame indices at which label i has been assigned to the query marker during its trajectory. $|T_i|$ is the cardinality of T_i. p and q are hyperparameters which are chosen during validation step. The second term for $p = 0$ is defined as $|T_i|$. $c_{i,j}^{(t)}$ represents the degree of confidence for assigning the label i to the marker j at frame t. The details of $c_{i,j}^{(t)}$ formulation are discussed in Sect. 3.4.

3.4   Degree of Confidence

During the running phase, each column of the outputted DSM matrix represents a distribution over labels for the corresponding marker which can be interpreted as the model's belief in each label. When the model is confident in labelling all markers, the estimated DSM matrix is close to the true permutation matrix on the polytope surface and all of these distributions peak at the true label. On the other hand, when a marker is hard to label, the corresponding distribution might not have a sharp peak at the true label. We compute a degree of confidence for each predicted label i assigned to marker j at frame t as the distance between the model's belief for label i and the highest belief, as follows:

$$c_{i,j}^{(t)} = D_{i,j}^{(t)} - \max_{\substack{1 \le k \le N \\ k \ne i}} D_{k,j}^{(t)}, \tag{3}$$

where $D^{(t)}$ is the DSM matrix produced by Sinkhorn normalization at frame t. Note that the defined $c_{i,j}^{(t)}$ can be negative in the situations where the assigned label and the index of maximum value in the distribution are not the same. Therefore, we use a min-max normalized version of it ($c_{i,t} \leftarrow \frac{c_{i,t}+1}{2}$) in Eq. 2 to make sure its range is between 0 and 1.

4   Experiments and Evaluations

4.1   Data

To evaluate our method we used a subset of Biomotion dataset [20] recorded from 115 individuals at 120 frames per second using Vicon system. The subset includes four types of actions namely walking, jogging, sitting, and jumping, where each recording contains the 3D trajectories of 41 markers. Some actions where recorded multiple times from the same individual. On average, we used 11.5 sequences per subject for a total of 1329 sequences. The total number of frames in our dataset is around 630k frames. Data from 69 individuals were used for training, while the data from 46 different individuals were held out for testing and validation (23 each).

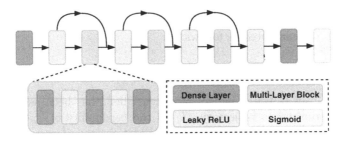

Fig. 3. Schematic diagram of the feed-forward deep residual neural network used for permutation learning.

4.2   Training

The feed-forward residual network implemented as our learning module was designed with three residual blocks where each block contains three dense layers followed by a Leaky ReLU activation (see Fig. 3). The residual connections showed a smoothing behavior on our optimization landscape. Hyper-parameters of the network were chosen using a random search scheme [2].

The original training set was constructed by applying 16 random permutations on each of the 378k training frames resulting in around 6.4 million shuffled training frames. Then, to augment the training data with the occlusions, up to 5 markers in each generated shuffled frame were randomly occluded by replacing the 3D position values by the center location $(0.5, 0.5, 0.5)$. Both the numbers of occlusions and the index of occluded markers were drawn from uniform distributions.

For training the model, we used an Adam optimizer with batches of size 32. The learning rate was initially set to 5×10^{-5} and was reduced by a factor of 2 after each epoch when the validation loss increased. Our model was trained for 100 epochs using a cross-entropy loss function. The number of Sinkhorn iterations was set to 5 since for each additional iteration the improvement in performance was very small while the running time was increased linearly. By performing these 5 Sinkhorn iterations on our unconstrained matrix, the sum of squared distances between 1 and the row- and column-wise sums of the resulting matrix was less than 10^{-17}.

4.3   Permutation Learning Model Evaluation

To evaluate our permutation learning model, we synthesized an evaluation set by applying 16 random permutations followed by randomly introducing 0 to 5 occlusions into each frame of the test set. Table 1 shows the performance of our model in different setups and compares them with the initialization steps proposed by Holzreiter et al. [9] and Maycock et al. [12]. First and second rows in the Table 1 show the accuracy results when the model was trained on the original training set and the occlusion augmented set, respectively. As anticipated, introducing occlusions into the training data improves the results for the test frames with occluded markers, which is usual in real scenarios. On the other hand, when the model is trained without occlusions the performance on occluded frames significantly decreases.

To evaluate the influence of Sinkhorn normalization, we replaced the Sinkhorn layer with a Softmax function over the rows of outputted DSM matrix and trained the parameters from scratch. The results for this setups are illustrated in the third row of Table 1. Without Sinkhorn normalization, the output matrix ignores the inherent structure of permutation matrices resulting in a drop in the labelling performance.

Table 1. A comparison of performance of different models in labelling a single test frame as an initialization step in the presence of a varying number of occlusions in the test frames (show in each column). The first and second rows illustrates the performance when the model is trained with and without occlusions, respectively. Third row, shows the results when the Sinkhorn layer is replaced by a Softmax function. It can be seen that the model trained on occlusion augmented training set outperforms the rest when having occlusions in the frames.

Method	# Occs					
	0	1	2	3	4	5
Ours + Occs	97.11%	**96.56%**	**96.13%**	**95.87%**	**95.75%**	**94.9%**
Ours + No Occs	**98.72%**	94.41%	92.15%	88.75%	86.54%	85.0%
Ours w/o SN	94.03%	91.12%	88.1%	84.27%	81.62%	77.78%
Maycock et al.	83.18%	79.35%	76.44%	74.91%	71.17%	65.83%
Holzreiter et al.	88.16%	79.0%	72.42%	67.16%	61.31%	52.1%

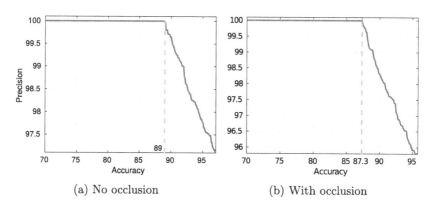

(a) No occlusion   (b) With occlusion

Fig. 4. Plot of accuracy-precision curves for labelling frames without and with occlusions. In the latter case an average of 2.5 markers was missing in each frame.

Table 2. The performance of trajectory labelling with different settings of p and q in our scoring function

Method	Occs ratio					
	0	2%	4%	6%	8%	10%
No trajectory labelling	97.13%	96.55%	96.17%	95.91%	95.68%	94.82%
$p = 0,\ q = 0$	97.52%	96.81%	96.55%	96.09%	96.51%	95.43%
$p = 1,\ q = 0$	98.77%	98.01%	97.78%	97.32%	97.12%	96.85%
$p = 1,\ q = -1$	97.35%	96.51%	96.42%	96.06%	95.89%	94.37%
$p = 2,\ q = -1/2$	**99.85%**	**99.54%**	**99.47%**	**99.25%**	**99.07%**	**98.76%**

Having defined the degree of confidence, there is the option to only assign a label to a marker if the corresponding degree of confidence is higher than a threshold. Otherwise, the marker is left unlabelled. This allows the model to set a trade-off between the precision (the fraction of correctly labelled markers over labelled markers) and accuracy (the fraction of correctly labelled markers over all markers). Figure 4 shows the accuracy-precision curves. It can be seen that a high proportion of the markers can be labelled with no error (89% when there is no occlusion and 87.3% with an average of 2.5 markers occluded in each frame) and leaving less than 12.7% markers to be labelled manually.

4.4   Trajectory Labelling Evaluation

So far, we looked at frames individually. In the next stage, we integrate frame-by-frame labelling with information about the temporal order of the frames in an effort to label continuous trajectories. To evaluate the trajectory labelling stage, we used the original unlabelled test set and introduced occlusions to each motion sample with different occlusion ratios. Here, the occlusions are introduced as gaps with different lengths into trajectories. As a result, the motion of the marker is fragmented into two or more trajectories. Table 2 shows the performance of trajectory labelling with different settings of p and q in our scoring function. When $p = 0$ and $q = 0$, this stage acts as a voting function ($S_i = |T_i|$). Thus, the degree of confidence does not have an influence on the final result. For $p = 1$ and $q = 0$, the scoring function computes the sum of confidences for the frames that the label has been assigned to the marker. Also, when $p = 1$ and $q = -1$, the score for each label is considered as the average of confidences. Therefore, the number of times that a label is assigned to a marker is neutralized by averaging. Best performance in our hyper-parameters search was achieved when $p = 2$ and $q = -1/2$. In this case, the influence of N_i on the score is less than when $q = -1$. Also, since p is set to 2, the role of the high degree of confidences is more than other settings.

5   Conclusion

In this paper, we presented a method to address the problem of auto-labelling markers in optical motion capture pipelines. The essence of our approach was to frame the problem of single-frame labelling as a permutation learning task where the ordered set of markers can be recovered by estimating the permutation matrix from a shuffled set of markers. We exploited the idea of using DSMs to represent a distribution over the permutations. Also, we proposed a robust solution to correct the mislabelled markers by utilizing the temporal information where the label with a higher confidence score is assigned to the whole trajectory. We demonstrated that our method performed with very high accuracy even with only single-frame inputs, and when individual markers were occluded. Furthermore, the trajectory labelling will further improve if longer gap-free trajectories are available. Our method can be considered as both initialization and tracking. Once the model is trained, it easily runs on a medium-power CPU at 120 frames per second and can therefore be used for real time tracking.

6   Future Works

Our model makes fast and robust predictions and is easy to train. However, it should be trained on a training set with the same marker layout. One solution could be to synthesize desired training sets by putting virtual markers on the animated body meshes from labelled data using body and motion animating tools such as [11] and to record the motion of virtual markers.

We have addressed the problem of single-subject marker labelling, but have not considered multi-subject scenarios. Future work could explore using clustering approaches and multi-hypothesis generative approaches to separate the subjects and apply the model on each of them.

Here, we have used a completely data-driven approach to label motion capture trajectories. The model could be further improved by integrating both anthropometric and kinematic information into our method where they can serve as priors that further constrain the model.

References

1. Adams, R.P., Zemel, R.S.: Ranking via Sinkhorn propagation. ArXiv, pp. 1106–1925 (2011)
2. Bergstra, J., Bengio, Y.: Random search for hyper-parameter optimization. J. Mach. Learn. Res. **13**, 281–305 (2012)
3. Birkhoff, G.: Three observations on linear algebra. Univ. Nac. Tacuman, Rev. Ser. A **5**, 147–151 (1946)
4. Etemad, S.A., Arya, A.: Expert-driven perceptual features for modeling style and affect in human motion. IEEE Trans. Hum.-Mach. Syst. **46**(4), 534–545 (2016)
5. Han, S., Liu, B., Wang, R., Ye, Y., Twigg, C.D., Kin, K.: Online optical marker-based hand tracking with deep labels. ACM Trans. Graph. **37**(4), 166 (2018)

6. He, K., Zhang, X., Ren, S., Sun, J.: Deep residual learning for image recognition. In: IEEE Conference on Computer Vision and Pattern Recognition (2016)
7. Herda, L., Fua, P., Plänkers, R., Boulic, R., Thalmann, D.: Using skeleton-based tracking to increase the reliability of optical motion capture. Hum. Mov. Sci. **20**(3), 313–341 (2001). https://doi.org/10.1016/S0167-9457(01)00050-1
8. Holden, D.: Robust solving of optical motion capture data by denoising. ACM Trans. Graph. **38**(1), 1–12 (2018). https://doi.org/10.11499/sicejl1962.40.735
9. Holzreiter, S.: Autolabeling 3D tracks using neural networks. Clin. Biomech. **20**(1), 1–8 (2005)
10. Ionescu, C., Papava, D., Olaru, V., Sminchisescu, C.: Human3.6M: large scale datasets and predictive methods for 3d human sensing in natural environments. IEEE Trans. Pattern Anal. Mach. Intell. **36**(7), 1325–1339 (2014)
11. Loper, M., Mahmood, N., Black, M.J.: MoSh: motion and shape capture from sparse markers. ACM Trans. Graph. **33**(6), 220 (2014)
12. Maycock, J., Röhlig, T., Schröder, M., Botsch, M., Ritter, H.: Fully automatic optical motion tracking using an inverse kinematics approach. In: IEEE/RAS International Conference on Humanoid Robots, pp. 2–7 (2015). https://doi.org/10.1109/HUMANOIDS.2015.7363590
13. Meyer, J., Kuderer, M., Muller, J., Burgard, W.: Online marker labeling for fully automatic skeleton tracking in optical motion capture. In: Proceedings of IEEE International Conference on Robotics and Automation, pp. 5652–5657 (2014). https://doi.org/10.1109/ICRA.2014.6907690
14. Pons-Moll, G., Romero, J., Mahmood, N., Black, M.J.: Dyna: a model of dynamic human shape in motion. ACM Trans. Graph. (TOG) **34**(4), 120 (2015)
15. Rezatofighi, S.H., et al.: Deep perm-set net: learn to predict sets with unknown permutation and cardinality using deep neural networks. arXiv preprint arXiv:1805.00613 (2018)
16. Santa Cruz, R., Fernando, B., Cherian, A., Gould, S.: DeepPermNet: visual permutation learning. In: Proceedings of the IEEE Conference on Computer Vision and Pattern Recognition, pp. 3949–3957 (2017)
17. Schubert, T., Gkogkidis, A., Ball, T., Burgard, W.: Automatic initialization for skeleton tracking in optical motion capture. In: Proceedings of IEEE International Conference on Robotics and Automation, pp. 734–739. IEEE (2015)
18. Sigal, L., Balan, A.O., Black, M.J.: HumanEva: synchronized video and motion capture dataset and baseline algorithm for evaluation of articulated human motion. Int. J. Comput. Vis. **87**(1–2), 4 (2010)
19. Sinkhorn, R.: A relationship between arbitrary positive matrices and doubly stochastic matrices. Ann. Math. Stat. **35**(2), 876–879 (1964)
20. Troje, N.F.: Retrieving information from human movement patterns. In: Shipley, T.F., Zacks, J.M. (eds.) Understanding Events: How Humans See, Represent, and Act on Events. Oxford University, New York, vol. 1, pp. 308–334 (2008)
21. Yu, Q., Li, Q., Deng, Z.: Online motion capture marker labeling for multiple interacting articulated targets. Comput. Graph. Forum **26**(3), 477–483 (2007). https://doi.org/10.1111/j.1467-8659.2007.01070.x

A Simple Algorithm for Hard Exudate Detection in Diabetic Retinopathy Using Spectral-Domain Optical Coherence Tomography

Maciej Szymkowski[1]($\boxtimes$), Emil Saeed[2], Khalid Saeed[1], and Zofia Mariak[2]

[1] Faculty of Computer Science, Białystok University of Technology, 45A Wiejska Street, 15-351 Białystok, Poland
{m.szymkowski,k.saeed}@pb.edu.pl
[2] Faculty of Medicine, Department of Ophthalmology, Medical University of Białystok, 24A Curie-Skłodowskiej Street, 15-276 Białystok, Poland
emilsaeed1986@gmail.com, mariakzo@umb.edu.pl

Abstract. Hard exudates are usually seen in the course of diabetic retinopathy. This illness is one of the most common reasons for blind registration in the world. Due to the data presented by World Health Organization (WHO) the number of people who lose sight because of undetected diabetes will be doubled by 2050. The purpose of this paper is to introduce an enhanced algorithm for hard exudates detection in Optical Coherence Tomography images. In these samples, dangerous pathological changes can be observed in the form of yellow-red spots. During the experiments more than 150 images were used to calculate the accuracy of the proposed approach. We created an algorithm that was implemented in development environment with Java Programming Language and Maven Framework. Classification was done on the basis of authors' own algorithm results and compared with ophthalmologist decision. The experiments have shown the proposed approach has 97% of accuracy in hard exudates detection.

Keywords: Hard exudates ·
Spectral-Domain OCT (Optical coherence Tomography) · Retina ·
Automated analysis · Pattern recognition

1 Introduction

Currently, worldwide diabetes affects over 425 million people [1]. All sufferers are at a risk of developing pathological complications such as hard exudates. Diabetes mellitus is an important cause of visual impairment. Some complications in diabetes mellitus seem to appear early and might lead to blindness at late stages of the disease. It is also predicted that 80% of them will have a diabetic retinopathy after around 20 years of having the disease [2]. The most significant aspect in diagnosing pathway is to find the early symptoms of the illness. It is needed because ophthalmologist can stop malady development or even completely eliminate the possibility of its occurrence. Physicians can

© Springer Nature Switzerland AG 2019
M. Gavrilova et al. (Eds.): CGI 2019, LNCS 11542, pp. 179–189, 2019.
https://doi.org/10.1007/978-3-030-22514-8_15

observe the early stage of the diabetic retinopathy by hard exudates appearance. Unfortunately, sometimes these pathological changes are so small that ophthalmologist cannot notice them in retina color images. It is there where computer-aided solutions are needed.

In the literature we can observe different approaches to medical images processing and analysis. Automated detection and assessment of disease severity is, nowadays, a kind of a trend. Diversified worldwide scientific teams are working under solutions connected with this task – especially under detection of neoplastic lesions in their early stages.

In this paper, the authors present their novel approach to detect hard exudates in images obtained by Optical Coherence Tomography (OCT). The proposed algorithm is an improvement of the solution described in [3]. In this work, the Authors prepared a multimodal system that decides whether changes are dangerous on the basis of two images: OCT and retina color images. OCT image is first processed and, pathological changes are primarily detected, whilst retina color image analysis is used to detect hard exudates and confirm those retrieved from OCT image. In the approach described in this work, the authors also took into consideration hard exudates; no other pathological changes are of interest and hence they are not detected. Our solution is based on image processing algorithms. This approach allowed us to achieve good results with very high efficiency. Each photo is processed in no more than 30 s.

The novelty of the proposed solution lies in using OCT images and applying simple image processing methods for diabetic lesion detection. Moreover, our approach returns satisfactory results with low computational complexity of the prepared method.

The manuscript is organized as follows: in the first chapter methodology and the proposed solution are presented. The second chapter contains information about the performed experiments. In the third section, a discussion of the results obtained from authors' experiments is presented. Finally, conclusions and future work are given.

2 How Others See It

In the literature we can find different approaches to process OCT images a little number of them is connected with hard exudates detection. Most of the approaches are connected with simple image processing and analysis. Only a few of them use artificial intelligence for pathological changes detection [4, 5].

An interesting approach was presented in [4]. The experiments were connected with hard exudates detection, though they do not use any computer-aided tools. 238 participants took part and the results showed there is a correlation between hard exudates and lipid serum levels in type 2 diabetes.

The authors of [5] used Optical Coherence Tomography images of retina for different disease observation. They also do not use any computer algorithms. The results presented by the authors were also connected with medical analysis of the OCT retina image. It was claimed there is association between hard exudates (shown in the course of diabetes) and chorioretinal folds.

The most common approach in observation of the hard exudates in retina is connected with retina color images. Hard exudates are visible in the form of small discolorations in these samples. An approach that uses retina color images for this aim was presented in [6, 7]. The authors also dealt with the problem of hard exudates detection, but they do not use OCT images. Due to this fact, no comparison was done between the results of our approach and those described in [6, 7].

Another interesting algorithm was presented in [8]. In it, the authors processed OCT images to find huge lesions. In this case, patient did not see or had very limited eyesight. Their approach was based on measuring the thickness of the tissue. This task was realized on the basis of image processing methods. The results have shown their solution accuracy is more than 80%.

If it comes to hard exudates detection in retina color images, we can also easily find multiple research papers in which the Authors used different soft computing techniques to detect pathological changes. The most popular is artificial neural network. It was used in [9, 10]. These approaches differ from each other by the mathematical models of Neural Network and the way in which significant data was obtained. In the literature we can also find deep learning [11] and machine learning [12] approaches to hard exudates detection in the retina color images. Their main drawback is long learning time and a very large sample database needed to complete this task. Image processing approaches are much easier and have lower computing complexity.

3 Proposed Methodology

In the proposed approach, the authors used images from Spectral-Domain OCT. Some hospitals and Medical Universities use Heidelberg OCT for image retrieval. These samples are then analyzed by ophthalmologists. Images obtained with Spectral-Domain OCT are the base for scientific experiments. Results retrieved with these samples can also be applied in Heidelberg OCT images.

During our experiments a total of 150 photos were included in the analysis. The database was collected after patient consent in Medical University of Białystok. It comprises 75 healthy and 75 sick eyes. 67 patients - 39 females and 28 males with an age ranging between 50 and 64 were examined. The sample photo is presented in Fig. 1.

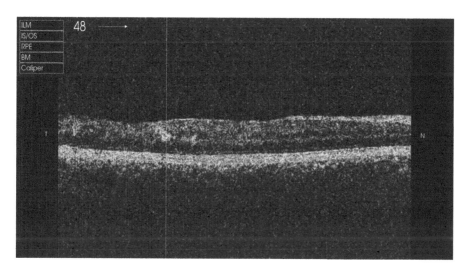

Fig. 1. Original image obtained by the Optical Coherence Tomography device

Our approach consists of a few consecutive steps. Activity diagram of the proposed solution is presented in Fig. 2.

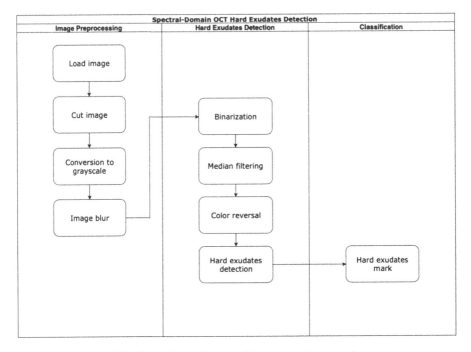

Fig. 2. Activity diagram of the proposed approach

The first stage of the authors' algorithm is to cut image from both sides by 24%. In all of the pictures that form our base, two black rectangles (from both sides of the image) are visible. It can be observed that they do not provide any necessary or valuable information. Moreover, we know it is highly possible that hard exudate will occur in the middle part of the retina than in its extreme areas. This information allowed to remove side parts of the image.

The second step of the proposed algorithm is median filtering. It is used due to the fact that the original image contains a large number of small distortion parts that can be detected and removed by median filters. The processed image after both of these steps is presented in Fig. 3. The third algorithm used in the proposed solution is image conversion to greyscale. The authors have tried different methods based on RGB channels (red, green, blue and average) though the best result was obtained with red channel. It means this method outcome was most precise – whole structure was clearly visible, and image was prepared to further processing.

The next step was image blur. It was done with a small 3 × 3 mask and Gaussian model. This operation was repeated three times to remove small points that still might be visible after conversion to grayscale. The image after steps three and four is presented in Fig. 4.

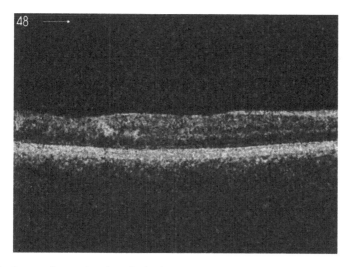

Fig. 3. Image after cutting from both sides and median filtering (Color figure online)

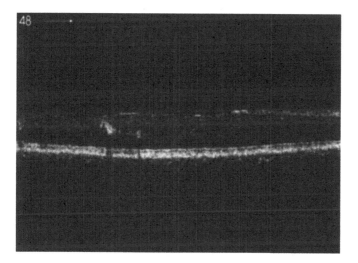

Fig. 4. Image after conversion to grayscale and blur.

Another step of the proposed approach was binarization. The authors, as mentioned above tried a few different approaches like: binarization with manual thresholding, Niblack algorithm [13], Otsu binarization [14] and Bernsen local binarization method [15]. The best results were obtained with Otsu approach. This algorithm allowed the authors to precisely receive as an output the hard exudates or other lesions. In our algorithm, white elements are connected with hard exudates or the retina tissue. The result obtained with the selected algorithm is presented in Fig. 5.

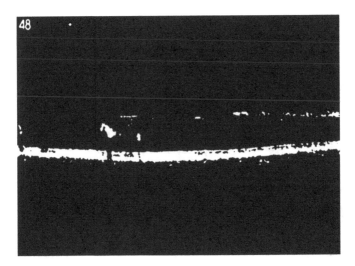

Fig. 5. Image after Otsu binarization

After binarization observed small spots are removed by median filtering. This filter is used for image denoising. We can conclude that these small additional points can be classified to this kind of distortion. The next step in our solution was connected with color reversal. Right now, all black pixels are correlated with hard exudates or the retina layers. The result of these operations is presented in Fig. 6.

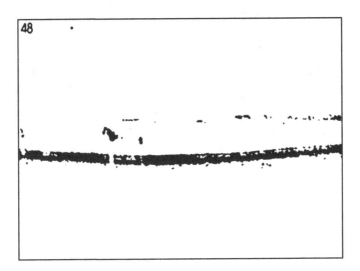

Fig. 6. Image after additional median filtering and color reversal.

The last stage of the proposed algorithm is the removal of tissue points. The authors used their own algorithm to deal with this problem. Its main idea is connected with the detection of the retina borders and removing all points that are too close to them. We then easily detect tissue elements. The result obtained with the proposed approach is presented in Fig. 7.

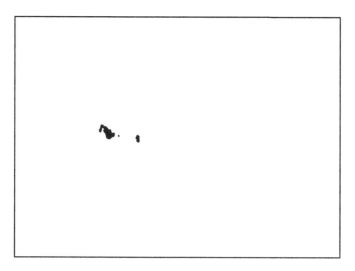

Fig. 7. Hard exudates detected in the analyzed image.

The algorithm pseudocode is presented in Algorithm 1.

```
Tissue removal: {
    for each pixel in image {
        up = pixel.findUpperBorder();
        down = pixel.findLowerBorder();
        if(up != -1 && down != -1) {
            pixel.markAsInsideRetina();
        } else if (up != -1) {
            pixel.markAsLowerBorder();
        } else if (down != -1) {
            pixel.markAsUpperBorder();
        }
    }
    for each border in borders {
        border.removeTissue(threshold);
    }
}
```

The final step of the approach is to mark the possible hard exudates in white color in the image. The final result is presented in Fig. 8.

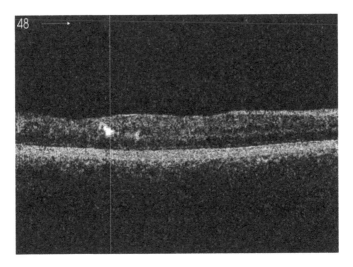

Fig. 8. Possible hard exudates marked in white color in the OCT image.

4   Results and Discussion

The most important parameter in our experiments is the algorithm efficiency. It was calculated on the basis of the algorithm decision (healthy - 1 or pathological/suspected - 0) compared with the diagnosis of the ophthalmologist. This comparison has shown that the proposed approach was on 97% accuracy level. We also observed that in the case of four not properly classified images, our algorithm pointed they contain pathological changes (even they present healthy samples). The ophthalmologist asserted that it is sometimes better to classify healthy sample as the one with pathological changes and check it with an ophthalmologist rather than miss them. It is better for a patient to check his health with experienced physician rather than to have small non-recognized pathological changes and be in danger of diabetic retinopathy. The summary of our results is presented in Table 1.

Table 1. The summary of the experiments conducted on the authors database

Type of photo	Correct classification	Incorrect classification
Healthy retina (75 images)	71	4
Retina with pathological changes (75 photos)	75	0
Total	146	4

We also checked how our algorithm is performing in different computer environments. We took into consideration different parameters like: type of CPU, RAM capacity, and type of hard drive. The most important parameter that we measured was the time needed to collect the results. The best result was obtained in 30 s. The summary of this experiment is shown in Table 2.

Table 2. The summary of comparison between different machine configurations

CPU	RAM	Hard drive type	Measured time
Intel Core i5	4 GB	SSD	41 s
Intel Core i7	8 GB	HDD	38 s
Intel Core i9	16 GB	SSD	30 s

It was really hard to compare our idea with other similar methodologies because most of the approaches connected with Optical Coherence Tomography are not dealing with hard exudates detection. We have found interesting approaches connected with retina color image processing in the course of pathological changes detection [16–20]. As far as it concerns the OCT images, and to the authors' state of the art knowledge, there is no research in this field. Hence, there was no possibility for our results comparison with the works of other researchers of similar approaches. They simply do not use OCT images.

Despite the fact that there are no other approaches to detect hard exudates in OCT images, the authors compared their results with the ones obtained on the basis of retina color images [17, 19]. Morphological operations described in [17, 19] were used in retina color images that correspond to OCT images analyzed by us. It was clearly visible that both solutions could give satisfactory results. In both of the cases hard exudates in their advanced stage were detected although small pathological changes in their early form were only (partially) marked by our novel algorithm in OCT images and solution described in [17]. We also tried to use morphological operations-based solutions in OCT images. The summary of these experiments is that we cannot use algorithms for hard exudates detection in retina color images for the same task in OCT images. It is mostly connected with the fact that these samples are completely different, and these solutions have to be adapted (by additional image processing steps) for this kind of images. Table 3 contains summary of the experiments.

Table 3. The summary of comparison between different algorithms

Algorithm	Early stage of hard exudates	Advanced stage of hard exudates
Joshi and Karlue [17]	Partially detected	Detected
Kekre et al. [19]	Non-detected	Detected
Authors' approach	Partially detected	Detected

5 Conclusions and Future Work

The conducted experiments have shown that automatic detection of hard exudates in Optical Coherence Tomography images can be done with high accuracy in a short time. It is possible even if the image has low resolution and it is processed by the computer implemented algorithm and program with small resources.

The experiments conducted by the authors have also shown it is much more useful to diagnose small pseudopathological changes as pathological ones rather than ignoring them. Our algorithm misidentified only in 4 cases out of 150 images. In all of these four cases the algorithm found hard exudates in healthy samples.

Currently, the authors are increasing the number of samples in the database and working on extending the algorithm capabilities to apply artificial intelligence for hard exudates detection. Moreover, we are in the phase of collecting samples from Heidelberg OCT. These images have much higher resolution.

Acknowledgments. This work was supported by grant S/WI/3/2018 from Białystok University of Technology and funded with resources for research by the Ministry of Science and Higher Education in Poland.

References

1. James, B., Chew, C., Bron, A.: Lecture Notes. Ophthalmology, pp. 172–173 (2007)
2. Klein, B.E.: Overview of epidemiologic studies of diabetic retinopathy. Ophthalmic Epidemiol. **14**(4), 179–183 (2007)
3. Szymkowski, M., Saeed, E., Saeed, K.: Retina tomography and optical coherence tomography in eye diagnostic system. In: Chaki, R., Cortesi, A., Saeed, K., Chaki, N. (eds.) Advanced Computing and Systems for Security. AISC, vol. 666, pp. 31–42. Springer, Singapore (2018). https://doi.org/10.1007/978-981-10-8180-4_3
4. Davoudi, S., et al.: Optical coherence tomography characteristics of macular edema and hard exudates and their association with lipid serum level in type 2 diabetes. Retina **36**(9), 1622–1629 (2018)
5. Tuncay, T., Eyup, D.: Chorioretinal folds associated with different etiologies. Biomed. J. Sci. Tech. Res. **2**(4) (2018)
6. Sasaki, M., Kawasaki, R., Noonan, J.E., Wong, T.Y., Lamoureux, E., Wang, J.J.: Quantitative measurement of hard exudates in patients with diabetes and their associations with serum lipid levels. Invest. Ophthalmol. Vis. Sci. **54**(8), 5544–5550 (2013)
7. Raman, R., Nittala, M.G., Gella, L., Pal, S.S., Sharma, T.: Retinal sensitivity over hard exudates in diabetic retinopathy. J. Ophthalmic Vis. Res. **10**(2), 160–164 (2015)
8. Szymkowski, M., Saeed, E.: A novel approach of retinal disorder diagnosing using optical coherence tomography scanners. In: Gavrilova, M.L., Tan, C.J.K., Chaki, N., Saeed, K. (eds.) Transactions on Computational Science XXXI. LNCS, vol. 10730, pp. 31–40. Springer, Heidelberg (2018). https://doi.org/10.1007/978-3-662-56499-8_3
9. Anitha, G.J., Maria, K.G.: Detecting hard exudates in retinal fundus images using convolutional neural network. In: Proceedings of International Conference on Current Trends Towards Converging Technologies (ICCTCT) (2018). https://doi.org/10.1109/icctct.2018.8551079

10. Bharkad, S.: Morphological and neural network based approach for detection of exudates in fundus images. In: Second International Conference on Computing Methodologies and Communication (ICCMC) (2018). https://doi.org/10.1109/iccmc.2018.8487517
11. Avula, B., Chakraborty, C.: Detection of hard exudates in retinal fundus images using deep learning. In: 7th International Conference on Informatics, Electronics & Vision (ICIEV) and 2018 2nd International Conference on Imaging, Vision & Pattern Recognition (icIVPR) Proceedings (2018). https://doi.org/10.1109/iciev.2018.8641016
12. Long, S., Huang, X., Chen, Z., Pardhan, S., Zheng, D.: Automatic detection of hard exudates in color retinal images using dynamic threshold and SVM classification: algorithm development and evaluation. BioMed. Res. Int. **2019**(6a), 1–13 (2019)
13. Saxena, L.P.: Niblack's binarization method and its modifications to real-time applications: a review. Artif. Intell. Rev. 1–33 (2017)
14. Otsu, N.: A threshold selection method from gray-level histograms. IEEE Trans. Syst. Man Cybern. **9**(1), 62–66 (1979)
15. Eyupoglu, C.: Implementation of Bernsen's locally adaptive binarization method for gray scale images. In: 7th International Science and Technology Conference (ISTEC), Vienna, Austria, Proceedings (2016)
16. Rokade, P., Manza, R.: Automatic detection of hard exudates in retinal images using haar wavelet transform. Int. J. Appl. Innov. Eng. Manag. **4**(5), 402–410 (2015)
17. Joshi, S., Karlue, P.T.: Detection of hard exudates based on morphological feature extraction. Biomed. Pharmacol. J. **11**(1), 215–225 (2018)
18. Deep Learning for Hard Exudates Detection (2018). https://arxiv.org/ftp/arxiv/papers/1808/1808.03656.pdf. Accessed 21 Nov 2018
19. Kekre, H., Sarode, T., Parkar, T.: Hybrid approach for detection of hard exudates. Int. J. Adv. Comput. Sci. Appl. **4**(1) (2013)
20. Eadgahi, M.G.F., Pourreza, H.: Localization of hard exudates in retinal fundus image by mathematical morphology operations. J. Theor. Phys. Cryptogr. **1**(2) (2012)

Multi-level Motion-Informed Approach for Video Generation with Key Frames

Zackary P. T. Sin$^{(\boxtimes)}$, Peter H. F. Ng, Simon C. K. Shiu,
Fu-lai Chung, and Hong Va Leong

The Hong Kong Polytechnic University, Hung Hom, Hong Kong
{csptsin, cshfng, csckshiu,
cskchung, cshleong}@comp.polyu.edu.hk

Abstract. Observing that a motion signal is decomposable into multiple levels, a video generation model which realizes this hypothesis is proposed. The model decomposes motion into a two-level signal involving a global path and local pattern. They are modeled via a latent path in the form of a composite Bezier spline along with a latent sine function respectively. In the application context, the model fills the research gap in its ability to connect an arbitrary number of input key frames smoothly. Experimental results indicate that the model improves in terms of the smoothness of the generated video. In addition, the ability of the model in separating global and local signal has been validated.

Keywords: Global motion path · Local motion pattern ·
Video generation with key frames · Latent path · Periodic latent function

1 Introduction

Motion could be modeled in different ways, among which optical flow is one well-known approach. More recently, Tulyakov et al. proposed using a string of motion codes to represent motion in the latent space [1]. In this paper, we observe that the motion signal could be decomposed and be represented as global and local signals. When a person moves, s/he moves from one place to another with a global trajectory, while exhibiting some repeating motion locally, such as arm and leg swinging. There may also be subtle movements for fingers and hair. To model this hierarchical motion structure, we propose to decompose the motion into a multi-level signal spanning from the top global level to the fine local level.

In this paper, we validate our motion decomposition approach with two levels: a global path signal and a local pattern signal. The former represents the motion that makes an object move in the environment while the latter represents the motion by a local part of the moving object. This is analogous to computer graphics concepts: the global path resembles the translation of an object while the local pattern its rotation.

In order to achieve a separation of global and local motion, some key problems need to be addressed. We model the properties in a latent space [1]. Since a global path is representing a global movement to model an object going from one place to another, an intuitive modeling could be a latent path drawn in the latent space. A local pattern

M. Gavrilova et al. (Eds.): CGI 2019, LNCS 11542, pp. 190–202, 2019.
https://doi.org/10.1007/978-3-030-22514-8_16

represents a repeating motion, which could intuitively be modeled with periodic functions in the latent space (e.g. sine function).

Modeling motion as a global path and local pattern opens up a new avenue for applications. For a controllable global signal, an intuitive application comes from the animation industry. It is well accepted that senior animators draw out some key frames as a rough video. Junior animators will fill out the frames in-between. Global path could be easily adapted to this application by ensuring that the latent path passes through the key frames specified by the user. Not only is this an intuitive method to control video generation, it also fills the research gap on using key frames for generating video. We currently adopt Bezier spline in the latent space.

With a controllable local motion signal, it would be ideal that the local motion could be tuned regardless of the global motion. An effect somewhat like moonwalking could be achieved, where a person's leg movement is seemingly detached with the person's movement. More research is needed to accurately replicate this with our current model. In summary, the contributions of this paper include the recognition of the motion signals being decomposable into multiple levels. We decompose the signal to facilitate automatic video frame generation in the latent space. We propose models for the global and local motions in the latent space and evaluate via experiments.

2   Literature Review

With the introduction of variational autoencoder (VAE) [2] and generative adversarial networks (GAN) [3], image and video generation problems have become robustly solvable. For example, VGAN adopts GAN to generate videos [4], which also implies that spatial and temporal dimensions have identical properties. TGAN was proposed to separately generate temporal codes and images from the said codes [5]. Since videos can be viewed as sequences of coherent images, they could be processed via recurrent neural networks (RNN) such as LSTM [6]. MoCoGAN is a good example [1].

There are also works in video generation. Mathieu et al. [7] worked on a loss function to improve the fidelity. Walker et al. [8] used human pose information to act as a higher-level abstraction for GAN. Liang et al. [9] and Liu et al. [10] adopted optical flow as additional feature for the generative model. Chan et al. [11] proposed a motion transfer method for human subjects with stick figure as an intermediate representation to enable a dancer's motion to be transferred to another person via video.

There seems to be relatively few works on video generation models controllable by multiple key frame inputs. VGAN, TGAN and MoCoGAN allow a video to be generated by a conditional image input. Motion codes in MoCoGAN could also be transferred from one video to another, but it is unclear how easy it is to control and get the motion codes. Wang et al. [12] proposed a video-to-video synthesis model that could translate a video from one domain to another. Although the result is impressive, it requires another video to generate a new video. Controllability of the video generation process via a few specific video key frames as in animation context remains lacking.

3 Methodology

The key idea of the proposed model is to separate motion into its global and local components. We will first discuss how the global path could be modelled, followed by the local pattern. With the global path, we can draw a smooth path in the latent space for generating a video. How this latent path could fit the input key frames will then be discussed. For the local pattern, we can use a periodic function to model.

3.1 Global Motion

For the global motion path, we have chosen a VAE framework [2]. A GAN-based solution does not quite work with the idea of latent path, perhaps due to the fact that GAN does not explicitly model the distribution of the latent space. On the other hand, VAE explicitly models the distribution of the latent space and hence, the distance between the points is meaningful. This allows us to easily apply Euclidean geometry techniques such as Bezier curves in the latent space. However, we make no claim that this is the reason why GAN fails in our experiments.

In order to model latent paths, we propose that the input key frames (images) x be projected first into the latent space via an encoder F_E such that $(z_c, z_g^{(t)}) = F_E(x^{(t)})$ where z_c is the content code, z_g is the global motion code [1] and t is the time step. Content code models the content in a video frame and therefore should be consistent throughout all the frames of a video while motion code models the motion in a video and therefore represents the changes between frames. z_c and z_g are both sampled from prior distributions P_{z_c} and P_{z_g}. Similar to [1], we make a distinction between content and motion by fixing z_c for generating all frames (by picking a z_c from one of the encoded key frames). Then the path could be drawn such that it passes through the latent space projection $z_g = \{..., z_g^{(t)}, ...\}$ of all input key frames. Let us first consider the simplistic case where only the starting and ending frames are the inputs such that $z_g = \{z_g^{(0)}, z_g^{(T-1)}\}$ (Fig. 1), where T is the total number of frames of the to-be-generated video. The latent path will simply be a line which samples the in-between global motion code $\widehat{z_g^{(t)}}$ such that $\widehat{z_g^{(t)}} = z_g^{(0)}\left(1 - \frac{t}{T-1}\right) + z_g^{(T-1)}\left(\frac{t}{T-1}\right)$. Each video frame could then be constructed by decoding the consecutive global motion code $\widehat{z_g} = \left\{\widehat{z_g^{(0)}}, ..., \widehat{z_g^{(t)}}, ..., \widehat{z_g^{(T-1)}}\right\}$ with the decoder F_D such that the video $v = F_D(z_c, \widehat{z_g})$.

For a three key frames scenario (Fig. 1), a quadratic Bezier curve in the latent space will be required. It is worth pointing out that although the first and last control points of the Bezier curve, $c^{(0)}, c^{(2)}$, lie on the curve, the middle one does not. Hence, the second control point $c^{(1)}$ needs to be computed for the curve to pass through the second key frame $x^{(M_k)}$, where M_k is the time step of the second key frame. This second control point $c^{(1)}$ is computed as in Eq. (1).

$$c^{(1)} = -\frac{c^{(0)}\left(1 - \frac{M_k}{T-1}\right)^2 + c^{(2)}\left(\frac{M_k}{T-1}\right)^2 - z^{(M_k)}}{2\left(1 - \frac{M_k}{T-1}\right)\left(\frac{M_k}{T-1}\right)} \tag{1}$$

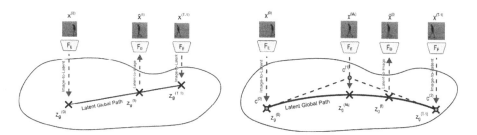

Fig. 1. Illustration of latent paths. The left and right are the latent paths drawn given two and three conditional key frames input respectively.

3.2 Local Motion Pattern

To model the local motion pattern, we propose using a periodic function in the latent space. Here, we have chosen the sine function. Although we will show that using a sine function is possible, it is not robust and requires a specific design in order to work. So, we will show here an architecture which we have found to be usable. That is, it is able to facilitate in the separation of the global and local motions.

Ideal Modeling. Since the original purpose of the periodic function in the latent space is to model the repeating local motion, ideally the local motion codes sampled from this function should be repeated every specific time interval. Therefore, the function should be temporal-based such that the latent local motion $z_l^{(t)} = sin\left(\frac{t}{T}\right)$. Using only one sine curve is too simplistic for modeling. Inspired by the Fourier transformation, we instead propose that there should be multiple sine curves. Internally, the neural network could be expected to combine the output of multiple sine curves (a sine curve for each dimension) to model more complex periodic functions.

In our first attempt, we allow the model to choose the amplitude, frequency and phase shift as in Eq. (2). Specifically for our case, $(z_c, z_g^{(t)}, z_s) = F_E(x^{(t)})$, where z_s is sampled from P_{z_s}. Our encoder now generates codes for the local motion, as shown in Eq. (2):

$$z_l^{(t)} = z_a sin\left(z_b\left(\frac{t}{T}\right) + z_u\right) \tag{2}$$

where $z_s = \{z_a, z_b, z_u\}$ and $sin(\cdot)$ is an element-wise sine function. The reason why the sine curve parameters z_s do not have a temporal component (t) is that the sine curve should remain the same throughout the entire video (i.e. picking a z_s from one of the encoded key frames, similar to how we treat z_c). Regardless, our experiments show that this ideal approach does not quite work as the model simply disregards the contribution from the local motion model. We suspect that the periodic nature of the sine curve could have led to local minima which could have trapped the search for the optimal solution during the training process.

Modeling with Forced Step Observing the deficiency of the ideal model with a number of free parameters, we would like to impose additional constraints, in our alternative model known as "forced steps" (see Fig. 2). This model tries to predict how far in a phase this time step should move with an RNN such that:

$$s^{(t)} = \sigma\left(z_u^{(t)}\right) + s^{(t-1)} \tag{3}$$

$$z_l^{(t)} = z_a sin\left(s^{(t)}\right) \tag{4}$$

where $z_s = \{z_a, z_u^{(t)}\}$ and $\sigma(\cdot)$ is a sigmoid function. Here, the frequency component is dropped. This is because if the model controls which phase is to be sampled for each time step (Fig. 2), effectively it is also controlling the frequency of the curve. We found that this model is capable of separating the global and local motions which we will show later. This solution is based on the assumption that the ideal model experiences difficulties crossing the local minima induced by the sine curves. Instead, we encourage the model to move across the local minima with forced phase steps.

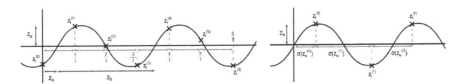

Fig. 2. The left is the ideal model while the right is the forced step model. In contrast to the ideal model which has fixed steps, the forced step model generates a step for each time step.

3.3 Latent Path

One of the key goals of this paper is to utilize a latent path to generate a smooth video given an arbitrary number of input key frames. It is possible that the latent path is immediately drawn based on the number of input key frames initially. For example, given five key frames we draw a quartic Bezier curve. However, this limits the flexibility of the latent path as the number of inputs needs to be known prior. Instead, it is proposed that it is better to use Bezier spline to draw the path. To utilize Bezier spline, we propose two strategies, extension and connection.

Extension. Given a path segment p_A and an additional key frame, we need to smoothly extend the latent path such that it could cross the latent representation of the newly added input key frame image $z_g^{(T_A + T_B - 1)}$, where T_B is the number of frames of the extended path p_B (Fig. 3). In order for the new composite path to be smooth throughout, there must not be sudden changes in the tangents of the path. Obviously, the point that would cause problem in this case is where the path is to extend. To ensure a smooth extension from that point, it is proposed that the extended path p_B be a quadratic Bezier curve and its second control point $c_B^{(1)}$ be computed as follows:

$$c_B^{(1)} = c_A^{(M_{c_A}-1)} + \frac{c_A^{(M_{c_A}-1)} - c_A^{(M_{c_A}-2)}}{\left| c_A^{(M_{c_A}-1)} - c_A^{(M_{c_A}-2)} \right|} \cdot \frac{\left| z_g^{T_A+T_B-1} - c_A^{(M_{c_A}-1)} \right|}{2} \tag{5}$$

where M_{cA} is the number of control points of path segment p_A. Note that since p_A and p_B meet at $z_g^{(T_A-1)}$, $c_B^{(0)} = c_A^{(M_c-1)}$.

Connection. Given two path segments p_A and p_C, we need to smoothly connect the two latent paths by drawing an in-between path p_B. Similar to extension, we need to consider the tangents. However this time, we need to consider tangents at the end of p_A and the start of p_C. We will connect the two latent paths with a cubic Bezier curve (Fig. 3). Its second and third control points could be computed similar to extension as:

$$c_B^{(1)} = c_A^{(M_{c_A}-1)} + \frac{c_A^{(M_{c_A}-1)} - c_A^{(M_{c_A}-2)}}{\left| c_A^{(M_{c_A}-1)} - c_A^{(M_{c_A}-2)} \right|} \cdot \frac{\left| c_A^{(0)} - c_C^{(M_{c_C}-1)} \right|}{2} \tag{6}$$

$$c_B^{(2)} = c_C^{(0)} + \frac{c_C^{(1)} - c_C^{(0)}}{\left| c_C^{(1)} - c_C^{(0)} \right|} \cdot \frac{\left| c_C^{(0)} - c_A^{(M_{c_C}-1)} \right|}{2} \tag{7}$$

Fig. 3. The extensions (left) and connections (right) of latent paths could be achieved by drawing a new path p_B with control points without causing a sudden change at the ends of the paths.

3.4   Proposed Model

We combine all the methods described above to complete our proposed model. In our experimental prototype, the global motion code z_g is computed as in Sect. 3.1. The local motion code z_l is computed as in Sect. 3.2. When we attempt to generate a video, we adopt the strategies in Sect. 3.3. Video frames are generated by the decoder from latent inputs such that a video frame $v^{(t)} = F_D(z_c, \widehat{z_g^{(t)}}, z_l^{(t)})$. The training objective of our proposed VAE model with parameters θ is as follow:

$$J_\theta = \sum_{m=0}^{M_c-1} D_{KL}\left[q_\theta\left(z^{(k^{(m)})}|k^{(m)}\right)||p_z(z)\right] \cdot \lambda_{latent}$$
$$+ E_{q_\theta(z^{(k)}|k)}\left[\sum_{t=0}^{T-1} L_2\left(F_{D_\theta}\left(R\left(z^{(k)}, \frac{t}{T-1}\right)\right), x\right)\right] \cdot \lambda_{rec} \tag{8}$$

where latent vector $z^{(t)}=\{z_c, z_g^{(t)}, z_l^{(t)}\}$, k is the set of key frames, $k^{(m)}$ is the mth key frame, R is a latent function that computes the latent code for each time step and λs are hyperparameters. The former term is the latent loss while the latter term is the reconstruction loss. To obtain $z_u^{(t)}$ for each time step, a string of GRU [13] cells as an RNN is used with the initial state $h_0=\{z_c, z_u^{(0)}\}$. Each GRU cell at time step t will be fed with the tangent of the latent path $z_{\Delta g}^{(t)}$ and the previous prediction $z_u^{(t-1)}$. An illustration of the model is shown in Fig. 4.

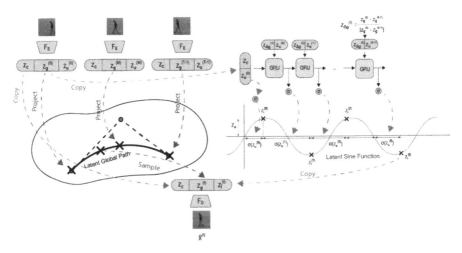

Fig. 4. The proposed model separates the global and local signals via a latent path and a latent sine curve. An encoder-decoder (F_E and F_D) pair is used to project an image to and from the latent space. A string of GRU cells is used to predict $z_u^{(t)}$ for each time step t.

4   Experiments

As our proposed model involves a global motion and a local motion component, we intend to evaluate them separately. The proposed model will be evaluated and compared with MoCoGAN [1] and VGAN [4]. Both MoCoGAN and VGAN models used spatio-temporal convolutional networks as discriminators. However, since the video generated does not have a fixed length here, we use a discriminator with spatial convolutional layers and GRU-based RNN for the temporal connection instead. Here, we also use two datasets in the evaluation, the walking videos in KTH action database [14] and the Weizmann Action database [15]. The KTH walking dataset consists of 75 videos with 25 people walking from left to right and right to left. Given a video length of 15, 11284 samples can be extracted from the dataset. The Weizmann Action dataset consists of 72 videos of 9 people performing 4 actions such as hand-waving and crouching. Given a video length of 15, 2069 samples can be extracted.

4.1 Three Conditional Images

We first evaluate the model given three conditional images, i.e. three input key frames. When evaluating, one of the questions we want to answer is whether the proposed model is able to generate a smooth video given arbitrary number of input frames. This is a question of interest as though models such as MoCoGAN or VGAN could only accept a fixed number of input images, we can still use them to generate video segments given two input key frames then merge all video segments together into a single video. However, it is hypothesized that since the models generate each segment independently, the transition before and after key frames will not be smooth. Thus, it is expected that the proposed model would produce an improved performance over models that do not consider arbitrary number of inputs.

Quantitatively, we make use of four metrics to evaluate the performance of our model. Average content distance (ACD) and mean-square error (MSE) are two common metrics. Nevertheless, since they are more useful in evaluating the content similarity between frames while we are more interested in evaluating the smoothness between frames, we propose two metrics, first-order optical flow distance (OFD) and angular-sensitive smoothness distance (ASD) to evaluate the smoothness of a video.

The OFD metric is defined as in Eq. (9):

$$OFD\left(f^{(t)}\right) = \frac{1}{N_I} \sum_i^{N_I} \left| f_i^{(t+1)} - f_i^{(t-1)} \right| \tag{9}$$

where f is the optical flow map, N_I the number of pixels and i the index of a pixel. OFD approximates the acceleration of pixel movements. The expectation is that this metric could detect sudden movement which may be perceptually viewed as unsmooth. However, the OFD leans towards measuring the change in speed. Two flow changes with the same magnitude, but different directions will be measured similarly. To make the direction carry a stronger influence on the metric, the ASD metric is introduced as in Eq. (10):

$$ASD\left(f^{(t)}\right) = \frac{1}{N_I} \sum_i^{N_I} \left(\frac{\left| f_{\theta_i}^{(t)} - f_{\theta_i}^{(t-1)} \right|}{\pi} + 1 \right) \left| f_{mi}^{(t)} - f_{mi}^{(t-1)} \right| \tag{10}$$

where f_θ is the angles on a flow map and f_m is the magnitudes on a flow map.

To evaluate whether the content is consistent, we followed [1] in adapting the ACD metric as in Eq. (11):

$$ACD\left(I^{(t)}\right) = \sqrt{\sum_c \left(\frac{1}{N_I}\left(\sum_i^{N_I} I_{i,c}^{(t)} - \sum_i^{N_I} I_{i,c}^{(t-1)}\right)\right)^2} \qquad (11)$$

where I is a video frame and c is the number of color channels. The MSE metric is similar to ACD. It compares each frame to the previous frame as in Eq. (12).

$$MSE\left(I^{(t)}\right) = \frac{1}{N_I}\sum_i^{N_I}\left(I_{i,c}^{(t)} - I_{i,c}^{(t-1)}\right)^2 \qquad (12)$$

In our evaluation, we give the proposed model three key frames and use it to generate a video. We evaluate the smoothness of the video by using OFD and ASD to check whether the frames before and after key frames are smooth transitions. Given each key frame with time step t_k, we use OFD at time step t_k and ASD at t_k and t_k+1. To verify the content consistency, we adopt ACD and MSE for each frame consecutively. As shown in Tables 1 and 2, the proposed model has achieved its intended effect on generating a video, that is, smoother, since it generally achieves a better OFD and ASD. However, it does not achieve a better score in terms of content consistency (ACD and MSE) in general. This outcome is expected as GAN architectures generally perform better than VAE in terms of content fidelity. Qualitatively, we can also see that the proposed model could maintain a better smoothness before and after the key frames as shown in Fig. 5.

Table 1. Model scores when conditioned on 3 key frames from the KTH walking dataset.

	OFD	ASD	ACD	MSE
Proposed model	0.03366	0.03385	0.0008766	0.008037
VGAN	0.05214	0.04689	0.0005443	0.007557
MoCoGAN	0.04096	0.03769	0.0006116	0.010060

Table 2. Model scores when conditioned on 3 key frames from the Weizmann dataset.

	OFD	ASD	ACD	MSE
Proposed model	0.01359	0.01629	0.00004677	0.001511
VGAN	0.01599	0.01558	0.00014130	0.001895
MoCoGAN	0.01604	0.01722	0.00011010	0.001661

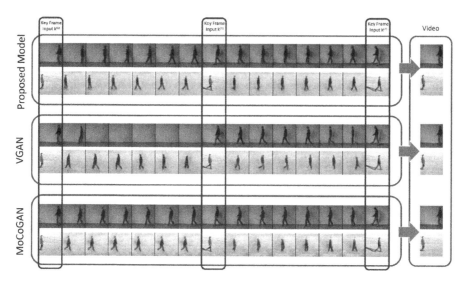

Fig. 5. Results of the three video generation models conditioned on three key frames. Each set contains two videos with the first, eighth and fifteenth frames as the key frames. From top to bottom, the sets represent videos generated by the proposed model, VGAN and MoCoGAN respectively. Readers can visit https://youtu.be/cj-HsAro_Zk for the video demonstration.

4.2   Extending and Connecting Latent Paths

Next, we evaluate the model with different number of input frames, two, three, four and five. For the four and five input key frames, we need to use the latent path strategies mentioned in Sect. 3.3. The results on extending and connecting the latent path are shown in Fig. 6.

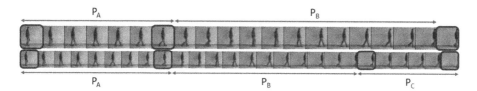

Fig. 6. Results of extending a latent path to pass through a key frame in the latent space (left) and connecting two latent paths by drawing an in-between latent path (right). The dark blue circle indicates the key frame inputs. (Color figure online)

As shown in Fig. 7, the proposed model is generally able to achieve a better smoothness given different number of input key frames. A noticeable exception is when the model is generating with only two key frames. This outcome is expected as the global path modeling only has an advantage when the number of input frames is more than two. This result shows that the latent path is a viable solution to the problem with an arbitrary number of input frames. There seems to be no trend between the number of inputs and the ASD. However, there seems to be a subtle negative correlation between the number of inputs and the OFD. We suspect that the reason is that given more conditional key frames, the in-between frames generated will become more constrained and therefore it will be more likely for the model to be able to generate video frames that could be coherent with all others.

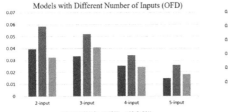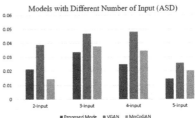

Fig. 7. The results when given different number of input key frames for the different models. The left is evaluated in OFD while the right is evaluated in ASD.

4.3 Separation of Global and Local Motion

To visualize the separation of the global and local motion, we have devised an experiment that manipulates the global and local latent space separately. Given a string of latent vector $z^{(t)} = \{z_c, z_g^{(t)}, z_l^{(t)}\}$, we generate two results where one locks $z_g^{(t)}$ such that $v^{(t)} = F_D(z_c, \widehat{z_g^{(0)}}, z_l^{(t)})$, and the other locks $z_l^{(t)}$ such that $v^{(t)} = F_D(z_c, \widehat{z_g^{(t)}}, z_l^{(0)})$. The results are depicted in Fig. 8. It is shown that our model is able to achieve a separation of the global and local motions. When z_l is locked, the local motion is missing while when z_g is locked, the global motion is missing.

Fig. 8. Video generated with global motion (above) and local motion (below) locked respectively. It can be seen that when global motion is locked, the model tries to keep the person in the same place while still generating the local motion. Readers can visit https://youtu. be/PYGC0jMa9vw for the video demonstration.

We also conduct an experiment to see if the local motion could be tuned to create special effects like a person moonwalking. To achieve that, we multiply the value with $\sigma\left(z_u^{(t)}\right)$ produced by the local motion component described in Sect. 3.2. Effectively, we have scaled the step to make it go further or vice versa. In Fig. 9, we multiply it by 1.5 and 0.5 to make it go faster and slower respectively. The results show that although the person indeed moves faster and slower, there are strong artefacts. To fully utilize local motion tuning for application, further work is needed.

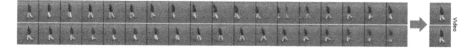

Fig. 9. The result of scaling with $\sigma\left(\mathbf{z}_u^{(t)}\right)$. The outcome is a video where the person walks faster or slower. The model tries to keep the person in the same global position regardless of local motion, but ultimately, the artefact is clearly visible. Readers can visit https://youtu.be/PYGC0jMa9vw for the video demonstration.

5   Conclusion and Future Work

Inspired by the observation that a motion signal could be decomposed into multi-level signals, we proposed a model to materialize our observation and conducted a feasibility study of the idea via decomposing a motion into a global path and a local pattern. We suggested that the global path could be represented as a latent Bezier spline while the local pattern could be represented as a latent sine function. To evaluate the smoothness of the generated video, two measurement metrics were also proposed. Our experiments showed that our proposed model was capable of generating a video given some conditional key frames with general improvement on smoothness. One of the experiments also demonstrated the decomposition of the global and local motion.

In the future, we will expand the number of motion levels to completely model the multi-level motion in representing a rich continuum that spans from the very global motion to the very local motion. This means that a hierarchy of motions could be formed to increase the controllability of the video generation. With human walking as an example, we could control from the movement of the whole body, to the movement of the legs, then to the ankles and further down to the feet, and so on to even more local parts. Instead of just a global motion parented to a local motion, each level of motion would be parented to another motion one level down in general.

References

1. Tulyakov, S., Liu, M.-Y., Yang, X., Kautz, J.: MoCoGAN: decomposing motion and content for video generation. In: CVPR Workshop (2017)
2. Kingma, D.P., Welling, M.: Auto-encoding variational bayes. In: Proceedings of ICLR (2013)
3. Goodfellow, I.J., et al.: Generative adversarial nets. In: Proceedings of NIPS (2014)
4. Vondrick, C., Pirsiavash, H., Torralba, A.: Generating videos with scene dynamics. In: Proceedings of NIPS (2016)
5. Saito, M., Matsumoto, E., Saito, S.: Temporal generative adversarial nets with singular value clipping. In: Proceedings of ICCV (2017)
6. Hochreiter, S., Schmidhuber, J.: Long short-term memory. Neural Comput. **9**(8), 1735–1780 (1997)
7. Mathieu, M., Couprie, C., LeCun, Y.: Deep multi-scale video prediction beyond mean square error. In: Proceedings of ICLR (2016)

8. Walker, J., Marino, K., Gupta, A., Hebert, M.: Video forecasting by generating pose futures. In: Proceedings of ICCV (2017)

9. Liang, X., Lee, L., Dai, W., Xing, E.P.: Dual motion GAN for future-flow embedded video prediction. In: Proceedings of ICCV (2017)

10. Liu, Z., Yeh, R.A., Tang, X., Liu, Y., Agarwala, A.: Video frame synthesis using deep voxel flow. In: Proceedings of ICCV (2017)

11. Chan, C., Ginosar, S., Zhou, T., Efros, A.A.: Everybody dance now. In: ECCV Workshop (2018)

12. Wang, T.-C., et al.: Video-to-video synthesis. In: Proceedings of NIPS (2018)

13. Cho, K., et al.: Learning phrase representations using RNN encoder-decoder for statistical machine translation. In: Proceedings of International Conference on Empirical Methods in NLP (2014)   ·

14. Schuldt, C., Laptev, I., Caputo, B.: Recognizing human actions: a local SVM approach. In: Proceedings of International Conference on Pattern Recognition (2004)

15. Gorelick, L., Blank, M., Shechtman, E., Irani, M., Basri, R.: Actions as space-time shapes. In: Proceedings of ICCV (2005)

Evaluating the Performance of Virtual Reality Navigation Techniques for Large Environments

Kurtis Danyluk$^{(\boxtimes)}$ and Wesley Willett

University of Calgary, Calgary, AB, Canada
{ktdanylu,wesley.willett}@ucalgary.ca

Abstract. We present results from two studies comparing the performance of four different navigation techniques (flight, teleportation, world-in-miniature, and 3D cone-drag) and their combinations in large virtual reality map environments. While prior work has individually examined each of these techniques in other settings, our study presents the first direct comparison between them in large open environments, as well as one of the first comparisons in the context of current-generation virtual reality hardware. Our first study compared common techniques (flight, teleportation, and world-in-miniature) for search and navigation tasks. A follow-up study compared these techniques against 3D cone drag, a direct-manipulation navigation technique used in contemporary tools like Google Earth VR. Our results show the strength of flight as a stand-alone navigation technique, but also highlight five specific ways in which viewers can combine teleportation, world-in-miniature, and 3D cone drag with flight, drawing on the relative strengths of each technique to compensate for the weaknesses of others.

Keywords: Human computer interaction (HCI) · Virtual reality ·
Digital maps · Navigation

1 Introduction

Recent advances in consumer-grade immersive virtual reality (VR) technology have made it increasingly easy to create large, open, and detailed virtual environments. Many fields already use these systems to accurately portray information that is challenging to present on traditional 2D flat displays. For example, urban informatics, geology, and infrastructure planning all benefit from the detailed and flexible perspectives provided by immersive virtual reality.

However, existing work has rarely compared navigation techniques for large spaces, instead focusing on novel navigation techniques like GiAnt [2] and cube-maps [12]. Those evaluations that do exist [6] consider a limited set of techniques [9] or focus on small virtual worlds [3]. Moreover, contemporary navigation techniques like 3D cone drag [8], which have been designed for large environments, remain largely unexamined in the research literature.

© Springer Nature Switzerland AG 2019
M. Gavrilova et al. (Eds.): CGI 2019, LNCS 11542, pp. 203–215, 2019.
https://doi.org/10.1007/978-3-030-22514-8_17

We present a direct comparison of four navigation techniques—flight, teleportation, world-in-miniature, and 3D cone drag (Figure 1)—in large immersive VR environments and discuss how they can be combined. To compare these approaches, we developed a test-bed that supports all four techniques and conducted studies in which participants performed navigation and search tasks within a virtual mountainous environment. We examined when each technique performed best, which techniques viewers preferred to use, and how their navigation behavior changed when using each technique, especially when they had access to several. Based on our evaluations, we contribute a comparison of flight, teleportation, world-in-miniature, and 3D cone drag that showcases the all-around effectiveness of flight, as well as the strengths and weaknesses of the other techniques. We also examine five specific ways in which participants combined these navigation techniques to overcome their individual weaknesses.

2   Related Work

Our work builds on a variety of prior examinations of interactive navigation in virtual reality environments, including early work on VR camera control, as well as more recent techniques for navigating in large environments. Ware and Osborne [18] introduced and evaluated several navigation metaphors, including techniques they referred to as "flying vehicle control" and "scene-in-hand". Due to the limitations of these early systems, scenes were limited to single objects and camera orientation was entirely controlled as part of the navigation technique, rather than by the viewer's head motion. Later work, including Stoakley et al.'s "Virtual reality on a WIM" [16] introduced worlds-in-miniature, which allowed viewers to navigate by manipulating a token placed in a miniature recreation of the scene. Much like earlier work, Stoakley et al.'s system still relied on token orientation rather than the viewer's head position to provide camera orientation.

In contrast, most contemporary VR systems use the viewer's head position to provide camera orientation, and rely on navigation techniques like flight or teleportation to change the viewer's position in the scene. Additionally, contemporary systems also use techniques like automatic scaling [2] or cubemaps [17] [12] to adjust navigation speed and reduce disorientation. Techniques like 3D cone drag [8] also extend the direct-manipulation metaphor of scene-in-hand to modern VR systems, allowing viewers to grab, manipulate, and move the scene.

Physical locomotion for navigation in VR is another popular navigation method, with many implementations of walking [15,19]. However, because of the large scale of map-like environments, most simple realizations of locomotion in VR are inadequate in large scenes. More complex imlplementations, such as redirected walking [14] or redirected teleportation [11], allow locomotion to function within large virtual spaces, but do not reduce the physical effort required to walk across a potentially kilometers-long scene. Scaling alternatives such as GulliVR [10] offer a solution to this problem, but drastically change the viewers' perspective of a scene. Other locomotion alternatives, such as virtual surfboards [7] or finger-walking [19] use locomotion as a controller for another navigation technique, normally flight.

Fig. 1. The four different VR navigation techniques: (a) flight, (b) teleport, (c) world-in-miniature, (d) 3D cone drag.

Early comparisons of basic flight and teleportation in relatively small environments show that teleportation can be faster than flight but causes greater disorientation [4]. Moreover, a large body of work suggests that constant velocity flight is less disorienting than accelerated flight, regardless of velocity [4]. However, there exists little work that directly compares techniques other then flight and teleportation [6].

3   Navigation in Large VR Spaces

Large VR spaces are a challenge because their sheer size rules out navigation techniques like locomotion, which most closely resemble navigation in the physical world. In large spaces, origins and destinations may be far apart, and viewers need mechanisms for transitioning these distances quickly yet precisely. Here, we introduce four common yet contrasting techniques we chose to compare in our studies.

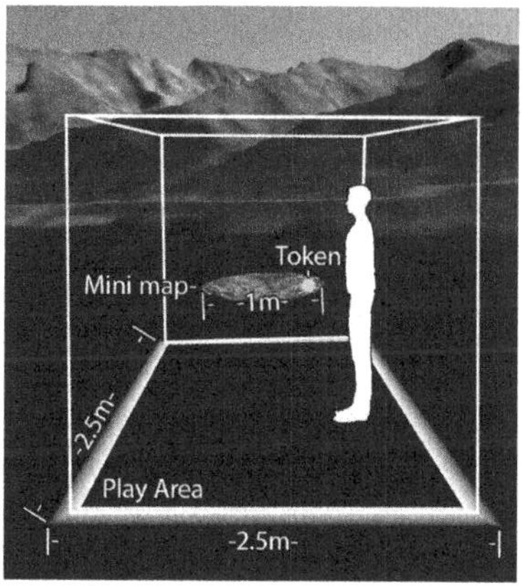

Flight is one of the earliest navigation techniques for VR [18]. When using this technique, a viewer moves through virtual environments as if they were controlling a flying vehicle, like a helicopter (Fig. 1a). Flight involves a smooth, predictable, continuous, and reversible translation.

Fig. 2. The 2.5 m play area and 1 m diameter mini-map configuration used in our test environment.

World-in-miniature allows the viewer to change their position by manipulating a version of themselves in a miniature version of the scene (Fig. 1c). We use a 1 m diameter mini-map, located at the center of the viewer's play area (Fig. 2).

3D Cone Drag allows the viewer to directly manipulate the scene as though they were directly grabbing and dragging the landscape. We examine 3D Cone

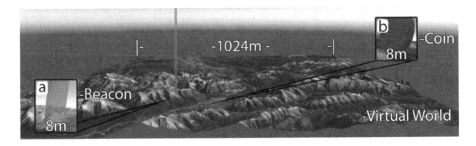

Fig. 3. Overview of the entire virtual world used during the study tasks. Insets show beacons (a) used for navigation tasks and coins (b) used for search tasks (Color figure online)

Drag because of its prominent use in Google Earth VR [8], a popular commercial application which involves exactly the type of large scene navigation tasks that we are interested in exploring.

Teleportation allows the viewer to specify a point in space and then directly and instantly move to it (Fig. 1b). The most obvious advantage of teleportation is that transit is instant. Further, because there are no intermediate transitions, users do not experience any velocity in navigation, avoiding a common cause of cybersickness.

Of these techniques, world-in-miniature requires an additional navigation aid–in this case, a mini-map showing a small-scale, version of the surrounding environment. However, mini-maps also provide an alternative perspective that can help viewers evaluate distances and see terrain outside of their immediate field of view. In particular, mini-maps may be a useful navigation aid when using teleportation, where they make it possible for viewers to teleport to parts of the virtual world that are not directly visible from their current location.

4   Studies

We conducted a pair of studies that examine the trade-offs between these techniques and how viewers might combine them. In both studies, we compared (1) which techniques allowed viewers to navigate and search more quickly in large virtual environments and (2) how each technique impacted viewers' sense of orientation. We also characterized (3) viewers qualitative preferences for and experiences with these four techniques, and (4) examined how viewers combined the approaches to compensate for their strengths and weaknesses.

4.1   Study Setup

Test Environment. We developed our study environment for the HTC Vive VR headset. The implementation used Unity 5.6 with C# and relied on elevation data from Amazon Web Services and satellite imagery from Bing Maps.

Using these we created large virtual worlds at scales between 1:78271 and 1:4.7. Our test map included a 124 km × 124 km region centered around the hamlet of Exshaw, Alberta. This area is situated at the edge of the Canadian Rockies, near Banff National Park, and features a diverse mix of flat, rolling, and mountainous terrain. We rendered this region at a scale of roughly 1:120, resulting in a 1024 m × 1024 m virtual terrain (Fig. 3). Within this virtual world, the viewer occupied a 2.5 m × 2.5 m play area (mirroring the size of the physical test area) within which they could move and interact freely (Fig. 2).

4.2   Tasks and Measures

Tasks. We asked participants to perform two different kinds of common spatial wayfinding and orientation tasks [13]. These included navigation tasks which required viewers to move as quickly as they could to a known location, and search tasks which required them to explore the virtual world in order to locate a hidden object. These are similar to the tasks used by Darken and Peterson [13]. Each trial consisted of one task.

Navigation tasks involved moving from a starting position to a large, clearly visible beacon placed at a random location in the environment (Fig. 3a). The beacons also appeared as bright yellow pins on the mini-map.

Search tasks involved finding and collecting a large red coin (Fig. 3b) placed randomly in the environment. Coins were not marked on the mini-map.

Measures. During both studies we tracked participants' position in the virtual environment We also collected timing data for each task, along with detailed notes on participants' behaviors and vocalizations.

To gauge participants' spatial awareness, we asked them to complete a point-back test immediately after they finished each task. Upon reaching a beacon or coin, the interface prompted participants to point back towards the location of the previous coin or beacon. We measured point-back error by calculating the acute horizontal angle between where the viewers pointed and the actual position of the previous beacon/coin.

After the study, participants completed a 5-point Likert survey rating the difficulty and enjoyability of the navigation techniques. Finally, we asked participants to discuss their favorite and least favorite navigation techniques.

4.3   Study 1: Flight, Teleportation, and World–in–Miniature

Study 1 compared flight, teleportation, and world-in-miniature. We also evaluated the effect of a mini-map in the flight and teleportation conditions and examined participants' behavior when they could combine all of the techniques.

Participants and Procedure. We recruited 10 Participants (2 female/8 male, ages 22–47). Their VR experience ranged between none (7), extensive gaming (2), and development experience (1). We refer to these participants using codes P1–P10.

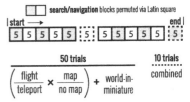

Participants performed 5 repetitions of the two task types in 6 different experimental conditions for a total of 60 trials. They alternated between 5-trial blocks of search and navigation tasks. In blocks 1–5 and 7–11 participants alternated between 5 different experimental conditions— flight and teleportation (each with/without mini-map) plus world-in-miniature. Blocks 6 and 12 used a combined interface where participants had access to flight, teleportation, world-in-miniature, and the mini-map simultaneously. We permuted both task and condition using a Latin square design. Participants could rest between each block, and we asked them to remove the VR headset and take an enforced break after every three blocks. Participants also performed a 10-minute training block where the experimenter familiarized them with all the navigation techniques and how to perform each task. After all the tasks, participants debriefed with the experimenter and completed a follow-up questionnaire. This took roughly 1 h to complete.

Quantitative Results. Due to growing concern in a variety of fields about the use of null hypothesis significance testing [5] we analyze our results using estimation techniques and report effect sizes with confidence intervals (CI) rather than p-value statistics. This reporting methodology is consistent with recent APA recommendations [1]. We first computed average scores for each participant, then computed averages and 95% confidence intervals using the aggregate scores, applying a Bonferroni correction to control for multiple comparisons. We also computed pairwise differences between conditions, again using 95% confidence intervals with a Bonferroni correction. Our complete analysis as well as additional explanatory figures can be viewed as supplementary material.[1]

Mini-Map. Although we included variations of flight and teleport both with and without a mini-map, the inclusion of a mini-map had little impact on task performance. For navigation tasks, pairwise comparisons (Fig. 4) showed no differences in task duration or point-back error between the map and no-map variations for either flight or teleportation. For search tasks, we only observed one clear case in which the map appeared to impact performance. Participants took an average of 16.5 s (CI = [14.3,18.9]) to complete search tasks while using flight with no-map, compared to 21.8 s (CI = [18.5,25.8]) with a map. We saw no clear difference in point-back error across any of the variations, and no clear interactions between the mini-map and any of the interaction techniques. In light of this, we combined data from the map and no-map conditions in all subsequent analysis of Study 1.

---

[1] https://www.dropbox.com/s/muyzsbge8zlwpi1/Submission%20Package.zip?dl=0.

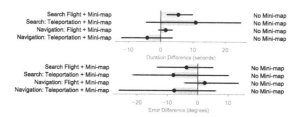

Fig. 4. Pairwise comparison of task duration (top) and point-back error (bottom) for flight and teleportation with and without a mini-map. Error Bars show 95% CIs.

Fig. 5. Pairwise comparisons of task duration between conditions for navigation tasks (left) and search tasks (right) in Study 1. All error bars show 95% CIs.

Task Duration. Participants using flight took an average of 15.9 s (CI = [12.1, 24.6]) to complete navigation trials and 19.1 s (CI = [15.5,23.1]) to complete search trials. World-in-miniature was slower, averaging 18.5 s (CI = [13.0,28.1]) for navigation trials and 37.0 s (CI = [28.4,50.8]) for search trials. Teleportation was also slower, averaging 21.1 s (CI = [16.2,27.3]) for navigation tasks and 56.9 s (CI = [40.6,84.3]) for search tasks.

Pairwise comparisons (Fig. 5) show that flight was faster than either teleportation or world-in-miniature for navigation tasks, but show no clear difference between teleportation and world-in-miniature. For search tasks, flight outperformed other approaches by a considerable margin, and world-in-miniature clearly outperformed teleportation. Although flight performed best, 3 of 10 participants noted that they felt world-in-miniature was as fast or faster than flight, even though they performed more slowly with it.

Orientation. Point-back error was comparable between flight and world-in-miniature for both task types. In navigation trials the average point-back error for flight was 16.9° (CI = [10.0,30.8]) while world-in-miniature averaged 21.1° (CI = [14.7,27.9]). For search trials flight averaged 17.7° (CI = [13.2,23.5]) and world-in-miniature 21.7° (CI = [12.7,32.5]). Teleportation introduced much more error, averaging 25.5° (CI = [17.4,38.0]) in navigation trials and 38.2° (CI = [27.5,48.7]) in search. Pairwise comparisons (Fig. 6) show similarity between flight and world-in-miniature and their divergence from teleportation.

Fig. 6. Pairwise comparisons of point-back error between conditions for navigation tasks (left) and search tasks (right) in Study 1. All error bars show 95% CIs.

Fig. 7. Pairwise comparisons of task duration (left) and point-back error (right) for Study 2. Error bars show 95% CIs.

4.4   Study 2: Comparison with 3D Cone Drag

The second study compared the techniques from the first study (flight, teleportation, and world-in-miniature) with 3D cone drag, the navigation technique used by Google Earth VR [7].

Participants and Procedure. We recruited 8 participants (2 female/6 male, ages 22–43), balancing four repeat participants (P6–P10) from Study 1, with four new participants (P11–14).

Because differences between the navigation techniques were more pronounced for search tasks, we did not include navigation tasks in Study 2. Instead, participants completed 50 search trials split across 10 blocks. To capture more data about the new condition while reducing participant fatigue, we biased the number of blocks allocated to 3D cone drag (4 blocks) and flight (2 blocks) and included only one block each of teleport and world-in-miniature to serve as training for the combined condition. We permuted block order using a Latin Square. To explore how participants combined all four techniques, we included two combined blocks at the end of the study.

As in Study 1, participants had the opportunity to rest between each block, and we asked them to remove the VR headset and take an enforced break after 4 blocks. We also used the same pre- and post-study procedures as in Study 1.

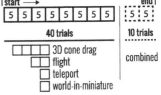

Task Duration. Participants performed the best with flight, taking an average of 19.2 s (CI = [16.3,23.5]) to complete tasks. This was faster than world-in-miniature which took on average 26.5 s (CI = [22.6,31.9]), 3D cone drag which took on average 31.0 s (CI = [24.7,38.4]) and teleportation which took on average 49.7 s (CI = [40.3,58.3]). Pairwise comparisons (Fig. 7-left) show that flight clearly outperformed 3D cone drag, world-in-miniature had comparable performance to 3D cone drag, and 3D cone drag outperformed teleportation.

Orientation. Participants again performed best with flight with an average of 16.3° (CI = [11.5,20.9]) of point-back error. This was close to world-in-miniature which had an average of 17.5° (CI = [13.1,21.9]) of error. 3D cone drag had an average of 25.3° (CI = [17.8,37.6]) of error which outperformed teleportation which had an average of 32.2° (CI = [27.7,36.8]) of error. Pairwise comparisons (Fig. 7-right) show that participants were consistently more accurate when using flight than 3D cone drag.

5 Discussion

Overall, participants found flight much easier to use than any other individual technique and preferred to use it when possible. However, participants also highlighted distinct advantages of each of the other techniques and frequently combined techniques to leverage their respective strengths.

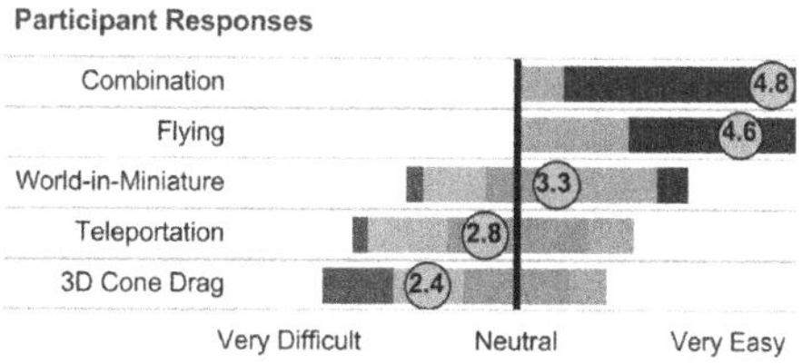

Participant Responses

Fig. 8. Likert responses on participants perceived difficulty of techniques. Circles show mean score. Staggered bars show stacked responses offset with positive responses to the right of the reference line and negative to the left.

5.1 Participant Feedback

Flight. Overall, participants articulated a strong preference for flight and found it very easy to use (Fig. 8). In Study 1, 7 participants rated flight as their favorite while 1 rated it as least favorite. In Study 2, five participants rated flight as their favorite and 0 as least favorite. Overall, participants found flight intuitive to use and effective at all tasks. The only complaints were that it could be nauseating at higher velocities and that movement could be a bit slow. P5 and P6 noted that they felt immersed in the environment while using flight.

World-in-Miniature. Participants were more divided in their opinion on world-in-miniature and opinions varied on whether it was easy or difficult (Fig. 8). This matches our study results where world-in-miniature ranked near the middle on both performance measures. In Study 1, 3 participants rated world-in-miniature as their favorite and 3 as least favorite. In Study 2, 1 participant rated it as their favorite if combined with flight and 2 as least favorite. Participants liked that they could use their whole body to control the token and found it to be a fast method for gaining an overview of the scene. However, they also found that precise control was challenging and participants would often spend a lot of time struggling with fine-grained navigation.

Teleportation. Participants disliked when they were forced to use teleportation and found it difficult to use (Fig. 8). This matches our study results that consistently found teleportation to perform poorly compared to other navigation techniques. In Study 1, 6 participants rated teleportation as their least favorite and 0 as favorite. In Study 2, 1 participant ranked teleportation combined with flight as their favorite and 2 participants ranked it as their least favorite. Participants felt that it was ill-suited for the tasks they were asked to perform. The main reason for this was that participants found it difficult to gain an overview of the scene. P8 and P12 expressed that teleportation—by forcing them to teleport up to high points on the mountains to survey the map for coins—felt that more like exploring a game world than the other two techniques. However, the instantaneous nature of teleportation for line-of-sight movements made it attractive as a supplementary technique.

3D Cone Drag. Participants responses to 3D cone drag were mixed but participants generally preferred other navigation techniques when given the choice (Fig. 8). Participants' difficulty rating for the technique was surprising, since 3D cone drag performed comparably to world-in-miniature in both performance measures but participants still ranked it as much more difficult. One participant ranked it as their favorite technique and 4 as least favorite. Participants liked that 3d cone drag was very precise, allowing for fine movements. Several participants found that using the technique was very fun and made them feel like "Tarzan or Spiderman" (P13). However, when grabbing from far away, some participants found that the velocity was too fast and could be nauseating. Two participants also found that the repeated arm motions were tedious and tiring to use for longer periods.

5.2   Combinations

Interestingly, when participants in our studies had access to all the techniques simultaneously, they tended to combine techniques to address the relative weaknesses of individual approaches. We observed five unique combinations of techniques across the two studies (Fig. 9) and suggest some combination guidelines.

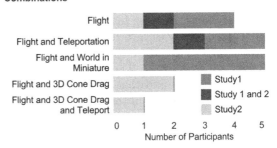

Fig. 9. Number of participants who used each combination of navigation techniques by study.

Teleportation + Flight. Five total participants combined these approaches, using teleportation for rapid, long-distance travel that might otherwise be tedious. Participants would fly directly up into the air to get a good view of the scene and their target, teleport as close to the destination as possible, then fly the remaining distance.

World-in-Miniature + Flight. Similarly, 5 participants used world-in-miniature to cover large distances, before shifting to flight for small precision movements. Participants would often move upward to get a good overview of the scene using world-in-miniature then use it to get as close as possible to their target, before shifting to flight for the final more difficult movements.

3D Cone Drag + Flight. In our second study, participants used 3D cone drag in a similar way—first moving up to gain an overview of the scene and then grabbing to move most of the way to their target before flying the last bit.

3D Cone Drag + Teleportation + Flight. One participant combined three techniques to great effect, using 3D cone drag to move up to a better vantage point, and then combining teleportation and flight to get close.

In all of these cases, participants used flight mostly for precise movements, while relying on teleportation, world-in-miniature, and 3D cone drag for longer transits across the environment. Participants found world-in-miniature and 3D cone drag especially useful for moving upward quickly to obtain an overview of the scene. Even when given access to all techniques, 5 of the 14 participants still relied exclusively on flight.

Pairing Navigation Techniques Effectively. Navigation in large VR environments requires the capacity for both precise local movements and large, quick movements through the scene. Mechanisms for obtaining an overview of the environment are also particularly valuable, especially when environments include complex terrain or obstructions. Many navigation techniques fit several of these three qualifications. For example, flight can be used for high precision movement and can easily be used to obtain an overview, making it the most reliable single technique out of those we evaluated. However, when used for long, protracted movements, it (as well as the other continuous techniques) may trigger nausea or discomfort. As a result, pairing flight with discrete teleportation and/or a continuous technique like world-in-miniature or 3D cone drag allows viewers to navigate efficiently and reducing their risk of disorientation.

6   Conclusion

When working in a large immersive virtual environment every navigation technique has its own strengths and weaknesses. We have highlighted some of these challenges and discussed how combinations can counteract technique-specific weaknesses and greatly increase user power and freedom. When considering which techniques to support in a system, designers confronted with large open environments will typically want to include some variant of flight (the most versatile stand-alone technique). However, complementing flight with techniques that support more rapid movement or easier access to overviews has the potential to create a more satisfying viewer experience.

Acknowledgement. We acknowledge the support of the Natural Sciences and Engineering Research Council of Canada (NSERC) [RGPIN-2016-04564] as well as our colleagues who helped test and give feedback on the techniques and paper.

References

1. Publication Manual of the American Psychological Association, 6th edn. American Psychological Association, Washington, D.C. (2017)
2. Argelaguet, F., Maignant, M.: GiAnt: stereoscopic-compliant multi-scale navigation in VEs. In: ACM VRST, pp. 269–277 (2016). https://doi.org/10.1145/2993369.2993391
3. Bowman, D.A., Johnson, D.B., Hodges, L.F.: Testbed evaluation of virtual environment interaction techniques. Presence: Teleoperators Virtual Environ. **10**, 75–95 (2001). https://doi.org/10.1162/105474601750182333
4. Bowman, D.A., Koller, D., Hodges, L.F.: Travel in immersive virtual environments: an evaluation of viewpoint motion control techniques. In: IEEEVR, pp. 45–52 (1997)
5. Cumming, G.: The new statistics: why and how. Psychol. Sci. **25**(1), 7–29 (2014)
6. Jankowski, J., Hachet, M.: Advances in interaction with 3D environments. In: Computer Graphics Forum, vol. 34, pp. 152–190. Wiley Online Library (2015)
7. Wang, J., Lindeman, R.W.: Comparing isometric and elastic surfboard interfaces for leaning-based travel in 3D virtual environments. In: IEEE 3DUI, pp. 31–38. IEEE (2012). https://doi.org/10.1109/3DUI.2012.6184181
8. Käser, D.P., et al.: The making of Google Earth VR. In: ACM SIGGRAPH 2017 Talks, pp. 63:1–63:2. ACM (2017). https://doi.org/10.1145/3084363.3085094
9. Kopper, R., Ni, T., Bowman, D.A., Pinho, M.: Design and evaluation of navigation techniques for multiscale virtual environments. IEEEVR **2006**, 175–182 (2006). https://doi.org/10.1109/VR.2006.47
10. Krekhov, A., Cmentowski, S., Emmerich, K., Masuch, M., Krüger, J.: GulliVR. In: CHI PLAY, pp. 243–256. ACM Press (2018). https://doi.org/10.1145/3242671.3242704
11. Liu, J., Parekh, H., Al-Zayer, M., Folmer, E.: Increasing walking in VR using redirected teleportation. In: ACM UIST, pp. 521–529 (2018). https://doi.org/10.1145/3242587.3242601
12. McCrae, J., Mordatch, I., Glueck, M., Khan, A.: Multiscale 3D navigation. In: I3D, pp. 7–14. ACM (2009). https://doi.org/10.1145/1507149.1507151
13. Montello, D.R.: Spatial cognition and architectural space: research perspectives. Architect. Des., 74–79 (2014). https://doi.org/10.1002/ad.1811
14. Peck, T.C., Fuchs, H., Whitton, M.C.: The design and evaluation of a large-scale real-walking locomotion interface. IEEE TVCG **18**(7), 1053–1067 (2012). https://doi.org/10.1109/TVCG.2011.289
15. Slater, M., Usoh, M., Steed, A.: Taking steps: the influence of a walking technique on presence in virtual reality. ACM TOCHI **2**, 201–219 (1995). https://doi.org/10.1145/210079.210084

16. Stoakley, R., Conway, M.J., Pausch, R.: Virtual reality on a WIM: interactive worlds in miniature. In: ACM SIGCHI, pp. 265–272 (1995). https://doi.org/10.1145/223904.223938

17. Trindade, D.R., Raposo, A.B.: Improving 3D navigation in multiscale environments using Cubemap-based techniques. In: ACM SAC, pp. 1215–1221 (2011). https://doi.org/10.1145/1982185.1982454

18. Ware, C., Osborne, S.: Exploration and virtual camera control in virtual three dimensional environments. SIGGRAPH Comput. Graph., 175–183 (1990). https://doi.org/10.1145/91394.91442

19. Yan, Z., Lindeman, R.W., Dey, A.: Let your fingers do the walking: a unified approach for efficient short-, medium-, and long-distance travel in VR. In: IEEE 3DUI, pp. 27–30 (2016). https://doi.org/10.1109/3DUI.2016.7460027

HMD-TMO: A Tone Mapping Operator for 360° HDR Images Visualization for Head Mounted Displays

Ific Goudé[1(✉)], Rémi Cozot[1], and Francesco Banterle[2]

[1] Univ Rennes, CNRS, IRISA, Rennes, France
ific.goude@irisa.fr
[2] Visual Computing Lab, ISTI-CNR, Pisa, Italy

Abstract. We propose a Tone Mapping Operator, denoted HMD-TMO, dedicated to the visualization of 360° High Dynamic Range images on Head Mounted Displays. The few existing studies about this topic have shown that the existing Tone Mapping Operators for classic 2D images are not adapted to 360° High Dynamic Range images. Consequently, several dedicated operators have been proposed. Instead of operating on the entire 360° image, they only consider the part of the image currently viewed by the user. Tone mapping a part of the 360° image is less challenging as it does not preserve the global luminance dynamic of the scene. To cope with this problem, we propose a novel tone mapping operator which takes advantage of both a view-dependant tone mapping that enhances the contrast, and a Tone Mapping Operator applied to the entire 360° image that preserves global coherency. Furthermore, we present a subjective study to model lightness perception in a Head Mounted Display.

Keywords: Head Mounted Display · High Dynamic Range · Tone Mapping Operator · 360° image

1 Introduction

Due to the growth of Virtual Reality (VR) technologies over the last years, the visualization of 360° images has become common. 360° images can have a higher dynamic range than classic 2D images. When considering natural outdoor images, the sun can arise in certain zones of the image while dark shadows can appear in other zones. High Dynamic Range (HDR) cameras are now used to capture the whole dynamic of a scene without any loss of information, thereby providing realistic panoramas. The main issue is that all the manufactured Head Mounted Displays (HMDs) still have Standard Dynamic Range (SDR) displays, which prevents them from displaying all the dynamic range of HDR images. To appreciate HDR contents through standard displays, the well known process of

Supported by the ANR project ANR-17-CE23-0020.

M. Gavrilova et al. (Eds.): CGI 2019, LNCS 11542, pp. 216–227, 2019.
https://doi.org/10.1007/978-3-030-22514-8_18

Tone Mapping is used to get a limited range corresponding to SDR displays. Many Tone Mapping Operators (TMOs) exist and can be divided into two main groups (global and local) and are often based on how the human perceives lightness. Each TMO can be more appropriated for a particular type of image and some user studies (see Sect. 2) have been conducted to determine which one is a better candidate for 360° images. These studies show that there is no preferred TMO, and emphasizes on the necessity of developing one dedicated to HMD. For this purpose, two TMOs have been proposed in the literature (see Sect. 2). There are several different approaches to the problem of tone mapping a 360° HDR image. One of them is to consider the content overall, the 360° image is processed at once, toward its entire dynamic range. The obtained result is globally coherent but, when considering a viewport of the entire 360° image, the contrast is reduced. However, as the user can only watch a limited part of the 360° image at a time, a TMO may be applied to the current viewport. Thus, the viewport contrast is enhanced while the global coherency is lost.

To overcome this problems, we propose a method that takes into account the results of two TMOs: one applied to the entire 360° image, and the other to the current viewport. As will be explained later, the viewport TMO provides a better contrast, while the global TMO preserves the spatial coherency. The main contributions of this paper are: (1) a subjective evaluation to model lightness perception on an HMD; (2) a novel TMO for 360° HDR images that ensures a spatial coherency and enhances contrasts by combining the luminances (physical quantity of light) provided by these two TMOs.

After introducing in Sect. 2 related works on TMOs dedicated to 360° images visualization on HMD, we present the user study we conducted to model lightness perception (subjective perception of light by the human eye) in Sect. 3. As a result, we show that the perception model of the lightness on a classic 2D display is still valid on an HMD. Then, we describe in details our HMD-TMO in Sect. 4. Next, in Sect. 5, we comment on our results and discuss the efficiency of our approach. Finally, Sect. 6 concludes the paper and presents some research avenues for future work.

2   Related Work

Two approaches have been considered to visualize 360° HDR images on HMDs. The first consists in applying existing TMOs to the entire 360° image and display the result on the HMD. Some studies performed a comparison of many TMOs for many 360° HDR images in order to find the most appropriated TMO. As for the second approach, a new TMO is proposed, it considers the specific visualization conditions on an HMD by applying a TMO to the viewport only. The first comparison of existing TMOs for 360° images using a subjective evaluation has been run by Perrin *et al.* [1]. However, none of the evaluated TMOs show a clear increase of perceived quality. Melo *et al.* [2] have ran another user study to compare four different TMOs on five 360° HDR images and found similar results. So, we cannot rely on existing TMOs in the case of visualization of 360° HDR images on HMD, a specific operator has to be developed. Yu [3] has adapted an existing operator to propose a TMO that takes advantage of the particularity of visualization on HMD. The main contribution was first to take into account the fact that a user only looks at a limited part of the 360° image at a time, and second to simulate the light and dark adaption of human vision to provide smooth transitions between successive views. When compared to previous evaluations, instead of applying the TMO to the entire 360° image, Yu's applies a TMO only to the current viewport. He has adapted the Photographic Tone Reproduction operator [4] accordingly to the specific key value (log-average luminance) of the viewport. Indeed, the key value can significantly change from a view to another. To prevent flickering, Yu proposed to smooth the key value between successive views to coarsely reproduce the human eye adaptation behavior. Cutchin and Li [5] proposed a method that performs a tone mapping on each viewport independently depending on its luminance histogram. The viewport histograms are divided into four groups corresponding to different TMOs. Authors noticed popping effects that happen when two successive views belong to different groups: as the TMO is different, the image shifts dramatically. Both methods benefit from view dependency on an HMD and provide a better perceptible quality, but they still present some limits we want to overcome. These two methods only perform a global operation on the viewport without worrying about the spatial coherency of the entire 360° image. We propose a method that takes advantage of the viewport dependent operation with smooth transitions between successive viewports to ensure a good contrast while maintaining a global coherency considering the luminance of the entire 360° image. Our method implement the logarithm of the luminance to mimic the human perception of the lightness. To ensure the validity of this representation in case of visualization on HMD, we conducted a subjective evaluation that models the human perception.

3   Lightness Perception on HMD

For classic 2D displays in a controled visualization environment, the lightness is modelled as the logarithm of the luminance. This result comes from Weber and Fechner [6] studies about lightness perception, and many TMOs are based on this work. We will show, thanks to a subjective evaluation, that this result holds for HMDs.

3.1   The Lightness Perception Model

Weber showed that the human capacity to distinguish a stimulus from the background is linearly proportional to the background luminance. In other words, the lighter the background L, the higher the difference ΔL should be (between stimulus and background) to perceive the stimulus. This ratio is commonly known as the Just Noticeable Difference (JND):

$$JND = \frac{\Delta L}{L} = k, \tag{1}$$

with ΔL the luminance difference between the stimulus and the background (in cd/m^2), L the background luminance (in cd/m^2) and k a constant (around 0.01 for traditional visualization condition on a 2D display [7]). Fechner integrated Weber's result to obtain the response of the visual system based on the luminance transducer:

$$\frac{dR}{dl}(L) = \frac{1}{\Delta L(L)}, \tag{2}$$

$$R(L) = \int_0^L \frac{1}{\Delta L(l)}dl = \frac{1}{k}ln(L), \tag{3}$$

where R is the lightness response for a given luminance L, and ΔL is actually the perceived difference measured by Weber's experiment. Accordingly, the subjective perception of lightness is assumed to be the logarithm response to the physical luminance.

3.2 User Study

In our experiment, our objective was to reproduce as closely as possible the Weber's experiment while following the CIECAM recommendations [8]. The CIECAM suggests a circular stimulus with a radius between 2° and 4° to match with the foveal vision. The background has an achromatic color with a radius of 20° to match with the peripheral vision. Finally, the surround field encompasses the rest of the vision field (see Fig. 1). Indeed, in case of visualization on HMD, the black plastic structure around the displays is interpreted as the surround. Recall that the CIECAM model has been determined for a background covering a 20° vision for a classic display, while this angle corresponds to all of the Field of View (FoV) of the HMD. We consider a stimulus of 4°, a background covering all the FoV of the used HMD (about 100°), and the surround field is ignored.

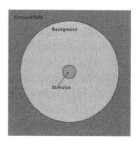

Fig. 1. CIECAM conditions recommendations.

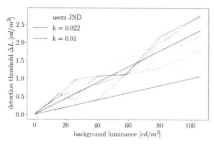

Fig. 2. ΔL as a function of L given the JND on an HMD.

Twenty participants have been presented with ten background luminance levels covering all the dynamic range of the HMD. For each background, a slightly lighter stimulus was displayed and incrementally increased until it gets perceived by the participant. This allows us to determine the JND. The test lasted about 15 min and our panel consisted of 20 participants (13 men and 7 women) with normal vision, from 20 to 57 years of age, with various socio-cultural backgrounds. After data fitting (see Fig. 2), we found the JND is equal to 2%. Despite of finding linear sensitivity (ΔL as a function of L) resulting in a logarithmic response by the Fechner's integration, in line with 2D visualization, the visual system perceives two times less contrast between the stimulus and the background. Indeed, the JND approaches 2%, while traditional visualization on a 2D display is usually around 1%. This result means that we can lose perceptible fine details when we watch an image on an HMD. This evaluation also emphasizes that the logarithmic lightness function (Eq. 3) is valid to model the human perception on an HMD. We designed our HMD-TMO accordingly to this result.

4   HMD-TMO

As seen in previous evaluations [1,2], applying a TMO to the entire 360° image does not produce a satisfying quality. A TMO applied to the entire 360° image takes into account all the luminance of the scene to produce the tone mapped result. Therefore, it maintains a global coherency but loses contrast in the viewports. Regarding a TMO applied to the viewport, it preserves the contrast but loses the global coherency of the scene. Since none of these methods produces a satisfying result when applied independently, we developed a TMO that combines both methods, global and viewport based, adapted to visualization on HMD in order to preserve global coherency and enhance contrast. Our operator consists in a pipeline with two branches (see Fig. 3). The input is a 360° HDR image and the output is a tone mapped image of the current viewport. The upper branch performs a tone mapping on the entire 360° image and thus preserves the spatial coherency, while the lower branch performs a tone mapping on the viewport image to enhance the contrast. Note that the time parameter t means the viewports succession due to the movement of the user who is wearing the HMD. The combination of the resulting luminances of these two TMOs (tone

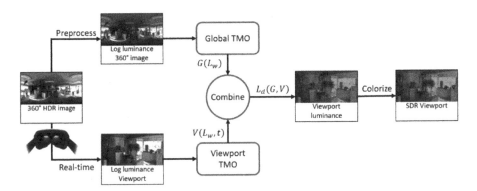

Fig. 3. Our operator combines a Global TMO $G(L_w)$ and a Viewport TMO $V(L_w, t)$. The Global TMO (upper branch) aims to preserve the global coherency of the scene while the Viewport TMO (lower branch) aims to enhances contrast. The combination of both produces our final HMD-TMO $L_d(G, V)$.

mapping of the entire 360° image $G(L_w)$ and tone mapping of the viewport image $V(L_w, t)$) is calculated by a geometric mean to compute the final tone mapped luminance $L_d(G, V)$. Note that luminance stands for the Y channel in the CIE XYZ color space. Each component of our pipeline (entire image tone mapping, viewport tone mapping, and combination) are detailed in the following subsections.

4.1 Global Tone Mapping

First, we tone map the entire 360° image in order to preserve the global coherency of the scene. Similarly to Ward *et al.* Visibility Matching Tone Reproduction operator [9], our method is based on the log-luminance histogram of the image represented by a *Cumulative Distribution Function (CDF)*. First, Ward *et al.* compute the normalized cumulative histogram of log-luminance value to find the *CDF*:

$$P(b) = \frac{\sum_{b_i < b} f(b_i)}{\sum_{b_i} f(b_i)}, \tag{4}$$

where $f(b)$ is the number of pixels for a bin b. The number of bins is set to 100 as proposed by the authors to avoid banding artifacts due to quantization. The tone curve G proposed by Ward *et al.* is a scaled version of $P(b)$:

$$G(L_w(x, y)) = exp(log(L_{dmin}) + (log(L_{dmax}) - log(L_{dmin})) \times P(L_w(x, y))), \tag{5}$$

where L_{dmin} and L_{dmax} are respectively the minimum and maximum luminance of the display, $L_w(x, y)$ is the world luminance of the pixel (x, y), $P(L_w(x, y))$ the *CDF* defined in Eq. 4, and $G(L_w(x, y))$ (our Global TMO) the resulting luminance of the pixel. To better match with human perception, Ward *et al.* add a pass of histogram adjustment in case of a too high contrast in the tone mapped image. Given the lightness perception values, the log-luminance histogram is clipped to avoid contrast exaggerations, which results in a flat *CDF*. Figure 4 shows the result of three TMOs applied to the entire 360° image: TMO based on Eq. 5 ($G(L_w(x, y))$), Ward *et al.*'s TMO [9] (with clipping), and Reinhard *et al.*'s TMO [4]. Reinhard *et al.*'s [4] TMO (first row) preserves the global coherency: the back of the store (red inset) appears dark while the storefront (green inset) is slightly lighted. Ward *et al.*'s [9] TMO (second row) better represents the difference between the dark and the bright zone but it is not enough for the expected result due to the histogram clipping. Finally, the TMO using Eq. 5 (third row) seems perceptually too contrasted (the difference between the red and the green inset is significant) but it is the most representative of the global coherency. As will be seen in the next subsection, the contrast is managed by the viewport TMO.

4.2 Viewport Tone Mapping

The objective of the viewport TMO is to enhance the contrast in the part of the 360° image currently viewed by the user (the viewport). We used an improved

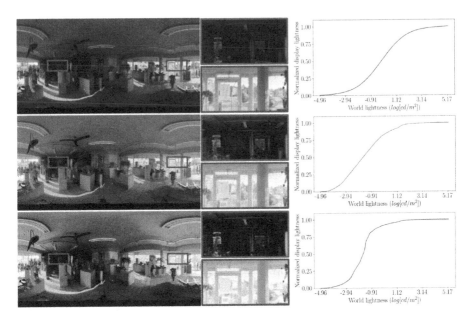

Fig. 4. From top to bottom: the Photographic Tone Reproduction operator [4], the Visibility Tone Reproduction operator [9], and the *CDF* (all are applied to the entire 360° image). To the right of each image, the corresponding tone mapping curves. (Color figure online)

version of the viewport TMO proposed by Yu [3]. His method relies on a simplified Photographic Tone Reproduction operator [4]. To avoid any flickering when changing view, Yu proposed to temporally smooth the key values to simulate the adaptation behavior of the human eye (see Fig. 5). This TMO is based on the log-average luminance of the image:

$$\bar{L}_w\big(V(t)\big) = \frac{1}{N} exp\bigg(\sum_{x,y} log\big(\delta + L_w(x,y)\big)\bigg), \tag{6}$$

where $\bar{L}_w\big(V(t)\big)$ is the viewport key value at a given time, $L_w(x,y)$ the pixel luminance, δ a small value to avoid singularity in case the image contains black pixels, and N the number of pixels in the viewport. Here, time t corresponds to an orientation of the camera due to the head movement. To ensure a smooth transition between two successive viewports, the key and the white values are interpolated as:

$$\bar{L}'_w(t) = \alpha \bar{L}_w\big(V(t)\big) + (1 - \alpha)\bar{L}'_w(t - 1), \tag{7}$$

$$L'_{white}(t) = \alpha L_{white}\big(V(t)\big) + (1 - \alpha)L'_{white}(t - 1), \tag{8}$$

where $\bar{L}'_w(t)$ and $L'_{white}(t)$ are respectively the smoothed key and white values between two successive views and α is a time dependent interpolation variable. Finally, the luminance is scaled and high values are attenuated to avoid clipping:

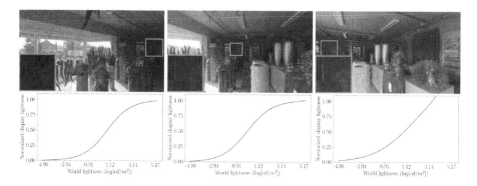

Fig. 5. Photographic Tone Reproduction operator [4] applied to a viewport sequence with smooth transitions. As the key value and the white value evolve from a view to another, the tone curve is modified and a same zone in the scene (red inset) becomes brighter or darker. (Color figure online)

$$L(x, y, t) = \frac{a}{\overline{L}'_w(t)} L_w(x, y), \qquad (9)$$

$$V\big(L_w(x, y), t\big) = \frac{L(x, y, t)\left(1 + \frac{L(x,y,t)}{L'^2_{white}(t)}\right)}{1 + L(x, y, t)}, \qquad (10)$$

where a is a user defined variable which scales the luminance (commonly 0.18), $L(x, y, t)$ the time dependent scaled luminance and $V\big(L_w(x, y), t\big)$ (our Viewport TMO) the displayed luminance. In his operator, Yu actually uses Eq. 9 that does not avoid clipping in high luminances. We have now the global coherency assured by the 360° image CDF $(G(L_w))$ and the viewport contrast $(V(L_w, t))$ we want to combine to obtain our final tone mapped image.

4.3   TMOs Combination

To recap, we want to display a tone mapped viewport of a 360° HDR image. In order to combine both luminances provided by the global and viewport TMOs, ensuring the global coherency to be preserved and the contrast to be enhanced, we propose to use a geometric mean to combine both luminances. After experimenting with different combinations (arithmetic mean, weighted sum and geometric mean), the geometric mean produces the best results (see Fig. 6). The resulting images produced by the weighted sum combination are perceptually unpleasant.

As the lightness is the logarithm of the luminance, this combination is interpreted as a perceptual mean:

$$\left(\prod_{i=1}^{n} a_i\right)^{\frac{1}{n}} = exp\left(\frac{1}{n} \sum_{i=1}^{n} ln(a_i)\right), \qquad (11)$$

$$L_d(G, V) = L_d(x, y, t) = \sqrt{V\big(L_w(x, y), t\big) \times G\big(L_w(x, y)\big)}, \qquad (12)$$

224   I. Goudé et al.

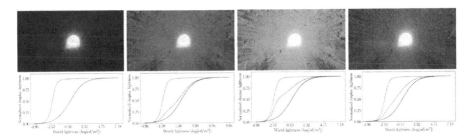

Fig. 6. Comparison between weighted sum and geometric mean combinations. Combinations are respectively: 100% Viewport, 80% Viewport + 20% Global, 50% Viewport + 50% Global, and the geometric mean. The green, blue and red curves below correspond respectively to the Global TMO, the Viewport TMO and the combination. (Color figure online)

where $L_w(x,y)$ is the world luminance of the pixel (x,y), t is the time, $V(L_w(x,y),t)$ is the viewport TMO defined in Eq. 10 and $G(L_w(x,y))$ is the global TMO defined in Eq. 5. $L_d(G,V)$ is our final tone mapped luminance we display on the viewport. In Fig. 7, we show the behavior of global, viewport and combined TMOs in both dark and bright areas of a 360° image. When only the viewport TMO is applied, the global coherency is lost, both zones seem equally enlightened. Contrarily, regarding the global TMO, the global coherency is preserved but the contrast in the viewport is exaggerated and unnatural. Finally, the combination of these two TMOs preserves global coherency and provides a proper contrast in the viewport.

Fig. 7. Two opposite views in a same scene, a dark side (top) and a bright side (bottom). From left to right: the viewport TMO $V(L_w(x,y),t)$ (blue curve), the combination of viewport and global TMOs $L_d(G,V)$ (red curve), and the global TMO $G(L_w(x,y))$ (green curve). (Color figure online)

5 Results

Once our TMO has calculated the tone mapped luminance, we compute the color of all the pixels of the tone mapped image using the Schlick's approach [10]:

$$C' = \left(\frac{C}{L_w}\right)^s L_d, \tag{13}$$

where C and C' are respectively the input and output trichromatic values (RGB), L_w the world luminance and L_d the tone mapped luminance. The saturation parameter s is set to 0.7 for our results.

We implemented our HMD-TMO using Unity3D because of its friendly interface for managing VR and its capacity to handle HDR. We used the HTC Vive Pro[1] as HMD. We benefited from GPU programming with shaders to compute 360° image histograms on the 2048 × 1024 equirectangular projection, and the 1440 × 1600 viewports (left and right views) key values in real time. Rendering (computation of the colored tone mapped image) is achieved with an image effect shader applied to the HDR viewport. The global TMO is computed once for all and takes less than one second. The navigation (calculation and display of successive viewport images) is performed in real-time: 90 frames are computed per second (Intel Core i7 vPro 7th Gen, NVidia Quadro M2200). We used a dataset of 90 views: 15 views for each of the six different 360° HDR images. We computed the Tone Mapped Image Quality Index (TMQI) [11] score of each view of each 360° image, which amounted to compute 90 scores. We calculated the average of the viewport scores for our method and three other TMOs. Overall, our method had the best mean score (see Table 1).

Table 1. The result of the TMQI quality test: mean value computed on 90 images (Reinhard *et al.*'s [4] and Ward *et al.*'s [9] TMOs are applied to the entire 360° image).

	Reinhard *et al.*	Ward *et al.*	Yu	Ours
TMQI quality	0.798	0.854	0.865	**0.887**

We also compared visually our results to those of Yu's [3] (see Fig. 8). In addition to preserving the global coherency, our TMO avoids clipping luminances out of the dynamic range of the HMD. This improvement is shown on the church wall in the tree image, and in the background and at the bottom left corner of the forest image. Furthermore, due to the exaggerated contrast produced by the *CDF*, our HMD-TMO enhances the fine details. Indeed, in the tree image, the contrast between the night sky and the tree leaves is higher with our method, which allows us to distinguish holes through the foliage. The branches lying on the ground are also more detailed in the forest image. The same phenomenon

---

[1] https://www.vive.com/fr/product/vive-pro/.

occurs in both examples of the village image and in the folds of the curtain in the florist image. However, an unwelcome effect appears in the florist image. The lighting of the box practically disappears when using our TMO because its luminance is not enough represented by the *CDF* which flattens the zone within the green inset.

Fig. 8. Yu's TMO [3] (left) compared to our HMD-TMO (right). Our method enhances fine details and removes the clipping in high luminance. (Color figure online)

6 Conclusion

HDR imaging enables to capture the whole dynamic of a $360°$ scene. Previous subjective studies have shown that naive tone mapping of the entire $360°$ image or tone mapping of a viewport does not provide convincing results. To overcome these limitations, we have proposed a new HMD-TMO. More precisely, our contribution is twofold: (1) a logarithmic model of lightness still valid on an HMD; (2) a novel TMO that combines both global and viewport TMOs. This new TMO doesn't tackle the limits of a viewport tone mapping but ensures a spatial coherency while navigating through the 360° HDR content. Our future work heads toward HDR video tone mapping for visualization on HMD. The main challenge will consist in accounting for: temporal coherency, sudden change in luminance range through time, naturalness of time adaptation, etc.

Acknowledgments. All 360° HDR images come from free SYNS and LizardQ datasets. This work has been supported by the ANR project ANR-17-CE23-0020. We would like to thank Kadi Bouatouch for his help and proofreading. Thanks to all experiment participants for their contributions.

References

1. Perrin, A.-F., Bist, C., Cozot, R., Ebrahimi, T.: Measuring quality of omnidirectional high dynamic range content. In: Optics+Photonics Optical Engineering+Applications Applications of Digital Image Processing XL, p. 38 (2017)
2. Melo, M., Bouatouch, K., Bessa, M., Coelho, H., Cozot, R., Chalmers, A.: Tone mapping HDR panoramas for viewing in head mounted displays. In: International Joint Conference on Computer Vision, Imaging and Computer Graphics Theory and Applications, pp. 232–239 (2018)
3. Yu, M.: Dynamic tone mapping with head-mounted displays. Standford University Report. 5 (2015)
4. Reinhard, E., Stark, M., Shirley, P., Ferwerda, J.: Photographic tone reproduction for digital images. In: Conference on Computer Graphics and Interactive Techniques, vol. 29, pp. 267–276 (2002)
5. Cutchin, S., Li, Y.: View Dependent Tone Mapping of HDR Panoramas for Head Mounted Displays. The Eurographics Association (2016)
6. Fechner, G.T., Howes, D.H., Boring, E.G.: Elements of psychophysics, vol. 1. Holt, Rinehart and Winston, New York (1966)
7. Reinhard, E., Heidrich, W., Debevec, P., Pattanaik, S., Ward, G., Myszkowski, K.: High Dynamic Range Imaging: Acquisition, Display, and Image-Based Lighting, vol. 238, 2nd edn. Elsevier, Amsterdam (2010)
8. Fairchild, M.D.: Color Appearance Models. Wiley, Hoboken (2013)
9. Larson, G.W., Rushmeier, H., Piatko, C.: A visibility matching tone reproduction operator for high dynamic range scenes. IEEE Trans. Vis. Comput. Graph. **3**(4), 291–306 (1997)
10. Schlick, C.: Quantization techniques for visualization of high dynamic range pictures. In: Sakas, G., Müller, S., Shirley, P. (eds.) Photorealistic Rendering Techniques. Focus on Computer Graphics (Tutorials and Perspectives in Computer Graphics), pp. 7–20. Springer, Heidelberg (1995). https://doi.org/10.1007/978-3-642-87825-1_2
11. Yeganeh, H., Wang, Z.: Objective quality assessment of tone mapped images. IEEE Trans. Image Process. **22**(2), 657–667 (2013)

Integrating Peridynamics with Material Point Method for Elastoplastic Material Modeling

Yao Lyu[1(✉)], Jinglu Zhang[1], Jian Chang[1], Shihui Guo[2], and Jian Jun Zhang[1]

[1] National Centre for Computer Animation, Bournemouth University,
Poole, Dorset, UK
{ylyu,zhangj,jchang,jzhang}@bournemouth.ac.uk
[2] School of Software, Xiamen University, Xiamen, China
guoshihui@xmu.edu.cn

Abstract. We present a novel integral-based Material Point Method (MPM) using state based peridynamics structure for modeling elastoplastic material and fracture animation. Previous partial derivative based MPM studies face challenges of underlying instability issues of particle distribution and the complexity of modeling discontinuities. To alleviate these problems, we integrate the strain metric in the basic elastic constitutive model by using material point truss structure, which outweighs differential-based methods in both accuracy and stability. To model plasticity, we incorporate our constitutive model with deviatoric flow theory and a simple yield function. It is straightforward to handle the problem of cracking in our hybrid framework. Our method adopts two time integration ways to update crack interface and fracture inner parts, which overcome the unnecessary grid duplication. Our work can create a wide range of material phenomenon including elasticity, plasticity, and fracture. Our framework provides an attractive method for producing elastoplastic materials and fracture with visual realism and high stability.

Keywords: Material Point Method · Peridynamics · Elastoplastic modeling

1 Introduction

Physically-based modeling of elastoplastic material has been an active research topic for many years in compute graphics, particularly for its appealing application in visual effects industry. Scenes involving elastoplastic deformation are very common, for example, clothes moving with wind, rubber toys bouncing on the floor, or plastic board damaged by high speed impact. In order to model such

This work is supported by National Natural Science Foundation of China (61702433, 61661146002), the Fundamental Research Funds for the Central Universities, the China Scholarship Council and Bournemouth University.

realistic behaviors under different circumstances, the robust simulation method needs to be capable of handling complex topological changes and various contact responses, such as collision and cohesion. To find the simulation method that can naturally model elastoplastic material along with complex topological changes is the current focus of the field.

Meshless simulation methods are powerful in dealing with complicated topological changes since it does not require high quality mesh and efforts to overcome the issues from severe mesh distortion. The MPM [23,24] is an extension of the particle-in-cell (PIC) method. It combines the Eulerian Cartesian grids and Lagrangian material points for tracking mass, momentum and deformation on particles [20]. It can naturally process material point distribution and self-collisions. It also has been proved to be especially suitable for animating materials that undergo large deformations [10]. Despite its physical realism and geometrical convenience, the traditional MPM solver has several disadvantages: (1) Due to the governing equation based on spatial derivatives of displacements, the results are sensitive to the underlying particle distribution [6]. Also it has difficulty in solving singularity along discontinuities. (2) To observe boundary details, MPM has to maintain a fine resolution grid which brings high computational costs for particle-grid transfer throughout the whole simulation domain. While researchers have extensively studied refining regions of particular interest by using adaptive grid [4], the ability to simulate detailed discontinuities dynamics, such as crack propagation, is still limited.

Recently, peridynamics has gained its popularity in meshless simulation for discontinuous deformation. It was originally proposed by Silling [16] and has been adopted mainly for studying fracture dynamics due to its integral based constitutive model. Peridynamics is not suitable for handling large deformation due to the fact that initial bond connections are not in consistent with the configuration where topological changes are severe. Based on this fact, there are not a lot of mature models and experiments in continuum mechanics being adopted by peridynamics methods for animating elastoplastic material [28]. Furthermore, its point-based nature leads additional efforts to handle contacts.

Aiming at alleviating above problems, we propose an integral-based MPM framework with peridynamics structure for modeling elastoplastic material and fractures. We present three main contributions:

Elasticity. We equip material point with virtual bonds and family points. The elastic energy density function is redefined in an integral way with this truss structure. Varied stiffness of elastic materials can be simulated with high realism and stability.

Plasticity. The virtual bond structure makes our model trivial to model plastic behaviors. We use a novel method to extract plasticity from the deviatoric part of constitutive model and accumulate plastic increment permanently at particle-grid transfer step.

Fracture. We handle crack definition and propagation through screening virtual bonds. The fracture criterion combines the deformation status of single material point and the grid cell. We update fracture surfaces and fracture inner parts in different time integration methods. Our method avoids the difficulty of duplicating grids and large computation cost brought by multiple particle-grid transfer process.

After discussing related work in Sect. 2, we outline our method and explain integral-based governing equation in Sect. 3. Section 4 describes the constitutive model for modeling elastoplastic material in details. Crack definition and propagation are discussed in Sect. 5. Experimental examples for evaluating our method and discussion of results are give in Sect. 6. In Sect. 7 we conclude the method and explain our future work.

2   Related Work

Elastoplastic Continuum Modeling. Terzopoulos and Fleischer [26,27] pioneered the plastic simulation methods in computer graphics. O'Brien and colleagues [14] incorporated finite element method (FEM) with multiplicative plasticity model and obtained realistic motion for a much wider range of materials. Later, Gerszewski et al. [5] adopted deformation gradient for animating elastic behaviors based on point method. Levin [11] rediscretized elasticity on a Eulerian grid, which is similar to MPM grid. Based on previous hybrid grid and particle modeling method, Stomakhin [21] incorporated energetically consistent invertible elasticity model into MPM for modeling snow varying phase effects. Recently, Chen [3] presented a novel elastoplastic constitutive model to handle brittle fracture and ductile fracture in peridynamics-based framework. At the same time, many researchers focused on developing the real time and haptic simulator. For example, Salsedo et al. [15] designed the HAPTEX system using dynamically variable spatial resolution to reduce the computational burden during rendering the fabrics, which was extended by Bottcher [1,2] by implementing separated computation threads for different simulation scales.

Material Point Method. MPM is a hybrid grid-particle method using a regular Eulerian Cartesian grid to treat self-collision and fracture naturally, proposed by Sulsky [23,24]. Later, Stomakhin et al. [21] introduced MPM into computer graphics and obtained a variety of snow phenomenon. Jiang and his colleagues proved that MPM is a useful method for granular materials by animating sand [9]. Tampubolon extended the MPM to simulate multi-phase behaviors through using multiple grids, such as porous sand and water interactions [25]. A majority of elastoplastic MPM works for computer graphics [8,22] focus on resolving intensive collision scenarios on the surface or the curve with millions degrees of freedom. Unlike above studies, our method incorporates integral-based constitutive model to replace typical partial derivative based model. This helps us alleviate the instability and difficulty issues from particle distribution of arbitrary elastoplastic deformation. With virtual bonds, constitutive model can demonstrate detailed topological changes smaller than grid cell.

Peridynamics. Silling proposed the peridynamics theory [16] as an efficient non-local continuum theory to uniformly solve problems involving both continuities and discontinuities [3,6,18]. Instead of using spatial differential formulations, peridynamics uses spatial integral equations as the governing equations. Its application sparked the engineering field, such as multiscale material modeling [19] and crack dynamics [17]. Later, Levine [12] introduced the peridynamics theory to computer graphics. He revisited brittle fracture studies by characterizing peridynamics as spring-mass systems. Currently, most research [3,6] focused on how to reformulate elastic constitutive models and produce persuasive effects. However, the theoretical equivalence of peridynamics compared to continuum mechanics remains unclear [28]. A lot of mature theories and experiments in continuum mechanics have not been adopted for peridynamics in computer graphic. This motivates us to define the integral-based constitutive model equipped with peridynamics structure within MPM framework for versatile elastoplastic deformation and self-collision detection.

3   Method

The governing equation of MPM arises from basic conservation of mass and momentum [21]. Back to weak formulation which is obtained by multiplying the balance of momentum and integrating the governing equation over initial volume, we propose an integral force density function $F^s(x_p)$ to replace spatial derivatives of displacement and redefine the weak formulation as:

$$\int_\Omega \rho a_p \delta u_p d\Omega + \int_\Omega \rho F^s(x_p) \delta u_p d\Omega = \int_\Omega \rho b_p \delta u_p d\Omega + \int_{\Gamma_\tau} \rho \delta u_p \overline{\tau_p} d\Gamma \quad (1)$$

where Ω denotes the integrating region in the current configuration, ρ is density, a_p is the acceleration of particle p, δu_p is the virtual displacement (infinitesimal feasible changes where constraints remain satisfied). b_p is the body force, for example, gravity. τ_p is the surface traction on part of the boundary Γ_τ.

$$F^s(x_p) = \int_{H_{x_p}} [T < x_p, x_p' > -T < x_p', x_p >]/\rho dH_{x_p} \quad (2)$$

$F^s(x_p)$ is the internal force density function constructed in an integral way. x_p' is the neighbor point of point x_p. When incorporating peridynamics theory, we construct the truss structure for each material point as: the neighbor material points H_{x_p} of material point x_p are referred as its family members. x_p has interaction with all its family members at same time. Each interaction is operated by a virtual bond. $T < x_p, x_p' >$ represents the interaction force between x_p and x_p'. The $F^s(x_p)$ avoids using the spatial derivatives of displacements $\frac{\delta u_{x_p}}{\delta x_p}$. We will discuss details of the constitutive model in Sect. 4.

   In the MPM framework, the material domain at t^n is discretised with particles at x_p^n. Each particle has volume V, mass m_p, velocity v_p^n, and other physical quantities, such as deformation matrix F_p, $Lam\acute{e}$ parameters μ_p and λ_p, plastic yield parameters ψ_p. In each time step, a new grid is generated. Grid node I is used to store nodal parameters, such as position x_I, mass m_I, velocity v_I, force f_I. Our framework adopts dyadic products of one-dimensional cubic B-splines as basic weight function in [21] during particle-grid transfer process. Here we outline the full update procedure:

(1) **Particle-to-grid transfer.** Transfer material point mass m_p and momentum $(mv)_p$ to the grid.

(2) **Compute internal forces.** The internal force of grid node I is calculated by the stress tensor of each point, presented as $f_I^{INT} = \sum_{Np} m_p N_I(x_p) F^s(x_p) V$. Our method presents this equation based on our integral-based energy function. The detailed description of the update rule for $F^s(x_p)$ is given in Sect. 4.

(3) **Update Grid Momentum.** Nodal velocities are updated by $\widehat{v}_i^{n+1} = v_i^n + \triangle t f_I/m_i^n$ for explicit time integration. f_I is the total force.

(4) **Grid-based body collisions.** Grid velocity v_I^{n+1} is updated by collision field and friction parameter from [21].

(5) **Grid-to-particle transfer.** Transfer updated nodal velocity v_I^{n+1} and momentum $(mv)_I^{n+1}$ to particle.

(6) **Particle collisions.** Modify v_p^{n+1} by collision field on particle level to obtain detailed deformation behaviors on the boundary.

(7) **Fracture.** Based on the current particle distribution and the deformation status of grid cell, we remove virtual bond that intersects with fracture plane. The fracture model is discussed in Sect. 5.

4   Constitutive Models

In this section, we describe our constitutive model in details. We start with elastic model, then incorporate plasticity in a consistent frame.

4.1   Elastic Model

When we only consider elasticity in continuum mechanics, the elastic energy density function [20] can be defined as:

$$E^s = \mu \|F_e - R_e\|^2 + \frac{\lambda}{2}(J_e - 1)^2 \tag{3}$$

where F_e is the deformation gradient tensor, R_e is rotation matrix and $J_e = det(F_e)$. We can decompose this equation into the combination of two parts in the view of different contributions to topological changes: $\mu \|F_e - R_e\|^2$ as deviatoric part; $\frac{\lambda}{2}(J_e - 1)^2$ as isotropic part. However, F_e is based on the spatial derivatives of displacement which leads to the inability of constitutive model to compute singularity issues, such as discontinuities. We adopt the concept of integral deformation matrix $\overline{F_p}$ in [6] to describe the local deformation which has similar meaning to F_e but is represented by the integration of displacement and peridynamics structure. When the initial bond state and deformed bond between material point x_p and $x_p{'}$ are $X = x_p - x_p{'}$ and $Y = y_p - y_p{'}$, deformation matrix F_p shown in Eq. 4 represents the average deformation status of point x_p. H_{x_p} represents all family members. $w(Y)$ is linear weight function. $\otimes$ is dyadic product operator defined by Silling [16]. Thus an average deformed bond is calculated as $\overline{Y} = \overline{F_i}X$.

$$F_p = [\sum_{H_{x_p}} w(Y)Y \otimes X][\sum_{H_{x_p}} w(Y) \otimes X]^{-1} \tag{4}$$

With these concepts, Eq. 3 is reformulated as the combination of deviatoric component and isotropic component:

$$E^s = \sum_{H_{x_p}} w(Y)(\mu E^{dev} + \frac{\lambda}{2} E^{iso}) \tag{5}$$

$E^{dev} = (\frac{|\overline{Y}|}{|X|} - 1)^2$ describes deformed energy similar to mass spring system but removes the influence from different bond length in order to simulate material with the same stiffness. It uses the average deformed bond length. Similarly, $E^{iso} = (\frac{|Y|}{|X|} - 1)^2$ represents single bond deformation energy.

Then the elastic force density function $T < x_p, x_p{'} >$ for the material point pair of x_p and $x_p{'}$ is obtained through $\frac{\partial \psi}{\partial y_p}$, as:

$$T < x_p, x_p{'} >= \frac{2\mu w}{|X|^2}(\overline{Y} - |X|dir\overline{Y}) + \frac{\lambda w}{|X|^2}(Y - |X|dirY) \tag{6}$$

where $\frac{2\mu w}{|X|^2}(|\overline{Y}| - |X|)dir\overline{Y}$ depends on all neighbours, so it presents the shear stress effects. $\frac{\lambda w}{|X|^2}(|Y| - |X|)dirY$ denotes spring force between by x_p and $x_p{'}$, so the direction follows the deformed bond. Using Eqs. 2 and 6, the internal force of grid node I for updating nodal momentum is:

$$f_I^{INT} = \sum m_p N_I(x_p)[\sum_{H_{x_p}} w(Y)(T < x_p, x_p{'} > -T < x_p{'}, x_p >)V] \tag{7}$$

Compared to many existing methods, our method only needs the current virtual bond state Y, so the local step is fast. Our method avoids the singular value decomposition (SVD) to extract elastic deformation gradient in [21]. The advantages of avoiding SVD are obvious: we obtain a better stability for simulation with large time steps as in [6]; also reduce the complexity of plasticity definition in MPM framework.

4.2 Plastic Model

Many methods [21, 29] take out the part of elastic deformation gradient tensor that exceeds the yield function and push it into plastic deformation gradient calculation. Due to the hybrid structure in our method, the plasticity can be extracted simply on our integral-based elastic model. Singularity issues can be overcome easily without any extra efforts.

Our plastic model is purely from deviatoric plastic flow [3] theory. Firstly, we reformulate our elastic model in Eq. 6 in order to adapt it for modeling plasticity. $|\overline{Y}| - |X|$ and $|Y| - |X|$ are average and single bond extension. When the deformation is smooth enough under small neighbor horizon, we predict $|\overline{Y}| - |X| \approx |Y| - |X|$. Then we have:

$$T < x_p, x_p' >= \frac{2\mu w}{|X|^2}(|Y| - |X|)dir\overline{Y} + \frac{\lambda w}{|X|^2}(|Y| - |X|)dirY \quad (8)$$

Based on the plastic flow theory, the unified displacement is decomposed into isotropic and deviatoric part, $e = (|Y| - |X|)/|X| = e^{iso} + e^{dev}$. Plastic deformation e^p is extracted from e^{dev}. Then we integrate the plasticity into Eq. 8:

$$T < x_p, x_p' >= \frac{2\mu w}{|X|}(e^{iso} + e^{dev} - e^p)dir\overline{Y} + \frac{\lambda w}{|X|}(e^{iso} + e^{dev} - e^p)dirY \quad (9)$$

We make the best use of our bond-particle-grid structure and define the yield function as $f(E_{dev})$:

$$E_{dev} = (\frac{2\mu w}{|X|} + \frac{\lambda w}{|X|})(e^{dev} - e^p), f(E_{dev}) = \frac{(E_{dev})^2}{2} - \psi_p \quad (10)$$

where ψ_p is controllable plastic material parameter. We use $f(E_{dev})$ to decide if the current configuration enters the plastic regime. If $f(E_{dev}) < 0$, the deformation is still within the elastic domain. If $f(E_{dev}) > 0$, part of deformation occurred as plasticity. We project the deformation back to yield surface and add plastic increment Δe^p to e^p permanently as Eq. 11.

$$\Delta e^p = \frac{|X|}{(\lambda)}[E_{dev} - \sqrt{2\psi_p}sign(E_{dev})] \quad (11)$$

This model is still valid for elastic when e^p varnishes in the equations. This constitutive model can be used for both elastic and elastoplastic materials in MPM.

5   Fracture

Crack simulation is a bottleneck of the MPM [13]. To processing the discontinuities at the interfaces, special treatments for creating cracks and partitioning fracture fragments into multigrid and multiple velocity fields are approaches [7]. When an excessive number of cracking interfaces are involved, the computation of multiple grid transferring can be very expensive. Additionally, the strategy to duplicate grid is limited because during simulation small fragments are numerous and randomly generated so it is hard to duplicate grid for each crack interface.

The dynamics with discontinuities is straightforward to compute in our MPM framework. If we simply remove over-deformed bonds like [3], it leads to numerous small fragments in deformed area rather than several crack lines after collision happens. We now propose to generate crack cut by fracture plane based on analyses of single point and global deformation status in gird cell.

Firstly, we define the fracture criterion by removing the plastic displacement as:

$$l = \frac{e - e^p}{|X|(1 + p_{inactive})} \qquad (12)$$

where $p_{inactive}$ is the percentage of broken bond in total bond numbers in the grid cell where the material point stays.

After screening the material points whose l exceeds the threshold, we use cluster method to sort these points into several deformed areas based on position and normal. For each area, we calculate the central point and the largest deformed bond. Next step we use the central point position and the bond direction as normal to construct fracture plane for each area. Any bond intersected by the fracture plane will be removed. That is how crack line occurs. With $p_{inactive}$, this method can effectively reduce the number of small fracture pieces. Because if one grid has too many broken bonds, the active bonds in this grid cell are less possible to be removed.

In the MPM, grid cell size decides the resolution of whole simulation. This also works for crack dynamics. In experiments, we transfer particle velocity to three grid cells in any direction to get stable, smooth results. When two sides of crack line are within this range, they will share another fragment information through transfer. Therefore using only one grid leads to "fracture sticky to each other" effects. We alleviate this problem by applying two time integration ways: material points on the crack surface are updated by its own bond forces; other material points which don't have any broken bonds (in the fragment inner parts) are updated by grids as normal. Thus we avoid the information mixture of different crack fragments.

6   Result and Discussion

We implemented our method and tested examples in this section. All our examples are run in Houdini software, including material point discretization, vorinoi fracture generation and rendering. We use Houdini Development Kit(HDK) tools to customise nodes for material point dynamics. Eigen library is equipped with dynamics nodes. We use explicit time integration for the ease of implementation.

Implementation. We list the modeling types, parameter settings and the performance data in Table 1 for all the examples presented in the paper. We add ghost particles on object boundary to guarantee that each material point have similar family density.

Elastoplastic Model Validation. We use several examples with different material properties to evaluate our method. Figure 1 shows the examples of garment anchored by clothespins. With varied bending stiffness parameters μ, the

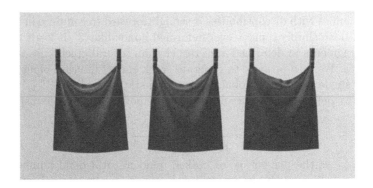

Fig. 1. The moving cloths with different material parameters show different bending stiffness. From left to right: $\mu = 2 \times 10^4$, $\mu = 1.5 \times 10^5$, $\mu = 1 \times 10^6$.

Fig. 2. Shooting ball to elastic and plastic boards show visibly different results. In the first row, elastic board can recover to initial shape after the collision. The second row shows that plastic board keeps deformed topology.

experiments present the realistic and fine wrinkles. Figure 2 shows the comparison of elastic board and plastic board collided by a ball. Our model can create correct behaviors. With complex topology objects, this method still works as in Fig. 3. Figure 4 shows the simulation of ductile plastic fracture. Figure 5 demonstrates the stretching beams deformation with different material stiffness.

Limitations and Future Work. This paper presents a lot of examples with elastic and plastic material. However, there are still some works which need to be achieved in the future. Firstly, we represent fracture with Houdini voronoi structure which is represented by polygon with random vertex number. It is unable to generate the arbitrary fracture shape. The resolution is limited to the number and size of voronoi pieces. Incorporating tetrahedron structure for embedded geometry modeling is the future option for cooking detailed cracking interfaces.

Fig. 3. The collision between two identical bunnies with different materials. This example demonstrates the different deformation of elastic bunny (in the first row) and plastic bunny (in the second row). Collision happens in (a) and (c). Elastic bunnies can recover as in (b). Plastic bunny deforms afterwards in (d).

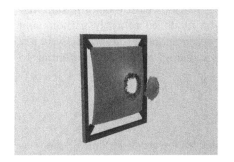 

Fig. 4. Simulation of plastic wall collided by a sphere.

Fig. 5. Stretch beams with different material parameters. From left to right, bending stiffness μ are: 0, 50, 500.

Secondly, we only apply plastic fracture models with deformed topology. Some important complex models should be covered in future work, such as brittle glass crack and complex crack propagation. Finally, we use explicit integration for its straightforwardness in HDK. It requires very small substeps for dealing with huge displacement. Alternatively, the current study implements projective dynamics implicit integration method for fast simulation. It can obtain stable and robust results under large substeps. Our future work will focus on addressing above limitations and obtaining versatile and realistic elastoplastic performance.

Table 1. Modeling information for all examples

	Type	Grid cell Size(cm)	λ(Kpa)	μ(Kpa)	ψ_p	Fracture threshold	Δt (ms)
Cloth	Mesh	0.005	1×10^6	2×10^4,1.5×10^5,1×10^6	1×10^{25}	1×10^{10}	0. 1
Elastic board	Mesh	0.02	3×10^6	1.5×10^5	1×10^{25}	1×10^{15}	0.02
Plastic board	Mesh	0.02	5×10^6	1.5×10^5	1000	1×10^{15}	0.0001
Elastic bunny	Particles	0.01	1×10^5	1×10^5	1×10^{25}	1×10^{25}	0.1
Plastic bunny	Particles	0.01	1×10^6	3×10^5	300	1×10^{25}	0.01
Broken board	Voronoi	0.005	1×10^6	5×10^4	500	0.05	0.001
Stretching beam	Mesh	0.05	500	0,50,500	1×10^{25}	1×10^{25}	100

7   Conclusion

We present an integral-based constitutive model within the Material Point Method framework. Our method demonstrates various elastic deformation and plastic deformation scenarios. Fracture can be modelled robustly without any singularity issues. Additionally, our method presents a novel integral-based view for multi-material modeling and fractures modeling, which has potential to inspire future research in the field.

References

1. Böttcher, G.: Haptic Interaction with Deformable Objects: Modelling VR Systems for Textiles. Springer, London (2011). https://doi.org/10.1007/978-0-85729-935-2
2. Bottcher, G., Allerkamp, D., Wolter, F.E.: Virtual reality systems modelling haptic two-finger contact with deformable physical surfaces. In: 2007 International Conference on Cyberworlds (CW 2007), pp. 292–299. IEEE (2007)
3. Chen, W., Zhu, F., Zhao, J., Li, S., Wang, G.: Peridynamics-based fracture animation for elastoplastic solids. In: Computer Graphics Forum, vol. 37, pp. 112–124. Wiley Online Library (2018)
4. Gao, M., Tampubolon, A.P., Jiang, C., Sifakis, E.: An adaptive generalized interpolation material point method for simulating elastoplastic materials. ACM Trans. Graph. (TOG) **36**(6), 223 (2017)
5. Gerszewski, D., Bhattacharya, H., Bargteil, A.W.: A point-based method for animating elastoplastic solids. In: Proceedings of the 2009 ACM SIGGRAPH/Eurographics Symposium on Computer Animation, pp. 133–138. ACM (2009)
6. He, X., Wang, H., Wu, E.: Projective peridynamics for modeling versatile elastoplastic materials. IEEE Trans. Vis. Comput. Graph. **24**(9), 2589–2599 (2018)
7. Homel, M.A., Herbold, E.B.: Field-gradient partitioning for fracture and frictional contact in the material point method. Int. J. Num. Methods Eng. **109**(7), 1013–1044 (2017)
8. Jiang, C., Gast, T., Teran, J.: Anisotropic elastoplasticity for cloth, knit and hair frictional contact. ACM Trans. Graph. (TOG) **36**(4), 152 (2017)

9. Jiang, C., Schroeder, C., Selle, A., Teran, J., Stomakhin, A.: The affine particle-in-cell method. ACM Trans. Graph. (TOG) **34**(4), 51 (2015)
10. Jiang, C., Schroeder, C., Teran, J., Stomakhin, A., Selle, A.: The material point method for simulating continuum materials. In: ACM SIGGRAPH 2016 Courses, p. 24. ACM (2016)
11. Levin, D.I., Litven, J., Jones, G.L., Sueda, S., Pai, D.K.: Eulerian solid simulation with contact. ACM Trans. Graph. (TOG) **30**(4), 36 (2011)
12. Levine, J.A., Bargteil, A.W., Corsi, C., Tessendorf, J., Geist, R.: A peridynamic perspective on spring-mass fracture. In: Proceedings of the ACM SIGGRAPH/Eurographics Symposium on Computer Animation, pp. 47–55. Eurographics Association (2014)
13. Liang, Y., Benedek, T., Zhang, X., Liu, Y.: Material point method with enriched shape function for crack problems. Comput. Methods Appl. Mech. Eng. **322**, 541–562 (2017)
14. O'brien, J.F., Bargteil, A.W., Hodgins, J.K.: Graphical modeling and animation of ductile fracture. ACM Trans. Graph. (TOG) **21**, 291–294 (2002)
15. Salsedo, F., et al.: Architectural design of the HAPTEX system. In: submitted to the Proceedings of this Conference (2005)
16. Silling, S.A.: Reformulation of elasticity theory for discontinuities and long-range forces. J. Mech. Phys. Solids **48**(1), 175–209 (2000)
17. Silling, S.A., Askari, A.: Peridynamic model for fatigue cracking. SAND2014-18590. Sandia National Laboratories, Albuquerque (2014)
18. Silling, S.A., Epton, M., Weckner, O., Xu, J., Askari, E.: Peridynamic states and constitutive modeling. J. Elast. **88**(2), 151–184 (2007)
19. Silling, S.A., Askari, A.: Practical peridynamics. Technical report, Sandia National Lab. (SNL-NM), Albuquerque, NM, United States (2014)
20. Stomakhin, A., Howes, R., Schroeder, C., Teran, J.M.: Energetically consistent invertible elasticity. In: Proceedings of the ACM SIGGRAPH/Eurographics Symposium on Computer Animation, pp. 25–32. Eurographics Association (2012)
21. Stomakhin, A., Schroeder, C., Chai, L., Teran, J., Selle, A.: A material point method for snow simulation. ACM Trans. Graph. (TOG) **32**(4), 102 (2013)
22. Stomakhin, A., Teran, J., Selle, A.: Augmented material point method for simulating phase changes and varied materials, 2 Jul 2015. US Patent App. 14/323,798
23. Sulsky, D., Chen, Z., Schreyer, H.L.: A particle method for history-dependent materials. Comput. Methods Appl. Mech. Eng. **118**(1–2), 179–196 (1994)
24. Sulsky, D., Zhou, S.J., Schreyer, H.L.: Application of a particle-in-cell method to solid mechanics. Comput. Phys. Commun. **87**(1–2), 236–252 (1995)
25. Tampubolon, A.P., Gast, T., Klár, G., Fu, C., Teran, J., Jiang, C., Museth, K.: Multi-species simulation of porous sand and water mixtures. ACM Trans. Graph. (TOG) **36**(4), 105 (2017)
26. Terzopoulos, D., Fleischer, K.: Modeling inelastic deformation: viscolelasticity, plasticity, fracture. In: ACM SIGGRAPH Computer Graphics, vol. 22, pp. 269–278. ACM (1988)
27. Terzopoulos, D., Platt, J., Barr, A., Fleischer, K.: Elastically deformable models. ACM SIGGRAPH Comput. Graph. **21**(4), 205–214 (1987)
28. Xu, L., He, X., Chen, W., Li, S., Wang, G.: Reformulating hyperelastic materials with peridynamic modeling. In: Computer Graphics Forum, vol. 37, pp. 121–130. Wiley Online Library (2018)
29. Zhu, B., Lee, M., Quigley, E., Fedkiw, R.: Codimensional non-Newtonian fluids. ACM Trans. Graph. (TOG) **34**(4), 115 (2015)

"Am I Talking to a Human or a Robot?": A Preliminary Study of Human's Perception in Human-Humanoid Interaction and Its Effects in Cognitive and Emotional States

Evangelia Baka[1]([⊠]), Ajay Vishwanath[2], Nidhi Mishra[2], Georgios Vleioras[3], and Nadia Magnenat Thalmann[1,2]

[1] MIRALab, University of Geneva, Rte de Drize 7, 1227 Geneva, Switzerland
ebaka@miralab.ch
[2] Institute of Media Innovation, Nanyang Technological University, 50 Nanyang Drive, Singapore, Singapore
[3] University of Thessaly, Argonafton Kai Filellinon, 38221 Volos, Greece

Abstract. The current preliminary study concerns the identification of the effects human-humanoid interaction can have on human emotional states and behaviors, through a physical interaction. Thus, we have used three cases where people face three different types of physical interaction with a neutral person, Nadine social robot and the person on which Nadine was modelled, Professor Nadia Thalmann. To support our research, we have used EEG recordings to capture the physiological signals derived from the brain during each interaction, audio recordings to compare speech features and a questionnaire to provide psychometric data that can complement the above. Our results mainly showed the existence of frontal theta oscillations while interacting with the humanoid that probably shows the higher cognitive effort of the participants, as well as differences in the occipital area of the brain and thus, the visual attention mechanisms. The level of concentration and motivation of participants while interacting with the robot were higher indicating also higher amount of interest. The outcome of this experiment can broaden the field of human-robot interaction, leading to more efficient, meaningful and natural human-robot interaction.

Keywords: Human-robot interaction · EEG · Speech · Social robots · Social cognition · Emotional communication

1 Introduction

The communication between human beings has been guided and facilitated by the existence of emotions. Emotions, as an inherent internal procedure, are the mirror of what we feel, allowing us to perceive and understand our environment, including ourselves. The importance of emotions in human communication has been supported since 1973 by Ekman [1], influenced by Darwin's work. Fast-forward to the 21st century, the focus has shifted towards the relationship between humans and machines, creating the broad area of affective computing, examining emotions and perception

M. Gavrilova et al. (Eds.): CGI 2019, LNCS 11542, pp. 240–252, 2019.
https://doi.org/10.1007/978-3-030-22514-8_20

evoked by human-computer interaction or the use of emotions for the emotional intelligence of the machines. The ultimate purpose is the facilitation of the smooth communication between humans and computer-generated characters or robots.

The study and comparison between emotions and neural processing in human-human and human-computer interaction have recently been in the focus of various research studies. Robots, until recently, were considered unable to have inner experiences and independent thought [2]. Towards this direction, research aims to develop robots which will be able to comprehend people [3]. Thus, an interesting question is whether interacting with them could trigger human-like responses. To that end, enriching robots with a degree of emotional intelligence could lead to more efficient, meaningful and natural human-robot interactions.

In order to develop such empathic social robots, it is important to consider human reactions derived from the interaction with them. Our purpose lies in examining the effects of human-humanoid interaction in humans' cognitive state and emotions, including the way the brain responds to such an interaction and consequently, the degree to which humans can perceive the difference of interacting with robots instead of other human beings. Most of the studies have tried to examine interactive tasks through observation, which means using video clips, or images [2, 4], highlighting the limitation of the physical interaction and the loss of the sense of embodiment.

The second step is the determination of the modalities that need to be used for the optimal emotion and perception recognition. Emotional information can be transmitted through verbal (speech and semantic content of a message) and non-verbal (facial and vocal expressions, gestures) communicative tools that can be influenced by several internal or external conditions, like the mood of the person or the environment [5]. However, a multimodal approach is preferred, avoiding the limitations each modality may have. For the purpose of our work, we decided to combine EEG data to include the physiological aspect, with voice detection and self-measurements for the personal and psychological factors.

1.1 State-of-the-Art

Researches on emotions have been based on the extraction of two kind of signals: the physiological (i.e. the Galvanic skin response (GSR), skin temperature (ST), electroencephalogram (EEG), Heart Rate (HR)) and the non-physiological ones (facial expressions, voice detection and gestures). The early works have been mainly based on the latter and especially face and voice recognition. Physiological signals though, in recent works, seem to have higher accuracy, with EEG being advantageous as the signal comes directly from the central nervous system and it can provide more accurate information about internal emotional states [6].

Studies that have used only EEG for emotion recognition have managed to correlate frequency bands and brains areas with some basic emotions [9, 10, 12]. Frontal lobe has been shown to be more related to Valence emotions [9]. Moreover, high frequency bands, like beta or gamma, are also related to Valence emotions compared to the lower ones [9–11]. In general, Frontal and Parietal areas have been proved to be the most dominant brain areas for emotion detection [11].

To increase the accuracy and the reliability of such estimations, a multimodal data fusion has recently started to be tested. At the beginning, studies started to combine non-physiological signals [7], like facial expressions, with audio features and text-based emotion recognition, while other studies tried physiological signals, like EEG and eye tracking [8]. Recently, data fusion of both kind of signals, like EEG and facial expressions [11] has increased the accuracy of the results.

Most of the studies though, examining human – robot interaction, have been based on the observation of images without a physical interaction. Urgen et al. [4] examined the difference in perception between humans and robots (mechanical and with physical appearance ones), using only EEG recordings for the sensorimotor mu rhythm (8–13 Hz) and the frontal theta (4–8 Hz). Wang et al. [2], one year later, examined such an interaction based on the observation of images of several social interactions with the mechanical robot Nao. In this study, functional Magnetic Resonance Imaging was used, and the outcome was that robot observation leads to lower MTN (mentalizing network) engagement. Thus, interaction between the robot and the human were considered less believable. Recently, Perez-Gaspar et al. worked again with the combination of voice and facial expressions [3], using cameras and a microphone, with real interaction between a small mechanical robot and a human.

One really important aspect is the one that Borst and Gelder [13] examined about how and if the perception during robot- or avatars-human interaction can differ from the one of human-human interaction, regarding the appearance and expressions of emotions. The most important features that can influence the perception are the human likeness, the naturalness of the movements and the emotions expressed by them [13].

There are a lot of studies investigating how the degree of human likeness can influence the perception and the feelings as well as cause differences in brain activity. Cheetham et al. [14, 15] found that perceptual discrimination was asymmetrical along the human likeness dimension and that familiarity increases with human likeness. Moser et al. [16] found a differentiation in the recognition of emotion provoked by an avatar and photographs of human faces between females and males. Chaminade et al. [17] examined the perception of different emotions expressed by a human and a mechanical robot through video clips, using fMRI. There are also some EEG studies examining differences in the perception while interacting with a human or a robot. Theta oscillations have been studied as they are supposed to be correlated with memory processes and can be used as a dependent measure to investigate responses to visual properties of artificial agents [4]. Regarding the frontal theta oscillations, a significant increase in the activity were found when observing a humanoid robot but not a mechanical one [4]. This suggests that frontal theta activity is modulated by the appearance of the agent being observed.

Lastly, we can mention some examples of some already used robot systems that can integrate emotion recognition for interaction tasks. Robot Kismet [18], and his recent extension Jibo, function as companion for commercial purposes and use voice and facial recognition accordingly. Moreover, MOUE [19] is able to capture physiological signals and gestures through a bracelet and a webcam.

1.2   Research Questions

To address the limitations of previous studies and to broaden the field of human-robot interaction, we conducted an experiment with three different types of interaction. Our main consideration is to examine if the brain can perceive the difference between a human and a robot which looks exactly like the human. For that purpose, we used one of the most human-like robots, Nadine and her creator, Nadia Magnenat-Thalmann, and we compared these two conditions with a neutral person.

To constrain as much as possible the subjectivity of the interaction, we introduced 4 specific areas of discussion to all participants (Table 1).

Table 1. Research questions intended to be answered in this study

Questions to be answered:
Is there a difference in the perception of a human and an identical human-like robot?
How brain reacts to a human-humanoid interaction and what brain areas can play the most important role?
Is there a difference in emotions and motivation when simply interacting with a human and an identical robot?

For the validation and the accuracy of our experiment, that is to properly examine the effect of such interactions, we used EEG recording to capture the brain activity, an audio recorder to capture voice and speech features and psychometric measures through a questionnaire which subjectively examined the emotional states of the participants.

2   Material and Methods

2.1   Participants

Twelve healthy adults (all of the participants were male aged from 20 to 35) participated voluntarily in this study. The subject took place in the Institute for Media and Innovation (IMI) at the Nanyang Technological University (NTU). We tried to ensure no previous experience of the participants with robots to avoid any bias in our results. A form of consent, based on the NTU requirements, was signed by all the subjects before the onset of the experiment. None of them mentioned any sign of discomfort.

2.2   Experimental Design

During the experiment, volunteers were exposed to three different types of interaction under the same scenario. The first case (A) constitutes the control case and participants interacted with a neutral person. We chose to put the control case first to avoid any discomfort that might be caused by the interaction with the robot and to enhance the sense of familiarity during the whole process. The second case (B) concerns the human-robot interaction and participants had the opportunity to communicate with Nadine. Nadine is modelled on Prof. Nadia Thalmann, she has very natural-looking skin and hair, and realistic hands, providing a strong human-likeness. We chose to use the interaction with the real identical person as the third and last case (C) to examine if the brain can directly perceive the differences between the two last conditions.

The thematic areas of the discussion were pre-defined and guided by the people or robot involved in the process, but the time of the interaction was up to the participants (Fig. 1).

Fig. 1. Participants during the three types of interaction. Left: Case A - participant with a natural person, Middle: Case B - participants interacting with Nadine, Right: Case C - participant discussing with Prof. Nadia Magnenat Thalmann

2.3   EEG Recordings and Analysis

EEG signals were recorded and amplified using a NuAmps amplifier (https://compumedicsneuroscan.com/applications/eeg/). 34 electrodes were attached on a Quick-Cap according to 10–20 system at the locations Fp, F, FT, FC, C, T, TP, CP, P, PO, O. Curry 8 X was used for the data acquisition and the online processing with a sample rate 1000 Hz per channel.

The analysis of the EEG data and the processing of the signal were carried in MATLAB. All data were carefully checked for artifacts, like eye blinks or head/body movements. Fast Fourier Transform was applied to the signal to transport it to the frequency domain and then the power spectra were calculated. The analysis was conducted in two set ups. The first one consists of 5 Regions of Interest (ROI) examining five brain areas: Prefrontal (Fp), Frontal (F), Parietal (P), Temporal (T) and Occipital (O) whereas the second one analyses the same areas but for each hemisphere (10 ROIs). Brain rhythms that we are mainly interested in are theta (3–7 Hz), alpha (8–12), beta (13–30 Hz) and low gamma (30–42 Hz).

Based on previous studies, we will focus our research in the frontal and parietal areas [11] and we will use the occipital region to investigate the recruitment of visual attention mechanisms. We will also consider the existence of frontal theta oscillations that some studies have already noticed during human-robot interaction [4].

2.4   Dialog and Audio Analysis

The whole conversation was in English. The human participants were from different cultural backgrounds with unique styles of conversation. The thematic areas though were specific no matter the choice of each interviewer. On the other hand, Nadine was operated in two modes: *control* and *free* mode.

Our humanoid in the *control* mode used the Wizard-of-Oz technique and the questions in the interviews were asked in an orderly fashion. The participants had to respond to each of those questions, followed by the free *mode*, where the participant was asked to ask RN anything. In the *free* mode, the answers are based on a chatbot with the architecture in Fig. 2. In our experiment, the episodic memory portion is ignored, since the participant was unfamiliar to Nadine.

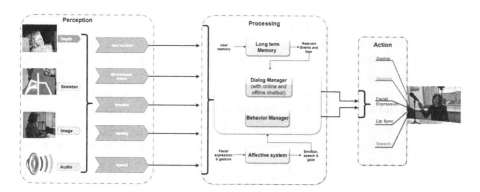

Fig. 2. Nadine's architecture

In our experiment, the episodic memory portion is ignored, since the participant was unfamiliar to Nadine. Therefore, once the speech of the participant is converted to text, it is sent to the chatbot. If the chatbot does not have an appropriate response, it is looked up online. If the online results are not available, a generic default response is given.

2.5   Psychometric Data

To provide our results with a higher validity, a reliable and validated questionnaire, including closed-ended Likert-scale questions, was used. The questionnaire consisted of questions regarding participants' demographic data, and mood states for each condition. The mood states scale was based on the Positive and Negative Affect Schedule, which comprises two mood scales: one measuring positive affect and the other measuring negative.

2.6 Statistics

Statistical analysis was carried out for the variables of the EEG and the questionnaire, through JASP. We conducted Repeated Measures ANOVAs and followed up statistically significant results with the Connover's post-hoc tests. When the data did not meet the sphericity requirement, the corresponding non-parametric Friedman test was used.

3 Results

Our first aim was to reveal the dominant frequencies, and consequently, the dominant brain states in different chosen brain areas, examining the possible effects a human-humanoid interaction may have. Moreover, we intended to correlate these frequencies with positive and negative emotions, comparing them with the psychometric and audio results. The purpose of this preliminary study is not to make a proper emotion recognition, but to study the effects human-humanoid interaction can have on human emotional states and behaviors, thus providing a first glance into this new field of research.

3.1 EEG Data

As we have already mentioned, we have focused on five brain areas. Thus, for the prefrontal area we noticed a general alpha rhythm, same for all the three conditions, with no significance difference ($F(2, 22) = .43$, $p = 0.654$). More than any other area of the brain, prefrontal cortex is fully associated with the personality, planning of complex and social behaviors, decision making and in general with the orientation of our behavior in line with our goals and values [20].

Regarding the frontal area, the analyses exhibited statistically significant differences, $F(2, 22) = 8.63$, $p = .002$. The post-hoc analyses exhibited that the two human cases differed from the one of the robot, $t = 3.76$, $p = .010$ and $t = 5.86$ for the A vs. B and the C vs. B comparisons, respectively. In both human-human interaction, we noticed a high alpha state whereas during the interaction with Nadine theta oscillations were observed (7.8 ± 0.6 Hz). Theta band power increases as a task becomes more demanding [21]. This can be attributed to the participants' bigger cognitive effort to get focused while discussing with Nadine.

Our results in the parietal area complements the above. A non-parametric Friedman test rendered a chi-square value of 7.45, $p = .024$. Connover's post-hoc comparisons exhibited that Control and Robot differed from Human, $t(22) = 2.97$, $p = .021$ and $t(22) = 2.38$, $p = .053$, respectively. In particular, we noticed beta oscillations in both human-human interaction (13.4 ± 3.8 Hz for the A and 14.7 ± 5.5 Hz for the C case) whereas in B case we found a clear alpha state with the 10.8 ± 2.6 Hz. Alpha rhythm in parietal cortex is mostly linked with perception processes [21] whereas beta rhythm is supposed to be an indicator of valence emotions [9] (Fig. 3).

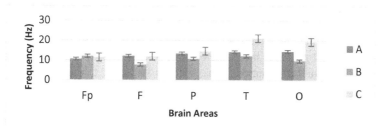

Fig. 3. Mean frequencies observed in each of the 5 ROIs, in response to each case. Power spectra was calculated as $PS = abs(filteredsignal)^\wedge 2$.

Regarding the temporal lobe we noticed again beta oscillations in both human-human interactions (A: 14.2 ± 4.8 Hz, C: 21.1 ± 5.3 Hz) and alpha in the human-robot case (B: 12.2 ± 2.8 Hz), F(2, 22) = 18.51, p < .001. However, the post-hoc analyses exhibited that case C differed from the case A and B t = -3.95, p = .007 and t = −5.35, p < .001, respectively. Temporal lobe, in general, is associated with processing of auditory information [21]. The presence of the alpha band in the human-robot interaction may indicate that participants put a higher effort to decipher Nadine's speech compared to the human's way of talking they are used to.

Lastly, regarding the occipital region, the analysis exhibited statistically significant differences, F(2, 22) = 8.06, p = .002. The post-hoc analysis exhibited that Nadine's case (B) presented an alpha rhythm (9.7 ± 2.3 Hz) differed from both A and C cases (A: 14.5 ± 5.7 Hz, C: 19.4 ± 7.6 Hz), t = −4.26, p = .004 and t = 2.49, p = .090, respectively. This result was more or less predicted and proves that, from a visual perspective, the brain can completely understand the difference between a human and a robot, whatever appearance the latter may have. The alpha band indicates the recruitment of visual attention mechanisms, which obviously were necessary for the processing of the new features. However, we also notice the higher value of the C case, which reveals a bigger familiarity compared to the A case. That may be explained by the fact that participants had first seen Nadine, so they already had created a memory image of this appearance.

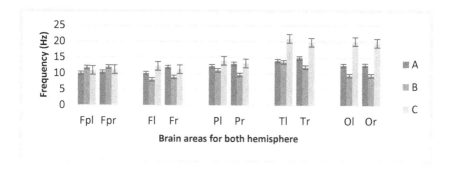

Fig. 4. Mean of frequencies for each brain area for both hemispheres in three conditions

For all these areas, we have also examined possible differences between the two hemispheres, investigating two main questions. Figure 4 presents the outcome of the first question regarding the differences among the three conditions for each hemisphere.

The second, and probably more interesting question regards the difference of each condition in the two hemispheres. Thus, we run statistical tests for the three cases separately and we concluded to the results depicted in Fig. 5. For the case A, we noticed a slightly bigger activation of the right hemisphere, but ANOVA tests revealed no significant differences between the two hemispheres. For the case B, we noticed exactly the opposite, with the left hemisphere to be in a higher activation. Parametric post-hoc tests showed though significant validity only for the frontal and parietal areas. For case C, we noticed again higher values of frequencies in the left hemisphere, but ANOVA tests revealed no statistically significance.

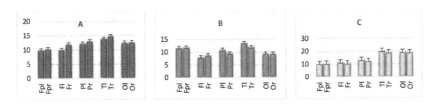

Fig. 5. Differences in frequencies of each case for the two hemispheres

3.2 Psychometric Data

Based on our questionnaire we noticed no negative emotions during the whole procedure. The most dominant emotional states were the Interested, Inspired and Confident which reveal also a sense of motivation. It is also worth mentioning that the state of inspiration appears from the case B and on, with an ascending value, which means that Nadine triggered this reaction to the participants, and they kept being inspired for the rest of the procedure. We can also justify this supporting that they found the similarity in the appearance interesting and motivating. The state of the interest is higher in case B which is normal if we assume that people are not yet so used to the existence of robots and they don't often have the chance to interact with them. The state of concentration was rising along the process. Lastly, the participants felt significantly active only in cases B and C. However, in the question of who was the most comfortable to discuss with, participants voted equally the two humans (Fig. 6).

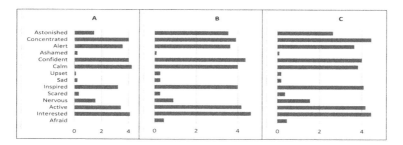

Fig. 6. Participants' emotional states for each condition. The questionnaire was completed at the end of the whole procedure

3.3   Dialog and Audio Data

We observed that the average pitch of the voice is the highest (133 Hz) in the humanoid conversation. Although the small sample size, it seems encouraging to explore the hypothesis where people speak with humanoids in a higher pitch. However, further analysis with more participants is undoubtedly required. In addition, the variable placement of microphone made difficult the comparison of the speech intensity among the participants. Nevertheless, among the questions asked to the participants, there is a peak in the question with regards to belief in the existence of God. This can be due to the emotional nature of the question. This was also verified by our EEG results, as we noticed a higher brain activation during that period of time. There was also noticeable delay in the speech of the conversation in case C. This is perhaps an indicator of *mirroring* by the participant. With accurate speaker diarization and better microphones, we could do a thorough quantitative analysis in the future.

Of interest is the longer duration of conversation in case C. It is in line with the results we acquired from our questionnaire where participants showed higher amount of inspiration and concentration during that case. We can clearly also see that the duration with neutral human was lower than humanoid that is also verified by the questionnaire results. Lastly, we can note that the conversation with the humanoid had no interruptions by the participant when compared to humans. This highlights the limitation of present generation humanoids which lack natural conversational abilities (Fig. 7).

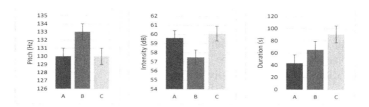

Fig. 7. Mean values for Pitch, Intensity and duration of the interaction for each condition, derived from the audio analysis

4 Discussion and Future Work

In this preliminary study we investigated the human's perception in human-humanoid interaction and its effects in cognitive and emotional states. We have used three cases where people face three difference types of interaction. To support our research, we have used EEG and audio recordings as well as a questionnaire to complement the above. To the best of our knowledge, there is no previous work that could compare a human with her identical humanoid and provide a physical interaction, supporting new insights in the human-robot interaction and the application of it.

Answering our first research question, our results revealed a difference in the perception of a human and an identical human-like robot mainly in the visual perception. However, this is normal as people are not yet used to interacting and physically seeing robots. This difference was uncovered by the existence of alpha state in the occipital lobe, which proves the activation of visual attention mechanisms compared to the human-human interaction where we noticed the existence of beta states and consequently, the sense of familiarity. The latter was more enhanced in the third case, where the human interacted with the human identical to the robot and thus, we are not sure if this familiarity is a result of the first contact of the person with the robot.

Regarding the brain activity, we concluded to some very interesting results. In the prefrontal cortex, we found no difference between the three cases, all of them synchronized in alpha brain state. However, we noticed frontal theta oscillation in case B, human-Nadine interaction, with a clear difference from the other two conditions where we saw the dominance of alpha state. This comes in line with previous studies [4] that have noted the existence of theta oscillations when a human interacts with a humanoid but not with a mechanical robot.

The same result was observed in the parietal area where, only in the human-robot interaction, we noticed the existence of the alpha state, which is associated with the perception process. In general, we conclude that during such an interaction, humans are unintentionally more concentrated to their tasks and we can attribute that to the existence of new, non-familiar elements people are forced to face. We have previously met this behavior in a previous study [22] where during a comparison between physical and virtual environments, it was found that people tend to unconsciously be more concentrated to environment they are not familiar with. This has also been supported by the results of the questionnaire used, where emotions related to motivational states are developed during the human-robot interaction.

Of great interest is the result of the temporal area, which is linked with the processing of auditory information, and is verified by the outcome of the audio analysis. We noticed the presence of the alpha power only in case B which can be attributed to a higher cognitive effort participant made to understand Nadine's voice. This can also be correlated with the higher pitch of the voice participants presented during their interaction with Nadine. It could also be a result of nervousness, but the results of the questionnaire didn't reveal any negative emotion.

We answer our third research question indicating that there is a motivation enhancement throughout our process, with no observation of negative feelings. Participants, in the beginning, were presented as calm, confident and concentrated and while interacting with Nadine new states appeared like inspired, active and interested. The values of all the emotional states were ascending, revealing the high level of motivation. The increasing duration of speech in the three scenarios verifies the same.

To sum up, we remind that the purpose of this study was to provide a first glance of this innovative approach of human-robot interaction and not to execute a proper emotion recognition. The latter is our upcoming goal with which we intend to address any limitation this preliminary work had. Robots and virtual characters are increasingly becoming ubiquitous in our daily lives. Therefore, it is paramount to study our behaviour and emotions to these technological transitions to aid in their humane development and to enhance their applications in several domains like education, rehabilitation or even entertainment.

Acknowledgments. This research is partly supported by the BeingTogether Centre, a collaboration between Nanyang Technological University (NTU) Singapore and University of North Carolina (UNC) at Chapel Hill. The BeingTogether Centre is supported by the National Research Foundation, Prime Ministers Office, Singapore under its International Research Centers in Singapore Funding Initiative. This research is partly supported by the European Commission through the project MINGEI.

References

1. Ekman, P.: Darwin and Facial Expressions. Academic Press, New York (1973)
2. Wang, Y., Quadflieg, S.: In our own image? Emotional and neural processing differences when observing human-human vs human-robot interactions. Soc. Cogn. Affect. Neurosci. **10** (11), 1515–1524 (2014). https://doi.org/10.1093/scan/nsv043
3. Perez-Gaspar, L.A., Caballero-Morales, S.O., Trujillo-Romero, F.: Multimodal emotion recognition with evolutionary computation for human-robot interaction. Expert Syst. Appl. **66**, 42–61 (2016). https://doi.org/10.1016/j.eswa.2016.08.047
4. Urgen, B.A., Plank, M., Ishiguro, H., Poizner, H., Saygin, A.P.: EEG theta and Mu oscillations during perception of human and robot actions. Front. Neurorobot. **7**, 1–13 (2013)
5. Esposito, A., Esposito, A.M., Vogel, C.: Needs and challenges in human computer interaction for processing social emotional information. Pattern Recogn. Lett. **66**, 41–51 (2015)
6. Nakisa, B., Rastgoo, M.N., Tjondronegoro, D., Chandran, V.: Evolutionary computation algorithms for feature selection of EEG-based emotion recognition using mobile sensors. Expert Syst. Appl. **93**, 143–155 (2018). https://doi.org/10.1016/j.eswa.2017.09.062
7. Poria, S., Cambria, E., Hussain, A., Huang, G.B.: Towards an intelligent framework for multimodal affective data analysis. Neural Netw. **63**, 104–116 (2015)
8. Zheng, W.-L., Dong, B.-N., Lu, B.-L.: Multimodal emotion recognition using EEG and eye tracking data. In: 2014 36th Annual International Conference of the IEEE Engineering in Medicine and Biology Society, pp. 5040–5043 (2014). https://doi.org/10.1109/EMBC.2014.6944757
9. Jatupaiboon, N., Pan-Ngum, S., Israsena, P.: Emotion classification using minimal EEG channels and frequency bands. In: 2013 10th International Joint Conference on Computer Science and Software Engineering (JCSSE), pp. 21–24 (2013). https://doi.org/10.1109/JCSSE.2013.6567313

10. Wan Ismail, W.O.A.S., Hanif, M., Mohamed, S.B., Hamzah, N., Rizman, Z.I.: Human emotion detection via brain waves study by using electroencephalogram (EEG). Int. J. Adv. Sci. Eng. Inf. Technol. **6**(6), 1005 (2016)
11. Jenke, R., Peer, A., Buss, M.: Feature extraction and selection for emotion recognition from EEG. IEEE Trans. Affect. Comput. **5**(3), 327–339 (2014)
12. Thammasan, N., Moriyama, K., Fukui, K., Numao, M.: Familiarity effects in EEG-based emotion recognition. Brain Inform. **4**(1), 39–50 (2017). https://doi.org/10.1007/s40708-016-0051-5
13. de Borst, A., de Gelder, B.: Is it the real deal? Perception of virtual characters versus humans: an affective cognitive neuroscience perspective. Front. Psychol. **6**, 576 (2015)
14. Cheetham, M., Pavlovic, I., Jordan, N., Suter, P., Jancke, L.: Category processing and the human likeness dimension of the uncanny valley hypothesis: eye tracking data. Front. Psychol. **4**, 108 (2013)
15. Cheetham, M., Suter, P., Jäncke, L.: The human likeness dimension of the uncanny valley hypothesis: behavioral and functional MFR findings. Front. Hum. Neurosci. **5**, 126 (2011)
16. Moser, E., Derntl, B., Robinson, S., et al.: Amygdala activation at 3T in response to human and avatar facial expressions of emotions. J. Neurosci. Methods **161**, 126–133 (2007)
17. Chaminade, T., Cheng, G.: Social cognitive neuroscience and humanoid robotics. J. Physiol. **103**, 286–295 (2009)
18. Breazeal, C.: Emotion and sociable humanoid robots. Int. J. Hum. Comput. Interact. **59**, 119–155 (2003)
19. Lisetti, C.L., Nasoz, F., Lerouge, C., Ozyer, O., Alvarez, K.: Developing multimodal intelligent affective interfaces for tele-home health care. Int. J. Hum.-Comput. Stud. Spec. Issue Appl. Affect. Comput. HCI **59**(1–2), 245–255 (2003)
20. Babiloni, C., Del Percio, C., Vecchio, F., et al.: Alpha, beta and gamma electrocortico-graphic rhythms in somatosensory, motor, premotor and prefrontal cortical areas differ in movement execution and observation in humans. Clin. Neurophysiol. **127**(1), 641–654 (2016)
21. Cavanagh, J.F., Frank, M.J.: Frontal theta as a mechanism of cognitive control. Trends Cogn. Sci. **18**(8), 414–421 (2014)
22. Baka, E., Stavroulia, K.E., Magnenat-Thalmann, N., Lanitis, A.: An EEG-based evaluation for comparing the sense of presence between virtual and physical environments. In: Proceedings of Computer Graphics International (CGI 2018), 10 p. ACM, New York (2018)

Transferring Object Layouts from Virtual to Physical Rooms: Towards Adapting a Virtual Scene to a Physical Scene for VR

Zackary P. T. Sin$^{(\boxtimes)}$, Peter H. F. Ng, Simon C. K. Shiu,
Fu-lai Chung, and Hong Va Leong

The Hong Kong Polytechnic University, Hung Hom, Hong Kong
{csptsin, cshfng, csckshiu, cskchung,
cshleong}@comp.polyu.edu.hk

Abstract. One crucial problem in VR is to establish a good correspondence between the virtual and physical scenes, while respecting the key structure and layout of the two spaces. A VR scene may well allow a user to move towards a certain direction, but in reality, a wall could block his/her path. The reason is that the virtual scene is often designed by designers for a large user population, being unable to consider individual physical constraints. Recent works involve redirected walking or additional VR hardware. We propose an alternative solution by adapting the virtual scene to the physical scene. The goal is to preserve the layout of the original design while allowing the virtual scene to be fully walkable. To move towards that goal, this paper proposes an object layout transfer mechanism to transfer an object layout from a virtual room to a physical room. A VR application can automatically transfer a designer's virtual scene to fit any household room. Our solution involves key object layout features extraction and a multi-stage algorithm to shuffle the objects in the physical space. A user study is conducted to demonstrate that the proposed model is able to synthesize transferred layouts that appear to be created by a human designer.

Keywords: Object layout transfer · Space adaptation ·
Layout discrepancy measure

1 Introduction

One of the double-edged swords of deploying virtual reality (VR) is the inherent spatial inconsistency between real and virtual environments, especially in the context of game playing and scene exploration. A virtual scene may contain a large explorable area which is good for players staying within small households. However, if the player wishes to explore by walking in reality, due to the limited space of a common physical room, s/he would eventually be blocked. Most games usually allow movement in virtual scenes via joystick controllers instead of actual walking to mitigate the constraint. The player is allowed to move via joystick control input, which is commonly known to induce motion sickness [1, 2]. Some games opt to use a point-to-point teleportation presentation to get around this nausea problem. However, this method is believed to limit the immersiveness of VR gaming.

© Springer Nature Switzerland AG 2019
M. Gavrilova et al. (Eds.): CGI 2019, LNCS 11542, pp. 253–265, 2019.
https://doi.org/10.1007/978-3-030-22514-8_21

Another approach is to use VR treadmill like Virtuix Omni by Virtuix Inc. or KAT WALK by KatVR. Via the additional hardware, the player would be able to walk indefinitely in reality and therefore also a virtual one. It is believed that this kind of hardware could provide a more immersive experience compared to joystick controllers. However, the costs and sizes of such devices may make it less desirable for home-use.

Due to the constraints of the solutions aforementioned, space warping [3] and redirected walking [4] are recently gaining attention. Instead of relying on additional hardware to bound the player, spaces are transformed from time to time such that s/he could explore freely by walking without fear of obstacles in reality. Current works achieved impressive results, but they do not guarantee a complete immersive experience as, for example, it is known for some redirecting techniques to send warning to the player to stop and to turn [5].

Previous methods in some sense attempted to "fit" a virtual environment into a physical one by avoiding the spatial inconsistency problem. An obviously preferable approach is to eliminate spatial inconsistency from the first place. If the virtual scene is spatially similar to the physical scene, the player would be able to explore freely without motion sickness or additional hardware/software to avoid physical obstacles. It is possible to design a virtual scene to spatially match that of a physical room. However, this would be a case-by-case approach that is only suitable for specific scenarios, such as a theme park creating a VR experience for a designated room. A more desirable application would be that a level designer could create a virtual room, and that virtual room would be tuned to match the physical room. Therefore, a designed virtual level could be played in any room, especially household ones.

A new perspective on addressing the spatial inconsistency is proposed. Instead of "fitting" a virtual environment to a physical one, a virtual environment could be synthesized from a physical one such that they are spatially similar. Aside from alleviating the spatial inconsistency, this methodology has an added benefit of "what you see is what you get". If the player sees a virtual wall, it is because there is actually a physical wall. This also means that the player could touch the wall, further enhancing the immersiveness of the VR experience and fun factor of the game via sensational feedback [6]. Our concept is closely related to and inspired by Simeone's substituting reality [7], but our's leans towards synthesizing the virtual space from the physical space while Simeone's focused on utilizing physical objects for interactions. We call our concept *scene adaptation*, i.e. adapting a virtual scene to a physical scene (see Fig. 1).

Fig. 1. The left illustrates the idea of scene adaptation while the right illustrates an object layout transfer model which is a step towards the mentioned idea.

In this paper, we propose a step towards the idea of scene adaptation. Specifically we aim to solve a sub-problem: transferring a designer's object layout to a physical room (Fig. 1). The outcome is that a designer could simply design a single virtual object layout and it could be transferred to any physical room. Concrete application examples include: a virtual museum could be transferred to anyone's living room for walkable visits; or a game level's monster placement where monsters start at specific locations of a room could be transferred to a player's bedroom to surround him/her.

We propose a model to transfer an object layout from a virtual to physical room by utilizing a set of selected features to compute an *Object Layout Discrepancy* (OLD) metric between the virtual and physical room. Via searching in an object placement space, a best placement for each object could be found. It is assumed that the lower the OLD, the more similar the physical room's object layout is to the original design. An illustration of this model is shown in Fig. 2. We highlight a specific process to achieve object layout transfer via the use of OLD metric. To conclude, the main contributions of this paper include: (1) a pipeline to adapt a designer's object layout to a given physical room, (2) a computational process which uses selected features to search for best placements for the virtual objects, and (3) a preliminary user study on the effectiveness.

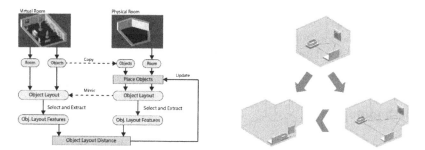

Fig. 2. The left is the proposed model while the right illustrates the result of the proposed model. The right also shows that by extracting object layout features and computing the OLD, a physical room could be placed with virtual objects such that the layout is similar to the original one from the virtual room. As can be seen, the object layout of the bottom-right is better than that of the bottom-left (which does not follow OLD at all) in mimicking the layout at the top.

2   Literature Review

VR treadmills are good hardware solutions for freely exploring virtual realities. However, their costs and sizes impose severe limitations on their home use. They may also require additional setup. Virtuix Omni by Virtuix Inc., for example, requires the player to wear a pair of Omni shoes and also a harness [8].

There is a growing body of literature in space transformation techniques which help players avoid hitting obstacles in the real environment while exploring in virtual reality. Redirection is one such technique which timely rotates the virtual camera [9]. Combined with saccade [10], it can achieve an impressive result that only requires a room of

12.25 m^2 for redirecting [3]. Another technique is to warp the virtual scene to guide the player away from physical obstacles [4]. A downside is that the virtual environment will be distorted and therefore does not reflect the original look and feel.

Our work in contrast does not attempt to allow the player to explore an unconstrained virtual reality in a limited physical space. Instead, we are interested in transferring object layout from a virtual room to any physical room which aids in creating a virtual scene based on an actual physical environment. Thus, our work is closer to furniture planning. Xu et al. [11] proposed a furniture layout system that utilizes pairwise relationships and constraints to help users place furniture quickly. Merrell et al. [12] proposed an interactive furniture layout system that uses internal interior design guidelines to rearrange furniture's placements to make them look more natural together. More recently, Wang et al. [13] has proposed using deep neural networks to iteratively place furniture in a room, creating novel room layouts. However, in contrast to these works that aim to place furniture in such a way that is either functional or aesthetically pleasing, our work aims to transfer the object layout from one room to another such that they look similar.

Regarding works that utilize a physical environment for mixed-reality, Simone et al. [7] is first to propose using real-life objects in the player's environment for interacting in virtual reality. Hettiarachchi and Wigdor [14] proposed a pipeline that pairs a virtual object to a real object in real-time, so that the user could wear an augmented-reality device to see and 'touch' the virtual object. Specific to control, Cheng et al. [15] demonstrated that daily objects could be used as novel controllers and Corsten et al. [16] has developed a tracker that enables user to assign novel objects as alternative controllers.

3   Methodology

In this section, the transfer mechanism for an object layout is discussed. The key idea is to use some selected features to compute an object layout discrepancy (OLD). The OLD metric is used to search for best placement of virtual objects in a physical room. In our prototype, each virtual object is paired with one another forming a relation and the object layout feature is the collection of captured relations. To simplify the computational problem by limiting the search space, we have also divided objects into three categories. Each of them has a different placement space to search. In this section, we divide the content into three parts. We will first discuss what exactly the object layout features are; then what exactly the virtual objects are; finally what exactly the method to place virtual objects in a physical room is.

3.1   Object Layout

In a broad sense, an object layout describes the spatial relations between objects (Fig. 2). Hence, it is useful to model the spatial relations between objects. First, the relation between object O_i and O_j is defined as $R(i, j)$, where i and j are object indexes such that $i \neq j$. We picked two relational features that could be used to form the object layout feature.

The first relational feature is the normalized distance $R_r(i, j)$ between two objects.

$$R_r(i,j) = \frac{\|\vec{O}_i - \vec{O}_j\|}{\min_{u,v} \|\vec{O}_u - \vec{O}_v\|} \tag{1}$$

where u and v are also object indexes such that $u \neq v$ and we present the position of an object O as a vector in the Euclidian space.

This distance term is useful to depict whether the relative distance of each object is maintained in the physical room. The reason why relative distance is picked over absolute distance is because there will be varying room sizes. The second relational feature is the direction $R_\theta(i, j)$. It is the direction of an object with respect to another.

$$R_\theta(i,j) = \frac{\vec{O}_j - \vec{O}_i}{\|\vec{O}_j - \vec{O}_i\|} \tag{2}$$

As mentioned, object layout discrepancy (OLD) is used to find the most suitable placements of objects such that the physical room's object layout is similar to that of the original. The OLD is measuring the difference between each relation pair, one from the virtual room V and its correspondence from the physical room P such that

$$OLD(V, P) = \frac{1}{N(N-1)} \sum_i^N \sum_{j \neq i}^N (|R_{r_V}(i,j) - R_{r_P}(i,j)| \cdot \lambda_r$$
$$+ |R_{\theta_V}(i,j) \cdot R_{\theta_P}(i,j) - 1| \cdot \lambda_\theta + \left| \|\vec{O}_{V_i} - \vec{O}_{V_j}\| \cdot \sqrt{\frac{Size(P)}{Size(V)}} - \|\vec{O}_{P_i} - \vec{O}_{P_j}\| \right| \cdot \lambda_s) \tag{3}$$

where λ is a parameter that controls the weight of a term and N is the number of objects. The first term is comparing the difference in R_r. This term helps us to preserve the relative distance between each object such that if two objects are far away from each other in V, it will also try to be so in P. The second term is comparing the difference in R_θ. This term preserves the directional relations of objects such that if an object O_a is on the right of O_b in V, it will also try to be so in P. The dot product term is transformed such that if the directions are dissimilar, a positive cost value is produced. The third and last term is what we refer to as the size term. It takes into account of the sizes of the rooms by scaling the corresponding distance measures in the two rooms in such a way that the proposed model will not cluster all the objects in one part of the room simply to minimize OLD. A square root is imposed on the size ratio of the two rooms because the area grows quadratically with the length. It should be noted here that since V and P could be of different shapes, the relations from V cannot be guaranteed to be preserved in P. Experimental results in Sect. 4.2 suggest that OLD will become larger when the dissimilarity between the shapes of the two rooms increases.

3.2 Virtual Objects

In an ideal case, it should be possible to simply optimize OLD by finding the best possible positions for all objects. However, our experiments show that this is difficult to achieve practically as the large placement space has many local minima. Instead, a specific process is proposed to find an improved solution. The objects will first be separated manually into three categories, major-walled objects, minor-walled objects and non-walled objects. The main purpose of this categorization is to limit the placement space for each object. The designer would need to manually categorize the objects. Since this is a one-off process, we believe this is an acceptable tradeoff.

Major-Walled Object. Objects in this category (O_M) are objects that are walled and deemed important by the designer. They could be objects that are critical to the layout. It is expected that they are usually objects with greater sizes or simply deemed to be of greater importance by the designer. For example, when recreating a virtual museum, the virtual paintings of Mona Lisa and The Coronation of Napoleon I are likely to be of this category. By placing objects in this category, the proposed method would take precedence in finding the most suitable placements for them. Since these are walled objects, their search spaces are limited to the physical room's walls H_w as shown in Fig. 3. Hence, the search space for a major-walled object is $S_M = [0, 1]$ where 0 and 1 denote the starting and ending point of the room's wall respectively. Since the room is enclosed, 0 and 1 are equivalent in that they are representing the same point of the room. If a major-walled object indexed i, $O_M^{(i)}$, is located midway along the room's walls, we denote that $H_w(O_M^{(i)}) = 0.5$.

Fig. 3. Illustrations on major-walled objects (O_M), minor-walled objects (O_m) and non-walled objects (O_o), from left to right with gradual inclusion.

Minor-Walled Object. The minor-walled object (O_m) category is for walled objects that are not major-walled objects. Since they are deemed less important to the designer, these objects compared to the major-walled objects are given secondary priority in finding the most suitable placements. It is assumed that a minor-walled object is bounded by two major-walled objects. So, not only is its search space simply of one dimension, it is also bounded by the two closest major-walled objects along the wall. So, if $O_m(i)$ has $O_M^{(j)}$ and $O_M^{(k)}$ as neighbours, we denote that $Flk(O_m^{(i)}) = (O_M^{(j)}, O_M^{(k)})$. It means that $O_m^{(i)}$ is flanked by $O_M^{(j)}$ and $O_M^{(k)}$ such that $H_w(O_M^{(j)}) < H_w(O_m^{(i)}) < H_w(O_M^{(k)})$. An illustration of minor-walled objects is also provided in Fig. 3.

Non-walled Object. This category as its name implied contains objects (O_o) that are simply not walled. They are the last type of objects to search for best placements. The reason is that walled objects are used as reference to find the best placement. As the objects are non-walled, their search spaces are not simply along the wall but within the entirety of the room. However, it is proposed that the search space could be limited to one dimension via drawing a line that cut the room in half. We refer to such a line as the half room line C. The object could then simply move along the line to find its best placement. So, the search space for non-walled objects is $S_o = [0, 1]$. But unlike S_M, 0 and 1 do not meet at the same point in the spatial space. To avoid abrupt positional change along C, smoothing could also be considered. An illustration of non-walled objects is given in Fig. 3 as well.

3.3 Object Placement

There are two intuitions for layout transfer and they are: (1) we could approximate a virtual object's placement then fine-tune it, and (2) we could make assumptions regarding the dependencies between virtual objects of different categories.

The exact method to approximate the placement of an object depends on the category, but for fine-tuning, the strategy is fundamentally the same. Figure 4 showcases the step by step result of the proposed object layout transfer procedure.

Fig. 4. Illustration of the proposed object layout transfer procedure. Left to right: empty room, after major-walled object placement (approximation and fine-tuning), after minor-walled object placement and after non-walled object placement.

Major-Walled Object Approximation. Major-walled objects O_M are relatively few in numbers and are considered as a noticeable part of the designer's layout. So, they are given priority in searching for the best placements. To approximate O_M's placement, it is proposed that each object $O_M^{(i)}$ in O_M first searches for a wall W in P to attached on that would minimize the object layout discrepancy (OLD). That is, we are trying to find the best (O_M, W) pair for Eq. (4):

$$min_{(O_M^{(i)}, W_j)} OLD(V, P) \tag{4}$$

where W_j denotes a W indexed j. Note that at this moment, since only O_M have been copied from V to P, the relations to compute OLD are only the ones between each O_M.

Major-Walled Object Fine-Tuning. Searching which W is best for an O_M does not minimize OLD. It is proposed that the second step is to fine-tune the position of all O_M along the room's encircled wall for improving the cost function. Thus, the goal is to minimize

$$min_{H_w(O_M^{(i)})} OLD(V,P).\qquad(5)$$

Note that since we are trying to find all $H_w(O_M^{(i)})$ that minimize OLD, the placement of an object in O_M is not bounded to the paired wall in the previous step. Although that is the case, the previous approximation step should find a good enough placement for each O_M such that the topological relationship among objects in O_M remains the same.

Minor-Walled Object Approximation. Once the best placement for O_M has been found, the search space of a minor-walled object O_m, S_m can be limited. We make an intuitive assumption that if $O_m^{(i)}$ is flanked by $O_M^{(j)}$ and $O_M^{(k)}$ in the virtual room, $O_m^{(i)}$ will also be flanked in the physical room. Given $Flk(O_m^{(i)})=(O_M^{(j)}, O_M^{(k)})$, for approximating its rough placement, we simply compute

$$H_{wP}\left(O_m^{(i)}\right) = H_{wP}\left(O_M^{(j)}\right) + \frac{H_{wV}(O_m^{(i)}) - H_{wV}(O_M^{(j)})}{H_{wV}(O_M^{(k)}) - H_{wV}(O_M^{(j)})} \cdot \left(H_{wP}\left(O_M^{(k)}\right) - H_{wP}\left(O_M^{(j)}\right)\right).$$

$$(6)$$

Minor-Walled Object Fine-Tuning. Similar to fine-tuning placement of objects in O_M, fine-tuning the placement of objects in O_m is to minimize the OLD. The main difference is that the search space is limited such that

$$min_{H_w(O_m^{(i)})} OLD(V,P)\qquad(7)$$

where $H_w(O_M^{(j)}) < H_w(O_m^{(i)}) < H_w(O_M^{(k)})$. However, the OLD computation does not only involve relations between O_M, but also O_m and across the two categories.

Non-walled Object Approximation. To approximate the placement of a non-walled object $O_o^{(i)}$, we need to first make use of the half room line of the virtual room V, C_V, to find where roughly an object in O_o should be. $C_V(O_o) = (x, y)$ gives us the room width ratio x and room length ratio y of the object O_o. Both x and y are bounded by 0 and 1. For x, 0 represents one side of the room, while 1 represents the other side. Similar for y, 0 represents the start of the room while 1 represents the end of the room. The O_o's approximation is done by copying $C_V(O_o)$ to $C_P(O_o)$ such that

$$C_P\left(O_o^{(i)}\right) = C_V\left(O_o^{(i)}\right).\qquad(8)$$

Non-walled Object Fine-Tuning. The fine-tuning for non-walled objects is also similar to the other two:

$$min_{C_P(O_o^{(i)})} OLD(V,P).\qquad(9)$$

So, we simply consider searching along the room line to fine-tune a non-walled object's placement.

4   Evaluation

We first showcase the results of the proposed model compared with two other models. Then, to give better insight on the limitations of the proposed model, the result of transferring the object layout to rooms with different shapes is shown.

4.1   User Study

We followed [11] in conducting a user study to evaluate the effectiveness of our proposed model. The purpose of the user study is to see if a human considers the proposed model and its associated implementation are capable of transferring the object layout in a convincing way. We have compared three different models (Fig. 5): our proposed model based on the method mentioned in Sect. 3; a baseline random placement model which randomly picks placements for objects; and a bounding box placement model which scales the virtual room to fit into the physical room.

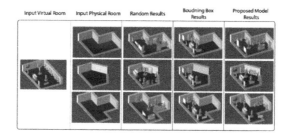

Fig. 5. Comparing the proposed model to random placement and bounding box placement with L-shape, D-shape and T-shape physical room.

In the survey, we inform the respondents that we have developed a model that could transfer object layout from one room to another. We ask them in a 5-point Likert scale question format regarding their certainty as to whether a resulting object layout is coming from a human designer. A score of 5 represents that they are most convinced that the object placement is done by a designer, while a score of 1 represents that they are most convinced that it is done by a computer instead. In the survey, we have indicated to the respondents the original object layout and the three empty rooms that the layout will transfer to. Each of the three rooms will be filled via the three afore-mentioned models. So, for each room-model pair, the respondent is asked regarding their certainty on whether the room's layout is created by the designer. The assumption is that, the more convincing a model is, the more its result is able to fake a human on that it is created by a human designer. It should be noted that none of the three rooms have their objects actually placed by a human. In total, we have received 33 responses. A snippet of the survey could be found in Fig. 6.

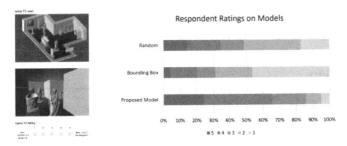

Fig. 6. The left is an example of a question in the survey. A first-person view is also given to help a respondent feel what the room would look like being physically inside it. The right is the chart on how certain the respondent believes that the resulting placement is created by a human designer.

As shown in Fig. 6, compared with the other two models, it is much more likely for respondents to choose the proposed model as the probable designer. To statistically compare whether the proposed model is more convincing than the other two models, two matched paired t-tests are performed. In Table 1, the rating of each model is shown on the left column while the rating difference of a model to the proposed model (meaning, how much higher/lower a respondent rate a model against the proposed model) is shown on the middle column. As shown in Table 1, it is statistically significant ($p < 0.05$) that the respondents rate the proposed model higher compared to the other two. This result indicates that the respondents believe that the proposed model could transfer the layout most convincingly out of the three. It should be noted that although the bounding box model could achieve a lower OLD as shown in Table 2, since it did not fully utilize the entire room, it generally fails to convince the respondents. This shows that simply copying the layout is insufficient for a good layout transfer.

Table 1. Respondent answer statistics.

	Mean score (SD)	Mean score difference (SD) with proposed model	p-value (t-test with proposed model)
Random	2.798 (1.102)	0.909 (1.799)	0.0066600
Bounding Box	2.091 (1.094)	1.616 (1.446)	0.0000003
Proposed Model	3.707 (0.920)	–	–

Table 2. The object layout discrepancy result for each model-room pair.

	L-Shape	D-Shape	T-Shape
Random	31.492	28.921	41.100
Bounding Box	13.541	8.408	10.676
Proposed Model	9.527	13.793	10.349

4.2   Properties of the Proposed Model

To make it easier to observe its properties, the proposed model is tasked to transfer an object layout to different rooms similar to the user study. However this time, the focus is on comparing the different OLDs for each room shape. In Fig. 7, we first deploy the model on regular polygonal rooms with different number of sides. As the result indicates, a larger number of sides would result in a higher value of OLD. This is expected as when there are more sides, the less likely the model could find a placement that fits the directional requirement of the original layout (for example, that an object is supposed to be on the exact right of another according to the virtual room).

Fig. 7. Comparison of the OLD when transferring an object layout to regular polygonal rooms with different numbers of sides (left) and transferring to rooms with 'peculiar' shapes (right).

We are also interested in testing the proposed model on rooms with 'peculiar' shapes. They are a cross-shape room, a u-shape room, a double-u room and a triple-u room as shown in Fig. 7. The result seems to indicate that the more complex a room is, the higher the OLD would be. For this case, since the rooms offer more corners for the proposed model to work with, the higher OLD seems to be related to the fact that the growth of the in-between object distances could not catch up with that of the growth in the room sizes.

Both of these results show an inherent problem with the proposed model that when the physical room is significantly different from the virtual room, the algorithm would simply have difficulty transferring the object layout. This outcome could be attributed to the fact that the algorithm has no component of creativity and therefore could not internalize the layout. It could simply attempt to seek for object placements which would make it as similar to the original one as possible. However, for some scenarios, it is suggested that the physical room could be segmented into smaller areas. The area most suitable for object layout transfer could be used. Although this approach could not utilize all of the rooms, it could improve the OLD of the transferred layout. This is also in line with the better OLD generated by the bounding box approach.

It is worth noting here that the proposed model does not consider whether the sizes of the objects are suitable with respect to the size of the physical room. If only using the proposed implementation here, a very large physical room will have large distances between objects due to the relatively small sizes of the objects. However, it is believed that this problem could be easily resolved by resizing the transferred objects in accordance to the size of the physical room as much as possible.

5   Conclusion and Future Work

One of the main problems in VR is how we could physically walk to explore a much larger virtual environment while residing in a household room. In this paper, we suggested that the virtual scene could be adapted in accordance to the physical room. Spatially speaking, the virtual environment is similar to that of the physical one and therefore the player could freely walk around in the virtual environment. We proposed a step towards this direction with object layout transfer, which could transfer the designed object layout from a virtual room to any physical room. This is useful because many games involve a specific virtual object layout created by a designer. Our method involves selecting a set of object layout features to compute an object layout discrepancy (OLD). The best placement for a virtual object could then be determined via minimizing the discrepancy. To evaluate the proposed object layout transfer model, a user study is conducted on whether the transferred layout could fool respondents that it is more likely created by a designer. The result seems to imply that the proposed model is rather successful in placing objects in a convincing way.

Currently, the algorithm only considers the room's walls to help constrain the search space. It is believed that the next step to this line of work could be considering also physical obstacles. By strategically placing virtual objects where physical obstacles are, it could help the player prevent colliding with them. Once this is achieved, a virtual scene would be directly applicable to any home room and the player could play without any consideration of his/her room's physical constraints. Thus, a player would be able to enjoy a more immersive VR experience where s/he can physically walk and interact with the virtual environment.

The physical rooms currently shown in this paper are simply simulations to test the feasibility of the proposed model. The user study only evaluates whether the generated layout is more convincing. The important question regarding how users will actually feel in a virtual space generated from a real physical room when playing VR is not known. Therefore, another important research direction would be to study and capture the user experience in interacting with a virtualized physical room. By using a scanned physical room and transferring an object layout to it, the user playing in VR could report his/her own feeling regarding safety, fun and immersiveness.

References

1. Ohyama, S.: Automatic responses during motion sickness induced by virtual reality. Auris Nasus Int. J. ORL&HNS **34**(3), 303–306 (2007)
2. Kennedy, R.S., Drexler, J., Kennedy, R.C.: Research in visually induced motion sickness. Appl. Ergon. **41**(4), 494–503 (2010)
3. Sun, Q., et al.: Towards virtual reality infinite walking: dynamic saccadic redirection. ACM Trans. Graph. **37**(4), 67 (2018)
4. Dong, Z.-C., Fu, X.-M., Zhang, C., Wu, K., Liu, L.: Smooth assembled mappings for large-scale real walking. ACM Trans. Graph. **36**(6), 211 (2017)
5. Azmandian, M., Grechkin, T., Suma, E.: An evaluation of strategies for two-user redirected walking in shared physical spaces. In: IEEE Virtual Reality, Los Angeles (2017)
6. Hunicke, R., LeBlanc, M., Zubek, R.: MDA: a formal approach to game design and game research. In: AAAI Workshop on Challenges in Game AI (2004)
7. Simeone, A.L., Velloso, E., Gellersen, H.: Substitutional reality: using the physical environment to design virtual reality experiences. In: ACM Conference on Human Factors in Computing Systems, Seoul (2015)
8. Avila, L., Bailey, M.: Virtual reality for the masses. IEEE Comput. Graph. Appl. **34**(5), 103–104 (2014)
9. Steinicke, R., Bruder, G., Jerald, J., Frenz, H., Lappe, M.: Estimation of detection thresholds for redirected walking techniques. IEEE Trans. Vis. Comput. Graph. **16**(1), 17–27 (2010)
10. Burr, D.C., Morrone, M.C., Ross, J.: Selective suppression of the magnocellular visual pathway during saccadic eye movements. Nature **371**(6497), 511–513 (1994)
11. Xu, K., Stewart, J., Fiume, E.: Constraint-based automatic placement for scene composition. In: Graphics Interface, Calgary (2002)
12. Merrell, P., Schkufza, E., Li, Z., Agrawala, M., Koltun, V.: Interactive furniture layout using interior design guidelines. In: SIGGRAPH, Vancouver (2011)
13. Wang, K., Savva, M., Chang, A.X., Ritchie, D.: Deep convolutional priors for indoor scene synthesis. ACM Trans. Graph. **37**(4), 70 (2018)
14. Hettiarachchi, A., Wigdor, D.: Annexing reality: enabling opportunistic use of everyday objects as tangible proxies in augmented reality. In: ACM Conference on Human Factors in Computing Systems, San Jose (2016)
15. Cheng, K.-Y., Liang, R.-H., Chen, B.-Y., Liang, R.-H., Kuo, S.-Y.: iCon: utilizing everyday objects as additional, auxiliary and instant tabletop controllers. In: ACM Conference on Human Factors in Computing Systems, Atlanta (2010)
16. Corsten, C., Avellino, I., Mollers, M., Borchers, J.: Instant user interfaces: repurposing everyday objects as input devices. In: ACM International Conference on Interactive Tabletops and Surfaces, St. Andrews (2013)

Fast Simulation of Crowd
Collision Avoidance

John Charlton$^{(\boxtimes)}$ⓘ, Luis Rene Montana Gonzalezⓘ, Steve Maddockⓘ,
and Paul Richmondⓘ

University of Sheffield, Sheffield S10 2TN, UK
{j.a.charlton,lrmontanagonzalez1,s.maddock,p.richmond}@sheffield.ac.uk

Abstract. Real-time large-scale crowd simulations with realistic behavior, are important for many application areas. On CPUs, the ORCA pedestrian steering model is often used for agent-based pedestrian simulations. This paper introduces a technique for running the ORCA pedestrian steering model on the GPU. Performance improvements of up to 30 times greater than a multi-core CPU model are demonstrated. This improvement is achieved through a specialized linear program solver on the GPU and spatial partitioning of information sharing. This allows over 100,000 people to be simulated in real time (60 frames per second).

Keywords: Pedestrian simulation · Real-time rendering ·
GPU-computing

1 Introduction

Crowd simulations are important for many applications, such as safety studies for communal transport hubs and flows within sports stadiums and large buildings [29]. Such simulations require believable dynamics that match observed behavior, including correct collision avoidance, or steering behavior. The Optimal Reciprocal Collision Avoidance (ORCA) algorithm [4] is an agent-based solution that can simulate many real crowd behaviors. Currently, implementations of the ORCA algorithm have been made for single- and multi-core CPU. This paper presents a GPU implementation, supporting real-time simulations and interactivity for very large populations of order 5×10^5.

Computer models that contain inherent parallelism are suitable candidates for GPUs. This applies to agent-based pedestrian simulation models, where all agents follow the same rules. Using steering techniques that lend themselves well to implementation on GPU architecture can result in much faster performance [2,5]. By increasing performance, greater numbers of people can be simulated and/or a more accurate, possibly more time-consuming, algorithm can be used for the simulation.

This paper presents a GPU implementation of the ORCA model for agent-based pedestrian simulation. We parallelize as much of the data and computation as possible, choosing data parallel algorithms and spatial partitioning to allow

M. Gavrilova et al. (Eds.): CGI 2019, LNCS 11542, pp. 266–277, 2019.
https://doi.org/10.1007/978-3-030-22514-8_22

communication between people to provide speedup. Our solution makes use of a novel low-dimension linear program solver developed for the architecture of a GPU [8], and a grid-based spatial partitioning scheme of information transfer between GPU threads [22]. Grid partitioned data structures are an efficient form of spatial partitioning on the GPU [17]. Our GPU implementation shows performance increases of up to 30 times over the original CPU multi-core version [4,26] with these changes. In addition, it consistently outperforms the CPU version for sufficiently large amounts of people.

The organization of the paper is as follows. Section 2 covers background information and related work. Section 3 explains in detail the implementation of the ORCA model on the GPU. Section 4 presents results and discussion of the multicore CPU and GPU ORCA models. Finally, Sect. 5 gives the conclusions.

2   Background

Many types of models have been proposed to generate local pedestrian motion and collision avoidance [20,21,27]. The simplest separation of steering models is between continuum models and microscopic models. Continuum models attempt to treat the whole crowd in a similar way to a fluid, allowing for fast simulation of larger numbers of people, but are lacking in accuracy at the individual person scale [18]. Moving part of the calculation to the GPU has shown performance improvements [9]. Overall, however, the model is not ideal for solving on the GPU due to the large sparse data structures. In comparison, microscopic models tend to be paired with a global path planner to give people goal locations and trajectories. Such models specify rules at the individual person scale, with crowd-scale dynamics being an emergent effect of the rules and interactions, and easily allow for non-homogeneous agents and behavior.

Popular microscopic models are cellular automata (CA), social forces [14] and velocity obstacles (VO) [10]. CA are popular due to the ability to reproduce observable phenomena [6,7], but a downside is the inability to reproduce other behaviors due to using discrete space. CA models are computationally lightweight and lend themselves well to specify certain complex behavior. However, CA pedestrian models tend to use discrete spatial rules, where the order of agent movements are sequential, which does not lend itself to parallelism and GPU implementations [24]. Social forces models use a computationally lightweight set of rules that allows for crowd-scale observables such as lane formation. They are well suited to parallelizing on the GPU since all agents can be updated simultaneously, with good performance for many simulated people [15,23]. However, generated simulations can result in unrealistic looking motion and produce undesirable behavior at large densities.

Velocity obstacles (VO) work by examining the velocity and position of nearby moving objects to compute a collision-free trajectory. Velocity-space is analyzed to determine what velocities can be taken which do not cause collisions. VO models lend themselves to parallelization since agents are updated simultaneously and navigate independently of one another with minimal explicit communication. It tends to be more computational and memory intensive than social forces models, but the large throughput capability of the GPU for such parallel tasks make it a very suitable technique for GPU implementation. Early models assumed that each person would take full responsibility for avoiding other people. Several variations include the reactive behavior of other models [1, 11, 16]. One example is reciprocal velocity obstacles (RVO), where the assumption is that all other people will take half the responsibility for avoiding collisions [3, 12]. This model has been implemented on the GPU [5] and has shown credible speedup over the multi-core CPU implementation through use of hashing instead of naive nearest neighbor search. Group behavior has also been included in VO models [13, 30] allowing people to be joined into groups. Such people attempt to remain close to other members of the group and aim for the same goal location. A further extension is optimal reciprocal collision avoidance (ORCA). It provides sufficient conditions for collision-free motion. It works by solving low-dimension linear programs. Freely available code libraries have been implemented for both single- and multi-core CPU [26].

VO techniques are very suitable candidates for GPU implementation. The RVO model and implementation by Bleiweiss [5] show notable performance gains against multi-core CPU equivalent models. However, these methods must perform expensive calculations to find a suitable velocity. They tend to perform slower and are not guaranteed to find the best velocity. ORCA is deemed more suitable because of its performance relative to other VO models and collision-free motion, theoretically providing "better" motion (i.e. less collisions).

Linear programming is a way of maximizing an objective function subject to a set of constraints. For ORCA, linear programming is used to find the closest velocity to a person's desired velocity which does not result in collisions. It is important to choose a solver that is efficient on the GPU at low dimensions. A popular solver type is the Simplex method. This is best suited for large dimension problems and struggles at lower dimensions. The incremental solver [25] is efficient at low dimensions but suffers on the GPU due to load balance: not all GPU threads have the same amount of computation, which reduces the performance on such parallel architecture. The batch GPU two-dimension linear solver [8] is an efficient way to solve the numerous linear problems simultaneously. We make use of this approach, demonstrating its use for large-scale pedestrian simulations.

3   The Algorithm

The proposed algorithm is based on the multi-core ORCA model and applies GPU optimizations. This section provides an overview of the algorithm as well as important changes and optimizations that need to be made to make the simulation efficient for running on the GPU. For more in-depth description of the ORCA algorithm, see the work of van den Berg et al. [4]. The main changes are the use of an efficient linear program made for GPUs and an efficient method of communication between GPU cores for people to "observe" properties of other people.

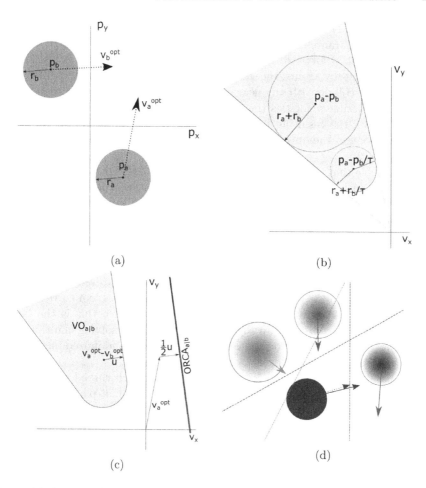

Fig. 1. (a) A system of 2 people a and b with corresponding radius r_a and r_b. (b) The associated velocity obstacle $VO_{a|b}$ in velocity space for a look-ahead period of time τ caused by the neighbor b for a. (c) The vector of velocities $v_a^{opt} - v_b^{opt}$ lies within the velocity obstacle $VO_{a|b}$. The vector u is the shortest vector to the edge of the obstacle from the vector of velocities. The corresponding half-plane $ORCA_{a|b}$ is in the direction of u, and intersects the point $v_a^{opt} + u$. (d) A view of a blue agent and its neighbors, as well as the generated half-planes caused by the neighbors interacting with the blue agent. The solid blue arrow shows the desired velocity of the blue agent. The dotted blue arrow is the resulting calculated velocity that does not collide with any neighbor in time τ. (Color figure online)

As an overview to the ORCA model, each person in the model has a start location and an end location they want to reach as quickly as possible, subject to an average speed and capped maximum speed. For each simulation iteration, each agent "observes" properties of nearby people, namely radius, the current position and velocity. For each nearby agent a half-plane of restricted velocities is calculated (Fig. 1). By selecting a velocity not restricted by this half-plane, the two agents are guaranteed to not collide within time τ, where τ is the *lookahead time*, the amount of forward time planning people make to avoid collisions. By considering all nearby agents, the set of half-planes creates a set of velocities that, if taken, do not collide with any nearby agents in time τ. The agent then selects from the permissible velocities the one closest to its desired velocity and goal. Figure 1d shows the resulting half-planes caused by neighboring agents on an example setup, and the optimal velocity that most closely matches the person's desired velocity.

It is possible that the generated set of half-planes does not contain any possible velocities. Such situations are caused by large densities of people. The solution is to select a velocity that least penetrates the set of half-planes induced by the other agents. In this case, there is no guarantee of collision-free motion.

The computation of velocity subject to the set of half-planes is done using linear programming. The problem for the linear program is defined with the constraints corresponding to the half-plane $ORCA_{a|b}$ of velocities, attempting to minimize the difference of the suitable velocity from the desired velocity. Since each agent needs to find a new velocity, there is a linear problem corresponding to each agent, each iteration. The algorithm used to solve this is the batch-GPU-LP algorithm [8]. It is an algorithm designed for solving multiple low-dimensional linear programs on the GPU, based on the randomized incremental linear program solver of Seidel [25].

This batch-LP solver works by initially assigning each thread to a problem (i.e. one pedestrian). Each thread must solve a set of half-plane constraints, subject to an optimization function. Respectively, these are that the person should not choose a velocity that collides with other people, and the person wants to travel as close to their desired velocity as possible.

Each half-plane constraint is considered incrementally. If the current velocity is not satisfied by the currently considered constraint a new valid velocity is calculated. The calculation of a new velocity is one of the most computationally expensive operations. It is also very branched, as only only some of the solvers require a new valid velocity and others can maintain their current value. This branching calculation causes the threads that do no need to perform a calculation to remain idle while the other threads perform the operation. This is an unbalanced workload on the GPU device and can vastly reduce the throughput as many threads do not perform any calculations, exacerbated by the fact that those threads performing the operation must take a lot of time to complete the operation.

The implementation of this calculation uses ideas from cooperative thread arrays [28] to subdivide the calculation into *"work units"*, blocks of equal size computation. These work units can be transferred to and computed by different threads, allowing for a balanced work load and good performance. If the thread does not need to compute a new velocity, then it can aid in another problem's calculation. This algorithm shows performance improvements over state-of-the-art CPU LP solvers and other GPU LP solvers [8].

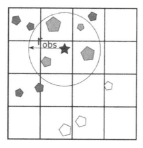

Fig. 2. FLAME message partitioning. The simulation is discretized into spatial bins and people save their message to the corresponding bin. For a given person (blue star), it does not read messages of those in non-neighboring bins (white pentagons). For those within the same or neighboring partitioning bins, it calculates whether they are within the observation radius r_{obs}. If not, they are ignored (grey pentagons). If they are within the observation radius (green pentagon) the person is aware of them and will attempt to avoid them accordingly, by generating corresponding ORCA half-planes of valid velocities. (Color figure online)

The other main improvement is concerning the communication between people. Some information must be observed by people in the model. Examples are the radius, speed and position of others nearby. In order to communicate this information between people we use the idea of messages from the FLAME GPU framework [22], which is demonstrated in Fig. 2. Each agent creates a message which contains information on observables about themselves. Each message is assigned a spatial location equal to the position of the agent in the simulation. These messages are organized into spatial bins. Each agent will then read the messages from its associated bin, and those neighboring. This method is far faster than a brute-force read all approach for large spaces and many people/messages. The associated overhead in organizing messages into bins outweighs the cost of reading all messages and discarding those far away. A possible alternate implementation, that is used by the CPU model, uses a KD-tree spatial partitioning. It is expected, from the work of Li and Mukundan [17], that this grid based spatial partitioning is faster than a KD-tree implementation on the GPU.

4   Results

This section presents the results of two experiments. The first experiment is composed of two test cases to demonstrate the appearance and correctness of the model. The first test case is a two-way crossing and the second test case is an eight-way crossing. The second experiment demonstrates the performance compared to the equivalent multi-core CPU version [4, 26].

For the first experiment, all the test cases are set up in a similar way. Multiple associated start and end regions are chosen, such that people are spawned in a start region with a target in an associated end region. Random spawn locations are chosen so that there is no overlap with other people within a certain time period based on person size and speed. Within a simulation, each agent has a goal location to aim for. The agent's velocity is in the direction of the goal location, scaled to the walking speed. Once a person reaches the goal location they are removed from the simulation. Once all people have reached their goal the simulation is ended.

The first test case was a 2-way crossing, with the two crowds attempting to pass amongst each other to reach their destination. Two variations of this were simulated. The first involves all people with the same size and speed parameters. The second version varies the size and speed parameters of each individual. Figure 3 shows the first variation for 2.5×10^3 people. The starting region of one group of people is the same area as the goal region of the other, forcing the two groups to navigate past each other. All agents have the same parameters, namely radius = 0.5 m, desired speed = 1.0 m/s and maximum speed = 1.33 m/s. Various expected behaviors such as lane formation can be observed. The visualizations of the results are done by saving the agent data for each simulation step to a binary file and passing this to the Unreal engine.

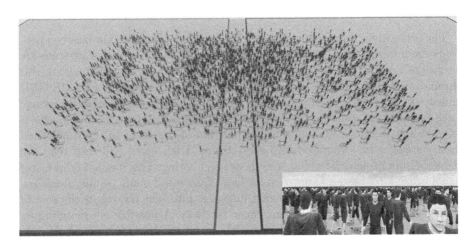

Fig. 3. Visualization of 2,500 people in Unreal. Two crowds navigate past each other, one heading from left to right and the other heading from right to left. Left: scene view from above. Colored arrows show the direction of travel. One pedestrian is highlighted with a green circle; Inset: view from the perspective of the pedestrian in the green circle (Color figure online)

In the second variation of the first test case, people have different sizes and different maximum speeds. Figure 4 illustrates this. In this example all people have an equal chance of being of radius 0.5 m, 0.75 m or 1 m (shown by person size in the figure, as well as S, M and L on their tops) and, independently, an equal chance of a desired speed of 1 m/s, 1.33 m/s or 2 m/s. The maximum speed is adjusted to be 125% of the desired speed. In Fig. 4, people moving in the x direction (left to right) have red tops, and people moving in the negative x

direction (right to left) have blue tops. Brighter shaded tops indicate the largest desired speed, 2 m/s, and the darkest tops indicate the slowest speed, 1 m/s.

Fig. 4. Visualization of 2,500 people in Unreal. Two crowds navigate past each other, one heading from left to right (blue clothes) and the other from right to left (red clothes). People are color coded according to their maximum speeds (using three shades of red or blue, respectively) and have varying radii (indicated by their actual size and also using S, M and L on their tops). Top: scene view from above; One pedestrian is highlighted with a green circle; Inset: view from the perspective of the pedestrian in the green circle (Color figure online)

The second test case was an 8-way crossing, visualized in Fig. 5. Each crowd must navigate 135° across the environment, resulting in a vortex-like pattern around the center.

The second experiment was designed to test the performance of the GPU implementation in comparison to the multi-core CPU implementation. Figure 6 shows the results that varying numbers of people have on the frame time. Various test cases (e.g. 2-way and 8-way crossings) with different agent parameters were run, and the timings averaged between them. In this experiment no visualisation was used so as to ensure the timings were due to the algorithm only. The GPU solution gives speed increases of up to 30 times compared to the multi-core CPU implementation. Results for the single-core CPU version are not given as for any sizeable number of agents the multi-core CPU implementation always out-performs the single-core CPU implementation. This is due to better utilization of the CPU device. The colored bars of Fig. 6 correspond to the primary (left) vertical axis, which uses a logarithmic scale. The relative time taken between the charts corresponds to the secondary (right) vertical axis, with linear scale.

The results show that the speed increases proportionally to the number of people. Greater relative speed-up occurs for even larger numbers of people, but the time taken per frame is below real time. The GPU simulations ran at close

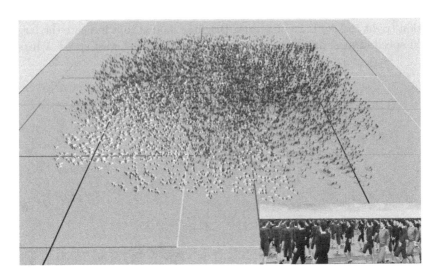

Fig. 5. Visualization of 10,000 people in Unreal. Eight crowds attempting to navigate to the opposite end of the environment. Different colors are used for each crowd. Top: scene view from above; One pedestrian is highlighted with a green circle; Inset: view from the perspective of the pedestrian in the green circle (Color figure online)

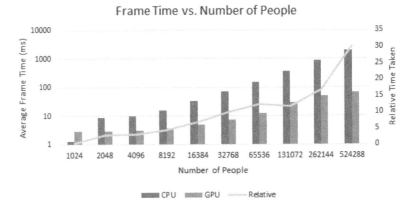

Fig. 6. Frame time (in ms) for multi-core CPU and GPU ORCA models with varying numbers of people. Logarithmic scale on primary (left) vertical axis. Relative timing is given on the secondary (right) vertical axis, in linear scale. Simulation time only without visualisation of the pedestrians. (Color figure online)

to 30 frames a second (33 ms per frame) for up to 5×10^5 agents. The CPU version performs better for smaller number of agents, with a crossover occurring at approximately 2×10^3 agents. This is due to the GPU device not being fully utilized for smaller simulations and the reduced throughput being outperformed by the CPU. The experiments were run on an NVIDIA GTX 970 GPU card with 4 GB dedicated memory and a 4-core/8-thread Intel i7-4790K with 16 GB

RAM. The GPU was connected by PCI-E 2.0. The GPU software was developed with NVIDIA CUDA 8.0 on Windows 10. On the GPU tested, there was a limit on the amount of usable memory of 4 GB, which corresponded to approximately 5×10^5 people. It is expected that relative performance increases will continue to be obtained for larger numbers of people for the GPU implementation for GPUs with larger memory capacity.

5   Conclusions

We have introduced a GPU-optimized version of the ORCA model. It shows substantial performance increases for large numbers of people compared to the multi-core CPU version. We demonstrated the performance gains through real-time visualizations that would not be possible on similar level CPU hardware.

Our model is currently limited in the number of people in the simulation size due to GPU memory. The models use large amounts of memory for storing the ORCA half-planes of each person. Memory usage could be reduced by considering fewer people. This would reduce the memory of each person but may result in less realistic motion with greater chance of collisions. A solution to the lack of memory is with Maxwell and later architectures, which can use managed memory [19] to page information from CPU to GPU on demand. This would allow for many more people to be simulated, up to the computer's RAM capacity. It is expected that greater relative speedups between multi-core CPU and GPU will continue to be obtained for even larger amounts of simulated people.

It is expected that the more computationally expensive steering models would include more realistic motion such as side-stepping, more realistic densities, and less probability of collisions. In comparison, it is expected that the model in this paper would have greater performance and larger numbers of simulated people.

The current work involves writing the data from the simulation to a file before visualization using Unreal. The data is copied from the GPU to the CPU, then loaded into Unreal and copied back to the GPU in Unreal for visualization. This is expensive. Future work will look at how to use the Unreal engine to visualize a simulation as it is calculated, which could be done by sharing GPU buffer information between the simulation program and the Unreal Engine.

Acknowledgements. This research was supported by the Transport Systems Catapult and the National Council of Science and Technology in Mexico (Consejo Nacional de Ciencia y Tecnología, CONACYT).

References

1. Abe, Y., Yoshiki, M.: Collision avoidance method for multiple autonomous mobile agents by implicit cooperation. In: Proceedings 2001 IEEE/RSJ International Conference on Intelligent Robots and Systems. Expanding the Societal Role of Robotics in the the Next Millennium (Cat. No. 01CH37180), vol. 3, pp. 1207–1212, October 2001. https://doi.org/10.1109/IROS.2001.977147
2. Barut, O., Haciomeroglu, M., Sezer, E.A.: Combining GPU-generated linear trajectory segments to create collision-free paths for real-time ambient crowds. Graph. Models **99**, 31–45 (2018). https://doi.org/10.1016/j.gmod.2018.07.002
3. van den Berg, J., Lin, M., Manocha, D.: Reciprocal velocity obstacles for real-time multi-agent navigation. In: 2008 IEEE International Conference on Robotics and Automation, ICRA 2008, pp. 1928–1935, May 2008. https://doi.org/10.1109/ROBOT.2008.4543489
4. van den Berg, J., Guy, S.J., Lin, M., Manocha, D.: Reciprocal n-body collision avoidance. In: Pradalier, C., Siegwart, R., Hirzinger, G. (eds.) Robotics Research. Springer Tracts in Advanced Robotics, vol. 70, pp. 3–19. Springer, Heidelberg (2011). https://doi.org/10.1007/978-3-642-19457-3_1
5. Bleiweiss, A.: Multi agent navigation on the GPU. White paper, GDC, vol. 9 (2009)
6. Blue, V., Adler, J.: Emergent fundamental pedestrian flows from cellular automata microsimulation—request PDF. Transp. Res. Rec. J. Transp. Res. Board **1644**, 29–36 (1998). https://doi.org/10.3141/1644-04
7. Blue, V., Adler, J.: Cellular automata microsimulation of bidirectional pedestrian flows. Transp. Res. Rec. J. Transp. Res. Board **1678**, 135–141 (1999). https://doi.org/10.3141/1678-17
8. Charlton, J., Maddock, S., Richmond, P.: Two-dimensional batch linear programming on the GPU. J. Parallel Distrib. Comput. **126**, 152–160 (2019). https://doi.org/10.1016/j.jpdc.2019.01.001
9. Fickett, M., Zarko, L.: GPU Continuum Crowds. CIS Final Project Final report, University of Pennsylvania (2007)
10. Fiorini, P., Shiller, Z.: Motion planning in dynamic environments using velocity obstacles. Int. J. Rob. Res. **17**(7), 760–772 (1998). https://doi.org/10.1177/027836499801700706
11. Fulgenzi, C., Spalanzani, A., Laugier, C.: Dynamic obstacle avoidance in uncertain environment combining PVOs and occupancy grid. In: Proceedings 2007 IEEE International Conference on Robotics and Automation, pp. 1610–1616. IEEE, Rome, April 2007. https://doi.org/10.1109/ROBOT.2007.363554
12. Guy, S.J., et al.: ClearPath: highly parallel collision avoidance for multi-agent simulation. In: Proceedings of the 2009 ACM SIGGRAPH/Eurographics Symposium on Computer Animation, SCA 2009, pp. 177–187. ACM, New York (2009). https://doi.org/10.1145/1599470.1599494
13. He, L., Pan, J., Narang, S., Wang, W., Manocha, D.: Dynamic Group Behaviors for Interactive Crowd Simulation. arXiv:1602.03623 [cs], February 2016
14. Helbing, D., Molnár, P.: Social force model for pedestrian dynamics. Phys. Rev. E **51**(5), 4282–4286 (1995). https://doi.org/10.1103/PhysRevE.51.4282
15. Karmakharm, T., Richmond, P.: Agent-based large scale simulation of pedestrians with adaptive realistic navigation vector fields. EG UK Theor. Pract. Comput. Graph. **10**, 67–74 (2010)

16. Kluge, B., Prassler, E.: Recursive probabilistic velocity obstacles for reflective navigation. In: Yuta, S., Asama, H., Prassler, E., Tsubouchi, T., Thrun, S. (eds.) Field and Service Robotics: Recent Advances in Research and Applications. Springer Tracts in Advanced Robotics, vol. 24, pp. 71–79. Springer, Berlin (2006). https://doi.org/10.1007/10991459_8

17. Li, B., Mukundan, R.: A Comparative Analysis of Spatial Partitioning Methods for Large-Scale, Real-Time Crowd Simulation. Václav Skala - UNION Agency (2013)

18. Narain, R., Golas, A., Curtis, S., Lin, M.C.: Aggregate dynamics for dense crowd simulation. In: ACM SIGGRAPH Asia 2009 Papers, SIGGRAPH Asia 2009, pp. 122:1–122:8. ACM, New York (2009). https://doi.org/10.1145/1661412.1618468

19. Nvidia: Tuning CUDA Applications for Maxwell (2018). http://docs.nvidia.com/cuda/maxwell-tuning-guide/index.html

20. Pettré, J., Kallmann, M., Lin, M.C.: Motion planning and autonomy for virtual humans. In: ACM SIGGRAPH 2008 Classes, SIGGRAPH 2008, pp. 42:1–42:31. ACM, New York (2008). https://doi.org/10.1145/1401132.1401193

21. Pettré, J., Pelechano, N.: Introduction to crowd simulation. In: Bousseau, A., Gutierrez, D. (eds.) EG 2017 - Tutorials. The Eurographics Association (2017). https://doi.org/10.2312/egt.20171029

22. Richmond, P.: Flame GPU Technical Report and User Guide. Department of Computer Science Technical report CS-11-03, University of Sheffield (2011)

23. Richmond, P., Romano, D.M.: A high performance framework for agent based pedestrian dynamics on GPU hardware. In: Proceedings of EUROSIS ESM 2008 (2008)

24. Schönfisch, B., de Roos, A.: Synchronous and asynchronous updating in cellular automata. Biosystems 51(3), 123–143 (1999). https://doi.org/10.1016/S0303-2647(99)00025-8

25. Seidel, R.: Small-dimensional linear programming and convex hulls made easy. Discrete Comput. Geom. 6(3), 423–434 (1991). https://doi.org/10.1007/BF02574699

26. Snape, J.: Optimal Reciprocal Collision Avoidance (C++). Contribute to snape/RVO2 development by creating an account on GitHub, March 2019

27. Thalmann, D.: Populating virtual environments with crowds. In: Proceedings of the 2006 ACM International Conference on Virtual Reality Continuum and Its Applications, VRCIA 2006, p. 11. ACM, New York (2006). https://doi.org/10.1145/1128923.1128925

28. Wang, Y., Davidson, A., Pan, Y., Wu, Y., Riffel, A., Owens, J.D.: Gunrock: a high-performance graph processing library on the GPU. In: Proceedings of the 21st ACM SIGPLAN Symposium on Principles and Practice of Parallel Programming, p. 11. ACM (2016)

29. Xu, M.L., Jiang, H., Jin, X., Deng, Z.: Crowd simulation and its applications: recent advances. J. Comput. Sci. Technol. 29, 799–811 (2014). https://doi.org/10.1007/s11390-014-1469-y

30. Yang, Z., Pan, J., Wang, W., Manocha, D.: Proxemic group behaviors using reciprocal multi-agent navigation. In: 2016 IEEE International Conference on Robotics and Automation (ICRA), pp. 292–297 (2016). https://doi.org/10.1109/ICRA.2016.7487147

Improved Automatic Speed Control
for 3D Navigation

Domi Papoi[1] and Wolfgang Stuerzlinger[2(✉)]

[1] York University, Toronto, ON M3J 1P3, Canada
[2] SIAT, Simon Fraser University, Vancouver, BC V3T 0A3, Canada
w.s@sfu.ca

Abstract. As technology progresses, it is possible to increase the size and complexity of 3D virtual environments. Thus, we need deal with multiscale virtual environments today. Ideally, the user should be able to navigate such environments efficiently and robustly, which requires control of the user speed during navigation. Manual speed control across multiple scales of magnitude suffers from issues such as overshooting behaviors and introduces additional complexity. Most previously presented methods to automatically control the speed of navigation do not generalize well to environments with varying scales. We present an improved method to automatically control the speed of the user in 3D virtual environment navigation. The main benefit of our approach is that it automatically adapts the navigation speed in a manner that enables efficient navigation with maximum freedom, while still avoiding collisions. The results of a usability test show a significant reduction in completion time for a multiscale navigation task.

Keywords: 3D navigation · Virtual environments

1 Introduction

Virtual navigation, i.e., movement within a *virtual environment* (VE), is a common interactive task in *three-dimensional* (3D) VE. During such navigation, users need to maintain their orientation and interact to move their viewpoint. Thus, 3D navigation involves two main tasks: wayfinding and travel, but we only focus on the later here.

Travel is the motor component of navigation. It can be defined as the actions that the user makes through the user interface to control the position and orientation of their viewpoint. In VEs, travel techniques enable the user to control their viewpoint and direction, and other attributes of movement, such as the speed. Here, we present a new method to control the speed of travel in *multi-scale virtual environments* (MSVEs).

Generally, the user can move in all 6 degrees of freedom (6DOF) in VEs. Yet, direct control of all 6DOFs is challenging. Compare the skills required to pilot a car or plane (which many can master) to those required to control a helicopter (which fewer possess). One can also observe this in most computer games, where navigation typically involves control over four or fewer DOF, typically rotate left/right and up/down, move forward/backward and both ways sideways, all at predefined speeds.

© Springer Nature Switzerland AG 2019
M. Gavrilova et al. (Eds.): CGI 2019, LNCS 11542, pp. 278–290, 2019.
https://doi.org/10.1007/978-3-030-22514-8_23

Many 3D *user interfaces* (UIs) ignore the aspect of changing the speed of the travel and simply use a reasonable constant velocity. This works reasonably well as long as the size and detail of the environment do not vary much. In MSVEs, a fixed speed leads to problems because a constant speed will always be too slow in some situations and too fast in others. If the speed is too slow, user frustration can set in quickly. If the speed is too fast, the user can overshoot the target, forcing the user to turn around or back up, to navigate back to the intended destination. On the other hand, allowing the user to explicitly control the speed across multiple scales adds complexity to the interface, and the user then even more easily overshoots or undershoots the target [21] and might be forced to again take corrective actions [20]. Another issue with manual control is that users can fly into objects when they do not stop in time or when backing up. This can lead to usability issues, as especially novice users do not know how to recover quickly from being inside an object [7]. A potential solution for this problem is to slow the user down when they get close to an object. Another aspect of VE immersion that needs to be considered is cybersickness. Recent work aims to reduce such symptoms [11].

There are many options for a user to control their speed, including buttons, sliders, or various attributes of the users' pose. A discrete technique for speed control might use buttons, which increases/decreases the speed by a predefined amount (say by 50%) and allows backward travel, while a slider-based control might use a linear mapping. All these controls give the user direct control over the speed of travel. The main drawback is that this choice adds complexity to the user interface, as the user has to constantly monitor their speed and adapt it to the current environment.

Ideally, a navigation control scheme should be as simple as possible, to make the user interface easy to learn. Another constraint is that each navigation functionality requires some physical control or a widget, which consumes either display space, requires dedicated buttons, or introduces modes. That means that fewer controls are typically better. This design trade-off is directly visible in touchscreen user interfaces, where space for widgets is at a premium, and multi-touch interaction possibilities are limited to, e.g., one-/two-/three-finger-based controls. There, a system-controlled speed technique might be more appropriate. Another ideal use case for automatic speed control are MSVEs where the user has to repeatedly travel between regions with radially varying spatial complexity, such as tight corners that necessitate short, slow, and precise movements, while open spaces can benefit from higher speeds. In such cases, the user can benefit much from automatic changes to the speed depending on the surrounding geometry. This idea is the main motivation for our research.

As example consider a VE for a star system, where the user is on a planet's surface and looks up into the vast empty space between planets. Launching, the user into space at very high speeds seems a good choice but can lead to a loss of control if the user steers in the wrong direction. Instead, we could take the (invisible) geometry behind the user into account and start slow, but keep increasing the speed, if the user keeps moving towards free space. In contrast, when the user approaches an object with high speeds, the system will slow the user down, which avoids overshooting. This is especially important if the user aims just beside the planet to get to the other side of the planet. Yet, as noted by Trindade [21], directly using the proximity of geometry can slow the user down too much in certain scenarios. For example, if the user navigates through a tunnel the system will reduce the speed drastically based on the close proximity to the walls, which could lead to speeds that are perceived as frustratingly slow.

1.1 Previous Work

In VEs, user actions must be mapped in some more or less intuitive way to travel. Mine [17] presented an overview of motion specification interaction techniques and, similar to Robinett [19], also discussed issues relevant to their implementation of travel techniques. Several studies of immersive travel techniques have been described in the literature, for instance comparing different travel modes and metaphors for specific VE applications, e.g., [5, 15]. Bowman et al. [3] discussed various ways to control travel speed. Yet, allowing the user to explicitly control the speed across multiple scales adds complexity to the interface, and the user then even more easily overshoots or under-shoots the target [21] and might be forced to take corrective actions [20].

A common approach to scaling the user during navigation is to allow the user to actively control the scale of the world. One of the earliest was the 3DM immersive modeler [4], which enables the user to "grow" and "shrink". SmartScene [14] also allowed the user to control the scale of the environment to allow both rapid navigation and manipulation of objects at all scales. The scaled-world grab technique [18] scales the user in an imperceptible way when an object is selected. While active scaling enables the user to specify the scale of the world, it requires additional interface components to do so. In contrast, a 3D UI could also change the scale of the world automatically based on the user's current task or position. This automated approach obviates the need for the user to specify a scale. An example of an automated scaling approach is "Multi-scale Virtual Environments" [12]. This approach allows the user to concentrate on navigating instead of scaling while still benefitting from having the world scale up or down. However, such VEs require careful design, as the hierarchy of objects and scales need to be intuitive and usable for the user.

The speed control of a travel technique is at least weakly linked with the scale of the environment and the user's preferences. The maximum allowed speed is dictated by the scale of the environment, while the minimum sensible speed corresponds to the finest detail. Users can manually adjust the speed through a travel interface by various input commands [10] or speed mappings [1]. If the scale and level of detail of the environment is known a priori, then the maximum and minimum speed can be set accordingly. Freitag et al. [9] identify locations that maximize scene visibility, based on predefined region importance scores and real-time tracking of the exploration status of scene regions.

Mackinlay [13] first observed that the current distance to a target point is an appropriate way to control viewer speed. Ware and Fleet [22] investigated this further and found that in most situations, the minimum distance to any visible point generally works best, but noted also that average distances were competitive.

An improved version of Ware and Fleet's interface [22] is the approach proposed by McCrae et al. [16], which uses a six-sided distance map, the *cubemap*, which encodes the distance to all visible parts of the surroundings of the user through six depth maps from the camera viewpoint. These depth maps are generated by rendering six images in the six main axial directions, each one corresponding to a side of the cube. Every time the camera viewpoint changes, the cubemap is updated in real time. Based on the cubemap, McCrae et al.'s method then computes a vector that displaces the camera in a way that adjusts both speed and direction, similar to the distance-dependent speed control presented by Ware and Fleet [22]. Through the weighting by distance, the direction of the vector adjusts the travel direction to avoid collisions.

Trindade et al. [21] improved McCrae's et al.'s approach to facilitate travel in a MSVEs. In their flying technique, they also include collision avoidance and automatic navigation speed adjustment with respect to the scale of the environment. They identified that when flying close to geometry, speed control via the global minimum can unnecessarily slow the user down. For example, when the user is flying through a tunnel that has no geometry straight ahead, the nearby walls reduce the speed (too) much, and therefore the user would fly very slowly. Their solution is to use the distance along a ray in the view direction to detect situations where the viewer could speed up. Using an exponentially weighted average between the distance along the view direction and the global minimum distance, they smooth out the resulting rough speed changes. Despite this weighted average approach, a speed computed for a distance of infinity or equivalent will overwhelm any other terms. This can cause the user to move at huge speeds very close to geometry, which is undesirable. Moreover, the discrete nature of using a sampling ray can cause abrupt speed changes, if said ray falls on/off geometry. Another variation of the cubemap was used by Duan et al. [6] to control a flying vehicle model.

Argelaguet [2] proposes a new method of speed control that aims to keep optical flow constant. Yet, they found that there is no strong difference between distance-based speed control and a method that keeps optical flow constant. In contrast, Freitag et al. [8] adjust the travel speed automatically based on the informative quality of the viewpoint. When the viewpoint has a high visual quality, the navigation speed is decreased and vice versa.

1.2 Contributions

Our contributions are:

- A new, efficient, and robust way to automatically adapt the user's speed depending on the camera's direction and the surrounding environment by smoothly attenuating the effect of geometry in the view direction different from the surround.
- A user study evaluating our new automatic speed control method relative to two other methods from previous work.

2 Automatic Speed Control for 3D Travel

In this chapter, we first explain the technical details of our automatic speed control technique. Our speed control method applies to all 3D travel interfaces where the user controls their motion through specifying a direction and then flying or traveling in (or reversing based on) said direction. Similar to McCrae et al. [16], we compute the distances to all objects around the viewer by generating a cube map of all objects. Instead of using a world space aligned cube map we use a view aligned cube map, as suggested by Trindade et al. [21]. After all, a world space aligned cube does not encode directly where geometry is relative to the viewer and their view direction. This makes it (a bit) harder to tell where an object is relative to the viewer.

We propose an improvement to the equation for computing the displacement vector proposed by McCrae et al. [16], by scaling it with a smoothing function. We first compute the average displacement vector from the cubemap over all its pixels:

$$\vec{d}\,isp = \frac{1}{6N_xN_y} \sum_{x,y,i} w(dist(x,y,i)) \cdot norm(\vec{p}\,os(x,y,i) - \vec{e}\,ye)$$

In the above equation i is an integer value between 1 and 6 and represents one side of the cube map. The horizontal and vertical resolutions are represented by N_x and N_y. While the sum appears to involve only 2 dimensions, there are 3D vectors involved and the final result is also a vector. To give a larger weight to geometry closer to the viewer, McCrae et al. used an exponential soft penalty function. To reduce computational effort, we present here a simpler option for the weighting function that uses a smooth-step or an improved version of the smoothfunction wro 1st and 2nd order derivatives at $t = 0$ and $t = 1$ to determine how nearby geometry influences the viewer:

$$smoothstep(t) = 6t^5 - 15t^4 + 10t^3$$

$$w_1(dist) = \begin{cases} 1, if \left(\frac{min(dist,\delta)}{\delta} < \alpha\right), else \\ 1 - smoothstep\left(2\frac{min(dist,\delta)}{\delta} - 1\right) \end{cases}$$

Where δ represents the bound radius within which objects should affect the user and α. is a dynamic penalty control variable within [0, 1]. As δ. is constant across samples, the viewer's collision boundary is then a sphere with radius δ. The bound radius δ can be modulated by a scale estimate, which is the minimum distance from the cubemap. In our work, we choose 0.5 for the dynamic penalty control variable α. McCrae et al.'s technique then uses the minimum distance across the cubemap to control the speed and applies the displacement vector to the viewer position to avoid collisions.

As mentioned above in the review of previous work, this computed speed may be too low in long narrow passages [21]. To address this issue in a better way than Trindade et al.'s ray-based solution [21], we propose to *add* a second weighting term $w_2(dist)$ to the sum, which increases the weight of the contribution of geometry close to the view direction with a smooth fall off for geometry orthogonal or behind the viewer. Based on pilot experiments, we use the 16th power of the cosine of the angle relative to the view direction and redefine the weighting function accordingly.

$$w_2(dist) = \max(\cos^{16}(\theta), 0)$$

$$w(dist) = w_1(dist)w_2(dist)$$

Without the weighing term, all directions have equal influence. As shown in Fig. 1, applying the second weighting term $w_2(dist)$ reduces the influence of geometry that is not in front of the viewer on the final result. To compute the final speed, we scale the length of the final displacement vector so that the user can never collide with objects.

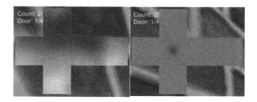

Fig. 1. Illustration of depth buffer without and with a second weighting term.

3 Evaluation

To evaluate our proposed automatic speed control and to compare it with the speed control via the global minimum described by McCrae et al. [16] as well as the automatic speed adjustment developed by Trindade et al. [21] we performed a user study.

We chose to evaluate our new technique with the mouse as input device, as we wanted to investigate one-handed operation (which frees the second hand for other operations). This keeps our navigation method open for other devices, such as touch screens and VR-style controllers. Similar to many games, any mouse movement without a button held down controls the user's view direction in our control scheme, while holding the left mouse button down will move the viewer forward, with mouse movements mapped to steering. The right mouse button is mapped to backward movement. We used only two buttons, to keep the user interface as simple as possible and to leave other buttons free for other purposes, such as object selection and manipulation.

3.1 Participants

We recruited 14 participants (11 male, 3 female) for this study, aged from 23 to 45 (mean age 31.8 years, *SD* 8.35). In the practice session, one participant found the task too difficult and declined to continue and another seemed to experience strong motion sickness symptoms and needed to be excluded. All remaining 12 participants had used VEs before, played FPS games, or 3D race car games.

Fig. 2. VE used for the travel task. The VE is composed of 2 different sections replicated across three different levels of scale (1:1, 1:2 and 1:10).

3.2 Setup

The experiments were conducted on a generic PC with a nVidia GeForce GTX 970 on a 24" wide screen monitor (HP ZR24w) at 1920 × 1200, with a Microsoft Intelli-Mouse mouse as the input device. We did not use stereoscopic display.

To evaluate our new navigation technique, we were inspired by Argelaguet's experimental design and the VE they used [2]. Thus, our VE also includes a maze-like and a geometry-filled section, repeated across three different scales (1:1, 1:2 and 1:10).

To guide users we painted arrows on the maze walls to show the direction of the path to be followed. This helps if a user gets disoriented. We used textured walls (brick, stone) to enhance depth cues within the environment. To encourage all users to follow the same path we added rotating red cubes that users had to pick-up (see Fig. 3). Once the user collided with such a cube it was removed from the environment and the pick-up event was convoyed by a positive acoustic sound. Within the second geometry section of the VE these pick-up cubes were connected through thin rays, so that participants could always easily tell where to go next. The (previous) thin ray was always removed whenever the user reached a cube (see Fig. 3).

Fig. 3. (Left) First section of the environment, the maze, with directional arrows pointing towards pick-up objects and textured walls. (Right) Second section of the environment with geometry objects showing pick-up objects connected through thin rays.

3.3   Procedure

First, each participant was given a brief questionnaire about their background. The questionnaire recorded gender, age, and previous experience with 3D VEs. Then, the participant was instructed to use the UI and encouraged to practice until they felt comfortable. The mouse was the only means to navigate the environment. The left mouse button was mapped to forward movement, while the right mouse button initiated backward movement. With no button pressed the users could orient their view in the VE.

The order of the speed control techniques was counterbalanced with a Latin square design across all participants to minimize learning effects. The order of the sections (Maze, Geometry) and the scale factors was fixed due to the design of the VE (see Fig. 1). We did not counterbalance the sections, as the maze was easier to navigate. And, the smaller mazes might be more difficult to navigate. All three techniques shared settings for the collision radius, smoothing term, and near and far plane distances.

Once the participants were comfortable with the VE, they were instructed to traverse the VE following the path marked by the pick-up cubes. Each participant was instructed to hit these target cubes as quickly and accurately as possible but not to be overly concerned if any given pick-up was not successful. To encourage participants to follow the path, we introduced a somewhat unpleasant audio cue for any missed pick-up.

At the end of the experiment, we gave participants a short questionnaire on their perceptions on the ease of use and navigation smoothness for all three techniques using 5-point Likert scales. Overall, the study took about half an hour per participant.

3.4   Results

Data was first filtered for clear participant errors, such as deviating from the sequence of cubes to pick up or pausing in the middle of the navigation sequence. We removed such errors by eliminating results with more than three standard deviations from the mean as outliers. This amounted to less than 3% of the total data.

3.5   Task Completion Time

The data for task completion time was not normally distributed. Levene's test for homogeneity revealed that the data did not have equal variances. We used the Aligned Rank Transform for nonparametric factorial data analysis [23] and then performed a repeated measures parametric ANOVA on the transformed data.

There was a significant effect of completion time on technique ($F_{2,22} = 8.14$, p < .01). See Fig. 4 for task completion times for across all scales. A Tukey-Kramer post-hoc test revealed that our technique had a smaller completion time than both other techniques. Figure 4 also shows task completion times for each scale of the environment.

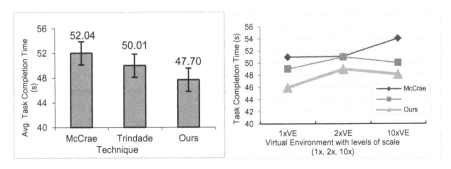

Fig. 4. (Left) Graph depicting the average task completion time for each technique, with standard deviations. (Right) Graph depicting the task completion time (s) for each VE scale.

An ANOVA test on group effect was not significant ($F_{5,6} = 0.652$), which confirmed that the counterbalancing cancelled out any potential learning effects. Further, we detected no significant learning effects across participants.

3.6 Average Speed

To analyze the average speed across all three scales, we multiplied the speeds from the half-scale environment by two and the speeds from the 1:10 scale by ten. After this adjustment the data was normally distributed.

The one-way ANOVA of technique versus speed showed a main effect on technique ($F_{2,22} = 3.39$, $p < .05$). See Fig. 5 for the average speeds.

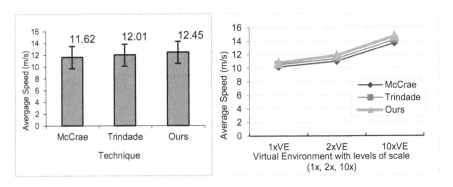

Fig. 5. (Left) Mean speed across all scales, with standard deviations. (Right) Average speed in m/s for each scale and technique.

A Tukey-Kramer test showed that the mean speed for our new technique was significantly higher than for Trindade's version, which in turn was higher than for McCrae's. Figure 5 also shows that the ordering was consistent across techniques and scales.

From our observations of the participants and their comments during the experiment, we were able to identify that our new technique was perceived to be the best option. The data from the user questionnaire on the ease of use and the smoothness of the speed changes corroborates this insights. The outcomes confirm our observations (see Fig. 6). None of our 12 main participants reported discomfort or simulator sickness symptoms.

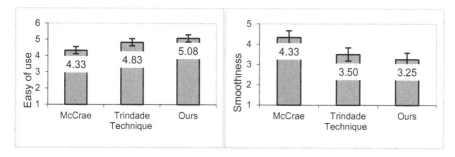

Fig. 6. (Left) Graph showing average user feedback for ease-of-use for each technique (higher is better), with standard deviations. (Right) Graph showing user feedback regarding the smoothness of speed changes for each technique (lower is better), with standard deviations.

4   Discussion

The overall conclusion from this study is that our implementation allowed for smooth navigation with a performance improvement over the state-of-the-art travel speed control approaches. In comparison to two previously presented methods that are directly comparable, our method demonstrated a reduced completion time and improved speed, allowing the users to achieve the navigation goal in less time.

In general, our new solution seems to better address the issue that excessive slowdowns can occur with previous methods for automatic speed control, e.g., when the viewer slides along walls or navigates through tunnels. Our automatic speed control method takes the geometry that is in front of the viewer more strongly into account, instead of the whole surroundings (such as McCrae et al. [16]). In contrast to Trindade et al.'s work [21], we use an average over an area in front of the viewer, which eliminates the downsides of using only a single point. Our approach weights the influence of geometry behind or beside the viewer less than that of geometry directly ahead, with a smooth interpolation to guarantee smooth transitions. In essence, this allows the user to navigate parallel to an existing plane at a higher speed than would be achievable if navigating perpendicular towards the plane. By combining the influence of the surround geometry in a more robust way with the forward one, the navigation speed is adequate when navigating away from geometry, but still results in a smooth "takeoff" behavior.

The system presented here also generalizes to navigation on touchscreen systems used with a single hand, where a single finger touch/drag controls the look direction, while a 2-finger touch-and-hold will move the user forward based on the current user's view for the duration of the hold. Steering is then achieved by dragging both fingers in the desired direction. Backward movement can be mapped to a 3-finger touch event. Because the navigation techniques require only 2D input, our new method can also be easily used on other input devices, such as with a pen or a VR style controller.

We did not record sufficient data to analyze the participant's motion trails for signs of temporary disorientation. Yet, the lack of corresponding observations by the experimenter make it unlikely that this was a notable issue. Moreover, we observed only very few episodes with overshooting and subsequent backwards movements, or participants turning around. We believe that the root cause of this lack of overshoot is that the automatic speed control methods already reduce the speed of the participants sufficiently far in advance to enable them to adjust their path before they run into problems.

4.1 Limitations

As mentioned above, the computations result in a single displacement vector that pushes the user away from the nearest geometry. As mentioned by McCrae et al. [16] this will move the viewer towards the center of any cavity and can push the user out of rooms with openings. As the environment scale decreases, the magnitude of this vector increases and will start moving the user stronger away from nearby geometry, which can lead to surprising results and frustrating situations, e.g., when the viewer is extremely close to a surface while looking parallel to it. Then McCrae's algorithm will create a local "drift", even though the path in front of the user is clear, which could be addressed through a threshold that depends on the scale or another dynamically calculated value adapted to the desired use case.

Considering the size of the world relative to the smallest detail and the three different scales, we only explored up to a range of 5,000:1 in our experiment, with the speed decreasing at most by a factor of ten compared with the 1:1 scene. Initial experiments with larger scenes at approximately 1,000,000:1, revealed implementation-specific issues. The vector computations of McCrae et al.'s main equation [16] suffered quickly from lack of floating-point precision, which caused undesirable "jitter" effects. If we scale the environment up even further, i.e., explore scale differences of (say) 1 billion:1, a speed based on the minimum distance would in theory still adjust itself, but will likely also run into depth value precision issues.

The overall computing overhead of our (not fully optimized) shader-based implementation of our new automatic speed control method per frame was small: 2.88 ms compared to 2.52 ms for McCrae's and Trindade's versions, an increase of 12%.

5 Conclusion

In summary, the main contribution of this work is a method for automatic speed control for 3D travel in multi-scale virtual environments. We proposed a new and efficient way to automatically adapt a user's speed. This new method derives its benefit by taking the geometry that is in in front of the user better into account. By using shaders, this technique has also low overhead relative to CPU-based techniques. Future work will focus on applying the ideas behind our technique to navigation in vast empty spaces, such as a star system. Specifically, we will look at situations where the distance between objects is (far) beyond what can be represented on graphics hardware with floating-point number precision. We will also explore optimizations through clipping planes at the bounding radius.

References

1. Anthes, C., Heinzlreiter, P., Kurka, G., Volkert, J.: Navigation models for a flexible, multi-mode VR navigation framework. Virtual Reality Continuum Appl. Ind. 476–479 (2004)
2. Argelaguet-Sanz, F.: Adaptive navigation for virtual environments. In: Symposium on 3D User Interfaces 2014, pp. 91–94 (2014)
3. Bowman, D.A., Koller, D., Hodges, L.: A methodology for the evaluation of travel techniques for immersive virtual environments. Virtual Reality: Res. Dev. Appl. **3**, 120–131 (1998)
4. Butterworth, J., Davidson, A., Hench, S., Olano, M.T.: 3DM: a three dimensional modeler using a head-mounted display. In: Symposium on Interactive 3D Graphics, pp. 135–138 (1992)
5. Chung, J.C.: A comparison of head-tracked and non-head-tracked steering modes in the targeting of radiotherapy treatment beams. In: Symposium on Interactive 3D Graphics 1992, pp. 193–196 (1992)
6. Duan, Q., Gong, J., Li, W., Shen, S., Li, R.: Improved Cubemap model for 3D navigation in geo-virtual reality. Int. J. Digit. Earth **8**(11), 877–900 (2015)
7. Fitzmaurice, G., Matejka, J., Mordatch, I., Khan, A., Kurtenbach, G.: Safe 3D navigation. In: Symposium on Interactive 3D Graphics, pp. 7–15 (2008)
8. Freitag, S., Weyers, B., Kuhlen, T.W.: Automatic speed adjustment for travel through immersive virtual environments based on viewpoint quality. In: Symposium on 3D User Interfaces (3DUI), pp. 67–70 (2016)
9. Freitag, S., Weyers, B., Kuhlen, T.W.: Interactive exploration assistance for immersive virtual environments based on object visibility and viewpoint quality. In: IEEE Virtual Reality Conference, pp. 355–362. IEEE (2018)
10. Galyean, T.A.: Guided navigation of virtual environments. In: Symposium on Interactive 3D Graphics, pp. 103–104 (1995)
11. Kemeny, A., George, P., Merienne, F., Colombet, F.: New VR navigation techniques to reduce cybersickness. In: The Engineering Reality of Virtual Reality, pp. 48–53 (2017)
12. Kopper, R., Ni, T., Bowman, D.A., Pinho, M.: Design and evaluation of navigation techniques for multiscale virtual environments. In: IEEE Virtual Reality Conference, pp. 175–182 (2006)
13. Mackinlay, J.D., Card, S.K., Robertson, G.G.: Rapid controlled movement through a virtual 3D workspace. In: SIGGRAPH 1990, pp. 171–176 (1990)
14. Mapes, D.P., Moshell, J.: A two-handed interface for object manipulation in virtual environments. Presence: Teleoperators Virtual Environ. **4**(4), 403–416 (1995)
15. Mercurio, P.J., Erickson, T., Diaper, D., Gilmore, D., Cockton, G., Shackel, B.: Interactive scientific visualization: an assessment of a virtual reality system. In: INTERACT, pp. 741–745 (1990)
16. McCrae, J., Mordatch, I., Glueck, M., Khan, A.: Multiscale 3D navigation. In: Symposium on Interactive 3D Graphics, pp. 7–14 (2009)

17. Mine, M.: Virtual environment interaction techniques. UNC Chapel Hill computer science technical report, TR95-018 (1995)
18. Mine, M.R., Brooks Jr., F.P., Sequin, C.H.: Moving objects in space: exploiting proprioception in virtual-environment interaction. In: SIGGRAPH 1997, pp. 19–26 (1997)
19. Robinett, W., Holloway, R.: Implementation of flying, scaling and grabbing in virtual worlds. In: Symposium on Interactive 3D Graphics, pp. 189–192 (1992)
20. Stuerzlinger, W., Wingrave, C.A.: The value of constraints for 3D user interfaces. In: Brunnett, G., Coquillart, S., Welch, G. (eds.) Virtual Realities, pp. 203–224. Springer, Vienna (2011). https://doi.org/10.1007/978-3-211-99178-7_11
21. Trindade, D.R., Raposo, A.B.: Improving 3D navigation in multiscale environments using cubemap-based techniques. In: Symposium on Applied Computing 2011, pp. 1215–1221 (2011)
22. Ware, C., Fleet, D.: Context sensitive flying interface. In: Symposium on Interactive 3D Graphics, pp. 127–130 (1997)
23. Wobbrock, J.O., Findlater, L., Gergle, D., Higgins, J.J.: The aligned rank transform for nonparametric factorial analyses using only anova procedures. In: ACM CHI Conference, pp. 143–146 (2011)

Efficient Rendering of Rounded Corners and Edges for Convex Objects

Simon Courtin[1(⊠)], Sébastien Horna[1], Mickaël Ribadière[1], Pierre Poulin[2], and Daniel Meneveaux[1]

[1] Univ. Poitiers, CNRS, XLIM, UMR 7252, Poitiers, France
`simon.courtin@univ-poitiers.fr`
[2] LIGUM, Dept. I.R.O., Université de Montréal, Montréal, Canada

Abstract. Many manufactured objects and worn surfaces exhibit rounded corners and edges. These fine details are a source of sharp highlights and shading effects, important to our perception between joining surfaces. However, their representation is often neglected because they introduce complex geometric meshing in very small areas. This paper presents a new method for managing thin rounded corners and edges without explicitly modifying the underlying geometry, so as to produce their visual effects in sample-based rendering algorithms (e.g., ray tracing and path tracing). Our method relies on positioning virtual spheres and cylinders, associated with a detection and acceleration structure that makes the process more robust and more efficient than existing bevel shaders. Moreover, using our implicit surfaces rather than polygonal meshes allows our method to generate extreme close views of the surfaces with a much better visual quality for little additional memory. We illustrate the achieved effects and analyze comparisons generated with existing industrial software shaders.

Keywords: Rounded edges · Bevel · Chamfer · Shading ·
Implicit surface representation

1 Introduction

The realism of computer-generated images can be greatly improved with the representation of detailed features, such as dust, hair, or imperfect surfaces [12]. However, such thin structures are often neglected because (i) their impact affects only small portions of image pixels, (ii) their representation highly increases scene complexity in terms of geometry and appearance modeling, and (iii) their associated processing results in high complexity, both in terms of computation time and memory requirements.

This paper focuses on the rendering of thin rounded corners and edges. As shown by previous authors [15], managing the effects resulting from rounded corners and edges improves the observed realism. They produce specular highlights and appearance changes that improve shape perception. Real objects almost never exhibit perfect sharp edges, and their borders appear as brighter or darker

© Springer Nature Switzerland AG 2019
M. Gavrilova et al. (Eds.): CGI 2019, LNCS 11542, pp. 291–303, 2019.
https://doi.org/10.1007/978-3-030-22514-8_24

(a) No chamfer   (b) Photograph   (c) Our method

Fig. 1. Visual comparison of real and virtual objects with and without a rounding operation: (a) Virtual objects with sharp edges; (b) Photo of real play blocks; (c) Same virtual objects with our rounded spheres and cylinders. Notice the top red and cyan blocks on the two structures, with their darker adjacent rounded edges. (Color figure online)

than the rest of the surface, as illustrated in Fig. 1. Such rounded edges are often due in real life to imprecisions or desired intentions caused by the manufacturing process, e.g., in material cutting, moulding, sculpting, etc., or due to the wear of surfaces in their physical environment.

Rounding operations have been studied for a long time in geometric modelling, and many software packages offer robust operations [1,2]. Beveling operations rely on explicit chamfering [10,17] or on subdivision surfaces [4,7,16]. The process generates a polygonal mesh that approximates rounded chamfers. However, this is usually not applied to all objects of a 3D scene because of the high complexity associated with the resulting mesh. In addition, even with very detailed meshes, some information is lost on rounded shapes because of the discretization process, thus resulting in limited shading effects. Mesh discontinuities may also be visible depending on the observer point of view and lighting configurations.

The rendering of round edges can also be rendered using bevel shaders, to avoid generating explicit geometry. For instance, Saito et al. [15] propose a rendering system dedicated to rasterization, where reflected radiance is integrated analytically on the curvature of rounded spheres and cylinders. Three rendering passes are performed, in which corners and edges are processed separately, and added to the final image. Tanaka and Takahashi [18] extend this method with cross-scanline [15], thus reducing artifacts on thin curves. More recently, Wei et al. [19] propose an extension for GPU real-time rendering. These three methods have proven efficient, but their extension to global illumination remains complex since illumination on edges is performed locally and mapped directly on the final image. Several industrial software packages have an implementation of bevel shaders for managing rounded edges (e.g., Cycle [3], V-Ray [9], and Corona [8]). However they are mostly based on interpolation of normals, that is unfortunately not robust to many simple configurations (several examples are illustrated in the additional material). These methods remain unsuitable for handling the shrinking due to chamfering, and they fail with thin structures.

This paper focuses on the visual appearance of rounded corners and edges without explicitly generating a detailed mesh. We aim at defining a method that can be integrated efficiently in a ray tracing renderer (and more generally in a path tracing renderer), with an analytic description of spheres for corners and cylinders for edges. The goal is to be able to naturally generate smooth-to-sharp highlights within the rendering process, including correct geometry (volumetric shrinking on corners and edges) and normals. Our method consists of placing automatically spheres on corners and cylinders on edges of convex objects. Our method does not modify the original geometry representation (it is not invasive), since it operates in parallel with the existing data and rendering process. We propose a new structure that handles the geometric modifications due to the rounding operation, while explicitly taking an analytic representation of smoothness with spheres and cylinders, ensuring C^1 continuity at the junctions of surface and rounded features. We also define a structure that serves for the detection of rounded corners and edges, and for acceleration with topological links. The main contributions of our work can be summarized as follows:

- Automatic positioning of rounding spheres and cylinders to generate a C^1 smooth continuous surface, that accounts for accurate and fast ray-object intersection in many geometric cases. The resulting shape and rendering process account for volume shrinking due to chamfering.
- A geometric structure that allows for efficient detection and intersection of rounded corners and edges, including a graph for managing vertex and edge adjacencies useful for handling rays at grazing angles.
- A noninvasive structure, defined in parallel with the existing 3D data and accelerating structure, that integrates well in a sampling-based renderer. The structure has a small impact both on memory and computation cost.

Our method has been integrated in the *Cycles* rendering system and in *Blender* [5,6]. The achieved results illustrate configurations with many rounded objects in virtual environments. Applying our rounding operations and updating our detection structures are performed in only a few seconds. It has been used in path tracing [11,14], and results illustrate substantially visible differences and quality improvements compared to existing bevel shaders.

This paper is organized as follows. Section 2 presents an overview of our method. Section 3 provides technical details of positioning rounding geometry as well as of our detection and acceleration structure. Section 4 describes the ray intersection process with our structure. Section 5 discusses the implementation techniques and the achieved results. Section 6 concludes and presents insights into future investigations.

2 Overview

The goal of this work is to introduce smooth chamfer effects on object corners and edges, with as few geometric primitives as possible, and efficient ray-object intersection. With our method, the original scene geometry is not modified, which makes it easy to edit chamfer radii, without much impact on a potentially complex mesh geometry. The efficiency of our approach comes from a detection and acceleration structure, located on the chamfer boundaries.

Figure 2 illustrates the general idea of the structure construction and on the rendering process. First, each edge in the original geometry is processed with its two adjacent faces to determine the positions of a rounding cylinder and a detection cylinder (Fig. 2(a)). When a ray is traced in the 3D scene, the resulting intersection is with the original geometry (Fig. 2(b)). This intersection is tested with the detection cylinders (Fig. 2(c)) using a Kd-tree structure. If the intersection lies within one or more detection cylinders, the associated interior rounding cylinder is used for ray intersection (Fig. 2(d)). Finally, the origin of a reflected or shadow ray is placed at the correct point on the original geometry.

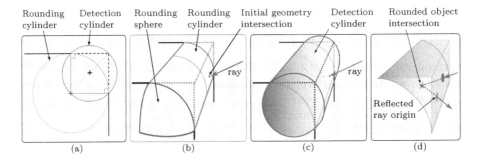

Fig. 2. (a) A rounding cylinder and a detection cylinder are associated to a rounded edge. (b) The ray tracing process intersects the original geometry of the 3D scene. (c) The corresponding intersection point is used to determine if its position lies within a detection cylinder using a Kd-tree structure. (d) If the intersection point lies within a detection cylinder, the intersection is computed with the corresponding rounding cylinder. If a reflected or shadow ray follows this intersection point, its origin is placed accordingly on the original geometry.

Note that in some cases, the ray does not intersect the rounding geometry (spheres and cylinders). The ray should continue its path through the scene, as explained in Sect. 4. We introduce a topological structure to allow rays to travel through rounding spheres and cylinders, and efficiently perform the intersection tests.

3   Rounding and Detecting

Positioning rounding spheres and cylinders at corners and edges of polygonal meshes has been addressed before [15,18]. This section briefly recalls the main principles and provides the notations used in the remainder of this paper.

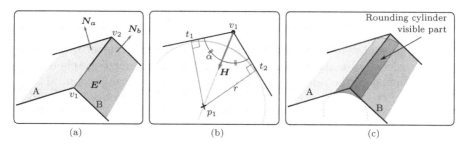

Fig. 3. A rounding cylinder for an edge (v_1, v_2) is associated with adjacent faces A and B. (a) A and B have respective normals $\boldsymbol{N_a}$ and $\boldsymbol{N_b}$, $\boldsymbol{H} = -(\boldsymbol{N_a} + \boldsymbol{N_b})/|\boldsymbol{N_a} + \boldsymbol{N_b}|$. (b) p_1 (resp. p_2) is defined from vertex v_1 (resp. v_2) and $\boldsymbol{H}$; (c) The visible area of the rounding cylinder defined by the axis (p_1, p_2) and the cylinder radius r is defined by the user.

Using spheres for corners and cylinders for edges presents several advantages: (i) they correspond to smooth analytic primitives with well-known ray intersection processing, and (ii) continuity between surfaces, spheres, and cylinders is straightforwardly ensured for an identical radius [13].

Figure 3 illustrates the positioning methodology for cylinders. Let us consider a rounding cylinder of radius r (user-defined), associated with an edge (v_1, v_2), shared by two faces of normal $\boldsymbol{N_a}$ and $\boldsymbol{N_b}$ respectively. Let $\boldsymbol{E} = v_2 - v_1$ ($\boldsymbol{E'} = \boldsymbol{E}/|\boldsymbol{E}|$). The cylinder axis crosses the line defined by the half-vector direction $\boldsymbol{H} = -(\boldsymbol{N_a} + \boldsymbol{N_b})/|\boldsymbol{N_a} + \boldsymbol{N_b}|$. The axis of the rounding cylinder is defined by two points $p_1 = v_1 + d\boldsymbol{H}$ and $p_2 = v_2 + d\boldsymbol{H}$, with $d = r/\sin\alpha$.

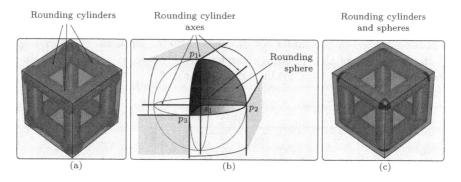

Fig. 4. (a) Set of rounding cylinders for a cube. (b) Axes of cylinders cross at a point, defining a rounding sphere center (s_1 is the sphere center associated with p_1, p_2, and p_3). (c) Final configuration with rounding spheres and rounding cylinders.

As illustrated in Fig. 4, rounding a corner consists in placing a sphere with the same radius r (as the cylinder), centered at the intersection between all axes of adjacent rounding cylinders [13]: p_1 and p_2 are respectively replaced by the sphere centers s_1 and s_2, thus ensuring C^1 continuity between the rounding spheres, cylinders, and surfaces.

This representation is suitable for any convex object, whatever the number of edges incident to a vertex, as illustrated in Fig. 5, for rounding spheres and cylinders having all the same radius. The rendering system can be applied from both sides of the chamfer (i.e., observed from outside or from inside a rounded object).

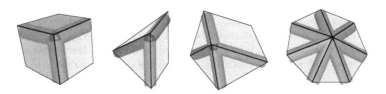

Fig. 5. Various configurations of positioning rounding cylinders, with different number of edges incident to one vertex.

Our goal is to perform robust and efficient ray intersection tests for ray/path tracing applications. The rounding primitives are placed *inside* an object geometry, that would not be reached by (exterior) rays. This is why an additional structure is mandatory for determining the intersection point and associated normal on the rounding primitive.

3.1 Detection Cylinders

The structure defined in this section aims at finding the potential rounding cylinder for a given intersection point on the original geometry. On a polygon, the area concerned by a chamfer corresponds to the region between a face edge and the beginning of the rounding cylinder. We propose to define a *detection cylinder* that precisely delimits this region (see Fig. 6).

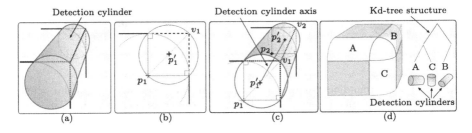

Fig. 6. Detection structure associated with three bevel areas: (a) A detection cylinder delimits the chamfer area. (b) The axis is placed so as to precisely fit the chamfer borders. (c) The representation in 3D. (d) Detection cylinders are organized into a Kd-tree.

The detection cylinder axis associated with an edge (v_1, v_2) is defined by two points $p'_1 = (v_1 + p_1)/2$ and $p'_2 = (v_2 + p_2)/2$ (illustrated in Fig. 6(c)). The detection cylinder radius r_d is equal to $|v_1 - p'_1|$.

One detection cylinder is associated to each edge; its central axis is parallel to the edge, and they are of equal length. These detection cylinders precisely delimit the region corresponding to the chamfer on the adjacent faces. Therefore, when a ray intersects a face at a 3D point I, a first test is performed to determine if I is within a detection cylinder (see Fig. 7(a)). If so, the associated rounding cylinder is considered for intersection with the ray. An adjacency graph is also defined for managing grazing ray directions. A rounding cylinder is linked to its two end rounding spheres, and a rounding sphere is linked to all its connected rounding cylinders.

This detection structure has several advantages: (i) It completely contains and exactly fits the bevel region. (ii) It is defined by one axis and a radius. (iii) Determining if an intersection point is inside a cylinder is straightforward and fast. (iv) The adjacency graph allows finding the chamfer intersection along a series of rounded edges and corners traversals without renewing the search in the Kd-tree.

3.2 Kd-Tree Structure

Because we aim at managing scenes with a large number of rounded edges, an acceleration structure is mandatory. We have chosen an organization of detection cylinders based on a Kd-tree, which is faster in this case than a bounding volume hierarchy (BVH) since the number of tests is smaller. We use a classical binary split along the longest axis, but any heuristic can be used (surface area heuristics, middle cut, etc.). The leaves of the Kd-tree contain the set of detection cylinders. This choice favors a fast construction with a balanced tree. In our implementation, a Kd-tree is constructed for each object or a group of simple objects, so as to benefit from moderate tree depths.

Our structure is independent from any path tracing structure, since it does not rely on the same geometry. When a ray-object intersection I is identified, it is located within the Kd-tree structure, and for each detection cylinder belonging to the corresponding Kd-tree leaf, the algorithm tests if I lies in the corresponding volume. If the test is positive, the intersection with the enclosed rounding cylinder can be performed, as explained below.

4   Ray Tracing Process

Let us consider a scenario in path tracing, and the corresponding ray intersection process. Our method can be applied for paths issued from the observer or from light sources. Thus, it could be used in any modern rendering method based on stochastic path construction: photon mapping, bidirectional path tracing, Metropolis light transport, etc. For a given intersection point I on the original

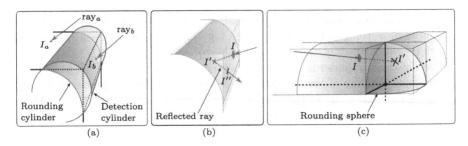

Fig. 7. Ray-object intersection using the original mesh. (a) With ray_a, the intersection I_a is located on the original geometry and outside all detection cylinders: the ray tracing process can be continued. For ray_b, I_b lies inside a detection cylinder and the intersection has to be tested with the rounding cylinder. (b) A ray intersects the rounding cylinder in I', and the reflected ray origin is set to I'' on the original mesh. (c) The ray does not hit the rounding cylinder, but the rounding sphere of I'.

geometry, our method determines if such an intersection exists, and if so, computes the intersection point and associated normal off the rounding primitive.

Figure 7 illustrates the possible cases for an intersection point I. The Kd-tree identifies if I is located within a detection cylinder. If no detection cylinder is identified, I is directly used as the intersection point for the global illumination process (Fig. 7(a)). Otherwise, every rounding cylinder containing I is used as a geometric primitive for ray intersection. Two configurations are possible:

- An intersection is found on the rounding cylinder, between the limits defined by s_1 and s_2. In this case, the resulting intersection point and its normal are used for further processing instead of I (Fig. 7(b)).
- An intersection is found on the rounding cylinder between the limits defined by s_1 and p_1 (resp. s_2 and p_2). This area corresponds to a corner, and the rounding sphere is tested to determine the potential intersection (Fig. 7(c)).

Given an intersection point I' on a rounding primitive (sphere or cylinder), the associated normal is computed. Since I' is located beneath the object surface, secondary rays must start on the original geometry mesh. They are first defined by their origin I' and a direction $\boldsymbol{D}$ fixed by the path tracer, but actually traced from an origin I'' located on the mesh surface. If no intersection is found on the rounding structure, the ray carries on its traversal in the adjacency structure.

5   Implementation and Results

The results presented in this section have been computed on an Intel Core 17-4790 3.60 GHz processor, with 8 threads and 16 GB of RAM. The code is completely integrated into *Blender* [5] and *Cycles* renderer [6], in order to provide fair comparisons with existing bevel shaders and modifiers. All images and statistics are for a resolution of 1920 × 1080 with 512 paths per pixel.

(**a**) Scene 1: 43.6k edges, 23.5k vertices, 23.3%   (**b**) Scene 2: 106k edges, 57.5k vertices, 30.4%

(**c**) Scene 3: 259k edges, 140k vertices, 29.2%   (**d**) Blocks: 182k edges, 122k vertices, 1.89%

Fig. 8. Number of rounded spheres/edges and percentage of rays impacted by chamfers for four test scenes. (a) Cylinders generated in 1.5 s, Kd-tree in 17 ms. (b) Cylinders generated in 3.6 s, Kd-tree in 44 ms. (c) Cylinders generated in 9.7 s, Kd-tree in 111 ms. (d) Cylinders generated in 9.5 s, Kd-tree in 0.004 ms.

Figure 8 illustrates the main scenes used in this paper, with worst cases corresponding to Fig. 8(a)–(c), where many corners and edges are defined on small objects. In practice, the user selects a set of objects in *Blender*, and our process automatically places the rounding and detection cylinders for all the corners and edges, as well as builds a Kd-tree structure per object.

The data structure associated with corners and edges is provided in the supplementary material. Note that data for rounding spheres are not explicitly stored since all the necessary information is already contained in the cylinder data structure: rounding cylinders axes are defined by the two associated sphere centers.

When a ray-object intersection occurs with the original object, the object index is returned by the rendering system with the corresponding data. The index is used for accessing the correct Kd-tree and its associated rounding spheres and cylinders. Figure 9 shows the visual importance of rounded edges. Without rounded edges (zoomed-in red frame), individual blocks blend together, contrary to clear demarcations (darker at junctions, brighter on highlights, between real blocks). Note also highlights on the rounded knobs on top of each block. Even when observed from a distance (zoomed-in blue frame), the edges greatly affects the perception of object shapes. The left image looks flatter.

Figure 10 compares our method with standard rounding meshes, with various levels of subdivision for the rounded corners and edges. The rendering time for

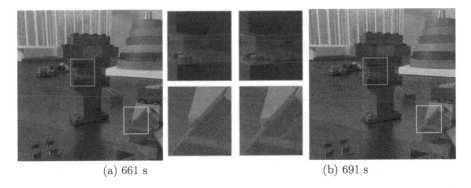

(a) 661 s   (b) 691 s

Fig. 9. Without rounded edges, blocks look flat, contrary to the appearance of real blocks. The total time difference between the two images is less than 5%. In this example, 2.65% of rays are affected by rounded edges. (Color figure online)

our method in this image corresponds to a subdivision level of 10, but with much less memory consumption (as shown in Table 1). In addition, our method is not prone to edge flickering when the light source (or viewpoint) moves, as shown in the video from the supplementary material.

(**a**) Sharp edges, 601 s   (**b**) 1 subdivision, 602 s   (**c**) 3 subdivisions, 654 s

(**d**) 5 subdivisions, 664 s   (**e**) 10 subdivisions, 729 s   (**f**) Our method, 727 s

Fig. 10. Close-up view of Scene 2 from Fig. 8(b) for a comparison between our method and different levels of mesh subdivisions. Rounded corners and edges affect 28.9% of rays in this image.

Table 1 compares computation time and memory requirements for a number of configurations: our method, including all the rounding spheres and cylinders, detection cylinders, and the Kd-tree acceleration structure, has only a minor impact on memory. In terms of computation time, the worst case we have observed concerns Scene 2, for which almost 30% of rays are affected by bevel corners and edges. In this case, our method is as fast as a subdivision of level 10, but memory consumption is much lower.

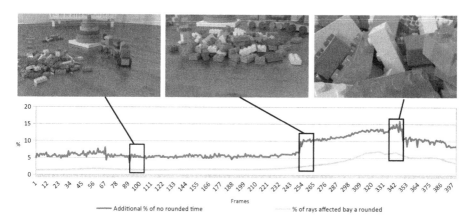

Fig. 11. Variations of computation time for a path traced animation of a moving viewpoint in the scene Blocks (Fig. 8d). The red curve indicates the percentage of rays that hit chamfers, while the blue one shows computation time increases. (Color figure online)

Using rounding cylinders instead of sharp edges requires additional computation time: respectively 3.2%, 1.9%, 34.5%, and 3.4% for Scenes 1, 2, 3, and Blocks. Our method is slightly faster than a subdivision of level 10 for the meshing method, but with far less memory requirements, and with a smoother appearance. The computation time highly depends on the number of rays that are affected by chamfers. This is why computation time increases very differently for our tested scenes or depending on the viewpoint as illustrated in Fig. 11 extracted from the video in the additional material. Figure 12 illustrates internal rounded corners and comparisons between meshed chamfers and our method.

Table 1. Number of triangles, rendering time, and memory consumption for the four test scenes of Fig. 8.

	Scene 1			Scene 2			Scene 3			Blocks		
	# tri	time	MB	# tri	time	MB	# tri	time	GB	# tri	time	MB
No rounding	42k	386 s	128	103k	639 s	478	252k	656 s	2,42	276k	1010 s	122
Our method	**42k**	**493 s**	**132**	**103k**	**823 s**	**487**	**252k**	**882 s**	**2.44**	**276k**	**1050 s**	**138**
1 subdivision	108k	396 s	143	267k	686 s	516	664k	695 s	2.51	507k	1022 s	182
3 subdivisions	364k	436 s	201	909k	716 s	662	2.26M	746 s	2.86	1.01M	1029 s	299
5 subdivisions	777k	452 s	296	1.93M	746 s	900	4.85M	793 s	3.48	1.54M	1045 s	439
10 subdivisions	2.49M	509 s	690	6.24M	839 s	1889	15.6M	909 s	5.96	2.9M	1068 s	780
Bevel shader	42k	628 s	128	103k	1106 s	478	252k	1148 s	2.42	276k	1585 s	122

Memory consumption with our method is much lower than with mesh subdivision. Bevel shaders also have very little impact on memory, but the rendering quality fails in many cases. This is due to the normal interpolation, not always adapted to geometric configurations, and that does not account for volume removal due to chamfering.

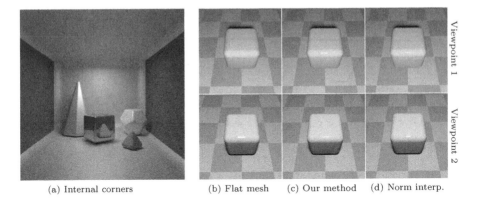

(a) Internal corners (b) Flat mesh (c) Our method (d) Norm interp.

Fig. 12. (a) A Cornell box with rounded corners, containing objects chamfered with our method. The rounded corners and edges of the Cornell box itself seen from the interior. (b), (c), and (d) Two frames from a video provided in supplementary material. (b) Subdivision of level 10 without interpolation of normals. (c) Our method. (d) Subdivision of level 10 with interpolation of normals.

Our method offers a simple control on the chamfer radius, with a the same visual quality when observed from any viewpoint in the scene. It also can be easily integrated in an existing rendering system based on ray sampling.

6   Conclusion and Future Work

This paper presents a method dedicated to the efficient rendering of rounded corners and edges on convex objects with ray tracing based renderers. The process consists in automatically positioning rounding spheres and cylinders of a given radius within objects. It does not affect the object original geometry and does not require much change to the rendering system.

A detection and acceleration structure allows us to determine whether an intersection point is located on a rounded corner or edge. The actual intersection on the rounded primitive is performed only if required, making the method robust, with a small memory consumption compared to regular and subdivision meshes, while offering a simple control.

Our method does not account for nonconvex objects because convexity changes around a corner imply complex changes of curvature that cannot be handled by a simple sphere.

In the future, we aim at improving the method with arbitrary geometric configurations while maintaining C^1 continuity. Some technical improvements could also reduce computation times, because for instance parts of the method have not been implemented using SSE instructions.

References

1. Autodesk: 3DS Max chamfer modifier. www.help.autodesk.com
2. Blender Foundation: Bevel geometry tool in Blender. www.docs.blender.org/manual
3. Blender Foundation: Blender shader for round edges. www.docs.blender.org/manual
4. Blender Foundation: Subdivision tool in Blender. www.docs.blender.org/manual
5. Blender Foundation: Blender (2018). www.blender.org
6. Blender Foundation: Cycles (2018). www.cycles-renderer.org
7. Catmull, E., Clark, J.: Recursively generated B-spline surfaces on arbitrary topological meshes. Comput.-Aided Des. **10**(6), 350–355 (1978)
8. Chaos group: Corona round-edges shader. www.coronarenderer.freshdesk.com
9. Chaos group: V-RAY round-edges shader. www.docs.chaosgroup.com
10. Chiyokura, H.: An extended rounding operation for modeling solids with free-form surfaces. In: Kunii, T.L. (ed.) Computer Graphics 1987, pp. 249–268. Springer, Tokyo (1987). https://doi.org/10.1007/978-4-431-68057-4_16
11. Kajiya, J.T.: The rendering equation. In: ACM SIGGRAPH Computer Graphics, vol. 20, pp. 143–150. ACM (1986)
12. Loubet, G., Neyret, F.: Hybrid mesh-volume LoDs for all-scale pre-filtering of complex 3D assets. In: Computer Graphics Forum, vol. 36, pp. 431–442. Wiley Online Library (2017)
13. Max, N.: Cone-spheres. In: ACM SIGGRAPH Computer Graphics, vol. 24, pp. 59–62. ACM (1990)
14. Pharr, M., Jakob, W., Humphreys, G.: Physically Based Rendering: From Theory to Implementation. Morgan Kaufmann, Burlington (2016)
15. Saito, T., Shinya, M., Takahashi, T.: Highlighting rounded edges. In: Earnshaw, R.A., Wyvill, B. (eds.) New Advances in Computer Graphics, pp. 613–629. Springer, Tokyo (1989). https://doi.org/10.1007/978-4-431-68093-2_40
16. Stam, J., Loop, C.: Quad/triangle subdivision. In: Computer Graphics Forum, vol. 22, pp. 79–85. Wiley Online Library (2003)
17. Szilvasi-Nagy, M.: Flexible rounding operation for polyhedra. Comput.-Aided Des. **23**(9), 629–633 (1991)
18. Tanaka, T., Takahashi, T.: Precise rendering method for exact anti-aliasing and highlighting. Vis. Comput. **8**(5), 315–326 (1992)
19. Wei, L.Y., Shi, K.L., Yong, J.H.: Rendering chamfering structures of sharp edges. Vis. Comput. **31**(11), 1511–1519 (2015)

Convenient Tree Species Modeling
for Virtual Cities

Like Gobeawan[1]([✉])[iD], Daniel Joseph Wise[1][iD], Alex Thiam Koon Yee[2],
Sum Thai Wong[1][iD], Chi Wan Lim[1][iD], Ervine Shengwei Lin[2], and Yi Su[1][iD]

[1] Institute of High Performance Computing, A*STAR, Singapore, Singapore
`gobeawanl@ihpc.a-star.edu.sg`
[2] National Parks Board, Singapore, Singapore

Abstract. Generating large scale 3D tree models for digital twin cities
at a species level-of-detail poses challenges of automation and maintenance of such dynamically evolving models. This paper presents an
inverse procedural modeling methodology to automate the generation of
3D tree species models based on growth spaces from point clouds and
pre-formulated L-system growth rules. The rules capture the botanical
tree architecture at a species level in terms of growth process, branching pattern, and responses to external stimuli. Users only need to fill in
a species profile template and provide the growth space derivable from
the point clouds. The parameters involved in the rules are automatically optimised within the growth space to produce the species models
to represent actual trees. This methodology enables users without 3D
modeling skills to conveniently produce highly representative 3D models
of any tree species in a large scale.

Keywords: Tree fractal models · Procedural modeling · L-system ·
Tree species profile · Tree architecture · Optimisation

1 Introduction

Motivation. Virtual cities, especially digital twins of actual cities, are full
of urban component models that represent actual objects such as buildings,
streets, and trees. Being the most dynamic components in the cities, trees grow
and respond to environmental stimuli over time. They vary across thousands of
species and span the cities in large scale, often in millions. Clearly, generating
tree models for a virtual city to keep up with their real counterparts are very
challenging. In practice, tree models generated in a large scale tend to be copies
of generic, static models or at a low level of detail, in contrast to other urban
objects especially buildings. Closing the gap in the level of detail between the tree
models and the building models will bring virtual cities to a new level of uses in
environmental simulations, city planning, agriculture, education, entertainment,
among others.

© Springer Nature Switzerland AG 2019
M. Gavrilova et al. (Eds.): CGI 2019, LNCS 11542, pp. 304–315, 2019.
https://doi.org/10.1007/978-3-030-22514-8_25

Problem Statement. This work seeks to address the challenges of generating dynamic tree models for virtual cities: tree growth, automated large scale generation, ease of maintenance, species-level representation, and convenient modeling of additional species. Specifically, given tree point clouds and species information, we aim to automatically generate dynamically growing 3D tree models at a species level of detail. The species models are differentiated with respect to their botanical architecture and morphology, of especially woody organs such as trunk, branch, and root. Non-woody components such as leaf, flower, and fruit only appear seasonally, hence not essential in the species representation.

Proposed Approach. We present a procedural methodology to generate tree models at a species level of detail based on pre-formulated L-system [15] biological growth rules and known physical measurement values derived from point clouds. The growth rules dictate the tree evolution from a seed into next stage components such as root, trunk, branch, leaf, flower, fruit, and so on. The rules were constructed specifically to match the tree architecture of a target species. We designed the rules to allow general users to model a new species by providing known biological facts of the species. Users need not be 3D artists to generate a tree model. By an automated optimisation to solve for unknown parameters, a tree model is grown to fill up a growth space, which is the space occupied by the point cloud. This results in a tree model similar to the actual tree species in terms of growth process, branching pattern, and morphology.

Potential Contributions. This work contributes the following.

1. A novel convenient mechanism to generate species models based on known biological and physical facts of species to fit point cloud growth space
2. A set of growth rules and parameters applicable to all known tree species
3. A non-graphical species profile template to model new, additional species
4. An effective optimisation to fit a tree model on a given growth space

2   Literature Review

Depending on their purposes, many different 3D tree modeling techniques have been proposed, mainly in the categories of interactive approach [16,18,26], image-based approach [11,22], point cloud reconstruction [10,17,27], stochastic procedural approach [12,26,28], non-stochastic simplistic procedural approach [7,14], inverse procedural approach [2,4,24], or non-stochastic procedural botanical approach of functional structural plant modeling (FSPM) [8,23,25].

Among all, non-procedural approaches tend to produce realistic tree models manually, hence they are not scalable to model all trees in virtual cities. On the other hand, procedural approaches produce a vast variety of trees with believable branching structure automatically based on a relatively small set of rules. They are potentially suitable for large scale modeling in virtual cities. However, most procedural approaches are stochastic in nature, making stochastic procedural approaches unsuitable to control the outcome to represent actual trees in digital twin cities.

Non-stochastic procedural models are generally suitable for representing actual individual trees in a large scale setting of a virtual city. The works of [7,14] generate static, simplified, low resolution models of real trees for a virtual city at a level of detail that represent crown shapes and tree heights. Boudon et al. [4] as well as Bernard and McQuillan [2] constructed tree skeletons which match those of the point clouds of trees with sparse foliage. Similarly, Stava et al. [24] formulated a generic parameterised model to generate a similar tree skeleton through semi-stochastic Monte Carlo Markov Chain optimisation [13], which also worked well for trees with sparse foliage. The resulting models are realistic and dynamically growing, eventhough they do not capture actual species' branching pattern or other botanical species features. In addition, most FSPM-based works produce dynamic, accurate tree models, although they tend to be valid only for a particular species to simulate trees' internal processes and require extensive biomass data. Our proposed methodology is a FSPM-based species modeling to fit within the given point cloud growth space. In our case, the FSPM-based growth rules focus on species architecture facts which users can readily provide based on a simple field observation, and the resulting models are optimised to match the growth space and known measurement values of point cloud data.

3   Methodology

The proposed methodology comprises of two components: pre-processing (formulation of tree growth rules and their parameters) and runtime (parameter optimisation within growth space constraint to produce species models similar to actual trees).

In modeling the tree species for this paper, we make a few assumptions. Non-woody components of trees such as leaf, flower, and fruit are not modelled faithfully (either randomly generated or absent) as they are seasonal, unstable, and easily shed based on environment conditions, which can be handled accordingly in an established simulation context. The woody components of the tree models are generated without any randomness in order to allow users to have full control on the model outcome. The generated models are grown without external or environment effects, except for the gravity that constantly affects a tree standing. This implies that the woody components such as branches will never fall off or be pruned away. They will continue to grow longer until their apical buds abort or transform. When these models are actually used in, say, simulations, then only external environmental factors will affect the models. For the sake of simplicity, we assume uniformity throughout the whole tree for growing process, branching pattern, and response to external stimuli, e.g., same branching angles for all branches of the tree, one growth model throughout the lifespan of the tree. In nature, trees usually have different growth models at different life stages (e.g., seedling, sapling, mature, decline) or size/orientation variations due to environment conditions. A more detailed, accurate model with various growth changes can be produced when the corresponding data are available.

4   Species Growth Rules and Parameters

4.1   L-System Growth Rules

L-System rules [21] govern the evolution of various tree components which can be controlled by a set of parameters. In this work, tree growth rules are formulated as L-system rules according to aspects of the tree architecture as described in [1]. When these aspects are combined differently, they will form the fundamental 23 tree architecture models found in all (tropical) tree species in nature [9]. We constructed each aspect of the tree architecture as seen in Fig. 1 in form of L-system growth rules. This allows our model to adopt a configuration of the tree architecture aspects based on its species profile.

4.2   Tree Parameters

All tree parameters are configured in the growth rules to generate a certain species models. There are essentially constraint parameters and growth parameters.

Constraint parameters are the parameters measurable from actual individual tree point cloud data which are used as constraints to generate models similar to actual trees. At the same time, such constraint parameter values of many individual trees form the tree statistics to provide a reliable guess of a parameter value when it is unknown. Examples of constraint parameters are trunk height, trunk diameter, branching angle, and growth space. On the other hand, growth parameters are the parameters that determine the tree growth in general or for a certain species. Their values can be derived from knowledge, statistics, biological facts, field measurements, or observation. Examples of growth parameters are bud lifespan, rhythmic growth pattern, internode length, number of new nodes per bud per year, and diameter growth rate. Diameter growth rate, in particular, vary greatly among different species. We use the relative growth rate (RGR) to represent the diameter growth rate across the tree body, taking one of the growth models commonly used by ecologists [5]: linear, exponential, power law, monomolecular, three-parameter logistic, four-parameter logistic, and Gompertz models. In our field experiment work [14], we measure the trunk diameter at 1.3-m breast-height in field measurement to represent the tree biomass in calculating RGR. We then apply the growth model to estimate the diameters of all branches at any point of time. When field measurement data are not available, users can adopt one of the growth models and let the system estimate the parameters.

In fact, for all parameters in the system, users only need to provide known range values (including the growth space derived from point cloud data, if any), and the system will solve for the unknowns by an optimisation in order to generate the target species models within reasonable ranges based on existing statistics and facts. In this work, we optimise ten parameters in Table 1 while keeping the values of other parameters (profile parameters) fixed according to the user-specified tree species profile and the growth space.

Users may add new species to model by providing any known species information into a species profile template (Table 2). Examples of completed species
profiles are given in Table 3.

Table 1. List of optimised parameters

No	Parameter name	Unit	Description
1	Age	Year	Time lapse from seed to current state
2	Trunk pitch angle	Year	Angle between up vector and trunk direction at bottom
3	Trunk roll angle	Degree	Counter-clockwise (CCW) angle from North to trunk on ground
4	Trunk height	Meter	Shortest distance from ground/flare to lowest crown or first branching point
5	Number of first order branches	-	Order counted from bottom to top
6	Branching pitch angle	Degree	From parent's head down to start of branch
7	Branching roll angle	Degree	Rotate CCW around parent's head
8	Diameter growth rate	-	Normalised RGR variable of a growth model
9	Number of new nodes per bud	/year	Number of nodes a bud produces in a year
10	Internode length	Meter	Length of a segment between two conse-cutive nodes

5   Parameter Optimisation

Optimisation Strategy. In this work, ten unknown parameters are solved
using a genetic algorithm [20]. An initial population of 1000 possible parameter
configuration solutions is generated using Latin hypercube sampling [19] over
ranges of possible values specified in the species profile. The cost function is
evaluated for each solution and the solution-cost entry is appended to a database.
After testing the initial population, the algorithm iteratively selects a number
of best solutions (of lowest cost) as well as a number of random solutions from
the database, collectively as the parent solutions. They are combined in pairs,
and their parameter values are mutated (slightly modified) to form a successive
generation of 4 child solutions. The successive generations are then evaluated
for their costs, and the solution-cost entries are appended to the database. The
algorithm terminates after a specified number of generations or when a solution
is under a specified cost threshold, whichever is earlier.

Cost Function. The cost function E for the optimisation is a linear weighted
distances between a proposed solution and the target tree constraints. The constraints are a combination of the macroscopic shape of the target tree (i.e., crown

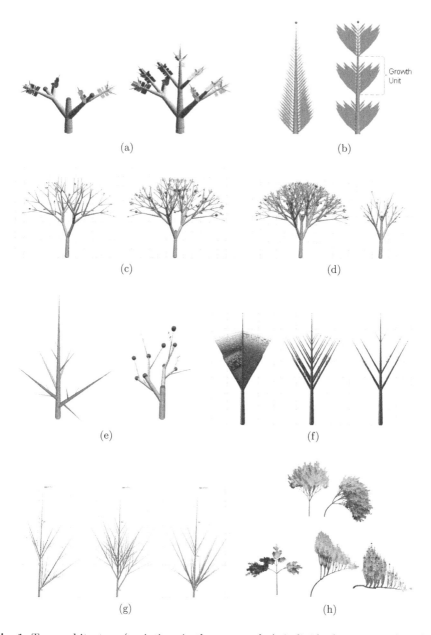

Fig. 1. Tree architecture (variations in the same order): individual structures based on (1) growth process: (a) determinate/indeterminate growth, (b) continuous/rhythmic growth, (2) branching patterns: (c) terminal/lateral branching, (d) immediate/delayed branching, (e) monopodial/sympodial branching, (f) continuous/rhythmic/diffuse branching, (g) acrotonic/mesotonic/basitonic branching, (3) response to external stimuli: (h) orthotropy/plagiotropy. Red spheres at the tips of branches indicate buds that have aborted or transformed to terminal organs such as flowers. (Color figure online)

Table 2. Species profile template

No.	Parameter name	Format	Unit	Description
1	Phyllotaxy	$\frac{c}{n}$	-	c is number of circles for a round of n orthostichies
2	Bud lifespan	≥ 0	Year	Lifespan of a bud, 0 if indeterminate
3	Rhythmic growth period	≥ 0	Year	Period of rhythmic growth to produce 1 GU, zero if continuous growth
4	Growth unit shape	A choice	-	Options: unspecified, acrotonic, mesotonic, or basitonic
5	Branching rhythm	A choice	-	Options: continuous, rhythmic, diffuse
6	Branching rhythmic pattern	xxx	-	Binary rhythmic pattern of 0s and 1s pattern for rhythmic branching
7	Terminal/lateral branching	A choice	-	New branches are formed by growing lateral buds (lateral branching) or splitting apical bud (terminal branching)
8	Branching delay	≥ 0	Year	New branches grow out immediately (0) or after some delay
9	Monopodial/sympodial branching	A choice	-	Apical stem remains dominant with emergence of lateral branches (monopodial) or stops growing with emergence of dominant lateral branches (sympodial)
10	Number of apices	A choice	-	Sole or multiple number of dominant apices (scaffolds) at a time
11	Axis morphology	An array	-	Characteristics of tropism (stimuli field or vector, plagiotropy angle, axis elasticity) for proximal and distal parts
12	Leaf compound size	≥ 0	Meter	Length of a single or compound leaf

Table 3. Examples of species profiles

No	Parameter name	P. pterocarpum	H. odorata	K. senegalensis
1	Phyllotaxy	1/6	1/4	1/4
2	Bud lifespan	10	20	3
3	Rhythmic growth period	2	3	1
4	Growth unit shape	Unspecified	Unspecified	Unspecified
5	Branching rhythm	Rhythmic	Rhythmic	Rhythmic
6	Branching rhythmic pattern	$0^{55}1$	$0^{31}10^{21}1$	$0^{44}1$
7	Terminal/lateral branching	Lateral	Lateral	Lateral
8	Branching delay	1	2	1
9	Monopodial/sympodial	Sympodial	Monopodial	Monopodial
10	Number of apices	Multiple	Sole	Sole
11	Axis morphology	Proximal orthotropic, Distal plagiotropic	Proximal orthotropic, distal plagiotropic	Orthotropic
12	Leaf compound size	0.4	0.1	0.6

shape and dimension) and the microscopic structure of the target tree (i.e., measurements, growth space). Specifically, the growth space is a set of voxels within a uniform grid in the 3D space. Each voxel represent a space containing at least a threshold number of points of the point cloud.

$$E = \sum_{i=1}^{5} w_i E_i \tag{1}$$

$$E_1 = 1 - \frac{|C_L \cap C_G|}{|C_G|} \tag{2}$$

$$E_2 = \frac{|C_G \backslash C_L| + |C_L \backslash C_G|}{|C_G|} \tag{3}$$

$$E_3 = \frac{|\mathbf{B}_{L_{max}} - \mathbf{B}_{G_{max}}| + |\mathbf{B}_{L_{min}} - \mathbf{B}_{G_{min}}|}{|\mathbf{B}_{G_{max}} - \mathbf{B}_{G_{min}}|} \tag{4}$$

$$E_4 = \frac{|g_L - g_G|}{max(g_L, g_G)} \tag{5}$$

$$E_5 = \sum_i \frac{|a_{i_L} - a_{i_G}| + |b_{i_L} - b_{i_G}|}{a_{i_G} + b_{i_G}} \tag{6}$$

w_i is the weight of the error cost component E_i, which captures a certain geometrical difference between the solution tree and the growth space.

E_1 measures the empty space unfilled by the solution tree within the growth space. C_L is the set of voxels occupied by the tree and C_G is the set of voxels in the growth space.

E_2 measures the extra space occupied by the solution tree outside the growth space.

E_3 measures the difference between the bounding boxes of the tree and the growth space. $\mathbf{B}_{L_{min}}$ and $\mathbf{B}_{L_{max}}$ are two diagonally-opposite corner points of the boundary box of the tree, while $\mathbf{B}_{G_{min}}$ and $\mathbf{B}_{G_{max}}$ are those of the growth space, correspondingly.

E_4 measures the difference in the trunk girths of the tree and the growth space at a certain height. g_L and g_G are the trunk girths of the tree and the growth space, respectively.

E_5 measures the difference in the overall shape of the crown by comparing the radii of the smallest horizontal ellipses which bound the crowns of the tree and the growth space at various heights of the crown. a_{i_L}, b_{i_L}, a_{i_G}, and b_{i_G} are the radii a and b of the ellipses at the height i of the crown of the tree L and the growth space G.

6   Results and Discussions

The L-System growth rules were implemented in Python using L-Py [4] and tested to generate 10 tropical tree species models with average parameter values obtained from actual field measurements. The resulting species tree models are shown in Fig. 2.

Based on our processed point cloud data [7], the species profile, and the growth space of actual tree inputs, we also experimented to generate species models that fit within given growth spaces by optimising the ten unknown parameters, within a limited runtime (12 h per task thread with 100 GB memory on an i7-7800X CPU) or until the error E falls below 10%. The optimised parameter results are shown in Table 4, and their corresponding tree models within given growth spaces (voxel spacing of 50 cm, minimum of 5 points per voxel) are in Fig. 3. The results show that relatively similar, realistically structured species models can be automatically generated given the growth spaces of actual trees of known species without any measurement information. The branching topology of the generated models does not necessarily match that of actual trees, but the branching patterns are those typical of their species.

We showed that our models can represent actual trees with a constant growth model. Some species such as *Tabebuia rosea* undergo different modes of growth [3], hence users need to indicate this in its species profile to model the species more accurately.

Fig. 2. L-System models for ten tree species (left to right per row): *Archontophoenix alexandrae, Samanea saman, Peltophorum pterocarpum, Hopea odorata, Swietenia macrophylla, Khaya senegalensis, Syzygium grande, Tabebuia rosea, Syzygium myrtifolium, Sterculia parviflora*

Table 4. Optimised parameters for various tree samples

Parameters	P. pterocarpum	H. odorata	K. senegalensis
Age	30.00	30.00	27.00
Trunk pitch angle, roll angle	0.50, 358.83	359.92, 359.07	0.74, 359.19
Trunk height	2.03	2.72	4.47
Number of 1st order branches	3.00	3.00	2.00
Branch pitch angle, roll angle	20.00, 210.12	21.40, 350.41	33.21, 214.83
Diameter growth rate	0.01	0.01	0.01
Number of new nodes per bud	31.00	29.00	35.00
Internode length	0.02	0.01	0.05

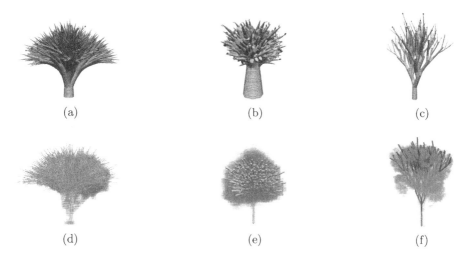

(a)   (b)   (c)

(d)   (e)   (f)

Fig. 3. Optimised species models and superimposed with growth spaces of actual trees: (a, d) *P. pterocarpum* ($E = 14.06\%$), (b, e) *H. odorata* ($E = 11.37\%$), (c, f) *K. senegalensis* ($E = 35.84\%$)

7   Conclusions

Our methodology works to model dynamic trees in a large scale at the species level by pre-formulated L-system growth rules and species profiles. Users can conveniently model actual trees by providing their growth space inputs which can be derived from point cloud data. Our methodology will optimise the generated models to fit around the growth space. To model new, additional species, user fill in known facts of the species into the species profile, and the system will automatically generate the species models.

Our methodology enables users without 3D modeling skills to easily produce species models, especially for actual trees in digital twin cities. This will create a better usage of digital twin cities with botanically representative tree models especially in areas of urban planning and simulation such as [6]. Through simulation, the generated models will transform in reaction to environment stimuli such as sunlight, walls, touch, wind, and pruning.

The current work has many potential future improvements. We plan to fully incorporate tree reiteration and responses to external stimuli to further shape the tree models. To produce models with naturally falling branches, a good mechanism can be proposed to minimise random components. The current optimisation technique could be improved to fit tree models within growth space more tightly with a better bottom up search along the growth direction. Finally, this methodology can be extended to non-tree vegetation (e.g., shrubs, vines) by formulating its growth structure.

Acknowledgement. This work is supported by National Research Foundation Singapore, Virtual Singapore Award no. NRF2015VSG-AA3DCM001-034. Authors thank colleagues at IHPC (A*STAR), NParks, and GovTech for their valuable input and support.

References

1. Barthélémy, D., Caraglio, Y.: Plant architecture: a dynamic, multilevel and comprehensive approach to plant form, structure and ontogeny. Ann. Bot. **99**, 375–407 (2007)
2. Bernard, J., McQuillan, I.: A fast and reliable hybrid approach for inferring l-systems. In: The 2018 Conference on Artificial Life: A Hybrid of the European Conference on Artificial Life (ECAL) and the International Conference on the Synthesis and Simulation of Living Systems (ALIFE), vol. 30, pp. 444–451 (2018)
3. Borchert, R., Honda, H.: Control of development in the bifurcating branch system of tabebuia rosea: a computer simulation. Bot. Gaz. **145**(2), 184–195 (1984)
4. Boudon, F., Pradal, C., Cokelaer, T., Prusinkiewicz, P., Godin, C.: L-Py: an l-system simulation framework for modeling plant architecture development based on a dynamic language. Front. Plant Sci. **3**, 76 (2012)
5. Paine, C.E.T., et al.: How to fit nonlinear plant growth models and calculate growth rates: an update for ecologists. Methods Ecol. Evol. **3**, 245–256 (2012)
6. Ge, Z., Poh, H.J., Wise, D.J., Lim, C.W., Gobeawan, L., Lou, J.: Drag force prediction with CFD full closure model simulation on scaled fractal tree in wind tunnel. In: Proceedings of The Eighth International Symposium on Physics of Fluids (2019)
7. Gobeawan, L., et al.: Modeling trees for virtual Singapore: from data acquisition to cityGML models. Int. Arch. Photogrammetry Rem. Sens. Spat. Inf. Sci. XLII-4/W10, 55–62 (2018)
8. Godin, C., Sinoquet, H.: Functionalstructural plant modelling. New Phytol. **166**(3), 705–708 (2005)
9. Hallé, F., Oldeman, R.A.A., Tomlinson, P.B.: Tropical Trees and Forests: An Architectural Analysis. Springer, New York (1978)
10. Hu, S., Li, Z., Zhang, Z., He, D., Wimmer, M.: Efficient tree modeling from airborne LiDAR point clouds. Comput. Graph. **67**(C), 1–13 (2017)
11. Kamal, M., Phinn, S., Johansen, K.: Object-based approach for multi-scale mangrove composition mapping using multi-resolution image datasets. Rem. Sens. **7**(4), 4753–4783 (2015)

12. Kang, M., Hua, J., De Reffye, P., Jaeger, M.: Parameter identification of plant growth models with stochastic development, pp. 98–105, November 2016
13. Kass, R.E., Carlin, B.P., Gelman, A., Neal, R.M.: Markov chain monte carlo in practice: a roundtable discussion. Am. Statist. **52**(2), 93–100 (1998)
14. Lin, E.S., Teo, L.S., Yee, A.T.K., Li, Q.H.: Populating large scale virtual city models with 3D trees. In: 55th IFLA (International Federation of Landscape Architects) World Congress (2018)
15. Lindenmayer, A.: Mathematical models for cellular interactions in development I. Filaments with one-sided inputs. J. Theor. Biol. **18**(3), 280–299 (1968)
16. Lintermann, B., Deussen, O.: Interactive modeling of plants. IEEE Comput. Graph. Appl. **19**(1), 56–65 (1999)
17. Livny, Y., et al.: Texture-lobes for tree modelling. ACM Trans. Graph. **30**(4), 53:1–53:10 (2011)
18. Longay, S., Runions, A., Boudon, F., Prusinkiewicz, P.: Treesketch: interactive procedural modeling of trees on a tablet. In: Kara, L., Singh, K. (eds.) EUROGRAPHICS Symposium on Sketch-Based Interfaces and Modeling, Cagliari, Italy (2012)
19. McKay, M.D.: Latin hypercube sampling as a tool in uncertainty analysis of computer models. In: Proceedings of the 24th Conference on Winter Simulation, WSC 1992, pp. 557–564. ACM, New York (1992)
20. Mitchell, M.: An Introduction to Genetic Algorithms. MIT Press, Cambridge (1998)
21. Prusinkiewicz, P., Lindenmayer, A.: The Algorithmic Beauty of Plants. Springer, Berlin (1996)
22. Reche-Martinez, A., Martin, I., Drettakis, G.: Volumetric reconstruction and interactive rendering of trees from photographs. ACM Trans. Graph. **23**(3), 720–727 (2004)
23. Sievänen, R., Godin, C., Dejong, T., Nikinmaa, E.: Functional-structural plant models: a growing paradigm for plant studies. Ann. Bot. 114, 599–603, September 2014
24. Stava, O., et al.: Inverse procedural modelling of trees. Comput. Graph. Forum **33**(6), 118–131 (2014)
25. Vos, J., Evers, J.B., Buck-Sorlin, G.H., Andrieu, B., Chelle, M., de Visser, P.H.B.: Functional structural plant modelling: a new versatile tool in crop science. J. Exp. Bot. **61**(8), 2101–2115 (2010)
26. Weber, J., Penn, J.: Creation and rendering of realistic trees. In: Proceedings of the 22nd Annual Conference on Computer Graphics and Interactive Techniques, SIGGRAPH 1995, pp. 119–128. ACM, New York (1995)
27. Xu, H., Gossett, N., Chen, B.: Knowledge and heuristic-based modeling of laser-scanned trees. ACM Trans. Graph. **26**(4), 19 (2007)
28. Xu, L., Mould, D.: Procedural tree modeling with guiding vectors. Comput. Graph. Forum **34**(7), 47–56 (2015)

On Visualization of Movements for Monitoring Older Adults

Shahram Payandeh$^{(\boxtimes)}$ and Eddie Chiu

Networked Robotics and Sensing Laboratory, School of Engineering Science,
Simon Fraser University, 8888 University Drive, Burnaby, BC V5A 1S6, Canada
payandeh@sfu.ca

Abstract. It is a well-known statistics that the percentage of population of older adults will globally surpass the other age categories. It is also observed that a majority of older adults would prefer to stay at their own place of residence for as long as they can. In support of such an independent living life style, various ambient sensor technologies have been designed which can be deployed for long-term monitoring of movements and activities. Depending on the required level of detail associated with such a monitoring system, spatiotemporal data can be collected during various intervals of daily activities for detecting any on-sets of anomalies. The greater granularity, the deeper the level of detail associated with the movement patterns for instances of time and collective durations. This paper we first presents an overview of various visualization techniques which can be employed for monitoring movement patterns. The paper further presents our results of movement visualization experiments using two sample datasets which can be used as a basis for determining movement anomalies. The first dataset is associated with the global movement patterns between various locations in an ambient assisted living environment (AAL) and the other dataset is associated with movement tracking using wearable sensing technologies.

Keywords: Ambient assisted living · Movement data · Older adults · Spatiotemporal visualization · Activity monitoring

1 Introduction

The 2011 Census of Population counted nearly 5 million seniors aged 65 and over in Canada. Of these individuals, 92.1% lived in private households or dwellings (as part of a couple or with others) while 7.9% lived in collective dwellings, such as residences for senior citizens or health care and related facilities [1,2]. The percentage of elderly living in special care facilities reaches 30% by the age of 85. British Columbia's share of seniors 65 and older was 15.7%, above the Canadian national average of 14.8% in 2011 [3]. These trends are also shared with similar statistics all across the globe.

© Springer Nature Switzerland AG 2019
M. Gavrilova et al. (Eds.): CGI 2019, LNCS 11542, pp. 316–326, 2019.
https://doi.org/10.1007/978-3-030-22514-8_26

Older adults who live alone are at risk of accidents at home as a consequence of three main factors: external, physical (due to age), or diseases (chronic or sudden). Loss of consciousness leading to a fall and aberrant behavior associated with certain brain diseases (e.g. Frontotemporal dementia) are examples of possible risks. In recent years, AAL (ambient assisted living) systems have been proposed to deal with home risk detection [4]. AAL systems essentially acquire data from the environment (house) using a network of sensors, in order to provide monitoring or a service to the user without involving direct interaction. One of the objectives of these systems is to detect potential risk scenarios such as: a) fatigue which can be associated with one of the main effects of chronic cardiovascular diseases, characterized by physical weakness and slow activity, especially at the end of the day, and b) aberrant behavior, which may be symptomatic of brain diseases like Fronto temporal Dementia (characterized by the involuntary repetition of movements).

In general, any AAL unit stores a large amount of temporal data collected from a network of sensors or IoT modules which can be interpreted in representing the movements and activity of older adults [5]. Any analysis for understanding and interpreting the stored data requires exploring various approaches which can enable care-givers or physician to better understand and visualize such movements and activities for determining any onset of anomalies. In general, and depending on the state of mental or physical health of an older adult, various levels of sensing details can be deployed [6]. This data can be divided into (a) global presence of movements and activities at various sensing stations located in the living area; (b) trajectory of movements between the sensing stations and (c) the gait patterns along the trajectory in the living space. Each of these levels introduces various degrees of granularity in what can be defined as the movement patterns of the older adults. At the lowest level of sensing granularity is the presence of movement of older adults between various sensing stations. Sensing technology for this case are usually proximity type sensors which can detect the presence or absence of the person in a particular room or at a particular location within the room.

In this paper we first present an overview of current methods for visualizing the movement data and then we presents our own data visualization experiments of using two movement monitoring datasets. The first study uses global motion data of people in their place of residence available through the Center for Advanced Studies in Adaptive System (CASAS) [17]. The second datasets is associated with indoor tracking movements of people using wearable sensors available through the University of South Florida (UoSF) [19].

2   An Overview of Movement Visualization

In general, the expressiveness and effectiveness of a temporal information display (such as movement) can be a function of many factors, such as scale or arrangements [8]. The most simple and widely used solution is the time line representation. In time lines, events are represented as geometric figures, arranged horizontally according to the time they occurred and displayed in one or multiple rows depending on their categories, such as in Gantt charts [7]. The spiral arrangement have been proposed to better distinguish recurrent (cyclic) scenarios in movement patterns or daily activities. The spiral proposals usually represent their rings as a fixed duration (like a clock). [9] proposed a spiral layout to arrange an event sequence in two and three dimensions (Fig. 1a). The spiral time series model of [10] extends this idea by adjusting the length of its cycle and representing multiple records in different rings of the same spiral (Fig. 1b). SpiraClock [11] has an interval sequence in the spiral, representing future and near past, simulating a clock. Other authors also proposed a spiral display to visualize spatiotemporal patterns of cartography in 3 dimensions [12]. An approach for visualizing changes in spatial data over time by plotting a number of non-overlapping pixels, close to sensor positions is proposed by [13]. The approach encode the amount of time that a subject spent at a particular sensor to the number of plotted pixels.

 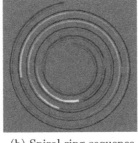 

(a) Event sequence   (b) Spiral ring sequence   (c) Time-line sequence

Fig. 1. Spiral visualization of recurrent data associated with movement patterns or daily activities.

Some efforts in AAL consider finite state machines for modeling and visualizing movement patterns and behavior [14]. These approaches visualize patterns as a state diagram (Fig. 2a) [15]. Similar efforts have been carried to visualize information in the form of graphs, Fig. 2(b), e.g. [16]. Recently [17] has proposed a model referred to as multiple temporal axes which offers a visual representation of temporal information of a person at different locations, Fig. 2(c). Other approaches for interactive exploration of spatiotemporal data using the a space-time cube was propose by [18].

3   Our Visualization Case Studies

In general, it is difficult to determine the degree of frailty associated with the movements and activities of older adults. This would also be associated with the amount of actual information that can be collected from the deployed ambient

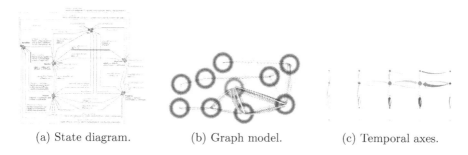

(a) State diagram.   (b) Graph model.   (c) Temporal axes.

Fig. 2. Finite state machine visualization of patterns and behaviors.

sensors in the living environment of the elderly. In addition, without assistant of physicians or care-giving personnel, it is more challenging to establish what can be considered as normal patterns of movements, the health of elderly, and the selected coarseness of sensing modalities; the monitoring information that should be collected. As stated, the tracking of motion and activities can be sampled, clustered, and analyzed at three levels given the locations, distributions, and types of ambient sensors used [5,6]. Analytics associated with each level can further be used in order to establish guidelines for further anomaly detection.

This section presents movement visualization experiments using two classes of datasets. The first dataset is associated with the detection of movements using ambient motion sensing technology distributed in a living environment. The second dataset is associated with the movement trajectory data where subjects are using wearable motion sensing technology.

3.1   CASAS Datasets

At the first level of monitoring, the global movement events between various predefined key sensing points located in the living environment of older adults are collected. These sensing stations are generally used to detect the presence or absence of a person within their operating ranges. Figure 3(a) shows the floor plan of the observation area and the locations of motion sensors associated with the CASAS dataset [17]. Figure 3(b) shows an example of reducing overall sensing granularity through clustering various representative sensors associated with the area. For this example case study, a trivial clustering is used where the collective information from sensors belonging to a particular room is used as an indication of the presence of motion. In this case, the objective of monitoring is to detect movements of older adult between the rooms where groups of sensors are clustered together. The data can also be used in order to associate some global statistics of movements over a required monitoring period. This can be considered as the first level of health monitoring based on movement statistics.

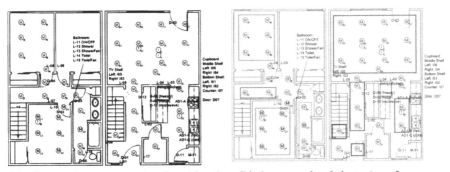

(a) Sensor layout associated with the dataset.   (b) An example of clustering of sensors.

Fig. 3. Physical sensor layout associated with the CASAS datasets and an example of clustering of sensors. [17].

The visualization approach taken in this paper is to define the clustered sensing information associated with each of the room as a node in a directed movement graph. The edges of this graph represent the observed directions of motion between each of the rooms. A moving window of observation can be defined where the time instances and activations of various sensors within the clustered area can be recorded. This information can then be normalized within each nodal points of the graph in order to define a probability distribution of the movements between any of the connected nodes. For example, Fig. 4(a) shows the probabilistic directed graph of the movement data for a three-day observation period (First day (2008-06-24-25) from 7:49:21 PM to 2:41:42 AM, the second day (2008-06-29) from 6:13 AM to 1:56 AM of the next day, and the third day from 6:04 AM to 1:48 AM on of the following day (July 1st)). Depending on the required constraints imposed on the probability distribution, one can associated various colors to the information display [20]. The edges which represent the highest probability of movements between the connecting nodes are shown with darker shades. For example as shown in the Figure, there is a high probability in going from the living room to the bottom bedroom.

General daily movement activity can also be visualized using circular visualization. Circular visualization is selected where the period of 24 h is divided into hourly intervals. For example, Fig. 4(b) shows the activity level for the datasets associated with 2008-06-29.

The hourly total counts of movements can be further visualized for each room as shown in Fig. 5(a). This Figure further splits the hours between the day-time and night-time where color-bars are associated with the movement activities within each room. This approach can also be extended to visualize differences between activities of a given day and previously defined normal activities (Fig. 5b). This is important for cases where it is required to visualize changes in movements and activities patterns for mental health observations.

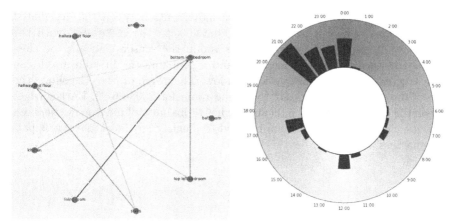

(a) Visualization using probabilistic directed graph   (b) Daily circular visualization of activies

Fig. 4. Results of our movement visualization experiments. (a) Probabilistic directed graph model with nodes presenting the rooms and edges representing the probability of movements between the nodes. Darker edges corresponds to high probability of movements between the connecting nodes. (b) Daily circular visualization of movements for (2008-06-12).

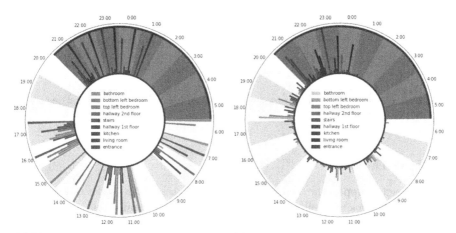

(a) Movement activities within each room. (b) Differential circular visualization with a reference model.

Fig. 5. Results of our circular visualization of daily movement activities associated with each room using CASAS datasets.

Similar approaches can be followed in order to visualize movement and activities associated with the sensing range of a single room. For example, Fig. 6(a) shows movement activity patterns for the living room for day 2008-06-29 of datasets. Darker arrows indicate increase movements between the designated sensor locations. The Figure shows dominated activities associated with the central part of the living room. For this room, the sensors can also be clustered together within various locations and a probabilistic directed graph can be constructed within an observation window. The graph of Fig. 6(b) shows the graph of movement activities for the living room for 2008-06-29. Darker edges between the connected nodes indicates higher probability of movements between the nodes. Such visualizations can be used to identify any local movement pattern behaviors.

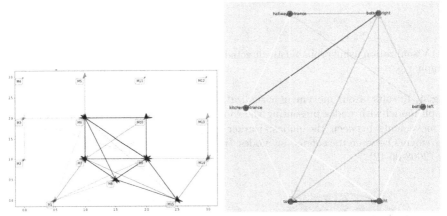

(a) Visualization of movement in the living room. (b) Probabilistic directed graph visualization of movements in living.

Fig. 6. Our graph visualization of movement activities for a living room for day 2008-06-29 of CASAS datasets.

3.2 UoSF Datasets

These datasets supply the tracking information associated with older adults using wearable sensing technology. The person wears a transponders where an ultra-wideband sensor network can measure daytime movements in an assisted living facility [19]. The objective of this tracking system is to detect path tortuosity (irregular movements) of older adults which can be associated with cognitive impairment and potential signs of dementia. The temporal and spatial components of wandering behavior is defined as repetitive or random variations in unconstrained voluntary movements. The datasets are associated with the observation area which is an open 25.6 m by 9.3 m rectangular hallway. In the following, we investigate various visualization approaches which can be explored to further identify possible irregularities in movement patterns of the data associated with a single older adult.

Figure 7(a) shows a basic directional arrow visualization of the movements within a one day cycle of observation. Data points were drawn with a low opacity to show areas of greater activity. Figure 7(b) shows a visualization of movement patterns of the same person over a period of one week. This approach for visualization of the movements can be used in order to identify areas in the observation area which have a high probability of being visited by the older adult.

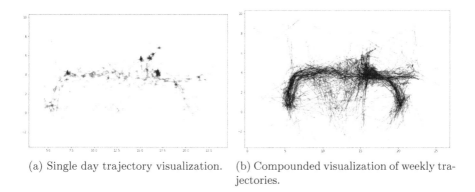

(a) Single day trajectory visualization.   (b) Compounded visualization of weekly trajectories.

Fig. 7. Results of our trajectory visualization of a single older adult using wearable sensor in UoSF datasets.

The next set of visualization experiments were carried in order to include the temporal instances of observations in addition to the spatial information associated with the movement trajectory. This can allow visualization of both the time and location of when and where various irregularities in movement occur. For example, Fig. 8(a) shows an example of an interactive 3D visualization of the

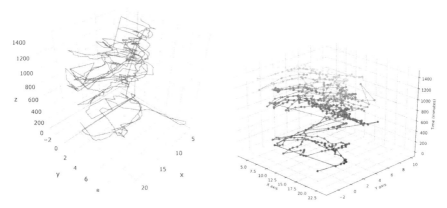

(a) Interactive spatiotemporal trajectory visualization.   (b) Time-lapsed spatiotemporal visualization.

Fig. 8. Our interactive visualization of spatiotemporal movement of trajectory data using UoSF datasets.

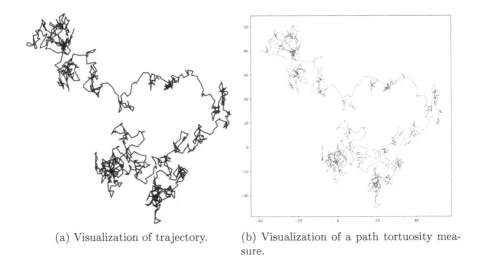

(a) Visualization of trajectory.   (b) Visualization of a path tortuosity measure.

Fig. 9. Visualization of time and locations of path intersections.

raw movement data. Here it is possible to interactively change the viewing angle of the data for identifying various properties of the trajectory of the individual. Figure 8(b) shows another interactive visualization of the trajectory data which indicates the visualization of time axes and the location on the trajectory where the subject deviated from the straight line trajectory.

An extension of results of Fig. 8 is further simulated in order to visualize a measure of path tortuosity based on the number of intersections along the path trajectory during an observation cycle [21] (Fig. 9).

4   Conclusions

Aging in place is commonly defined as the ability for older adults to live in one's own home and community safely, independently, and comfortably. In support of this notion, various commodity grade sensors are being developed with the intention of being easily deployed in one's place of residence for monitoring movements and activities. Depending on their specific sensing features in regard to protection of privacy and sensing resolutions, their output can be processed and collected in a form of historical movement datasets which can be used for health monitoring purposes. In order to make these datasets more usable for care-givers and physicians, various forms of data visualization methodologies need to be explored and studied. This can for example applied to the cases of determining any onsets of anomalies in movements and activities. This paper presents our preliminarily results on movement data visualization study using two publicly available datasets. In these experiments, various basic forms of movement data visualization were presented for the case where the motion sensing is accomplished through various discrete locations in the living environment and for the case of using wearable sensing technologies. One of the main purpose of the movement data visualization is to offer a tool which can easily be used by care-givers and physicians in order to identify any on-sets of anomalies. A prototype system is being developed which can be deployed in residence of healthy older adults for such monitoring purposes and for further evaluation and usability studies. Comparative studies of various movement visualization techniques and their effectiveness are also part of the future work.

References

1. Health Care in Canada (2011), Canadian Institute for Health Information. https://secure.cihi.ca/free_products/HCIC_2011_seniors_report_en.pdf. Accessed Apr 2018
2. Living arrangements of Seniors, Statistics Canada. http://www12.statcan.ca/census-recensement/2011/as-sa/98-312-x/98-312-x2011003_4-eng.cfm. Accessed Apr 2018
3. BCStats. http://www.bcstats.gov.bc.ca/StatisticsBySubject/Census/2016Census.aspx. Accessed Apr 2018
4. Van Den Broek, G., Cavallo, F., Wehrmann, C.: AALiance Ambient Assisted Living Roadmap. IOS press, Amsterdam (2010)
5. Payandeh, S.: On visulizing movements and activities of healthy seniors: an overview. In: Proceedings of the 10th International Conference on Computer Graphics Theory and Applications, pp. 517–522 (2015)
6. Payandeh, S.: Level of detail in motion science associated with older adults. In: Proceedings of the International Conference on Control, Automation, Robotics and Vision (2018)
7. Cousins, S., Kahn, M.: The visual display of temporal information. In: Proceedings of Conference on Graphics Interface, pp. 141–148 (1994)
8. Aigner, W., Miksch, S., Schumann, H., Tominski, C.: Visulization of Time-Orineted Data. Human-Computer Interaction Series. Springer, London (2011). https://doi.org/10.1007/978-0-85729-079-3
9. Carlis, J.V., Konstan, J.A.: Interactive visualization of serial periodic data. In: Proceeedings of ACM Symposium on User Interface Software and Technology, pp. 29–38 (1998)
10. Weber, M., Alexa, M., Mller, W.: Visualizing time-series on spirals. In: Proceedings of IEEE INFOVIS, pp. 7–14 (2001)
11. Dragicevic, P., Huot, S.: SpiraClock: a continuous and non-intrusive display for upcoming events. In: Proceedings of the SIGCHI Conference on Human Factors in Computing Systems, pp. 604–605 (2002)
12. Priyantha, H.K., Hirakawa, M., Ichikawa, T.: Interactive visualization of spatiotemporal patterns using spirals on a geographical map. In: Proceedings of the IEEE Symposium on Visual Languages, p. 296 (1999)
13. Bak, P., Mansmann, F., Janetzko, H., Keim, D.: Spatiotemporal analysis of sensor logs using growth ring maps. IEEE Trans. Visual. Comput. Graphics **15**(6), 913–920 (2009)
14. Navarrete, I., Rubio, J.A., Botía, J.A., Palma, J.T., Campuzano, F.J.: Modeling a risk detection system for elderly's home-care with a network of timed automata. In: Bravo, J., Hervás, R., Rodríguez, M. (eds.) IWAAL 2012. LNCS, vol. 7657, pp. 82–89. Springer, Heidelberg (2012). https://doi.org/10.1007/978-3-642-35395-6_11

15. Blaas, J., Botha, C., Grundy, E., Jones, M., Laramee, R., Post, F.: Smooth graphs for visual exploration of higher-order state transitions. IEEE Trans. Visual. Comput. Graphics **16**(6), 969–976 (2009)
16. Wattenberg, M.: Visual exploration of multivariate graphs. In: Proceedings of the SIGCHI Conference on Human Factors in Computing Systems, pp. 811–819 (2006)
17. Cook, D., Crandall, B., Thomas, B., Krishnan, N.: CASAS: a smart home in a box. Computer **46**(7), 62–69 (2013)
18. Gatalsky, P., Andrienko, N., Andrienko, G.: Interactive analysis of event data using space-time cube. In: Proceedings of IEEE International Conference on information Visualization (2004)
19. Kearns, W., Nams, V., Fozard, J.: Tortuosity in movement paths is related to cognative impairment: wireless fractal estimation in assisted living facility residents. J. Methods Inf. Med. **49**(6), 592–598 (2010)
20. Payandeh, S., Chiu, E.: Application of modified pagerank algorithm for anomaly detection in movements of older adults. Int. J. Telemed. Appl. **2019**, Article ID 8612021, 9 p. (2019)
21. Li, A., Payandeh, S.: An overview of path tortuosity measures for tracking and monitoring. In: Proceedings of IEEE Conference on Information Technology, Electronics and Mobile Communication (2016)

CGI'19 Short Papers

Create by Doing – Action Sequencing in VR

Flavien Lécuyer[1](✉), Valérie Gouranton[1], Adrien Reuzeau[1], Ronan Gaugne[2], and Bruno Arnaldi[1]

[1] Univ Rennes, INSA Rennes, Inria, CNRS, IRISA, Rennes, France
flavien.lecuyer@irisa.fr
[2] Univ Rennes, Inria, CNRS, IRISA, Rennes, France

Abstract. In every virtual reality application, there are actions to perform, often in a logical order. This logical ordering can be a predefined sequence of actions, enriched with the representation of different possibilities, which we refer to as a scenario. Authoring such a scenario for virtual reality is still a difficult task, as it needs both the expertise from the domain expert and the developer. We propose to let the domain expert create in virtual reality the scenario by herself without coding, through the paradigm of *creating by doing*. The domain expert can run an application, record the sequence of actions as a scenario, and then reuse this scenario for other purposes, such as an automatic replay of the scenario by a virtual actor to check the obtained scenario, the injection of this scenario as a constraint or a guide for a trainee, or the monitoring of the scenario unfolding during a procedure.

1 Introduction

Virtual reality has a strong positive impact for the learning of procedures [1], as with serious games [8]. Virtual reality also tends to make students more interested during the learning process, because they can interact with the knowledge presented to them, they get a better understanding of it and feel more involved [3]. Those serious games can benefit from the use of a scenario, which divides the learning into different steps, for a better understanding of each concept that is presented. When we know in advance what are the actions allowed by the scenario, and what is supposed to be the timeline for those actions, the scenario can take the form of an action sequence, with possible choices or repetitions changing the final outcome of the scenario. However, such scenarios are difficult to implement for trainers that are not experts in the domain of computer science, since there is a need for a certain knowledge of coding to author a scenario for virtual reality. At the very least, someone wanting to create a scenario needs to learn how the scenario representation works to be able to use it. This requires time and effort that could be avoided thanks to a higher level authoring tool. Because

This work is part of the ANR-16-FRQC-0004 INTROSPECT project, and the SUNSET project funded by the ANR-10-LABX-07-01 "Investing for the Future" program.

© Springer Nature Switzerland AG 2019
M. Gavrilova et al. (Eds.): CGI 2019, LNCS 11542, pp. 329–335, 2019.
https://doi.org/10.1007/978-3-030-22514-8_27

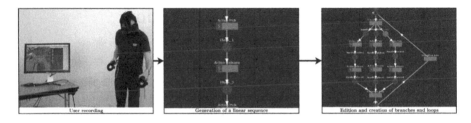

Fig. 1. The proposed workflow starts from the action recording to generate a straight scenario, which can then be edited for a more complex sequence

of this, it is very often a developer who integrates the scenario in the virtual environment. This often leads to a wrong interpretation of the scenario, making it less efficient, and even in the worse case counter productive. On the contrary, explaining a procedure in real life can be easy. A common way of explaining to someone what should be the sequence of actions in a procedure is to show the procedure to the person learning it. This is particularly efficient, since it shows how each action leads to the following one, and at the same time, helps in the achievement of the final goal. It is also a good way to demonstrate the feasibility of the procedure.

We propose to use this metaphor of showing the procedure to explain it, to create scenarios for a virtual environment from this virtual environment. In this paper, after the analysis of the related work in Sect. 2, we present a concept for the generation of a scenario through the recording of users in a virtual environment, through three points:

- The *create by doing* concept to author scenarios, presented in Sect. 3
- The presentation of a proof of concept based on this paradigm, in Sect. 4
- The creation of a use case demonstrating our approach in Sect. 5

2 Related Work

Some works proposed to provide a replay function in virtual environments, which can be seen as a way to record the user actions to generate a scenario, or at least a trace of what the user has been doing. For instance, Chan et al. captured the movements of the user to replay them in virtual reality, which allowed to highlight more efficiently the mistakes during the learning of dance moves [2]. However, movements are recorded as a continuous data, without any interpretation or cutting into separate steps. Because of this, the replay is only a video separated from the virtual environment, which cannot be used later if the environment is meant to be modified even the slightest. The video format can only be used to provide indications to the user of an application, making it impractical if the scenario is supposed to constrain and guide the actions of the user. Similarly, Bailenson et al. [1] used the possibility of virtually going back in time, to help the users in the learning of martial arts. For an efficient analysis of the movements of the user, the participants were asked to wear specific clothes in order to help the computer vision algorithm. This is a strong constraint, since it forces the user to have access to a specific equipment to use the application. Another interesting work is the one done by the MIT Education Arcade with *Mystery at the Museum* (*M@M*) [4] and *Environmental Detectives* [5], in which replaying the previous actions is possible, and provided as a means to remind the players of what already happened. Unfortunately, their approach is not really detailed, and the replay function seems to rely more on a log of the events than on a reusable scenario. A scenario that is generated through the execution can also be reused to generate a final product, as done by Paiva et al. [7]. In this application, the child can influence the evolution of the story. Those choices are recorded in order to produce a movie taking into account every choice made by the user. This means that, if a user makes the correct decisions and unfolds the best scenario possible, this unfolding will be reusable for other people only in a passive way. A better possibility would be to create a mixed reality application through an immersive environment, as proposed in [6]. However, the creation of a scenario for a virtual reality application is a tedious task for a non-developer.

3   Scenario Creation

The authoring of scenarios for virtual reality is a tedious task, because the necessary knowledge is shared between the domain expert and the developer.

Before we present our approach, it is important to define what we call a "scenario". In our context, a scenario is a sequence of actions, linked in a given order so as to describe a logical progression through time. Of course, this sequence can be enriched with branches, for which the choices of the user will influence how the rest of the scenario unfolds. It should also be possible to repeat the same action or group of actions multiple times, which would be translated by a loop in the sequence of actions.

To make the *create by doing* process possible, the actions must be as atomic as possible, but also discrete in time. Indeed, we focus more on the consequences of an action, rather than on how this action is done. An illustration of this is given in Fig. 2. In this precise example, we first take the object, triggering the recording of the `Take` action. Then, we move it as we want, until it go through a given point in space, which triggers the `Move to` action regarding this point. Of course there could also be other points in space triggering this action. Finally, we release the object on a given spot, with the `Place` action.

We propose to use the *create by doing* paradigm, which is based on the automatic recording of the actions done by a user. Thanks to this, the authoring of a scenario becomes as natural as possible, since it is the very execution of the procedure that generates the corresponding action sequence.

The main steps of our approach are summarized in Fig. 1. There are four main steps for the authoring of a scenario with our method:

1. Define a set of possible actions in the virtual environment
2. Run the application in a free mode, with the tool recording the performed actions. At the end of this step, the expert gets a linear sequence corresponding to the actions she performed.
3. Edit the action sequence to make it more complex, by adding branches/loops.

Our paradigm of creating the action sequence by doing actions mostly improves the recording of straight procedures. Indeed, this part can be done by letting the expert choose some actions and execute them freely, to generate the according scenario with the sequence of selected actions. The best way to let the expert select the actions to record in the scenario is to actually let her *do* those actions from within the virtual environment, which is why the recording is done from the application itself. In order to make the actions recorded in the generated scenario easier to recognize, we limit the actions to the ones that are already defined in the environment. This way, the actions can themselves notify the authoring tool, which can in turn generate the action sequence. For the creation of more complex scenarios, with branches and tools, we let the expert modify a straight scenario from a graphic editor. The use of a graphic editor for the final modification of the action sequence is also an efficient way to let the averted user add finer modifications to the scenario. Indeed, it is also possible to add other steps, independent from the actions of a user, and to add direct consequences for the execution of an action, directly from the editor.

4   Proof of Concept

In order to verify the practical feasibility and the usefulness of our approach, we built a proof of concept, under the form of a scenario authoring tool.

The authoring tool can be integrated in a virtual environment that is already created. This is done through an automatic generation of the scenario according to the actions that are done by the application designer. For an action to be recognized, it has to be defined beforehand in the environment. In fact, an action is considered as a given behaviour the application executes when asked to. If the actions are continuous over a given period of time, we will prefer to log the beginning and the end of the action. For instance, we will not take into account the fact that a user holds an object in the hand, but rather the moment when the object is taken, and the moment when the same object is released.

Each time an action is recognized, it is logged in the form of a new transition and state, with the transition being triggered by the said action. The scenario

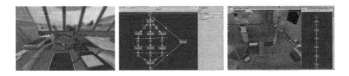

Fig. 2. On the left, the actions recorder for a pick and place task. On the middle, a scenario in the editing tool. On the right, a scenario performed by a virtual agent.

being created changes dynamically according to the events in the virtual environment. Because of this, it should not be saved or reused before the end of the recording. However, it is still possible to modify it from the editor at any moment.

In our proof of concept, we provide three main features, according to the main steps we presented in Fig. 1. The first one, which is the core of our *create by doing* paradigm, is the free execution of actions from within the virtual environment to generate a scenario. The user will have two options for the interactions. First, it is of course possible to interact in the ways that have been explicitly defined with the objects in the environment. Instead, the actions define what they can do on some properties. To be involved in specific actions, the objects have to possess those properties. This way, an action can be defined only once, independently of the objects involved. For instance, plugging the outlet of a fridge on the wall is the same action as plugging the outlet for the oven.

When the creation of the linear scenario is done, the expert can move on to the creation of branches on loop on the scenario. To do this, we use the same interface as for the display of the scenario during the authoring, which is the one illustrated in Fig. 2. On this interface, the expert can modify the structure of the scenario simply by moving nodes, and by creating/deleting edges.

In order to facilitate the creation of branches, we also propose to use an undo function that can be used from the virtual environment. In the scenario, the undo will change the last state selected in the sequence, to go to the previous step. The actions already recorded will be kept in the scenario as an additional branch. Whenever another action is recorded, the scenario will then create a new branch, starting from the selected state followed by said action.

To help the domain expert to check the scenario, we propose to make a virtual agent automatically play it, action by action, in the virtual environment, as shown in Fig. 2. When there are choices to make in the scenario, the virtual agent can be customized to modify how it chooses the actions to perform.

5   Medical Procedure Training

In the medical domain, the knowledge of the procedures is extremely important, since every member of an intervention must know his/her next action, in order not to slow down the entire group. To help the students in learning the procedures inherent to the preparation of a surgical intervention, we created an application,

Fig. 3. On the left, the preparation table in the virtual operating room. On the middle, a scrub nurse interacting with the application. On the right, the corresponding scenario

dedicated to scrub nurses, in which the trainee has to prepare the operating table before the intervention.

In this use case, the trainee has to take some instruments and to place them on the table in a very specific manner according to the nature of the intervention. For different interventions, different tools and dispositions might be appropriate, which is why different scenarios can be needed. Even though the virtual environment is a powerful tool for learning, it is by nature supposed to be used for one person at a time. To show more efficiently the correct procedure to a group of students, showing the virtual agent evolving in the virtual environment would be more adequate, as it would be easy to transpose the knowledge gained from seeing the movie, and it is also easy to show a movie to a group. The application simulates an operating room, with the table to prepare, on a HMD. During the learning process, the trainee is helped by the scenario, which highlights the possible actions in the environment to make her move forward in the simulation.

To design the procedure in the virtual environment, the trainer can use the scenario authoring tool to record the correct sequence of actions, to create for instance the scenario provided in Fig. 3. This creates a scenario in which the trainee starts from the table with no instrument, and finishes with the table ready for the operation. In fact, the trainer can use the application as a tool in which the students can *learn by doing*, but the trainer can also benefit from the scenario being played at the same time as the trainee executes the tasks to *monitor* her. An overview of the setup, with a real scrub nurse unfolding the scenario, can also be seen in Fig. 3.

6 Discussion

Through the creation of our use cases, we noted that our scenario authoring tool could also be easily used for other purposes, illustrated in Fig. 4.

Learn by doing When the scenario is done, it can be reused for an application in which a trainee has to complete the tasks described by the scenario.

Learning by seeing The scenario can be automatically replayed by a virtual agent to demonstrate the procedure.

Collaborate by doing Multiple users can collaborate to perform the scenario, possibly with an assignation of roles.

Monitor by seeing The scenario provides two feedbacks: the execution in real-time of the scenario can be displayed on-screen, and the replay can be used afterwards as a tool to repeat a previous execution.

Fig. 4. The additional uses of the scenario, from top left to bottom right: learning by doing, collaborating by doing, learning by seeing, monitoring by seeing

7   Conclusion

In this paper, we presented a tool to easily create scenarios for virtual reality without having to write a single line of code, through the principle of *"creating by doing"*. This way, the application designer can start from a simple virtual environment enriched with objects and interactions, and create a scenario through the execution of a simulation in which every action adds a step in a scenario. More functions are also provided in our tool to help in building more complex scenarios, to add choices to the simulation.

The scenario created through this tool can then be used in the virtual environment. Thanks to this, a trainee can then be immersed in an environment with given tasks to complete. Through the completion of these tasks, the student can *learn by doing*, or even *collaborate by doing* when there are multiple students. Furthermore, the scenario can be used to make a virtual agent execute the scenario automatically, which is a great help to demonstrate how the sequence of actions is supposed to be. This demonstration can be done to help the trainees, who can then *learn by seeing* someone else do the work.

References

1. Bailenson, J.N., Yee, N., Blascovich, J., Beall, A.C., Lundblad, N., Jin, M.: The use of immersive virtual reality in the learning sciences: digital transformations of teachers, students, and social context. J. Learn. Sci. **17**(1), 102–141 (2008). https://doi.org/10.1080/10508400701793141
2. Chan, J.C.P., Leung, H., Tang, J.K.T., Komura, T.: A virtual reality dance training system using motion capture technology. IEEE Trans. Learn. Technol. **4**(2), 187–195 (2011). https://doi.org/10.1109/TLT.2010.27
3. Fletcher, J.D.: Does this stuff work? A review of technology used to teach. Tech-Knowlogia **Jan–Mar**, 10–14 (2003)
4. Klopfer, E., Perry, J., Squire, K., Jan, M.F., Steinkuehler, C.: Mystery at the museum: a collaborative game for museum education. In: Proceedings of the 2005 Conference on Computer Support for Collaborative Learning, pp. 316–320. International Society of the Learning Sciences (2005). http://dl.acm.org/citation.cfm?id=1149293.1149334
5. Klopfer, E., Squire, K.: Environmental detectives-the development of an augmented reality platform for environmental simulations. Educ. Technol. Res. Dev. **56**, 203–228 (2007)
6. Lee, G.A., Nelles, C., Billinghurst, M., Kim, G.J.: Immersive authoring of tangible augmented reality applications. In: Proceedings of the 3rd IEEE/ACM International Symposium on Mixed and Augmented Reality, ISMAR 2004, pp. 172–181. IEEE Computer Society, Washington, DC (2004). https://doi.org/10.1109/ISMAR.2004.34
7. Paiva, A., Machado, I., Prada, R.: Heroes, villians, magicians, & dramatis personae in a virtual story creation environment. In: Proceedings of the 6th International Conference on Intelligent User Interfaces, IUI 2001, pp. 129–136. ACM, New York (2001). https://doi.org/10.1145/359784.360314
8. Zyda, M.: From visual simulation to virtual reality to games. Computer **38**(9), 25–32 (2005). https://doi.org/10.1117/12.703906

Deep Intrinsic Image Decomposition
Using Joint Parallel Learning

Yuan Yuan[1,2], Bin Sheng[1(✉)], Ping Li[3(✉)], Lei Bi[4], Jinman Kim[4],
and Enhua Wu[5,6]

[1] Department of Computer Science and Engineering, Shanghai Jiao Tong University,
Shanghai 200240, China
shengbin@sjtu.edu.cn
[2] School of Marine Science and Technology, Northwestern Polytechnical University,
Xi'an 710072, China
[3] Faculty of Information Technology, Macau University of Science and Technology,
Macau 999078, China
pli@must.edu.mo
[4] Biomedical and Multimedia Information Technology Research Group,
School of Information Technologies, The University of Sydney,
Sydney, NSW 2006, Australia
[5] Faculty of Science and Technology, University of Macau,
Macau 999078, China
[6] State Key Laboratory of Computer Science, Institute of Software,
Chinese Academy of Sciences, Beijing 100190, China

Abstract. Intrinsic image decomposition is a highly ill-posed problem
in computer vision referring to extract albedo and shading from an image.
In this paper, we regard it as an image-to-image translation issue and
propose a novel thought, which makes use of parallel convolutional neural networks (ParCNN) to learn albedo and shading with different spatial features and data distributions, respectively. At the same time, the
energy is preserved as much as possible under the constraint of image
reconstruction loss shared by the two networks. Moreover, we add the
gradient prior based on the traditional image formation process into the
loss function, which can lead to a performance improvement of our basic
learning model by jointing advantages of the physically-based method
and the data-driven method. We choose MPI Sintel dataset for model
training and testing. Quantitative and qualitative evaluation results outperform the state-of-the-art methods.

Keywords: Intrinsic image decomposition · ParCNN · Gradient priors

This work was supported in part by the National Natural Science Foundation of China
under Grant 61872241 and Grant 61572316, in part by the Macau Science and Technology Development Fund under Grant 0027/2018/A1, in part by the National Key
Research and Development Program of China under Grant 2017YFE0104000 and Grant
2016YFC1300302, and in part by the Science and Technology Commission of Shanghai
Municipality under Grant 18410750700, Grant 17411952600, and Grant 16DZ0501100.

© Springer Nature Switzerland AG 2019
M. Gavrilova et al. (Eds.): CGI 2019, LNCS 11542, pp. 336–341, 2019.
https://doi.org/10.1007/978-3-030-22514-8_28

1   Introduction

Intrinsic image decomposition addresses the problem of separating an image into its albedo and shading components (see Fig. 1). Albedo is invariant to camera viewpoint and illumination conditions; while shading is dependent on the illumination effects due to geometry, shadows and inter-reflectance. Some prior work tackles the ill-posed problem by optimizing the summation of a series of pre-defined energy functions which are used to force albedo and shading to obey some local or global priors such as reflectance is piece-wise constant and shadings are smooth [2]. With the advent of artificial intelligence, deep learning methods have become a favorite in the field, especially the convolutional neural network. The common CNNs consist of a shared encoder and several separated decoders, but only the decoders can extract uncoupled features of different intrinsic components. Different from them, we propose a parallel learning network which uses two variant U-Nets to learn albedo and shading, respectively, and the image reconstruction loss function is shared by the two nets so that the result can satisfy reconstruction consistency as far as possible. Considering the gradient information is a quintessence to express the edge structure of the object in images and variations of light and shadows, we incorporate the gradient loss into our data-driven learning method to attenuate typical generative CNN artifacts like blur, color bleeding and contrast oscillations. We choose the synthetic MPI Sintel dataset to train and test our model. The evaluation shows a comparable decomposition results with previous state-of-the-art methods.

2   Method

The global summary of our method is illustrated in Fig. 1. We employ two parallel variant U-Nets to learn different subspace features of albedo and shading from the original image, respectively. At the same time, by means of result sharing, the identical image reconstruction loss keeps the energy conservation possible. Moreover, we add gradient prior to the loss function to guide a learned solution.

2.1   Intrinsic Image Decomposition Model

Intrinsic decomposition task is typically formulated as finding decomposition of an image where the albedo and shading pair multiply to give the original image. Formally, given an RGB image $\mathbf{I}$, we should solve for albedo layer $\mathbf{A}$ with RGB channels and shading layer $\mathbf{S}$ satisfying:

$$\mathbf{I} = \mathbf{A} \times \mathbf{S} \tag{1}$$

where $\times$ denotes the element-wise product, $\mathbf{I}, \mathbf{A}, \mathbf{S} \in \mathbf{R}^{w \times h \times 3}$ are vectors in RGB space, w and h indicate the width and height of the images. We use $\mathbf{I}_i$, $\mathbf{A}_i$, and $\mathbf{S}_i$ to indicate the pixel observed at location i of the input image, the albedo image, and the shading image, respectively. Note that shading is three-channel which means that the color illumination can be included in the shading component.

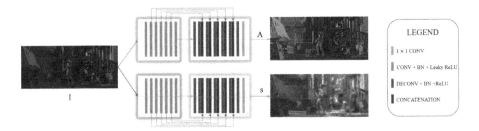

Fig. 1. Network architecture. The CNNs learn albedo and shading in parallel with same image reconstruction loss and other individual relevant losses. Details of the network structure and loss function are elaborated in Sects. 2.2 and 2.3, respectively.

2.2 Network Architecture

We learn albedo and shading components from the original images simultaneously with two identical networks which are variant of the "U-Net" architecture. Each of our network has one encoder and one decoder with skip connections. The two networks are trained for exporting log albedo and log shading, respectively. Each layer of the encoder consists mainly of a 4×4 stride-2 convolutional layer followed by batch normalization and leaky ReLu. For the decoder, each layer is composed of a 4×4 deconvolutional layer followed by batch normalization and ReLu, and a 1×1 convolutional layer is appended to the final layer of it (see Fig. 1).

2.3 Loss Function

The learning problem for the MPI Sintel dataset equipped with a full ground truth decomposition can be formulated as a direct regression problem from input image I to output images A and S. Let $\hat{\Phi}$ be the prediction of the U-Net and Φ be the ground truth intrinsic image, that's to say, $\hat{\Phi} \in \{\hat{A}, \hat{S}\}$ and $\Phi \in \{A, S\}$. Our objective is to make $\hat{\Phi}$ and Φ as close as possible. Formally, we define the loss L of each variant U-Net as follows, including a data loss, a gradient loss and a reconstruction loss.

$$L(\hat{\Phi}) = L_{data}(\hat{\Phi}) + L_{grad}(\hat{\Phi}) + L_{rec}(\hat{A}, \hat{S}) \tag{2}$$

Data Loss. Data loss defines the similarity between the predicted image and the ground truth at the pixel-level and we express it as a scale-invariant L_2 norm:

$$L_{data}(\hat{\Phi}) = \frac{1}{N} \sum_{i=1}^{N} (\hat{\Phi}_i - p_\phi \Phi_i)^2 \tag{3}$$

where N is the number of valid pixels in Φ. The scale factor $p_\phi \in \{p_a, p_s\}$ are computed via least squares.

Gradient Loss. Edge is the place where image information is most concentrated and the attributes of image region mutate. Inspired by traditional Retinex algorithm, we use multi-scale gradient loss to preserve sharp edges in both albedo and shading components, as well as encourage the piecewise smoothness. The formula is expressed as follows:

$$L_{grad}(\hat{\Phi}) = \sum_{l=1}^{L} \frac{1}{N_l} \sum_{i=1}^{N_l} \left\| \nabla \hat{\Phi}_{l,i} - p_\phi \nabla \Phi_{l,i} \right\|_1 \tag{4}$$

where l is the scale of an image pyramid and N_l is the number of valid pixels at scale l, L is equal to 4.

Reconstruction Loss. In order to follow the constraint of consistent decomposition, we design a reconstruction loss for the two networks, so that the results of parallel learning can be restored to the original image:

$$L_{reconstruct}(\hat{R}, \hat{S}) = \frac{1}{N} \sum_{i=1}^{N} (I_i - \hat{A}_i \hat{S}_i)^2 \tag{5}$$

3 Evaluations

In this section, we elaborate on the processing of training dataset, details of the network training and the qualitative results.

3.1 Dataset

MPI Sintel dataset is available for 18 scenes with 50 frames each (one of the scenes has only 40 frames), for a total of 890. The albedo images have been rendered without illumination. The ground truth shading images are created by rendering all the scenes with uniform grey albedo on all objects. As opposed to [2] using the "clean pass" images as input, we restructure the original images to respect Eq. (1).

We use two-fold cross validation procedure to produce the results, and we implement both image split (randomly sampling half of the images for training, and the rest for testing) and scene split (placing an entire scene (all images it contains) either completely in training or completely in testing) to evaluate the generalization ability of our model comprehensively.

3.2 Network Training Details

We implement our method in Pytorch. For the dataset, we use data augmentation techniques by random horizontal mirroring, rotating, resizing and crops. In addition, we use Adam optimizer for model optimization with $\beta_1 = 0.9$, $\beta_2 = 0.999$, initial learning rate 0.0005 and mini-batch size 16.

3.3   Results

We quantitatively and qualitatively evaluate the model on MPI Sintel dataset. Compared with previous state-of-the-art work, our model shows better generalization ability.

We follow [4], and utilize the scale-invariant metrics (si-MSE and si-LMSE), perceptually-motivated metrics(DSSIM) and the image split test images first to quantitatively measure the performance of the proposed approach. The conclusion shows that our method has generally achieved better performance compared to [1–3,5], and the qualitative results are presented in Fig. 2. We can see that our intrinsic images have less blur comparing to the other methods. Moreover, our albedo image seems to be more natural and harmonious which shows the success of our approach. And then we implement the evaluation on scene split images which shows a comparable generalization ability of our network compared with DI [5]. It is noteworthy that our recovered reflectance images have less errors which explains the hypothesis that larger gradients in an image usually correspond to reflectance changes.

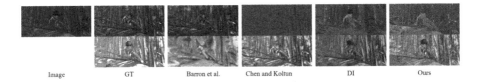

Image   GT   Barron et al.   Chen and Koltun   DI   Ours

Fig. 2. Qualitative results on the Sintel image split.

4   Conclusion

We propose a ParCNN architecture to recover albedo and shading for single image intrinsic decomposition in parallel for the sake of learning spatial characteristics in different domains without entangled. Through shared image reconstruction loss, the consistent decomposition is guaranteed. Integration of gradient information into the CNN-based model allows us to make full use of the advantages of physically-based priors to handle complex natural world cases and achieve better results. Evaluation on both synthetic and real images outperforms state-of-the-art methods. However, the limitation is that there is a small domain shift which affects the generalization ability of our model. We hold the view that training models on more realistic datasets can help solve this problem, and we hope our work can facilitate further research.

References

1. Barron, J.T., Malik, J.: Shape, illumination, and reflectance from shading. IEEE Trans. Pattern Anal. Mach. Intell. **37**(8), 1670–1687 (2015). https://doi.org/10.1109/TPAMI.2014.2377712
2. Chen, Q., Koltun, V.: A simple model for intrinsic image decomposition with depth cues. In: 2013 IEEE International Conference on Computer Vision, pp. 241–248, December 2013. https://doi.org/10.1109/ICCV.2013.37
3. Grosse, R.B., Johnson, M.K., Adelson, E.H., Freeman, W.T.: Ground truth dataset and baseline evaluations for intrinsic image algorithms. In: 2009 IEEE 12th International Conference on Computer Vision, pp. 2335–2342 (2009)
4. Lettry, L., Vanhoey, K., Gool, L.V.: DARN: a deep adversarial residual network for intrinsic image decomposition. In: 2018 IEEE Winter Conference on Applications of Computer Vision (WACV), pp. 1359–1367 (2018)
5. Narihira, T., Maire, M., Yu, S.X.: Direct intrinsics: learning albedo-shading decomposition by convolutional regression. In: Computer Science, pp. 2992–2992 (2015)

Procedurally Generating Biologically Driven Feathers

Jessica Baron[(⊠)] and Eric Patterson[(⊠)]

Clemson University, Clemson, SC, USA
{jrbaron,ekp}@clemson.edu

Abstract. Computer-generated feathers are of interest for both research and digital production, but previously proposed modeling methods have been user controlled rather than shaped by actual data. This work demonstrates a new, biologically informed model for individual feathers that uses techniques from computer vision and computer graphics to derive and control shapes. The method reduces the amount of user effort and influence and provides an accurate means of using natural variation of real feathers to synthesize photo-realistic feather assets.

Keywords: Procedural · Feather · Curves · Modeling · Computer vision

1 Introduction

The motivation to improve modeling of feathers stems from their use for both productions and scientific research. In the entertainment industry, feathered creatures are often engaging characters such as the owls from *Legend of the Guardians* (2011) [11]. Computer-generated feathers can also aid scientific inquiry through visualization where active research includes the origin of birds and feathered dinosaurs in ornithological and paleontological studies as well as the development of biological and material-science understanding concerning the strength, aerodynamic, and insulating properties of feathers [2,10].

This paper proposes a method to extract data from images of real feathers and use it to model geometry that matches natural shape variation. The Feather Atlas [19] was used for its well-cataloged variety of images of multiple feathers from various types of birds, though the techniques could work on most images of most types of feathers. The novel contributions of this work include (1) a new model for the shape of an individual feather, (2) a pipeline for extracting and retrieving data of actual feathers, and (3) the means to incorporate gathered data to improve production and visualization.

2 Brief Biological Background

Feathers are present in birds and are studied in multiple disciplines for properties such as flight and water repellency [2,10,13]. Recent paleontological studies also focus on the bridge between modern birds and extinct dinosaurs [10].

© Springer Nature Switzerland AG 2019
M. Gavrilova et al. (Eds.): CGI 2019, LNCS 11542, pp. 342–348, 2019.
https://doi.org/10.1007/978-3-030-22514-8_29

A *feather's anatomy* primarily consists of three branching components: shaft, barbs, and barbules. The *shaft* is the central structure from which extend thin *barbs*. The *rachis* is a part of the shaft where barbs connect, and the *calamus* is the shaft's bare part. From the tube-like *ramus* of each barb branch smaller *barbules* that may possess hooklets, or *barbicels* [2]. Barbules are often visible to the unaided human eye, but barbicels are microscopic. *Pennaceous barbs*, those that hook together, form the *vanes* of a feather which appear as smooth surfaces extending from the shaft. Barbules on fluffy, *plumaceous barbs* lack barbicels [16].

The six main *feathers types* are flight, contour, down, semiplume, filoplume, and bristle; each varies in function, placement, and anatomical composition [16]. This study focuses on flight feathers due to their visibility, their distinct shapes, and the Feather Atlas's data, but the techniques can be applied for the others.

3   Related Work

3.1   Computer-Graphics Research

Early publications in creating feather geometry are curve-based. The work of Chen et al. incorporates Bézier curves into L-system modules to define the rachis and barbs, but barbules are present only via textures [3]. Further studies are similar though not organized using L-systems [8,17]. Others expand on these by generating multiple feathers and encoding their ontogeny, but the model for a single feather is not improved [12,18]. No barbule geometry is created in these works, and model decisions are not supported by real feather measurements.

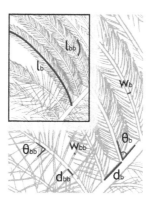

Fig. 1. Barb and barbule lengths l_b l_{bb}, angles θ_b θ_{bb}, widths w_b w_{bb}, spacing d_b d_{bb}.

3.2   Production Tools

Film studios often develop proprietary software tools for procedural content generation. Studios have published some descriptions of artist-driven feather tools. Animal Logic's feather system, Quill, is notable for use in the film *Legend of the Guardians*. Quill provides artist control of individual feather parameters related to the shaft, vanes, and barbs, but there is no mention of barbules [11,14]. Rzankowski [15] developed a feather plug-in for Houdini that allows user control of a shaft curve and barbs with some level-of-detail output options. Some tools such as Rzankowski's use systems created for hair rendering to create feather models [4,15]. Real feather structures are quite different from hair or fur.

3.3 Ornithological Studies

In both research and production, there has been a lack of use of actual feather data. Several ornithological studies exist, however, with some statistics on variation in specific sets of feathers. Related variable attributes are visualized with labels in Fig. 1 and findings summarized in Table 1. These studies include Feo and Prum's observation of vane asymmetry in a variety of feathers and measured barb angle θ_b, barb length l_b, and vane width w_v. Barb angle, between the rachis and the barb, shows a range of 5 to 50 but mostly in 20 to 40°. Vane width w_v is dependent upon barb length l_b and barb angle θ_b, estimated as $w_v = l_b sin\theta_b$ [6,7], incorporated in this work. Rijke investigated the diameters w_b of and spacing d_b between barbs of aquatic birds [13]. Broggi et al. observed differences in barb and barbule densities to study insulation [1]. Greenewalt discusses iridescence in terms of feather growth and reflection angles and measured the barbule angle θ_{bb} as the rotation of the barbule away from the barb [9].

Table 1. A sample of a summary of data gathered from several ornithological studies.

Data summary from ornithological studies					
Attribute	Symbol	Feather type(s)	Bird(s)	Value	Unit
Barb angle	θ_b	3 Primaries	60 Species	5–50	degrees
Barb angle	θ_b	Covert, Rectrex	Parrots	10–40	degrees
Barb length	l_b	3 Primaries	60 Species	10–60	mm
Barb length	l_b	Covert, Rectrex	Parrots	5–25	mm
Vane width	w_v	Covert, Rectrex	Parrots	5–15	mm
Barb diameter	w_b	Contour	Ducks, Cormorants	56	μm
Barb spacing	d_b	Contour	Ducks, Cormorants	271	μm
Barbule angle	θ_{bb}	unknown	Hummingbirds	0–70	degrees
Barbule length	l_{bb}	unknown	Hummingbirds	100	mm
Barbule diameter	w_{bb}	unknown	Hummingbirds	15	mm
Penn. barb density	d_b	Contour	Tits	1.47	per mm
Penn. barbule density	d_{bb}	Contour	Tits	2.17	per 0.1 mm

4   Method and Implementation

The proposed method extracts, organizes, and uses structural information from real feathers to model digital ones. It consists of three main steps as roughly depicted in Fig. 2: (1) data collection, (2) data extraction using image analysis, and (3) the use of data in modeling. Firstly, images of multiple feathers and their metadata are the initial input. Next, the multi-feather images are segmented into images of individual feathers; shape information from each is extracted using statistical analysis for landmarking and eventual curve regression to represent key shapes of the feather. Finally, the collected and extracted data is used for parameters in procedurally modeling geometry for a feather.

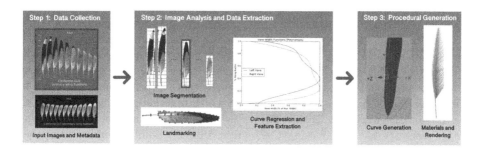

Fig. 2. Chart depicting the main workflow as three core steps.

4.1   Data Collection and Representation

The Feather Atlas, a database of scans of flight feathers, was used [19]. Each multi-feather scan consists of ordered feathers of one type with metadata such as bird name, taxonomic rank, and feather lengths. Key selections based on taxonomic order (*Charadriiformes*, *Galliformes*, and *Passeriformes*) were chosen. Feather data is organized by bird and by feather through Python dictionaries stored as Javascript Object Notation (JSON) files.

4.2   Image Analysis and Data Extraction

Each multiple-feather image is segmented into individual feather images using OpenCV's implementation of the Watershed algorithm as shown in Part 2 of Fig. 2. Each is then landmarked with fifty-two (chosen as a fairly minimal number to record shape) points placed to outline the shaft as well as the outer edges of the vanes. Landmarks are used to build Active Appearance Models (AAMs) that can extract and encode shape and appearance information for a particular class of objects [5]. AAMs aid here in automatically landmarking additional images and also provide a parameterized model that can provide information for future analysis. Both polynomial and spline curve fittings of varying order are considered for the vane outlines, shaft, barbs, and barbules. NumPy and

SciPy libraries are used for regression to find the coefficients of a polynomial of given degree or the coefficients and knots of a cubic B-spline that best represent landmarks for a particular part. Figure 3 displays curves regressed using both and vane-width functions on a single feather with resulting synthetic feathers. A curve to represent the shape of the *shaft* is found and is scaled to a normalized space along the feather rather than image. *Width functions* per vane are created relative to the shaft curve and treated as functions that take the progress along the rachis as input and output the perpendicular vane width w_v at that point. Degree, coefficients, and knots (if applicable) per curve along with additional attributes such as the rachis-start parametric value are stored.

4.3   Data-Driven Generation of Feather Geometry

Data stored is used as parameters for procedural geometry generation. This includes the name and type of feather; curve widths (diameters) for the shaft, barbs w_b, and barbules w_{bb}; barb and barbule densities d_{bb} and d_{bb}; and the barb and barbule rotation angles θ_b and θ_{bb} from the tangent of their parents. Other data retrieved includes feather length in centimeters l_f, rachis start, shaft-curve polynomial, maximum width per vane, and width function per vane w_v. Python for Maya 2018 with RenderMan 22 are used to model and render. The *shaft curve* geometry is created using the regressed curve. Points sampled from the curve function are scaled by the feather length to values in centimeters before being passed as edit points (EPs) to create a curve in Maya that connects them. *Barbs curves* are generated evenly spaced along the rachis. The local orientation axes (the tangent along the shaft, the normal perpendicular to the shaft and the vanes, and the bitangent orthogonal to the other two axes) are calculated at the point to which a barb attaches to the rachis. Using the vane-width function, the vane width w_v perpendicular to the shaft is calculated and scaled by the feather length l_f. The length of the barb l_b is found using the barb angle θ_b

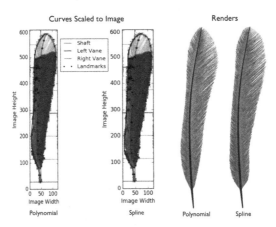

Fig. 3. Polynomial versus spline regression for outer-vane curves drawn on the images along with corresponding renders for a Blue Jay's tail feather.

to rotate from the shaft tangent about the normal. Using displacements along the tangent and bitangent, several EPs for a curve may be generated, and the distance between the endpoints is equal to the barb length. The interior EPs may be subtly distorted using noise or chosen pattern. The barbule length l_{bb} is computed as fraction of barb spacing d_b, and a barbule spacing d_{bb} per barb is set. Starting from the base of the barb on the shaft towards the tip of the barb, a pair of barbules generated similarly to the barb curves using angle and length.

5 Discussion and Conclusion

This section discusses results, the contributions to visual-computing research and production, and areas for continued work. Figure 4 are final images of the process. Per render, the input argument is the feather name (California Gull primary and Wild Turkey secondary); the resulting shapes reflect results from the image analysis process in Part 2 of Fig. 2. Other inputs such as barb and barbule angles were designed based on ornithology and set to 45° for these results. A main *contribution* of this work is the use of real-world data of feathers to informal procedural generation. This work also presents a workflow that can be used to find patterns. Including barbules in modeling contributes to the overall appearance and allows for future work in studying feather reflectance and physical simulation. Other fields of study may be interested in this process, too, such as paleontology in predicting the appearance of fossilized feathers.

Areas of *future work* include collecting, extracting, and employing more data; improving rendering; and external collaboration. All of the scans from the Feather Atlas and other sources could be incorporated. Statistics could be derived based on feather type, bird taxonomy, and other categories with an AAM built from a larger dataset. *Additional geometric features* may be extracted from higher-resolution images, too, such as barb angles. *Generating a realistic layout* of feathers could also be driven by feather-shape statistics rather than artist control and interpolation. *Improvements in rendering* can increase by using appearance information from an AAM to generate texture maps and with the development of a new light-scattering model for shading. Lastly, a *public Maya*

Fig. 4. Renders using shaft curve and width-function polynomials from a gull feather (top) and splines from a turkey feather with a projected, diffuse texture (bottom).

plug-in based on this work with the collected data may be released to promote collaboration for further data collection and analysis as well as improved usability and accuracy for visualization and production tools.

References

1. Broggi, J., Gamero, A., Hohtola, E., Orell, M., Nilsson, J.K.: Interpopulation variation in contour feather structure is environmentally determined in great tits. PLoS One **6**(9) (2011)
2. Chandler, A.C.: A study of the structure of feathers, with reference to their taxonomic significance **3**(11) (1916). https://www.biodiversitylibrary.org/item/51770
3. Chen, Y., Xu, Y., Guo, B., Shum, H.Y.: Modeling and rendering of realistic feathers. In: Proceedings of the 29th Annual Conference on Computer Graphics and Interactive Techniques, SIGGRAPH 2002, pp. 630–636 (2002)
4. Choi, W., Kim, N., Jang, J., Kim, S., Yang, D.: Build your own procedural grooming pipeline. In: ACM SIGGRAPH 2017 Talks, SIGGRAPH 2017, pp. 54:1–54:2 (2017)
5. Cootes, T.F., Edwards, G.J., Taylor, C.J.: Active appearance models. In: Burkhardt, H., Neumann, B. (eds.) ECCV 1998. LNCS, vol. 1407, pp. 484–498. Springer, Heidelberg (1998). https://doi.org/10.1007/BFb0054760
6. Feo, T.J., Prum, R.O.: Theoretical morphology and development of flight feather vane asymmetry with experimental tests in parrots. J. Exp. Zool. **322B**, 240–255 (2014)
7. Feo, T., Field, D., Prum, R.: Barb geometry of asymmetrical feathers reveals a transitional morphology in the evolution of avian flight. Proc. Roy. Soc. B **282**, 20142864 (2015)
8. Franco, C.G., Walter, M.: Modeling and rendering of individual feathers. In: Proceedings of the 15th Brazilian Symposium on Computer Graphics and Image Processing, SIBGRAPI 2002, pp. 293–299 (2002)
9. Greenewalt, C.H.: Hummingbirds. Doubleday, New York (1960)
10. Hanson, T.: Feathers: The Evolution of a Natural Miracle. Basic Books, New York (2011)
11. Heckenberg, D., Gray, D., Smith, B., Wills, J., Bone, C.: Quill: birds of a feather tool. In: ACM SIGGRAPH 2011 Talks, SIGGRAPH 2011, pp. 34:1–34:1 (2011)
12. Newport, M.: Start to Finish Feathers Solution. Master's thesis, N.C.C.A. Bournemouth University (2005)
13. Rijke, A.M.: The water repellency and feather structure of cormorants, phalacrocoracidae. J. Exp. Biol. **48**, 185–189 (1968)
14. Robertson, B.: In fine feather. Computer Graphics World (2010). http://www.cgw.com/Publications/CGW/2010/Volume-33-Issue-9-October-2010-/In-Fine-Feather.aspx. Accessed 01 Oct 2018
15. Rzankowski, T.: Feather tools. SideFX Tutorials, August 2017. https://www.sidefx.com/tutorials/author/trzanko/
16. Scott, D., McFarland, C.: Bird Feathers. A Guide to North American Species. Stackpole Books, Mechanicsburg (2010)
17. Streit, L., Heidrich, W.: A biologically-parameterized feather model. In: Eurographics 2002, vol. 21. The Eurographics Association and Blackwell Publishers (2002)
18. Strett, L.M.: Modelling of feather coat morphogenesis for computer graphics. Ph.D. thesis (2004)
19. Trail, P.: The feather atlas (2015). https://www.fws.gov/lab/featheratlas/

A Unified Algorithm for BRDF Matching

Ron Vanderfeesten[(✉)] and Jacco Bikker

Departement of Geometrical Computing, Universiteit Utrecht,
Princetonplein 5 (4.21), 3584 CC Utrecht, The Netherlands
`r.g.f.p.vanderfeesten@uu.nl`
`http://uu.nl`

Abstract. This paper generalizes existing BRDF fitting algorithms presented in the literature that aims to find a mapping of the parameters of an arbitrary source material model to the parameters of a target material model. A *material model* in this context is a function that maps a list of parameters, such as roughness or specular color, to a BRDF. Our conversion function approximates the original model as close as possible under a chosen similarity metric, either in physical reflectivities or perceptually, and calculates the error with respect to this conversion. Our conversion function imposes no constraints other than that the dimensionality of the represented BRDFs match.

Keywords: BRDF · Fitting · Material model

1 Introduction

In the game and movie industry, a multitude of 3D applications are used for rendering. Each application internally uses similar, yet different material models for their shading [9]. Eventually, these shading models need to be converted to a single rendering pipeline for production, which ideally maintains the visual fidelity of the source model. In practice, this conversion is often done manually, which is time consuming and imprecise.

In academia, new material models are often evaluated using the *quality of fit* of the model onto measurements. A multitude of such quality of fit algorithms exist, and direct comparison between these algorithms is difficult as they are all tied to their specific BRDF or implementation. While each approach is different, they are all, in essence, running the same procedure.

2 Contributions

This paper introduces a generalized procedure MODEL-MATCH that abstracts the target BRDF, distance metric, minimization algorithm, and integration algorithm of many existing algorithms (see Table 1).

© Springer Nature Switzerland AG 2019
M. Gavrilova et al. (Eds.): CGI 2019, LNCS 11542, pp. 349–355, 2019.
https://doi.org/10.1007/978-3-030-22514-8_30

Table 1. Components used in BRDF fitting algorithms in the literature. *Model* is the target model of the fit, *metric* is the distance metric used, *min* is the minimization algorithm chosen (B&B: Branch-and-bound, QM: Quadratic Programming, LM: Levenberg-Marquardt), *int* is the integration or sampling function chosen (ID: Inlier detection, Q: Quadrature, A: Analytical, MC: Monte-Carlo), *dep* is yes when the minimization depends on the choice of BRDF, *options* are whether the paper uses perceptual or cosine weighting. A '*' indicates that the paper does not explicitly state the way samples are summed, but in these cases, it is inferred from the algorithm.

Paper	Model	Metric	Min	Int	Dep?	Options
Lee et al. [7]	Lafortune	L_2	B&B	ID	No	
Chanki et al. [15]	Cook-Torrance	L_2, L_∞	B&B	Q*	No	
Wang [14]	Cook-Torrance	L_2	Genetic	Q*	No	
Renhorn and Boreman [3]	Cook-Torrance	L_2	FindFit	A	Yes	
Pacanowski et al. [11]	Rational BRDF	L_2	QP	Q	Yes	Fixed sampling
Yu et al. [16]	B-Splines	L_2	LM	Q	Yes	
Bagher et al. [1]	Shifted Gamma	L_2	LM	MC	Yes	
Ngan et al. [10]	Any	L_2	QP	Q*	No	Perceptual
Guarnera et al. [4]	Any	L_2	Genetic	Q*	No	Image-based
ALTA Analysis Library	Any	L_1, L_2	Various	Q/LM	Yes	

This procedure provides a formalism for BRDF matching and allows direct comparison between the quality of fit, performance and convergence across different BRDF matching algorithms. Additionally, the formalism can be used to generate a conversion algorithm of a material model from one render system to another. To reduce the runtime of any conversion, we present a method to precalculate a conversion using a look-up table.

3 Framework

To formalize the concept of BRDF matching we first define a *material model*. Such a material model is a function M that maps a parameter list $p \in P$ to a specific BRDF. An (isotropic) BRDF is a function $f_r(\theta_i, \theta_r, \phi)$ that assigns a *reflectivity*, which is the ratio of irradiance to radiance for an infinitesimal point on the surface, to each combination of incident zenith angle $\theta_i \in [0 \ldots \frac{1}{2}\pi)$, reflected zenith angle $\theta_r \in [0 \ldots \frac{1}{2}\pi)$, and azimuthal difference $\phi \in [0 \ldots \pi)$.

A parameter list p can contain any number of *parameters* such as roughness, diffuse color, or specular intensity, and forms an n-space vector. We require that each parameter is bounded (which many material parameters intrisically are), which together forms a bounded, non-zero subspace containing all possible instances of parameters $p \in P$ for M. A parameter that is not bounded can be coerced to a finite interval using a function like $1 - e^{-|p|}$ where p is an unbounded material parameter, or another appropriate function.

As material models are uniquely defined in terms of their parameter vector we can represent a *material model match* as a function:

$$\text{MM}_D : P \to \varPhi \tag{1}$$

Fig. 1. Left: The blue metallic paint measurement from the MERL database. **Right**: A Rational BRDF from the literature matched onto the BRDF rendered in the left image, using genetic optimization instead of the Mathematica FINDFIT function as used in the paper of Pacanowski et al. [11]. The maximum normalized error of the match is 0.028. The optimization searches a 150 dimensional problem space. (Color figure online)

that maps a parameter list P of a *source material model* to a parameter list Φ of a *target material model.*

The BRDF matching problem can now be formulated as follows: given two material models S and T, which have a parameter vector p_1 of length n and a parameter vector p_2 of length m respectively, find a function $\mathrm{MM}_D(p_1)$ that maps p_1 of S to the model parameters p_2 of T, such that it has the smallest similarity measure:

$$\mathrm{MM}_D(p_1) = \mathrm{argmin}_{p_2}\left(D(S(p_1), T(p_2))\right) \tag{2}$$

We introduce the concept of *similarity* to generalize the notion of the perceived differences between reflectances. It always consists of a *distance metric* $L_1, L_2, \ldots, L_\infty$, and may also include a color distance function such as CIELAB ΔE, and a weighting function W for certain angles.

The L_p-norm of a vector v with n elements is defined as:

$$||v||_p \leftarrow \left(\sum_{i=1}^{n} |v_i|^p\right)^{\frac{1}{p}} \tag{3}$$

of which the L_1 (Manhattan distance), L_2 (Euclidean distance) and L_∞ (maximum norm) are most often used.

To implement perceptual matching a tone-mapping function G can be included [12]. G contains parameters such as the color temperature and exposure settings. Matching two tonemapped values essentially compares two material models under a given imaging system.

We can use W to modify the matching algorithm in such a way that it essentially compares two rendered images of BRDFs. We first calculate exactly which input and output angles occur within a given rendered image of an object with the BRDF applied. We then restrict W to sample only those in- and output

angles (W is zero at any angle other than those), in this way we greatly reduce
the number of samples that need to be taken.

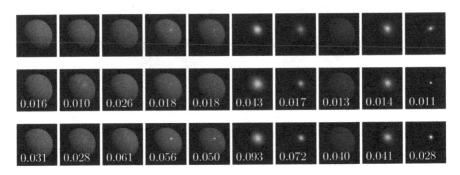

Fig. 2. A set of material matches made with the MODEL-MATCH algorithm, with materials taken from the MERL database [8] against a white GGX [13] with a Lambertian diffuse component. **Top**: MERL measurement, **Middle**: Physical match, **Bottom**: Perceptual. The normalized error is indicated in white.

Assuming that the BRDFs used are energy preserving, the similarity measure is bounded, with a maximum of $2 \cdot \pi$ under L_1, which is also a bound for L_2. Using these bounds we can normalize all similarities to the range $[0 \dots 2]$, which ensures that the normalized similarity between a maximally reflective Lambertian reflector and a perfect absorber is 1, and not 0.5, which fits better with intuition. In practice, values will be in the range $[0 \dots 1]$. We can now interpret this normalized value as an absolute measure of error, which we can use to compare the mean error of different choices of BRDF fitting algorithms.

4 Matching Algorithm

We can now present the unified matching algorithm in functional notation as follows:

$$\text{MODEL-MATCH}(S, T, p, m) := minimize \; \text{SIMILARITY}(S_p, T, m) \qquad (4)$$

$$\text{SIMILARITY}(S_p, T, m) := \begin{cases} \max \; \text{DIST}(S_p, T) \; \text{over} \; \alpha & \textbf{if } m = L_\infty \\ \text{integrate} \; \text{DIST}(S_p, T, m) \; \text{over} \; \alpha & \textbf{otherwise} \end{cases} \qquad (5)$$

$$\text{DIST}(S_p, T, m, \alpha) := \begin{cases} W(\alpha) \cdot C(G(S_p(\alpha)), G(T(\alpha))) & \textbf{if } m = L_\infty \\ (W(\alpha) \cdot C(G(S_p(\alpha)), G(T(\alpha))))^{e(m)} & \textbf{otherwise} \end{cases} \qquad (6)$$

This description is an implementation of Eq. 2, where S is the source material model, T is the target material model. p is the parameter list to be applied to

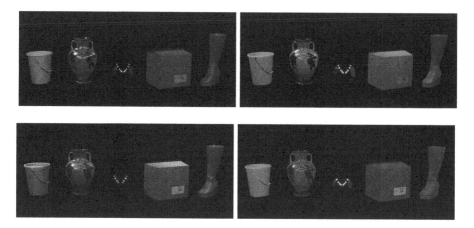

Fig. 3. Scenes from several rendering systems containing materials with varying roughnesses, such as plastic, porcelain, chrome, cardboard and leather. **Top left**: A scene created in iRay® using the Ashikhmin-Shirley material model, that serves as the input for the matching algorithm. **Top right**: The same scene in Unreal Engine 4 where the materials have been matched using the unified matching algorithm. **Bottom left**: The same scene in Unity, where the materials have been matched onto the Unity standard shader. **Bottom right**: The scene rendered in Arnold, with those materials matched to the scene created in iRay®.

S, m is the distance metric L_e, S_p is the source material model with p applied, $T(q)$ gives the parameter set q for the angles α, G is the tonemapping function, C is the color distance function, W is the weighting function, and e is a function that takes the exponent from some distance metric L_e. The maximum and integration is taken over the bound variables $\alpha = \theta_i, \theta_r, \phi$ and yields q, not the calculated value. This description can be directly entered in a language that supports functional notation or can be converted to an appropriate imperative version.

5   Results

To show that the unified matching algorithm is indeed a generalization of the different matching algorithms presented in the literature we have made several instances of the unified matching algorithm, one that uses the Rational BRDF model from Pacanowski et al. [11] but matches using Genetic Optimization from different papers [2,4]. As in the original publication, the Rational BRDF was matched against the `blue-metallic-paint` measurement from the MERL database and uses 250 coefficients for the polynomial. Figure 1 shows that the Unified Matching algorithm is able to get very similar results when matching the same BRDF under the same circumstances. This is supported by the value of the normalized L_2 error of the match. The different choice of optimization algorithm enables us to quickly search the high dimensional problem space.

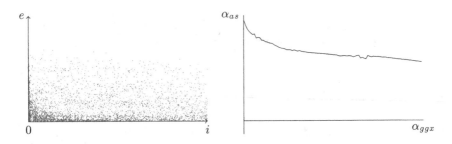

Fig. 4. Left: Convergence of Simulated Annealing and Artificial Bee Colonoy optimization, x-axis indicate the number of iterations, y-axis indicates the error. **Right**: The dependency between the Ashikhmin-Shirley roughness α_{as} and the GGX roughness α_{ggx} between $0 \ldots 100$ and $0 \ldots 1$ respectively.

As a second example (See Fig. 2) we have implemented the Cook-Torrance (GGX) shading model and matched it to several measurements from the MERL database. By choosing to instantiate the procedure with and without a tonemapping function G we have performed model matching with both physical reflectances and perceptual color values, and we can easily compare the two using the normalized error. Half of these matches were made using Artificial Bee Colony Optimization [14] while the rest were made using Simulated Annealing [5].

As a third example (See Fig. 3) of the MODEL-MATCH procedure we instanced the unified matching algorithm with different parametrized models. The source model is the Ashikhmin-Shirley model as used in the NVidia iRay© (top-left) and the target models are various implementations of Cook-Torrance (Unreal, Unity and Arnold).

The proposed unified matching algorithm provides a tool to compare the run-time performance of matching algorithms as well. In Fig. 4 (left) we have plotted the current error of two different optimization algorithms.

We can now also precalculate the dependency between model parameters (See Fig. 4 (right). We can represent the MM_D function as a look-up table with discrete entries and find all intermediate values using multilinear interpolation [6], or use a polynomial approximation. This way we can quickly convert many material model instances without having to run the entire MODEL-MATCH procedure many times.

6   Conclusion

We have presented a procedure MODEL-MATCH that is able to emulate many BRDF fitting algorithms in the literature, and can be used to generate an algorithm that is able to convert material models from one pipeline to another by selecting appropriate implementations for the abstract functions. We showed how we can compare the performance of BRDF matching algorithms using this general procedure and proposed an error metric that can be used to compare across different matching algorithms, as well as a method to inspect the convergence of a particular BRDF fitting algorithm.

References

1. Bagher, M.M., Soler, C., Holzschuch, N.: Accurate fitting of measured reflectances using a Shifted Gamma micro-facet distribution. Comput. Graph. Forum **31**, 1509–1518 (2012)
2. Brady, A., Lawrence, J., Peers, P., Weimer, W.: genBRDF: discovering new analytic BRDFs with genetic programming. ACM Trans. Graph. **33**, 114:1–114:11 (2014)
3. Renhorn, I.G.E., Boreman, G.D.: Analytical fitting model for rough-surface BRDF. Opt. Express **16**, 12892–12898 (2008)
4. Guarnera, D., et al.: Perceptually validated cross-renderer analytical BRDF parameter remapping. IEEE Trans. Vis. Comput. Graph. 1 (2018)
5. Kirkpatrick, S., Gelatt, C.D., Vecchi, M.P.: Optimization by simulated annealing. Science **220**, 671–680 (1983)
6. Kreyszig, E., Kreyszig, H., Norminton, E.J.: Advanced Engineering Mathematics. Wiley, Hoboken (2011)
7. Lee, Y., Yu, C., Lee, S.W.: Sequential fitting-and-separating reflectance components for analytical bidirectional reflectance distribution function estimation. Appl. Opt. **57**, 242–250 (2018)
8. Matusik, W., Pfister, H., Brand, M., McMillan, L.: A data-driven reflectance model. ACM Trans. Graph. **22**, 759–769 (2003)
9. Montes, R., Urena, C.: An Overview of BRDF Models, February 2012
10. Ngan, A., Durand, F., Matusik, W.: Experimental analysis of BRDF models. In: Eurographics Symposium on Rendering 2005 (2005)
11. Pacanowski, R., Salazar Celis, O., Schlick, C., Granier, X., Poulin, P., Cuyt, A.: Rational BRDF. IEEE Trans. Visual. Comput. Graph. **18**, 1824–1835 (2012)
12. Sinha, P., Russell, R.: A perceptually based comparison of image similarity metrics. Perception **40**, 1269–1281 (2011)
13. Walter, B., Marschner, S.R., Li, H., Torrance, K.E.: Microfacet models for refraction through rough surfaces. In: the 18th Eurographics Conference on Rendering Techniques, EGSR 2007, pp. 195–206 (2007)
14. Wang, Q., Zhao, J., Gong, Y., Hao, Q., Peng, Z.: Hybrid artificial bee colony algorithm for parameter optimization of five-parameter bidirectional reflectance distribution function model. Appl. Opt. **56**, 9165–9170 (2017)
15. Yu, C., Seo, Y., Lee, S.W.: Global optimization for estimating a multiple-lobe analytical BRDF. Comput. Vis. Image Underst. **115**, 1679–1688 (2011)
16. Yu, J., Tu, W., Wang, Z.: A BP training fitting method about multivariate BRDF based on B-spline function. In: 2012 Fifth International Conference on Information and Computing Science (ICIC), pp. 30–32 (2012)

Multi-layer Perceptron Architecture for Kinect-Based Gait Recognition

A. S. M. Hossain Bari[(⊠)] and Marina L. Gavrilova

University of Calgary, Calgary, AB T2N 1N4, Canada
{asmhossain.bari,mgavrilo}@ucalgary.ca

Abstract. Accurate gait recognition is of high significance for numerous industrial and consumer applications, including virtual reality, online games, medical rehabilitation, video surveillance, and others. This paper proposes multi-layer perceptron (MLP) based neural network architecture for human gait recognition. Two unique geometric features: joint relative cosine dissimilarity (JRCD) and joint relative triangle area (JRTA) are introduced. These features are view and pose invariant, and thus enhance recognition performance. MLP model is trained using dynamic JRTA and JRCD sequences. The performance of the proposed MLP architecture is evaluated on publicly available 3D Kinect skeleton gait database and is shown to be superior to other state-of-the-art methods.

Keywords: Gait recognition · Human motion ·
Joint relative triangle area · Joint relative cosine dissimilarity ·
Neural network · Biometrics

1 Introduction

Gait recognition is one of the tasks commonly used in a multitude of industrial and consumer applications, such as virtual reality, medical rehabilitation, video surveillance, and others. Biometric gait is a unique behavioral biometric, which provides one of the most popular unobtrusive means of remote authentication. Since biometric gait is acquired from the distance, identity, intention or even emotion of an individual can be recognized remotely based on gait. Therefore, gait recognition system can be used for person authentication [2], human action recognition [5], gender recognition [10], surveillance [12], and emotion recognition [11]. Though physical injuries and tiredness may affect the walking pattern of an individual, it is still quite difficult to imitate another person's gait [4].

Deep learning methodology is the emerging machine learning (ML) technique which opens new doors for advanced analysis of human motion detection. This research introduces a multi-layer perceptron (MLP) based neural network architecture for gait recognition. The system utilizes human 3D body joint data as an input acquired by Kinect sensor. The major contributions of this paper can be outlined as follow. First, two unique view and pose invariant geometric features: joint relative triangle area (JRTA) and joint relative cosine dissimilarity (JRCD)

© Springer Nature Switzerland AG 2019
M. Gavrilova et al. (Eds.): CGI 2019, LNCS 11542, pp. 356–363, 2019.
https://doi.org/10.1007/978-3-030-22514-8_31

are introduced. Then, JRTA and JRCD features are fused in such a way that resulting feature vector is compatible as input to the proposed MLP architecture. Second, a MLP based neural network architecture is designed for gait recognition. All the hyper-parameters of the proposed MLP model are tuned so that it gives the best performance specially for the gait recognition. Third, the MLP model is optimized by the RMSProp optimizer. Publicly available UPCV 3D gait database [10] is used to evaluate the performance of the proposed gait recognition method. Results of cross-validation experimentation demonstrate that the proposed system clearly outperforms all other recently proposed state-of-the-art gait recognition methods in terms of recognition accuracy.

2   Related Work

Gait analysis relies on video sequence recorded by the motion capture system. Motion-based gait recognition can be either model-based or model-free [7]. In the model-free approach, segmented version of the silhouette of the gait sequence is generated to analyze the changes of the motion of the human body [6]. However, model-free approaches are not very effective in real-life scenarios. In the model-based approach, the model is constructed and updated over time by estimating changes of parameters of the model considering different body parts. Since the accuracy of the 3D skeleton image generation system of Kinect is comparable with the marker-based system, 3D data acquisition using Kinect can be utilized for model-based gait recognition. Preis et al. [13] extracted anthropometric features from the Kinect skeleton image and used traditional classifier for person identification. Ball et al. [3] applied unsupervised K-means clustering on the motion data extracted from the lower body part. On the other hand, Dikovski et al. [4] utilized MLP model, not specialized for gait recognition. MLP based model using a single hidden layer was designed by Andersson and Araujo [2]. In this study, we propose one of the first MLP based neural network specialized for gait recognition.

3   Methodology

There are several key contributions of our proposed method. We introduce two unique geometric features: joint relative cosine dissimilarity and joint relative triangle area. These dynamic spatio-temporal features are extracted over the frame of a gait cycle or over multiple gait cycles. We design MLP based neural network which is specialized for gait recognition using Kinect skeleton data. Since the length of the gait cycle is different from person to person, features are resampled to a vector of fixed size. Then we train the proposed MLP model after merging these two dynamic geometric features. Moreover, we propose to use RMSProp optimizer for the MLP model. Figure 1 shows the flowchart of the enrollment and recognition system of the proposed method.

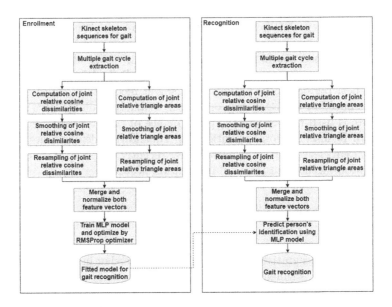

Fig. 1. Overall system flowchart of the proposed method

3.1 Multiple Gait Cycle Extraction

During walking, the motion of the different joints of the human body has a resemblance to a cyclic pattern. As a result, each frame of a gait cycle exhibits classifying recurrent features. Features extracted from each frame of a gait cycle comprise a unique gait identification for the subject. Euclidean norm is calculated between left and right ankles for determining a gait cycle. A complete gait cycle consists of three successive maxima. The first maxima is the beginning of a gait cycle and the gait cycle is ended by the third maxima. Euclidean distances between two ankles of a gait sequence are shown in Fig. 2a. Firstly, we apply a moving average filter and secondly a median filter to suppress the noise in the distance vector, as shown in Fig. 2b. Local maxima and minima are shown in Fig. 2c. We extract more than one gait cycle if a gait sequence has multiple gait cycles. In Fig. 2c, P_1, P_2, P_3, P_4, P_5, and P_6 represent the local maxima of the distance vector. Therefore, we extract four gait cycles from this distance vector such as $P1$ to P_3, P_2 to P_4, P_3 to P_5, and P_4 to P_6. The inclusion of multiple gait cycle and feature extraction from multiple gait cycles act as a data augmentation for model training.

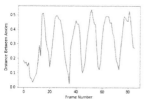 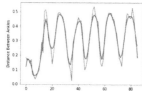 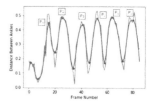

(a) Distances between left and right ankle

(b) After smoothing on distance vector

(c) Local maxima and minima

Fig. 2. Steps of gait cycle detection algorithm tracking the euclidean distance between two ankles

3.2 Novel Gait Features

Distinctive feature extraction is crucial for gait recognition. In prior researches, various degrees of success were achieved in locating motion of body joints. Very effective features based on the relationship of distance and angle of body joints were introduced by Ahmed et al. [1]. We make one step further through extracting more robust and generic features to find the distinctive motion of human body joints. These features are JRTA and JRCD—extracted from different body joints. We identify the dynamic motion of different body joints while walking using these dynamic features. Consider N_g is the number of the gait cycle in a gait sequence and N_f is the number of frames in a complete gait cycle, N_C is the length of the JRCD feature vector and N_T is the length of the JRTA feature vector. We extract $N_f * N_C$ numbers of JRCD and $N_f * N_T$ numbers of JRTA features. In Table 1, it is established that new features are better than in [1].

Joint Relative Triangle Area (JRTA). We determine area of triangle considering three 3D coordinates in 3D space. We represent three body joints as $A(x_1, y_1, z_1)$, $B(x_2, y_2, z_2)$, and $C(x_3, y_3, z_3)$ Cartesian 3D points. Here, B is the reference point. We compute area of triangle as follows:

$$\triangle ABC = \frac{\|\overrightarrow{AB} \times \overrightarrow{BC}\|}{2} \tag{1}$$

Fluctuation of the spine body joint in Kinect is the least among all other body joints. Therefore, spine body joint is chosen as the reference point for determining the JRTA feature. If there are total N_b body joints in the skeleton of Kinect, length of a JRTA (N_T) feature vector is $((N_b - 1) * (N_b - 2))$.

Joint Relative Cosine Dissimilarity (JRCD). Joint relative cosine dissimilarity is the cosine distance between two points. Consider A and B are the 3D coordinates of two body joints. Cosine dissimilarity between $\vec{A}$ and $\vec{B}$ is defined by the Eq. 2.

$$\delta_{cosine}(A, B) = 1 - \frac{\vec{A} \cdot \vec{B}}{\|\vec{A}\|\|\vec{B}\|} \tag{2}$$

We calculate cosine dissimilarities of each of the body joints comparing with the rest of the body joints; these body joints can be connected or not. The directional motions of each of the body joints with respect to the rest of the body joints are identified by the JRCD features. If there are total N_b body joints in the skeleton of Kinect, length of a JRCD (N_C) feature vector is $(N_b * (N_b - 1))/2$.

3.3 Multi-layer Perceptron Architecture

This paper presents a MLP based neural network architecture for gait recognition. In the pre-processing step, JRTA and JRCD features are normalized to eliminate the effect of outliers. We transform the feature vector to make the mean equal to 0 and variance equal to 1 of the normalized feature vector. Normalized feature vectors are fed into hidden blocks for training the model. Hidden units of four hidden blocks are stacked in such a way that the output of one layer becomes the input of the next layer. There are 128, 256, 256, and 128 fully connected dense nodes in the first, second, third, and fourth hidden block respectively. We initialize the weights of each of the dense layers of all hidden blocks using *He normal* initializer [8]. We successively add the batch normalization layer, activation layer, and dropout layer after the fully connected layer. The order of dense layer, batch normalization layer, activation layer, and dropout layer is similar to other hidden blocks. Purpose of the addition of batch normalization layer is for performance improvement by reducing the oscillation of gradient descent and thus improves the accuracy of the model [9]. We use hyperbolic tangent activation (tanh) instead of logistic activation because the derivatives of tanh are bigger than derivatives of logistic activation. We also apply the rectifier linear unit (ReLU) activation function and compare the performance of ReLU activation with tanh activation. In order to subdue the high-variance problem in the MLP model, we introduce dropout regularizer by setting weights to zero to random hidden units. Thus, the co-dependency of each of the hidden units is prevented. We achieve this task by setting 10%, 20%, 20%, and 20% dropout rate in the dropout layer of first, second, third, and fourth hidden block respectively. In order to classify a person's identity in a multi-class gait recognition system, we apply the Softmax activation function in the decision layer. Then, we optimize the proposed MLP model using RMSProp optimizer. The categorical cross-entropy loss function is applied to minimize the training loss iteratively. We add callback function for reducing the learning rate by a factor if learning does not change for a number of epochs. Thus, the learning rate reduction method is adaptive in nature.

4   Experimental Results

We validate the proposed MLP model using the benchmark UPCV gait dataset [10]. The gait sequences of 30 subjects are available in this dataset. Subjects are directed to walk normally in a straight direction. Kinect sensor is placed at a position which is 1.70 m above the ground level. Videos are recorded at the

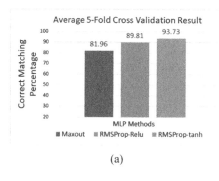 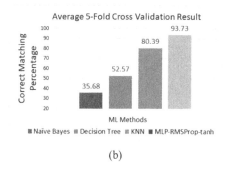

(a) (b)

Fig. 3. (a) Average 5-fold cross-validation recognition performance of neural network methods. (b) Average 5-fold cross-validation recognition performance for traditional ML and proposed MLP method

speed of 30 fps from the left side of the person's walking direction. There are five walking sequences for each of the subjects. Multiple gait cycles are detected from the gait sequences. JRTA and JRCD features are extracted from every gait cycles. Proposed MLP model is trained using these feature vectors. Fitted model is stored and in the identification phase, the trained model is used for predicting the person's identification. We evaluate the MLP model using the 5-fold cross-validation experiment. Data samples are chosen randomly for each of the folds of the 5-fold cross-validation experiment. We arrange multiple experiments to evaluate the proposed neural network architecture. First, proposed MLP model, where the dense layer is replaced by the Maxout network, is evaluated. Second, we apply ReLU and tanh activation functions. Third, we optimize the proposed MLP model by using RMSProp optimization method. In Fig. 3a, average performance results of 5-fold cross-validation of Maxout network, MLP model with ReLU activation and RMSProp optimizer, MLP model with ReLU activation and RMSProp optimizer, MLP model with tanh activation and RMSProp optimizer are shown. MLP Maxout network achieves on average 81.96% recognition accuracy. MLP model with ReLU activation and RMSProp optimizer achieves on average 89.81% recognition accuracy. In addition, the MLP model with tanh activation and RMSProp optimizer achieves on average 93.73% recognition accuracy. This architecture secures the best performance result among all neural network configurations studied.

On the other hand, we compare results of neural network methods with traditional machine learning (ML) methods such as Naïve Bayes (NB), Decision Tree (DTree), and K-Nearest Neighbors (KNN). We re-implement NB, DTree, and KNN as is and we find out the optimal values of the parameters of NB, DTree, and KNN using the exhaustive grid-search method. Performance comparison of average 5-fold cross-validation results between traditional ML method and MLP model with tanh activation and RMSProp optimizer is shown in Fig. 3b. NB performs the worst with the accuracy percentage on average 35.68%. DTree achieves on average 52.57% and KNN achieves on average 80.39% recognition accuracy. KNN achieves the highest recognition accuracy among traditional ML

Table 1. Performance comparison among gait recognition methods

Methods	Recognition accuracy (%)
Proposed features + DTree	52.57
Ball et al	57.0
Preis et al	78.0
Proposed features + KNN	80.39
Proposed features + Maxout	81.96
Proposed features + MLP + ReLU + RMSProp	89.81
JRA and JRD features + MLP + tanh + RMSProp	91.37
Proposed features + MLP + tanh + RMSProp	**93.73**

methods and performance of KNN is close to the performance of Maxout network whereas the highest performance of new features with the proposed neural network model is 93.73%. In order to demonstrate that the new features are more effective, we extract JRA and JRD features according to [1] and train proposed MLP model with tanh activation and RMSProp optimizer. We also evaluate this method using 5-fold cross-validation experiment. In Table 1, the average recognition accuracy of JRA and JRD features is compared with the performance of proposed features. JRTA and JRCD features provide better recognition accuracy than JRA and JRD feature set. The average recognition accuracy by JRA and JRD features is 91.37% whereas average recognition accuracy by the proposed features is around 93.73%. Recognition performance comparison among previous state-of-the-art methods, proposed features with classical ML model (KNN and DTree) and proposed features with neural network architecture and its variants is summarized in Table 1. Proposed features with traditional KNN classifier outperform methods presented in [3] and [13] by around 23.4% and 2.40% respectively. Each of the proposed neural network architectures performs significantly better than the methods presented in [3] and [13]. MLP model with ReLU activation and RMSprop optimization achieves 89.81% accuracy, which is 11.81% higher than Preis et al. and 32.81% higher than Ball et al. The highest recognition accuracy of the proposed neural network architecture is 93.73%, achieved when the proposed features are used with MLP architecture with tanh activation and RMSProp optimization. We also establish that neural network architecture outperforms all of the traditional machine learning methods. It achieves 41.16% higher accuracy than the DTree based method and 13.34% higher recognition accuracy over KNN based method.

5   Conclusion and Future Work

This research presents two unique geometric features JRTA and JRCD to increase the accuracy of gait recognition. Data augmentation is performed by extracting multiple gait cycles from a gait sequence and JRTA and JRCD features are extracted from each cycle. A multi-layer perceptron architecture is designed specially for gait recognition and is enhanced by the tanh activation and RMSProp optimization method. The highest accuracy obtained by the proposed MLP model, trained with the new geometric features, is around 93.73% on average after 5-fold cross-validation. In the future, an evolutionary algorithm for optimizing the feature set can be studied in the context of the proposed neural network architecture.

Acknowledgments. Authors would like to acknowledge partial support from NSERC DG "Machine Intelligence for Biometric Security", NSERC ENGAGE on Gait Recognition and NSERC SPG on Smart Cities funding.

References

1. Ahmed, F., Paul, P.P., Gavrilova, M.L.: DTW-based kernel and rank-level fusion for 3D gait recognition using kinect. Vis. Comput. **31**(6–8), 915–924 (2015)
2. Andersson, V.O., de Araújo, R.M.: Person identification using anthropometric and gait data from kinect sensor. In: AAAI, pp. 425–431 (2015)
3. Ball, A., Rye, D., Ramos, F., Velonaki, M.: Unsupervised clustering of people from 'skeleton' data. In: ACM/IEEE HRI, pp. 225–226. ACM (2012)
4. Dikovski, B., Madjarov, G., Gjorgjevikj, D.: Evaluation of different feature sets for gait recognition using skeletal data from kinect. In: Information and Communication Technology, Electronics and Microelectronics, pp. 1304–1308. IEEE (2014)
5. Gavrilova, M.L., Wang, Y., Ahmed, F., Paul, P.P.: Kinect sensor gesture and activity recognition: new applications for consumer cognitive systems. IEEE Consum. Electron. Mag. **7**(1), 88–94 (2018)
6. Han, J., Bhanu, B.: Individual recognition using gait energy image. IEEE Trans. Pattern Anal. Mach. Intell. **2**, 316–322 (2006)
7. Han, J., Bhanu, B.: Statistical feature fusion for gait-based human recognition. In: CVPR 2004, vol. 2, p. 2. IEEE (2004)
8. He, K., Zhang, X., Ren, S., Sun, J.: Delving deep into rectifiers: surpassing human-level performance on imagenet classification. In: IEEE International Conference on Computer Vision, pp. 1026–1034 (2015)
9. Ioffe, S., Szegedy, C.: Batch normalization: accelerating deep network training by reducing internal covariate shift. arXiv:1502.03167 (2015)
10. Kastaniotis, D., Theodorakopoulos, I., Theoharatos, C., Economou, G., Fotopoulos, S.: A framework for gait-based recognition using kinect. Pattern Recogn. Lett. **68**, 327–335 (2015)
11. Maret, Y., Oberson, D., Gavrilova, M.: Identifying an emotional state from body movements using genetic-based algorithms. In: Rutkowski, L., Scherer, R., Korytkowski, M., Pedrycz, W., Tadeusiewicz, R., Zurada, J.M. (eds.) ICAISC 2018. LNCS (LNAI), vol. 10841, pp. 474–485. Springer, Cham (2018). https://doi.org/10.1007/978-3-319-91253-0_44
12. Popa, M., Kemal Koc, A., Rothkrantz, L.J.M., Shan, C., Wiggers, P.: Kinect sensing of shopping related actions. In: Wichert, R., Van Laerhoven, K., Gelissen, J. (eds.) AmI 2011. CCIS, vol. 277, pp. 91–100. Springer, Heidelberg (2012). https://doi.org/10.1007/978-3-642-31479-7_16
13. Preis, J., Kessel, M., Werner, M., Linnhoff-Popien, C.: Gait recognition with kinect. In: International Workshop on Kinect in Pervasive Computing, New Castle, UK, pp. 1–4 (2012)

New Three-Chemical Polynomial Reaction-Diffusion Equations

Do-yeon Han[1], Byungmoon Kim[2], and Oh-young Song[1]([✉])

[1] Sejong University, Seoul, South Korea
`hando715@gmail.com`, `oysong@sejong.ac.kr`
[2] Adobe Research, San Jose, USA
`bmkim@adobe.com`

Abstract. Reaction-diffusion (RD) generates time-varying patterns or noises, used to create beautiful patterned or noisy variations in colors, bumps, flow details, or other parameters. RD can be relatively easily solved on various domains: image, curved surface, and volumetric domains, making their applications popular. Being widely available, most of the patterns from known RD have been well explored. In this paper, we move on this field, by providing a large number of new reaction equations. Among the vast space of new equations, we focus on three-chemical polynomial reactions as the three chemicals can be easily mapped to any colors. We propose a set of new equations that generate new time-varying patterns.

Keywords: Reaction-diffusion · Pattern generation · PDE · Texture synthesis · Time-varying noise

1 Introduction

Reaction-diffusion (RD) is known as a chemical process model that, in large part, generates natural patterns such as cheetah dots, tiger stripes, etc. [19]. Turing [19], Gray-Scott [15], FitzHugh-Nagumo [6], Barkley [2], Gierer-Meinhardt [7] and Brusselator [16] models are all known two-chemical reaction-diffusion equations. Belousov-Zhabotinsky equation [3,24] that biochemist Belousov formulated in an unpublished paper is three-chemical reactions. Meinhardt introduced five-chemical reaction equations [13]. In the equations, however, three chemicals play auxiliary roles in the reaction of two main chemicals. Similar to RD, Sims [18] searched patterns using cellular automata and Walter et al. [21] created mammalian patterns using cell division and cell-to-cell interactions.

"This research was supported by the MSIP (Ministry of Science, ICT & Future Planning), Korea, under the National Program for Excellence in SW (2015-0-00938) supervised by the IITP (Institute for Information & communications Technology Planning&Evaluation)".
"This work was supported by the faculty research fund of Sejong University in 2019".

M. Gavrilova et al. (Eds.): CGI 2019, LNCS 11542, pp. 364–370, 2019.
https://doi.org/10.1007/978-3-030-22514-8_32

These known reaction equations generate interesting time-varying patterns, and these are used for texture synthesis or simulation effects [11,20,22], for visualizations [9,17,23] and for image processing [1,4,5]. Ready [8] is a software that integrates existing reaction equations, in particular, multi-layer forms that combine multiple reaction equations to allow larger number of chemicals. For example, some models allow up to seven chemicals. Otherwise, the generated time varying noise can be treated in various ways, e.g., considering chemicals as material properties, heights, or to produce beautiful patterns and structures by adding more layers.

Reaction is to evaluate an algebraic formula at each grid location, very simple to understand and easy to implement. Despite this advantage, the fundamental limitation of RD is that the known reaction equations are only a few. Therefore, new reaction equations would re-lit the study on RD.

Most known reaction equations are either designed to model real-world chemical reactions or used to generate patterns in graphics applications. However, if the application is focused to generate patterns and noises, reaction equations do not have to be chemically based. Any free form equations that generate interesting patterns would be useful. So, it would be reasonable to assume that there exist ample nonlinear PDEs that generate interesting patterns.

In this paper, we search for new types of reaction equations. We model reactions as polynomials and search for parameters (polynomial and diffusion coefficients) that generate interesting patterns. Since few three-chemical reaction equation is known, the space of three-chemical reaction equations is vastly unexplored. Therefore, we search for three-chemical RD.

2   Previous Works

In this section, we explore some known reaction equations. Alan-Turing [10,19] first described the way in which stable patterns such as stripes, spots and spirals may arise naturally. Gray-Scott equations are the most popular reaction equation family [15]. These equations generate splitting dots behavior that eventually fills the domain with dots or fingerprint like patterns. Gierer-Meinhardt [7] shows periodic dot, stripe or cell patterns[1]. Both FitzHugh-Nagumo [6,12] and Brusselator [16] generate fingerprint patterns. Barkley model [2] generates '3'-shape patterns similar to Belousov patterns. Belousov-Zhabotinsky model [14] is a three-chemical RD that is known to model oscillating chemical reaction[2]. Since Barkley model has two chemicals while Belousov model has three chemicals, Belousov has richer colored patterns. Our search of generalized three-chemical equation often produced this '3'-shape patterns with more broad variations in shapes and blending patterns than Barkley and Belousov equations.

---

[1] For the results of Gierer-Meinhardt, refer https://imc.zih.tu-dresden.de/wiki/morpheus/doku.php?id=examples:reaction-diffusion.

[2] For the results of Belousov-Zhabotinsky, refer https://en.wikipedia.org/wiki/Belousov-Zhabotinsky_reaction, https://scipython.com/blog/simulating-the-belousov-zhabotinsky-reaction/.

3 Three-Chemical Reaction Diffusion

A typical RD is made of both a reaction part and a diffusion part. In the diffusion part, chemicals are simply diffused. In the reaction part, chemicals react to each other and then the concentrations increase or decrease. Equation (1) is for an arbitrary chemical a and C_a is a reaction equation.

$$\frac{\partial m_a}{\partial t} = \mu_a \nabla^2 m_a + C_a(m_a, m_b, m_c) \tag{1}$$

For the diffusion part, we just simply used the convolution kernel size to be 3×3 with 9-point stencil $[[0.05, 0.2, 0.05], [0.2, -1.0, 0.2], [0.05, 0.2, 0.05]]$. For the reaction part, we composed the equations with polynomial coupling terms up to order three and it uses 192 reaction coefficients. Since our end goal is finding visually interesting patterns, we consider each chemicals as color state r, g, b(red, green and blue), so the results already mapped to color space[3]. We simulated about 58,000 random coefficients set, and found 303 patterns. This is about 0.5% of success rate.

$$C_r(r, g, b) = \sum_{i,j,k=0}^{3} \alpha_{ijk} r^i g^j b^k$$

$$C_g(r, g, b) = \sum_{i,j,k=0}^{3} \beta_{ijk} r^i g^j b^k \tag{2}$$

$$C_b(r, g, b) = \sum_{i,j,k=0}^{3} \gamma_{ijk} r^i g^j b^k$$

4 Results

We set the time interval $1/60$, the resolution is 256×256. For each simulation, we set the initial concentration to be a color noise image, reaction-diffusion coefficients to be random and use periodic boundary condition. The range of diffusion coefficients is 0.0 to 1.0, and the reaction coefficients is -1.0 to 1.0. We consider all patterns interesting except when all pixels on the domain have the same color. Basically, we performed 5,000 iterations per simulation. However, if all pixels on the domain are the same color after 300 frames, the simulation is automatically terminated. If the color of each pixel has no change for 1,000 frames, we consider the reaction-diffusion reached a static equilibrium state.

In Fig. 1, there are '3'-shape patterns similar to the ones from Barkley and Belousov-Zhabotinsky model. Patterns appear to be slightly different from previous equations due to sharp color transition (#000101) and deep dark valleys (#002355). Some patterns' shapes are simplified (#000081), colors are mixed

---

[3] These PDE's correspond to the additive color mixing. Of course, arbitrary color states and the subtractive color mixing can be applicable.

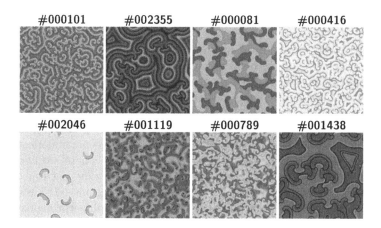

Fig. 1. '3'-shape patterns similar to the ones from Barkley and Belousov-Zhabotinsky model. (Color figure online)

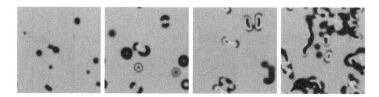

Fig. 2. This is a recursive boundary formation pattern that spreads out and eventually develops in to oscillating noise pattern. (Color figure online)

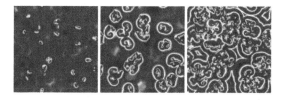

Fig. 3. Patterns evolve into steady-state oscillation. (Color figure online)

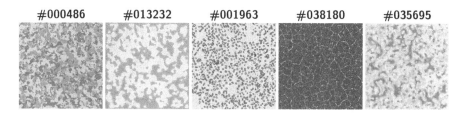

Fig. 4. Reaction-diffusion reached to static equilibrium states where patterns stop changing (#000486, #013232), developing some structure (#001963, #038180) or showing two-patterns (#035695). (Color figure online)

(#000416) or become sparser (#002046). Also, we have doublet flow patterns with slight (#001119), more color mixing amounts (#000789), and thinner red zones compared to green and blue zones (#001438).

Figure 2 shows recursive boundary formation that spreads out and eventually develops in to oscillating noise patterns and as you can see in Fig. 3, some patterns evolve into steady-state oscillations.

In Fig. 4, there are some cases that reaction-diffusion reached to static equilibrium states where patterns stop changing (#000486, #013232). Reaction-diffusion developed to particles (#001963) or red and green components shrink to thin films revealing a foam-like structure (#038180). There are two-pattern cases where a pattern grows and then freezes, leaving some patterned masks, while another pattern is oscillatory in the unmasked regions (#035695). Also, you can see more various patterns in Fig. 5, especially a fingerprint-like pattern was found (#032174).

We implemented a real-time simulator for reaction-diffusion (Fig. 6). With this, it is possible to test various coefficients values, modify provided coefficients sets or give some concentration on specific area of the domain.

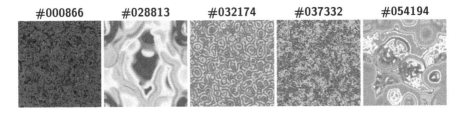

Fig. 5. More selected various patterns. (Color figure online)

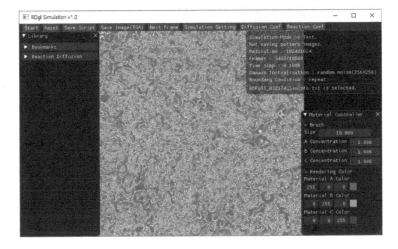

Fig. 6. A real-time simulator for reaction-diffusion. (Color figure online)

5 Conclusions

We formulated three-chemical reaction-diffusion equations with the simple 3×3 kernel convolution and polynomial coupling terms up to order three. We then searched coefficients generating visually interesting patterns. We found new three-chemical polynomial reaction-diffusion equations that generate new colored patterns.

With the previous equations, the reaction-diffusion patterns are composed of small circle points, lines or curly shapes, and the almost patterns are static after the completion of pattern formation. With our equations, we can get curly shapes patterns similar to Barkley or Belousov-Zhabotinsky equations and various modified curly shapes patterns. Also, we can find some cases that the patterns are evolving into steady-state oscillations or seems to have two layers. These cases are not found with the previous equations. Compared to the traditional RD patterns, our method can generate constantly changing colors while maintaining shapes and patterns.

The reaction equations with arbitrary coefficients lead to the r, g or b values outside the range easily. Sometimes, this makes reaction-diffusion system blow up even if an interesting pattern is found. In order to keep the system stable all the time, we constrained the values in the range to $[0, 1]$ by clamping. According to our experiments, the types of reaction-diffusion patterns with clamping don't have big difference from the ones without clamping.

We obtained a large number of interesting time varying noise patterns that even drift slowly over time. These new patterns can be used as input sources for various applications. As future work, we will expand the search space of the RD patterns including various nonlinear terms. Also, we will search feasible sets of patterns using machine learning approach and analyze the relation of patterns and coefficients for the classification of patterns. Furthermore, based on the classification, we will study on how to provide proper coefficients with user specification.

References

1. Acton, S.T., Mukherjee, D.P., Havlicek, J.P., Bovik, A.C.: Oriented texture completion by AM-FM reaction-diffusion. IEEE Trans. Image Process. **10**(6), 885–896 (2001)
2. Barkley, D.: A model for fast computer simulation of waves in excitable media. Physica D: Nonlinear Phenom. **49**(1–2), 61–70 (1991)
3. Belousov, B.P.: Radiates. Med. **145** (1959)
4. Chen, Y., Pock, T.: Trainable nonlinear reaction diffusion: a flexible framework for fast and effective image restoration. IEEE Trans. Pattern Anal. Mach. Intell. **39**(6), 1256–1272 (2017)
5. Cottet, G.H., Germain, L.: Image processing through reaction combined with nonlinear diffusion. Math. Comput. **61**, 659–673 (1993)
6. FitzHugh, R.: Mathematical Models of Excitation and Propagation in Nerve. Publisher Unknown (1966)

7. Gierer, A., Meinhardt, H.: A theory of biological pattern formation. Biol. Cyberne. **12**(1), 30–39 (1972)
8. Tim, H., Munafo, R., Trevorrow, A., Rokicki, T., Wills, D.: Ready, a cross-platform implementation of various reaction-diffusion systems (2012). https://github.com/GollyGang/ready
9. Kindlmann, G., Weinstein, D., Hart, D.: Strategies for direct volume rendering of diffusion tensor fields. IEEE Trans. Visual. Comput. Graph. **6**(2), 124–138 (2000)
10. Kondo, S., Miura, T.: Reaction-diffusion model as a framework for understanding biological pattern formation. Science **329**(5999), 1616–1620 (2010)
11. Lo, K.Y., Li, H., Fu, C.W., Wong, T.T.: Interactive reaction-diffusion on surface tiles. In: 15th Pacific Conference on Computer Graphics and Applications, PG 2007, pp. 65–74. IEEE (2007)
12. Malevanets, A., Kapral, R.: Microscopic model for Fitzhugh-Nagumo dynamics. Phys. Rev. E **55**(5), 5657 (1997)
13. Meinhardt, H.: Models of Biological Pattern Formation. Academic Press, Cambridge (1982)
14. Murray, J.: Mathematical Biology II: Spatial Models and Biochemical Applications, vol. II. Springer, New York (2003). https://doi.org/10.1007/b98869
15. Gray, P., Scott, S.K.: Autocatalytic reactions in the isothermal, continuous stirred tank reactor: isolas and other forms of multistability. Chem. Eng. Sci. **38**(1), 29–43 (1983)
16. Pena, B., Perez-Garcia, C.: Stability of Turing patterns in the Brusselator model. Phys. Rev.E **64**(5), 056213 (2001)
17. Sanderson, A.R., Johnson, C.R., Kirby, R.M.: Display of vector fields using a reaction-diffusion model. In: Proceedings of the Conference on Visualization 2004, pp. 115–122. IEEE Computer Society (2004)
18. Sims, K.: Interactive evolution of dynamical systems. In: Toward a Practice of Autonomous Systems: Proceedings of the First European Conference on Artificial Life, pp. 171–178 (1992)
19. Turing, A.M.: The chemical basis of morphogenesis. Philos. Trans. Roy. Soc. Lond. B: Biol. Sci. **237**(641), 37–72 (1952)
20. Turk, G.: Generating textures on arbitrary surfaces using reaction-diffusion. ACM SIGGRAPH Comput. Graph. **25**, 289–298 (1991)
21. Walter, M., Fournier, A., Reimers, M.: Clonal mosaic model for the synthesis of mammalian coat patterns. Graph. Interface **98**, 82–91 (1998)
22. Witkin, A., Kass, M.: Reaction-diffusion textures. ACM SIGGRAPH Comput. Graph. **25**(4), 299–308 (1991)
23. Yang, L., Epstein, I.R.: Oscillatory turing patterns in reaction-diffusion systems with two coupled layers. Phys. Rev. Lett. **90**(17), 178303 (2003)
24. Zhabotinsky, A.M.: Dokl. Akad. Nauk SSSR 157. **392** (1964)

Capturing Piecewise SVBRDFs
with Content Aware Lighting

Xiao Li[1,3]([✉]), Peiran Ren[2], Yue Dong[3], Gang Hua[4], Xin Tong[3],
and Baining Guo[3]

[1] University of Science and Technology of China, Hefei, China
pableetoli@gmail.com
[2] Alibaba Inc., Hangzhou, China
[3] Microsoft Research Asia, Beijing, China
[4] Wormpex AI Research, Beijing, China

Abstract. We present a method for capturing piecewise SVBRDFs over
flat surfaces that consist of piecewise homogeneous materials with arbitrary geometric details. To achieve fast and simple capture, our method
first evaluates the piecewise material distribution over the surface from
an image taken with uniform lighting and then find an suitable 2D light
pattern according to the material's spatial distribution, which combines
both step edge and gradient lighting patterns. After that, we capture
another image of the surface lit by the optimized light pattern and reconstruct the SVBRDF and normal details from two captured images. The
capturing only takes two photographs and the light pattern optimization
is executed in real time, which enables us to design a simple device setup
for on-site capturing. We validate our approach and demonstrate the
efficiency of our method on a wide range of synthetic and real materials.

Keywords: Appearance capture · Adaptive capture · SVBRDF

1 Introduction

Real world surfaces exhibit rich spatial details and appearance variations under
different lighting and viewing conditions. Capturing and modeling the detailed
surface reflectance (i.e. SVBRDFs) is important to the realism of computer generated imagery. Early works [5,9] directly capture the 6D SVBRDFs with both
angular and spatial details, which requires dedicated device setup and long capturing time. Recent methods [2,6–8,10,12] simplify the device setup and reduce
the number of measurements for SVBRDF acquisition by exploiting the spatial
coherence and using simplified BRDF models at each surface point. However,
most of them, if not all, still require specialized device setups or tens of measurements, making them difficult to use by end-users for on-site capturing.

We present a method for capturing and reconstructing SVBRDFs of a flat
surface from only *two* images captured by a camera mounted on a LCD screen.
Instead of developing a general capturing method for all kinds of materials, we

© Springer Nature Switzerland AG 2019
M. Gavrilova et al. (Eds.): CGI 2019, LNCS 11542, pp. 371–379, 2019.
https://doi.org/10.1007/978-3-030-22514-8_33

aim to simplify the capturing process as much as possible by restricting our method for flat surfaces that are composed of piecewise homogeneous isotropic material regions with per-pixel normal details. To this end, we first combine the gradient lighting [11] with step-edges [13] and design a 2D near field light pattern for estimating homogeneous BRDF with arbitrary normal details. For surfaces contain multiple piecewise homogeneous materials, we tile the designed 2D patterns to cover each individual material and optimize their layout so that every material is illuminated by both step-edges and gradient patterns for best SVBRDF and normal recovery. To make the lighting pattern specifically adapted to the given material, we first capture an image of the material sample under uniform lighting and segment the material into several homogeneous material regions. Based on the segmentation, we compute the adaptive 2D light pattern via optimization and then capture a second image of the material illuminated with the computed content aware lighting. Finally, we reconstruct the SVBRDF and normal details by iteratively solving the SVBRDF and normal details as well as refining the registration between the light pattern and the surface from the aligned light pattern and images. We validate and demonstrate the effectiveness and efficiency of our method with a set of examples composed of a wide range of synthetic and real materials.

2   Overview

Device Setup. Our device setup only consists of a DSLR camera mounted on a LCD screen. Before capturing, we calibrate the geometric and radiometric properties of our device setup. For geometric calibration, we follow the method in [14] to calibrate the camera's intrinsic and extrinsic parameters. For radiometric calibration, we calibrate the radiometric properties of the LCD screen by measuring the three color response curves of the LCD screen w.r.t. pixel values.

SVBRDF Capturing. To capture the SVBRDF and normal of a material sample, A user is asked to hold the flat sample in front of our device and makes the material surface roughly parallel to the LCD screen. Then we take an image of the sample under a 2D uniform lighting by displaying a uniform white image on the LCD screen. Our method then segments the material sample into a set of homogeneous regions by applying mean-shift [3] clustering on the histogram of the uniformly lit image. After that we optimize a 2D light pattern so that every homogeneous region is well illuminated by both a step-edge and a gradient lighting (Sect. 3). Then we capture the second image of the material with this computed light pattern. During capture, we determine an initial value of position and orientation of the target material by reflected checkerboard through a flat PMMA mirror frame on the top of the material sample.

SVBRDF Reconstruction. We model the BRDF of each region with a Cook-Torrance BRDF model [4] parameterized by the diffuse coefficient k_d, specular coefficient k_s, and specular roughness α. The geometric details is modeled as a per-pixel normal map $\mathbf{n_p}(\mathbf{p})$. Given the second image I captured under the

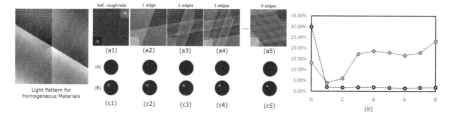

Fig. 1. Left: the 2D light pattern designed for homogeneous materials. Right: the importance of adaptive lighting design. For a synthetic material BRDF spatial distribution shown in (a1), (a2–a5) shows a set of naive tiled light patterns with different number of edges. (b) plots the roughness reconstruction error w.r.t. number of repeated light patterns, with the solid line corresponding to sharp regions (A) and dash line to rough regions (B). A single light pattern that misses light edge in corner regions (a2) results in large reconstruction errors; while arbitrarily increasing the number of light edges (a3–a5) increases the reconstruction error of rough materials. (c1–c5) visualized solved roughness (bottom row) and its correspond ground truth (top row).

designed light pattern L, we recover the BRDF model parameters for each region and per-pixel normal by minimize the rendering error between captured image and reconstructed image. We develop a robust solver to iteratively solve the SVBRDF and normal as well as refine the registration between the LCD screen and the material samples (Sect. 4).

3   Lighting Pattern Optimization

Given the material distribution over the sample surface, our method optimize a suitable light pattern for SVBRDF acquisition. For homogeneous materials, we proposed a suitable light pattern by combining two lighting patterns used in previous methods for normal and BRDF reconstruction: the step-edge lighting for homogeneous BRDF acquisition [13] and the multiple gradient lighting for normal estimation [11]. Specifically, we replace the constant lighting at each side of the step edge with two periodic gradient lighting patterns:

$$l(q) = \begin{cases} h_r \sin(2\pi q) & 0 \leq q < 0.5 \\ 1.0 - h_r \sin(2\pi(q - 0.5)) & 0.5 \leq q \leq 1 \end{cases}, \quad (1)$$

which is determined by parameter h_r. We choose $h_r = 0.5$ for the light pattern which achieves good balance between BRDF and normal reconstruction; to make a light pattern for robust normal estimation, we multiplex the 1D lighting pattern above in different color channels to form our final light pattern. Figure 1 demonstrates the designed multiplex light patterns used for homogeneous material samples.

For materials that consist of piecewise homogeneous material regions, using the same light pattern above or simply tiling the patterns without optimization may make the capturing fail: if the step edges are too sparse, the specular reflection of some regions may miss the step edge and thus result in large roughness error; if the step edge are too dense, the accuracy of the estimated roughness also degraded, especially when the width between step edges became smaller than the BRDF lobe size (See Fig. 1(a2) and (a5)). Therefore, we optimize the light pattern layout and its orientation to the underlying material sample so that each homogeneous material region can be covered by at least one step edge in each color channel, while the number of the step edges along each direction is minimized and their distances are maximized. Specifically, the light pattern layout is determined by several parameters: the angle φ of each light pattern; the number of the step edges in each color channel $N_e^C, C \in \{R, G, B\}$, and the position of each step edge e, represented by the distance d_e^C from the edge to the material center. Given a material sample distribution, we optimize the light pattern layout with a cost function f:

$$f = \sum_{C \in \{R,G,B\}} \sum_j^{N_m} \left[w_j^C \left(E_v(C, j) + E_s(C, j) \right) \right], \tag{2}$$

which sums the cost of the step edges in all three color channels. For step edges in each color channel, the cost function sums the region coverage cost E_v and the edge sparseness cost E_s for each clustered material region j in N_m. w_j^C is the weight for the costs of step edges of each color channel in the material region j; we give higher weights to the dominant color channal by setting $w_j^C = \alpha_j^C / \sum_C \alpha_j^C$, where α_j^C is the average intensity of color channel C for all pixels of the region j. The region coverage cost E_v for the step edges in color channel C is defined by:

$$E_v(C, j) = \left(\frac{1}{\max(0.01, \min(1, m_v/\eta_v))} - 1 \right)^2, \tag{3}$$

which measures the number of pixels m_v crossed by the step edges in current region j. $\eta_v = 100$ is the number of pixels that is sufficient for a robust BRDF estimation. Given a pattern layout, we first determine the step edge segments in color channel C that cross this region and then count m_v as the number by pixels that within 1.0 pixel distance to the edge segments. E_v decreases with the increasing m_v, encouraging more pixels crossed by edges. The edge sparseness cost E_s of the step edges in color channel C is computed by:

$$E_s(C, j) = \frac{1}{N_d} \sum_i^{N_d} \left(1 - \min(1, m_{s_i}/\eta_s) \right)^2, \tag{4}$$

which is determined by the distribution of distances between the pixels in region j and their nearest step edges. In order to count pixels with different distance to an edge, we first discretized the distance into N_d slots, and count the number of pixels in the region $m_{s,i}$ that lie in each slot. The distance range for each slot i is increased exponentially and the number of slots N_d is then determined with the furthest distance covering the whole input image. We define the upper bound

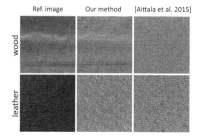

Fig. 2. Normal reconstruction result comparison with Aittala's method [1]. For stationary materials (leather), both method result reasonable reconstruction. Aittala's method [1] (right image) fails to capture the non-stationary variations exhibits in the wood example, while our method reproduces those global structures well.

Fig. 3. Effect of our registration refinement on a real example. (a): input image. (b) & (c): Solved result without (b) and with (c) registration refinement; Corresponding solved spec and roughness are visualized in left corner of images. Note the region that have sharp light edge crossed (marked in green) is blurred (b) and is fixed by our refinement (c) The corresponding roughness are: (a) 0.070, (b) 0.083, (c) 0.065 (Color figure online)

$\eta_s = 50$ for each slot to avoid overweighting. The edge sparseness function E_s decreases as m_s increasing, and then is clamped to 0 after the m_s exceeds η_s.

To solve the above highly non-linear optimization as fast as possible, we initialize the optimization with different combinations of pattern angles φ and step edge numbers N_e^C in each color channel. For each initialization we optimize distances between step edges by minimizing the cost function defined in Eq. 2 via gradient decent. Finally, we choose the light pattern with the minimal cost function value as the result.

4 SVBRDF Reconstruction

With our piecewise constant BRDF model, the goal for SVBRDF reconstruction is determining the BRDF parameters for each cluster $B^i(k_d^i, k_s^i, \gamma^i)$ and the surface normal for each surface point $\mathbf{n_p}(\mathbf{p})$.

Iterative Solving Between BRDF and Normals. We solve the SVBRDF by iteratively optimize BRDF parameters and the normal directions. We initialize the optimization by setting the diffuse coefficient of each BRDF is set as the average color of clustered region, with specular coefficient as $(0.5, 0.5, 0.5)$ and roughness as 0.1. Then we alternately optimize per-cluster BRDF parameters and per-pixel normals until convergence with Levenberg-Marquardt (LM) method. To speed up the computation and avoid local minimal, for solving per-pixel normals we perform a sparsely brute-force search on 20×20 directions and find the best fit normal directions as the initialization for the LM solver.

Registration Refinement. Although we perform optical calibration of material positions during capturing, the registration process is still not perfect accurate and may affects the result accuracy. We thus refine the rotation and translation of the material sample after each iteration. To the end, we parameterize the material position with six parameters accounting for yaw, pitch and roll angles as well as 3D translation, and minimize re-rendering error with current BRDF and normal. Figure 3 demonstrates our refinement on a real captured case compared with no refinement.

5   Experimental Results

System Performance. We implemented our material clustering and light pattern optimization with C++; the reconstruction algorithm with Python except the rendering equation is evaluated on GPU with CUDA. The material clustering and light pattern optimization take less than 0.1 s, enabling fast capture. For

Table 1. Typical types of synthetic data and their corresponding light pattern; for each type of materials we show one example with the computed light pattern (top) and other material input images (bottom). (Left) Homogeneous BRDF with stationary normal variations; (Middle) wallpaper example with piecewise constant SVBRDF; (Right) natural wood SVBRDF with non-stationary normal map. For every material, from left to right: rendered image under light pattern, designed light pattern and clustering results.

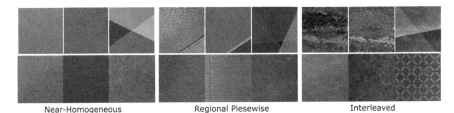

Near-Homogeneous   Regional Piesewise   Interleaved

Table 2. Numerical comparisons of adaptive and non-adaptive method (a single fixed lighting pattern at the center of the image), on a synthetic dataset with 12 materials. Error metrics are mean per-pixel relative MSE w.r.t ground truth for diffuse albedo/specular albedo/roughness, and mean per-pixel degree deviation for bump normal, averaged on each type of materials (See main texts for description). Typical material samples of each type is shown as in above Figure.

Material type	Average error (adaptive)				Average error (non-adaptive)			
	Diff. Albedo	Spec. Albedo	Roughness	Normal	Diff. Albedo	Spec. Albedo	Roughness	Normal
Near-Homogeneous	0.59%	0.80%	0.69%	1.94°	0.55%	0.88%	1.07%	2.82°
Regional	1.39%	3.05%	2.39%	1.54°	1.59%	3.29%	3.96%	1.71°
Interleaved	0.69%	2.25%	1.60%	1.90°	1.05%	2.53%	3.07%	2.08°

an input of 1500×1500, the SVBRDF optimization takes about 45–60 min on a workstation computer with Geforce 980 GPU card.

Method Validation. We validate the effectiveness of out light pattern optimization scheme by comparing our method with a naive tiled 2D light pattern, on a selected synthetic dataset with 12 materials from the Adobe Stock dataset. To evaluate our method on with different type of spatial variations, we grouped the synthetic material into three different types with 4 materials for each, namely *near-homogeneous*, *regional piecewise* and *interleaved*. Figure 1 illustrates typical kind of materials in each type as well as their corresponded adaptive light pattern, where the designed light pattern adapts to different material distributions and guarantees each material cluster could be "lit" by at least one sharp edge of lighting. Table 1 listed the numerical error of reconstructed BRDF coefficients and normal maps w.r.t each type of materials using our adaptive lighting scheme, as well as the results obtained with non-adaptive lighting. For near-homogeneous material, both adaptive and non-adaptive achieve similar accuracy with low errors; while for interleaved and regional materials, our adaptive lighting scheme provides benefit on the reconstruction of corner material regions and achieves lower error.

Comparison with Aittala et al. [1]. We compare our method with Aittala et al.'s approach [1] which also use two images for reconstruction of stationary materials (Fig. 2). For the non-stationary wood example, [1] fails to recover the large scale bumps while our method can successfully reconstruct the normal variations; the average per-pixel normal derivation by [1] is $2.28°$, while our method is $0.74°$.

Results of Real Materials. We captured SVBRDF and normals for a number of real material samples that have variant BRDF and normal distributions. Figure 4 illustrates the input images of all samples under adaptive lighting, together with the recovered material maps and novel renderings. Our method

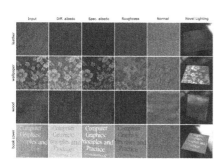

Fig. 4. Real captured materials, with material name shown on the left.

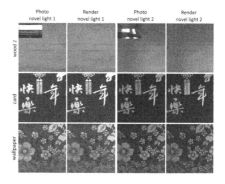

Fig. 5. Relighting results vs. photographs, under novel illuminations; Corresponding environment lightings are shown in left corner.

faithfully reconstructs BRDFs and normals of all real samples from image lit with optimized light pattern; Note that non-trivial material patterns are also successfully illuminated and recovered with our adaptive light patterns, such as the material residing on the bottom right region of the *wood* sample. Figure 5 shows side-by-side comparisons between photographs of materials lit with novel illumination rendering results of the recovered BRDFs and normals under the same lighting. The rendering results fit the reference photograph well, with few missing BRDF details resulting from our piecewise constant assumption.

6   Conclusion

We present a fast, on site acquisition method for capturing piecewise homogeneous SVBRDFs and arbitrary normal details of piecewise homogeneous materials with two images lit by 2D adaptive lighting. The first image is used to segment the materials and guide the light pattern design, while the second image of the material lit with the optimized lighting pattern well captures the specular reflectance of each material region. A reconstruction method is developed to robustly recover the SVBRDFs and the detailed normal maps from the two images. We validate our method with a wide range of materials with variant SVBRDFs and normal details on both synthetic data and real data.

References

1. Aittala, M., Weyrich, T., Lehtinen, J.: Two-shot SVBRDF capture for stationary materials. ACM Trans. Graph. **34**(4), 110 (2015)
2. Chen, G., Dong, Y., Peers, P., Zhang, J., Tong, X.: Reflectance scanning: estimating shading frame and BRDF with generalized linear light sources. ACM Trans. Graph. **33**(4), 117 (2014)
3. Cheng, Y.: Mean shift, mode seeking, and clustering. IEEE Trans. PAMI **17**(8), 790–799 (1995)
4. Cook, R.L., Torrance, K.E.: A reflectance model for computer graphics. ACM Trans. Graph. **1**(1), 7–24 (1982)
5. Dana, K.J., van Ginneken, B., Nayar, S.K., Koenderink, J.J.: Reflectance and texture of real-world surfaces. ACM Trans. Graph. **18**(1), 1–34 (1999)
6. Dong, Y., et al.: Manifold bootstrapping for SVBRDF capture. ACM Trans. Graph. **29**(4), 98 (2010)
7. Goldman, D., Curless, B., Hertzmann, A., Seitz, S.: Shape and spatially-varying BRDFs from photometric stereo. IEEE Trans. PAMI **32**(6), 1060–1071 (2009)
8. Kang, K., Chen, Z., Wang, J., Zhou, K., Wu, H.: Efficient reflectance capture using an autoencoder. ACM Trans. Graph **37**, 127 (2018)
9. Lawrence, J., et al.: Inverse shade trees for non-parametric material representation and editing. ACM Trans. Graph. **25**(3), 735–745 (2006)
10. Lensch, H.P.A., Kautz, J., Goesele, M., Heidrich, W., Seidel, H.P.: Image-based reconstruction of spatial appearance and geometric detail. ACM Trans. Graph. **22**, 234–257 (2003)
11. Ma, W.C., Hawkins, T., Peers, P., Chabert, C.F., Weiss, M., Debevec, P.: Rapid acquisition of specular and diffuse normal maps from polarized spherical gradient illumination. In: EGSR 2007, pp. 183–194 (2007)

12. Ren, P., Wang, J., Snyder, J., Tong, X., Guo, B.: Pocket reflectometry. ACM Trans. Graph. **30**(4), 45:1–45:10 (2011)
13. Wang, C.P., Snavely, N., Marschner, S.: Estimating dual-scale properties of glossy surfaces from step-edge lighting. ACM Trans. Graph. **30**(6) (2011)
14. Zhang, Z.: Flexible camera calibration by viewing a plane from unknown orientations. In: ICCV 1999, vol. 1, pp. 666–673. IEEE (1999)

VRSpineSim: Applying Educational Aids Within A Virtual Reality Spine Surgery Simulator

Ahmed E. Mostafa[1]([☒])[ID], Won Hyung Ryu[1], Sonny Chan[1],
Kazuki Takashima[2], Gail Kopp[1], Mario Costa Sousa[1], and Ehud Sharlin[1]

[1] University of Calgary, Calgary, AB T2N 1N4, Canada
ezzelden.ahmed@gmail.com
[2] Tohoku University, Sendai, Miyagi 980-8577, Japan

Abstract. We contribute VRSpineSim, a stereoscopic virtual reality surgery simulator that allows novice surgeons to learn and experiment with a spinal pedicle screw insertion (PSI) procedure using simplified interaction capabilities and 3D haptic user interfaces. By collaborating with medical experts and following an iterative approach, we provide characterization of the PSI task, and derive requirements for the design of a 3D immersive interactive simulation system. We present how these requirements were realized in our prototype and outline its educational benefits for training the PSI procedure. We conclude with the results of a preliminary evaluation of VRSpineSim and reflect on our interface benefits and limitations for future relevant research efforts.

Keywords: Immersive simulation · Spine surgery · Education

1 Introduction

Three-dimensional (3D) surgical simulation systems are becoming increasingly important to educate and train medical students about critical procedures [3]. However, medical students are faced by many challenges when using such educational tools due to technical and user experience limitations. In particular, existing simulation systems have focused primarily on accurate implementation of the surgical procedure (e.g., supporting haptic feedback or high-resolution rendering), while optimizing the user experience and interaction have been often weakly considered leading to limited adoption by some medical experts [6]. Therefore, there is a need to mitigate the aforementioned challenges to widen the adoption of 3D simulation technology, and support medical experts with a learning environment that better satisfies their needs and expectations.

We focus on this work on the education and training of spine surgery and specifically the common task of pedicle screw insertion (PSI). In this context, we studied existing systems (e.g., [7]), collaborated with medical experts and identified key limitations that pertain to interaction and user experience aspects.

© Springer Nature Switzerland AG 2019
M. Gavrilova et al. (Eds.): CGI 2019, LNCS 11542, pp. 380–387, 2019.
https://doi.org/10.1007/978-3-030-22514-8_34

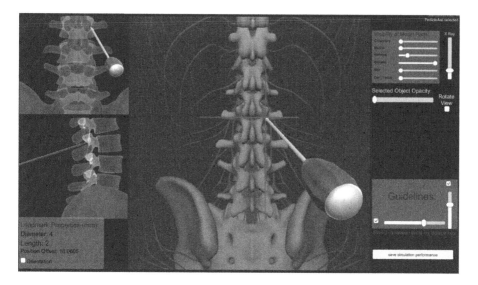

Fig. 1. VRSpineSim interface: X-ray views (left), contextual visualization around the spine showing yellow nerves and green guidelines (center), and GUI controls (right) (Color figure online)

As a result, we propose VRSpineSim, a 3D stereoscopic virtual reality simulation with unique educational features and simplified interactions, enriching surgeons when they learn about and practice the procedure of PSI. We also report on the results of a preliminary evaluation conducted reflecting on the efficacy of our prototype in assessing the technical skills of surgical experts.

The contributions of this paper are as follows:

– Insight derived from participatory collaboration with medical experts regarding the design of spine surgery simulators.
– VRSpineSim, an immersive simulation prototype with educational features that facilitate learning about and practicing the PSI procedure.
– The results of a preliminary evaluation of the developed prototype including reflections on benefits and limitations that could support future design efforts of spine surgery simulations.

2   Related Work

Virtual reality simulations are common in surgical education and training [13], and particularly spine surgery and the PSI procedure (e.g., [14], and [10]). Such simulations have been shown to improve surgeons' skills [19] and operation room performance [17]. A recent survey has studied the effect of 3D simulation on neurosurgical skill acquisition and performance [3]. The authors highlighted that 3D simulations are useful supplement to training programs and stressed the need for continuous improvement to warrant large-scale adoption of this technology.

Clearly, effective visualization in surgical simulations is critical as well as haptic feedback that is becoming increasingly important [4]. Unfortunately, usability and user experience elements are often poorly explored in the design of surgical simulation [6]. Thus, our work extends existing research and focuses on improving usability aspects to support novice surgeons when using simulation.

3   Research Approach

We followed a user-centred iterative participatory approach [16], involving collaboration with medical and educational experts gathering their feedback and suggestions about our implementation. We also strived to follow existing usability guidelines [18] and design recommendations [15].

3.1   Task Description

We focused on the task of pedicle screw insertion (PSI) that pertains to back surgery for its simplicity. Key task steps are: (1) identifying landmarks or entry points for screw insertion to support particular vertebrae, (2) drilling pilot holes over the previously identified landmarks, and (3) placing screws of particular size/diameter in the created holes [11]. For effective task completion, spinal anatomy knowledge with x-ray guidance is needed. The unfortunate mistake during this surgery (e.g., touching a nerve or misplacing the screw so it skips the bone) may paralyze the patient or destroy the spine. Therefore, a simulated environment enriched with simplified interaction capabilities would benefit medical practitioners and allow them to better learn and train the PSI procedure.

3.2   Design Rationale

We studied and experimented with many of the existing back-surgery simulation systems (e.g., [8,9], and [7]). We identified that the limitations of current systems stem partially from the complexity of interaction and the lack of educational features for supporting simple and effective simulation. For instance, the visualization of the anatomical context is often limited and lacks support of visual guidelines. Also, the reported numeric performance score may poorly hint at specific improvement aspects. Finally, user interaction often requires simultaneous use of a variety of devices (e.g., hand controller and foot pedal), a complication that can be avoided with improved design. These issues were also highlighted by our medical collaborators and thus we focus our work on addressing the aforementioned limitations.

For our design, we focused on supporting specific usability criteria [12]. We aimed for *Learnability* (easy usage with no prior knowledge), *Feedback* (handling errors and reporting performance), *Efficiency* (simplicity and flexibility of interaction capabilities), and *Satisfaction* (intuitive interface and visualization).

Towards achieving *Learnability* and *Efficiency*, our prototype enables users to explore and customize the visualization of the anatomy around the spine (e.g., nerves and blood vessels) as shown in Fig. 1.

In terms of supporting *Feedback*, we decided to keep the user informed at all interaction steps. For instance, visual blinking occurs upon touching critical parts (e.g., nerves) around the spinal bones. We also support visual guidelines and 3D visual trajectory (following [11]) to guide users align insertion landmarks (Fig. 1). This GUI is only shown on-demand to simplify clutter and reflect an adaptive interface. Finally, after completing the procedure, simulation is frozen and ideal interaction paths, as defined by expert surgeons, can be shown for reflection and examination. Those designed features allow novice users to use the simulation without significant back-end technical support or a steep learning curve.

4   VRSpineSim

We propose VRSpineSim (VRSS) as an educational simulation prototype for spinal surgery. VRSpineSim supports visualization of the spinal context, haptic interaction capabilities, and X-ray views for guiding user interaction within the simulation similarly to real operation room (Fig. 1).

4.1   Implementation

We used a machine with Nvidia GTX 980 graphics card, NVIDIA 3D Vision (v2) with active 3D stereoscopic glasses and a 3D monitor from Asus for stereo rendering. For haptic feedback, we first explored Novint Falcon, but it was limiting by only having three degrees of freedom. Thus, we switched to using Touch 3D stylus from 3DS Systems that supports six degrees of freedom and feels more natural with a pen-like interface. For software integration, we used the Unity3D and Geomagic plug-in v1.7 to simplify accessing the haptic device interface.

The 3D patient data we used is organized into sub-models each representing an anatomical category (nerves, bones, etc). In VRSpineSim, a unique material is assigned to each sub-model to enable independent visualization and interaction. Also, special render-to-target cameras are used to enable fluoroscopy (X-ray) visualization of the spinal model (Fig. 1). Finally, haptic feedback is supported by adjusting properties such as stiffness and puncture-level based on user interaction. For example, when a rendered surgical tool collides with the bone, we update the haptic parameters to makes it feel harder or impossible to penetrate the structure, essentially providing the feeling of bone versus soft tissue.

5   Evaluation

We conducted a preliminary study to assess the usability of our prototype as an educational tool especially for supporting novice medical trainees. Our evaluation involved the use of VRSpineSim and ImmersiveTouch[TM] (IT) [7], which is a commercial simulator used in many surgical education-based simulation scenarios [2] including the procedure of PSI.

We implemented a survey and semi-structured interview, and recruited two groups of participants gathering feedback from domain experts and user interface specialists. The first group involved 6 independent surgeons (5M/1F) of varying expertise including junior and senior residents as well as staff neurosurgeons. Two of our medical participants were familiar with the IT simulator, but not with the specific PSI task we focused on. The other group consisted of 6 design experts (3M/3F); computer science grad students working on visualization, design, and/or human-computer interaction.

We used a within-subjects design approach where participants were asked to perform a simplified PSI task on both simulators in randomized sequence to avoid learning bias. Then, participants completed the survey and the post-study interview questions during the one hour study session. The study protocol is identical for both groups, but we asked the design group to additionally complete a system usability questionnaire (SUS) [1] as we wanted their feedback on the interface design of the simulation rather than its context of use.

6   Results and Discussion

Most participants liked the simplified interaction elements of VRSS and regarded our simulation as an educational tool. As one medical participant said, *"If I am a professor, I will get that tool [VRSS] because it is very easy to handle than this one [IT]"*. Also with regards to the capability of VRSS to customize the visualization, one expert expressed, *"having anatomical features that can be manipulated by making some parts transparent may be very beneficial to anatomical education"*. Such positive comments reflect on the potential of our simulator to address the *learnability* factor, and achieve face and content validity.

The medical participants rated how both simulators may support skill transfer to the operating room. The ratings were 4.1 and 4.6 out of 5 for the IT and VRSS respectively. Also, the participants rated key simulation features as reported in Fig. 2, which shows both simulators to be almost identical with slightly better rating of our simulator for most features except the haptic feedback. The design participants who completed the SUS questionnaire reported average scores of 80.41 and 37.5 out of 100 for VRSS and IT respectively. This seemingly large difference in scores is also reflected by qualitative feedback we received, and may reflect better usability and *learnability* of our prototype.

Many participants mentioned the dispersed controls and the various devices for controlling the IT simulator as one of its key limitations, hinting at the difficulty of interacting with it. Another limitation is about how the IT reports post-simulation performance. As one medical expert stated, *"The [performance] measurement [of VRSS] are better than just the [IT] score as it tells us what angle was wrong and it shows us where we entered [the bone] as compared to the ideal trajectory, which is very useful for getting oriented"*. Most participants, however, highlighted that the haptic feedback was more realistic in IT. As another medical participant expressed, *"The haptic feedback [in IT] was not perfect but comparably better than this one [VRSS]"*. We argue that the limited haptics in VRSS is

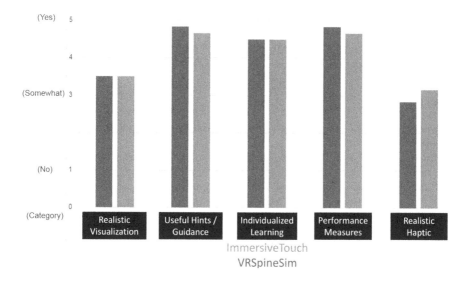

Fig. 2. Rating of simulator features by our medical participants

in part due to the expensive high-quality haptic device of the IT simulator (e.g., roughly 30 times more costly), and because the focus of this work is not about improving the haptic feedback. Nonetheless, we aim as part of our future work to improve our implementation of the haptic feedback. On the positive side, we received various comments about our simulation and the integrated educational elements. For example, one medical participant stated, *"The interactive thing [of VRSS] is quite helpful, with being able to see, I guess, bones and where the nerves are . . . , it just gives you a better idea of the anatomy"*. Such results reflect on the usability aspects of our prototype.

Our study had a small sample size, so we refrain from making any significance claims. We highlight our focus on usability aspects and claim that our approach gives more value to the subjective results received from the domain experts, and this rationale aligns with the argument proposed by Greenberg and Buxton [5].

7   Conclusion and Future Work

We proposed VRSpineSim, a 3D stereoscopic virtual reality spine simulation designed to support surgeons with a convenient environment to learn about and train the procedure of pedicle screw insertion (PSI). Our prototype was developed following an iterative design approach in collaboration with medical experts. We presented a preliminary evaluation highlighting the potential benefits of our 3D simulation in supporting education and training for the PSI spine surgery procedure. We argue that by including educational aids and following the feedback of medical collaborators, as we demonstrated in this work, the usability and the training quality of immersive medical simulation can be improved.

For future work, we are considering the feedback we received, for instance, to support loading and displaying patient-specific data for enhanced contextuality. We also plan to conduct a formal expanded study with more participants and with additional focus on quantitative measurements.

References

1. Brooke, J., et al.: SUS - a quick and dirty usability scale. Usability Eval. Indus. **189**(194), 4–7 (1996)
2. Brunozzi, D., Shakur, S.F., Kwasnicki, A., Ismail, R., Charbel, F.T., Alaraj, A.: Role of immersive touch simulation in neurosurgical training. In: Alaraj, A. (ed.) Comprehensive Healthcare Simulation: Neurosurgery. CHS, pp. 185–198. Springer, Cham (2018). https://doi.org/10.1007/978-3-319-75583-0_14
3. Clark, A.D., Barone, D.G., Candy, N., Guilfoyle, M., et al.: The effect of 3-dimensional simulation on neurosurgical skill acquisition and surgical performance: a review of the literature. Surg. Educ. **74**, 828–836 (2017)
4. Coles, T.R., Meglan, D., et al.: The role of haptics in medical training simulators: a survey of the state of the art. IEEE Trans. Haptics **4**(1), 51–66 (2011)
5. Greenberg, S., Buxton, B.: Usability evaluation considered harmful (some of the time). In: Proceedings of SIGCHI, CHI 2008, pp. 111–120. ACM (2008)
6. Henriksen, K., Patterson, M.D.: Simulation in health care: setting realistic expectations. Patient Saf. **3**(3), 127–134 (2007)
7. ImmersiveTouch: A leader in simulation based surgical training. http://www.immersivetouch.com/ (2017)
8. Klein, S., Whyne, C.M., et al.: CT-based patient-specific simulation software for pedicle screw insertion. Clin. Spine Surg. **22**(7), 502–506 (2009)
9. Mostafa, A.E., Ryu, W.H.A., Takashima, K., et al.: ReflectiveSpineVR: an immersive spine surgery simulation with interaction history capabilities. In: the 5th Symposium on Spatial User Interaction, SUI 2017, pp. 20–29. ACM (2017)
10. Mostafa, A.E., Ryu, W.H.A., et al.: Designing NeuroSimVR: a stereoscopic virtual reality spine surgery simulator. Technical report, University of Calgary (2017)
11. Naddeo, F., Cataldo, E., Naddeo, A., Cappetti, N., Narciso, N.: An automatic and patient-specific algorithm to design the optimal insertion direction of pedicle screws for spine surgery templates. Med. Biol. Eng. Comput. **55**, 1549–1562 (2017)
12. Nielsen, J.: Usability metrics: tracking interface improvements. IEEE Softw. **13**(6), 12 (1996)
13. Pelargos, P.E., Nagasawa, D.T., Lagman, C., Tenn, S., et al.: Utilizing virtual and augmented reality for educational and clinical enhancements in neurosurgery. Clin. Neurosci. **35**, 1–4 (2017)
14. Pfandler, M., Lazarovici, M., Stefan, P., Wucherer, P., Weigl, M.: Virtual reality based simulators for spine surgery: a systematic review. Spine J. **17**, 1352–1363 (2017)
15. Ryu, W.H.A., Mostafa, A.E., Dharampal, N., et al.: Design-based comparison of spine surgery simulators: optimizing educational features of surgical simulators. World Neurosurg. **106**, 870–877 (2017)
16. Schuler, D., Namioka, A.: Participatory Design: Principles and Practices. CRC Press, Boca Raton (1993)
17. Seymour, N.E., Gallagher, A.G., Roman, S.A., et al.: Virtual reality training improves operating room performance: results of a randomized, double-blinded study. Ann. Surg. **236**(4), 458 (2002)

18. Stanney, K.M., Mollaghasemi, M., et al.: Usability engineering of virtual environments (VEs): identifying multiple criteria that drive effective VE system design. Int. J. Hum.-Comput. Stud. **58**(4), 447–481 (2003)
19. Xiang, L., Zhou, Y., Wang, H., et al.: Significance of preoperative planning simulator for junior surgeons' training of pedicle screw insertion. Spinal Disord. Tech. **28**(1), E25–E29 (2015)

Visual Analysis of Bird Moving Patterns

Krešimir Matković[1]([⊠]) [ID], Denis Gračanin[2], Michael Beham[1][ID],
Rainer Splechtna[1], Miriah Meyer[3], and Elena Ginina[1][ID]

[1] VRVis Research Center, Vienna, Austria
{Matkovic,Beham,Splechtna,elena.ginina}@VRVis.at
[2] Virginia Tech, Blacksburg, VA, USA
gracanin@vt.edu
[3] University of Utah, Salt Lake City, UT, USA
miriah@cs.utah.edu

Abstract. In spite of recent advances in data analysis techniques, exploration of complex, unstructured spatial-temporal data could still be difficult. An interactive approach, with human in the analysis loop, represents a valuable add on to automatic analysis methods. We describe an interactive visual analysis method to exploration of complex spatio-temporal data sets. The proposed approach is illustrated using a publicly available data set, a collection of bird locations recorded over an extended period of time. In order to explore and comprehend complex patterns in bird movements over time, we provide two new views, the centroids scatter plot view and the distance plot view. Successful analysis of the birds data indicates the usefulness of the newly proposed approach for other spatio-temporal data of a similar structure.

Keywords: Visual analytics · Spatio-temporal data ·
Patterns in movement data

1 Introduction

Recent technology advancements make it easier than ever to capture or generate complex data. The same is the case about the analysis techniques. Still, when it comes to analyzing complex, unstructured data, readily available algorithms and techniques are not always present. In this paper, we introduce an interactive visual exploration tool for analyzing complex spatial-temporal data. The data set used to exemplify our approach originates from the IEEE VAST Challenge 2018—Mini-Challenge 1 [7] and consists of a local bird songs collection recorded over several decades. However, the same approach could be applied to other data sets with a similar structure.

Our data set consists of recordings of bird positions for 19 different bird species, taken at specific place and time, over a period of 32 years. The analysts are interested in patterns of bird movements. In order to meet the analysts' needs, we deploy an interactive visual analysis solution, relying on the well known

© Springer Nature Switzerland AG 2019
M. Gavrilova et al. (Eds.): CGI 2019, LNCS 11542, pp. 388–394, 2019.
https://doi.org/10.1007/978-3-030-22514-8_35

coordinated multiple views paradigm, and exploiting exploratory capabilities of human analysts. We describe the entire workflow, from raw data processing to the final analysis. We also describe and justify our design decisions. Two new views are introduced, the centroids scatter plot view and the distance plot. Along the new views we also extensively use standard views such as histograms or scatter-plots. The scatter-plots are enriched by descriptive statistics in order to make the analysis results easier to communicate.

The main contributions of the paper can be summarized as follows: (1) analysis workflow including discussion on the decisions made during the design process, (2) two new views integrated into a coordinated multiple views system—the centroids scatter plot view and the distance plot view.

2   Related Work

We deploy interactive visualization techniques and use coordinated multiple views extensively [11]. The spatio-temporal context is made feasible by a number of technologies, such as Global Positioning System (GPS), Radio-frequency identification tags (RFID), and mobile phones. A widespread use of these technologies resulted in ability to collect large amounts of location and mobility data. A comprehensive coverage of the analysis of movement data is provided in [1].

Chen et al. [2] provide a survey of traffic visualization system to analyze large amounts of spatio-temporal multi-dimensional traffic trajectory data. Cibulski et al. [3] present an integrated solution for interactive visual analysis and exploration of events along trajectories data. Orellana et al. [9] describe automatic analysis of visitor movement patterns in natural recreational areas.

Ferreira et al. [4] describe BirdVis, an interactive visualization system that supports the analysis of spatio-temporal bird distribution models. Ferreira et al. [5] discuss exploration of taxi traffic using a visual query model that allows users to quickly select data slices and explore large amounts of spatio-temporal data.

In this paper we focus on understanding on patterns of movement. We do not have birds trajectories, just information on positions collected in large time intervals.

3   Data and Tasks

The data we are dealing with presents a fictitious scenario of possible endangerment of the Rose-crested blue pipit, a beloved bird species living in the Mistford natural Preserve [7]. Recent disclosures indicate an alarming reduction of the birds' nesting pairs and point out to the local manufacturing company Kasios, as a possible culprit. Kasios denies any fault and supplies a collection of bird calls/songs, consisting of 15 anonymous audio files, for which the company claims to be records of healthy pipits taken only recently among the preserve. On the other hand, the Mistford College provides a large collection of bird calls/songs from all over the Preserve that has been inspected by various ornithology groups to confirm accurate identifications. To find out whether the two collections are consistent and if the claims of the alleged company are credible, further investigation is needed.

The collection provided by the Mistford College describes the 19 known bird species living in the Wildlife Preserve, and consists of recordings that were made during the period 1986–2018. The relevant data is assembled in a large csv file and includes information about the type of the recording (call or song), position, date, and time of the recordings, as well as their quality.

In this particular case, the main analysis tasks are to find and characterize any patterns of the bird species, and to check if Kasios claims are plausible. In a more general case, the analysis tasks can be abstracted as:

1. Characterize movements of items of interest (persons, animals, objects, ...) in space and time.
2. Compare and analyse selected cases.

In order to analyze data, we have to structure it somehow. As a recording represents an item of interest in our case, we decided to structure the data so that each record corresponds to a recording. The record contains all data provided as well as derived data which is necessary for the analysis. In the beginning, the meta data is cleaned, and various additional attributes are derived. For example, the angle of sunlight (differentiating daylight and night), or centroids of birds positions per year, represent some of the derived data. We describe the new views along with design requirements and justifications in the next section.

4   Visualization Design

In order to support identified tasks, the following requirements on the visualization can be abstracted:

R1. Show spatial distribution of recordings.
R2. Enable comparison of different species.
R3. Enable temporal comparisons.
R4. Examine temporal changes for different species.

We describe the newly introduced views which are designed to fulfil above listed requirements.

4.1   Centroids Scatter Plot View

The identified analysis tasks mostly correspond to the analysis tasks which are usually solved with a scatter plot [12]. Therefore, we choose a scatter plot as an underlying design of our centroids scatter plot view. The first step is depicting all recordings in a scatter plot (Fig. 1a). We see that the birds are recorded all around the natural preserve area, but we don't know anything about their individual species or years of the recordings. The first, straight forward approach,

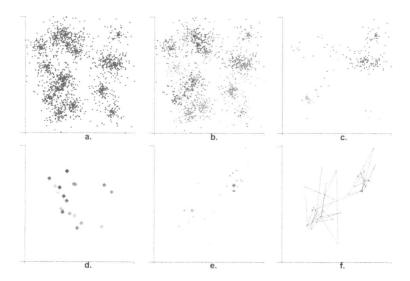

Fig. 1. Evolution of the centroids scatter plot. (a) All audio recordings shown at once. Clusters are clearly seen, but there is no notion of individual bird species or temporal component. (b) Color coding of individual bird species solves the species problem. Due to over-plotting it is hard to see individual bird species. (c) Filtering helps, only Rose-crested blue pipit and Blue-collared zipper are shown. (d) A centroid for each bird species is computed. (e) A centroid for each year and bird species is computed. Only two bird species are shown. (f) Yearly centroids are connected based on time.

is to color the points (recording locations) corresponding to the recorded bird species (Fig. 1b).

There are 19 different bird species, so choosing an easily distinguishable color scheme is not easy. We used the Colorbrewer tool [6] to select 19 colors. Further, following the design guidelines proposed by Lin et al. [8] we have tried to mach the colors with bird names. We assign orange to the Orange-Pine-Plover, e.g. With 19 bird species it is still not easy to have a mental map of all color mappings. If we drill down to several bird species it becomes much simpler to relate them to the names if colors are semantically assigned. Figure 1c shows data for Rose-Crested-Blue-Pipit and Blue-Collared-Zipper only. Due to the semantic mapping it is clear which points correspond to which species.

Showing all recordings, even for a subset of bird species cannot help us in spotting spatial or temporal trends. We augment the scatter plot with centroids. They are simply computed as average x and y coordinates of individual record-ings. In addition, we compute centroids for each of the years separately. These centroids make it possible to see the moving trends. It is also possible to compute monthly centroids, if movements within a year and not over many years are of interest. Figures 1d and e show yearly and monthly centroids.

The centroids scatter plot view is integrated in a coordinated multiple views environment. It is easy to drill down by means of composite brushing in all views. Figure 1f shows Rose-Crested-Blue-Pipit yearly centroids as context, and last three years (2016, 2017, and 2018) as context.

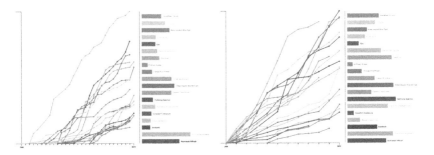

Fig. 2. Left: The newly introduced distance plot view shows how much do centroids move (in absolute amount) from year to year. We see significant differences in the total amount moved, and we see different patterns—some centroids change position every year, while some remain almost constant for some periods in time. Right: The change of position is depicted from month to month. The January centroid, e.g., represents an average of all Januaries in the data set. (Color figure online)

4.2 Distance Plot View

Visualizing the centroid trails helps to see the moving pattern. However, it is not yet easy to see which bird species move more and which move less. In order to further support spatio-temporal patterns analysis we design the distance plot view. The main idea is to depict movement of a centroid over years. Only absolute distance to the previous year is shown.

Figure 2 left shows the distance plot view for all bird species from 1986 until 2018. If the yearly centroids would have remained at the same position for a certain bird species, the corresponding line would be horizontal. The slope of the line correlates with the distance which a centroid moved. We can clearly see the grouping of distance lines. We also can see changes that happen for some bird species—significant differences in line slopes.

Figure 2 right shows the months based distance plot view. We see how the average position changes from month to month. The bird species that moved the most on the monthly bases is that Darkwing-Sparrow (red line). At the same time this bird species moves very little on the yearly basis. We could reason that it moves a lot from month to month, but the movement patterns remain the same over the years.

4.3 Overall System

As stated above, the new views are integrated in a coordinated multiple views solution. In addition to the new views, it is also possible to deploy standard views such as histograms or scatter plots, for example.

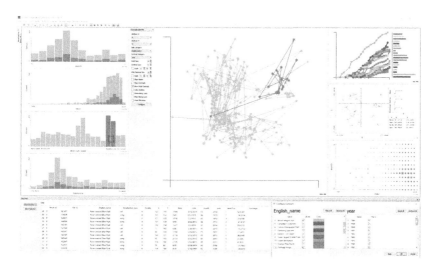

Fig. 3. A screenshot from an analysis session. The histograms on the left show the meta data and can be used for an efficient drill-down during the analysis. The centroids scatter plot view is shown in the middle. The views on the right show different aspects of the data. The table at the bottom shows details for the brushed audio recordings. The view in the lower right corner is used to filter bird species and years of interest.

Figure 3 shows a screenshot from an analysis session. It reassembles the most used view configuration. On the left, four histograms show the months when recordings are taken, the years, bird species names, and sunlight angle. These four views are often use for brushing. Composite brushing is also supported, which makes creation of complex queries fast and intuitive. In the picture two bird species are selected in the histogram.

The newly proposed centroid scatter plot view is placed in the middle of the screen. As this is the central view, it gets the most of the screen space and a dominant position. There are three additional views on the right hand side. The distance view on top, the statistics scatter plot inspired by work of Radoš et al. [10], shows statistics and bounding rectangle of brushed data. Finally, the scatter plot in the lower right corner shows years (x-axis) and months (y-axis) of all recordings. The size of point corresponds to the recording count for certain months. It is easy to see how frequency of recordings changes over time.

Using the new system we have identified several interesting patterns. Green-Tipped-Scarlet-Pipit, for example, has been recorded all over the preserve. Ordinary Snape and Qax are the bird species which do not move much. Scrawny-Jay bird species lives basically at two locations. We could not find a temporal pattern which would correspond to those two locations, so we reason that there are two communities of the Scrawny-Jay in the preserve. We also noticed that some bird species do not appear between October and January (cold months). There are less recordings in these months for most of the bird species. Two exceptions are Qax and Carries-Champagne-Pipit since these two bird species are recorded more often in cold months. As we have no information about the location of the preserve, we can only reason that this seasonal variations are due to bird species which leave the preserve in winter.

5   Conclusions

We described an interactive visual analysis workflow for spatio-temporal recordings. Two new views were designed and implemented to supported the analysis workflow, the centroids scatter plot view and the distance plot view. The interactive visualization makes it possible to efficiently explore the data and helps the analysts to create a mental model of birds' moving patterns. Due to the complexity and different granularity of the data (monthly or yearly cycles, for example), an interactive visual exploration speeds up the analysis process significantly.

Acknowledgements. VRVis is funded by BMVIT, BMDW, Styria, SFG and Vienna Business Agency in the scope of COMET - Competence Centers for Excellent Technologies (854174) which is managed by FFG.

References

1. Andrienko, G., Andrienko, N., Bak, P., Keim, D., Wrobel, S.: Visual Analytics of Movement. Springer, Berlin (2013). https://doi.org/10.1007/978-3-642-37583-5
2. Chen, W., Guo, F., Wang, F.Y.: A survey of traffic data visualization. IEEE Trans. Intell. Transp. Syst. **16**(6), 2970–2984 (2015)
3. Cibulski, L., et al.: ITEA-interactive trajectories and events analysis. Vis. Comput. **32**(6), 847–857 (2016)
4. Ferreira, N., et al.: BirdVis: visualizing and understanding bird populations. IEEE Trans. Visual. Comput. Graph. **17**(12), 2374–2383 (2011)
5. Ferreira, N., Poco, J., Vo, H.T., Freire, J., Silva, C.T.: Visual exploration of big spatio-temporal urban data: a study of New York city taxi trips. IEEE Trans. Visual. Comput. Graph. **19**(12), 2149–2158 (2013)
6. Harrower, M., Brewer, C.A.: ColorBrewer.org: an online tool for selecting colour schemes for maps. Cartograph. J. **40**(1), 27–37 (2003)
7. IEEE VIS 2018 Conference: VAST Challenge 2018: Mini-challenge 1 (2018). http://www.vacommunity.org/VAST+Challenge+2018+MC1
8. Lin, S., Fortuna, J., Kulkarni, C., Stone, M., Heer, J.: Selecting semantically-resonant colors for data visualization. Comput. Graph. Forum **32**(3), 401–410 (2013)
9. Orellana, D., Bregt, A.K., Ligtenberg, A., Wachowicz, M.: Exploring visitor movement patterns in natural recreational areas. Tour. Manag. **33**(3), 672–682 (2012)
10. Radoš, S., Splechtna, R., Matković, K., Djuras, M., Gröller, E., Hauser, H.: Towards quantitative visual analytics with structured brushing and linked statistics. Comput. Graph. Forum **35**(3), 251–260 (2016)
11. Roberts, J.C.: State of the art: coordinated amp; multiple views in exploratory visualization. In: Fifth International Conference on Coordinated and Multiple Views in Exploratory Visualization (CMV 2007) (2007)
12. Sarikaya, A., Gleicher, M.: Scatterplots: tasks, data, and designs. IEEE Trans. Visual. Comput. Graph. **24**(1), 402–412 (2018)

GAN with Pixel and Perceptual Regularizations for Photo-Realistic Joint Deblurring and Super-Resolution

Yong Li[1], Zhenguo Yang[1,2(✉)], Xudong Mao[3], Yong Wang[1(✉)],
Qing Li[3], Wenyin Liu[1(✉)], and Ying Wang[1]

[1] School of Computer Science and Technology,
Guangdong University of Technology, Guangzhou, China
yonglicutter@gmail.com, yzgcityu@gmail.com,
13928887919@126.com, liuwy@gdut.edu.cn,
1625748226@qq.com
[2] Department of Computer Science, City University of Hong Kong,
Kowloon, Hong Kong
[3] Department of Computing, The Hong Kong Polytechnic University,
Hong Kong, China
xudong.xdmao@gmail.com, csqli@comp.polyu.edu.hk

Abstract. In this paper, we propose a Generative Adversarial Network with Pixel and Perceptual regularizations, denoted as P^2GAN, to restore single motion blurry and low-resolution images jointly into clear and high-resolution images. It is an end-to-end neural network consisting of deblurring module and super-resolution module, which repairs degraded pixels in the motion-blur images firstly, and then outputs the deblurred images and deblurred features for further reconstruction. More specifically, the proposed P^2GAN integrates pixel-wise loss in pixel-level, contextual loss and adversarial loss in perceptual level simultaneously, in order to guide on deblurring and super-resolution reconstruction of the raw images that are blurry and in low-resolution, which help obtaining realistic images. Extensive experiments conducted on a real-world dataset manifest the effectiveness of the proposed approaches, outperforming the state-of-the-art models.

Keywords: Image deblurring · Super-resolution · GANs · Pixel loss · Contextual loss

1 Introduction

In reality, the low-quality images are not limited to just one case and can be more complex. There exists a little work can deal with both low-resolution and blurry images jointly. Some works [3–5] indicate that if we simply concatenate a deblurring module and a super-resolution module sequentially, the output images will be deteriorated. To this end, Zhang et al. [4] proposed a seminal work with a deep encoder-decoder network (ED-DSRN) for joint images deblurring and super-resolution. However, they focus on low-resolution images degraded by uniform Gaussian blur, which may not be

© Springer Nature Switzerland AG 2019
M. Gavrilova et al. (Eds.): CGI 2019, LNCS 11542, pp. 395–401, 2019.
https://doi.org/10.1007/978-3-030-22514-8_36

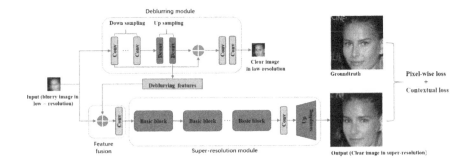

(a)   Generator

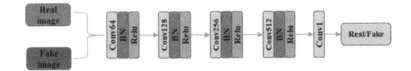

(b)   Discriminator

Fig. 1. Overview of the framework.

effective in motion-blurred images. Furthermore, the authors proposed Gated Fusion Network (GFN) [5] to focus on images degraded by motion blur, which achieves the state-of-the-art performance on GOPRO dataset.

Although some works using pixel-wise loss like GFN achieve quite high PSNR scores, the output images may be seemed to be vague in practice. As pointed out by some researchers [9, 12, 13], the improvement on reconstruction accuracy like pixel-wise loss, is not always accompanied with improvement in visual quality. A main reason may be that the pixel-wise loss doesn't have much correlation with semantic similarity among images.

In this work, we propose an end-to-end neural network for joint deblurring and super-resolution, denoted as P²GAN which is showed in Fig. 1. Figure 1a shows the Generator and Fig. 1b shows the Discriminator. Instead of concatenating deblurring and super-resolution models in a straight-forward manner, P²GAN firstly deblurrs the input images and extracts the deblurring features in the deblurring module. Furthermore, images and deblurring features are concatenated, which are used as the input of the super-resolution module. To generate realistic images with low distortion and high perceptual quality, we integrate pixel loss, contextual loss [14, 15], and adversarial loss to train the network. The main contributions of this paper are summarized in two aspects:

(1) We devise a neural network for joint deblurring and super-resolution integrates contextual loss, pixel-wise loss and adversarial loss simultaneously, and can be trained in an end-to-end manner.

(2) We propose to exploit both raw images and deblurring features achieved with the guidance of multiple loss terms, and unify the deblurring and super-resolution modules in a framework.

2 Related Work

The aforementioned approaches improve the quality of images focusing on either deblurring or super-resolution, while the low-quality images in practice may be more complicated. Michaeli et al. [11] proposed a framework to deblur and conducted super-resolution on the images suffering from simple blurry kernel simultaneously. Xu et al. [3] proposed deconvolution layers to up-sample the feature maps during extracting deblurring features and used Generative Adversarial Networks to train the network, denoted as SCGAN. However, it can only deal with images or texts suffering from simple blurry kernels, due to the limitation of simplicity of the network structure. Zhang et al. [4] proposed a deep encoder-decoder network, denote as EDDSRN, for joint image deblurring and super-resolution. This network is only effective for the images degraded by uniform Gaussian blur. Furthermore, the authors proposed Gated Fusion Network (GFN), which separated consisting of deblurring feature-extraction and super-resolution-extraction into two modules. GFN has achieved the state-of-the-art performance on solving non-uniform motion deblurring and generic single-image super-resolution. However, it may not be effective when for reconstructing the severely blurry images. Moreover, GFN only uses single pixel-wise loss to train the network, which results in vague images.

3 Methodology

In this section, we introduce the proposed neural network, followed by the introduction on loss terms being used for training.

Like regular Generative Adversarial Networks (GANs), the proposed P^2GAN consists of a Generator and a Discriminator as shown in Fig. 1, where the Generator consists of two components, i.e., a deblurring module and a super-resolution module. The Discriminator aims to distinguish the generated images from the real images. More specifically, the main modules are detailed as follows.

(1) Deblurring Module in Generator. Inspired by [5], we adopt an asymmetric residual encoder-decoder architecture, which extracts effective features of motion deblurring images. In particular, the input images in the context of joint deblurring and super-resolution are low-resolution and blurry images.

(2) Super-resolution Module in Generator. Instead of using the input images directly, we integrate the input images with the features extracted by the deblurring module together, and adopt the neural network similar to the Enhanced Super-Resolution Generative Adversarial Networks (ESRGAN) [10], which uses the structure of Residual-in-Residual Dense Block (RRDB). In order to preserve the feature information of the original images, we take both the input images and features extracted by the deblurring module as the input of the super-resolution module.

(3) Loss Terms. The Generator of P^{2}GAN exploits pixel-wise loss, contextual loss and adversarial loss jointly. The Discriminator of P^{2}GAN tries to distinguish the generated images from the real images, and guides on training the Generator, which is the thought of adversarial training. For implementations, we add Batch Normalization (BN) after each convolution layer and use leakyRelu as the activation function except for the last layer as shown in Fig. 1b.

In summary, combining with the pixel-wise loss, contextual loss, and adversarial loss in the previous subsections, the objection of the Generator in the proposed P^{2}GAN can be summarized as follows:

$$L(G) = \lambda_{CX} \cdot L_{CX} + \lambda_{pixel} \cdot L_{pixel} + \lambda_{GAN} \cdot L_{GA} \tag{1}$$

where L_{CX}, L_{pixel}, L_{GA} denote the contextual loss, pixel-wise loss and adversarial loss respectively and λ_{CX}, λ_{pixel}, λ_{GAN} denote the weights of each loss.

4   Experiments

In this section, we introduce our training details and analyze the experimental results on a real-world dataset.

4.1   Baseline

The baselines include the seminal work on joint deblurring and super-resolution, i.e., GFN, and its variants. Intuitively, the task of joint deblurring and super-resolution can be addressed by a deblurring model [2, 5] and then a super-resolution model [6, 10], and vice versa. Therefore, we compare the proposed P^{2}GAN with the approaches by combining the different models directly, such as DB [2] + SR [10], SR [10] + DB [2], DB [2] + SR [6], etc., thus we have eight more baselines. In addition, to show the difference between the proposed P^{2}GAN and GFN, we extend GFN with combining multiple loss terms like P^{2}GAN, i.e., pixel-wise loss, contextual loss, and adversarial loss, and we denote it as GFN++ for comparisons.

4.2   Dataset

We evaluate the performance of the above approaches on the CelebA dataset, and use center cropping method to crop the images to the size of 128 × 128. We use blurred algorithm provided in [1] to generate motion blurred images. Furthermore, we use bicubic interpolation to down sample both blurred images and target images for 4 times to gain the 32 × 32 blurred images as the input of model. In addition, the 32 × 32 sharp images can be used as the target images of deblurring model for calculating the deblurring loss.

4.3   Experimental Results

To show the effectiveness of the proposed P²GAN, we conduct both qualitative and quantitative evaluations.

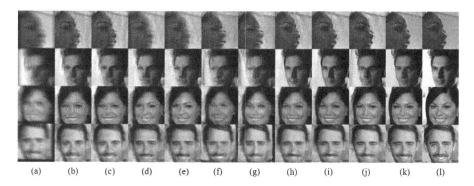

    (a)   (b)   (c)   (d)   (e)   (f)   (g)   (h)   (i)   (j)   (k)   (l)

Fig. 2. Examples of output images by the approaches. Columns (a) are input images, columns (b) to (k) are the output images of DB [5] + SR [10], DB [5] + SR [6], DB [2] + SR [10], DB [2] + SR [6], SR [10] + DB [5], SR [6] + DB [5], SR [10] + DB [2], SR [6] + DB [2], GFN, the proposed P²GAN, and column (l) are groundtruth images, respectively. Note that the input images are both in low-resolution and blurry, and we use Nearest Interpolation to scale them to 128 × 128 for visualizations.

Qualitative Evaluations. Intuitively, we visualize some examples of images generated by the approaches in Fig. 2, from which we can conclude some observations. Firstly, the eight approaches (from (b) to (i)) using the combinations of deblurring and super-resolution models are not in high quality, suffering from problems like distortion and vagueness. In contrast, GFN and the proposed P²GAN achieve high-quality images, benefiting from the joint training of the modules for deblurring and super-resolution. Secondly, the P²GAN outperforms the baselines, benefiting from the integration of the pixel and perceptual regularizations with GANs.

As mentioned above, we extend GFN by incorporating both pixel level and perceptual level regularization, i.e., pixel-wise loss, contextual loss, and adversarial loss, denoted as GFN++. The examples of the images obtained by GFN++ and our P²GAN are shown in Fig. 3. From the figures, we can observe that vagueness has almost vanished in the images generated by GFN++, while there may exist some downgraded pixels that are enlarged, causing some noise in the images. In contrast, our P²GAN works well and generates more natural images.

Quantitative Evaluations. As discussed by [7], though the PSNR values of two image pairs are the same, their degree of distortion may be different. Therefore, we use SSIM as a metric considering the degree of distortion. In addition, we use NRQM [8] as a metric to measure perceptual quality.

The Image Quality Assessment (IQA) on the approaches are summarized in Table 1, from which we can conclude some observations. Firstly, the images generated by the sequential-deblur-super-resolution networks or vice versa usually achieve low performance, and the images are in low quality as shown in Fig. 2. Secondly, P^{2}GAN obtains the realistic images in high perceptual quality, and decreases the distortion.

(a) Input   (b) GFN++   (c) P^{2}GAN   (d) Groundtruth

Fig. 3. Examples of the images obtained by the approaches.

Table 1. IQA on the approaches

Method	Loss term	SSIM	NRQM
DB [5] + SR [10]	The same as the references	0.7133	4.5718
DB [5] + SR [6]		0.7484	3.5883
DB [2] + SR [10]		0.7065	4.5525
DB [2] + SR [6]		0.7436	3.4643
SR [10] + DB [5]		0.6767	3.7051
SR [6] + DB [5]		0.7052	3.5005
SR [10] + DB [2]		0.7309	4.7258
SR [6] + DB [2]		0.7723	3.8856
GFN	L_{pixel}	**0.7792**	3.6848
GFN++	$L_{pixel} + L_{CX} + L_A$	0.7268	6.2855
P^{2}GAN	$L_{pixel} + L_{CX} + L_A$	0.7480	**6.3641**

5 Conclusion

In this paper, we propose a neural network for joint images deblurring and super-resolution, which integrates pixel-wise loss, contextual loss, and adversarial loss from the perspectives of pixels and perception. With the guidance of the multiple loss terms that can be optimized in an end-to-end manner, we can generate realistic and high-quality images from the low-quality images that are blurry and in low-resolution. Both qualitative and quantitative evaluations have been conducted on a real-world dataset. The experimental results show the effectiveness of the proposed approach for the current task.

Acknowledgment. This work is supported by the National Natural Science Foundation of China (No. 61703109, No. 91748107), and the Guangdong Innovative Research Team Program (No. 2014ZT05G157).

References

1. Kupyn, O., Budzan, V., Mykhailych, M., Mishkin, D., Matas, J.: Deblurgan: blind motion deblurring using conditional adversarial networks. In: Proceedings of the IEEE Conference on Computer Vision and Pattern Recognition, pp. 8183–8192 (2018)
2. Tao, X., Gao, H., Shen, X., Wang, J., Jia, J.: Scale-recurrent network for deep image deblurring. In: Proceedings of the IEEE Conference on Computer Vision and Pattern Recognition, pp. 8174–8182 (2018)
3. Xu, X., Sun, D., Pan, J., Zhang, Y., Pfister, H., Yang, M.H.: Learning to super-resolve blurry face and text images. In: Proceedings of the IEEE Conference on Computer Vision and Pattern Recognition, pp. 251–260 (2017)
4. Zhang, X., Wang, F., Dong, H., Guo, Y.: A deep encoder-decoder networks for joint deblurring and super-resolution. In: 2018 IEEE International Conference on Acoustics, Speech and Signal Processing (ICASSP), pp. 1448–1452. IEEE (2018)
5. Zhang, X., Dong, H., Hu, Z., Lai, W.S., Wang, F., Yang, M.H.: Gated fusion network for joint image deblurring and super-resolution. arXiv preprint arXiv:1807.10806 (2018)
6. Li, J., Fang, F., Mei, K., Zhang, G.: Multi-scale residual network for image super-resolution. In: Proceedings of the European Conference on Computer Vision (ECCV), pp. 517–532 (2018)
7. Wang, Z., Bovik, A.C., Sheikh, H.R., Simoncelli, E.P.: Image quality assessment: from error visibility to structural similarity. IEEE Trans. Image Process. **13**(4), 600–612 (2004)
8. Ma, C., Yang, C.Y., Yang, X., Yang, M.H.: Learning a no-reference quality metric for single-image super-resolution. Comput. Vis. Image Underst. **158**, 1–16 (2017)
9. Ledig, C., et al.: Photo-realistic single image super-resolution using a generative adversarial network. arXiv preprint (2017)
10. Wang, X., et al.: ESRGAN: enhanced super-resolution generative adversarial networks. In: Leal-Taixé, L., Roth, S. (eds.) ECCV 2018. LNCS, vol. 11133, pp. 63–79. Springer, Cham (2019). https://doi.org/10.1007/978-3-030-11021-5_5
11. Michaeli, T., Irani, M.: Nonparametric blind super-resolution. In: Proceedings of the IEEE International Conference on Computer Vision, pp. 945–952 (2013)
12. Blau, Y., Michaeli, T.: The perception-distortion tradeoff. In: CVPR (2017)
13. Zhang, R., Isola, P., Efros, A.A., Shechtman, E., Wang, O.: The unreasonable effectiveness of deep features as a perceptual metric. arXiv preprint (2018)
14. Mechrez, R., Talmi, I., Zelnik-Manor, L.: The contextual loss for image transformation with non-aligned data. arXiv preprint arXiv:1803.02077 (2018)
15. Mechrez, R., Talmi, I., Shama, F., Zelnik-Manor, L.: Maintaining natural image statistics with the contextual loss. arXiv preprint arXiv:1803.04626 (2018)

Realistic Pedestrian Simulation Based on the Environmental Attention Model

Di Jiao[1,2], Tianyu Huang[1,2(✉)] (iD), Gangyi Ding[1,2] (iD), and Yiran Du[1,2]

[1] Beijing Institute of Technology, Beijing 100081, China
huangtianyu@bit.edu.cn
[2] Beijing Key Lab of Digital Performance and Simulation Technology,
Beijing 100081, China

Abstract. This paper addresses the problem of crowd simulation while maintaining the attention behaviors. We set up an environmental attention model, which simulates various attention targets of virtual characters influenced by the surrounding environment. According to the investigation and analysis of crowd behaviors, the virtual character attention attributes are divided into the intrinsic attributes and the attention tendency. Based on the various environmental attributes and character attributes, the attention target of a virtual character can be calculated during the walk. Different attention targets lead to different moving heads' behaviors of characters with different attributes. In this way, we implement the attention individualization of virtual characters, and thereby, improve the diversity of crowd animation.

Keywords: Environmental attention model · Crowd animation · Crowd diversification · Realistic pedestrian simulation

1 Introduction

Crowd simulation is a study of the collective behavior of people in real life and the simulation of virtual characters in computer [1]. The particularity of individuals in a crowd, that is, crowd diversity, has become one of the research focuses of crowd simulation methods. In Computer Graphics, crowd diversity includes appearance diversity and animation diversity. However, in terms of the diversity of crowd animation, current methods are mostly aimed at the simulation of the diversity of virtual characters' own behavior, while ignoring the impact of environment on individuals. In both environmental psychology and environmental behavior science, it is pointed out that the environment has an important impact on human behaviors. However, there is a lack of related research in the field of crowd simulation.

This paper mainly focuses on the study of simulation of the influence of the surrounding environment on individuals during the movement. We simulated different head movements and behaviors of different pedestrians according to the environment and personal preferences. Through investigation and analysis, we set up an Environment Attention Mode, and proposed a crowd simulation method based on the environmental attention model. Because virtual characters had different personalities, the gazing targets were different, which improved the randomness and diversity of

© Springer Nature Switzerland AG 2019
M. Gavrilova et al. (Eds.): CGI 2019, LNCS 11542, pp. 402–409, 2019.
https://doi.org/10.1007/978-3-030-22514-8_37

behaviors, thereby improving the realism of crowd simulation. The experiment showed that this method can be applied in the scene of large-scale crowd simulation, such as the crowd background in the production of movies.

2 Related Work

Crowd simulation includes construction of crowd simulation systems and simulation of virtual characters. Many researchers have constructed systems using different methods [2–4]. The crowd diversity includes appearance diversity and animation diversity [5]. Jonathan et al. improved the color diversity of characters by adjusting appearance colors [6]. Referring to Laban Movement Analysis and psychologically validated OCEAN personality factors, Funda et al. developed an expressive human motion generation system [7]. Jason et al. constructed a crowd evacuation simulation tool under the influence of emotional infection [8]. Helena and Daniel proposed a framework which added gaze attention behaviors to crowd animations [9].

In 1970, Harold M. proposed the concept of environmental psychology [10]. It studied the relationship between the environment and human psychological activities. Environment-behavior study is the science which studies the interrelationship between human behaviors and the surrounding environment [11]. According to environmental psychology and environment-behavior studies, both the natural and social environment have an important impact on human behaviors [12].

In recent years, group animation has been applied in the fields of film, 3D games. For example, large-scale group scenes appear in movies and animations such as Zootopia and Coco. Behind these shocking scenes is the technical support of the group animation. However, the animation in films and TVs created by existing group animation methods still needs the fine adjustment by animators. Despite all these, the behaviors of virtual characters still lack of autonomy. Our work makes a step in attention behaviors of virtual characters autonomously.

3 Environmental Attention Model

In general, pedestrians will gaze at something when the line of sight is affected by the surrounding environment during the walk. We take various factors into account and build the environmental attention model. The interest that pedestrians have in the surrounding environment is defined as environmental attention. The degree of pedestrians' interest in environmental factors is the degree of environmental attention. The environmental object that attracts the character is the attention target. During a strolling process, the pedestrian's attention target is mainly determined by the character's attributes, environment attributes and the distance. Therefore, we obtain the original function of the environmental attention model, and we summarize our environmental attention force F as: $F = f(\delta, \mu, \sigma)$, where δ is the character attribute, μ is the environmental attribute, and σ is the attention distance coefficient.

3.1   Characters Attention Tendency

The tendency of having an interest in the environment is called attention tendency, which is related to the individual's personality, etc. The virtual character attribute definition is expressed as: $\delta = g(a, t)$. δ is the character attribute. Here, intrinsic attribute a contains the character factors of the gender, personality, etc. Attention tendency t contains the attention tendency to factors of static environment, dynamic environment and the small-scale group. The personality factor is derived from the five-factor model (OCEAN). The currently definition is in the NEO-P1 test manual [13]. The Personality-Effort matrix NPE applied is defined by Funda et al. [3].

Based on our investigation, according to the characteristics of the environmental factors and the states of the character, the attention tendency are classified into three categories: the attention tendency α for the static environment, such as buildings; the attention tendency β for the dynamic environment such as street performers; the attention tendency γ of the small-scale group which the character is located. We construct the attention tendency t as $t = \{\alpha, \beta, \gamma\}$. Buildings are the representative of the static environment. $\alpha = \{\alpha_1, \alpha_2\}$, α_1, $\alpha_2 \in [0, 10]$, where α_1, α_2 respectively represent the character's attention tendency for functional and appearance attributes. According to the occurrence possibility of dynamic factors, β has two categories: the tendency β_1 for ordinary factors, and β_2 for unconventional factors. $\beta = \{\beta_1, \beta_2\}$, β_1, $\beta_2 \in [0, 10]$. In addition, when a character is in a small-scale group, its attention tendency can be affected by the group. γ is escribed as the internal tendency γ_1 and the external tendency γ_2. $\gamma = \{\gamma_1, \gamma_2\}$, γ_1, $\gamma_2 \in [-1, 0]$, and $\gamma_2 \in [0, 1]$. γ_1 is the tendency of reducing the character's attention to the environment. For example, conversations could reduce their attention to the outside world. γ_2 is the increasing tendency. If someone in the group points to something, others will have a stronger tendency for it. Their summation result is the attention tendency γ.

3.2   Environmental Attention Force

In daily life, many things attract pedestrians, and people gaze at the most interesting thing. Meanwhile they are more likely to notice the closer things. As a result, there is a negative correlation between the environmental attention and the attention distance. The formulation of the environmental attention force is $F = \boldsymbol{max}\{\delta * \mu_i * \sigma\}$, where δ is the character attribute. μ_i are the environmental attributes corresponding to the related attributes in δ, $i \in [1, n]$, and n is the count of environmental factors. σ is the attention distance coefficient. After the calculation, the attention degree of each environmental factor corresponds to the rank of its attention value. For example, the thing with the highest attention value has the highest attention degree. And it will be the current attention target. If the attention value reaches the threshold, the character will complete a series of behaviors such as the gaze.

3.3   Attention Distance

The attention distance coefficient represents the influence degree of the attention distance on virtual characters. In general, the closer the object is to the character, the greater the influence on the character, and the greater the distance coefficient. The distance can be an Euclidean distance S or an egocentric distance D [15]. Assume that all things within the scope of the character's eyesight in the virtual environment can be attention targets. $S = |p_c - p_t|$, $\sigma = S^{-1}$, where p_c is the character's current position and p_t is the position of the target. The egocentric distance refers to the estimated judgment of people on the distance between themselves and a target, and $D = S * A/(A + S)$, where A is the farthest distance the observer can perceive [14]. In this way, $\sigma = 1 - \left(\frac{S}{A+S}\right)$. Using the attention distance, the closer the target, the greater the weight it occupies in the psychology of the character, and vice versa.

4 Surveys and Analysis of Pedestrians' Environmental Attention Tendency

The questionnaire survey named pedestrians' attention tendency in the city environment was conducted on the street and online. We added the pictures to the online survey. For static environmental factors, functional attributes were shopping malls, etc.; appearance attributes were color, etc. According to the results, shopping malls were the easiest to be noticed. The top three static factors were malls, restaurants, and supermarkets. Pedestrians' intrinsic attributes had less impact on the attention tendency of functional attributes. Instead, as shown in Table 1, it had a certain influence on the attention tendency of appearance attributes:

Table 1. Pedestrians' attention tendency to appearance attributes in different genders and ages

Gender	Male				Female			
Attribute	Age							
	12–18	19–44	45–60	61–75	12–18	19–44	45–60	61–75
Bright color (%)	2.1	42.3	39.4	8.1	1.9	39.7	36.9	6.3
Dark color (%)	0.2	3.1	3.3	1.5	0.3	6.8	6.7	1.4
High (%)	1.9	42.7	40.1	8.3	1.8	43.3	39.8	7.2
Short (%)	0.4	2.7	2.6	1.3	0.4	3.2	3.8	0.5
Classical (%)	1.7	31.9	27.7	9.2	1.5	33.4	32.7	7.3
Modern (%)	0.6	13.5	15.0	0.4	0.7	12.1	10.9	0.4
Big sign (%)	2.1	33.5	29.9	7.7	2.0	39.1	36.8	7.6
Small sign (%)	0.2	11.9	12.8	1.9	0.2	7.4	6.8	0.1

The ordinary dynamic environment includes billboards, etc.; the unconventional dynamic environment includes disputes, etc. Table 2 shows the survey result.

In the table, DE is dynamic environment, BB is billboard, NL is neon light, MV is moving vehicle, PP is passing pedestrian, SP is street performance, PD is pedestrian dispute, BP is business performance, and EG is emergency. It can be seen that pedestrians with different genders and age have different attention tendencies to

Table 2. Pedestrians' attention tendency to the dynamic environment

Gender		Male				Female			
DE		Age							
		12–18	19–44	45–60	61–75	12–18	19–44	45–60	61–75
Ordinary environment	BB (%)	8.8	11.1	10.9	6.7	9.1	10.2	7.7	6.3
	NL (%)	13.4	8.0	7.6	8.2	13.2	7.9	6.2	10.6
	MV (%)	7.6	6.8	7.7	7.9	2.1	0.3	0.4	3.1
	PP (%)	0.5	0.7	1.3	1.7	1.3	3.1	2.4	0.8
Unconventional environment	SP (%)	23.6	19.5	20.9	18.9	24.5	16.6	15.9	14.2
	PD (%)	10.3	15.3	16.2	16.7	11.1	23.2	25.3	25.7
	BP (%)	20.7	17.9	15.4	18.3	21.4	14.3	15.7	14.9
	EG (%)	15.1	20.7	20.0	21.6	19.4	24.4	26.4	24.4

different appearance factors. For example, dark buildings were more noticeable to female pedestrians. Personality factors weren't considered in the survey. According to the survey, most pedestrians' attention tendency is unconventional dynamic environment > ordinary dynamic environment.

5   Experiments

We built a crowd system and a virtual scene under the hardware environment of PC, with NVIDIA GeForce GTX 980 Ti, 32.0G RAM, 4.00 GHz CPU, and Unity 3D ADAPT Core [28]. The IK method was used to realize the animation of virtual characters. The strolling simulation effects were experimented mainly from three aspects: attention distance, attention tendency and attention distance model. Finally, a strolling simulation of an urban scene experiment was conducted to verify the running effect of the environmental attention model in the case of multiple virtual characters.

Under the same conditions of the character's attributes, different walking paths were planned for it. The changing process of environmental attention values and degrees are shown in Fig. 1. In (a), the ordinate is the attention value to different objects in the environment. (b) shows the environmental attention degree of objects.

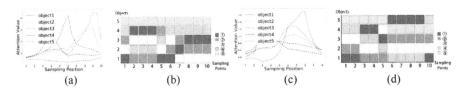

(a)   (b)   (c)   (d)

Fig. 1. The changing processes of the virtual character in different paths. (a) is the result of the environmental attention value in path1. (b) is the result of its attention degree in path1. (c) and (d) are the results in path2. (Color figure online)

① to ⑤ are degrees, and the red one is the attention target with the highest attention value. The experiment results of strolling along path2 are shown in Fig. 1(c), (d).

The result that virtual character's attention target was different due to different paths, indicates that the distance affect the character's choice of the attention target. But for the object with high attention tendency, the impact of the distance is less. The experiment results were different under other different aspects.

As to attention tendency, two virtual characters with different attention tendencies walked along the same path. As a result, their attention targets were pretty different at the same position. It shows that the attention tendency has a great impact on the selection of attention targets. With the same conditions of virtual character attributes, the character walked along the same path. Two kinds of attention distances were used to calculate the attention targets. Using the Euclidean distance, the virtual character's attention targets were more dispersed and averaged. Using the egocentric distance, the targets were more concentrated. As a result, Euclidean distance highlights the impact of the distance, and Euclidean distance highlights the attention tendency.

Finally, we built a virtual urban scene, and the buildings were categorized into different types: hotels, etc. And the distribution is shown in Fig. 2(a).

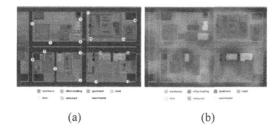

(a)   (b)

Fig. 2. (a) is the building distribution and sampling points in the virtual urban. (b) is the distribution of the pedestrians' attention tendency.

The intrinsic attributes of virtual characters were randomly assigned according to the investigation results. The environmental attention model was used to calculate the environmental attention during strolling. Then we obtained their attention targets, and realized the gazing action. The simulating results are shown in Fig. 3. And Fig. 2(b) demonstrates the distribution of the pedestrians' attention tendency.

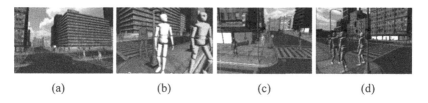

(a)   (b)   (c)   (d)

Fig. 3. The simulating results of virtual characters in the virtual urban.

6   Conclusions and Discussions

Based on the investigation and analysis of pedestrian psychology and behavior in real life, this paper proposed a crowd simulation method based on the environmental attention model. According to the attributes of virtual characters in the crowd and the environmental attributes in the virtual scene, the virtual character's attention target in the process of strolling can be calculated in real time using this method. As a result, the virtual character behavior is personalized due to the diversity of virtual character attributes, thereby improving the animation diversity. The experiment results show that this method can effectively improve the randomness of crowd movements, and thus improve the realism of crowd simulation. But our current classification of the environment is relatively simple. So refining the environment classification is one of our future work directions. Furthermore, our present work focuses on the attention behavior diversities of the crowd. Other diversity like appearance simulation methods will be added to the system for improving the appearance diversity of the crowd.

Acknowledgment. We appreciated the comments and suggestions of those who reviewed this paper. We also appreciated the supply of the ADAPT Core.

References

1. Thalmann, D.: Crowd simulation. Wiley Encyclopedia of Computer Science and Engineering (2007)
2. Wagner, N., Agrawal, V.: An agent-based simulation system for concert venue crowd evacuation modeling in the presence of a fire disaster. Expert Syst. Appl. **41**(6), 2807–2815 (2014)
3. Durupinar, F., Pelechano, N., Allbeck, J., Gudukbay, U., Badler, N.I.: How the ocean personality model affects the perception of crowds. IEEE Comput. Graph. Appl. **31**(3), 22–31 (2011)
4. Braun, A., Musse, S.R., de Oliveira, L.P.L., Bodmann, B.E.: Modeling individual behaviors in crowd simulation. In: Computer Animation and Social Agents. IEEE (2003)
5. Thalmann, D., Musse, S.R.: Crowd Simulation. Springer, London (2013). https://doi.org/10.1007/978-1-4471-4450-2
6. Maïm, J., Yersin, B., Thalmann, D.: Unique character instances for crowds. IEEE Comput. Graphics Appl. **29**(6), 82–90 (2009)
7. Durupinar, F., Kapadia, M., Deutsch, S., Neff, M., Badler, N.I.: PERFORM: perceptual approach for adding OCEAN personality to human motion using Laban movement analysis. ACM Trans. Graph. (TOG) **36**(1), 6 (2017)
8. Tsai, J., et al.: ESCAPES: evacuation simulation with children, authorities, parents, emotions, and social comparison. In: The 10th International Conference on Autonomous Agents and Multiagent Systems, vol. 2, pp. 457–464 (2011)
9. Grillon, H., Thalmann, D.: Simulating gaze attention behaviors for crowds. Comput. Animation Virtual Worlds **20**(2–3), 111–119 (2009)
10. Proshansky, H.M.: The pursuit of understanding. In: Altman, I., Christensen, K. (eds.) Environment and Behavior Studies. Springer, Boston (1990). https://doi.org/10.1007/978-1-4684-7944-7_2

11. Moore, G.T.: New directions for environment-behavior research in architecture. Center for Architecture and Urban Planning Research, University of Wisconsin-Milwaukee (1981)
12. Moore, G.T., Tuttle, D.P., Howell, S.C.: Environmental Design Research Directions: Process and Prospects. Praeger Publishers (1985)
13. John, O.P., Naumann, L.P., Soto, C.J.: Paradigm shift to the integrative big five trait taxonomy. Handb. Pers.: Theory Res. **3**(2), 114–158 (2008)
14. Ooi, T.L., He, Z.J.: A distance judgment function based on space perception mechanisms: revisiting Gilinsky's (1951) equation. Psychol. Rev. **114**(2), 441 (2007)

Fast Superpixel Segmentation
with Deep Features

Mubinun Awaisu[1], Liang Li[1,2($\boxtimes$)], Junjie Peng[1], and Jiawan Zhang[1]

[1] College of Intelligence and Computing, Tianjin University, Tianjin, China
amubinun@yahoo.com, {liangli,jwzhang}@tju.edu.cn,
jiongjiongpeng@yeah.net
[2] Hubei Key Laboratory of Intelligent Vision Based Monitoring for Hydroelectric
Engineering, China Three Gorges University, Yichang 443002, China

Abstract. In this paper, we propose a superpixel segmentation method which utilizes extracted deep features along with the combination of color and position information of the pixels. It is observed that the results can be improved significantly using better initial seed points. Therefore, we incorporated a one-step k-means clustering to calculate the positions of the initial seed points and applied the active search method to ensure that each pixel belongs to the right seed. The proposed method was also compared to other state-of-the-art methods quantitatively and qualitatively, and was found to produce promising results that adhere to the object boundaries better than others.

Keywords: Superpixel · Deep feature extraction · Active search

1 Introduction

Superpixels are becoming increasingly important in the field of computer vision. They are widely used in applications such as object detection [9], semantic segmentation [2], saliency estimation [3], and optical flow estimation [7]. Essentially, superpixel is a technique used to group image pixels into smaller sub-regions [1] based on the pixels similarity. State-of-the-art overview can be found in [8]. Superpixels can be used as the fundamental units instead of pixels to reduce computational complexity. Useful superpixels must produce high quality segmentations that adhere to the edges well. To fulfill this demand, researchers have tried many features. For instance, recently, the 5-D features consisting of the L, a, b values from CIELAB color space and the x, y pixel coordinate has been popular choice. However, relying only on appearance and spatial information is not enough to segment the edges accurately when the objects in the image share similar color with the background, which is very common when the scene is highly cluttered.

This work was supported by National Natural Science Foundation of China under Grants 61602338, Hubei Foundation for Innovative Research Groups under Grants 2015CFA025.

M. Gavrilova et al. (Eds.): CGI 2019, LNCS 11542, pp. 410–416, 2019.
https://doi.org/10.1007/978-3-030-22514-8_38

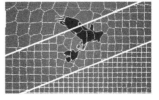

Fig. 1. Images segmented using our algorithm into 100, 200 and 400 superpixels. The superpixels are compact and adhere well to the region boundaries.

Therefore, researchers have recently resorted to the convolutional neural network (CNN) to extract features with more representability [5]. Due to the strong capability of CNN to learn the high-level representations for natural images, these methods often achieve better adherence to boundaries (Fig. 1).

It is important to note that superpixels are usually used as a preprocessing step in other applications. Therefore, running speed is a critical factor affecting the usefulness of superpixel algorithm. In this paper, we propose a superpixel segmentation algorithm that can produce superpixels with better boundaries adherence while being time efficient. There are two stages in our algorithm. In the first stage, we modified the initialization step in [10] by first measuring the distance between the seeds center and neighboring pixels. This makes each seed to contain almost similar pixels and also makes the active search less computational since most of the pixels are similar. Then we applied the active search to the initial superpixels to ensure that each pixel belongs to the right superpixel. The initial superpixels and modified active search approach have low computational cost and satisfy all the properties of good superpixels.

2   Proposed Method

In the proposed method, deep features were extracted from pre-trained network designed by [4] and concatenated with $LabXY$ for better representation of the image pixels. Superpixel Sampling Network (SNN) is mainly designed for feature extraction, and we extracted features for each image with a deep CNN originally trained over the BSDS500. Figure 2 shows an overview of the proposed method. Multidimensional vector is used to represent each pixel in our algorithm: $I_i = [l_i \ a_i \ b_i \ x_i \ y_i \ F_i]^T$, where $[l_i \ a_i \ b_i]$ is the pixel color vector in CIELAB color space, $F_i = [f_{i1} \ f_{i2}...f_{iT}]$ are the extracted features from deep network and $[x_i \ y_i]$ is the pixel position.

Details on getting the initial superpixels are explained in Algorithm 1. The nearest seed center is computed by a distance function D defined by the following equation,

$$D(I_i, S_k) = \sqrt{\lambda \left(d_c + \alpha d_s\right)^2 + d_F^2}, \tag{1}$$

where I_i represents the pixel, S_k represents the seed center, λ is the weight for controlling $LabXY$ and $\alpha = \frac{m}{N}$; m is the compactness variable and N is the

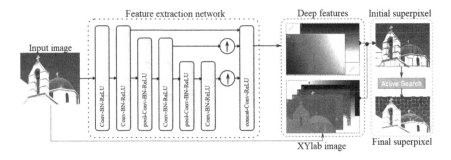

Fig. 2. Deep-FLIC flow chart. We used pre-trained network for extraction of features in each image, then we concatenated these features and the original image features in CIELAB color space. Finally we generated the initial superpixels and applied the active search method used in [10] to get the final superpixels segmentation.

number of pixels in an image. The variables d_c, d_s and d_F are the *lab* color distance, xy plane distance, and deep feature distance, respectively. They are defined by the following equations.

$$d_c = \sqrt{(l_i - l_j)^2 + (a_i - a_j)^2 + (b_i - b_j)^2}, \tag{2}$$

$$d_s = \sqrt{(x_i - x_j)^2 + (y_i - y_j)^2}, \tag{3}$$

$$d_F = \sqrt{(F_i - F_j)^2} = \sqrt{\sum_{t=1}^{T} (f_{it} - f_{jt})^2}. \tag{4}$$

2.1   Active Search

The active search strategy enables each of the current pixel to actively search for the superpixel it should belong to, based on it's neighbouring pixels. We computed the distances between the current pixel and the seeds of its four adjacent pixels. The assignment principle for pixel I_i is given by the equation below,

$$L_i = \arg \min_{L_j} D(I_i, S_{L_j}), I_j \in A_i, \tag{5}$$

where A_i consists of I_i and its four neighboring pixels, S_{L_j} is I_j's corresponding initial superpixel seed. Equation (1) was used to measure the distance $D(I_i, S_{L_j})$.

The back and forth strategy [10] is applied to traverse the initial superpixels and get the pixels processing sequence. Minimum bounding box for all the initial superpixels is defined. The scanning process for all pixels in the corresponding minimum bounding box is performed, and then the pixels are processed within the initial superpixels. When the label of the current pixel L_i changes to any seed of its neighbouring pixels L_j, the seeds are updated instantly using the following equations,

$$S_{L_i} = \frac{S_{L_i} * |P_{L_i}| - I_i}{|P_{L_i}| - 1}, \tag{6}$$

Algorithm 1. Superpixel Initialization

Input: $I_i = [l_i, a_i, b_i, x_i, y_i, F_i]$ for each pixel.
Initialization: The initial seed points $S = [S_1, \cdots, S_k]$ and the centers in each of the seeds $S_k = [l_k\ a_k\ b_k\ x_k\ y_k\ F_k]^T$ with the corresponding feature F_{S_k};
Set label $L_i = -1$, distance $d_i = \infty$ for each pixel and $itr = 0$;
for *each seed center S_k* **do**
    for *each pixel in a $2S \times 2S$ region around S_k* **do**
        Compute the distance D between S_k and I_i;
        if $D < d_i$ **then**
          | set $d_i = D$ and $L_i = k$
        end
    end
end
Output: Initial superpixels.

---

where $|P_{L_i}|$ is the number of pixels in the initial superpixel P_{L_i}, and S_{L_j} is updated using the below equation,

$$S_{L_j} = \frac{S_{L_j} * |P_{L_j}| + I_i}{|P_{L_i}| + 1}, \tag{7}$$

the bounding box is also updated. This process changes the seeds of the initial superpixels adaptively and allows the assignment and update to happen jointly.

3 Experiments

The proposed algorithm is implemented in C++ and runs on a PC with CPU, 4.0 GHz, 8 GB RAM, and 64 bit operating system. Our method is compared with existing four state-of-the-art algorithms, namely, FLIC [10], SLIC [1], LSC [6] and SSN [4]. Publically available implementations provided by the original authors are used for fair comparison. All the experiments are conducted on the BSD Berkeley Segmentation Dataset. This dataset consists of five hundred 321×481 images, together with human-annotated ground truth segmentations. The effectiveness of our method is demonstrated by providing visual and quantitative results with the existing superpixel methods. We experimented with the following default parameters: The number of superpixel, K, was set as desired, the spatial distance weight, $m = 5$ (as default), number of iterations, $itr = 2$, and $\lambda = 0.5$ (λ is a weighting value that balances the $LabXY$ features and deep features. Its value varies between $[0; 1]$).

3.1 Visual Results

Figure 3 shows segmentation results of our method and the compared existing algorithms. Looking closely at the characteristics of good superpixel algorithm, it can be seen that, our method performed well compared to the competing

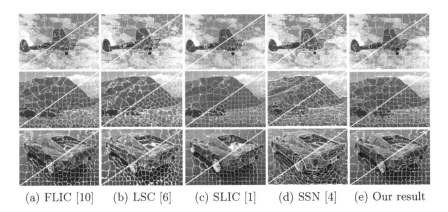

(a) FLIC [10]   (b) LSC [6]   (c) SLIC [1]   (d) SSN [4]   (e) Our result

Fig. 3. Visual comparison with SOTA algorithms with 100 and 300 superpixels.

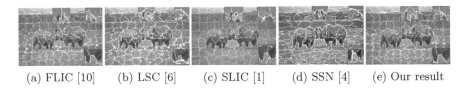

(a) FLIC [10]   (b) LSC [6]   (c) SLIC [1]   (d) SSN [4]   (e) Our result

Fig. 4. Superpixels segmentation results and magnified regions. The number of super-pixels in all the results is 100.

state-of-the-art algorithms. Furthermore, in Fig. 4 more visual results with magnified regions can be seen, thereby indicating that our method obtained a certain improvement in boundary adherence compared to FLIC, LSC and SLIC methods.

3.2 Quantitative Results

The most important feature of good superpixel algorithm is the boundary adherence. To determine how well the superpixels adhere to the boundaries of an object, it is required to use some criteria for quantitative comparison. Boundary recall (BR) and under-segmentation error (UE) are the standard criteria for measuring the quality of the boundary adherence. Figure 5(a) shows a graph of the boundary recall as a function of the number of superpixels generated by the algorithms. Our method performs favorably in both higher and lower superpixel numbers. Under-segmentation error and Achievable segmentation accuracy of all the methods are illustrated in Table 1. Looking at Table 1, its clearly seen that SSN has the best UE of all the comparison algorithms. However our method is the best compared to FLIC, LSC and SLIC.

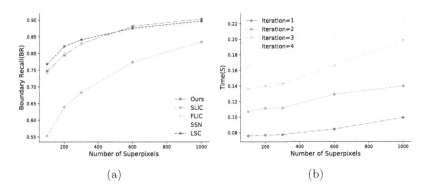

Fig. 5. Quantitative comparison with the state-of-the-art methods. (a) Boundary recall vs superpixel number. (b) Time comparison in different iterations.

Table 1. Comparison for 1000 superpixels (BR, UE) and 300 superpixels (ASA).

Existing methods	FLIC [10]	LSC [6]	SLIC [1]	SSN [4]	OURS
Boundary Recall (BR)	0.890	0.897	0.834	0.892	**0.900**
Under-segmentation Error (UE)	0.181	0.252	0.200	**0.108**	0.154
Achievable Segmentation Accuracy (ASA)	**0.949**	0.923	0.925	0.947	0.948

4   Discussion

Good superpixel segmentation method should have high BR as well as low UE. It is seen from Table 1 that the method developed in this study performs well compared to several algorithms. In comparison to FLIC, LSC, and SLIC, our method has lower UE. This advantage is due to the addition of more features in to the distance measure. The BR measure of our method (Table 1) and Fig. 4 further indicate the favorable performance of our algorithm compared to other methods especially when the number of superpixels is high. However, SSN has the best BR below 600 supepixels. The initial superpixels introduced in our method increased the efficiency of the running time by making the active search less computational. It ensures that each of the initial superpixel contained almost similar pixels. In Fig. 5(b) we compared the time required for our method to generate superpixels for different iterations with different number of superpixels. When processing an image with 600 superpixels the time taken for first and second iterations are 0.0852 s and 0.125 s, respectively, which can be used efficiently in image preprocessing.

5   Conclusions

In this research, we proposed a modified superpixel algorithm, that takes into account images with weak object boundaries to increase the boundary adherence of the superpixels. FLIC algorithm is extended to incorporate deep features along with color and spatial properties of the pixels. Visual and quantitative results show that the developed method is able to generate more semantically-coherent superpixels compared to the other state-of-the-art methods. Future work will involve the use of end to end trainable deep network with the active search method to improve both the lower and higher superpixels and also reduce the computational time.

References

1. Achanta, R., Shaji, A., Smith, K., Lucchi, A., Fua, P., Süstrunk, S.: SLIC superpixels compared to state-of-the-art superpixel methods. IEEE Trans. Pattern Anal. Mach. Intell. **34**(11), 2274–2282 (2012)
2. Gould, S., Rodgers, J., Cohen, D., Elidan, G., Koller, D.: Multi-class segmentation with relative location prior. Int. J. Comput. Vision **80**(3), 300–316 (2008)
3. He, S., Lau, R.W.H., Liu, W., Huang, Z., Yang, Q.: SuperCNN: a superpixelwise convolutional neural network for salient object detection. Int. J. Comput. Vision **115**(3), 330–344 (2015)
4. Jampani, V., Sun, D., Liu, M.-Y., Yang, M.-H., Kautz, J.: Superpixel sampling networks. In: Ferrari, V., Hebert, M., Sminchisescu, C., Weiss, Y. (eds.) ECCV 2018. LNCS, vol. 11211, pp. 363–380. Springer, Cham (2018). https://doi.org/10.1007/978-3-030-01234-2_22
5. Krizhevsky, A., Sutskever, I., Hinton, G.E.: ImageNet classification with deep convolutional neural networks. In: NIPS, pp. 1097–1105 (2012)
6. Li, Z., Chen, J.: Superpixel segmentation using linear spectral clustering. In: CVPR (2015)
7. Lu, J., Yang, H., Min, D., Do, M.N.: Patch match filter: efficient edge-aware filtering meets randomized search for fast correspondence field estimation. In: CVPR (2013)
8. Stutz, D., Hermans, A., Leibe, B.: Superpixels: an evaluation of the state-of-the-art. Comput. Vis. Image Underst. **166**, 1–27 (2018)
9. Yan, J., Yu, Y., Zhu, X., Lei, Z., Li, S.Z.: Object detection by labeling superpixels. In: CVPR (2015)
10. Zhao, J.X., Bo, R., Hou, Q., Cheng, M.M.: FLIC: fast linear iterative clustering with active search. In: AAAI (2018)

BricklAyeR: A Platform for Building Rules for AmI Environments in AR

Evropi Stefanidi[1], Dimitrios Arampatzis[1], Asterios Leonidis[1(✉)],
and George Papagiannakis[1,2]

[1] Institute of Computer Science (ICS),
Foundation for Research and Technology – Hellas (FORTH), Heraklion, Greece
{evropi, arabatzis, leonidis, papagian}@ics.forth.gr
[2] Department of Computer Science, University of Crete, Heraklion, Greece

Abstract. With the proliferation of Intelligent Environments, the need for configuring their behaviors to address their users' needs emerges. In combination with the current advances in Augmented and Virtual Reality and Conversational Agents, new opportunities arise for systems which allow people to program their environment. Whereas today this requires programming skills, soon, when most spaces will include smart objects, tools which allow their collaborative management by non-technical users will become a necessity. To that end, we present BricklAyeR, a novel collaborative platform for non-programmers, that allows to define the behavior of Intelligent Environments, through an intuitive, 3D building-block User Interface, following the Trigger-Action programming principle, in Augmented Reality, with the help of a Conversational Agent.

Keywords: Augmented Reality · Ambient Intelligence ·
Chatbot conversational agent · End user programming ·
Graphical human-computer interaction

1 Introduction

The need to manage the behavior of Internet of Things (IoT) devices is becoming increasingly apparent, as by 2020 their installed base is forecast to grow to almost 31 billion worldwide[1]. To that end, intuitive end-user programming interfaces are necessary to allow everyone - not just programming experts - to manage the emerging intelligent spaces [1, 2], including residents, who must be able to configure their own technologically-enhanced house [3]. The popular "if *trigger*, then *action*" programming technique [4] along with tangible programming for constructing simple programs [5], allows inexperienced users to express most desired behaviors regarding the control of a variety of digital "everyday objects".

Nevertheless, programming Ambient Intelligence (AmI) environments can be considered by its nature as a collaborative task, since its outcome is destined to affect multiple users. Additionally, collaboration can facilitate learning with guidance and

---

[1] https://www.statista.com/statistics/471264/iot-number-of-connected-devices-worldwide.

© Springer Nature Switzerland AG 2019
M. Gavrilova et al. (Eds.): CGI 2019, LNCS 11542, pp. 417–423, 2019.
https://doi.org/10.1007/978-3-030-22514-8_39

encouragement from a skilled partner [6, 7] and has the ability to produce better results than individual work [8], allowing for sharing of resources, accessibility of multilevel interaction, and higher order thinking activities [9].

In this paper we present BricklAyeR, which utilizes these concepts to deliver an intuitive immersive programming platform allowing non-programmers to collaborate and configure Intelligent Environments. Our system fuses uniquely the concepts of Augmented Reality (AR), AR interactive virtual characters [10, 11] with situated 3D programming, as users create rules dictating the behavior of smart artifacts, transferring the tangible blocks from the physical to the digital world, as 3D virtual programming bricks. This enables to harness the benefits of tangible programing (e.g. easier to understand, remember, and explain), while overcoming some of its challenges (e.g. large puzzles that correspond to complex programs can be represented as single blocks that can be expanded in their own virtual space). Additionally, BricklAyeR employs the concept of digital twins [12], to enable real-time collaboration between local and remote users, via appropriate visualizations. For example, a local user can physically trigger an event (i.e. open a door) and remote users can experience the same effect virtually through their devices (i.e. see that door opening). Finally, a 3D animated Conversational Agent (CA) intervenes and helps the user as needed.

2   Related Work

End-User development (EUD) has already been applied in various domains, including commercial software where users can incorporate their own functionality (e.g., recording macros in word processors, defining e-mail filters). Moreover, the proliferation of web-enabled devices and services in domains such as the smart home [13], has led to the application of various programming principles that enable non-technical users to create complex automation scenarios using sequence-based approaches [14] or if-this-then-that rules (e.g. IFTTT[2], Zapier[3]). Recently, this type of programming has been applied in the domain of AmI, where users can create simple "if trigger, then action" rules to specify the behavior of intelligent spaces [15] and classrooms [16].

From an interaction perspective, AR is extensively used in many EUD systems to increase task-related intuitiveness [17] by providing a more natural interface [18] that enables users to interact straightforwardly with spatial information [19]. For example, the Reality Editor [20] and Smarter Objects [21] allow programming and operating of physical objects by associating them with virtual ones, while Hammer [22] and RPAR [23] enable intuitive robot programming by non-skilled operators. Finally, with respect to collaboration, studies in group dynamics [24] support that teams can achieve goals more effectively, while the integration of AR ensures location awareness [25].

Built on top of such technologies, BricklAyeR, delivers a unique, intuitive and immersive interface that allows non-programmers to collaborate and create rules that define the behavior of their intelligent environment. In more detail, BricklAyeR

---

[2] https://ifttt.com/discover.

[3] https://zapier.com.

provides solutions to various challenges of previous 3D and tangible programming approaches (e.g. 3D bricks can easily be moved, scaled and reused to overcome physical space requirements since the whole augmented "world" is the user's canvas). Moreover, via AR, it simplifies the artifact collection task by enabling users to easily explore their physical environment, instead of having to navigate over "ambiguous" lists, so as to directly select which smart devices to use. This becomes especially important in emerging AmI environments that include a plethora of IoT devices. Moreover, by being immersed, users can get a better understanding of all the available programmable artifacts, their actions, and their locations.

3   The BricklAyeR Platform

Users, following the trigger-action paradigm, can use their tablet or other mobile devices to create rules, defining how the available smart objects will respond to contextual stimuli (e.g. user actions, time-based conditions, environmental factors), with the guidance of a CA (Fig. 1a). Every rule is composed of one or multiple triggers and one or multiple actions, represented as virtual blocks (i.e. 3D bricks), that users can combine as desired in the AR Environment. For the low-level management and configuration of the behavior of Intelligent Environments and its smart devices, the AmI-Solertis platform [26] is utilized, providing the necessary data (e.g. location, description, actions, parameters). Moreover, the trigger-action paradigm is facilitated by the LECTOR framework [27], which offers a rule-based mechanism that identifies behaviors and triggers interventions. Following that convention, BricklAyeR uses the term "behavior" for the trigger part of a rule (i.e. the way that a user or an artifact acts, e.g. *when the door opens*), and the term "intervention" for the action part (i.e. the system-guided actions aiming to support users in their activities, e.g. *then sound the alarm*).

BricklAyeR is actively used in the "Intelligent Home" simulation space located at the AmI Facility Building (http://ami.ics.forth.gr/) within the FORTH-ICS campus. Inside this environment, everyday activities are enhanced with the use of innovative interaction techniques, Artificial Intelligence, sophisticated middleware, commercial equipment and technologically augmented custom-made artifacts [15]. To build and deploy a rule in that Environment, users must execute the following process:

Artifact Collection. The smart artifacts are represented as virtual blocks and are collected manually; a user can direct the camera towards a real-world object and a digital twin in the form of a 3D block will be created. Users can create workgroups to collaborate not only during rule creation, but also when capturing the smart artifacts, i.e. remotely select objects, share common inventories and detailed information regarding the capabilities of their components (i.e. triggering events, actions).

Rule Building. The trigger and action parts that compose a rule are represented as 3D bricks that get connected like puzzle pieces. This metaphor can be beneficial to novice programmers, since such a visualization can offer easy access to the whole vocabulary as well as a graphical overview of the control flow [28]. Since the rule creation process resembles connecting physical bricks in order to build a concrete 3D structure, it takes place over a designated, LEGO-like, brick building baseplate. To create rules, users have at their disposal five types of bricks (Fig. 1b): (a) **artifact bricks**: the smart objects users collect from the intelligent environment, (b) **command bricks**: the available coding commands (i.e. WHEN, THEN, AND, OR), (c) **behavior bricks**: reusable partial rules containing only the trigger(s), (d) **intervention bricks**: reusable partial rules containing only the action(s), (e) **complete rule bricks**: complete rules, and (f) **literal bricks**: auto-generated bricks that display when an artifact brick is connected to a command brick and represent either the value that will trigger a condition (e.g. door opens) or the action that the artifact will take (e.g. turn the light on).

Fig. 1. (a) BricklAyeR in action. (b) Available 3D bricks. (c) Deployment options.

Rule Simulation and Deployment. A syntactically correct and complete rule can be deployed in the Intelligent Environment according to the user's preferences (i.e. run once, run periodically, run always) as depicted in Fig. 1c. Before actual deployment, users can experience the effects of a rule via simulating it. They can "manipulate" the virtual reality so as to verify the behavior of a rule in a sandboxed environment without actually distorting the reality or identify potential improvements. While in simulation mode, users can apply any of the following combinations: (i) **virtual-to-virtual**: artificially trigger a rule and view its effects virtually through their screen, (ii) **virtual-to-physical**: virtually trigger a rule and view its effects on the physical environment or (iii) **physical-to-virtual**: physically manipulate devices to trigger a rule and view its effects virtually through their screen.

Conversational Agent-Helper. In order to facilitate the whole rule creation process, an agent, powered by the ParlAmI platform [15], in the form of an animated 3D character [7, 10] appears in the virtual environment, interacting via natural language (voice). The CA helps either (i) on demand (e.g. the user asks which services are provided by an artifact) or (ii) automatically by inferring when a user is "confused" (e.g. a mistake is repeated, the user remains idle for a long time). Moreover, by being context-aware, the agent can understand queries of the form "what is this?" by taking into account where a user is looking via their tablet. In addition to assistance, the agent can be asked to configure part(s) of a rule via voice (e.g. "select the turn-on action for the lamp on the left"). Finally, the CA can serve as an announcer across different sessions when multiple users are collaborating; e.g. dictate, upon request, the (parts of the) rule that they are supposed to build.

4 Results

In order to assess the usability of BricklAyeR, a cognitive walkthrough expert-based evaluation [29] was conducted to acquire feedback on whether tasks could be carried out easily by users who had no previous interaction with our system[4]. A total of five HCI experts of ages 25–40 years participated in the experiment. According to Nielsen[5], testing a system with five users permits the detection of approximately 85% of the problems, increasing the benefit-cost ratio, while heuristic evaluation can uncover most major usability issues [30], before moving to a user-based evaluation.

During the evaluation experiment, the evaluators had to follow a simple scenario where a novice user was asked to create a rule that would automate their "returning home from work" routine (e.g. when the main door opens, turn-on the living room lights, set the TV on their favorite channel, open the blinds and lock the main door). All evaluators expressed a positive opinion about the system; they found it fun and engaging. The experience of using AR and 3D blocks was appealing in general. They agreed that live collaboration makes the process easier, is especially helpful for novice users and our approach is intuitive. Moreover, they found the interaction natural, and that the metaphor used improves the overall usability over time, after creating a couple of rules and getting more acquainted with the system and its features. Generally, no important problems were uncovered regarding the concept and the interaction paradigm. Most of the issues found were related to the UI, e.g. the need for a tutorial for first-time users, or perhaps also for multiple UIs based on users' expertise.

5 Discussion

This paper has presented BricklAyeR, a novel system in AR that allows non-experts to program the behavior of Intelligent Environments, through an intuitive, situated 3D-block programming interface, aided by a CA. A key innovation of our system is its collaborative nature, allowing users to create complex rules faster and more efficiently. The results of an expert-based evaluation validated these premises. Our immediate plans include a full-scale user-based evaluation. Future improvements involve: (i) context-sensitive guidance to help users benefit from the advanced functionality offered by BricklAyeR (e.g. encapsulate chained actions into a reusable "intervention"

---

[4] https://www.interaction-design.org/literature/article/how-to-conduct-a-cognitive-walkthrough.

[5] https://www.nngroup.com/articles/why-you-only-need-to-test-with-5-users.

block), (ii) a map with the location of the available smart objects in the home in order to facilitate their discovery, (iii) the introduction of a supplementary textual representation of rules in natural language, which will be dynamically updated as the creation process progresses, aiming to provide appropriate feedback regarding its current state in a user-friendly manner; and (iv) the incorporation of an extensive training mode where the CA introduces BricklAyeR facilities to its first-time users via interactive demos. Finally, appropriate strategies for conflict resolution will be applied (e.g. rule prioritization, MRU policies, real-time user-guided resolution).

References

1. Dahl, Y., Svendsen, R.-M.: End-user composition interfaces for smart environments: a preliminary study of usability factors. In: Marcus, A. (ed.) DUXU 2011. LNCS, vol. 6770, pp. 118–127. Springer, Heidelberg (2011). https://doi.org/10.1007/978-3-642-21708-1_14
2. Dey, A.K., Sohn, T., Streng, S., Kodama, J.: iCAP: interactive prototyping of context-aware applications. In: Fishkin, K.P., Schiele, B., Nixon, P., Quigley, A. (eds.) Pervasive 2006. LNCS, vol. 3968, pp. 254–271. Springer, Heidelberg (2006). https://doi.org/10.1007/11748625_16
3. Truong, K.N., Huang, E.M., Abowd, G.D.: CAMP: a magnetic poetry interface for end-user programming of capture applications for the home. In: Davies, N., Mynatt, E.D., Siio, I. (eds.) UbiComp 2004. LNCS, vol. 3205, pp. 143–160. Springer, Heidelberg (2004). https://doi.org/10.1007/978-3-540-30119-6_9
4. Ur, B., McManus, E., Pak Yong Ho, M., Littman, M.L.: Practical trigger-action programming in the smart home. In: Proceedings of the SIGCHI Conference on Human Factors in Computing Systems, pp. 803–812. ACM, New York (2014)
5. McNerney, T.S.: Tangible programming bricks: an approach to making programming accessible to everyone (1999)
6. Vygotsky, L.S.: Mind in Society. Harvard University Press, Cambridge (1978)
7. Zidianakis, E., Papagiannakis, G., Stephanidis, C.: A cross-platform, remotely-controlled mobile avatar simulation framework for AmI environments. In: SIGGRAPH Asia 2014 Mobile Graphics and Interactive Applications, p. 12. ACM (2014)
8. Nosek, J.T.: The case for collaborative programming. Commun. ACM 41, 105–108 (1998)
9. Oliveira, I., Tinoca, L., Pereira, A.: Online group work patterns: how to promote a successful collaboration. Comput. Educ. 57, 1348–1357 (2011)
10. Vacchetti, L., et al.: A stable real-time AR framework for training and planning in industrial environments. In: Ong, S.K., Nee, A.Y.C. (eds.) Virtual and Augmented Reality Applications in Manufacturing, pp. 129–145. Springer, London (2004). https://doi.org/10.1007/978-1-4471-3873-0_8
11. Kateros, S., et al.: A comparison of gamified, immersive VR curation methods for enhanced presence and human-computer interaction in digital humanities. Int. J. Heritage Digit. Era. 4, 221–233 (2015)
12. Söderberg, R., Wärmefjord, K., Carlson, J.S., Lindkvist, L.: Toward a Digital Twin for real-time geometry assurance in individualized production. CIRP Ann. 66, 137–140 (2017)
13. Stojkoska, B.L.R., Trivodaliev, K.V.: A review of Internet of Things for smart home: challenges and solutions. J. Clean. Prod. 140, 1454–1464 (2017)
14. Walch, M., Rietzler, M., Greim, J., Schaub, F., Wiedersheim, B., Weber, M.: homeBLOX: making home automation usable. In: Proceedings of the 2013 ACM Conference on Pervasive and Ubiquitous Computing Adjunct Publication, pp. 295–298. ACM (2013)

15. Stefanidi, E., et al.: ParlAmI: a multimodal approach for programming intelligent environments. Technologies **7**, 11 (2019)
16. Korozi, M., Leonidis, A., Antona, M., Stephanidis, C.: LECTOR: towards reengaging students in the educational process inside smart classrooms. In: Horain, P., Achard, C., Mallem, M. (eds.) IHCI 2017. LNCS, vol. 10688, pp. 137–149. Springer, Cham (2017). https://doi.org/10.1007/978-3-319-72038-8_11
17. Neumann, U., Majoros, A.: Cognitive, performance, and systems issues for augmented reality applications in manufacturing and maintenance. In: 1998 Proceedings of IEEE Virtual Reality Annual International Symposium, pp. 4–11. IEEE (1998)
18. Kasahara, S., Niiyama, R., Heun, V., Ishii, H.: exTouch: spatially-aware embodied manipulation of actuated objects mediated by augmented reality. In: Proceedings of the 7th International Conference on Tangible, Embedded and Embodied Interaction, pp. 223–228. ACM (2013)
19. Zaeh, M.F., Vogl, W.: Interactive laser-projection for programming industrial robots. In: 2006 IEEE/ACM International Symposium on Mixed and Augmented Reality. ISMAR 2006, pp. 125–128. IEEE (2006)
20. Heun, V., Hobin, J., Maes, P.: Reality editor: programming smarter objects. In: Proceedings of the 2013 ACM Conference on Pervasive and Ubiquitous Computing Adjunct Publication, pp. 307–310. ACM, New York (2013)
21. Heun, V., Kasahara, S., Maes, P.: Smarter objects: using AR technology to program physical objects and their interactions. In: CHI 2013 Extended Abstracts on Human Factors in Computing Systems, pp. 961–966. ACM (2013)
22. Mateo, C., Brunete, A., Gambao, E., Hernando, M.: Hammer: an android based application for end-user industrial robot programming. In: 2014 IEEE/ASME 10th International Conference on Mechatronic and Embedded Systems and Applications (MESA), pp. 1–6. IEEE (2014)
23. Chong, J.W.S., Ong, S.K., Nee, A.Y.C., Youcef-Youmi, K.: Robot programming using augmented reality: an interactive method for planning collision-free paths. Robot. Comput.-Integr. Manuf. **25**, 689–701 (2009)
24. Greenlee, B.J., Karanxha, Z.: A study of group dynamics in educational leadership cohort and non-cohort groups. J. Res. Leadersh. Educ. **5**, 357–382 (2010)
25. Brown, B., et al.: Lessons from the lighthouse: collaboration in a shared mixed reality system. In: Proceedings of the SIGCHI Conference on Human Factors in Computing Systems, pp. 577–584. ACM, New York (2003)
26. Leonidis, A., Arampatzis, D., Louloudakis, N., Stephanidis, C.: The AmI-Solertis system: creating user experiences in smart environments. In: Proceedings of the 13th IEEE International Conference on Wireless and Mobile Computing, Networking and Communications (2017)
27. Korozi, M.: Empowering intelligent classrooms with attention monitoring and intervention cycles (2017)
28. Weintrop, D., Wilensky, U.: To block or not to block, that is the question: students' perceptions of blocks-based programming. In: Proceedings of the 14th International Conference on Interaction Design and Children, pp. 199–208. ACM (2015)
29. Blackmon, M.H., Polson, P.G., Kitajima, M., Lewis, C.: Cognitive walkthrough for the web. In: Proceedings of the SIGCHI Conference on Human Factors in Computing Systems, pp. 463–470. ACM (2002)
30. Nielsen, J.: Enhancing the explanatory power of usability heuristics. In: Proceedings of the SIGCHI Conference on Human Factors in Computing Systems, pp. 152–158. ACM (1994)

Fine-Grained Color Sketch-Based Image Retrieval

Yu Xia[(⊠)], Shuangbu Wang, Yanran Li, Lihua You, Xiaosong Yang,
and Jian Jun Zhang

National Centre for Computer Animation,
Bournemouth University, Bournemouth, UK
yxia@bournemouth.ac.uk

Abstract. We propose a novel fine-grained color sketch-based image
retrieval (CSBIR) approach. The CSBIR problem is investigated for the
first time using deep learning networks, in which deep features are used to
represent color sketches and images. A novel ranking method considering
both shape matching and color matching is also proposed. In addition,
we build a CSBIR dataset with color sketches and images to train and
test our method. The results show that our method has better retrieval
performance.

Keywords: Color sketch · Image retrieval · Deep learning ·
Triplet network

1 Introduction

Sketch-based image retrieval (SBIR) is a fundamental computer vision problem
in recent years [1–4]. To differentiate fine-grained variations of objects, the concept of fine-grained retrieval is first proposed by [5]. After that, fine-grained SBIR
techniques [6–8] attract an increase attention due to its outstanding retrieval
performance. However, almost all of the current studies only focus on the shape
details matching between the black-and-white sketch and the retrieved image,
ignoring color matching.

Inspired by the work of Bui and Collomosse [9], this paper aims to solve
the problem of fine-grained image retrieval based on color sketch, and make
the retrieval results consider both shape details matching and color matching.
Solving this problem is particularly important in commercial applications such
as searching a specific item on the online shopping platform by color finger-
sketching using a touchscreen device. For example, when users draw a sketch of
female wedding shoe with white color, they will obtain an image of white female
wedding shoe rather than other color shoes even the shapes of these shoes are
closer to the sketch.

Recent existing color sketch-based image retrieval methods mainly focus on
the extraction and comparison of hand-designed features of color sketches and

© Springer Nature Switzerland AG 2019
M. Gavrilova et al. (Eds.): CGI 2019, LNCS 11542, pp. 424–430, 2019.
https://doi.org/10.1007/978-3-030-22514-8_40

images based on gradients [1,2]. In this paper, we propose a novel CSBIR method based on the multi-branch deep convolutional neural network. The network consists of three identical branches, one of which takes color sketches as input and the other two take images as input during training. For achieving the optimal performance of the neural networks, a lot of training data are needed. Since the deep FG-SBIR model [8] provided a suitable CNN foundation for black-and-white sketch-based image retrieval, we build our pre-training model based on the deep FG-SBIR model.

We make the following contributions: (1) A color sketch-image dataset is created which contains 419 color sketch-image pairs of shoes; (2) A deep learning model is developed to implement fine-grained image retrieval based on color sketches; (3) A new color similarity comparison method with Hellinger distance is proposed to rank retrieval images after shape matching process.

2   Fine-Grained Instance-Level CSBIR Dataset

We create a CSBIR dataset specifically which contains a total of 419 shoe color sketch-image pairs to meet the requirements of our proposed method based on the Shoe Dataset [6]. Color edge maps are extracted from the corresponding images using 11 most common shoe colors, i. e., black, blue, brown, grey, green, orange, pink, purple, red, white and pale gold, and taken as inputs of the image branches during model training. Similarly, the color sketch corresponding to every image is created by using the defined 11 colors to color the original black-and-white sketch. Figure 1 shows some examples of color sketch-image pairs in CSBIR dataset.

Fig. 1. Examples of the CSBIR dataset (Color figure online)

3   Methodology

The deep convolutional neural network used in this paper is a Triplet network and the three branches in the network are identical which are homogeneous. A soft attention model and two shortcut connection architectures are adopted to improve the retrieval precision of the network.

3.1 Triplet Network and Triplet Loss

Triplet network [10] has three convolutional neural networks. Three branches of Triplet network have three different inputs. Note that the second and the third branches share the same parameters. Given a triplet of a query sketch A, a similar image P and a dissimilar image N, the Triplet network needs to satisfy:

$$d(A, P) - d(A, N) + \alpha \leq 0 \tag{1}$$

where $d(\cdot)$ is Euclidean distance, α is a margin which means the distance between $d(A, P)$ and $d(A, N)$.

To achieve this goal, Triplet Loss is defined as:

$$L(A, P, N) = max(d(A, P) - d(A, N) + \alpha, 0) \tag{2}$$

Considering all triplets in the dataset, the ultimate optimization goal is:

$$\min_{\theta_1, \theta_2} \sum_{i=1}^{m} L(A^{(i)}, P^{(i)}, N^{(i)}) \tag{3}$$

where m is the total number of triplets, θ_1 and θ_2 represent the parameters of the sketch and image input branches respectively.

By minimizing Eq. (3), the distance between A and P will be narrowed while the distance between A and N will be widened. Triplet network can acquire the representations of inputs with detailed information if there are sufficient triplet annotations. We apply Triplet network with Triplet Loss to carry out detail matching and achieve fine-grained color sketch-based image retrieval.

3.2 Network Structure

In order to avoid overfitting and alleviate domain discrepancy, we select homogeneous network which means the first branch shares the same set of parameters with the second and third branches and process our dataset by extracting color edge maps which are used as inputs of the second and third branches instead of images. Inspired by the work of Song et al. [8], we implement a soft attention model in every branch of the triplet homogeneous network to improve the retrieval accuracy and shortcut connection architectures to solve the problem of gradient disappearance in deep networks.

3.3 Shape Matching and Color Matching

To achieve CSBIR, we need to solve two matching problems, i. e., the shape matching and the color matching. Since a color sketch and the color edge map of an image are represented by the feature vectors which are outputted from the networks, we apply Eq. (1) to estimate the shape similarity of the color sketch and image. After shape matching process, we use histograms to describe the three RGB channels of the color sketch and image respectively, and then apply Hellinger distance to calculate the color similarity between the histograms of the color sketch and image. Hellinger distance is widely used to study the convergence of likelihood ratios between two distributions [11], which can be expressed as:

$$H_k(D^k, E^k) = 1 - \left(\sum_{i=1}^{n} \sqrt{D_i^k E_i^k} \right)^{\frac{1}{2}} \qquad (4)$$

where D^k and E^k are the histogram vectors of k (k is R,G or B) channel of the color sketch and the image, respectively, and D_i^k and E_i^k are the ith bin in D^k and E^k, respectively. The Hellinger distance of three RGB channels is defined as:

$$dist = \frac{1}{3}[H_R(D^R, E^R) + H_G(D^G, E^G) + H_B(D^B, E^B)] \qquad (5)$$

3.4 Matching Color Sketches and Images Using Triplet Homogeneous Network

After obtaining the CSBIR model trained by the training set of CSBIR dataset, we apply it to the testing set to verify the retrieval accuracy of our method (see Sect. 4). The pipeline of our proposed CSBIR is illustrated in Fig. 2.

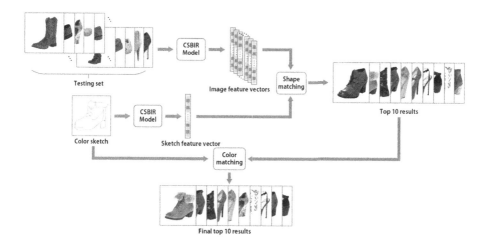

Fig. 2. Pipeline of the CSBIR method (Color figure online)

In the pipeline of the CSBIR method, the feature vector representations of all shoe images in the testing set have been obtained through pre-processing to improve the speed of real-time retrieval. The CSBIR method includes three steps. First, the user inputs a color sketch of a shoe as probe into the CSBIR model and gets its feature vector representation in real time. Second, the shape matching is applied to estimate shape similarity between the sketch feature vector and all the image feature vectors and find the top ten retrieval results which are the most similar to the shoe sketch in the dataset. Third, the color matching is used to estimate the color similarity between the color sketch and the top ten results of shape matching, and reorder the ten results according to the color similarity.

4   Experiments

We fine-tune the pre-trained model [8] using our CSBIR dataset. The CSBIR dataset contains 419 shoe color sketch-image pairs. It is split into two parts: 304 pairs as the fine-tuning training set and 115 pairs as the testing set.

4.1   Results

We compare our method with other two fine-grained sketch-based image retrieval methods, i. e., DTRM [6] and FG-SBIR [8], which apply DCNN for feature extraction. The DTRM was the first to use DCNN for fine-grained SBIR. To improve the retrieval accuracy, the FG-SBIR applied a soft attention model and shortcut connection architectures based on DTRM. We test our method, DTRM and FG-SBIR on our CSBIR testing set and calculate the retrieval accuracies within top K ($K = 1, 2, ..., 10$) retrieval results. We use accuracy @ K to describe the retrieval accuracy which is the percentage of the amount of times when the true-match image of a color sketch is ranked in the top K retrieval results.

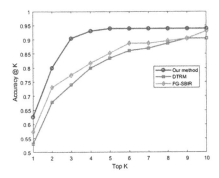

Fig. 3. Retrieval accuracy @ K for $K = 1$ to 10 of DTRM, FG-SBIR and our method

The results of the comparison for $K = 1$ to 10 are shown in Fig. 3. Compared with the DTRM and FG-SBIR methods, our method has the best retrieval accuracy within top K ($K = 1, 2, ..., 10$).

4.2   Visualizing Retrieval Results

We visualize part of the retrieval results to show the better retrieval accuracy of our method compared with the DTRM and FG-SBIR. In Fig. 4, the first row is the retrieval results of our method with query color sketch, the second row is the retrieval results of FG-SBIR with black-and-white sketch which has the same contour lines with the color sketch, and the third row is the retrieval results of DTRM using the same black-and-white sketch as input.

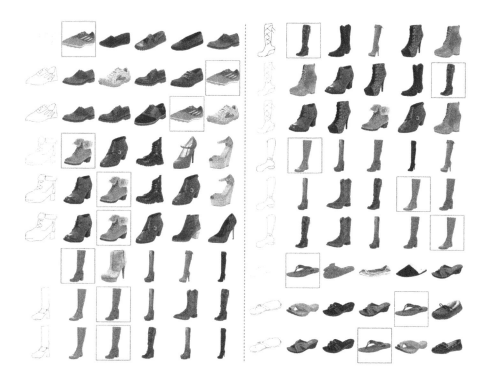

Fig. 4. The top five retrieval results by our method, FG-SBIR and DTRM. The true matches are highlighted in blue. (Color figure online)

By comparing the visual retrieval results, our method performs better in appearance matching including detailed shape matching and color matching. Unlike DTRM and FG-SBIR, our model can move the images with similar color up to the top of the retrieval results. For example, on the top shoe example in the right column, since the input color sketch is a long black boot sketch, the black boots are moved up to the top while boots of other colors are moved behind.

5   Conclusion

In this paper, we propose a novel fine-grained color sketch-based image retrieval method based on multi-branch deep convolutional neural networks, and first use a triplet homogeneous network to solve the fine-grained CSBIR problem. In addition, we have created a CSBIR dataset of color sketch-image pairs and proposed a novel ranking method combined with the shape similarity matching and color similarity matching which makes the retrieval results get the best matching in appearance. Extensive experiments have been implemented to demonstrate the effectiveness and verify better retrieval performance of our proposed approach.

Acknowledgements. This research is supported by the PDE-GIR project which has received funding from the European Union's Horizon 2020 research and innovation programme under the Marie Skłodowska-Curie grant agreement No 778035. Yanran Li has received research grands from the South West Creative Technology Network.

References

1. Eitz, M., Hildebrand, K., Boubekeur, T., Alexa, M.: Sketch-based image retrieval: benchmark and bag-of-features descriptors. IEEE Trans. Vis. Comput. Graph. **17**(11), 1624–1636 (2011)
2. Hu, R., Collomosse, J.: A performance evaluation of gradient field hog descriptor for sketch based image retrieval. Comput. Vis. Image Underst. **117**(7), 790–806 (2013)
3. Kiran Yelamarthi, S., Krishna Reddy, S., Mishra, A., Mittal, A.: A zero-shot framework for sketch based image retrieval. In: ECCV, pp. 300–317 (2018)
4. Huang, F., Jin, C., Zhang, Y., Weng, K., Zhang, T., Fan, W.: Sketch-based image retrieval with deep visual semantic descriptor. Pattern Recogn. **76**, 537–548 (2018)
5. Li, Y., Hospedales, T.M., Song, Y.Z., Gong, S.: Fine-grained sketch-based image retrieval by matching deformable part models. In: British Machine Vision Conference (2014)
6. Yu, Q., Liu, F., Song, Y.Z., Xiang, T., Hospedales, T.M., Loy, C.C.: Sketch me that shoe. In: Proceedings of the IEEE Conference on Computer Vision and Pattern Recognition, pp. 799–807 (2016)
7. Sangkloy, P., Burnell, N., Ham, C., Hays, J.: The sketchy database: learning to retrieve badly drawn bunnies. ACM Trans. Graph. (TOG) **35**(4), 119 (2016)
8. Song, J., Yu, Q., Song, Y.Z., Xiang, T., Hospedales, T.M.: Deep spatial-semantic attention for fine-grained sketch-based image retrieval. In: Proceedings of the IEEE International Conference on Computer Vision, pp. 5551–5560 (2017)
9. Bui, T., Collomosse, J.: Scalable sketch-based image retrieval using color gradient features. In: Proceedings of the IEEE International Conference on Computer Vision Workshops, pp. 1–8 (2015)
10. Schroff, F., Kalenichenko, D., Philbin, J.: FaceNet: a unified embedding for face recognition and clustering. In: Proceedings of the IEEE Conference on Computer Vision and Pattern Recognition, pp. 815–823 (2015)
11. Le Cam, L., Yang, G.L.: Asymptotics in Statistics: Some Basic Concepts. Springer, New York (2012). https://doi.org/10.1007/978-1-4684-0377-0

Development and Usability Analysis of a Mixed Reality GPS Navigation Application for the Microsoft HoloLens

Renan Luigi Martins Guarese$^{(\boxtimes)}$ (iD) and Anderson Maciel$^{(\boxtimes)}$ (iD)

Institute of Informatics, Federal University of Rio Grande do Sul (UFRGS),
Porto Alegre, Brazil
{rlmguarese,amaciel}@inf.ufrgs.br

Abstract. Navigation in real environments is arguably one of the primary applications for the mixed reality (MR) interaction paradigm. We propose a wearable MR system based on off-the-shelf devices as an alternative to the widespread handheld-based GPS navigation paradigm. Our system uses virtual holograms placed on the terrain instead of the usual heads-up display approach where the augmentations follow the line of sight. In a user experiment, we assessed performance and usability. We monitored user attention through EEG while performing a navigation task using either the MR or the handheld interface. Results show that users deemed our solution to offer a higher visibility to both the oncoming traffic and the suggested route. EEG readings also exposed a significantly less demanding focus level for our prototype. An easiness to learn and use was also indicated for the MR system.

Keywords: Mixed and augmented reality ·
Human-computer interaction · GPS navigation

1 Introduction

When using a Personal Navigation Device (PND) while driving or riding to follow a suggested route, vehicle operators have to often take their eyes off the road ahead and onto the GPS navigation screen. Studies have shown that distraction by a navigation device was significantly associated with the most serious incidents, pointing out that among the 44 deadly incidents researched, 21 involved distraction [5].

In this paper, we present the development of a GPS navigation system using virtual elements placed at the surface of the road using Mixed Reality (MR). By projecting a path onto the surface of the road, MR objects can be placed on

This study was partly funded by the Coordenação de Aperfeiçoamento de Pessoal de Nível Superior - Brasil (CAPES) - Finance Code 001, and partly by CNPq. We also acknowledge FAPERGS (project 17/2551-0001192-9) and CNPq-Brazil (project 311353/2017-7) for their financial support.

top of their proper geo-located analogous places, such as minimal curves of the road, round-abouts and corners. With the help of these virtual elements, users can be guided throughout the extent of a route without the need to take their focus away from the road. Despite having an ultimate use in motorized vehicles, this preliminary development and subsequent tests were aimed at pedestrians in order to validate the technology before inserting it into more accident-prone scenarios.

2   Related Work

Using either a smartphone or an HMD (Head-Mounted Display), several AR indoor navigation studies have been accomplished. The most relevant ones present AR-based applications that use pre-scanned environmental features to guide users inside buildings. Rehman [7] claims that the 3D scanning during the pre-deployment stages was time consuming and complicated, which hampered their ability to conduct large scale tests. Aside from that, their study also exposes that, when using the AR solutions, subjects presented the lowest workload of their tests. Bagling [1] mentions that people using the Hololens (HL) indoors, in a finding objects task, performed better than smartphone and paper maps.

Prior to commercial Head-Up Display (HUD) navigation systems, Madenica et al. [6] compared the use of an AR HUD PND with two other common PND methods by using a high-fidelity driving simulator. A thorough usability study was made. The results exposed that the HUD option provided for more visual attention at the road ahead. Their AR solution, besides being purely simulated, presented a yellow path projected above the center of the road at a height of about 2 meters. In our work, we reproduced their simulated AR solution in a real world MR setting.

3   Methodology

3.1   Design and Implementation

Arguably, a GPS navigator is meant to work ubiquitously, making it intrinsic not to require markers. This can be accomplished with the HL[1], an Optical See-through MR HMD. Since the HL does not provide all hardware necessary, a regular smartphone was used as a second device in our design, supplying it with GPS data and access to the Google Maps Platform. Regarding the development of the mobile application *per se*, it creates a TCP server and broadcasts a message containing the aforementioned information. We developed the holoNav using the Unity 3D Engine. This MR application receives a route graph that leads users from their current location to a requested destination, generating virtual holograms to guide the user along the path in a turn-by-turn manner. The latitude and longitude of these objects are mapped onto the 3D space around the user, according to their real analogous points in space.

---

[1] https://docs.microsoft.com/en-us/windows/mixed-reality/hololens-hardware-deta ils.

Fig. 1. Examples of route holograms generated by the holoNav application (Color figure online).

Several methods exist to calculate distances between two pairs of coordinates, such as the Haversine Formula [4]. This method was simplified in order to reduce the overhead of the algorithm based on the notion that one degree of latitude can be roughly approximated to 111111 m [2]. Thus, it is possible to use the GPS position of the user as an origin point and map all points of a received route graph onto the X and Y-axis distances away from the user, in a two-dimensional manner. The farther the points, the larger the error. Hologram positions are updated occasionally to fix any misplacements done by the HMD, which may also happen when the depth is hard to perceive. To do so, the application requests a new route, using the current GPS location and resets all path objects. Aside from fixing accumulated spatial displacements, resetting also suggests a more relevant route in case the user goes off track.

The exact front of the user is firstly assumed to be the north direction. In this fashion, a yaw rotation is necessary to align it, equivalent to the number of degrees this direction is divergent from the factual north. The magnetic north heading received from the smartphone magnetometer is a good starting point measurement. However, the deviation between the true north pole of the Earth and its magnetic equivalent is not constant across the Earth[2]. A transient design choice was made to keep this value *ad hoc*, using the deviation angle pertaining to our city. As to facilitate with the particular positioning of the phone, the user is suggested to place it according to a hologram in the form of a red arrow pointing ahead. This process has to be done only once, since the HL's accelerometers and gyroscope ensure that all object positions and rotations are maintained.

Relative to the holograms that indicate the suggested route, two kinds of objects are generated. At first, green arrows similar to Fig. 1-right are placed in each step of the route, one for each node of the graph. A different 3D arrow object was designed for each kind of *maneuver* the mapping API presents, e.g. an arrow pointing right for *turn-right* and a roundabout figure with an arrow head pointing left for *roudabout-left*. A textual description of the current turn is also displayed on the arrow body. The second type of object generated is a regular 2D blue plane parallel to the ground, as in Fig. 1-left. These planes are rectangles that link all of the *turns* present in the route together, thus showing a virtual path for the user to follow between arrows.

---

[2] https://www.ngdc.noaa.gov/geomag/WMM/.

3.2   Experimental Evaluation

Although an MR interface has intrinsic advantages due to egocentric navigation, a user study is necessary to properly assess its practical use. Our test design compares the proposed MR solution with a well established navigation tool. Being reasonable to assume it as the golden standard, we intend to assess the usability and performance gap between our prototype and the widely used navigation application. In the effort of accomplishing an impartial test, the order of the two tests was alternated for each subject. Tests were taken by users walking on the sidewalk, for the sake of avoiding any possible accidents.

Regarding the quantitative dependent variables, both route time and displacement were measured. Attention efficiency was measured by means of a Brain-Computer Interface (BCI) headset[3], which reads electroencephalography (EEG) signals and filters them into focused attention data, exposing the user concentration efficiency over time. The number of times each user checked the handheld device was also counted.

As for the qualitative attributes, users were asked to answer a survey comprised of three questionnaires for each test. The first two were traditional multi-dimensional assessment tools, namely the NASA TLX[4] (Task Load Index) and the SUS[5] (System Usability Scale). The third set of questions was adapted based on the *Mobile or Projector* questionnaire [3], since its comparison is similar to ours. All three questionnaires followed the Likert scale [8].

The same route of 350 m was chosen for both tests, a 4 min walk with two 90-degree turns. One at a time, users were taken to the starting point. The system was preset with the route as to not require any previous knowledge from subjects. Subjects were given the device to be tested and minimal instructions. Once at the destination, they were asked to answer the survey. After completion, the procedure was done again using the remaining of the two systems.

4   Results

In total, twelve subjects participated in user assessments (two female), varying from 21 to 35 years of age, average being 26.23 and the standard deviation (SD) 3.21. No effect of eye condition, age or gender was found on the resulting data. Some subjects performed their tests under very bright sun light, which was partially redressed by attaching a piece of dark cellophane sheet to the visor. Five subjects had problems with the EEG headset coming loose during the tests, which made it present a gap amidst the readings. These EEG samples were discarded.

---

[3] http://neurosky.com/biosensors/eeg-sensor/biosensors/.
[4] https://humansystems.arc.nasa.gov/groups/TLX/.
[5] https://www.usability.gov/how-to-and-tools/methods/system-usability-scale.html.

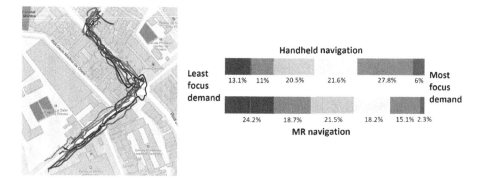

Fig. 2. Left: Geo-located paths performed by subjects using the MR application. Right: Subject average percentage of time spent in each focused attention level.

4.1   Quantitative Results

Figure 2-left displays the GPS data regarding the path test participants trod. Disregarding the second trial for each user, i.e., accounting only for the tests in which the subject was not familiar with the path beforehand, the respective times were 3 min 42 s (SD 31.09), and 4 min 51 s (SD 59.84). These results expose a roughly 31% increase in time for the MR application.

The number of times users looked away from the route in order to check the navigator application in their handheld device varied from 3 to 14 times. The average being 8.15 (SD 3.48) or 2.71 glances away from the road every 100 m. Regarding the EEG results, the averages of each level of focused attention was accounted in Fig. 2-right. Joining together the three higher levels of attention, users spent an average of 55.38% of the time at a high level of focus while using the smartphone application. This percentage dropped to 35.64% while using the HMD solution.

4.2   Qualitative Results

Figure 3 displays the average score for each statement subjects responded to. Both raw NASA TLX and SUS results are grouped together and indicated by name. The remaining statements represent the third questionnaire used. The unweighted TLX score was evaluated as 29.81 for the mobile navigator and 39.42 for the HMD application. Meanwhile, SUS final scores were 86.6 for the smartphone application, dropping to 66.6 regarding the MR solution, respectively an A and a C, according to SUS standards.

4.3   Discussion

Users attributed a higher score to the MR solution both in "route attentiveness" and in "traffic visibility", categorizing how easy or seamless it was to perceive the suggested route and how low it affected the capacity of users to see the

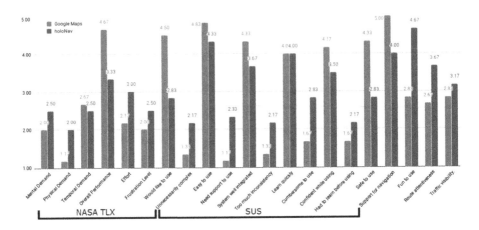

Fig. 3. Qualitative questionnaire results.

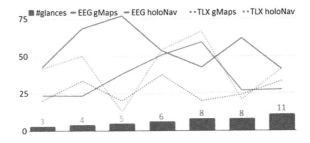

Fig. 4. Number of glances at the handheld device vs. EEG efficiency and NASA TLX

oncoming traffic and aspects of the road. The substantial increase in route time could be explained, for instance, by the "fun to use" aspect, being arguable that users demonstrated a considerably higher interest in the novelty aspect of the holoNav solution.

Ratings such as inconsistency, complexity and system integration could be improved refining the coordinates mapping algorithms and increasing the screen brightness. However, the least favorable aspects of the proposed solution are largely related to the UX of the HMD *per se*. Mental and physical demand, effort and inconvenience, likeness to use again and safety are all heavily dependant on the HMD paradigm. Nonetheless, as demand increases and the industry adjusts to it, it is customary for devices to get smaller and faster over time.

Six out of the seven subjects displayed a significantly higher level of attention during the handheld device trial. Disregarding the odd one out, an increase of 1.94 times was measured, virtually doubling the average attention level of the user. Arguably, the higher attention required means a greater cognitive load, which would possibly interfere in other attention seeking activities, such as driving or riding a bicycle. The high number of times subjects glanced at their phones could explain peaks in attention, since mentally translating the route seen in a 2D map into the user real surroundings requires some level of concentration.

However, no correlation could be observed between these two pieces of data, as seen in Fig. 4. Despite a couple of outliers, NASA TLX results shows some relation to EEG efficiency results, validating user responses to a certain degree. Regardless, further studies should be held with a larger population and in more demanding guiding conditions in order to obtain a less biased set of data.

5   Conclusion

The present study focused on comparing the map navigation task using a smartphone versus an original proposed solution. The conception, design and development of an MR application for an HMD was illustrated, which enables users to request, perceive and follow a geo-located route in the form of virtual holograms.

We demonstrated the performance and usability of the proposed application in objectively guiding subjects throughout an entire real-world route. Such an accomplishment provides an interesting advantage, whereas mentally interpreting a two dimensional map (allocentric) into the actual streets surrounding the user (egocentric) is not a trivial task, specially in inner-city locations with complex crossroads and traffic. The MR HMD proved to be a great interface for freeing user attention, mainly visual, since it follows the HUD paradigm. Despite its limitations, it was feasible to build a working prototype capable of day-to-day navigation. This is a highly significant aspect for the current state-of-the-art both in augmented reality and navigation, since new technologies might emerge with more capable and less effort-consuming devices.

References

1. Bagling, M.: Navigating to real life objects in indoor environments using an augmented reality headset. Master's thesis, Umea University, Umea, Sweden (2017)
2. Beding, S.: The Christopher Columbus Encyclopedia. Palgrave Macmillan, Basingstoke (2016)
3. Dancu, A., Franjcic, Z., Fjeld, M.: Smart flashlight: map navigation using a bike-mounted projector. In: Proceedings of the SIGCHI Conference on Human Factors in Computing Systems. CHI 2014, pp. 3627–3630 (2014)
4. Inman, J.: Navigation and Nautical Astronomy for the Use of British Seamen. C. and J. Rivington, London (1835)
5. Lin, A.Y., Kuehl, K., Schöning, J., Hecht, B.: Understanding "death by GPS": a systematic study of catastrophic incidents associated with personal navigation technologies. In: Proceedings of the 2017 CHI Conference on Human Factors in Computing Systems. CHI 2017, pp. 1154–1166 (2017)
6. Medenica, Z., Kun, A.L., Paek, T., Palinko, O.: Augmented reality vs. street views: a driving simulator study comparing two emerging navigation aids. In: Proceedings of the 13th International Conference on Human Computer Interaction with Mobile Devices and Services. MobileHCI 2011, pp. 265–274 (2011)
7. Rehman, U.: Augmented reality for indoor navigation and task guidance. Master's thesis, University of Waterloo, Waterloo, Ontario, Canada (2016)
8. Robinson, J.: Likert scale. In: Michalos, A.C. (ed.) Encyclopedia of Quality of Life and Well-Being Research, pp. 3620–3621. Springer, Dordrecht (2014). https://doi.org/10.1007/978-94-007-0753-5_1654

A Synthesis-by-Analysis Network with Applications in Image Super-Resolution

Lechao Cheng(ID) and Zhangye Wang$^{(\boxtimes)}$(ID)

State Key Lab of CAD&CG, Zhejiang University,
Hangzhou 310058, People's Republic of China
liygcheng@zju.edu.cn, zywang@cad.zju.edu.cn

Abstract. Recent studies have demonstrated the successful application of convolutional neural networks in single image super-resolution. In this paper, we present a general synthesis-by-analysis network for super-resolving a low-resolution image. Unlike Laplacian Pyramid Super-Resolution Network (LapSRN) that progressively reconstructs the sub-band residuals of high-resolution images, our proposed network breaks through the sequential dependency to expand the input and output into multiple disjoint bandpass signals. At each band, we perform the nonlinear mapping in truncated frequency interval by applying a carefully designed sub-network. Specifically, we propose a validated network substructure that considers both efficiency and accuracy. We also perform exhaustive experiments in existing commonly used dataset. The recovered high-resolution image is competitive or even superior in quality compared to those images produced by other methods.

Keywords: Super-resolution · Synthesis-by-analysis · Bandpass

1 Introduction

Single image super-resolution is a popular technique in computer vision that aims to reconstruct a high-resolution (I^H) image from their low-resolution (I^L) counterparts. However, the results of these techniques are far from being satisfactory for a variety of computer vision applications [20], ranging from surveillance to medical imaging [13].

Traditional studies on image super-resolution usually adopt interpolation mechanisms to super-resolve a I^L image. However, this method often generates overly smooth results with unbearable artifacts. These results tend to be blurry and lack high-frequency details when the input image precision is limited or when the magnification factor is large. Therefore, various natural image priors, such as edge prior [3] and gradient profile [14], are being exploited. Besides, sparse representation [17] is also one of the popular methods which learn the overcomplete dictionary of patches that are randomly sampled from similar images. several methods for mapping regression have been introduced including but not limited to neighbor embedding [1,2], decision tree [11], random forest [12], and

© Springer Nature Switzerland AG 2019
M. Gavrilova et al. (Eds.): CGI 2019, LNCS 11542, pp. 438–444, 2019.
https://doi.org/10.1007/978-3-030-22514-8_42

convolutional neural network based method, which is known for its excellent performance [5,8].

In this paper, we propose a synthesis-by-analysis network that learns the nonlinear transformation in a bandpass fashion. Recent laplacian-based [9] and wavelet-based works [6] have performed hierarchical analysis to obtain good results. In contrast to these works, we extend the decomposition process to a more general version where we split the input/output signal into multiple disjoint bands and establish predictive relationships in each band. We also treat the in-band mapping as an image-to-image translation problem and approximate this with a carefully defined network.

We quantitatively and qualitatively explore the effectiveness of the proposed model and block architecture by conducting experiments on an existing benchmark dataset. The final results achieve state-of-the-art performance in both SSIM and PSNR and present more reasonable visual effects.

2   Synthesis-by-Analysis Network

In this section, we describe our proposed synthesis-by-analysis framework that aims to super-resolve an input image I^L to an output image I^H. We first present a general overview of this framework and then describe our model reformation process that exploits this property to our final network structure with applications in image super-resolution.

The proposed framework can be divided into the analysis, nonlinear mapping, and synthesis stages. In the analysis stage, the input image I^L is transformed into multiple sub-band signals. After that, the transformation in each branch learns the inband relation independently. It has been well demonstrated that deep convolutional neural networks are a general and practical parametrization and optimization framework for a variety of such mapping relations. In the synthesis stage, the result of each branch are integrated to form the final prediction I^H.

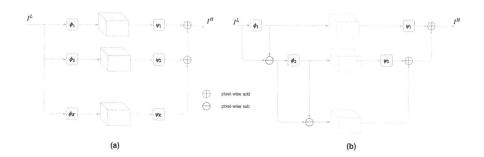

Fig. 1. Parallel structure (a) vs. Hierarchical structure (b)

2.1   Reformation

We write the outputs of analysis stage and inband mapping as $[I_0^L, I_1^L, ..., I_K^L]$ and $[I_1^H, ..., I_K^H]$ respectively, where $I_0^L = I^L$ and K is the total number of layers. We denote the analysis and synthesis filters with respect to ith level as ϕ_i and ψ_i.

First, let us consider a simple *parallel structure* framework: for each level, the input image I^L was delivered into a learnable decomposition filter to obtain a sub-band image, that is $I_i^L = \phi_i(I^L)$. Then sub-network bridges domain gap to transfer the distribution of frequency from blurred image to high definition image. With the synthesis filter ψ_i, we finally obtain the target by summing over all components by $I^H = \sum_{i=1}^K \psi_i(I_i^H)$. Fig. 1(a) describes overall structure.

A critical transition is from *parallel structure* to *hierarchical structure* - as it turns to be possible to restrict the orthogonality over the distribution in frequency domain. Thus the input of i-th sub-network I_i^L becomes the residual of previous input I_{i-1}^L and its filtered version $\phi_{i-1}(I_{i-1}^L)$ except for the first layer. The synthesis stage happens to be the corresponding inverse process. More precisely, we denote the complete reconstruction output at i-th level as $I_i^{H'}$ and therefore $I^H = I_1^{H'}$. We formulate this process (Fig. 1(b)) as:

$$I_i^L = \begin{cases} I^L, & i = 0 \\ I_{i-1}^L - \phi_{i-1}(I_{i-1}^L), & 1 \le i \le K \end{cases} \tag{1}$$

$$I_i^{H'} = \begin{cases} I_{i+1}^{H'} + \psi_i(I_i^H), & 1 \le i \le K-1 \\ I_i^H, & i = K \end{cases} \tag{2}$$

We implement both parallel and hierarchical architectures in the experiments, and the results indicate that the hierarchical structure outperforms the parallel structure. Therefore, we mainly focus on the hierarchical version of the proposed network in the next section. All of the parameters of the ψ_i and ϕ_i, $i \in \{1, ..., K-1\}$, are learned in network. Noted that all of the sub-networks share the same architectural topology, which we refer as residual blocks and describe in detail in Sect. 2.2.

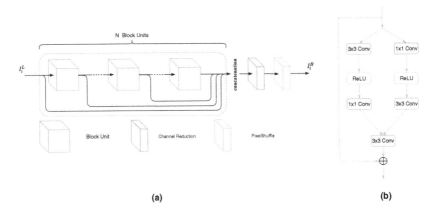

Fig. 2. Illustration of our Residual Blocks (a) and Block Unit (b).

2.2   Residual Blocks

The residual blocks are end-to-end convolutional sub-network that transform the input in different scales to the corresponding frequency components. Supposing that we have N sequential connected block units, the output for the last block is computed as the concatenation of all previously feature maps:

$$x_i = [I_i^L, x_i^1, ..., x_i^{N-1}, x_i^N] \tag{3}$$

where [.] denotes the concatenation operation. To guarantee efficiency, we add a channel reduction operation after the last block unit. This is implemented by a 1 × 1 convolution layer followed by PReLU. Further, we add a transposed convolution layer to match the size of the I^H image.

Several effective block units for image super-resolution have been proposed over the past few years. In this work, we develop the aggregated separable residual block (ASRB) (Fig. 2(b)) for the consideration of efficiency as well as accuracy. For the first bypass, we perform channel-wise convolution followed ReLU and then pass the output to a pixel-wise convolution layer. And the other bypass changes the order of convolution layers.

3   Experiments

In this section, we first introduce some common datasets for image super-resolution and then present the details of training setting.

3.1   Experiments Settings

We implemented our model in the PyTorch framework with a mini-batch size of 32. Following the research trend, we generate LR images by using bicubic downsampling method at scales of ×2, ×3, and ×4. During the training, we augment the input image by randomly cropping patches with a size of 48 × 48. We further augment the training data by randomly rotating the image by 90, 180, and 270 degrees and by randomly flipping the image horizontally/vertically with a probability of 0.5. we follow the trend to train our model on dataset DIV2K [15] and test on *Set5, Set14, BSD100, Urban100*, and *Manga109* with metrics PSNR and SSIM in the luminance channel of the YCbCr color space.

3.2   Results Analysis

Difference from LapSRN. Fig. 4 illustrates the convergence in terms of PSNR on dataset *BSD100* for ×3. The experiment that our framework converges to a better result has demonstrated its improvement.

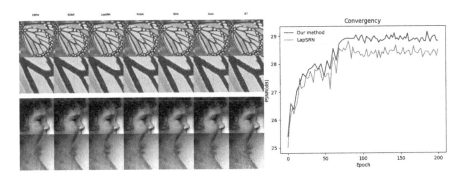

Fig. 3. Visual comparison of our pro-posed method with other methods.

Fig. 4. Convergence analysis compared to LapSRN

Table 1. Quantitative results compared to state-of-the-art methods. Noted that the red marked values show best performance and the blue marked values are in second place (Color table online)

Method	Scale	Set5		Set14		B100		Urban100		Manga109	
		PSNR	SSIM	PSNR	SSIM	PSNR	SSIM	PSNR	SSIM	PSNR	SSIM
SRCNN [4]	x2	36.71	0.9536	32.32	0.9052	31.36	0.8880	29.54	0.8962	35.74	0.9661
SCN [16]	x2	36.52	0.9530	32.42	0.9040	31.24	0.8840	29.50	0.8960	35.47	0.9660
SelfExSR [7]	x2	36.60	0.9537	32.46	0.9051	31.20	0.8863	29.55	0.8983	35.82	0.9671
FSRCNN [5]	x2	37.06	0.9554	32.76	0.9078	31.53	0.8912	29.88	0.9024	36.67	0.9694
VDSR [8]	x2	37.53	0.9583	33.05	0.9107	31.92	0.8965	30.79	0.9157	37.22	0.9729
EDSR [10]	x2	38.10	0.9599	33.93	0.9193	32.31	0.9009	32.93	0.9351	39.10	0.9773
LapSRN[9]	x2	37.44	0.9581	32.98	0.9115	31.76	0.8939	30.39	0.9092	37.19	0.9731
RDN [19]	x2	38.14	0.9603	33.99	0.9203	32.29	0.9007	32.84	0.9344	39.07	0.9770
RCAN [18]	x2	38.17	0.9604	34.10	0.9207	32.37	0.9017	33.30	0.9376	39.33	0.9776
SANet(ours)	x2	38.15	0.9606	34.04	0.9208	32.21	0.9012	32.94	0.9360	39.34	0.9762
SelfExSR [7]	x3	32.66	0.9089	29.34	0.8222	28.30	0.7839	26.45	0.8124	27.57	0.7997
FSRCNN [5]	x3	33.18	0.9140	29.37	0.8240	28.53	0.7910	26.43	0.8080	31.10	0.9210
VDSR [8]	x3	33.67	0.9210	29.78	0.8320	28.83	0.7990	27.14	0.8290	32.01	0.9340
EDSR [10]	x3	34.65	0.9280	30.52	0.8462	29.25	0.8093	28.80	0.8653	34.17	0.9476
LapSRN[9]	x3	33.82	0.9227	29.87	0.8320	28.82	0.7980	27.07	0.8280	32.21	0.9350
RDN [19]	x3	34.66	0.9285	30.55	0.8460	29.24	0.8084	28.77	0.8644	34.09	0.9473
RCAN [18]	x3	34.70	0.9288	30.63	0.8474	29.30	0.8102	29.07	0.8694	34.40	0.9488
SANet(ours)	x3	34.34	0.9286	30.64	0.8466	29.31	0.8097	28.89	0.8645	34.41	0.9471
SRCNN [4]	x4	30.49	0.8620	27.61	0.7540	26.91	0.7120	24.53	0.7240	27.66	0.8580
SCN [16]	x4	30.39	0.8620	27.48	0.7510	26.87	0.7100	24.52	0.7250	27.39	0.8560
SelfExSR [7]	x4	30.33	0.8610	27.54	0.7560	26.84	0.7120	24.82	0.7400	27.82	0.8650
FSRCNN [5]	x4	30.71	0.8650	27.70	0.7560	26.97	0.7140	24.61	0.7270	27.89	0.8590
VDSR [8]	x4	31.35	0.8820	28.03	0.7700	27.29	0.7260	25.18	0.7530	28.82	0.8860
EDSR [10]	x4	32.46	0.8970	28.80	0.7880	27.71	0.7420	26.64	0.8030	31.02	0.9150
LapSRN[9]	x4	31.47	0.8852	28.03	0.7689	27.31	0.7258	25.20	0.7547	29.09	0.8884
RDN [19]	x4	32.40	0.8976	28.77	0.7865	27.71	0.7412	26.60	0.8021	30.99	0.9141
RCAN [18]	x4	32.56	0.8989	28.82	0.7883	27.75	0.7429	26.81	0.8080	31.20	0.9163
SANet(ours)	x4	32.42	0.8988	28.83	0.7886	27.74	0.7438	26.75	0.8045	32.22	0.9132

3.3   Comparison with State-of-the-Art Results

Visual Effects. Figure 3 visually compares the aforementioned methods on the image *Butterfly*, on a scale of ×4. The prediction images generated by the other methods are obviously producing the over-smooth area. While the prediction image generated by our method recovers much more sharp details.

Quantitative Results. Table 1 summarizes the quantitative results obtained on five common datasets. Our model achieves state-of-the-art results and even outperforms most of the aforementioned methods. Specifically, when compared with LapSRN [9], our method shows the best performance among all datasets and scale factors, thereby highlighting the superiority of our independent bandpass sub-network. It is worth noting that our method offers few advantages over RCAN [18] but our results exhibit good detail restoration property and are visually close to the ground truth (see Fig. 3).

4   Conclusions

In this work, we propose a novel *synthesis-by-analysis* network for image super-resolution and explore the bandpass constraints for its network architecture. We approach this goal by decoupling the network into a cascade manner and achieve excellent results both quantitatively and qualitatively. Our proposed framework can also be easily adapted to other image-to-image translation problems.

Acknowledgements. This research work was supported partially by National Key R&D Program of China under grant No. 2017YFB1002703, Natural Science Foundation of China under Grant No. U1736109 and 863 Program of China under Grant No. 2015AA016404.

References

1. Bevilacqua, M., Roumy, A., Guillemot, C., Alberi-Morel, M.L.: Low-complexity single-image super-resolution based on nonnegative neighbor embedding (2012)
2. Chang, H., Yeung, D.Y., Xiong, Y.: Super-resolution through neighbor embedding. In: Proceedings of the 2004 IEEE Computer Society Conference on Computer Vision and Pattern Recognition, CVPR 2004, vol. 1, p. I. IEEE (2004)
3. Dai, S., Han, M., Xu, W., Wu, Y., Gong, Y.: Soft edge smoothness prior for alpha channel super resolution. In: 2007 IEEE Conference on Computer Vision and Pattern Recognition, CVPR 2007, pp. 1–8. IEEE (2007)
4. Dong, C., Loy, C.C., He, K., Tang, X.: Learning a deep convolutional network for image super-resolution. In: Fleet, D., Pajdla, T., Schiele, B., Tuytelaars, T. (eds.) ECCV 2014. LNCS, vol. 8692, pp. 184–199. Springer, Cham (2014). https://doi.org/10.1007/978-3-319-10593-2_13
5. Dong, C., Loy, C.C., Tang, X.: Accelerating the super-resolution convolutional neural network. In: Leibe, B., Matas, J., Sebe, N., Welling, M. (eds.) ECCV 2016. LNCS, vol. 9906, pp. 391–407. Springer, Cham (2016). https://doi.org/10.1007/978-3-319-46475-6_25

6. Huang, H., He, R., Sun, Z., Tan, T., et al.: Wavelet-SRNet: a wavelet-based CNN for multi-scale face super resolution. In: Proceedings of the IEEE Conference on Computer Vision and Pattern Recognition, pp. 1689–1697 (2017)
7. Huang, J.B., Singh, A., Ahuja, N.: Single image super-resolution from transformed self-exemplars. In: Proceedings of the IEEE Conference on Computer Vision and Pattern Recognition, pp. 5197–5206 (2015)
8. Kim, J., Kwon Lee, J., Mu Lee, K.: Accurate image super-resolution using very deep convolutional networks. In: Proceedings of the IEEE Conference on Computer Vision and Pattern Recognition, pp. 1646–1654 (2016)
9. Lai, W.S., Huang, J.B., Ahuja, N., Yang, M.H.: Deep Laplacian pyramid networks for fast and accurate super resolution. In: IEEE Conference on Computer Vision and Pattern Recognition, vol. 2, p. 5 (2017)
10. Lim, B., Son, S., Kim, H., Nah, S., Lee, K.M.: Enhanced deep residual networks for single image super-resolution. In: The IEEE Conference on Computer Vision and Pattern Recognition (CVPR) Workshops, July 2017
11. Salvador, J., Perez-Pellitero, E.: Naive Bayes super-resolution forest. In: Proceedings of the IEEE International Conference on Computer Vision, pp. 325–333 (2015)
12. Schulter, S., Leistner, C., Bischof, H.: Fast and accurate image upscaling with super-resolution forests. In: Proceedings of the IEEE Conference on Computer Vision and Pattern Recognition, pp. 3791–3799 (2015)
13. Shi, W., et al.: Cardiac image super-resolution with global correspondence using multi-atlas patchmatch. In: Mori, K., Sakuma, I., Sato, Y., Barillot, C., Navab, N. (eds.) MICCAI 2013. LNCS, vol. 8151, pp. 9–16. Springer, Heidelberg (2013). https://doi.org/10.1007/978-3-642-40760-4_2
14. Sun, J., Xu, Z., Shum, H.Y.: Image super-resolution using gradient profile prior. In: 2008 IEEE Conference on Computer Vision and Pattern Recognition, CVPR 2008, pp. 1–8. IEEE (2008)
15. Timofte, R., et al.: NTIRE 2017 challenge on single image super-resolution: methods and results. In: 2017 IEEE Conference on Computer Vision and Pattern Recognition Workshops (CVPRW), pp. 1110–1121. IEEE (2017)
16. Wang, Z., Liu, D., Yang, J., Han, W., Huang, T.: Deep networks for image super-resolution with sparse prior. In: Proceedings of the IEEE International Conference on Computer Vision, pp. 370–378 (2015)
17. Yang, J., Wright, J., Huang, T.S., Ma, Y.: Image super-resolution via sparse representation. IEEE Trans. Image Process. **19**(11), 2861–2873 (2010)
18. Zhang, Y., Li, K., Li, K., Wang, L., Zhong, B., Fu, Y.: Image super-resolution using very deep residual channel attention networks. arXiv preprint arXiv:1807.02758 (2018)
19. Zhang, Y., Tian, Y., Kong, Y., Zhong, B., Fu, Y.: Residual dense network for image super-resolution. In: The IEEE Conference on Computer Vision and Pattern Recognition (CVPR) (2018)
20. Zou, W.W., Yuen, P.C.: Very low resolution face recognition problem. IEEE Trans. Image Process. **21**(1), 327–340 (2012)

Towards Moving Virtual Arms Using Brain-Computer Interface

Jaime Riascos$^{(\boxtimes)}$ (ID), Steeven Villa$^{(\boxtimes)}$ (ID), Anderson Maciel(ID), Luciana Nedel(ID), and Dante Barone

Institute of Informatics, Federal University of Rio Grande do Sul (UFRGS), Porto Alegre, Brazil
{jarsalas,dsvsalazar,amaciel,nedel,barone}@inf.ufrgs.br
http://inf.ufrgs.br/~jarsalas, http://inf.ufrgs.br/~dsvsalazar,
http://inf.ufrgs.br/~amaciel, http://inf.ufrgs.br/~nedel

Abstract. Motor imagery Brain-Computer Interface (MI-BCI) is a paradigm widely used for controlling external devices by imagining bodily movements. This technology has inspired researchers to use it in several applications such as robotic prostheses, games, and virtual reality (VR) scenarios. We study the inclusion of an imaginary third arm as a part of the control commands for BCI. To this end, we analyze a set of open-close hand tasks (including a third arm that comes out from the chest) performed in two VR scenarios: the classical BCI Graz, with arrows as feedback; and a first-person view of a human-like avatar performing the corresponding tasks. This study purpose is to explore the influence of both time window of the trials and the frequency bands on the accuracy of the classifiers. Accordingly, we used a Filter Bank Common Spatial Patterns (FBCSP) algorithm for several time windows (100, 200, 400, 600, 800, 1000 and 2000 ms) for extracting features and evaluating the classification accuracy. The offline classification results show that a third arm can be effectively used as a control command (accuracy > 0.62%). Likewise, the human-like avatar condition (67%) outperforms the Graz condition (63%) significantly, suggesting that the realistic scenario can reduce the abstractness of the third arm. This study, thus, motivates the further inclusion of non-embodied motor imagery task in BCI systems.

Keywords: Brain-Computer Interface · Virtual reality · Rubber hand illusion

1 Introduction

Along the years, researchers have sought different alternatives to allow human-machine communication. In this context, Brain-Computer Interface (BCI) plays

---

This study was partly funded by the Coordenação de Aperfeiçoamento de Pessoal de Nível Superior - Brasil (CAPES) - Finance Code 001, and partly by CNPq.

M. Gavrilova et al. (Eds.): CGI 2019, LNCS 11542, pp. 445–452, 2019.
https://doi.org/10.1007/978-3-030-22514-8_43

a major role, motivated by overcoming the difficulties experienced by impaired people [9] or just by providing a non-mechanical user interface [5].

Motor Imagery BCI (MI-BCI) has been widely used and explored in active BCI [14]. MI-BCI employs sensorimotor rhythms (SMRs) that can be modulated voluntarily through the mental representation of physical motor actions. These patterns are called event-related de-synchronization (ERD/ERS) and have been successfully used for controlling different devices in BCI [5,6,9,11].

As BCI is a relatively new research area, establishing metrics to objectively assess BCI systems (e.g., classification accuracy plus usability) is still a task to be done. Potential user identification is a mandatory step to design suitable BCI applications. However, this requires additional resources and developments of wearable recording equipment. Finally, the training and feedback should consider human factors and include the user inside the BCI loop through a more realistic, natural and intuitive training and feedback.

Skola and Liarnokapis [13] carried out a recent work using an embodied VR training for MI-BCI. A human-like avatar performs the motor actions in synchrony with the user's actions. This neurofeedback-guided motor imagery training reports improvements in classification rates in comparison with the Graz paradigm. Even though it has not reached a significant difference, the authors report that ERD in VR subjects is stronger than the control group.

In that vein, this work studies an offline exploration of the classification of a third arm task in a BCI system. In order to explore as much as possible the differences in the classification of this task, several time windows were used in a Filter-Bank Common-Spatial Pattern (FBCSP) [1] for extracting features to train three classifiers: Support Vector Machine (SVM), K-Nearest Neighbors (KNN) and Linear Discriminant Analysis (LDA). Throughout such effort, we compared two training conditions: the traditional Graz paradigm and a realistic human-like feedback. In light of the results, we argue the feasibility of including the virtual third arm into a BCI system, and in line with the literature, the realistic training enhances the modulation of ERS/ERD patterns, and consequently, the performance of the user in motor imagery tasks.

2   Methods

2.1   EEG Signal Processing

EEG Pre-processing. The recorded data is imported and processed into EEGLAB (14.1) [4] (under Matlab 2017b). After down-sampling at 115 Hz, the signals are band-pass filtered at range 1–35 Hz using a finite impulse response (FIR) filter. Usually, a notch filter is used for line noise, but this method generally creates band-holes, and distortions close the cut-off frequency. Therefore, the Cleanline plugin, which uses multi-taper regression for removing sinusoidal artifacts, is used at 50–115 Hz instead. Likewise, Cleanraw plugin is set-up for rejecting bad channel. The rejected channels are then interpolated using a spherical function. Finally, EEG signals are re-referenced using common average referenced (CAR).

This study aims to explore as much as possible the influence of both time window of the trials and the frequency bands on the accuracy of the classifiers. Therefore, we used a Filter Bank Common Spatial Patterns (FBCSP) algorithm [1] for several time windows (100, 200, 400, 600, 800, 1000 and 2000 ms) for extracting features and evaluating the classification accuracy. The bank with the MI frequency bands is comprised of μ (8–12 Hz), low β (12–16 Hz), middle β (16–24 Hz), high β (24–30 Hz), and whole β (12–30 Hz) bands. The reason of splitting the β band into sub-bands is for getting enough variables for the FBCSP algorithm to work.

Feature Extraction. The ERS/ERD patterns are predominant in μ (8–12 Hz), and β (13–30 Hz) rhythms and in its onset goes from 500 ms up to three seconds after the movement execution [12]. Inspired by these facts, we built a framework to obtain the best combination of window size, frequency band, and classifier for each user. For obtaining a pool of possible combinations, we ran the Filter Bank Common Spatial Pattern (FBCSP) algorithm [1] in seven time-window sizes of the signal (100, 200, 400, 600, 800, 1000 and 2000 ms)) and five frequency bands (8–12 Hz,12–16 Hz, 16–24 Hz,24–30 Hz,12–30 Hz).

The method employs a greedy algorithm to heuristically find the best combination based on the classification error rates of all possibilities. We focused on the variability that exists across the users in their performance. So, with this approach, we were able to create a suitable and user-centered BCI classification.

The FBCSP approach has demonstrated successful performance in BCI applications [1]. This method extracts the most relevant spectral and spatial features using a CSP filter for each frequency band. CSP is one of the most known and widely used methods for extracting features in a two classes BCI application [3,8]. CSP computes the project matrix $\mathbf{W} \in \mathbb{R}^{c \times c}$ that linearly transforms the band-pass filtered data $\mathbf{E} \in \mathbb{R}^{c \times t}$ into a spatial filtered signal $\mathbf{Z} \in \mathbb{R}^{c \times t}$ (with c being the number of channels and t the EEG samples per channel) as follows:

$$\mathbf{Z} = W^T E \tag{1}$$

Thus, the power of $\mathbf{Z}$ effectively discriminates two mental states (classes), maximizing the variance under one condition meanwhile it is minimizing for the other [3]. In order to get the most discriminative patterns, the first and last m ($m = 3$) columns of $\mathbf{W}$ were used to create the spatial-filtered signal $\mathbf{Z}$. The m-dimensional feature vector is then formed from the logarithm of the normalized variance of $\mathbf{Z}$:

$$v_i = \log\left(var(Z_i)\right), \quad i = 1, 2, ..., 2m. \tag{2}$$

This results in 30 features (six CSP filters per each frequency bands) for each EEG trial in the specific window. From these features, the maximum Relevance Minimum Redundancy (mRMR) feature selection algorithm is used to extract the most relevant features [10]. This algorithm minimizes the redundancy meanwhile maximize the relevance of the features using mutual information. As the size of v_i depends on the frequency bands, the number of selected features was progressively increased (step = 3) from the minimum amount (6) up to the total size of v_i. Hence, the selected features for each time window is used to separately train three common BCI classifiers [7]: Support Vector Machine (SVM), K-Nearest Neighbor (KNN), and Linear Discriminant Analysis (LDA).

2.2 Classification

We used two of the most popular linear approaches (SVM and LDA) and a non-parametric method (KNN). These methods were trained to classify independently four binary imaginary tasks: Third and Left hand (TH\LH); Third and Right hand (TH\RH); Third hand and Resting State (TH\RS); and Left and Right hand (LH\RH). The reader can notice that the real movements are not included in the classification. The intention of including the real movements in the experiment was to reduce the abstractness of the three imaginative tasks and have a fresh mental representation of the action.

The miss-classification error was computed using the usual k-fold cross-validation approach. This method randomly divides the data into k equal size partitions and uses k−1 sets to train the model and one set to validate it. In this study, we used ten times the 10-fold cross-validation. Finally, the above classifiers were implemented using the Statistics and Machine Learning Toolbox of Matlab. Both SVM and LDA used the default parameters (linear kernel and standardize predictor data for SVM and LDA without hyperparameter optimization). KNN used a Euclidean distance with $k = 5$.

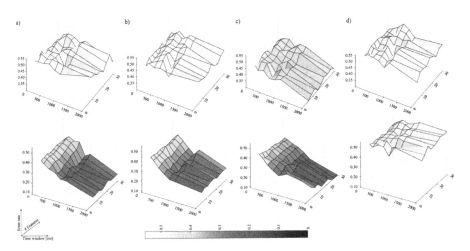

Fig. 1. Error rates over number of features and time window size for all users. Top: Graz condition. Bottom: Hands condition. The four binary classification are represented by (a) TH/LH; (b) TH/RH; (c) TH/RS; and (d) LH/RH.

3 Results

Figure 1 shows the error rates in function of the number of features and the size of the time windows for the KNN in each binary classification. We obtained these surfaces for both Graz (top) and Hands (bottom) conditions as well as for each classifier (SVM, KNN, LDA). Initially, we can see that Hands condition reached lower error rates than Graz for KNN. Likewise, the error rates are better in the classification that includes the third arm ((a), (b), (c) in the Fig. 1) than the left and right classification ((d) in the Fig. 1); in effect, the RH/LH classification reached error rates close to 0.5, which means a classification by chance. Finally, the tendency in both conditions is that as the size of the time window increases the error rates decrease but in the number of features the tendency is unclear.

Following the error mean values of each window\feature, we built a greedy algorithm to find the optimal global choice. Thus, we can obtain for each subject, the best combination of the three conditions (i.e. number of features (NF), size of the window (SW) and classifier (C)) to get the best miss classification rate (error). The Table 1 shows these values in Graz (G) and Hands (H) conditions among the subjects.

Table 1. The best combinations of number of features, time window and classifier and the error rates reached with them across the subjects for both conditions. The asterisks indicate the subjects that began the experiment with the Hands condition.

Subject	Condition	TH-RH				TH-LH				TH-RS				LH-RH			
		NF	SW	C	Error	NF	SW	C	Error	NF	SW	C	Error	NF	SW	C	Error
1*	G	6	2000	KNN	**0.18**	6	2000	KNN	**0.18**	6	800	LDA	**0.24**	9	2000	LDA	0.42
	H	9	2000	LDA	**0.17**	12	2000	KNN	0.28	15	1000	SVM	0.27	12	2000	SVM	0.41
2	G	6	800	SVM	0.26	24	100	KNN	0.40	9	2000	SVM	**0.16**	6	2000	KNN	0.30
	H	6	2000	KNN	0.19	6	2000	LDA	**0.13**	24	2000	SVM	**0.24**	21	800	KNN	0.39
3	G	6	800	LDA	0.42	6	800	KNN	0.41	12	2000	KNN	0.35	21	600	KNN	0.45
	H	12	1000	SVM	0.40	9	2000	KNN	0.34	12	2000	KNN	0.27	6	100	KNN	0.48
4*	G	30	100	KNN	0.42	6	800	LDA	0.41	24	1000	KNN	0.37	6	100	SVM	0.46
	H	15	100	KNN	0.47	6	400	LDA	0.45	18	600	KNN	0.37	6	1000	SVM	0.36
5	G	30	800	SVM	0.31	6	100	LDA	0.46	12	600	KNN	0.28	15	100	KNN	0.45
	H	12	2000	KNN	0.34	24	800	SVM	0.41	15	400	KNN	0.42	12	2000	KNN	0.38
6*	G	21	2000	KNN	0.40	6	100	LDA	0.42	18	2000	SVM	0.26	6	800	KNN	0.45
	H	18	2000	SVM	**0.10**	6	2000	SVM	**0.16**	30	2000	KNN	**0.09**	21	400	SVM	0.42
7	G	15	2000	SVM	0.38	18	800	SVM	0.38	21	400	SVM	0.37	21	2000	KNN	0.41
	H	21	200	LDA	0.28	30	1000	KNN	0.38	9	1000	SVM	0.34	6	800	SVM	0.44
8*	G	6	800	LDA	0.36	9	800	SVM	0.40	18	2000	SVM	0.31	6	200	SVM	0.46
	H	9	800	SVM	0.39	12	800	LDA	0.41	6	800	LDA	0.35	21	800	LDA	0.37
9	G	12	800	KNN	0.38	6	100	SVM	0.48	27	2000	KNN	0.34	15	600	LDA	0.40
	H	21	1000	KNN	0.31	9	1000	SVM	**0.22**	27	800	KNN	0.37	9	800	LDA	0.37
10*	G	12	800	KNN	0.32	9	800	LDA	0.34	6	2000	KNN	**0.22**	6	100	SVM	0.46
	H	6	800	SVM	**0.25**	6	2000	KNN	**0.21**	9	2000	LDA	**0.22**	6	2000	SVM	0.36

We merged the data of each run into a single dataset for thus training the classifiers. The tablshows that there are several variations across the subjects

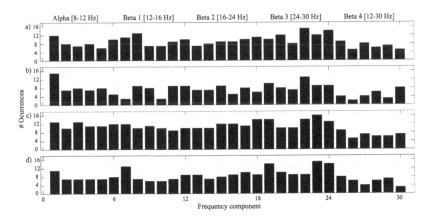

Fig. 2. Relevant frequency components over all subjects. (a) TH\LH; (b) TH\RH; (c) TH\RS; d) LH\RH.

and conditions. Only in TH/RS task, the number of features was widespread. Otherwise, the distribution was concentrated frosix up to 21, precisely, the Fig. 2 shows the histogram of selection of eacfrequency component over all subjects for the four binary classifications. In the figure can be seethat frequency components in the μ and $\beta 3$ were selected for most of the participants, ieffect, the clear peaks are inside these ranges. Meanwhile, the whole β band ($\beta 4$) was feused, showing how the β sub-bands can be used more than the whole band itself. In the other sidefor the size of the time window, the classification that includes the third arm (TH-RH, TH-LH anTH-RS) was superior of the 800 ms up to 2 s (maximum time). Finally, the KNN was the most used amonthe participants and conditions.

The mean error obtained over all participants (n = 10) in Hands condition was approx 32% (i.eTH-LH: 0.29±0.03, TH-RH: 0.29±0.03, TH-RS: 0.29±0.03, and LH-RH: 0.39±0.01 and around 36% in Graz condition (i.e. TH-LH: 0.34±0.02, TH-RH: 0.38±0.02, TH-RS0.29±0.02, and LH-RH: 0.42±0.01). Pairwise comparison using paired Wilcoxon signed rantest with Bonferroni correction reveals a significant (V = 0, p-value = 0.048) between conditionsLikewise, Dunn's Kruskal-Wallis Multiple Comparisons with Bonferroni correction show significandifference among groups, exactly in both TH-LH (z = −2.49, p-value = 0.03) and TH-RS (z = −3.92, p-value = 0.0003) against LH-RH for Graz, and in Hands only for TH-RS (z = −2.44, p-value = 0.04).

In summary, the Hands condition significantly outperforms (0.32) the Graz (0.36) in thclassification. Intriguingly, the classification of TH-LH was better than the other two motoimagery condition (TH-RH, LH-RH) in both conditions (Graz = 0.34, Hands = 0.29).

4   Conclusion

This study investigated the possibility of using an imaginary third arm and the differences of the EEG patterns and classification rates of using a realistic visual feedback. The benefits presented by this feedback are reflected in the enhanced of the ERS signals that consequently produces an improvement of the classification. Supernumerary MI-BCI systems are prominent and possible uses should be explored, especially for VR applications, where customized avatars could be controlled using imaginary non-body signals.

The high error rates reached by the left-right hand classification (LH/RH) in both conditions (Hands: 0.39 ± 0.01, Graz: 0.42 ± 0.01) could suggest that the inclusion of the third arm would cause the reduction of its accuracy because the users could interpret either left and right hand as the third arm. Whereas, the third arm is distinguished from the left hand than the right with better accuracies. It could support the fact that the TH task follows the activity based on the handedness. Unfortunately, all of our subjects were right-handed, so we can not evaluate the handedness thoroughly in this experiment.

Unfortunately, this work lacks in studies about ownership of the third-arm in both subjectively, with questions about the sense of agency and sense of ownership, and objectively, using galvanic skin response (GSR), following the work of Bashford and Mehring [2]. These data could give some insights regarding the use of supernumerary BCI and how it could be used in real application, coming from the answers of the users. Also, it would be necessary to perform the experiment with left-handed people, in order to study the handiness of the third arm.

References

1. Ang, K.K., Chin, Z.Y., Zhang, H., Guan, C.: Filter bank common spatial pattern (FBCSP) in brain-computer interface. In: 2008 IEEE International Joint Conference on Neural Networks (IEEE World Congress on Computational Intelligence), pp. 2390–2397 (2008). https://doi.org/10.1109/IJCNN.2008.4634130
2. Bashford, L., Mehring, C.: Ownership and agency of an independent supernumerary hand induced by an imitation brain-computer interface. PLoS One 11(6), 1–15 (2016). https://doi.org/10.1371/journal.pone.0156591
3. Blankertz, B., Tomioka, R., Lemm, S., Kawanabe, M., Muller, K.: Optimizing spatial filters for robust EEG single-trial analysis. IEEE Sig. Process. Mag. 25(1), 41–56 (2008). https://doi.org/10.1109/MSP.2008.4408441
4. Delorme, A., Makeig, S.: EEGLAB: an open source toolbox for analysis of single-trial EEG dynamics including independent component analysis. J. Neurosci. Methods 134(1), 9–21 (2004). https://doi.org/10.1016/j.jneumeth.2003.10.009
5. Gert, P., Leeb, R., Faller, J., Neuper, C.: Brain-computer interface systems used for virtual reality control. In: Kim, J.J. (ed.) Virtual Reality, Chap. 7, pp. 1–19. InTech (2011)
6. He, B., Baxter, B., Edelman, B.J., Cline, C.C., Ye, W.W.: Noninvasive brain-computer interfaces based on sensorimotor rhythms. Proc. IEEE 103(6), 907–925 (2015). https://doi.org/10.1109/JPROC.2015.2407272
7. Lotte, F., et al.: A review of classification algorithms for EEG-based brain-computer interfaces: a 10 year update. J. Neural Eng. 15(3), 031005 (2018)

8. Lotte, F.: A tutorial on EEG signal-processing techniques for mental-state recognition in brain–computer interfaces. In: Miranda, E.R., Castet, J. (eds.) Guide to Brain-Computer Music Interfacing, pp. 133–161. Springer, London (2014). https://doi.org/10.1007/978-1-4471-6584-2_7. https://hal.inria.fr/hal-01055103

9. Neuper, C., Muller, G., Kubler, A., Birbaumer, N., Pfurtscheller, G.: Clinical application of an EEG-based brain-computer interface: a case study in a patient with severe motor impairment. Clin. Neurophysiol. **114**(3), 399–409 (2003). https://doi.org/10.1016/S1388-2457(02)00387-5

10. Peng, H., Long, F., Ding, C.: Feature selection based on mutual information criteria of max-dependency, max-relevance, and min-redundancy. IEEE Trans. Pattern Anal. Mach. Intell. **27**(8), 1226–1238 (2005). https://doi.org/10.1109/TPAMI.2005.159

11. Pfurtscheller, G., Neuper, C.: Motor imagery and direct brain-computer communication. Proc. IEEE **89**(7), 1123–1134 (2001). https://doi.org/10.1109/5.939829

12. Pfurtscheller, G.: Quantification of ERD and ERS in the Time Domain, pp. 89–105, 6th edn. Elsevier B.V., Netherlands (1999). Revised edition

13. Skola, F., Liarokapis, F.: Embodied vr environment facilitates motor-imagery brain-computer interface training. Comput. Graph. **75**, 59–71 (2018). https://doi.org/10.1016/j.cag.2018.05.024

14. Wolpaw, J.R., Birbaumer, N., McFarland, D.J., Pfurtscheller, G., Vaughan, T.M.: Brain-computer interfaces for communication and control. Clin. Neurophysiol. **113**(6), 767–791 (2002). https://doi.org/10.1016/S1388-2457(02)00057-3

ODE-Driven Sketch-Based Organic Modelling

Ouwen Li[1]([✉]), Zhigang Deng[2], Shaojun Bian[1], Algirdas Noreika[3],
Xiaogang Jin[4], Ismail Khalid Kazmi[5], Lihua You[1], and Jian Jun Zhang[1]

[1] National Centre for Computer Animation, Bournemouth University,
Bournemouth, Dorset, UK
oli@bournemouth.ac.uk
[2] University of Houston, Houston, Texas, USA
[3] Indeform Ltd., K. Petrausko g. 26, 44156 Kaunas, Lithuania
[4] State Key Lab of CAD & CG, Zhejiang University, Hangzhou 310058, China
[5] Teesside University, Middlesbrough, Tees Valley, UK

Abstract. How to efficiently create 3D models from 2D sketches is an
important problem. In this paper we propose a sketch-based and ordinary differential equation (ODE) driven modelling technique to tackle
this problem. We first generate 2D silhouette contours of a 3D model.
Then, we select proper primitives for each of the corresponding silhouette
contours. After that, we develop an ODE-driven and sketch-guided deformation method. It uses ODE-based deformations to deform the primitives to exactly match the generated 2D silhouette contours in one view
plane. Our experiment demonstrates that the proposed approach can
create 3D models from 2D silhouette contours easily and efficiently.

Keywords: Organic models · Sketch-guided modelling ·
ODE-driven deformations

1 Introduction

Mainstream modelling approaches such as polygon and NURBS can create
detailed 3D models. However, they require good knowledge and skills to use
them, involve heavy manual operations, and take a lot of time to complete modelling tasks. In order to address these problems, various sketch-based modelling
(SBM) approaches have been developed in the past several decades [13].

Ordinary Differential Equations (ODE) have been widely used to describe
various physical laws in scientific computing and engineering applications. For
example, fourth-order ODEs have been used to describe the lateral bending
of elastic beams in structural engineering. Therefore, ODE-driven modelling is
physics-based and able to generate more realistic appearances and deformations
[19]. In order to generate such physically realistic surfaces, in this paper we introduce ODE-based modelling to develop primitive deformers to deform primitives
to match user's drawn sketches.

© Springer Nature Switzerland AG 2019
M. Gavrilova et al. (Eds.): CGI 2019, LNCS 11542, pp. 453–460, 2019.
https://doi.org/10.1007/978-3-030-22514-8_44

The main contributions of our approach is that we develop an efficient, ODE-driven, and sketch-guided deformation method to create 3D models quickly. It can deform primitives to exactly match the generated silhouette contours. Compared to existing methods, it automates shape manipulation, avoids tedious manual operations, can deform primitives to match the generated silhouette contours quickly, and is effective in achieving different shapes of a primitive.

2   Related Work

The work proposed in this paper is related to sketch-based modelling, especially the primitive-based systems, and ODE-based geometric processing. In the following, we briefly review the existing work in these fields.

Sketch-Based Modelling. Sketch-based-modelling (SBM) can be broadly divided into direct mesh generation and primitive-based mesh creation.

In the category of direct mesh generation, several systems have been proposed to generate organic models. The surface inflation technique extrudes a polygonal mesh from a given skeleton outwards and does a good job in modelling stuffed toys. One trend is to inflate free-form surfaces to create simple stuffed animals and other rotund objects in a SBM fashion [9,10,12]. BendSketch [11] complements those works by enabling complex curvature patterns on surfaces. In order to give the bending information, users need to draw a set of lines that comply with what BendSketch system has specified, which mimics the hatching technique artists often utilise to express the sense of volume and curvature information on the surfaces.

Unlike the inflating systems, primitives-based systems decompose the modelling task as a process of creating a certain set of geometry primitives and further editing the primitives [5,14,17]. The idea of assembling simple geometric primitives to form 3D models is commonly used in CSG (Constructive Solid Geometry) modelling [5,14]. Structured annotations for 2D-to-3D modelling [8], on the other hand, focus on organic modelling.

ODE-Based Geometric Processing. ODEs have been widely applied in scientific computing and engineering analyses to describe the underlying physics. For example, fourth-order ODEs have been used to describe the lateral bending deformations of elastic beams. Introducing ODEs into geometric processing can create physically realistic appearances and deformations of 3D models. ODE-based sweeping surfaces [19], ODE-based surface deformations [4,20], and ODE-based surface blending [18] have also been developed previously. Although researchers studied ODE-based geometric surface creation and deformations, how to use ODE-based modelling to deform geometric primitives and create new shapes from the user's drawn sketches has been under-explored to date.

3   System Overview

As shown in the Fig. 1, one can extract 2D silhouette contours from sketches, or to directly draw 2D silhouette contours.

After generating 2D silhouette contours, the next step is to set super-ellipsoid as 3D primitives. We sample the silhouette contours into point cloud and we use radial Euclidean distance to format the global distortion [6] to determine the parameters of the super-ellipse(ϵ_z, r_x, r_y). If one only feeds the system with the 2D sketch in one view not providing z-axis depth information, then the radius of z-axis r_z and ϵ_{xy} requires users to manually set, and any necessary translations in z-axis should be done manually. Since the parameter determination took place in object space, when we transform the superellipsoid primitives into the world space, they will align with its silhouette in world space.

Then the ODE-driven deformation method described in Sect. 4 is applied to deform the primitives to exactly match the corresponding 2D silhouette contours.

Fig. 1. System overview.

4   Primitive Deformers

Here we propose an ODE-driven and sketch-guided primitive deformation method. It is developed from a simplified version of the Euler-Lagrange PDE (Partial Differential Equation), which is widely used in physically-based surface deformations and briefly reviewed below.

As discussed in [1], the main requirement for physically-based surface deformations is an elastic energy which considers the local stretching and bending of two-manifold surfaces called thin-shells. When a surface $\mathbb{S} \subset \mathbb{R}^3$, parameterized by a function $\mathbf{P}(u, v) : \Omega \subset \mathbb{R}^2 \mapsto \mathbb{S} \subset \mathbb{R}^3$, is deformed to a new shape $\mathbb{S}'$ through adding a displacement vector $\mathbf{d}(u, v)$ to each point $\mathbf{P}(u, v)$, the change of the first and second fundamental $I(u, v)$, $\Pi(u, v) \in \mathbb{R}^{2 \times 2}$ forms in differential geometry [7] yields a measure of stretching and bending, as described in [15]:

$$E_{shell}(\mathbb{S}') = \int_{\Omega} k_s \|I' - I\|_F^2 + k_b \|\Pi' - \Pi\|_F^2 \, du \, dv, \qquad (1)$$

where I' and Π' are the first and second fundamental forms of the surface $\mathbb{S}'$, $\|.\|$ indicates a (weighted) Frobenius norm, and the stiffness parameters k_s and k_b are used to control the resistance to stretching and bending.

Generating a new deformed surface requires the minimization of the above Eq. 1, which is non-linear and computationally expensive for interactive applications. In order to avoid the nonlinear minimization, the change of the first and second fundamental forms is replaced by the first and second order partial derivatives of the displacement function $\mathbf{d}(u, v)$ [2, 16], i. e.,

$$\tilde{E}_{shell}(\mathbf{d}) = \int_{\Omega} k_s(\|\mathbf{d}_u\|^2 + \|\mathbf{d}_v\|^2) + k_b(\|\mathbf{d}_{uu}\|^2 + 2\|\mathbf{d}_{uv}\| + \|\mathbf{d}_{vv}\|^2) \, du \, dv,$$
(2)

where $d_x = \frac{\partial}{\partial x}$ and $d_{xy} = \frac{\partial^2}{\partial x \partial y}$. The minimization of the above equation can be obtained by applying variational calculus, which leads to the following Euler-Lagrange PDE:

$$-k_s \triangle \mathbf{d} + k_b \triangle^2 \mathbf{d} = 0,$$
(3)

where $\triangle$ and $\triangle^2$ are the Laplacian and the bi-Laplacian operators, respectively,

$$\triangle \mathbf{d} = div \nabla \mathbf{d} = \mathbf{d}_{uu} + \mathbf{d}_{vv},$$
$$\triangle^2 \mathbf{d} = \triangle(\triangle \mathbf{d}) = \mathbf{d}_{uuuu} + 2\mathbf{d}_{uuvv} + \mathbf{d}_{vvvv}.$$
(4)

Using the sketched 2D silhouette contours shown in Fig. 2 to change the shape of the primitive can be transformed to the generation of a sweeping surface which passes through the two sketched 2D silhouette contours. The generator that creates the sweeping surface is a curve of the parametric variable u only, and the two silhouette contours are trajectories. If Eq. (3) is used to describe the generator, the parametric variable v in Eq. (3) drops, and we have $\mathbf{d}_{vv} = 0$ and $\mathbf{d}_{vvvv} = 0$. Substituting $\mathbf{d}_{vv} = 0$ and $\mathbf{d}_{vvvv} = 0$ into Eq. (4), we obtain the following simplified version of the Euler-Lagrange PDE, seen as (5), which is actually a vector-valued ODE.

$$k_b \frac{\partial^4 \mathbf{d}}{\partial u^4} - k_s \frac{\partial^2 \mathbf{d}}{\partial u^2} = 0.$$
(5)

As pointed out in [3], the finite difference solution to ODEs is very efficient, we here investigate such a numerical solution to Eq. (5). For a typical node i, the central finite difference approximations of the second and fourth order derivatives can be written as:

$$\frac{\partial^2 \mathbf{d}}{\partial u^2}|_i = \frac{1}{\triangle u^2}(\mathbf{d}_{i+1} - 2\mathbf{d}_i + \mathbf{d}_{i-1}),$$
$$\frac{\partial^4 \mathbf{d}}{\partial u^4}|_i = \frac{1}{\triangle u^4}[6\mathbf{d}_i - 4(\mathbf{d}_{i-1} + \mathbf{d}_{i+1}) + \mathbf{d}_{i-2} + \mathbf{d}_{i+2}].$$
(6)

Introducing Eq. (6) into Eq. (5), the following finite difference equation at a representative node i can be written as:

$$(6k_b + 2k_s h^2)\mathbf{d}_i + k_b \mathbf{d}_{i-2} + k_b \mathbf{d}_{i+2} - (4k_b + k_s h^2)\mathbf{d}_{i-1} - (4k_b + k_s h^2)\mathbf{d}_{i+1} = 0.$$
(7)

For organic models, the 3D shape defined by two silhouette contours is closed in the parametric direction u as indicated in Fig. 2b. Therefore, we can extract some closed curves each of which passes through the two corresponding points on the two silhouette contours. Taking the silhouette contours in Fig. 2a as an example, we find two corresponding points $\mathbf{C}_{13}$ and $\mathbf{C}_{23}$ on the original silhouette contours $\mathbf{c}_1$ and $\mathbf{c}_2$, and two corresponding points $\mathbf{C}'_{13}$ and $\mathbf{C}'_{23}$ on the deformed silhouette contours $\mathbf{c}'_1$ and $\mathbf{c}'_2$ as shown in Fig. 2b. Then, we extract a closed curve $\mathbf{c}(u)$ passing through the two corresponding points $\mathbf{C}_{13}$ and $\mathbf{C}_{23}$ from the 3D model in Fig. 2a and depict it as a dashed curve in Fig. 2b. Assuming that the deformed shape of the closed curve $\mathbf{c}(u)$ is $\mathbf{c}'(u)$, the displacement difference between the original closed curve and the deformed closed curve is $\mathbf{d}(u) = \mathbf{c}'(u) - \mathbf{c}(u)$.

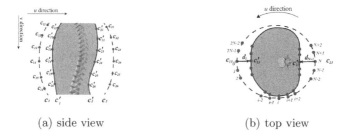

(a) side view   (b) top view

Fig. 2. Finite difference nodes for local shape manipulation from sketches in top and side view planes, respectively.

In order to use the finite difference method to find the displacement difference $\mathbf{d}(u)$, we uniformly divide the closed curve into $2N$ equal intervals as indicated in Fig. 2b. With the displacement difference at node 0 and node N already known, i. e. $\mathbf{d}_0 = \mathbf{C}'_{13} - \mathbf{C}_{13}$ and $\mathbf{d}_N = \mathbf{C}'_{23} - \mathbf{C}_{23}$, we can form a $2N$ linear algebra equations derived from (7) for each of these nodes' displacement. Solve the equations and add all the displacement differences to the original curve $\mathbf{c}(u)$, we can then obtain the deformed curve $\mathbf{c}'(u)$, and depict it as a solid curve in Fig. 2b. Repeating the above operations for all other points on the two silhouette contours, we obtain all deformed curves that describe a new 3D deformed shape. This method also applies to deformations responding to free form curves, which can be seen from the creation of a human leg shown in Fig. 3b.

The aforementioned method was developed in python on the Houdini FX Education Edition 16.5.323 package, and ran on a dual boot Linux PC with 23 GB memory and 64 bits Intel(R) Xeon(R) CPU E5-1650 0 @ 3.20 GHz CPU. The average time for deforming a primitive is 0.17 s, which ensures a smooth real-time modelling user experience.

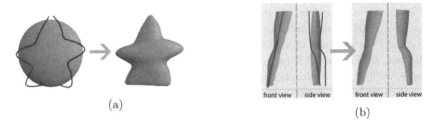

(a)   (b)

Fig. 3. ODE-driven Sketch-based deformations: (a) the deformation process of an organic shape represented by an ellipsoid and its 2D silhouette contour, and the deformed shape of the ellipsoid, (b) a leg that has been deformed by single-view sketch strokes before, now get further deformed in accordance with free form red-colored curves (Color figure online)

5   Conclusion and Future Work

In this paper, we present an ODE-driven and sketch-based modelling approach to create 3D models from 2D sketches efficiently, more examples are displayed in Fig. 4. By introducing ODE-driven geometric modelling, we proposed a primitive deformation method to deform primitives to match the input 2D silhouette contours exactly. Our approach has the advantages of: (1) easiness for beginners to use, (2) avoiding heavy manual operations, and (3) high efficiency in creating sketch-based 3D organic models.

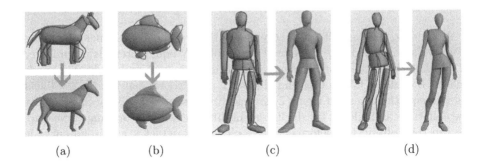

(a)   (b)   (c)   (d)

Fig. 4. Examples of the primitive deformation method

Acknowledgements. This research is supported by the PDE-GIR project which has received funding from the European Unions Horizon 2020 research and innovation programme under the Marie Skodowska-Curie grant agreement No 778035, and Innovate UK (Knowledge Transfer Partnerships Ref: KTP010860). Xiaogang Jin is supported by Science and Technology Project on Preservation of Cultural Relics, Cultural Heritage Bureau of Zhejiang Province (Grant No. 2018009) and the National Natural Science Foundation of China (No. 61732015).

References

1. Botsch, M., Sorkine, O.: On linear variational surface deformation methods. IEEE Trans. Vis. Comput. Graph. **14**(1), 213–230 (2008)
2. Celniker, G., Gossard, D.: Deformable curve and surface finite-elements for free-form shape design. ACM SIGGRAPH Comput. Graph. **25**(4), 257–266 (1991)
3. Chaudhry, E., Bian, S., Ugail, H., Jin, X., You, L., Zhang, J.J.: Dynamic skin deformation using finite difference solutions for character animation. Comput. Graph. **46**, 294–305 (2015)
4. Chaudhry, E., You, L., Jin, X., Yang, X., Zhang, J.J.: Shape modeling for animated characters using ordinary differential equations. Comput. Graph. **37**(6), 638–644 (2013)
5. Chen, T., Zhu, Z., Shamir, A., Hu, S.M., Cohen-Or, D.: 3-sweep: extracting editable objects from a single photo. ACM Trans. Graph. (TOG) **32**(6), 195 (2013)
6. Chevalier, L., Jaillet, F., Baskurt, A.: Segmentation and superquadric modeling of 3D objects (2003)
7. Do Carmo, M.P., Fischer, G., Pinkall, U., Reckziegel, H.: Differential geometry. Mathematical Models, pp. 155–180. Springer, Wiesbaden (2017). https://doi.org/10.1007/978-3-658-18865-8_10
8. Gingold, Y., Igarashi, T., Zorin, D.: Structured annotations for 2D-to-3D modeling. In: ACM Transactions on Graphics (TOG), vol. 28, p. 148. ACM (2009)
9. Igarashi, T., Matsuoka, S., Tanaka, H.: Teddy: a sketching interface for 3d freeform design. In: Proceedings of the 26th Annual Conference on Computer Graphics and Interactive Techniques, pp. 409–416. ACM Press/Addison-Wesley Publishing Co. (1999)
10. Karpenko, O.A., Hughes, J.F.: Smoothsketch: 3D free-form shapes from complex sketches. ACM Trans. Graph. **25**(3), 589–598 (2006). https://doi.org/10.1145/1141911.1141928
11. Li, C., Pan, H., Liu, Y., Tong, X., Sheffer, A., Wang, W.: Bendsketch: modeling freeform surfaces through 2D sketching. ACM Trans. Graph. (TOG) **36**(4), 125 (2017)
12. Nealen, A., Igarashi, T., Sorkine, O., Alexa, M.: Fibermesh: designing freeform surfaces with 3D curves. ACM Trans. Graph. (TOG) **26**(3), 41 (2007)
13. Olsen, L., Samavati, F.F., Sousa, M.C., Jorge, J.A.: Sketch-based modeling: a survey. Comput. Graph. **33**(1), 85–103 (2009)
14. Shtof, A., Agathos, A., Gingold, Y., Shamir, A., Cohen-Or, D.: Geosemantic snapping for sketch-based modeling. In: Computer Graphics Forum, vol. 32, pp. 245–253. Wiley Online Library (2013)
15. Terzopoulos, D., Platt, J., Barr, A., Fleischer, K.: Elastically deformable models. In: ACM SIGGRAPH Computer Graphics, vol. 21, pp. 205–214. ACM (1987)
16. Welch, W., Witkin, A.: Variational surface modeling. In: ACM SIGGRAPH Computer Graphics, vol. 26, pp. 157–166. ACM (1992)
17. Xu, M., Li, M., Xu, W., Deng, Z., Yang, Y., Zhou, K.: Interactive mechanism modeling from multi-view images. ACM Trans. Graph. (TOG) **35**(6), 236 (2016)
18. You, L., Ugail, H., Tang, B., Jin, X., You, X., Zhang, J.J.: Blending using ode swept surfaces with shape control and c1 continuity. Vis. Comput. **30**(6–8), 625–636 (2014)

19. You, L., Yang, X., Pachulski, M., Zhang, J.J.: Boundary constrained swept surfaces for modelling and animation. In: Computer Graphics Forum, vol. 26, pp. 313–322. Wiley Online Library (2007)
20. You, L., Yang, X., You, X.Y., Jin, X., Zhang, J.J.: Shape manipulation using physically based wire deformations. Comput. Anim. Virtual Worlds **21**(3–4), 297–309 (2010)

Physical Space Performance Mapping for Lenticular Lenses in Multi-user VR Displays

Juan Sebastian Munoz-Arango$^{(\boxtimes)}$, Dirk Reiners, and Carolina Cruz-Neira

Emerging Analytics Center, UA, Little Rock, AR 72204, USA
eacinfo@ualr.edu

Abstract. One of the common issues of virtual reality systems regardless if they are head mounted or projection based is that they cannot provide correct perspective views to more than one user. This limitation increases collaboration times and reduces usability of such systems. Lenticular lenses have been previously used to separate users in multi-user VR systems. On this paper we present an assessment of the area of interaction of users in a multi-user VR system that uses lenticular lenses.

Keywords: Multi-user VR · Virtual Reality · Lenticular lens

1 Introduction

Virtual Reality is used in many fields nowadays. When the person who is working in VR is alone, HMDs work well to some extent. Unfortunately, in today's world collaborative groups are now the norm and VR suffers some issues. Previous research has been presented [14] showing that collaboration times get significantly larger when participants dont perceive perspective correct images in VR.

Lenticular lenses can be used for generating multiple views from a single screen. It has been shown that a lenticular lens that maximizes the amount of unique perceived pixels and minimizes ghosting is a lens that has a 50% lenticule radius increase from the minimum possible radius, covers 18 to 21 pixels per lenticule with a pixel spread of 9° [9,10].

User's positions are something that cannot be controlled from the point of view of the VR app but is something that can be manipulated knowing where to place content to be seen by the users. On this paper we are going to present a physical space mapping on how good or bad the area in front of an optical routing system that uses lenticular lenses performs.

2 Background

Lenticular lenses can be thought of a set of cylinders (lenticules) overlapping each other. One side of an extruded plastic sheet is embossed with columns of tiny corrugations (lenticules) and the other side smooth.

© Springer Nature Switzerland AG 2019
M. Gavrilova et al. (Eds.): CGI 2019, LNCS 11542, pp. 461–467, 2019.
https://doi.org/10.1007/978-3-030-22514-8_45

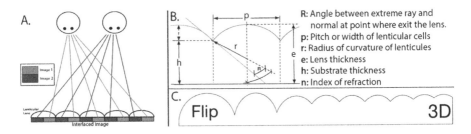

Fig. 1. A. Lenticular printing: 2 users, B. Lenticular lens details, C. Flip to 3D lenses.

Lenticular printing is one of the most common examples of lenticular lenses usage. Here, lenses are employed to give illusion of depth or to make images that change depending on the angle the print is looked from (Fig. 1A).

Lenticular lenses are classified by the number of lenticules that can be fit in an inch and measured in "Lenses per inch" (LPI), the higher the LPI is the smaller each lenticule is. Even though the lenticular classification of LPI is fairly basic, lenticular lenses have several parameters that generate different effects. Such parameters can be seen in Fig. 1B. These values change how lenses refract light, amount of viewing angle and how far/close they can seen from.

Lenticular lenses can produce several effects depending on how deep lenticules are (Fig. 1C). Theese effects that can be morphing, animations, flipping and 3D effects [4]. Following the same principle on how lenticular printing works; a multi-user VR system that generates perspective correct images depending on users' locations can be assembled by placing a lens on top of a screen.

3   Previous Work

In 1994, Little et present a design for an autostereoscopic, multiperspective raster-filled display [6]. They use an array of video cameras to capture multiple perspective views of a scene and feed the data to an array of LCTVs while projecting images to a special pupil-forming viewing screen. The screen is fabricated by crossed lenticular arrays and a holographic optical element.

Van Berkel et al. in [20,21] built a prototype display using a LCD and a lenticular lens from Philips Optics to display 3D images.

Matsumoto proposes a system that combines cylindrical lenses with different focal lengths, a diffuser screen and several projectors to create a 3D image [7].

Omura in [13], uses double lenticular lenses with moving projectors that move according to the tracked user's position to extend the viewable area.

Lipton proposed the Synthagram [5], a system that consists of an LCD Screen with a lenticular screen that overlays the LCD display.

Matusik proposes a system that consists of an array of cameras, clusters of PCs and a multi-projector 3D display with the purpose to transmit autostereoscopic realistic 3D TV [8]. The system consists of 16 NEC LT-170 projectors that are used for front or rear projection using lenticular lenses.

In [11,12] Nguyen et al. presented a special display which consists of a screen with 3 layers that has directional reflections for projectors so each participant sees a customized image from their perspective.

Takaki et al. presents a system that produces 72 views with lenticular lenses [16] and later on. In [17], Takaki discusses a multiple projection system that is modified to work as a super multiview display. They attach a lens to the display screen of a HDD projector and by combining the screen lens and the common lens they project an aperture array. This aperture array is placed on the focal plane of the common lens, and the display screen (a vertical diffuser) is placed on the other focal plane. Hence, the image of the aperture array is produced on the focal plane of the screen lens. Then, the produced image gets enlarged generating extended images that become viewpoints.

In 2009 Takaki and his team introduce a prototype panel that can produce 16 views [19]. They do this by building a LCD with slanted subpixels and a lenticular screen. Later in [18] they combine several 16-view flat-panels with slanted subpixels to create a system with 256 views.

Surman in [15] presents the Free2C display. The display accommodates head movement of the viewer by continually re-adjusting the position of a lenticular lens in relation to the LCD to create stereoscopic views for the viewer.

Similarly to Free2C, Brar et al. use image recognition to track users' to produce multiple steerable exit pupils for left and right eyes [1,2].

Kooima in [3] uses Alioscopy displays that come with lenticular lenses. They propose a system that consists of scalable tiled displays for large field of views and use a GPU based autostereoscopic algorithm for rendering in lenticular barriers.

Zang et al. proposes a frontal multi-projection autostereoscopic display [22]. Their approach consists of 8 staggered projectors and a 3D image guided screen. The 3D image screen is mainly composed of a single lenticular sheet, a retro-reflective diffusion screen and a transparent layer that is filled between them to control the pitch of the rearranged pixel stripe in interlaced images.

Some research has been presented throughout the past years that employs lenticular lenses to separate users. Still, none of these projects expose how the quality of the multiplexed images in the physical space changes depending on the movement of the participants.

4   Simulating Lenticular Lenses

To get to know how a specific lens/screen marriage performs, a lenticular lens simulator was created. This simulator tells us how many pixels are seen from a specific position in the physical space and shows us how many pixels of the perceived pixels are shared with other users (ghosting).

To assess how a lenticular lens works, a discretization of the light that comes from each subpixel is represented with a number of rays. These rays start from each subpixel, travel along the substrate of the lens and get refracted to the air from each lenticule. These rays are calculated in three phases: Substrate thickness contact, lenticular lens contact and finally lens refraction (Fig. 2).

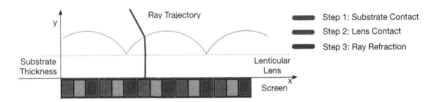

Fig. 2. Simulator steps for calculating refracted rays per user.

5　Experiment

To map the physical space of the multi-user VR display, we simulated lenses that fit 18–21 pixels per lenticule (PPL) and have a 50% minimum lenticule radius increase. For the screen we used a Samsung Q65Q900R 8k TV with pixel density of 137ppi, pixel size of 0.186 mm and 9° of simulated pixel spread.

Optimum lenticular lens parameters vary depending on the screen/lens marriage used. Factors like the minimum unique number of pixels seen by either of the users and maximum ghosting perceived need to be taken into account when mapping the physical space users interact in. To understand the aforementioned factors, a grid of possible positions was generated in front of a screen where users interact. The grid is spaced by 50 cm from the screen up to 2.5 m in 50 cm increments, horizontal separation of 2 m with a separation of 50 cm between cells.

The experiment was done with two, three and four users interacting in different positions at the same time. It is important to note that no user in the physical space occludes the other users (as is in front).

6　Data Analysis

Three different graphs where generated for assessing the proposed space: The number of pixels per lenticule (18–21) for three users, number of simultaneous users (2 to 4) and varying substrate thickness (0 mm to 1.5 mm). Each of the graphs contain the maximum generated ghosting by the system (top) and the minimum amount of unique seen pixels (bottom).

It is worth noting that the graphs are not correlated but are showing the worst cases. The proposed area for evaluation was 2.0 m by 2.5 m. since the display is only ∼1.5 m wide, its expected that on the corners the screen pretty much no unique pixels are perceived.

On Fig. 3 one can see how changing the amount of pixels per lenticule that the lenses have doesn't affect significantly the assessed factors. If the reader looks closely, the best area for using the system would be from the first 50 cm away from the screen up to 1.0 m without ghosting and up to 2 m with ∼1000 minimum unique perceived pixels.

If the reader notices on Fig. 4, with two users, participants can go back up to 2.5 m away from the screen and still perceive good amount of unique pixels

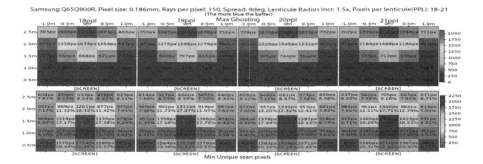

Fig. 3. Ghosting and unique seen pixels for 18 to 21 pixels per lenticule positions.

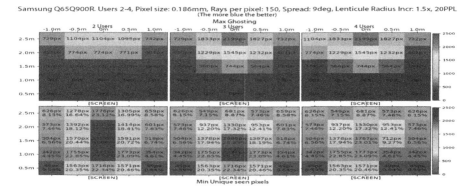

Fig. 4. Ghosting and unique seen pixels for 2, 3 and 4 simultaneous users.

(∼1200px) in the center. but with three and four users the experience rapidly gets affected by more ghosting and reduced unique pixels.

Finally, in Fig. 5 one can see that ghosting is lesser the more thin the substrate thickness is. Ghosting starts to appear in the first meter away from the screen when the substrate thickness is 0.5 mm but when the substrate thickness gets thicker more ghosting emerges. One could get away with a substrate thickness between 0 and 0.5 mm without affecting ghosting.

7   Conclusions

An overview on how lenticular lenses work and an experiment with two to four users moving in an area of 2×2.5 m with an analysis of the performance of lenticular lenses for a multi-user VR system was presented.

The optimum area that minimizes ghosting and maximizes unique pixels up to four users is in one meter away in the center of the screen. For 3 users one can expect an area of 1×1.5 m of movement from the center of the screen.

Content would be best seen closer to the screen up to 1 m without any ghosting. Up to 2 m, ∼1000 unique pixels can be seen. Enough to assemble an image.

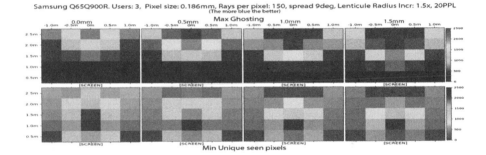

Fig. 5. Ghosting and unique seen pixels for 3 users with ranging substrate thickness.

The expected lens performance for minimum unique perceived pixels in this setup would be around ~20% of the resolution of the display.

Substrate thickness affects ghosting, but if its not possible to build a lens with 0 mm of thickness, one can get away with pretty much the same results with a lens up to 0.5 mm where ghosting starts to appear.

8 Future Work

Subpixel layout is something that changes from screen to screen; in this paper an evenly spaced/same size subpixel layout was presented. It is worth looking if results are affected with screens with uneven subpixel layout.

Color banding is a phenomenon that occurs when lenticules magnify enough pixels and produce separate red, green, blue bands. Color banding wasn't covered in this paper and is worth doing more research on it.

The experiment presented a lenticular lens optimized for 1 m away from the screen; it would be interesting to see how much one can push the specs of the lens to see if its possible to generate a lens that can further let users get away from the screen without affecting ghosting.

References

1. Brar, R.S., et al.: Laser-based head-tracked 3D display research. J. Display Technol. **6**(10), 531–543 (2010)
2. Brar, R.S., Surman, P., Sexton, I., Hopf, K.: Multi-user glasses free 3D display using an optical array. In: 2010 3DTV-Conference: The True Vision-Capture, Transmission and Display of 3D Video (3DTV-CON), pp. 1–4. IEEE (2010)
3. Kooima, R., Prudhomme, A., Schulze, J., Sandin, D., DeFanti, T.: A multi-viewer tiled autostereoscopic virtual reality display. In: proceedings of the 17th ACM Symposium on Virtual Reality Software and Technology, pp. 171–174. ACM (2010)
4. LenstarLenticular: Possible lenticular effects, December 2018. https://www. lenstarlenticular.com/lenticular-effects/. Accessed 15 Dec 2018

5. Lipton, L., Feldman, M.H.: New autostereoscopic display technology: the syntha-Gram. In: Stereoscopic Displays and Virtual Reality Systems IX, vol. 4660, pp. 229–236. Intl Society for Optics and Photonics (2002)
6. Little, G.R., Gustafson, S.C., Nikolaou, V.E.: Multiperspective autostereoscopic display. In: Cockpit Displays, vol. 2219, pp. 388–395. Intl Society for Optics and Photonics (1994)
7. Matsumoto, K., Honda, T.: Research of 3D display using anamorphic optics. In: Stereoscopic Displays and Virtual Reality Systems IV, vol. 3012, pp. 199–208. Intl Society for Optics and Photonics (1997)
8. Matusik, W., Pfister, H.: 3D TV: a scalable system for real-time acquisition, transmission, and autostereoscopic display of dynamic scenes. In: ACM Transactions on Graphics (TOG), vol. 23, pp. 814–824. ACM (2004)
9. Munoz-Arango, J.S., Reiners, D.: Analyzing pixel spread correlation with lenticular lens efficiency on multi user VR displays. In: WSCG, p. 10. ACM (2019)
10. Munoz-Arango, J.S., Reiners, D., Cruz-Neira, C.: Maximizing lenticular lens performance for multi user VR displays. In: Laval Virtual, p. 10. ACM (2019)
11. Nguyen, D., Canny, J.: Multiview: spatially faithful group video conferencing. In: Proceedings of the SIGCHI Conference on Human Factors in Computing Systems, pp. 799–808. ACM (2005)
12. Nguyen, D.T., Canny, J.: Multiview: improving trust in group video conferencing through spatial faithfulness. In: Proceedings of the SIGCHI Conference on Human Factors in Computing Systems, pp. 1465–1474. ACM (2007)
13. Omura, K., Shiwa, S., Miyasato, T.: Lenticular autostereoscopic display system: multiple images for multiple viewers. J. Soc. Inf. Disp. **6**(4), 313–324 (1998)
14. Pollock, B., Burton, M., Kelly, J.W., Gilbert, S., Winer, E.: The right view from the wrong location: depth perception in stereoscopic multi-user virtual environments. IEEE Trans. Vis. Comput. Graph. **4**, 581–588 (2012)
15. Surman, P., et al.: Head tracked single and multi-user autostereoscopic displays (2006)
16. Takaki, Y.: Thin-type natural three-dimensional display with 72 directional images. In: Stereoscopic Displays and Virtual Reality Systems XII, vol. 5664, p. 56. Intl Society for Optics and Photonics (2005)
17. Takaki, Y.: Super multi-view display with 128 viewpoints and viewpoint formation. In: Stereoscopic Displays and Applications XX, vol. 7237, p. 72371T. Intl Society for Optics and Photonics (2009)
18. Takaki, Y., Nago, N.: Multi-projection of lenticular displays to construct a 256-view super multi-view display. Opt. Express **18**(9), 8824–8835 (2010)
19. Takaki, Y., Yokoyama, O., Hamagishi, G.: Flat panel display with slanted pixel arrangement for 16-view display. In: Stereoscopic Displays and Applications XX, vol. 7237, p. 723708. Intl Society for Optics and Photonics (2009)
20. Van Berkel, C.: Image preparation for 3D LCD. In: Stereoscopic Displays and Virtual Reality VI, vol. 3639, pp. 84–92. Intl Society for Optics and Photonics (1999)
21. Van Berkel, C., Clarke, J.A.: Characterization and optimization of 3D-LCD module design. In: Stereoscopic Displays and Virtual Reality IV, vol. 3012, pp. 179–187. Intl Society for Optics and Photonics (1997)
22. Zang, S.F., Wang, Q.H., Zhao, W.X., Zhang, J., Liang, J.L.: A frontal multi-projection autostereoscopic 3D display based on a 3D-image-guided screen. J. Display Technol. **10**(10), 882–886 (2014)

Parallax Occlusion Mapping Using Distance Fields

Saad Khattak[1](✉) and Andrew Hogue[2]

[1] Tuque Games, Montreal, QC, Canada
saad@tuquegames.com
[2] Ontario Tech University, Oshawa, ON, Canada
andrew.hogue@uoit.ca

Abstract. Parallax occlusion mapping (POM) is a technique to introduce 3D definition using a depth map instead of adding new geometry. The technique relies on ray tracing with higher samples resulting in a better approximation, especially at steeper angles. The distance between each sample is constant and it is possible to skip over fine detail at lower sample count.

Our technique relies on a distance field (DF) instead of a depth map. This allows us to ray march through the field and lower the sample count considerably. We can get good results even with a single sample. Comparable results are obtained by less than half the samples of the industry standard POM approach.

Keywords: Parallax occlusion mapping · Video games · Computer graphics

1 Introduction

Aesthetics and realism play a big part in creating a believable and immersive 3D world. Video games and Virtual Reality simulations rely on texture mapping to add high frequency detail to objects that would otherwise require large amounts of geometry impacting performance. In addition to simple diffuse maps for color, modern game engines rely on multiple texture maps to approximate surface detail. Diffuse maps on their own results in a flat and featureless shading. A texture representing a rough surface will reflect light similar to a smooth surface. Bump mapping, introduced by Blinn [1] breaks up the smooth surface by scaling the intensity of the light, determined by a height map, and giving the illusion of roughness. Cohen et al. [2] introduced the technique of *normal mapping* where instead of a bump map, a texture containing surface normal information is used to calculate the amount and direction of reflected light. On shallow angles, normal mapping gives near perfect results. However, on sharper angles, the flatness of the texture is quite evident. Parallax Occlusion Mapping (POM) by Kaneko et al. [3] is a technique where the UV coordinates of the texture sample are displaced by a depth map taking into account the viewing

© Springer Nature Switzerland AG 2019
M. Gavrilova et al. (Eds.): CGI 2019, LNCS 11542, pp. 468–475, 2019.
https://doi.org/10.1007/978-3-030-22514-8_46

angle of the surface. The amount to displace the texture is determined by ray tracing a depth map with n samples. Higher number of samples result in a more convincing effect. Unlike normal maps, parallax maps give the illusion of displaced geometry even at steeper angles. Although visually the effect of POM is quite impressive, the added cost of requiring a loop in the pixel shader is quite dramatic. Hardware tessellation combined with actual displacement of hardware generated vertices is sometimes preferred. In this paper, we introduce a novel Parallax Occlusion Mapping technique that can produce similar or better quality results, as compared with the traditional Parallax Occlusion Mapping approach, with a lower sample count and fewer artifacts by using a distance field map generated from an existing depth map.

Normal mapping is a technique used to add more surface detail without using additional geometry. The technique relies on a texture map where each pixel of the map stores the surface normal. This surface normal is then used to influence the per pixel lighting and fake additional detail not defined by the underlying geometry. The technique is fairly effective, especially with high frequency detail with low surface displacement. Since the technique does not deform the surface itself, at steeper angles the result is no longer believable. Geometric surfaces are traditionally represented using a triangular *parametric surface*. In contrast, an *implicit surface* represents a surface implicitly through use of a by a continuous function sampled on a discrete grid [4]. This (distance) function is evaluated at each point on the grid. If the function returns zero the point lies on the surface. For all other points, the function returns a negative or positive value denoting the euclidean distance to the surface. The surface contour can then be extracted by assuming the surface lies on the inflection point. The surface contour can be assumed to be any constant, not just 0, thus deforming the original contour in a continuous manner. The signed field generated by the function is called a Signed Distance Field (SDF).

Parallax Occlusion Mapping (POM) is an advanced rendering technique to render complex surfaces without the added cost of geometric complexity. The technique relies on ray tracing a height field for each pixel in the scene [5]. A ray is traced from the origin (texture coordinates) along the view direction and the intersection of the ray with the surface is used to offset the texture coordinates. Multiple samples are required to accurately intersect with the surface defined by the depth map. Assuming that the delta between the samples is constant, steeper angles require higher samples. POM algorithms take into account the view direction and increase the number of samples on steeper angles. Although the results are quite compelling, the technique relies on discrete sampling and the resulting image has artifacts especially at steeper viewing angles when few samples are used. Unreal engine's POM shader has a default maximum of 32 samples per pixel.

2   Distance Field Texture Maps

Since a distance field function returns the distance to the closest point of a surface, the direction to the surface can be calculated using the gradient of the distance field. Distance field texture maps can be generated using depth maps by calculating the distance between the current point and the point closest on the surface of interest.

$$d(x, y) = |a - b| \tag{1}$$

where d defines the distance between points a and b. The distance can only be obtained if we are on the surface contour:

$$D(a, b) = \begin{cases} d(a, b) & \text{when } I(a) \leq C \\ 1 & \text{when } I(a) > C \end{cases} \tag{2}$$

where $I(a)$ returns the value of the depth map between $[0, 1]$ and C is a constant that defines the surface contour. We can then calculate the distance as follows:

$$f(x) = \max \{D^n(x, I_n)\} \tag{3}$$

where n is the number of pixels in image I.

3   Occlusion Mapping with Ray Marching

Using a distance field we can determine exactly how far the ray must traced to reach the surface contour. Depending on the direction of the ray, we can discard the trace altogether if the distance field gradient shows the surface to be in the opposite direction. Although multiple samples are still required, we no longer use a constant distance between samples. Instead, the delta between two samples is defined dynamically by the distance field. Once the intersection of the ray with the surface is found, the texture coordinates are offset similarly to POM. Depending on the complexity of the original depth map, this technique can drastically reduce the number of samples required to give the illusion of depth. Even with just a single sample, we get acceptable results at modest distances to the represented object.

4   Distance Field Occlusion Mapping

We introduce a new method for occlusion mapping we call Distance-Field Occlusion Mapping (DFOM). Similar to parallax mapping, in DFOM all calculations are done in tangent space. However, unlike POM where multiple samples have a constant interval, our technique relies on the distance information stored in the distance field map that was originally generated from a height map. Our technique deviates from POM with rays that have reached the maximum height without intersecting the surface defined by the original height map. We perform a ray-plane intersection where the ray is the view direction and the plane's offset in z is a user defined constant.

```
 1  for  i  in  range(numSamples):
 2        currDis  =  DFMap.r
 3        prevCoord  =  currCoord
 4        currCoord  =  prevCoord  +  (viewDirNorm  *  currDis)
 5
 6        if  (currDis  <  minDis):
 7              # interpolate
 8              w  =  currDis  /  (currDis  -  prevDis);
 9              coordToRet  =  prevCoord  *  w  +  currCoord  *  (1.0  -  w);
10              break
11
12        if  (abs(currCoord.z)  >  maxHeight):
13              # ray-plane  intersection
14              coordToRet  =  intersectionPoint.xy;
15              break
16
17        if  (0.0  <=  currTexCoord  <=  1.0):
18              coordToRet  =  saturate(currTexCoord)
19
20        if  (currDis  <  currMinDis):
21              currMinDis  =  currDis
22              coordToRet  =  currCoord
23
24  return  coordToRet
```

5   Results

Our technique is able to give convincing results with just 1 sample albeit with a maximum height after which too many artifacts begin to appear. We compared the results of the distance field occlusion mapping (DFOM) with the state of the art parallax occlusion mapping (POM) in Unreal Engine 4 (UE4). With just 3 samples, DFOM gives convincing results. Whereas UE4s POM (due to the low sample count) displays a staircase effect that can only be rectified by increasing the number of samples (Fig. 1d). Unreal Engine's current material and shader pipeline has a limitation where a pixel cannot be discarded. Thus, our technique and the POM shader supplied by Unreal, cannot account for the silhouette of the surface at the boundaries of the geometry.

6   Performance

The parallax effect from all parallax occlusion shaders rely on the viewing angle. If the viewing angle is perpendicular to the surface, a lower sample count can be sufficient. On steeper angles, a higher sample count is required to reduce the artifacts shown in Fig. 1d. UE4's Parallax Occlusion Mapping, by default, has a minimum sample count of 8 and a maximum sample count of 32. Our technique is capable of producing comparable results with just 1 sample. However, to produce

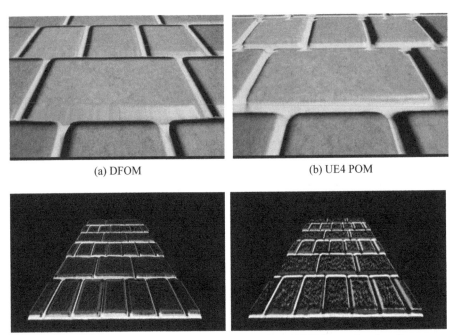

(a) DFOM

(b) UE4 POM

(c) DFOM (Our Method) error from baseline.

(d) UE4 POM error from baseline.

Fig. 1. Comparison between (a) our DFOM technique with 3 samples and (b) UE4's Parallax Occlusion Mapping with the 3 samples. Since POM relies on discrete samples taken at fixed intervals, lower sample counts produce unwanted artifacts. (c, d) Error maps between the methods and the baseline generated from the tessellation shader with height displacement.

a more pronounced effect at least 3 samples are required on steeper angles. Table 1 shows the cost of the 3 shaders with the Tessellation shader as a baseline. The tessellated quad has 8,192 triangles, where both the occlusion mapping shaders use a quad with 4 vertices. Due to the lower sample count requirement, our technique outperforms the UE4 POM shader. The lower triangle count helps our technique outperform the tessellation shader as well (Figs. 2 and 3).

7   Conclusion

Occlusion mapping is a great technique to add more detail to surfaces without additional geometry at the cost of one additional texture map. Current state-of-the-art approaches to occlusion mapping, such as the algorithm implemented in UE4 produce convincing results of geometry that appears to be displaced. However, the high sample requirements deter developers from using the technique often, especially with tessellation now supported on the GPU. We presented a technique where we replace the depth map with a distance field and ray march to find our ray intersection. As shown above, this technique can achieve results

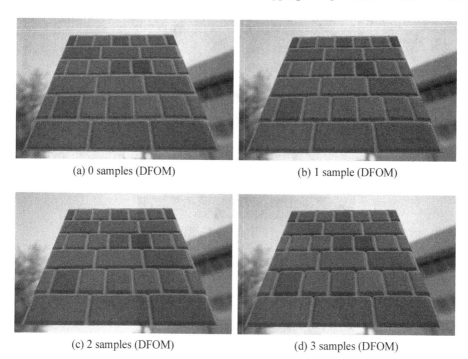

(a) 0 samples (DFOM)   (b) 1 sample (DFOM)

(c) 2 samples (DFOM)   (d) 3 samples (DFOM)

Fig. 2. Progression from 0 to 3 samples. Even with 1 sample results are comparable to Unreal's POM shader. More samples results in an increase in the maximum
displacement.

Table 1. Cost per frame of the 2 occlusion mapping techniques, and the tessellation baseline. Steeper angles require more samples to counteract the artifacts which
increases the cost per frame. The performance metrics were gathered on a machine
with a GTX 1060, 6 *GB* and Core i7 8750*H* CPU.

	Samples		ms/frame		
	Min	Max	View Angle (degrees)		
			0°	30°	75°
Tesselation	N/A	N/A	0.28 ms	0.31 ms	0.30 ms
DF Occlusion	1	3	0.12 ms	0.15 ms	0.21 ms
UE4 POM	8	32	0.15 ms	0.38 ms	0.67 ms

similar to that of parallax occlusion mapping with fewer than half the sample
count. Even with just 1 sample, the results are acceptable, especially when a
large displacement is not required.

(a) Tesselation (baseline)   (b) Distance Field (DFOM).

(c) Parallax Occlusion (UE4 POM)

Fig. 3. (a) Tesselation shader, (b) DFOM (3 samples), (c) UE4 POM (3 samples).

8   Limitations and Future Work

Our technique is currently limited to height maps with low frequency detail. The generation of the distance field map requires the surface to be defined by a constant to which the distance from a pixel is calculated. This limitation can be addressed by spatially partitioning the height map into regions where each region has its own constant based on the lowest depth value in the region. The sample count can further be reduced by using a direction vector calculated (or stored) using the distance field, which can be used to reason about the view direction of the ray's destination. For example, if the dot product of the ray and the distance field gradient is negative, the sample can be discarded earlier thus reducing the number of overall samples needed.

Acknowledgements. We gratefully acknowledge the financial support of the NSERC Discovery grant program.

References

1. Blinn, J.F.: Simulation of wrinkled surfaces. In: ACM SIGGRAPH Computer Graphics (1998)
2. Cohen, J., Olano, M., Manocha, D.: Appearance-preserving simplification. In: Proceedings of the 25th Annual Conference on Computer Graphics and Interactive Techniques, SIGGRAPH 1998, pp. 115–122. ACM, New York (1998)
3. Kaneko, T., et al.: Detailed shape representation with parallax mapping. In: Proceedings of the ICAT 2001 (2001)
4. Osher, S., Fedkiw, R., Piechor, K.: Level Set Methods and Dynamic Implicit Surfaces. Applied Mechanics Reviews (2004)
5. Tatarchuk, N.: Dynamic parallax occlusion mapping with approximate soft shadows. In: Proceedings of the 2006 Symposium on Interactive 3D Graphics and Games, I3D 2006, pp. 63–69. ACM, New York (2006)

Object Grasping of Humanoid Robot Based on YOLO

Li Tian[1] 🆔, Nadia Magnenat Thalmann[1], Daniel Thalmann[2(✉)],
Zhiwen Fang[3], and Jianmin Zheng[1]

[1] Nanyang Technological University, Singapore, Singapore
[2] EPFL, Lausanne, Switzerland
daniel.thalmann@epfl.ch
[3] A*STAR, Singapore, Singapore

Abstract. This paper presents a system that aims to achieve autonomous grasping for micro-controller based humanoid robots such as the Inmoov robot [1]. The system consists of a visual sensor, a central controller and a manipulator. We modify the open sourced objection detection software YOLO (You Only Look Once) v2 [2] and associate it with the visual sensor to make the sensor be able to detect not only the category of the target object but also the location with the help of a depth camera. We also estimate the dimensions (i.e., the height and width) of the target based on the bounding box technique (Fig. 1). After that, we send the information to the central controller (a humanoid robot), which controls the manipulator (customised robotic hand) to grasp the object with the help of inverse kinematics theory. We conduct experiments to test our method with the Inmoov robot. The experiments show that our method is capable of detecting the object and driving the robotic hands to grasp the target object.

Keywords: Robotics · Vision · Object detection · Motion control · Grasping

1 Introduction

Currently, robot technology is making it possible to introduce more automation service to our daily life. Intelligent and interactive robots could assist us in home or office. One of the most important tasks is to fetch objects. However, autonomous grasping is still a not completely solved problem in robotics. In order to archive autonomous grasping, robots should have abilities to recognise the target objects and determine the location of objects. Moreover, robots need to adjust their motion trajectory based on the information of the target objects, such as location and category. Nevertheless, there are still many uncertainties that need to be further studied. Therefore, how to deal with uncertain facts and improve the success rate of grabbing is a very worthwhile problem. Generally, the uncertainties in the grasping process mainly include the uncertainties of the shape of the target object, the pose of the object, the contact point of the manipulator and the quality of the object.

© Springer Nature Switzerland AG 2019
M. Gavrilova et al. (Eds.): CGI 2019, LNCS 11542, pp. 476–482, 2019.
https://doi.org/10.1007/978-3-030-22514-8_47

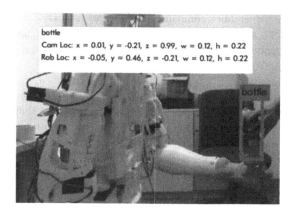

Fig. 1. Autonomous grasping with real-time object detection

To solve this problem, we establish a communication system, which includes a central controller, visual sensor and manipulator. We first collect the necessary information about the target, and then path-plan for the arm based on the position of the target. Finally, we actuate the robotic hand to grasp the target by preset grasp pose according to the categories and size of the targets. Figure 1 shows the screenshot of our object detection software. The water bottle has been detected and highlights within the blue rectangular box. The "x, y, z" after "Cam Loc" indicate the 3D coordinate of the bottle regarding the KINECT II. And the "x, y, z" after "Roc Loc" indicate the 3D coordinate of the bottle after transformation regarding the robot's position. "w" and "h", indicate the width and height of the detected object.

The rest of the paper is organized as follows: Sect. 2 gives an overview of existing related work about grasping of the humanoid robot. Section 3 presents our design and method in details. Section 4 reports the experiments of evaluating the performance with the Inmoov robot.

2   Related Work

2.1   Object Detection

For robot perception, category-specific object detection (COD) is one of the most fundamental yet challenging problems in the computer vision community [3]. The object detection is actually the progress of finding predefined objects among a large number of images. One existing solution uses regions with convolutional neural network features (R-CNN) and fast versions [4, 5]. In this solution, they solve the object localisation question in two parts: 1. Generate object proposal from an image and find where it is. 2. Classify each proposal into different categories and thus recognise the object. This progress brings a tremendous amount of repeated computing, and the speed of it is slow regarding the real-time automatic grasping.

In [6] and [2], the authors compared YOLO and YOLOv2 with other existing detection frameworks and showed that their methods are faster and more accurate. Regarding the perception of the robot, the speed is fulfilled for real-time grasping.

2.2   Grasping from a Humanoid Robot

There are two commonly used methods to deal with the uncertain shape objects when a manipulator is used for grasping. One is to rely on other sensors, such as the tactile sensor, the force sensor, the laser sensor, to feedback more information about the object, to compensate for the shape error caused by vision sensor (camera), and finally to control the multi-degree-of-freedom machine [7]. The other is to apply the method of machine learning to the manipulator grasping [3, 8]. A large amount of data obtained through enough grasping experiments can be used as a training set of feasible grasping configurations for manipulators, and a grasping model obtained from empirical data can be obtained. In [8], they create a complete framework for the iCub robot to let it learn how to roll affordances of the object and explore handheld tools, as well as learn how to use them and finally put the learned skill in real actions.

3   The Proposed Method

3.1   Object Perception in the RGB Image

How to grasp the object remains a very difficult task. Therefore, for safe grasping in a real environment, the target objects need to be recognised and localised accurately. We define the task of grasping as fetching objects from a static place. Firstly, the system collects depth and RGB images from KINECT II. Based on the RGB images, a CNN-based object detection method named as YOLO is adapted to extract CNN features, detect objects and recognise objects. The objects are marked by rectangular boxes and labelled using the object category. Secondly, according to the rectangular boxes including the target objects, the corresponding regions are cropped from the depth image. Finally, in the depth images, object segmentation is designed to obtain the pixels belonging to the target objects, which is used to calculate the location of objects.

Next, we will introduce the details about object perception for social robot grasping. In the vision-based grasping, an interested object should be perceived in the current image at real-time speed. To facilitate real-time object perception, we adopt YOLO [2] to detect and recognise the interesting objects.

YOLO is a unified pipeline, which treats object detection as a regression problem. It can output spatially separated bounding boxes and corresponding class probabilities simultaneously. Because the pipeline of object detection is a single network, it can be optimised end-to-end directly. Moreover, YOLO can process images as a real-time speed. The pipeline of YOLO is shown in Fig. 2. It can be observed that global image features are used by YOLO to detect the objects. This framework consists of three steps: (1) resize the input image to 544×544, (2) run a CNN-based network, and (3) output the results by the confidence of the network model.

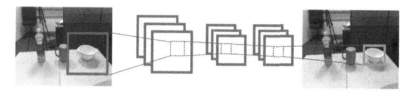

Fig. 2. The pipeline of YOLO: (1) resize the input image to 544 × 544, (2) run a CNN-based network, and (3) output the results by the confidence of network mode.

Next, we will briefly introduce YOLO. The input image is divided into a 7 × 7 grid. If a grid cell includes the centre of an object, that grid cell is used to detect that object. A bounding box and class probabilities are predicted using that grid. YOLO has 24 convolutional layers followed by two fully connected layers. It uses 1 × 1 layer followed by 3 × 3 convolutional layers and strode convolutions are used to replace the maxpooling layers.

3.2   Object Segmentation from the Depth Image

Having good segmentation information can be useful for grasping. It can help the social robot to estimate the location of target objects. Unlike previous methods, which only use RGB images, we take advantage of depth cues to get the pixels belonging to target objects. In order to segment the target objects from the depth image, we need to remove the background and the desk plane.

Because the length of humanoid robot arms is about 0.8 m, the background information can be filtered by a fixed threshold θ as Eq. 1

$$RGB(p) = \begin{cases} 0, & depth(p) > \theta \\ RGB(p), & other \end{cases},$$ (1)

where RGB(p) and depth(p) represent the RGB value and the depth value of pixel p; $\theta = 1000$ is the threshold. For removing the background. It means that the RGB value of pixels whose depth value are larger than 1 m will be set to 0. The distance-based filter can restrain the background. In order to segment objects, the depth map is also filtered as Eq. 2.

$$depth(p) = \begin{cases} 0, & depth(p) > \theta \\ depth(p), & other \end{cases},$$ (2)

Next, we need to get the pixels belonging to the desk. It can be observed that the plane of the desk is the biggest one because the background has been removed in the last step. In order to detect the plane, the first step is how to transform the depth image to point cloud data. IR camera intrinsic parameters, focal length and the principal point can be used to finish the transforming task [9]. The algorithm for converting the depth image to point cloud data is as Algorithm 1.

Algorithm 1: Transform the depth image to point cloud data
1: φ=1000; //Meter to MM
2: for vDepth = 1 to height
3:    for uDepth = 1 to weight
4:      z = depth(vDepth, uDepth)/φ
5:      x = (uDepth - cxd) * z / fxd
6:      y = (vDepth – cyd) * z / fyd
7:      pointcloud(vDepth,uDepth,1) = x;
8:      pointcloud(vDepth,uDepth,2) = y;
9:      pointcloud(vDepth,uDepth,3) = z;
10: end
11: end

where fxd, fyd are the focal length and cxd, cyd are the principal points. After point cloud data is obtained, we adopt a RANSAC [10]-based plane fitting method to discover planes in point cloud data efficiently. The plane fitting method can get the largest set of points which fit to plane. The plane equation is defined as:

$$ax + by + cz + d = 0 \tag{3}$$

where a, b and c are plane parameters and d is the distance from the origin to the plane. From the point cloud data, three points are selected by RANSAC which can calculate the parameters of the corresponding plane according to these points. Then a distance threshold is set to enlarge the plane. The distance threshold is set to 0.0 in our method. According to the segmentation result, the corresponding depth pixels of the desk plane are removed. Finally, we can obtain the target objects in the depth image. Based on the object detection in the RGB image and the object segmentation in the depth image, the object location (xc, yc, zc) in the camera space can be calculated by averaging the location information of pixels belonging to the target objects.

Aim to grasp the target objects, the location of the target objects should be transformed to the corresponding value in the robot space. The joint of the right arm is set as the origin of the coordinate plane in the robot space, and the formulation of the affine transformation is defined as Eq. 4

$$\begin{pmatrix} x_r \\ y_r \\ z_r \\ 1 \end{pmatrix} = Trans(\delta x, \delta y, \delta z)Rotz(\gamma)Rotx(\beta)Roty(\alpha)\begin{pmatrix} x_c \\ y_c \\ z_c \\ 1 \end{pmatrix} \tag{4}$$

3.3   Kinematics of the Arm

As Inmoov robot's arm has totally five DOFs, the kinematics calculation frame assignment is needed. After getting the position of the target object, the next task is to control the hand to approach the object. It is a typical inverse kinematics problem. It means that when a desired reachable position in the 3D space is given, the angle of each DOF can be calculated in order to move the robotic hand to the given location. It may have multiple solutions for one destiny position. The method proposed in [11] uses Eq. 5 to calculate inverse kinematics of robot arm to get the solution with the least possible movement.

$$\Delta \theta = J^T \left(JJ^T + \lambda^2 I \right)^{-1} \vec{e}$$ (5)

3.4 Robotic Hand Design

For a better grasping, with reference to previous work on humanoid robotic hand [12–15], we made a six DOFs 3D printable robotic hand via the processes of 3D scanning, segmentation, collision part removing and joints adding. It enables highly similar grasping when it works with artificial hand skin (Fig. 3).

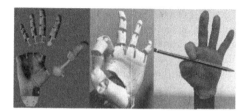

Fig. 3. Our robotic hand's 3D model and the final product

4   Experiments

We have tested our robotic hand on an open-sourced humanoid robot Inmoov with our customised robotic hand. The results showed that the robot could grasp the objects autonomously in real time. Figure 4 provides three screenshots of the robot grasp test. The procedure of our method is as follows:

1. Run our vision detection software on the controller PC. The linked KINECT II will start to detect the area in front of it.
2. When a pre-programmed target appeared, our software will send the category, location and size of the object to the humanoid robot (Fig. 1). In testing, we put a goblet in front of the robot with the human hand. Our software works fine in this case.
3. The humanoid robot will do the motion plan for the hand and fingers to grasp the target object (Fig. 4). In testing, the robot raises the left arm and hand to approach to the cup and eventually grasp the cup with wrap pose.

Fig. 4. Grasping test with Inmoov

Acknowledgements. This research is supported by the BeingTogether Centre, a collaboration between Nanyang Technological University (NTU) Singapore and University of North Carolina (UNC) at Chapel Hill. The BeingTogether Centre is supported by the National Research Foundation, Prime Minister's Office, Singapore under its International Research Centres in Singapore Funding Initiative.

References

1. Langevin, G.: Hand robot InMoov (2016)
2. Redmon, J., Farhadi, A.: YOLO9000: better, faster, stronger. In: Proceedings of the IEEE Conference on Computer Vision and Pattern Recognition (2017)
3. Han, J., et al.: Advanced deep-learning techniques for salient and category-specific object detection: a survey. IEEE Signal Process. Mag. **35**(1), 84–100 (2018)
4. Girshick, R.: Fast R-CNN. In: Proceedings of the IEEE International Conference on Computer Vision (2015)
5. Girshick, R., et al.: Rich feature hierarchies for accurate object detection and semantic segmentation. In: Proceedings of the IEEE Conference on Computer Vision and Pattern Recognition (2014)
6. Redmon, J., et al.: You only look once: unified, real-time object detection. In: Proceedings of the IEEE Conference on Computer Vision and Pattern Recognition (2016)
7. Roa, M.A., Suárez, R.: Grasp quality measures: review and performance. Auton. Robots **38**(1), 65–88 (2015)
8. Tikhanoff, V., et al.: Exploring affordances and tool use on the iCub. In: 2013 13th IEEE-RAS International Conference on Humanoid Robots (Humanoids). IEEE (2013)
9. Kurban, R., Skuka, F., Bozpolat, H.: Plane segmentation of kinect point clouds using RANSAC. In: The 7th International Conference on Information Technology (2015)
10. Fischler, M.A., Bolles, R.C.: Random sample consensus: a paradigm for model fitting with applications to image analysis and automated cartography. Commun. ACM **24**(6), 381–395 (1981)
11. Dakarimov, S., et al.: Study on the development and control of humanoid robot arm using MatLab/Arduino. 유공압건설기계학회 학술대회논문집, pp. 88–90 (2018)
12. Thalmann, N.M., Tian, L., Yao, F.: Nadine: a social robot that can localize objects and grasp them in a human way. In: Prabaharan, S.R.S., Thalmann, N.M., Kanchana Bhaaskaran, V.S. (eds.) Frontiers in Electronic Technologies. LNEE, vol. 433, pp. 1–23. Springer, Singapore (2017). https://doi.org/10.1007/978-981-10-4235-5_1
13. Tian, L., et al.: The making of a 3D-printed, cable-driven, single-model, lightweight humanoid robotic hand. Front. Robot. AI **4**, 65 (2017)
14. Tian, L., et al.: A methodology to model and simulate customized realistic anthropomorphic robotic hands. In: Proceedings of Computer Graphics International 2018. ACM (2018)
15. Tian, L., et al.: Nature grasping by a cable-driven under-actuated anthropomorphic robotic hand. TELKOMNIKA **17**(1), 1–7 (2019)

Bivariate BRDF Estimation Based on Compressed Sensing

Haru Otani[1], Takashi Komuro[1(✉)], Shoji Yamamoto[2], and Norimichi Tsumura[3]

[1] Saitama University, 255 Shimo-Okubo, Sakura-ku, Saitama 338-8570, Japan
otani@is.ics.saitama-u.ac.jp, komuro@mail.saitama-u.ac.jp
[2] Tokyo Metropolitan College of Industrial Technology,
8-17-1 Minami-senju, Arakawa-ku, Tokyo 116-8523, Japan
yamamoto@acp.metro-cit.ac.jp
[3] Chiba University, 1-33 Yayoi-cho, Inage-ku, Chiba 263-8522, Japan
tsumura@faculty.chiba-u.jp

Abstract. We propose a method of estimating a bivariate BRDF from a small number of sampled data using compressed sensing. This method aims to estimate the reflectance of various materials by using the representation space that keeps local information when restored by compressed sensing. We conducted simulated measurements using randomly sampled data and data sampled according to the camera position and orientation, and confirmed that most of the BRDF was successfully restored from 40% sampled data in the case of simulated measurement using a camera and markers.

Keywords: Reflectance estimation · Bivariate BRDF · Compressed sensing

1 Introduction

In recent years, the demand for 3DCG technology in video works is increasing. To create realistic CG, it is required to render objects with a similar reflectance to those of real objects. Many studies have been conducted for obtaining BRDFs (Bidirectional Reflectance Distribution Functions), which represents the reflectance of the surfaces of objects, to reproduce the appearance of real objects with CG.

In order to measure dense BRDFs, there are methods of mechanically moving a light source and a camera around the target object, or arranging a large number of light sources and cameras [2,9]. However, the former takes much time to measure, and the latter requires large and expensive equipment.

On the other hand, in order to reduce the number of measurements, there are methods of approximating arbitrary BRDFs using linear combination of known BRDFs [4,5] and methods of reducing the number of necessary parameters using an existing reflection model [1,6]. However, the former has a problem that it is

© Springer Nature Switzerland AG 2019
M. Gavrilova et al. (Eds.): CGI 2019, LNCS 11542, pp. 483–489, 2019.
https://doi.org/10.1007/978-3-030-22514-8_48

difficult to reproduce BRDFs with local changes, and the latter has limited capability to express reflectance of real objects.

Based on the related work, we propose a method to estimate a BRDF from a small number of sampled data using compressed sensing. Compressed sensing is a method of restoring all data from a smaller number of sampled data assuming that the data to be restored has few nonzero components in a representation space, that is, the data is sparse. The proposed method aims to estimate the reflectance of various materials by using the representation space that keeps local information when restored by compressed sensing.

2   BRDF Estimation

2.1   Expression of BRDF

BRDFs are generally expressed as functions of four variables: azimuth and elevation angles for incident light (θ_i, ϕ_i) and those for reflection light (θ_r, ϕ_r). Isotropic BRDFs assume rotational invariance around the normal and the number of variables is reduced to three $(\theta_h, \theta_d, \phi_d)$ as shown in Fig. 1.

Romeiro et al. [7] proposed to further reduce the number of variables of BRDFs to (θ_h, θ_d) with Eq. (1) by assuming that ϕ_d does not change even if both the incident and reflection directions are rotated around the half vector $\boldsymbol{h}$ as shown in Fig. 2.

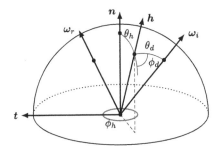
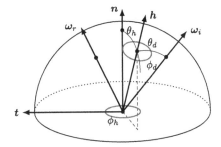

Fig. 1. Isotropic BRDF   **Fig. 2.** Bivariate BRDF [7]

$$\bar{f}(\theta_h, \theta_d) = \frac{1}{|\Phi(\theta_h, \theta_d)|} \sum_{\Phi(\theta_h, \theta_d)} f(\theta_h, \theta_d, \phi_d), \tag{1}$$

where $\Phi(\theta_h, \theta_d)$ is a set of the isotropic BRDF values.

We use this bivariable BRDF expression since compressed sensing is mainly applied to 1D or 2D data and also it is easy to visualize.

2.2   Compressed Sensing

The BRDF to be estimated has n RGB values. m values sampled from the BRDF are put to an input vector y, and a sampling matrix A is obtained from the indices of the sampled data. The BRDF x is not generally sparse, and compression sensing cannot be applied as it is. Therefore, we convert the data by applying Discrete Cosine Transform (DCT) to every 18×18 blocks of the 2D data. Estimation is performed by solving the optimization problem shown in Eq. (2).

$$W\hat{x} = \min\|Wx\|_1 \quad \text{subject to} \quad y = Ax \qquad (2)$$

W is a matrix that performs DCT. By applying the inverse DCT to the estimated $W\hat{x}$, an estimate $\hat{x}$ of x is obtained. Block DCT was used to enable estimation that keeps local changes in BRDFs.

3   Experiment

We used MERL BRDF Database [5], which contains isotropic BRDFs of various materials. The isotropic BRDF data were converted to bivariate BRDF data, which had 8,100 RGB values. When solving the optimization problem, we used CVXPY, an optimization library for Python.

3.1   BRDF Sampling

The BRDF was sampled in two ways. The first method was to randomly select a combination of variables (θ_h, θ_d) from the uniform distribution and sample the value of the BRDF at the position.

The second method was to simulate BRDF measurement using a camera and markers. Assuming that there is a moving light source and a planar object, the camera was moved by hand to capture the images of the object from various directions. In each frame, the camera pose was obtained using ArUco [3,8] which is an open source library for camera pose estimation using squared markers, and the variables (θ_h, θ_d) are calculated.

We used ChArUco (Chessboard + ArUco) markers which enable estimation of the camera pose even if a part of the marker is hidden. A rectangular box with the markers attached to five faces except the bottom was prepared and we assumed there was a planar object to be measured at the center of its upper face as shown in Fig. 3. The angle θ_i, which is the elevation angle in the direction of the light source, was moved by $\pi/12$ every 10 s within the range of $[0, \pi]$, since there are directions in which the samples of the bivariate BRDF cannot be obtained depending on the angle θ_i.

ChArUco obtains the position vector t and the rotation vector r of the marker on the top surface of the box in the camera coordinate system. In order to obtain the reflection direction ω_r, it is necessary to convert them to those in the marker coordinate system with the origin at the center of the top surface of the box. The rotation matrix R is obtained using Rodrigues' rotation formula having the

Fig. 3. Simulated measurement using a camera and markers

rotation axis r and the rotation angle $\|r\|_2$, and the position of the camera in the camera coordinate system c_{camera} can be written by Eq. (3) using the position of the camera in the marker coordinate system c_{marker}.

$$c_{\text{camera}} = Rc_{\text{marker}} + t \tag{3}$$

Since the camera position is equal to the origin of the camera coordinate system, $c_{\text{camera}} = 0$, Eq. (3) can be transformed to Eq. (4).

$$c_{\text{marker}} = -R^{-1}t \tag{4}$$

Since the reflection direction ω_r is parallel to the camera's position vector c_{marker} in the marker coordinate system, it can be obtained by normalizing the camera position as Eq. (3).

$$\omega_r = \frac{c_{\text{marker}}}{\|c_{\text{marker}}\|_2} = -\frac{R^{-1}t}{\|R^{-1}t\|_2} \tag{5}$$

A half vector h is obtained from ω_r and an incident direction ω_i, and (θ_h, θ_d) is obtained by Eq. (6).

$$\theta_h = \cos^{-1}(n \cdot h), \quad \theta_d = \cos^{-1}(h \cdot \omega_r) \tag{6}$$

Where n is the normal to the top face of the box.

3.2 Results

Figures 4 and 5 show the estimation result using the gold-metallic-paint BRDF in the database. Data was sampled with both sampling methods such that the percentage of known data became 10%, 20%, 40% and 80%.

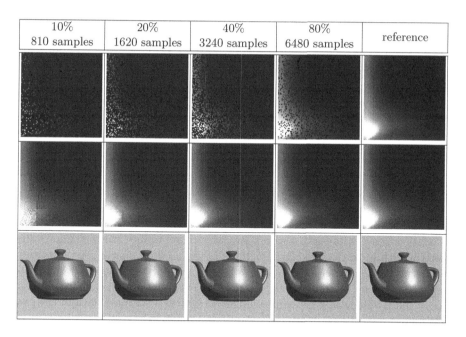

Fig. 4. Estimation results with random sampling (top: input, middle: output, bottom: rendering)

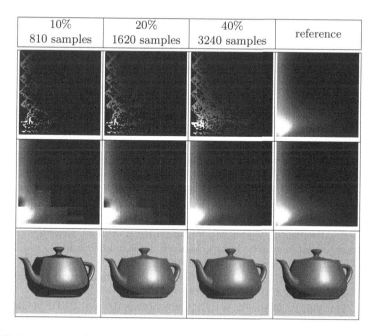

Fig. 5. Estimation results with camera sampling (top: input, middle: output, bottom: rendering)

Estimation results from 40% or more sampled data were mostly successful, but the results from 10% and 20% samples contained incorrect estimation with discontinuous region. This is probably because DCT was applied to each block and the minimum number of sampled data that was required to estimate the block could not be obtained.

When sufficient data could not be sampled, noticeable noise was seen in the highlight part, but it was estimated well in flat parts even with a small number of sampled data. This is probably because the highlight part contained large values and the estimation errors tend to increase in proportion to the values.

4   Conclusion and Future Work

We proposed a method to estimate a bivariate BRDF data from partially sampled data using compressed sensing. In order to reproduce the reflectance distribution with local changes, the block DCT was used for sparse representation. We conducted simulated measurements using randomly sampled data and data sampled according to the camera position and orientation, and confirmed that most of the BRDF was successfully restored from 40% sampled data in the case of simulated measurement using a camera and markers.

For future work, improvement of estimation accuracy is necessary. We used block DCT as a general sparse representation, but there are other sparse representations that can make more accurate estimation from less information. In addition, this study carried out only simulated measurement, and did not consider noise added in actual measurement. We will conduct an experiment using actual measurement data and verify the effectiveness of our proposed method in practical situations.

References

1. Bilgili, A., Öztürk, A., Kurt, M.: A general BRDF representation based on tensor decomposition. Comput. Graph. Forum **30**, 2427–2439 (2011)
2. Foo, S.C.: A gonioreflectometer for measuring the bidirectional reflectance of material for use in illumination computation. Ph.D. thesis, Citeseer (1997)
3. Garrido-Jurado, S., Muoz-Salinas, R., Madrid-Cuevas, F., Medina-Carnicer, R.: Generation of fiducial marker dictionaries using mixed integer linear programming. Pattern Recogn. **51** (2015). https://doi.org/10.1016/j.patcog.2015.09.023
4. Hullin, M.B., Hanika, J., Ajdin, B., Seidel, H.P., Kautz, J., Lensch, H.: Acquisition and analysis of bispectral bidirectional reflectance and reradiation distribution functions. ACM Trans. Graph. (TOG) **29**(4), 97 (2010)
5. Matusik, W., Pfister, H., Brand, M., McMillan, L.: A data-driven reflectance model. ACM Trans. Graph. **22**(3), 759–769 (2003)
6. Ngan, A., Durand, F., Matusik, W.: Experimental analysis of BRDF models (2005)
7. Romeiro, F., Vasilyev, Y., Zickler, T.: Passive reflectometry. In: Forsyth, D., Torr, P., Zisserman, A. (eds.) ECCV 2008. LNCS, vol. 5305, pp. 859–872. Springer, Heidelberg (2008). https://doi.org/10.1007/978-3-540-88693-8_63

8. Romero Ramirez, F., Muoz-Salinas, R., Medina-Carnicer, R.: Speeded up detection of squared fiducial markers. Image Vis. Comput. **76** (2018). https://doi.org/10.1016/j.imavis.2018.05.004
9. Schwartz, C., Sarlette, R., Weinmann, M., Klein, R.: DOME II: a parallelized BTF acquisition system. In: Material Appearance Modeling, pp. 25–31 (2013)

Nadine Humanoid Social Robotics Platform

Manoj Ramanathan[1]([✉])([iD]), Nidhi Mishra[1], and Nadia Magnenat Thalmann[1,2]

[1] Institute for Media Innovation, Nanyang Technological University,
Singapore, Singapore
{mramanathan,nidhi.mishra,nadiathalmann}@ntu.edu.sg
[2] MIRALab, University of Geneva, Geneva, Switzerland
thalmann@miralab.ch

Abstract. Developing a social robot architecture is very difficult as
there are countless possibilities and scenarios. In this paper, we introduce the design of a generic social robotics architecture deployed in
Nadine social robot, that can be customized to handle any scenario or
application, and allows her to express human-like emotions, personality,
behaviors, dialog. Our design comprises of three layers, namely, perception, processing and interaction layer and allows modularity (add/remove
sub-modules), task or environment based customizations (for example,
change in knowledge database, gestures, emotions). We noticed that it
is difficult to do a precise state of the art for robots as each of them
might be developed for different tasks, different work environment. The
robots could have different hardware that also makes comparison challenging. In this paper, we compare Nadine social robot with state of art
robots on the basis of social robot characteristics such as speech recognition and synthesis, gaze, face, object recognition, affective system, dialog
interaction capabilities, memory.

Keywords: Social robotics · Generic robotics architecture ·
Nadine-social robot · Human-robot interaction

1 Introduction

Social robots are designed as autonomous systems with AI that allow them to
interact with humans, other robots and their environment. Their design is based
on cognitive computing, which includes data mining, pattern recognition, natural
language processing, so as to mimic a human brain, which allows social robots
to interact in socially acceptable and sophisticated manner. For example, they
can work as consumer guides [20], teachers [7], companions for the elderly [15].

Building a generic social robot platform that can be used for any workplace
is very difficult. Such a platform would need to be reusable and retrained easily for different context and environment. This also makes it inherently difficult
to compare two social robots as their applications, hardware can be completely

© Springer Nature Switzerland AG 2019
M. Gavrilova et al. (Eds.): CGI 2019, LNCS 11542, pp. 490–496, 2019.
https://doi.org/10.1007/978-3-030-22514-8_49

different. In this paper, we develop a generic social robot platform that is modular and allows retraining according to our requirements (context, environment). Also, we provide a comparison between social robots based on social interaction cues, characteristics to understand and provide an overview of the available social robots. As shown in Fig. 1, she has a realistic human-like appearance with very natural skin, hair. Nadine has a total of 27 degrees of freedom for facial expressions and upper body movements. With the proposed platform, Nadine is able to adapt and work at different workplaces.

The rest of the paper is organized as follows: In Sect. 2, we provide previous related work in the field of social robots and architecture proposed. In Sect. 3, we introduce our proposed generic social robot architecture that follows perception - processing - interaction layer framework. In Sect. 4, we discuss about essential social robot characteristics and compare Nadine with other state of art social robots based on the these characteristics to the best of our knowledge. We provide conclusions in Sect. 5.

Fig. 1. Nadine social robot

2   Related Work

Humanoid robots are an essential part of robotics, which have a body shape built to resemble the human body. The design may be for functional purposes, such as interacting with human tools and environments, for experimental purposes, such as the study of locomotion, or for other purposes [1]. Designing humanoid robots for specific tasks like playing ping pong [24], chess [16], health care social robot [5] is considerably easy. But developing a generic social robot architecture to consider all possible social situations, context, workplace and hardware available is very challenging. Especially understanding social context and social interaction cues is difficult. KISMET robot [4] can process visual, auditory and proprioceptive sensory inputs to understand social context and behave appropriately.

iCub [13], Nao [18] are general purpose robots that are widely used for several applications. Metta et al. [13] introduced an open platform for cognition studies for iCub humanoid robot, based on YARP libraries, where modules can be added/removed. Similarly, Nao [18] designed by Softbank robotics for playing soccer allows modularity to include modules such as speech recognition, multi lingual speech synthesis, facial and shape recognition. SURENA [2] is a humanoid social robot capable of reading sensory inputs, recognize objects and detect human face/motion, distinguish Persian commands, navigation, imitate human actions.

The appearance of robot is a deciding factor in people's perception. The realistic appearance of a humanoid robot increases expectations of people in its functionality and behavior. HRP-4C [11] introduced a biped humanoid robot that has a Japanese female face and skin. It can closely mimic human movements and can respond to voice commands by using speech recognition. Robots like Nadine, Sophia [23], Erica [9] have realistic human appearance compared to other previously mentioned humanoid robots. In these cases, the behavior, cognitive abilities, personalities have to be carefully designed to look and behave human-like to avoid uncanny valley effects. Goertzel et al. [6] published a pilot study on Sophia robot's social interaction. Zhang et al. [25,26] shows studies on Nadine social robot's memory, emotion and personality in a social interaction.

3   Social Robotics Architecture

An essential requirement for any social robot would be interactions with humans, environmental awareness, dynamically understanding social cues. The social robot needs to maintain a natural human-like tone and flow to any conversation with any user. Therefore, the design of generic social robot platform is a complex task that takes into account several factors like maintaining naturalness of conversation, generalization to any field, multi-lingual support. In this section, we briefly explain about our social robot, Nadine's architecture.

Figure 2 shows our proposed architecture. From the Fig. 2, we can see that our architecture consists of 3 layers, namely, perception, processing and interaction. Firstly, our platform perceives various stimuli which helps the robot understand user and its operating environment. 3D cameras, web cameras, and microphone are used as input devices to recognize the user identity, position, facial emotion, actions, speech, gender and objects in the environment. Then each of these stimuli are processed to decide upon an appropriate verbal or non-verbal response. The processing layer includes various sub-modules such as dialog processing (chatbot), affective system (emotions, personality, mood), Nadine's memory of previous encounters with users. Finally, the verbal or non-verbal responses have to be shown on the robot using the interaction layer. This layer is specific to Nadine's hardware but can be changed easily to fit other robots. The responses from the processing layer can be head movement to maintain eye gaze, gestures and facial expressions, dialog and tone (to show different emotions, personality). The main objectives of our design is to maintain human-like natural behavior even in complex situations and be generic to handle any kind of data. Each layer consists of several sub-modules for specific tasks. These sub-modules are connected using an independent platform framework [3] to facilitate module connections and development. Sub-modules can be added/removed into each layer based on our requirement. Currently, Nadine can support six languages including English, German, French, Chinese, Hindi and Japanese. See Wikipedia [22].

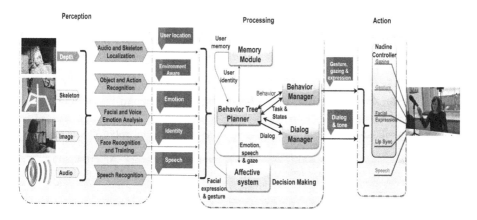

Fig. 2. Proposed social robots architecture of Nadine with perception-processing-interaction layers

4 Nadine Social Robot Characteristics - Discussion

In any setting, a social robot would require to gauge both verbal and non-verbal cues of people it meets and be able to change its own verbal and non-verbal behavior accordingly. Another requirement would be understanding its environment that would allow it perform different tasks and navigate if needed. Therefore, for robust functioning, Nadine has been equipped dedicated modules for face recognition, gaze behavior, speech recognition and synthesis, action recognition, object recognition, memory of users, affective system (to model her personality, emotion, mood), data processing or dialog system. Due to the generic nature of the platform, other modules can be added based on any requirement. Also each of the modules can be customized, modified and retrained according to the requirement.

Recently, several robots have been developed with different capabilities based on their work place, requirements, tasks and hardware itself. Due to this, there exists no fixed benchmark to compare the robots as well. But using the above-mentioned essential characteristics as a basis of comparison, in Table 1, we classify the available state of the art robots. To make this classification, it is necessary to know if a robotic platform can support these characteristics. But collection of such data is very difficult for commercial robots as they do not share proprietary data. Here, we have collected information based on the data sheets and online videos. In Table 1, √ indicates presence and × indicates absence of those characteristic in the robot. We have recorded 'NA' for entries were these characteristics could have been included by others or when we are not sure if such capabilities are present in the robot.

Another important factor considered is the human-like appearance of the robot including artificial skin. If a robot has more human-like appearance, the realism expected from it will be more. It also means the robot is expected to perform human-like tasks and behaviours in all scenarios. This can be attributed to the uncanny valley effect that users would experience. For this reason, realistic looking robots such as Nadine, Sophia [23], Erica [9] have to be designed to avoid uncanny valley effect. Due to this, Nadine has dedicated modules for the above-mentioned characteristics that allows her to behave in human-like manner.

Table 1. Classification of social robots based on essential social robot characteristics

Robot	Face recognition	Speech recognition	Speech synthesis	Gesture recognition	Object recognition	Memory	Affective system	Human appearance
Nadine	√	√	√	√	√	√	√	√
[5]	√	√	√	√	√	×	√	×
[8]	√	√	√	×	×	×	×	×
[17]	√	√	√	NA	NA	×	NA	×
[23]	√	√	√	×	×	×	×	√
[9]	×	√	√	×	×	×	NA	√
[12]	×	√	√	×	NA	×	×	×
[21]	√	√	√	√	√	×	×	×
[10]	×	×	√	×	√	×	×	×
[14]	×	√	√	×	√	×	√	√ (Only head)
[13]	×	√	×	×	√	×	×	×
[19]	√	√	√	×	√	×	√	×

5   Conclusion

Social robotics is a rapidly developing field with several applications in the real world. Each robot is required to operate in different work places, to perform different tasks making it difficult to develop a generic social robotics framework. In this paper, we provide a overview of the overall Nadine social robot platform. We also provide a comparison between Nadine social robot and state of the art robots based on social robot characteristics.

Acknowledgements. This research is supported by the BeingTogether Centre, a collaboration between Nanyang Technological University (NTU) Singapore and University of North Carolina (UNC) at Chapel Hill. The BeingTogether Centre is supported by the National Research Foundation, Prime Minister's Office, Singapore under its International Research Centres in Singapore Funding Initiative.

References

1. Humanoid robot (2018). https://en.wikipedia.org/wiki/Humanoid_robot
2. Surena III (2018). http://surenahumanoid.com/capabilitiess/
3. Beck, A., Zhijun, Z., Magnenat-Thalmann, N.: Motion control for social behaviors. In: Magnenat-Thalmann, N., Yuan, J., Thalmann, D., You, B.-J. (eds.) Context Aware Human-Robot and Human-Agent Interaction. HIS, pp. 237–256. Springer, Cham (2016). https://doi.org/10.1007/978-3-319-19947-4_11
4. Breazeal, C., Scassellati, B.: A context-dependent attention system for a social robot. In: Proceedings of the 16th International Joint Conference on Artificial Intelligence, IJCAI 1999, pp. 1146–1153. Morgan Kaufmann Publishers Inc., San Francisco (1999). http://dl.acm.org/citation.cfm?id=646307.687601
5. Ge, S., et al.: Design and development of Nancy, a social robot. In: International Conference on Ubiquitous Robots and Ambient Intelligence, pp. 568–573, November 2011
6. Goertzel, B., Mossbridge, J., Monroe, E., Hanson, D., Yu, G.: Humanoid robots as agents of human consciousness expansion. CoRR abs/1709.07791 (2017). http://arxiv.org/abs/1709.07791
7. Han, J., Park, I.W., Park, M.: Outreach education utilizing humanoid type agent robots. In: Proceedings of the 3rd International Conference on Human-Agent Interaction, HAI 2015, pp. 221–222 (2015). https://doi.org/10.1145/2814940.2814980
8. Holthaus, P., Pitsch, K., Wachsmuth, S.: How can I help? Spatial attention strategies for a receptionist robot. Int. J. Soc. Rob. 3(4), 383–393 (2011)
9. IshiguroLab: Erica (2018). https://eng.irl.sys.es.osaka-u.ac.jp/robot
10. Iwata, H., Sugano, S.: Design of human symbiotic robot TWENDY-ONE. In: IEEE International Conference on Robotics and Automation, pp. 580–586, May 2009
11. Kajita, S., et al.: Cybernetic human HRP-4C: a humanoid robot with human-like proportions. In: Pradalier, C., Siegwart, R., Hirzinger, G. (eds.) Robotics Research. Springer Tracts in Advanced Robotics, vol. 70, pp. 301–314. Springer, Heidelberg (2011). https://doi.org/10.1007/978-3-642-19457-3_18
12. Meghdari, A., Alemi, M., Khamooshi, M., Amoozandeh, A., Shariati, A., Mozafari, B.: Conceptual design of a social robot for pediatric hospitals. In: International Conference on Robotics and Mechatronics, pp. 566–571, October 2016
13. Metta, G., Sandini, G., Vernon, D., Natale, L., Nori, F.: The iCub humanoid robot: an open platform for research in embodied cognition. In: Proceedings of the 8th Workshop on Performance Metrics for Intelligent Systems, pp. 50–56, August 2008
14. Oh, J.H., Hanson, D., Kim, W.S., Han, I.Y., Kim, J.Y., Park, I.W.: Design of android type humanoid robot albert HUBO. In: IEEE/RSJ International Conference on Intelligent Robots and Systems, pp. 1428–1433, October 2006
15. Orejana, J.R., MacDonald, B.A., Ahn, H.S., Peri, K., Broadbent, E.: Healthcare robots in homes of rural older adults. Social Robotics. LNCS (LNAI), vol. 9388, pp. 512–521. Springer, Cham (2015). https://doi.org/10.1007/978-3-319-25554-5_51
16. PALROBOTICS: REEM-A: Robotics research (2018). https://en.wikipedia.org/wiki/REEMSpecifications
17. PALROBOTICS: REEM-C: Robotics research (2018). http://pal-robotics.com/en/products/reem-c/
18. Robotics, S.: Nao robot (2018). https://en.wikipedia.org/wiki/Nao_(robot)
19. Robotics, S.: Pepper (2018). https://www.softbankrobotics.com/emea/en/pepper
20. Sabelli, A.M., Kanda, T.: Robovie as a mascot: a qualitative study for long-term presence of robots in a shopping mall. Int. J. Soc. Rob. 8(2), 211–221 (2016). https://doi.org/10.1007/s12369-015-0332-9

21. Sakagami, Y., Watanabe, R., Aoyama, C., Matsunaga, S., Higaki, N., Fujimura, K.: The intelligent ASIMO: system overview and integration. In: IEEE/RSJ International Conference on Intelligent Robots and Systems, vol. 3, pp. 2478–2483, September 2002
22. Wikipedia: Nadine social robot (2018). https://en.wikipedia.org/wiki/Nadine_Social_Robot
23. Wikipedia: Sophia (robot) (2018). https://en.wikipedia.org/wiki/Sophia_(robot)
24. Wikipedia: Topio (2018). https://en.wikipedia.org/wiki/TOPIO
25. Zhang, J., Zheng, J., Magnenat Thalmann, N.: PCMD: personality-characterized mood dynamics model toward personalized virtual characters. Comput. Animation Virtual Worlds **26**(3–4), 237–245 (2015)
26. Zhang, J., Zheng, J., Magnenat Thalmann, N.: MCAEM: mixed-correlation analysis-based episodic memory for companion-user interactions. Vis. Comput. **34**(6–8), 1129–1141 (2018)

ENGAGE'19 Workshop Full Papers

Gajit: Symbolic Optimisation and JIT Compilation of Geometric Algebra in Python with GAALOP and Numba

Hugo Hadfield[1]([✉]) [iD], Dietmar Hildenbrand[2] [iD], and Alex Arsenovic[3] [iD]

[1] Cambridge University Engineering Department, Cambridge, UK
hh409@cam.ac.uk
[2] University of Technology Darmstadt, Darmstadt, Germany
dietmar.hildenbrand@gmail.com
[3] 810 Labs, Stanardsville, VA, USA
alex@810lab.com
http://810lab.com/

Abstract. Modern Geometric Algebra software systems tend to fall into one of two categories, either fast, difficult to use, statically typed, and syntactically different from the mathematics or slow, easy to use, dynamically typed and syntactically close to the mathematical conventions. Gajit is a system that aims to get the best of both worlds. It allows us to prototype and debug algorithms with the Python library clifford [1] which is designed to be easy to read and write and then to optimise our code both symbolically with GAALOP [2] and via the LLVM pipeline with Numba [3] resulting in highly performant code for very little additional effort.

Keywords: Geometric Algebra · Conformal geometry · Symbolic optimisation · Just in time compilation

1 Introduction

Geometric Algebra is syntactically concise and suited to algorithmic prototyping due to its intuitive embedding of geometry. Naturally these features pair well with dynamically typed, interpreted programming languages such as Python or JavaScript and this has lead to a proliferation of implementations. Notable examples of numerical packages in high level languages include ganja.js [4] and the clifford Python library [1]. Unfortunately while high level languages are fast for writing and reading code they are often slow for running code.

In this paper we aim to tackle this problem by investigating a dual symbolic optimisation and traditional Just In Time (JIT) compilation approach with GAALOP and Numba applied to the clifford Python library. First we will provide some background on the specific algebra of our examples, Conformal Geometric Algebra. Then we will describe the building blocks of our computational setup: the clifford Python package, GAALOP and Numba. Finally in

© Springer Nature Switzerland AG 2019
M. Gavrilova et al. (Eds.): CGI 2019, LNCS 11542, pp. 499–510, 2019.
https://doi.org/10.1007/978-3-030-22514-8_50

Sect. 5 we will provide the mechanism of operation of our final solution which we title the **gajit** compiler for geometric algebra just in time compiler.

1.1   Conformal Geometric Algebra

While the techniques and ideas presented here can generalise to arbitrary dimension algebras, in this paper we will focus on applying gajit to algorithms written in Conformal Geometric Algebra (CGA) as it is a well studied algebra and well suited to the realisation of engineering applications.

Conformal Geometric Algebra uses the three Euclidean **basis vectors** e_1, e_2, e_3 and two additional basis vectors e_+, e_- with positive and negative signatures, respectively, which means that they square to $+1$ as usual (e_+) and to -1 (e_-).

$$e_+^2 = 1, \qquad e_-^2 = -1, \qquad e_+ \cdot e_- = 0. \tag{1}$$

Another basis e_0, e_∞, with the geometric meaning

- e_0 represents the 3D origin,
- e_∞ represents infinity,

can be defined with the relations

$$e_0 = \frac{1}{2}(e_- - e_+), \qquad e_\infty = e_- + e_+. \tag{2}$$

Blades are the basic algebraic elements of Geometric Algebra. Conformal Geometric Algebra consists of blades with **grades** 0, 1, 2, ..., 5, where a scalar is a **0-blade** (a blade of grade 0) and the **1-blades** are the basis vectors. The **2-blades** $e_i \wedge e_j$ are blades spanned by two 1-blades, and so on. There exists only one element of the maximum grade 5, known as the **pseudoscalar**. A linear combination of k-blades is called a k-vector (or a vector, bivector, trivector. ...). The sum $e_2 \wedge e_3 + e_1 \wedge e_2$, for instance, is a bivector. A linear combination of blades with different grades is called a **multivector**. Multivectors are the general elements of a Geometric Algebra.

Conformal Geometric Algebra provides a great variety of basic geometric entities to compute with, namely points, spheres, planes, circles, lines, and point pairs, as listed in Table 1. These entities have two algebraic representations: the IPNS (inner product null space) and the OPNS (outer product null space) [5]. These representations are duals of each other. In Table 1, **x** and **n** are in bold type to indicate that they represent 3D entities obtained by linear combinations of the 3D basis vectors e_1, e_2, and e_3:

$$\mathbf{x} = x_1 e_1 + x_2 e_2 + x_3 e_3. \tag{3}$$

The $\{S_{I_i}\}$, $\{S_{O_i}\}$ represent different spheres, and the $\{\pi_{I_i}\}$, $\{\pi_{O_i}\}$ accordingly represent different planes (the subscripts I and O mean IPNS and OPNS). In the OPNS representation, the outer product "$\wedge$" indicates the construction of a geometric object with the help of points $\{P_i\}$ that lie on it. A sphere, for instance, is defined by four points $(P_1 \wedge P_2 \wedge P_3 \wedge P_4)$ on this sphere. In the IPNS representation, the meaning of the outer product is an intersection of geometric entities. A circle, for instance, is defined by the intersection of two IPNS spheres $S_{I_1} \wedge S_{I_2}$.

Table 1. The two representations (IPNS and OPNS) of conformal geometric entities. The IPNS and OPNS representations are dual to each other. The subscripts I for IPNS and O for OPNS can be omitted if is clear from the context which representation is meant.

Entity	IPNS representation	OPNS representation
Point	$P = \mathbf{x} + \frac{1}{2}\mathbf{x}^2 e_\infty + e_0$	
Sphere	$S_I = P - \frac{1}{2}r^2 e_\infty$	$S_O = P_1 \wedge P_2 \wedge P_3 \wedge P_4$
Plane	$\pi_I = \mathbf{n} + de_\infty$	$\pi_O = P_1 \wedge P_2 \wedge P_3 \wedge e_\infty$
Circle	$Z_I = S_{I_1} \wedge S_{I_2}$	$Z_O = P_1 \wedge P_2 \wedge P_3$
Line	$L_I = \pi_{I_1} \wedge \pi_{I_2}$	$L_O = P_1 \wedge P_2 \wedge e_\infty$
Point pair	$Pp_I = S_{I_1} \wedge S_{I_2} \wedge S_{I_3}$	$Pp_O = P_1 \wedge P_2$

2   The Clifford Python Package

Originally written by Robert Kern in the early 2000's, the clifford package is an open source, numerical GA library written in the Python programming language. Historically, there have been many Geometric Algebra (GA) software implementations in a range of languages, notable implementations include: C++ libraries versor [6], glucat [7] and garamon [8], the code generators Gaigen [9] and GAALOP [2] and the Javascript libary ganja.js [4].

Developing another GA library requires justification since each individual project splits both developer effort and community support. Given that Python has become the language of choice for scientific computing, data-science, and artificial intelligence, it is important to have a GA library in this domain. Additionally, Python is regularly used to teach programming, making it one of the most accessible languages. The clifford package is designed to be *pythonic*, meaning syntactically intuitive to write and concise to read. These characteristics are important for both accessibility and cost reasons, as developer time generally more expensive than CPU time.

The drawback of writing a computational library in Python is that performance has traditionally been poor compared to statically typed and compiled languages such as C. However, due to the widespread use of Python in scientific computing, several techniques to increase code performance have been developed. By combining clifford's ease of use with a high-performance computing backend driven by GAALOP and Numba we aim to both have our cake and eat it too.

2.1   Prototyping Algorithms with Clifford

Consider an example: we will take a 5D CGA vector x and apply a rotor R to it before adding one, multiplying the pseudoscalar $e1 \wedge e2 \wedge e3 \wedge e_{\text{inf}} \wedge e0$ and dotting the result with $e_1 \wedge e_2$:

$$Y = 1 + RX\tilde{R}$$
$$Y^* = Y(e_1 \wedge e_2 \wedge e_3 \wedge e_{\text{inf}} \wedge e_0)$$
$$F = Y^* \cdot (e_1 \wedge e_2)$$

we can directly translate this operation into a valid clifford python function with very few changes:

```
from clifford.g3c import *


def example_one(X, R):
    Y = 1 + (R * X * ~R)
    Ystar = Y * (e1 ^ e2 ^ e3 ^ einf ^ e0)
    F = Ystar | (e1 ^ e2)
    return F
```

Clearly this is a contrived example of an algorithm but it serves to highlight the syntax of the library and has a lot of potential for optimisation. The key differences from the mathematical syntax are that the $\cdot$ operator has been replaced with a | symbol, as in the python programming language (as in many languages) the . operator is considered a method accessing operator, and additionally we have changed Y^* to Ystar to prevent python considering the $*$ as an operator. Other than these two minor changes the code and the maths remain very similar. This is a key advantage of the clifford library when it comes to prototyping algorithms and implementing mathematics from scientific papers. Unfortunately there are some trade-offs that are made in order to achieve this level of simplicity. Under the hood the library is running run time type checking and each geometric, inner and outer product is implemented via operator overloading. These run time operations add significant overhead to the algorithm. Table 2 shows that it takes around 37.41 µs to run in a mid range laptop. If we are certain of the types of the inputs, i.e., they come from the algebra etc then we can hand optimise this code to bypass the checking at the expense of readability by accessing the raw array operations that implement the various products:

```
from clifford.g3c import *


gp = layout.gmt_func
op = layout.omt_func
ip = layout.imt_func
rev = layout.adjoint_func


e12_value = (e1 ^ e2).value
e12345_value = e12345.value


def example_one_faster(X, R):
    Y = gp(gp(R,X),rev(R))

    Y[0] += 1
    Ystar = gp(Y,e12345_value)
    F = ip(Ystar,e12_value)
    return F
```

These functions produce equivalent results. Table 2 shows the hand optimised code is significantly faster, over 4.5 times faster in fact, but it is much harder to read.

Table 2. Average taken over 10000 runs to execute example_one on a Acer Inspire V15 Nitro laptop. Gajit allows code to be written clearly and easily in python and to match or outperform hand optimised functions. This test was carried out with an Intel Core i5-4210U CPU @ 1.70 GHz, 2401 Mhz, 2 Core(s), 4 Logical Processor(s)

Unoptimised	Hand optimised	Hand optimised and Numba	Gajit
37.41 μs	7.66 μs	4.51 μs	3.31 μs

2.2 Representation of Multivectors in Clifford

Multivectors in the clifford library are stored a dense array of coefficients. While this storage is known to be computationally sub-optimal it is incredibly simple and easy to interface with external packages. Unfortunately in the case of calculating products there is very little that we can do to improve the speed of the operations as we store no sparsity information.

3 GAALOP

GAALOP [2] is an application written in the Java programming language that provides symbolic optimisation and code generation for Geometric Algebra algorithms. It has both a graphical and a command line interface, has a range of languages and frameworks as compilation targets and uses GAALOPScript as a source language.

The potential run time improvements achievable with symbolic optimisation are large as it fully exploits the sparsity of the multivector inputs. The inverse kinematics algorithm of [10,11] in 2006 which utilised this technology was to the authors knowledge the first Geometric Algebra application that was faster than the standard implementation. In this application more than 99% of computing time can be shifted to the precompiler symbolic optimisation step and less than 1% of the computational overhead is handled at runtime. In this computer animation application, the Geometric Algebra implementation based on symbolic simplification was three times faster than the conventional solution. In 2009 the optimised C-code generation capacity of GAALOP was used to significantly boost runtime performance for robot grasping [12], with a speedup of 14 times compared to the conventional implementation.

In the meantime, GAALOP has been extended to support many programming languages. It can be used as a stand-alone GA compiler or as a precompiler for languages such as C/C++, C++ AMP, OpenCL and CUDA [13,14].

3.1   Illustrative Ray Tracer Example

The paper [14] presents a ray tracing application based on GAALOP. One part of the corresponding algorithm is the computation of whether a ray intersects a (bounding) sphere or not. This can be expressed by the following GAALOP-Script.[1]

```
S = VecN3(Cx, Cy, Cz) - 0.5*r*r*einf;
O = VecN3(Ox, Oy, Oz);
L = VecN3(Lx, Ly, Lz);
R = *(O ^ L ^ einf);
PP = R ^ S;
?hasIntersection = PP.PP;
```

This example computes the sphere S and the ray R through the points O and L (VecN3 computes a conformal point based on its 3D coordinates). The intersection of the sphere S and the ray R can easily be expressed with the help of the outer product of these two geometric entities (Fig. 1). The result is the point pair PP. In the script we call its norm $hasIntersection$, since its sign indicates whether the ray and the sphere are really intersecting each other or not.

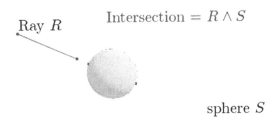

Intersection $= R \wedge S$

Ray R

sphere S

Fig. 1. Spheres and lines are basic entities of Geometric Algebra that one can compute with. Intersection of these objects are easily expressed with the help of their outer product.

A question mark at the beginning of a line indicates a multivector variable that has to be explicitly computed by GAALOP. This means that GAALOP is able to optimize not only single statements, but a number of Geometric Algebra statements. In the above script, the expressions for S, R, O, L and PP are used only by GAALOP, in order to compute an optimized result for the intersection indicator (see the question mark in the last line of the script).

---

[1] Here, all geometric objects are described in the IPNS representation according to Table 1.

4   The Numba Just In Time (JIT) Compiler

The trade off of readability for performance is typical in software engineering and has lead to the panoply of programming languages in use today. Popular modern programming languages can be broadly separated into two categories: dynamically typed, interpreted languages and statically typed, compiled languages. This is of course a gross simplification, for the sake of simplicity we are purposefully ignoring a host of other technologies that populate the middle ground including semi-compiled bytecodes and type inferring compilers [15].

Typically statically typed compiled languages require the user to specify information about the various variables and operations that are in use in the code and can pass this information to compilers allowing significant optimisations to be carried out before the code is run. These optimisations include loop unrolling, automatic SIMD vectorisation and a variety of other tricks [16]. Dynamically typed interpreted languages on the other hand rely on type checking at run time and very little optimisation can be done before the code is executed.

As a result of this problem many interpreted dynamically typed programming languages have Just In Time (JIT) compilation projects associated with them that attempt to bring some of the benefits of compilation to interpreted languages. For the python programming language PyPy [17] and Numba [3] are two such JIT compilation projects. PyPy is a implementation of the python language specification that brings with it a powerful JIT compiler. While the PyPy project is fantastic for accelerating pure Python code it has limited support for many of the numerical libaries such as numpy [18] and scipy [19] that have become hugely popular in the scientific community over the last few years.

Numba takes a different approach, it is a module for the cPython interpreter (the most commonly used language implementation) that processes the python abstract syntax tree (AST) and from it generates LLVM IR bytecode [20] allowing compilation to native machine code with modern highly optimising compilers. Numba has support for a very wide selection of numpy and scipy algorithms and has a very simple interface. This essentially allows a programmer to write a program once using normal tools, test that it works, profile it for bottlenecks and then JIT compile the bottlenecks directly. *Without modifying their source code.*

The clifford geometric algebra library relies on the Numba JIT compiler to speed up the basic array operations that underlie the library as well as to expose to users an easy way to improve the performance of their own code. Returning to our hand optimised GA algorithm from the previous section we can add a fair amount of speed by simply adding a decorator to our code:

```
from clifford.g3c import *
import numba

gp = layout.gmt_func
op = layout.omt_func
ip = layout.imt_func
rev = layout.adjoint_func

e12_value = e12.value
e12345_value = e12345.value

@numba.njit
def example_one_faster_jit(X, R):
    Y = gp(gp(R, X), rev(R))
    Y[0] += 1
    Ystar = gp(Y, e12345_value)
    F = ip(Ystar, e12_value)
    return F
```

In this case Table 2 shows that we have decreased our functions run time from $7.66\,\mu s$ for the hand optimised code to $4.51\,\mu s$ for the hand optimised *and* JITed code, not bad for a single line of code. This Numba acceleration technique is effective for operating on code that contains only simple language features and numpy operations. Ideally we would like to be able to combine the simple clean syntax of Python with the GA specific symbolic manipulation power of GAALOP and the advanced LLVM optimisation of Numba. We would like to write some nice looking maths and "just make it run fast".

5   Geometric Algebra JIT Compilation

5.1   Overview

Gajit, the Geometric Algebra JIT compiler is our solution to the problem of making simple GA code run fast. The interface for gajit is very simple we can take normal python code, add a decorator and perform symbolic and numeric optimisation:

```
from clifford.g3c import *
from gajit import *

@gajit(mask_list=[layout.grade_mask(1), layout.rotor_mask])
def example_one_gajit(X, R):
    Y = 1 + R*X*~R
    Ystar = Y*(e1^e2^e3^einf^e0)
    F = Ystar|(e1^e2)
    return F
```

Here two grade masks are passed to the function decorator corresponding to the two function inputs, this allows the user to specify the grade of the objects in the input and limits the number of symbols that need to be defined in GAALOP leading to faster, more concise code and lower compilation times. Table 2 demonstrates the speedup given by our simple decorator, we are now at $3.31\,\mu s$ which is 11.3x faster than the $37.41\,\mu s$ of the unoptimised function and beats the $4.51\,\mu s$ of our hand optimised and JITed function. To perform this speedup a fair amount of magic happens behind the scenes. In the rest of this section we will explain how gajit works and what this means in terms of runtime performance.

Python to GAALOPScript Translation. The first step of gajit is a direct source code translation from python to GAALOPScript, the subset of CLUSCRIPT [21] supported by GAALOP. At the same time as translation, the source of the python is analysed and the inputs, outputs and intermediate variables are extracted. The Python function is assumed to be a pure function, ie. to have no side effects, and is currently is restricted to a highly limited subset of Python due to the restrictions of support in GAALOPScript and the time requirements of designing robust source code translation systems.

GAALOP Symbolic Optimisation. Once we have a valid GAALOPScript program it is time to run the GAALOP symbolic optimisation. To run the GAALOP optimiser on our script we require GAALOP to be compiled in command line interface (CLI) mode and called such that it operates on a file CLUSCRIPT file and generates a C code file. Gajit sends the GAALOPScript to the CLI and instructs it to perform symbolic optimisation.

C to Python Translation. With our GAALOPScript successfully converted to C we now need a way to get that C code back into a form callable by Python. There are many ways to interface C code with Python, typically via wrappers or other direct means, in our case however we can exploit the simplicity of the functions generated to do a direct C to Python + Numpy translation.

Blade Order Remapping. Depending on the definition of the algebras in GAALOP the canonical blades may be ordered differently to the python implementation, to counteract this a blade remapping matrix can be applied in python to the results of the translated function.

Numba JIT Compilation. With a valid pure Python and Numpy function we can add an extra level of optimisation by wrapping the function in the Numba JIT compiler. This will allow it to be compiled down to LLVM-IR and from there to efficient native machine code at the function run time leading to very fast code.

5.2   Embedding GAALOPScript Directly in Python Programs

One of the downsides of the first step in our process, the current translation of Python to GAALOPScript is that it does not yet support all of the syntactic features of GAALOPScript and supports a very limited subset of Python. While the remaining functionality is implemented it may be worthwhile for users to be able to write functions directly in GAALOPScript and have them compiled to fast Python functions. As a byproduct of the way in which gajit operates we have already built in this functionality. Consider the raytracer example given in Sect. 3, we can directly embed some of the GAALOPScript from that example in our python code and can specify it in terms of multivector inputs rather than scalar inputs:

```python
from gajit import *
from clifford.tools.g3c import random_conformal_point, random_sphere

# The GAALOPScript function goes here
body = """
R = *(A ^ C ^ einf);
PP = R ^ (*S);
hasIntersection = PP.PP;
"""

# Create a python function from that GAALOPScript function
raytrace = Algorithm(
    inputs = ['S', 'A', 'C'],
    outputs = ['hasIntersection'],
    intermediates = ['R','PP'],
    body=body,
    function_name="raytracer",
    blade_mask_list = [layout.grade_mask(4),
                layout.grade_mask(1),
                layout.grade_mask(1)]
)

# We can now call the algorithm from python, passing in
# python multivectors and getting a python multivector back
S = random_sphere()
A = random_conformal_point()
C = random_conformal_point()
result = raytrace(S,A,C)
```

A pure python/clifford alternative could be written:

```python
def clifford_raytrace(S,A,C):
    PP = ((e12345 * (A ^ C ^ einf)) ^ (e12345 * S))
    hasIntersection = (PP | PP)
    return hasIntersection
```

The gajit compiled GAALOPScript takes $3.40\,\mu s$ while the pure clifford solution takes $30.97\,\mu s$. Of course for this simple example we could also simply wrap the python function in the gajit decorator:

```
@gajit([layout.grade_mask(4),layout.grade_mask(1),layout.grade_mask(1)])
def clifford_raytrace_gajit(S,A,C):
    PP = ((e12345 * (A ^ C ^ einf)) ^ (e12345 * S))
    hasIntersection = (PP | PP)
    return hasIntersection
```

the decorator results in the exact same function run time as GAALOPScript compilation.

6 Future Work

The most immediate work to do on gajit is to expand the support for GAALOP-Script language features in the Python translation code, improving this will allow much richer algorithms to be accelerated with very little effort as well as providing an additional front end for GAALOP. While this is a very specific instance of dual symbolic and traditional JITing, many modern high level programming languages have libraries for JIT compilation and symbolic manipulation, and as such it is easy to see how the concept may extend to other computing environments and languages. In the longer term we hope that further integration between the various GA software implementations can be achieved and the community can consolidate around a set of standard tools with mature codebases that are actively maintained and improved, while we don't claim that this is work is a panacea to the problems of everyone reinventing the wheel, we hope it is at least a promising step in the direction of interoperability in the community.

7 Conclusion

Python is a powerful tool for prototyping algorithms and implementing scientific papers. By combining it with symbolic and numeric optimisation in the form of GAALOP and Numba we can achieve high performance algorithms that are easy to read and write and syntactically close to the mathematics. For algorithms in CGA, gajit demonstrates order of magnitude speedups over unoptimised code and gajit even outperforms hand optimised, conventionally JITed, code in many cases.

References

1. Arsenovic, A., Hadfield, H., Kern, R.: The Pygae Team. pygae/clifford: v1.0.1, October 2018
2. Schwinn, C.: Gaalop 2.0 - a geometric algebra algorithm compiler (2010)

3. Lam, S.K., Pitrou, A., Seibert, S.: Numba: a LLVM-based python JIT compiler. In: Proceedings of the Second Workshop on the LLVM Compiler Infrastructure in HPC - LLVM 15, pp. 1–6. ACM Press (2015)
4. De Keninck, S.: ganja.js (2017)
5. Perwass, C.: Geometric Algebra with Applications in Engineering. Springer, Heidelberg (2009). https://doi.org/10.1007/978-3-540-89068-3
6. Colapinto, P.: VERSOR: spatial computing with conformal geometric algebra. Master's thesis, University of California at Santa Barbara (2011). http://versor.mat.ucsb.edu
7. Leopardi, P.C.: GluCat home page (2001). http://glucat.sourceforge.net/
8. Breuils, S., Nozick, V., Fuchs, L.: Garamon: Geometric algebra library generator. In: AGACSE 2018 (2018)
9. Fontijne, D.: Gaigen 2: a geometric algebra implementation generator. In: Proceedings of the 5th International Conference on Generative Programming and Component Engineering - GPCE06, p. 141. ACM Press (2006)
10. Hildenbrand, D., Fontijne, D., Wang, Y., Alexa, M., Dorst, L.: Competitive runtime performance for inverse kinematics algorithms using conformal geometric algebra. In: Eurographics Conference Vienna (2006)
11. Hildenbrand, D.: Geometric computing in computer graphics and robotics using conformal geometric algebra. Ph.D. thesis, TU Darmstadt, Darmstadt University of Technology (2006)
12. Woersdoerfer, F., Stock, F., Bayro-Corrochano, E., Hildenbrand, D.: Optimization and performance of a robotics grasping algorithm described in geometric algebra. In: Iberoamerican Congress on Pattern Recognition 2009, Guadalajara, Mexico (2009)
13. Hildenbrand, D.: Foundations of Geometric Algebra Computing. Springer, Heidelberg (2013). https://doi.org/10.1007/978-3-642-31794-1
14. Hildenbrand, D., Albert, J., Charrier, P., Steinmetz, C.: Geometric algebra computing for heterogeneous systems. Adv. Appl. Clifford Algebras J. (2016)
15. Aho, A.V., Lam, M.S., Sethi, R., Ullman, J.D.: Compilers: Principles, Techniques, and Tools, 2nd edn. Addison-Wesley Longman Publishing Co., Inc., Boston (2006)
16. Kennedy, K., Allen, J.R.: Optimizing Compilers for Modern Architectures: A Dependence-Based Approach. Morgan Kaufmann Publishers Inc., San Francisco (2002)
17. Bolz, C.F., Rigo, A.: How to not write virtual machines for dynamic languages. In: ESUG 2007 (2007)
18. Oliphant, T.E.: Guide to NumPy, 2nd edn. CreateSpace Independent Publishing Platform, Scotts Valley (2015)
19. Jones, E., Oliphant, T., Peterson, P., et al.: SciPy: open source scientific tools for Python (2001)
20. Lattner, C., Adve, V.: LLVM: a compilation framework for lifelong program analysis & transformation. In: International Symposium on Code Generation and Optimization, CGO 2004, pp. 75–86. IEEE (2004)
21. Perwass, C.: The CLU home page (2010). http://www.clucalc.info

Geometric Algebra Levenberg-Marquardt

Steven De Keninck[1(✉)] and Leo Dorst[2]

[1] Matrix Factory, Hingene, Belgium
steven@enki.ws,enkimute@gmail.com
[2] University of Amsterdam, Amsterdam, The Netherlands
L.Dorst@uva.nl

Abstract. This paper introduces a novel and matrix-free implementation of the widely used Levenberg-Marquardt algorithm, in the language of Geometric Algebra. The resulting algorithm is shown to be compact, geometrically intuitive, numerically stable and well suited for efficient GPU implementation. An implementation of the algorithm and the examples in this paper are publicly available.

Keywords: Geometric Algebra · Levenberg-Marquardt ·
Automatic differentiation · Non-linear estimation

1 Introduction

1.1 Motivation

Since its inception, the Levenberg-Marquardt algorithm (LMA) has become the go-to solution for a wide range of non-linear estimation problems. It is the default choice in a range of software applications and libraries, and as a result many variations and implementations exist (e.g. Eigen [3], MINPACK [4], Numerical Recipes [5]).

Without exception, these implementations depend heavily on methods and techniques from linear algebra, and using Levenberg-Marquardt in a different context will often require converting to and from matrix representations (see e.g. Tingelstad [1,6] and Lasenby [2]).

In this article we present a novel implementation of the LMA, using a Projective Geometric Algebra (PGA, see Gunn [8–10]) over the parameter space of a non-linear model function. We show how PGA offers an intuitive framework for the LMA, with a clear geometric interpretation and good numerical stability. While our algorithm works with all metrics, we additionally demonstrate the benefits of the degenerate metric of Euclidean PGA $R^*_{n,0,1}$, using its null vectors for the automatic differentiation of scalar valued functions, and its dual number extension $\mathbb{D}^{3*}_{3,0,1}$ for motor estimation.

© Springer Nature Switzerland AG 2019
M. Gavrilova et al. (Eds.): CGI 2019, LNCS 11542, pp. 511–522, 2019.
https://doi.org/10.1007/978-3-030-22514-8_51

1.2   The Linear Algebra Formulation

There is an abundance of detailed descriptions of the LMA available, so we limit ourselves to a quick overview, introducing the notation used throughout this paper. The LMA is an iterative procedure that aims to improve the parameter vector $\mathbf{p}$ of a non-linear function f of arguments x_i that minimizes (half of) the square of the residuals with the data samples y_i. It changes $\mathbf{p}$ to the value $\mathbf{p}+\mathbf{d}_*$ with optimal $\mathbf{d}_*$ given by:

$$\mathbf{d}_* = \underset{d}{\mathrm{argmin}} \sum_{i=1}^{N} \frac{1}{2}(y_i - f(\mathbf{p}+\mathbf{d}, x_i))^2,$$

where y_i is the i-th (of N) samples belonging to the argument x_i. The LMA starts with the assumption that the non-linear function f at a new estimate $\mathbf{p}+\mathbf{d}$ can reasonably be approximated by its first order Taylor expansion

$$f(\mathbf{p}+\mathbf{d}, x_i) \approx f(\mathbf{p}, x_i) + f'(\mathbf{p}, x_i) \cdot \mathbf{d}.$$

We switch to vector notation, where $\mathbf{y}$ is the vector of samples y_i, $\mathbf{x}$ is the vector of arguments x_i and J is the Jacobian of all gradients; the i-th row, for data item i, is $[J]_i = (\nabla f(\mathbf{p}, x_i))^\top$. Using this notation, we now solve the approximated minimization problem:

$$\begin{aligned}
\mathbf{d}_* &= \underset{d}{\mathrm{argmin}} \frac{1}{2}(\mathbf{y} - (f(\mathbf{p}, \mathbf{x}) + J\mathbf{d}))^2 \\
&= \underset{d}{\mathrm{argmin}} \frac{1}{2}(\mathbf{y} - f(\mathbf{p}, \mathbf{x}))^2 + (J\mathbf{d})^\top(\mathbf{y} - f(\mathbf{p}, \mathbf{x})) + \frac{1}{2}(J\mathbf{d})^\top J\mathbf{d}.
\end{aligned}$$

Therefore the optimal update step $\mathbf{d}_*$ is found by setting the derivative w.r.t $\mathbf{d}$ to zero, giving:

$$(J^\top J)\mathbf{d}_* = J^\top(\mathbf{y} - f(\mathbf{p}, \mathbf{x})).$$

The LMA avoids issues with ill-posed problems by applying a regularization factor. In the original formulation this is written:

$$(J^\top J + \lambda I)\mathbf{d}_* = J^\top(\mathbf{y} - f(\mathbf{p}, \mathbf{x})). \tag{1}$$

A popular improvement by Fletcher [7] replaces the identity matrix in the above formulation by the diagonal of $J^\top J$, improving convergence in directions of small gradient:

$$(J^\top J + \lambda \, \mathrm{diag}(J^\top J))\mathbf{d}_* = J^\top(\mathbf{y} - f(\mathbf{p}, \mathbf{x})). \tag{2}$$

Various strategies exist to update the λ factor at each step of the optimization. Our reformulation is compatible with all these strategies. Equation (2) is the one under consideration in this article. Therefore, the computational tasks to be performed at each iteration include:

- evaluating the partial derivatives on the model function, contained in J.
- calculating the modified Hessian $[J^\top J + \lambda \operatorname{diag}(J^\top J)]$ and residual vector $\mathbf{y} - f(\mathbf{p}, \mathbf{x})$.
- solving the system of n linear equations in the n variables $\mathbf{d}_*$.

We will handle these tasks in order, starting with two approaches to integrate automatic differentiation for the calculation of the derivatives that drive the optimization. In Sect. 3 we explore the geometry of the GA form of both the Jacobian and approximated Hessian. In the 4th Section we use this geometric form and present an outer product based alternative to the Cholesky, QR or Gaussian methods that are classically used to solve the system of equations at each step of the iteration. We present the implementation, examples and conclusion in Sects. 5 and 6.

2   Automatic Differentiation

2.1   Dual Numbers

Automatic differentiation based on Dual Numbers ($\mathbb{D}$) is a well-known technique (see e.g. [11]) that has recently gained popularity (e.g. back propagation in neural networks). Following Taylor's theorem we know that given the value of any (smooth) scalar function $f : \mathbb{R} \to \mathbb{R}$ at any point x, and its derivatives, we can calculate the value at a new point $x + e$ using:

$$f(x + e) = f(x) + \frac{f'(x)}{1!}e + \frac{f''(x)}{2!}e^2 + \frac{f'''(x)}{3!}e^3 + \ldots$$

If in the above, e is substituted by the dual unit ϵ (where $\epsilon^2 = 0$), all terms after the second will vanish, and we are left with the following equality:

$$f(x + \epsilon) = f(x) + f'(x)\epsilon. \tag{3}$$

We conclude that extending f to $f : \mathbb{D} \to \mathbb{D}$, extends its result to a dual number that has the function value as its real part, and the value of the function's derivative as its dual part.

2.2 $\mathbb{D}^n$: Multivariate Dual Numbers

To evaluate partial derivatives of a multivariate function $f : \mathbb{R}^n \to \mathbb{R}$, the dual numbers $(x + y\epsilon)$ are extended to the form $(x + y\epsilon_1 + z\epsilon_2 + \ldots)$, called multivariate dual numbers $\mathbb{D}^n$, where $\epsilon_i * \epsilon_j = 0$, for all i, j. The equation in (3) then generalizes to a function $f : \mathbb{D}^n \to \mathbb{D}^n$ of $a_1, \ldots, a_n$:

$$f(a_1 + \epsilon_1, \ldots, a_n + \epsilon_n) = f(a_1, \ldots, a_n) + \frac{\partial f(a_1, \ldots, a_n)}{\partial a_1}\epsilon_1 + \ldots + \frac{\partial f(a_1, \ldots, a_n)}{\partial a_n}\epsilon_n$$

Table 1 displays the Cayley table of the multivariate dual numbers with three dual components. In our motor estimation example we create a PGA over these multivariate dual numbers $\mathbb{D}^3$ to evaluate motor derivatives.

Table 1. Cayley table for multivariate dual numbers with three dual components (with PGA names between brackets).

$a*b$	1	$\epsilon_1(\mathbf{e}_{01})$	$\epsilon_2(\mathbf{e}_{02})$	$\epsilon_3(\mathbf{e}_{03})$
1	1	$\epsilon_1(\mathbf{e}_{01})$	$\epsilon_2(\mathbf{e}_{02})$	$\epsilon_3(\mathbf{e}_{03})$
$\epsilon_1(\mathbf{e}_{01})$	$\epsilon_1(\mathbf{e}_{01})$	0	0	0
$\epsilon_2(\mathbf{e}_{02})$	$\epsilon_2(\mathbf{e}_{02})$	0	0	0
$\epsilon_3(\mathbf{e}_{03})$	$\epsilon_3(\mathbf{e}_{03})$	0	0	0

2.3   Degenerate Metric of $\mathbb{R}^*_{n,0,1}$

With n parameters to determine in our function f, the parameter vector $\mathbf{p}$ is n-dimensional. We will soon introduce a projective, $(n+1)$-D (PGA) model where the residual and gradient combine into a residual plane. If, in that model, the degenerate metric is chosen for the extra homogeneous dimension $\mathbf{e}_0$, producing the algebra $\mathbb{R}^*_{n,0,1}$ (Gunn [8]), then the sub algebra formed by the scalars and null bivectors (i.e. bivectors of the form $\mathbf{e}_0 \wedge \mathbf{e}_i, i = 1,..,n$) is trivially isomorphic to the multivariate dual numbers $\mathbb{D}^n$ with n dual components. When optimizing a function of n scalar variables, the same algebra used to encode the residual planes can therefore be used for automatic differentiation (using these null bivectors as dual components). In this setup, both the residual value and the gradient are calculated by upgrading our function to $f : \mathbb{R}^*_{n,0,1} \rightarrow \mathbb{R}^*_{n,0,1}$. This will allow us to combine them into a single "residual hyperplane" (see Sect. 3.1). Our first example in Sect. 5.2 demonstrates this technique.

   This works well for a function with *scalar* parameters, since the null bivectors commute with those. When however optimizing a function of *multivectors* $f : \wedge \mathbb{R}^n \rightarrow \wedge \mathbb{R}$, none of multivector components, aside from the scalar, can be paired up with a null blade to produce a closed sub-algebra isomorphic to the dual numbers. To automatically calculate the derivative of each of the $\mathbf{e}_i$ basis blades, each blade needs a dual component with which it (and only it) commutes. We can accomplish this by creating our PGA not over $\mathbb{R}$, but over $\mathbb{D}^n$, as will be demonstrated in our motor estimation example in Sect. 5.3.

3   The Residual, Hessian and Jacobian Planes

3.1   The Residual Plane r_i

In the linear algebra formulation of Sect. 1.2, the residual value and the gradient of the cost function are two separate entities. We would like instead to suggest a unified, geometric view, using the Projective Geometric Algebra described above. In this algebra, we unify the gradient and residual into a residual plane, and represent it using a PGA 1-vector (for a detailed treatment of PGA, consult Gunn [8–10]). Denoting the basis vector in the extra dimension by $\mathbf{e}_0$, and the Euclidean dimensions by $\mathbf{e}_i$, the vector

$$a_1\,\mathbf{e}_1 + a_2\,\mathbf{e}_2 + ... + a_n\,\mathbf{e}_n + a_0\,\mathbf{e}_0$$

represents the hyperplane with equation $a_1x_1 + a_2x_2 + \ldots + a_nx_n = -a_0$. Clearly, this way of employing a PGA vector to denote a plane is akin to the usual homogeneous coordinates.

In this setup, using the gradient as the Euclidean coefficients and the (negative of) the residual value as the coefficient of $\mathbf{e}_0$, we form our *residual hyperplane* r_i for each sample i:

$$r_i = \frac{\partial f(\mathbf{p}, \mathbf{x}_i)}{\partial p_1} \mathbf{e}_1 + \frac{\partial f(\mathbf{p}, \mathbf{x}_i)}{\partial p_2} \mathbf{e}_2 + \ldots + \frac{\partial f(\mathbf{p}, \mathbf{x}_i)}{\partial p_n} \mathbf{e}_n + (y_i - f(\mathbf{p}, \mathbf{x}_i)) \mathbf{e}_0. \quad (4)$$

When the model function is a scalar function $f : \mathbb{R}^n \rightarrow \mathbb{R}$, and the degenerate metric is used for automatic differentiation, the following method calculates the partial derivatives and residual value to produce the residual plane vector:

$$r_i = \mathbf{e}_0{}^* (y_i - f(\mathbf{p} + \boldsymbol{\epsilon}, x_i))^*, \quad (5)$$

where star denotes the duality operator from PGA and $\mathbf{p}$ and $\boldsymbol{\epsilon}$ are the *scalar parameter vector* and the vector of dual elements $[\mathbf{e}_{01}, \mathbf{e}_{02}, \ldots, \mathbf{e}_{0n}]^\top$ respectively. This technique will be demonstrated in example Sect. 5.2.

3.2   The Hessian Planes H_j

For a single sample (or for a linear model function), it is clear that $J^\top J$ is rank one. The LMA avoids problems with rank deficiency by adding in a multiple of the identity matrix (similar to L2-regularization). It is customary to calculate both $J^\top (\mathbf{y} - f(\mathbf{p}, \mathbf{x}))$ and $J^\top J$ in one iteration over the samples. We employ the same strategy, and after calculating the residual hyperplane for each sample, we accumulate the *Hessian hyperplanes* H_j where $j = 1, 2, \ldots, n$ using:

$$H_j = \sum_{i=1}^{N} r_i^{\mathbf{e}_j} r_i, \quad (6)$$

where the superscript notation replaces the customary dot product to denote extraction of the indicated coefficient, independent of the metric. The resulting n hyperplanes are then regularized by adding in multiples of $\mathbf{e}_j$ to the j-th hyper plane (Marquardt):

$$H_j^{\text{Marquardt}} = \sum_{i=1}^{N} r_i^{\mathbf{e}_j} r_i + \lambda \mathbf{e}_j, \quad (7)$$

or by multiplying the coefficient of $\mathbf{e}_j$ of the j-th Hessian plane H_j by $(1 + \lambda)$ (Fletcher):

$$H_j^{\text{Fletcher}} = \sum_{i=1}^{N} r_i^{\mathbf{e}_j} r_i + \lambda (r_i^{\mathbf{e}_j})^2 \mathbf{e}_j.$$

Note that (7) combines the LHS and RHS of each row of Eq. (1). We have reasons not to combine these rows into a single entity, as we will explain in Sect. 4. The orange and red lines in the 2D example of Fig. 1 (with $\lambda = 0.2$) are the Hessian planes H_1 and H_2, in the Marquardt and Fletcher versions respectively, their intersection represents the update steps. In this formulation, our task of solving a system of equations reduces to an expression involving these H_j, to which we turn our attention in Sect. 4.

3.3 The Jacobian Plane J

It is also possible to construct a Jacobian plane, the projection onto which represents the update by gradient descent. In linear algebra notation, this plane can be characterized by:

$$J^\top (\mathbf{y} - f(\mathbf{p}, \mathbf{x})).$$

In PGA, the Jacobian plane can be extracted from the Hessian planes, or constructed from the residual planes:

$$J_{\text{plane}} = e_0 + \sum_{j=1}^{n} H_j^{\mathbf{e}_0} e_j = e_0 + \sum_{i}^{N} \sum_{j=1}^{n} r_i^{\mathbf{e}_j} r_i^{\mathbf{e}_0} e_j.$$

The method of Gradient Descent can now be seen as an orthogonal projection onto this hyperplane. This is illustrated in blue in Fig. 1.

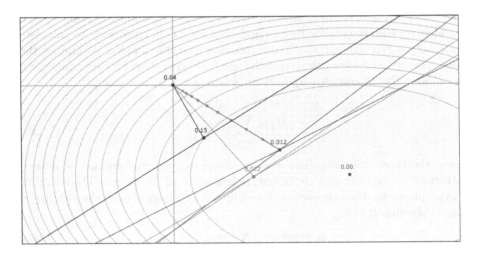

Fig. 1. Black - the current guess. Blue - the Jacobian plane, and the update with gradient descent. Orange - the Marquardt residual planes. Red - the Fletcher modified planes. Green - the true minimum. Light Red - solutions for increasing λ. (Color figure online)

4   Solving $A\mathbf{x} = \mathbf{y}$ by Outer Products

Having computed all ingredients of the system of n equations in (2), we need to solve them. Classically, implementations of the LMA use Gaussian Elimination, QR, or the faster Cholesky decomposition for this task. GA offers an alternative.

4.1   Casting into the Algebra of Planes

Our alternative is once again geometric and uses the same $(n + 1)$-dimensional PGA introduced in Sect. 3.1. Each row of the matrix equation $A\mathbf{x} = \mathbf{y}$ in n-D gives an equation of the form $A_j^\top \mathbf{x} = \mathbf{y}_j$ (where A_j is the j-th column of $A^\top$). As in Sect. 3.1, each of these equations corresponds in PGA to a 1-vector

$$a_j \equiv A_j - y_j\, e_0,$$

representing the j-th plane the solution $\mathbf{x}$ is required to lie on.

If the set of n equations in n variables has a unique solution, that solution corresponds to the intersection of the n planes specified by the n equations (since the point $\mathbf{x}$ should lie in each of them). In PGA, the linear subspace representing the intersection of n hyperplanes denoted by the 1-vectors a_j is their *outer product* $a_1 \wedge a_2 \wedge \cdots \wedge a_n$ (see e.g. [8]). For our n equations in the $(n + 1)$-dimensional representational space, this produces

$$\alpha\,(\mathbf{x} + e_0)^* = a_1 \wedge a_2 \wedge \cdots \wedge a_n. \tag{8}$$

The right-hand side is an n-vector, which is proportional by some factor α to the dual representation of a vector $\mathbf{x}$ in the $(n + 1)$-dimensional space. In practice, this means that we compute the outer product, and then read off the coefficients of the 1-vector $\mathbf{x}$ from those of the n-vector, after division by the coefficient of e_0^* (which is α). Note that for matrix equations with integer coefficients ($\in \mathbb{Z}$), the right-hand side is an integer computation, so that α is integer, and a rational $\mathbf{x}$ results, enabling an error-free approach.

We claim that this deceivingly straightforward formulation in (8) is a robust and intuitive alternative to the Cholesky decomposition.

4.2   Numerical Precision

To examine the numerical properties of this approach, we generate random matrices A, and random vectors $\mathbf{y}$, and solve $A\mathbf{x} = \mathbf{y}$ for $\mathbf{x}$. We use the Cholesky and outer product solver respectively and accumulate the error over M trials:

$$\sum_{i=1}^{M} \|A_i\mathbf{x}_i - \mathbf{y}_i\|.$$

In Table 2 we compare the average error of using Cholesky decomposition to that of our outer-product version. The Cholesky decomposition approach is known for its efficiency and uses substantially fewer elementary operations. As a result, the error for random A and $\mathbf{y}$ is, while in the same order of magnitude, approximately doubled in our outer product version (also included is the test of the above mentioned integer approach where our method is error-free).

Table 2. Average error on 100 million runs for 3×3 matrix A

Algorithm	$A_i, \mathbf{y} \in \mathbb{R}^n$	$A_i, \mathbf{y} \in \mathbb{Z}^n$
Cholesky	$1.5732 * 10^{-10}$	$1.6077 * 10^{-12}$
Outer Product	$3.0191 * 10^{-10}$	0

4.3   Performance

In Table 3 we summarize the computational cost of our algorithm and compare it to the Cholesky decomposition and Gaussian elimination. For our 3×3 test, the outer product solve uses almost 60% more operations, explaining the precision difference on random elements above.

We note however that the outer product solver lends itself particularly well to a GPU implementation, where it can leverage the similarity with the cross product to produce a highly efficient implementation. This is illustrated for the 3×3 case in Listing 1. (The applicability of this technique for higher n remains to be developed in detail.)

Table 3. Computational cost of solving $A\mathbf{x} = \mathbf{y}$ for 3×3 matrix A

Algorithm	Add	Mul	Div	Sqrt	Dot	Cross	Total
Gaussian Elimination	11	14	3				28
Cholesky	10	10	3	3			26
Outer Product (CPU)	14	24	3				41
Outer Product (GPU)			1		4	4	9

```
// Calculate !(a^b^c) for three 1-vectors a,b,c
vec4 DualWedgeWedge(vec4 a, vec4 b, vec4 c) {
  vec4 abc;
  abc.x = -dot(a.yzw,cross(b.yzw,c.yzw));
  abc.y =  dot(a.xzw,cross(b.xzw,c.xzw));
  abc.z = -dot(a.xyw,cross(b.xyw,c.xyw));
  abc.w =  dot(a.xyz,cross(b.xyz,c.xyz));
  return abc;
}
```

Listing 1: A GLSL version of the dual of $a \wedge b \wedge c$

5 Implementation and Examples

5.1 Implementation

Using the techniques introduced above, the Levenberg Marquardt algorithm, including automatic differentiation can be compactly implemented. Listing 2 is a JavaScript implementation using ganja.js [12]. It is the algorithm as used in our first example, that includes using PGA for the Automatic Differentiation of scalar model functions.

```
function LMA(par, y, func, terr=1E-12, nit=5000, step=10){
    var lambda=1E-4, err=y.reduce((sum,x,i)=>sum+(x-func(par,i))**2,0);
    for (var it=0; it<nit; it++) {
    // Calculate the Hessian Planes
        for (var Ri, H=[0,0,0],x=0; x<y.length; x++) {
        Ri = !1e0*!(y[x]-func(par+[1e01,1e02,1e03],x));          // eqn (4)
        H  = H+[Ri.e1,Ri.e2,Ri.e3]*Ri;                           // eqn (5)
        }
    // Intersect the Hessian planes, update parameters, re-evaluate error.
        while (it<nit) {
            for (var i=0; i<3; i++) H[i][2+i]*=(1+lambda);        // Fletcher
            var delta = !(H[0]^H[1]^H[2]);                        // eqn (6)
            var newpar = par.map((x,i)=>x+delta[i+2]/-delta.e0);  // Homog. divide.
            var newerr = y.reduce((sum,x,i)=>sum+(x-func(newpar,i))**2,0);
            var derr = newerr-err;
            if (derr>0) { lambda *= step; it++; } else break;
        }
    // Accept current best, Revert lambda. stop if desired precision reached.
        par = newpar; err = newerr; lambda /= step;
        if (-derr<terr) break;
    }
    return par;
}
```

Listing 2: The GALM implementation used for the example in 5.2

5.2 Law of Cooling Using $\mathbb{R}^*_{3,0,1}$

We begin with a simple example from physics. A bowl of water is being heated. Given a series of temperature measurements y_t, estimate the temperature of the heater T_h, the starting temperature of the water T_0 and a coefficient r, proportional to the heat transfer coefficient. Our model function is Newton's Law of cooling, a function $T : \mathbb{R} \to \mathbb{R}$ of time t, and the three scalar parameters $[T_0, T_h, r]$:

$$T(T_h, T_0, r; t) = T_h + (T_0 - T_h)e^{-rt}.$$

To calculate the derivatives of this model function, we upgrade T to a function $\mathbb{R} \to \mathbb{R}^*_{3,0,1}$, where additionally the parameters are also in $\mathbb{R}^*_{3,0,1}$. The derivatives w.r.t. the parameters are now found by evaluating T with an augmented parameter vector (see Sect. 2.3). We proceed and calculate the residual planes using (5), and the Hessian planes using (6). After applying the Fletcher regularization, the optimal step d_* is then found using (8). Figure 2 illustrates the samples (with 5% Gaussian Noise), initial guess, ground truth and estimate found after 8 iterations. These results are identical to the LA reference implementation in our test. Figure 3 displays the error manifold, and the path to the minimum.

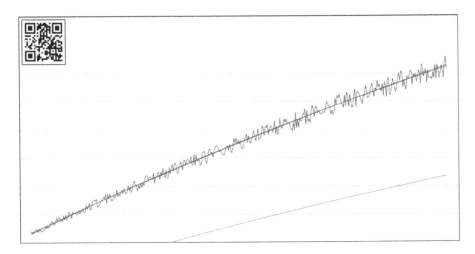

Fig. 2. Samples (black), Initial Guess (gray), GALM Estimate (red), ground truth (green) (Color figure online)

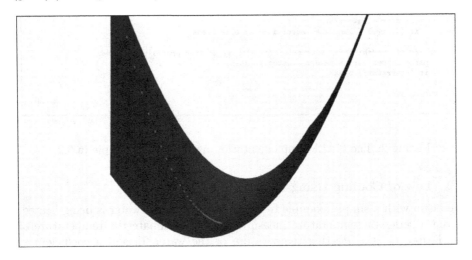

Fig. 3. The error manifold and the path to the minimum

5.3   Motor Estimation Using $\mathbb{D}_{3,0,1}^{3*}$

In our second example we estimate the translation and rotation between two point clouds x_i and y_i with given correspondence and 2% Gaussian noise. We choose 3D PGA for this problem as it offers a compact motion manifold, with an even sub-algebra isomorphic to the dual quaternions and a 6 component bivector B that compactly parametrizes the 3 rotational and 3 translational degrees of freedom. Our model function $f : \mathbb{R}_{3,0,1}^* \to \mathbb{R}_{3,0,1}^*$ is:

$$f(B, \mathbf{x}) = e^{-\frac{B}{2}} \, \mathbf{x} \, e^{\frac{B}{2}}.$$

We first upgrade f, this time to $\mathbb{D}_{3,0,1}^{3*}$, the 3D PGA over multivariate dual numbers with three dual coefficients. Note that we opt to estimate only three of the six parameters simultaneously, and instead alternate between translation and rotation at each iteration step of the LMA. For that reason, 3 dual numbers suffice at each step.

Using this algebra, we evaluate automatic derivatives, and proceed as before. Figure 4 illustrates the points and orbits of one such estimated motion. The algorithm performs both estimations in the examples in just a few iterations (an average of 4 steps for 30 points, zero initial guess and random bivector B). These results are the same as our linear algebra reference implementations, however without needing matrix conversions.

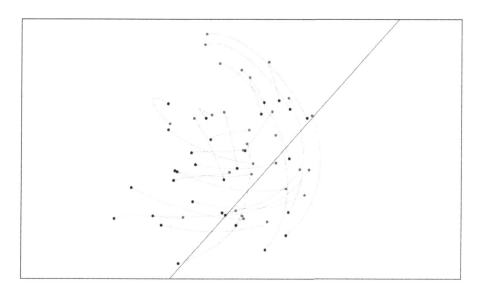

Fig. 4. Motor estimation between point clouds. Points x_i in frame A (black), y_i in frame B (red), and the helical orbit of the estimated motor between them (blue). (Color figure online)

6   Conclusion

This paper presented a matrix-free Geometric Algebra formulation of the Levenberg-Marquardt algorithm. As a part of this algorithm we have also explored a fresh view on solving a set of linear equations, and have explained the use of the degenerate metric for Automatic Differentiation. The presented algorithm was shown to be a numerically stable and viable alternative for existing implementations of the LMA in a wide range of situations. Additionally, when used to minimize multivector functions, our approach eliminates the need for otherwise inevitable conversions to and from matrix representations.

Acknowledgment. The authors would like to thank Charles Gunn for his valuable feedback on, and Hugo Hadfield and Vincent Nozick for their proofreading of an early version of this article.

References

1. Tingelstad, L., Egeland, O.: Motor parameterization. Adv. Appl. Clifford Algebras **28**, 34 (2018)
2. Lasenby, J., Fitzgerald, W.J., Lasenby, A.N., Doran, C.J.L.: New geometric methods for computer vision: an application to structure and motion estimation. Int. J. Comput. Vis. **26**(3), 191–213 (1998)
3. Guennebaud, G., Jacob, B. et al.: Eigen v3 (2010). http://eigen.tuxfamily.org
4. Moré, J.J., Sorensen, D.C., Hillstrom, K.E., Garbow, B.S.: The MINPACK project, in sources and development of mathematical software. In: Cowell, W.J. (ed.) pp. 88–111. Prentice-Hall (1984). http://www.netlib.org/minpack/
5. Press, W.H., Teukolsky, S.A., Vetterling, W.T., Flannery, B.P.: Numerical Recipes in C : The Art of Scientific Computing. Cambridge University Press, Cambridge (1992)
6. Tingelstad, L., Egeland, O.: Automatic multivector differentiation and optimization. Adv. Appl. Clifford Algebras **27**, 707 (2017). https://doi.org/10.1007/s00006-016-0722-6
7. Fletcher, R.: A modified marquardt subroutine for nonlinear least squares. Atomic Energy Research Establishment report R6799, Harwell, England (1971)
8. Gunn, C.: Geometry, Kinematics, and Rigid Body Mechanics in Cayley-Klein Geometries. Ph.D. thesis, Technical University, Berlin (2011). http://opus.kobv.de/tuberlin/volltexte/2011/3322
9. Gunn, C.: On the homogeneous model of Euclidean geometry. In: Dorst, L., Lasenby, J. (eds.) A Guide to Geometric Algebra in Practice, chapter 15, pp. 297–327. Springer, London (2011). https://doi.org/10.1007/978-0-85729-811-9_15, https://arxiv.org/abs/1101.4542
10. Gunn, C.: Geometric algebras for Euclidean geometry. Adv. Appl. Clifford Algebras **27**(1), 185–208 (2017). https://arxiv.org/abs/1411.650
11. Rall, L.B. (ed.): Automatic Differentiation: Techniques and Applications. LNCS, vol. 120. Springer, Heidelberg (1981). https://doi.org/10.1007/3-540-10861-0
12. De Keninck, S.: Ganja.js: Geometric Algebra - Not Just Algebra (2017). https://github.com/enkimute/ganja.js

Transverse Approach to Geometric Algebra Models for Manipulating Quadratic Surfaces

Stéphane Breuils[1]([✉]) [ID], Vincent Nozick[1] [ID], Laurent Fuchs[2] [ID],
and Akihiro Sugimoto[3] [ID]

[1] Laboratoire d'Informatique Gaspard-Monge, Equipe A3SI UMR 8049,
Université Paris-Est Marne-la-Vallée, Champs-sur-Marne, France
{stephane.breuils,vincent.nozick}@u-pem.fr
[2] XLIM-ASALI, UMR 7252, Université de Poitiers, Poitiers, France
Laurent.Fuchs@univ-poitiers.fr
[3] National Institute of Informatics, Tokyo 101-8430, Japan
sugimoto@nii.ac.jp

Abstract. Quadratic surfaces gain more and more attention in the geometric algebra community and some frameworks to represent, transform, and intersect these quadratic surfaces have been proposed. To the best of our knowledge, however, no framework has yet proposed that supports all the operations required to completely handle these surfaces. Some existing frameworks do not allow the construction of quadratic surfaces from control points while some do not allow to transform these quadratic surfaces. Although a framework does not exist that covers all the required operations, if we consider all already proposed frameworks together, then all the operations over quadratic surfaces are covered there. This paper presents an approach that transversely uses different frameworks for covering all the operations on quadratic surfaces. We employ a framework to represent any quadratic surfaces either using control points or the coefficients of its implicit form and then map the representation into another framework so that we can transform them and compute their intersection. Our approach also allows us to easily extract some geometric properties.

Keywords: Geometric algebra · Quadratic surfaces · Conformal geometric algebras

1 Introduction

Geometric algebra provides convenient and intuitive tools to represent, transform, and intersect geometric objects. Deeply explored by physicists, it has been used in quantum mechanics and electromagnetism [12] as well as in classical mechanics [13]. Geometric algebra has also found some interesting applications in geographic data manipulations [16,21]. Among them, geometric algebra is

© Springer Nature Switzerland AG 2019
M. Gavrilova et al. (Eds.): CGI 2019, LNCS 11542, pp. 523–534, 2019.
https://doi.org/10.1007/978-3-030-22514-8_52

used within the computer graphics community. More precisely, it is used not only in basis geometric primitive manipulations [20] but also in complex illumination processes as in [17] where spherical harmonics are substituted by geometric algebra entities. For image data analysis, on the other hand, we can find the usefulness of geometric algebra in mathematical morphology [6] and in neural networking [3,14]. In the geometric algebra community, quadratic surfaces gain more and more attention, and some frameworks to represent, transform, and intersect these quadratic surfaces have been proposed.

There exist three main approaches to deal with quadratic surfaces in geometric algebra. The first one, introduced in [9], is called double conformal geometric algebra (DCGA), $\mathbb{G}_{8,2}$. It is capable of representing quadratic surfaces from the coefficients of their implicit form. The second one is double projective geometric algebra (DPGA), $\mathbb{G}_{4,4}$, whose definition was firstly introduced in [11] and has been further developed in [8]. This approach is based on a duplication of $\mathbb{R}^4$ and it represents quadratic surfaces from the coefficients of their implicit form, as bivectors. However, it cannot construct quadratic surfaces from control points. The third one was introduced in [2] and is denoted as quadric conformal geometric algebra (QCGA), $\mathbb{G}_{9,6}$. QCGA allows to define any general quadratic surface from 9 control points, and to represent objects by only 1 or 2-vectors. QCGA is capable of constructing quadratic surfaces either using control points or implicit equations as 1-vector. QCGA also allows to efficiently intersect quadratic surfaces. However, it does not yet allow all geometric transformations over quadratic surfaces. In order to enhance the usefulness of geometric algebra for the geometry and the computer graphics communities, a new framework that allows to represent and manipulate quadratic surfaces has to be developed. It is the main purpose of this paper.

1.1 Contributions

We propose a new approach that transversely uses the three above mentioned geometric algebra models to compensate drawbacks of each model and show that it is possible to not only represent quadratic surfaces using either control points or implicit coefficients but also transform these quadratic surfaces using versors. More precisely, we employ a model that allows us to represent quadratic surfaces, and convert them into another model that allows us to transform them using versors, and then convert the result back into the original model. With our approach, the tangent planes to a quadratic surfaces and intersection of quadratic surfaces can be computed.

1.2 Notations

Following the state-of-the-art usage in [5] and [19], upper-case bold letters denote blades (blade **A**) whose grade is higher than 1. Multivectors and k-vectors are denoted with upper-case non-bold letters (multivector A). Lower-case bold letters refer to vectors and lower-case non-bold to multivector coordinates. The vector space dimension is denoted by 2^d, where d is the number of basis blades $\mathbf{e}_i$ of grade 1.

2   Geometric Algebra Models for Quadratic Surfaces

2.1   Measure for Evaluating Complexity of Models

This paper focuses on the most common operations on quadratic surfaces and their intersections, and aims at determining the most efficient geometric algebra model for each operation. These operations can be related to computer graphics or more general geometry and will mainly consist in:

- checking whether a point lies in a quadratic surface,
- intersecting quadratic surface and line,
- computing the normal vector (and the tangent plane) of a surface at a given point.

Indeed, these operations are precisely the minimal tools required to set up a ray-tracer [10]. According to these targeted operations, evaluating their complexity mostly consists in the estimation of the number of operations required for both the outer product of multivectors and the inner product between vectors and bivectors.

First, let us consider the outer product between two homogeneous multivectors whose numbers of components are u and v respectively, $u, v \in \mathbb{N}$. We then assume that an upper bound to the number of required products is at most uv products of scalars, as shown in the definition of the outer product [15].

Second, according to the target operations, we need to use the formula for inner products between 1-vector and 2-vector as well as the inner product between two 1-vectors. Considering that the first multivector has u non-zero components, and the second has v non-zero components, then the inner product between two 1-vectors will result in uv products. The inner product between 1-vectors and 2-vectors, on the other hand, requires two inner products for each pair of components of the two multivectors, that is to say $2uv$ products.

There exist three main geometric algebra frameworks to manipulate general quadratic surfaces: DCGA of $\mathbb{G}_{8,2}$ [9], DPGA of $\mathbb{G}_{4,4}$ [8,18], and QGCA of $\mathbb{G}_{9,6}$ [2]. The following sections present their specificities as well as their complexity for the targeted operations.

2.2   DCGA of $\mathbb{G}_{8,2}$

DCGA was presented by Hitzer and Easter [9] and aims at having entities representing both quartic surfaces and quadratic surfaces. In more details, DCGA of $\mathbb{G}_{8,2}$ is defined over a 10-dimensional vector space. The base vectors of the space are basically divided into two groups: $\{\mathbf{e}_{o1}, \mathbf{e}_1, \mathbf{e}_2, \mathbf{e}_3, \mathbf{e}_{\infty 1}\}$, corresponding to the CGA vectors, and a copy of this basis $\{\mathbf{e}_{o2}, \mathbf{e}_4, \mathbf{e}_5, \mathbf{e}_6, \mathbf{e}_{\infty 2}\}$. A point of DCGA whose Euclidean coordinates are (x, y, z) is defined as the outer product of two CGA points with coordinates (x, y, z).

Quadratic Surfaces: A general quadratic surface merely consists of defining some operators that extract the components of $\mathbf{x}$. A general quadratic surface is defined as:

$$ax^2 + by^2 + cz^2 + \mathrm{d}xy + eyz + fzx + gx + hy + iz + \mathrm{j} = 0. \tag{1}$$

In DCGA, 10 extraction operators $\{\mathbf{T}_{x^2}, \mathbf{T}_{y^2}, \mathbf{T}_{z^2}, \mathbf{T}_{xy}, \mathbf{T}_{xz}, \mathbf{T}_{yz}, \mathbf{T}_x, \mathbf{T}_y, \mathbf{T}_z, \mathbf{T}_1\}$ are defined (see [9]) such that the inner product of these operators and a point results in Eq. 1. DCGA not only supports the definition of general quadratic surfaces but also some quartic surfaces like Torus, cyclides (Dupin cyclides, etc.).

Complexity of Some Major Operations: Let us first evaluate the computational cost of checking whether a point is on a quadratic surface using the measure given in Sect. 2.1. $\mathbf{Q}_{\mathrm{DCGA}}$ has 10 basis bivector components in total. For each basis bivector, at most 3 inner products (bivector $\wedge$ bivector) are required. The number of point components is 25. Thus, the product $\mathbf{Q}_{\mathrm{DCGA}} \cdot \mathbf{X}$ requires $25 \times 3 \times 10 = 750$ products.

Now we detail the cost of the computation of the tangent plane to a quadratic surface, defined in [9] as:

$$\mathit{\Pi} = (\mathbf{n}_1 + \mathrm{de}_{\infty 1}) \wedge (\mathbf{n}_2 + \mathrm{de}_{\infty 2}). \tag{2}$$

The normal vector is defined as the commutator product of some differential operators and the quadratic surface resulting in a 7-component bivector. Each inner product with $\mathbf{X}$ then has the cost of $7 \times 25 = 175$ products. This latter computation is repeated for each axis; thus, this results in $175 \times 3 = 525$ products. The computation of the distance d, on the other hand, consists of merely 3 inner products. Both operands in this equation are 4-components 1-vector. Thus, the computational cost of the outer product is $4 \times 4 = 16$. Hence, the total cost of the computation of the tangent plane is $525 + 16 = 541$ products. The third operation is the intersection between a quadratic surface and a line. This computation is, unfortunately, not defined in DCGA.

2.3   DPGA of $\mathbb{G}_{4,4}$

DPGA was adapted from the approach of Parkin [18] in 2012 and firstly introduced in 2015 by Goldman and Mann [11] and further developed by Du and Goldman and Mann [8]. DPGA is defined over a 8-dimensional vector space. Similarly to DCGA, the base vectors of the space are divided into two groups: $\{\mathbf{w}_0, \mathbf{w}_1, \mathbf{w}_2, \mathbf{w}_3\}$, corresponding to the projective geometric algebra vectors, and a copy of this basis $\{\mathbf{w}_0^*, \mathbf{w}_1^*, \mathbf{w}_2^*, \mathbf{w}_3^*\}$ such that $\mathbf{w}_i \mathbf{w}_i^* = 0.5 + \mathbf{w}_i \wedge \mathbf{w}_i^*$, $\forall i \in \{0, 1, 2, 3\}$. In DPGA, the entity representing a point whose Euclidean coordinates are (x, y, z) has two definitions, namely, primal and dual. Both definitions are the base to construct quadratic surfaces by means of the sandwiching product. The definitions of the points are:

$$\mathbf{p} = x\mathbf{w}_0 + y\mathbf{w}_1 + z\mathbf{w}_2 + w\mathbf{w}_3, \qquad \mathbf{p}^* = x\mathbf{w}_0^* + y\mathbf{w}_1^* + z\mathbf{w}_2^* + w\mathbf{w}_3^*. \tag{3}$$

Note that the dual definition denotes the fact that

$$\mathbf{w}_i \cdot \mathbf{w}_j^* = \frac{1}{2}\delta_{i,j} \ (\forall i, j = 0, \cdots 3),$$ (4)

where $\delta_{i,j} = 1$ if $i = j$, 0 otherwise. This corresponds to the condition of the dual stated in Sect. 11 of [4].

Quadratic Surfaces: A quadratic surface in DPGA is the bivector Q_{DPGA} defined as follows:

$$\begin{aligned}
Q_{\mathrm{DPGA}} =\ & 4a\mathbf{w}_0^* \wedge \mathbf{w}_0 + 4b\mathbf{w}_1^* \wedge \mathbf{w}_1 + 4c\mathbf{w}_2^* \wedge \mathbf{w}_2 + 4j\mathbf{w}_3^* \wedge \mathbf{w}_3 \\
& +2d(\mathbf{w}_0^* \wedge \mathbf{w}_1 + \mathbf{w}_1^* \wedge \mathbf{w}_0) + 2e(\mathbf{w}_0^* \wedge \mathbf{w}_2 + \mathbf{w}_2^* \wedge \mathbf{w}_0) \\
& +2f(\mathbf{w}_1^* \wedge \mathbf{w}_2 + \mathbf{w}_2^* \wedge \mathbf{w}_1) + 2g(\mathbf{w}_0^* \wedge \mathbf{w}_3 + \mathbf{w}_3^* \wedge \mathbf{w}_0) \\
& +2h(\mathbf{w}_1^* \wedge \mathbf{w}_3 + \mathbf{w}_3^* \wedge \mathbf{w}_1) + 2i(\mathbf{w}_2^* \wedge \mathbf{w}_3 + \mathbf{w}_3^* \wedge \mathbf{w}_2).
\end{aligned}$$ (5)

A point (x, y, z) is in the quadratic surface Q_{DPGA} if and only if

$$\mathbf{p} \cdot Q_{\mathrm{DPGA}} \cdot \mathbf{p}^* = 0.$$ (6)

Table 1 summarises the computations involved in three main operations used for computer graphics.

Table 1. Formulas of DPGA involved in the main computations for computer graphics

Feature	DPGA
Point is on a quadratic surface	$\mathbf{p} \cdot Q_{\mathrm{DPGA}} \cdot \mathbf{p}^*$
Tangent plane	$Q_{\mathrm{DPGA}} \cdot \mathbf{p}^*$
Quadratic surface-line intersection	$(\mathbf{L}^* \wedge Q_{\mathrm{DPGA}} \wedge \mathbf{L}) \cdot \mathbf{I}$

Complexity of Some Major Operations: Q_{DPGA} has a total of 16 basis bivector components. For each basis bivector, 2 inner products are required. Thus, the first product $\mathbf{p} \cdot Q_{\mathrm{DPGA}}$ requires $4 \times 2 \times 16 = 128$ inner products. As previously seen, the resulting entity is a vector with 4 components. Hence, the second inner product requires $4 \times 4 = 16$ products. This results in 144 products in total.

Let us now evaluate the cost of the intersection between a quadratic surface Q_{DPGA} and a line $\mathbf{L}$ and $\mathbf{L}^*$. The line $\mathbf{L}^*$ is obtained by the outer product of two points $\mathbf{x}_1$ and $\mathbf{x}_2$ whose number of components is 4. Thus, a line $\mathbf{L}$ has 6 components. The number of components of the quadratic surface is 16 and the number of components of the line is 6. Then, the computational cost of the outer product $\mathbf{L}^* \wedge Q_{\mathrm{DPGA}}$ is $6 \times 16 = 96$ outer products. The result is a 4-vector and the resulting entity has 16 components. Furthermore, the line $\mathbf{l}$ has 6 components. Hence, the cost of the final outer product is $16 \times 6 = 96$ outer products. The total operation cost is thus $96 + 96 = 192$ products.

Considering the fact that the number of components of $\mathbf{p}^*$ is 4 and the number of components of Q_{DPGA} is 16, the computational cost of the computation of the tangent plane is $16 \times 4 = 64$ products.

2.4   QCGA of $\mathbb{G}_{9,6}$

QCGA was presented by Breuils et al. [2]. The base vectors are composed of Euclidean basis vectors and the 12 null basis vectors $\{\mathbf{e}_{oi}, \mathbf{e}_{\infty i}\}, i = 1 \cdots 6$. Firstly, a point is defined as the 12-component vector:

$$\mathbf{x} = \mathbf{x}_\epsilon + \tfrac{1}{2}(x^2 \mathbf{e}_{\infty 1} + y^2 \mathbf{e}_{\infty 2} + z^2 \mathbf{e}_{\infty 3}) + xy\mathbf{e}_{\infty 4} + xz\mathbf{e}_{\infty 5} + yz\mathbf{e}_{\infty 6} + \mathbf{e}_{o1} + \mathbf{e}_{o2} + \mathbf{e}_{o3}. \tag{7}$$

Secondly, the definition of a quadratic surface in QCGA is a 1-vector, called $\mathbf{Q}^*$, which has also a total of 12 basis vector components as:

$$\mathbf{q}^* = -\left(2a\mathbf{e}_{o1} + 2b\mathbf{e}_{o2} + 2c\mathbf{e}_{o3} + d\mathbf{e}_{o4} + e\mathbf{e}_{o5} + f\mathbf{e}_{o6}\right)$$
$$+ \left(g\mathbf{e}_1 + h\mathbf{e}_2 + i\mathbf{e}_3\right) - \frac{j}{3}(\mathbf{e}_{\infty 1} + \mathbf{e}_{\infty 2} + \mathbf{e}_{\infty 3}). \tag{8}$$

Let us evaluate the computational cost of checking whether a point is on a quadratic surface. Furthermore, the number of point component is 12. Thus, the product $\mathbf{x} \cdot \mathbf{Q}^*$ requires at most $12 \times 12 = 144$ products.

The computation of the tangent plane is performed by firstly computing the normal vector. This computation requires the inner product between a vector with 12 components and another vector with 4 components. This is repeated for each Euclidean basis vector; thus, the computation of the normal vector requires $3 \times 4 \times 12 = 144$ inner products.

Then, the tangent plane is computed using the normal vector as follows:

$$\boldsymbol{\pi}^* = \mathbf{n}_\epsilon + \frac{1}{3}(\mathbf{e}_{\infty 1} + \mathbf{e}_{\infty 2} + \mathbf{e}_{\infty 3})\sqrt{-2(\mathbf{e}_{o1} + \mathbf{e}_{o2} + \mathbf{e}_{o3}) \cdot \mathbf{x}}. \tag{9}$$

This computation requires the computation of an inner product of a vector with 3 components $(\mathbf{e}_1, \mathbf{e}_2, \mathbf{e}_3)$ with a 12 component-vector. This means $12 \times 3 = 36$ products. Thus, the total number of inner products required for computing the tangent plane is $144 + 36 = 180$ products.

The final computational feature is the quadratic surface-line intersection. In QCGA, this simply consists of computing the outer product:

$$\mathbf{C}^* = \mathbf{Q}^* \wedge \mathbf{L}^* \tag{10}$$

The number of components of $\mathbf{Q}^*$ is 12 as already seen. In QCGA, a line with the 6 Plücker coefficients is defined as:

$$\mathbf{L}^* = 3\,\mathbf{m}\,\mathbf{I}_\epsilon + (\mathbf{e}_{\infty 3} + \mathbf{e}_{\infty 2} + \mathbf{e}_{\infty 1}) \wedge \mathbf{n}\,\mathbf{I}_\epsilon. \tag{11}$$

The number of components of both $\mathbf{m}$ and $\mathbf{n}$ is 3. The outer product $(\mathbf{e}_{\infty 3} + \mathbf{e}_{\infty 2} + \mathbf{e}_{\infty 1}) \wedge \mathbf{n}\,\mathbf{I}_\epsilon$ yields a copy of the 3 components of $\mathbf{n}$ along $\mathbf{e}_{\infty 1}, \mathbf{e}_{\infty 2}, \mathbf{e}_{\infty 3}$ basis vectors. Thus, the number of components of $\mathbf{L}^*$ is $3 \times 3 + 3 = 12$. The cost of the outer product between $\mathbf{Q}^*$ and $\mathbf{L}^*$ is thus $12 \times 12 = 144$ products.

Table 2 summarises the complexity of DPGA, DCGA, and QCGA for computing features. We remark that the computation of the tangent plane is more efficient if we use DPGA whereas the intersection between a quadratic surface and a line requires less computations if we use QCGA. Furthermore, geometric transformations are not yet defined in QCGA.

Table 2. Numbers of operations required for computation in DPGA, DCGA, and QCGA.

Feature	DPGA	DCGA	QCGA
Point is on a quadratic surface	**144**	750	**144**
Tangent plane	**64**	541	180
Quadratic surface-line intersection	192	–	**144**

3   Mapping Between the Three Models for Quadratic Surfaces

As one of practical applications, we consider constructing a quadratic surface from 9 points then rotating this quadratic surface. To the best of our knowledge, QCGA is the only approach that can construct a quadratic surface from 9 points. But QCGA does not yet support all the transformations. Furthermore, as seen above, it is more computationally efficient to perform the quadratic surface-line intersection in the QCGA model whereas the computation of the tangent plane or the normal vector at a point of quadratic surface is more efficient in the DPGA model. Moreover, if we represent both a Dupin cyclide and a quadratic surface in a same way as [7], then we need DCGA. The above observation is our motivation for defining new operators that convert quadratic surfaces between the three models, see Fig. 1.

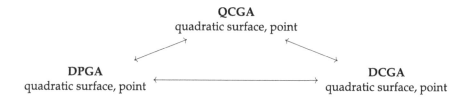

Fig. 1. Encapsulation of the three models of points and quadratic surfaces.

The key idea is that for any entities representing a quadratic surface in QCGA, DCGA, and DPGA, we convert the entity such that all the coefficients of the quadratic surface:

$$a x^2 + b y^2 + c z^2 + d x y + e y z + f z x + g x + h y + i z + j = 0 \qquad (12)$$

can be extracted easily.

3.1   DCGA Reciprocal Operators

We start by defining reciprocal operators for DCGA:

$$\mathbf{T}^{x^2} = \mathbf{e}_1 \wedge \mathbf{e}_4, \quad \mathbf{T}^{y^2} = \mathbf{e}_2 \wedge \mathbf{e}_5, \quad \mathbf{T}^{z^2} = \mathbf{e}_3 \wedge \mathbf{e}_6, \quad \mathbf{T}^1 = \mathbf{e}_{o1} \wedge \mathbf{e}_{o2}, \qquad (13)$$

along with the 6 following:

$$\mathbf{T}^x = \left(\mathbf{e}_1 \wedge \mathbf{e}_{o2} + \mathbf{e}_{o1} \wedge \mathbf{e}_4 \right), \ \mathbf{T}^y = \left(\mathbf{e}_2 \wedge \mathbf{e}_{o2} + \mathbf{e}_{o1} \wedge \mathbf{e}_5 \right),$$
$$\mathbf{T}^z = \left(\mathbf{e}_3 \wedge \mathbf{e}_{o2} + \mathbf{e}_{o1} \wedge \mathbf{e}_6 \right), \ \mathbf{T}^{xy} = \left(\mathbf{e}_1 \wedge \mathbf{e}_5 + \mathbf{e}_2 \wedge \mathbf{e}_4 \right), \quad (14)$$
$$\mathbf{T}^{xz} = \left(\mathbf{e}_1 \wedge \mathbf{e}_6 + \mathbf{e}_3 \wedge \mathbf{e}_4 \right), \ \mathbf{T}^{yz} = \left(\mathbf{e}_3 \wedge \mathbf{e}_5 + \mathbf{e}_2 \wedge \mathbf{e}_6 \right).$$

Given the DCGA extraction operators presented in Sect. 2.2, our defined reciprocal operators verify the following properties:

$$\mathbf{T}^{x^2} \cdot \mathbf{T}_{x^2} = 1, \ \mathbf{T}^{y^2} \cdot \mathbf{T}_{y^2} = 1, \ \mathbf{T}^{z^2} \cdot \mathbf{T}_{z^2} = 1, \ \mathbf{T}^{xy} \cdot \mathbf{T}_{xy} = 1, \ \mathbf{T}^{xz} \cdot \mathbf{T}_{xz} = 1,$$
$$\mathbf{T}^{yz} \cdot \mathbf{T}_{yz} = 1, \ \mathbf{T}^x \cdot \mathbf{T}_x \ = 1, \ \mathbf{T}^y \cdot \mathbf{T}_y \ = 1, \ \mathbf{T}^z \cdot \mathbf{T}_z \ = 1, \ \mathbf{T}^1 \cdot \mathbf{T}_1 \ = 1.$$
$$(15)$$

Then, given $\mathbf{Q}_{\mathrm{DCGA}}$, the entity representing a quadratic surface of DCGA, any coefficients of this quadratic surface (12) can be extracted as:

$$\mathbf{T}^{x^2} \cdot \mathbf{Q}_{\mathrm{DCGA}} = a, \ \mathbf{T}^{y^2} \cdot \mathbf{Q}_{\mathrm{DCGA}} = b, \ \mathbf{T}^{z^2} \cdot \mathbf{Q}_{\mathrm{DCGA}} = c, \ \mathbf{T}^{xy} \cdot \mathbf{Q}_{\mathrm{DCGA}} = d,$$
$$\mathbf{T}^{xz} \cdot \mathbf{Q}_{\mathrm{DCGA}} = e, \mathbf{T}^{yz} \cdot \mathbf{Q}_{\mathrm{DCGA}} = f, \ \mathbf{T}^x \cdot \mathbf{Q}_{\mathrm{DCGA}} \ = g, \ \mathbf{T}^y \cdot \mathbf{Q}_{\mathrm{DCGA}} \ = h, \quad (16)$$
$$\mathbf{T}^z \cdot \mathbf{Q}_{\mathrm{DCGA}} \ = i, \ \mathbf{T}^1 \cdot \mathbf{Q}_{\mathrm{DCGA}} \ = j.$$

The construction of a DCGA point is explained in Sect. 2.2 and defined in [9]. The reciprocal operation requires the computation of the normalized point $\hat{\mathbf{X}}$ of DCGA that we define as:

$$\hat{\mathbf{X}} = -\frac{\mathbf{X}}{\mathbf{X} \cdot (\mathbf{e}_{\infty 1} \wedge \mathbf{e}_{\infty 2})}. \quad (17)$$

The extraction of the Euclidean components (x, y, z) of a normalized point $\hat{\mathbf{X}}$ of DCGA can be performed as follows:

$$x = \hat{\mathbf{X}} \cdot (\mathbf{e}_1 \wedge \mathbf{e}_{\infty 2}), \qquad y = \hat{\mathbf{X}} \cdot (\mathbf{e}_2 \wedge \mathbf{e}_{\infty 2}), \qquad z = \hat{\mathbf{X}} \cdot (\mathbf{e}_3 \wedge \mathbf{e}_{\infty 2}). \quad (18)$$

3.2   DPGA Reciprocal Operators

Let us denote by $\mathbf{W}$ reciprocal operators for DPGA:

$$\mathbf{W}^{x^2} = \mathbf{w}_0^* \wedge \mathbf{w}_0, \ \ \mathbf{W}^{y^2} = \mathbf{w}_1^* \wedge \mathbf{w}_1, \ \ \mathbf{W}^{z^2} = \mathbf{w}_2^* \wedge \mathbf{w}_2, \ \ \mathbf{W}^{xy} = 2\mathbf{w}_1^* \wedge \mathbf{w}_0,$$
$$\mathbf{W}^{xz} = 2\mathbf{w}_2^* \wedge \mathbf{w}_0, \ \mathbf{W}^{yz} = 2\mathbf{w}_2^* \wedge \mathbf{w}_1, \ \mathbf{W}^x = 2\mathbf{w}_3^* \wedge \mathbf{w}_0, \ \mathbf{W}^y = 2\mathbf{w}_3^* \wedge \mathbf{w}_1, \ (19)$$
$$\mathbf{W}^z = 2\mathbf{w}_3^* \wedge \mathbf{w}_2, \ \mathbf{W}^1 = \mathbf{w}_3^* \wedge \mathbf{w}_3.$$

Given Q_{DPGA}, the entity representing a quadratic surface of DPGA, any coefficients of this quadratic surface (12) can be extracted as:

$$\mathbf{W}^{x^2} \cdot Q_{\mathrm{DPGA}} = a, \ \mathbf{W}^{y^2} \cdot Q_{\mathrm{DPGA}} = b, \ \mathbf{W}^{z^2} \cdot Q_{\mathrm{DPGA}} = c, \ \mathbf{W}^{xy} \cdot Q_{\mathrm{DPGA}} = d,$$
$$\mathbf{W}^{xz} \cdot Q_{\mathrm{DPGA}} = e, \ \mathbf{W}^{yz} \cdot Q_{\mathrm{DPGA}} = f, \ \mathbf{W}^x \cdot Q_{\mathrm{DPGA}} \ = g, \ \mathbf{W}^y \cdot Q_{\mathrm{DPGA}} \ = h, \quad (20)$$
$$\mathbf{W}^z \cdot Q_{\mathrm{DPGA}} \ = i, \ \mathbf{W}^1 \cdot Q_{\mathrm{DPGA}} \ = j.$$

As in projective geometry, the construction of a finite point of DPGA requires to add a homogeneous component 1 to the Euclidean components. The normalization of a point merely consists of dividing all the components by its $\mathbf{w}_3$ components (or $\mathbf{w}_3^*$ for the dual form) if it is a non-zero component.

3.3   QCGA Reciprocal Operators

For QCGA, quadratic surfaces can be represented using either the primal form or the dual form. We define the reciprocal operators for the dual form. When considering the primal form, we have only to compute the dual of the primal and then apply the following reciprocal operators:

$$\mathbf{Q}^{x^2} = \frac{1}{2}\mathbf{e}_{o1}, \quad \mathbf{Q}^{y^2} = \frac{1}{2}\mathbf{e}_{o2}, \quad \mathbf{Q}^{z^2} = \frac{1}{2}\mathbf{e}_{o3}, \quad \mathbf{Q}^{xy} = \mathbf{e}_{o4},$$
$$\mathbf{Q}^{xz} = \mathbf{e}_{o5}, \qquad \mathbf{Q}^{yz} = \mathbf{e}_{o6}, \qquad \mathbf{Q}^{x} = \mathbf{e}_{1}, \qquad \mathbf{Q}^{y} = \mathbf{e}_{2}, \qquad (21)$$
$$\mathbf{Q}^{z} = \mathbf{e}_{3}, \qquad \mathbf{Q}^{1} = \mathbf{e}_{\infty 1} + \mathbf{e}_{\infty 2} + \mathbf{e}_{\infty 3}.$$

Given a general quadratic surface $\mathbf{Q}^*$ whose coefficients are $(a, b, c, \cdots, j)$, the properties of these operators are as follows:

$$\mathbf{Q}^{x^2} \cdot \mathbf{Q}^* = a, \ \mathbf{Q}^{y^2} \cdot \mathbf{Q}^* = b, \ \mathbf{Q}^{z^2} \cdot \mathbf{Q}^* = c, \ \mathbf{Q}^{xy} \cdot \mathbf{Q}^* = d, \ \mathbf{Q}^{xz} \cdot \mathbf{Q}^* = e,$$
$$\mathbf{Q}^{yz} \cdot \mathbf{Q}^* = f, \ \mathbf{Q}^{x} \cdot \mathbf{Q}^* = g, \ \mathbf{Q}^{y} \cdot \mathbf{Q}^* = h, \ \mathbf{Q}^{z} \cdot \mathbf{Q}^* = i, \ \mathbf{Q}^{1} \cdot \mathbf{Q}^* = j. \qquad (22)$$

The reciprocal operation requires the computation of the normalized point $\hat{\mathbf{x}}$ of QCGA, which is missing in [2].

Proposition 3.1. *For a QCGA point* $\mathbf{x}$, *the normalization is merely computed through an averaging of* $\mathbf{e}_{o1}, \mathbf{e}_{o2}, \mathbf{e}_{o3}$ *components of* $\mathbf{e}_o$ *component as:*

$$- \frac{\mathbf{x}}{\mathbf{x} \cdot \mathbf{e}_{\infty}}. \qquad (23)$$

Proof. A scale α on $\mathbf{x}$ acts the same way on all null basis vectors of $\mathbf{x}$:

$$\alpha\mathbf{x} = \alpha\mathbf{x}_{\epsilon} + \tfrac{1}{2}\alpha(x^2\mathbf{e}_{\infty 1} + y^2\mathbf{w}\mathbf{e}_{\infty 2} + z^2\mathbf{e}_{\infty 3}) + xy\alpha\mathbf{e}_{\infty 4} + xz\alpha\mathbf{e}_{\infty 5} + yz\alpha\mathbf{e}_{\infty 6}$$
$$+ \alpha\mathbf{e}_{o1} + \alpha\mathbf{e}_{o2} + \alpha\mathbf{e}_{o3}. \qquad (24)$$

The metric of QCGA indicates (see [2]):

$$\alpha\mathbf{x} \cdot \mathbf{e}_{\infty 1} = -\alpha, \quad \alpha\mathbf{x} \cdot \mathbf{e}_{\infty 2} = -\alpha, \quad \alpha\mathbf{x} \cdot \mathbf{e}_{\infty 3} = -\alpha. \qquad (25)$$

Thus, if $\alpha \neq 0$:

$$\frac{-3\alpha\mathbf{x}}{\alpha\mathbf{x} \cdot (\mathbf{e}_{\infty 1} + \mathbf{e}_{\infty 2} + \mathbf{e}_{\infty 3})} \cdot \mathbf{e}_{\infty 1} = -\frac{-3\alpha\mathbf{x}}{-3\alpha} \cdot \mathbf{e}_{\infty 1} \qquad (26)$$
$$= \mathbf{x} \cdot \mathbf{e}_{\infty 1} = -1.$$

A similar result is obtained with $\mathbf{e}_{\infty 2}$ and $\mathbf{e}_{\infty 3}$:

$$\frac{-3\alpha\mathbf{x}}{\alpha\mathbf{x} \cdot (\mathbf{e}_{\infty 1} + \mathbf{e}_{\infty 2} + \mathbf{e}_{\infty 3})} \cdot \mathbf{e}_{\infty 2} = \mathbf{x} \cdot \mathbf{e}_{\infty 2} = -1. \qquad (27)$$

$$\frac{-3\alpha\mathbf{x}}{\alpha\mathbf{x} \cdot (\mathbf{e}_{\infty 1} + \mathbf{e}_{\infty 2} + \mathbf{e}_{\infty 3})} \cdot \mathbf{e}_{\infty 3} = \mathbf{x} \cdot \mathbf{e}_{\infty 3} = -1. \qquad (28)$$

Thus, we check that for any scaled points $\mathbf{x}_1, \mathbf{x}_2$:

$$\frac{\mathbf{x}_1}{\mathbf{x}_1 \cdot \mathbf{e}_\infty} \cdot \frac{\mathbf{x}_2}{\mathbf{x}_2 \cdot \mathbf{e}_\infty} = -\frac{1}{2} \left\| \mathbf{x}_{1\epsilon} - \mathbf{x}_{2\epsilon} \right\|^2. \tag{29}$$

The extraction of the Euclidean components (x, y, z) of a normalized point $\hat{\mathbf{x}}$ of QCGA can be performed as follows:

$$x = \hat{\mathbf{x}} \cdot \mathbf{e}_1, \qquad y = \hat{\mathbf{x}} \cdot \mathbf{e}_2, \qquad z = \hat{\mathbf{x}} \cdot \mathbf{e}_3. \tag{30}$$

3.4 How to Choose the Right Model?

Given a geometric operation and this general framework, a question arises that which model we should choose among QCGA, DPGA, and DCGA. To answer this question, we merely consider two criteria, namely, (1) if the operation is defined and (2) on which model it is the most computationally efficient. This is illustrated in Tables 2 and 3.

Table 3. Geometric operations allowed in either QCGA, DPGA or DCGA, where ✓means possible and ✗ means not.

Opération	DPGA	DCGA	QCGA
Quadratic surface from control points	✗	✗	✓
Point $\in$ quadratic surface	✓	✓	✓
Tangent plane	✓	✓	✓
Quadratic surface-line intersection	✓	✗	✓
Quadratic surface-quadratic surface intersection	✗	✗	✓
Transformations	✓	✓	✗
Quartic surfaces	✗	✓	✗

3.5 Example

We test our approach by defining an ellipsoid from 9 points using QCGA. Then we rotate it using DPGA and back-convert the rotated ellipsoid into QCGA. In terms of geometric algebra computations, first we compute the quadratic surface:

$$\mathbf{Q}^* = (\mathbf{x}_1 \wedge \mathbf{x}_2 \wedge \cdots \wedge \mathbf{x}_9 \wedge \mathbf{I}_o^{\triangleright})^*. \tag{31}$$

Then, we apply the extraction operators of QCGA to convert the QCGA quadratic surface to its corresponding DPGA quadratic surface.

$$
\begin{aligned}
Q_{\text{DPGA}} =& 4(\mathbf{Q}^{x^2} \cdot \mathbf{Q}^*)\mathbf{w}_0^* \wedge \mathbf{w}_0 + 4(\mathbf{Q}^{y^2} \cdot \mathbf{Q}^*)\mathbf{w}_1^* \wedge \mathbf{w}_1 + 4(\mathbf{Q}^{z^2} \cdot \mathbf{Q}^*)\mathbf{w}_2^* \wedge \mathbf{w}_2 \\
&+ 4(\mathbf{Q}^1 \cdot \mathbf{Q}^*)\mathbf{w}_3^* \wedge \mathbf{w}_3 + 2(\mathbf{Q}^{xy} \cdot \mathbf{Q}^*)(\mathbf{w}_0^* \wedge \mathbf{w}_1 + \mathbf{w}_1^* \wedge \mathbf{w}_0) \\
&+ 2(\mathbf{Q}^{xz} \cdot \mathbf{Q}^*)(\mathbf{w}_0^* \wedge \mathbf{w}_2 + \mathbf{w}_2^* \wedge \mathbf{w}_0) + 2(\mathbf{Q}^{yz} \cdot \mathbf{Q}^*)(\mathbf{w}_1^* \wedge \mathbf{w}_2 + \mathbf{w}_2^* \wedge \mathbf{w}_1) \\
&+ 2(\mathbf{Q}^x \cdot \mathbf{Q}^*)(\mathbf{w}_0^* \wedge \mathbf{w}_3 + \mathbf{w}_3^* \wedge \mathbf{w}_0) + 2(\mathbf{Q}^y \cdot \mathbf{Q}^*)(\mathbf{w}_1^* \wedge \mathbf{w}_3 + \mathbf{w}_3^* \wedge \mathbf{w}_1) \\
&+ 2(\mathbf{Q}^z \cdot \mathbf{Q}^*)(\mathbf{w}_2^* \wedge \mathbf{w}_3 + \mathbf{w}_3^* \wedge \mathbf{w}_2).
\end{aligned}
\tag{32}
$$

The rotation is now performed as follows:

$$
Q_{\text{DPGA}} = \mathbf{R} Q_{\text{DPGA}} \mathbf{R}^{-1}.
\tag{33}
$$

The rotor $\mathbf{R}$ is defined as:

$$
\mathbf{R} = \exp(\frac{1}{2}\theta \mathbf{w}_i \mathbf{w}_j^*),
\tag{34}
$$

where $i \neq j$. The final step is to convert the resulting quadratic surface back into QCGA. It is merely computed using the QCGA extraction operators as follows:

$$
\begin{aligned}
\mathbf{Q}^* = & -\big(2(\mathbf{W}^{x^2} \cdot Q_{\text{DPGA}})\mathbf{e}_{o1} + 2(\mathbf{W}^{y^2} \cdot Q_{\text{DPGA}})\mathbf{e}_{o2} + 2(\mathbf{W}^{z^2} \cdot Q_{\text{DPGA}})\mathbf{e}_{o3} \\
& + (\mathbf{W}^{xy} \cdot Q_{\text{DPGA}})\mathbf{e}_{o4} + (\mathbf{W}^{xz} \cdot Q_{\text{DPGA}})\mathbf{e}_{o5} + (\mathbf{W}^{yz} \cdot Q_{\text{DPGA}})\mathbf{e}_{o6}\big) \\
& + \big((\mathbf{W}^x \cdot Q_{\text{DPGA}})\mathbf{e}_1 + (\mathbf{W}^y \cdot Q_{\text{DPGA}})\mathbf{e}_2 + (\mathbf{W}^z \cdot Q_{\text{DPGA}})\mathbf{e}_3\big) \\
& - \frac{(\mathbf{W}^1 \cdot Q_{\text{DPGA}})}{3}(\mathbf{e}_{\infty 1} + \mathbf{e}_{\infty 2} + \mathbf{e}_{\infty 3}).
\end{aligned}
\tag{35}
$$

Note that the program can be found in the plugin folder of the git repository https://git.renater.fr/garamon.git.

4   Conclusion

In this paper, we focused on an approach to deal with quadratic surfaces. After presenting the main geometric algebras to represent and manipulate quadratic surfaces, we introduced an approach that transversely uses the main geometric algebras. This approach unifies all the models of geometric algebra into one more general approach that allows to represent and manipulate any quadratic surface either using control points or from the coefficients of its implicit form. For the following, we seek for a generalisation of this approach for the representation of quadratic and cubic surfaces. A potential drawback of the proposed approach is that the used algebras are all of high dimensions and, thus, are difficult to implement efficiently. The algebra generator Garamon [1] allows such efficient implementation and so, it will be interesting to compare the proposed approach to the usual way to represent and manipulate quadratic surfaces.

References

1. Breuils, S., Nozick, V., Fuchs, L.: Garamon: Geometric algebra library generator. Advances in Applied Clifford Algebras Submitted (2019)
2. Breuils, S., Nozick, V., Sugimoto, A., Hitzer, E.: Quadric conformal geometric algebra of $\mathbb{R}^{9,6}$. Adv. Appl. Clifford Algebras **28**(2), 35 (2018). https://doi.org/10.1007/s00006-018-0851-1

3. Buchholz, S., Tachibana, K., Hitzer, E.M.S.: Optimal learning rates for clifford neurons. In: de Sá, J.M., Alexandre, L.A., Duch, W., Mandic, D. (eds.) ICANN 2007. LNCS, vol. 4668, pp. 864–873. Springer, Heidelberg (2007). https://doi.org/10.1007/978-3-540-74690-4_88
4. Doran, C., Hestenes, D., Sommen, F., Van Acker, N.: Lie groups as spin groups. J. Math. Phys. **34**(8), 3642–3669 (1993)
5. Dorst, L., Fontijne, D., Mann, S.: Geometric Algebra for Computer Science: An Object-Oriented Approach to Geometry. Morgan Kaufmann, Burlington (2007)
6. Dorst, L., Van Den Boomgaard, R.: An analytical theory of mathematical morphology. In: Mathematical Morphology and its Applications to Signal Processing, pp. 245–250 (1993)
7. Druoton, L., Fuchs, L., Garnier, L., Langevin, R.: The non-degenerate dupin cyclides in the space of spheres using geometric algebra. Adv. Appl. Clifford Algebras **24**(2), 515–532 (2014). https://doi.org/10.1007/s00006-014-0453-5
8. Du, J., Goldman, R., Mann, S.: Modeling 3D geometry in the clifford algebra $\mathbb{R}^{4,4}$. Adv. Appl. Clifford Algebras **27**(4), 3039–3062 (2017). https://doi.org/10.1007/s00006-017-0798-7
9. Easter, R.B., Hitzer, E.: Double conformal geometric algebra. Adv. Appl. Clifford Algebras **27**(3), 2175–2199 (2017)
10. Glassner, A.S.: An Introduction to Ray Tracing. Elsevier, Amsterdam (1989)
11. Goldman, R., Mann, S.: R(4, 4) as a computational framework for 3-dimensional computer graphics. Adv. Appl. Clifford Algebras **25**(1), 113–149 (2015). https://doi.org/10.1007/s00006-014-0480-2
12. Gregory, A.L., Lasenby, J., Agarwal, A.: The elastic theory of shells using geometric algebra. Roy. Soc. Open Sci. **4**(3), 170065 (2017)
13. Hestenes, D.: New Foundations for Classical Mechanics, vol. 15. Springer, Heidelberg (2012)
14. Hitzer, E.: Geometric operations implemented by conformal geometric algebra neural nodes. Preprint arXiv:1306.1358 (2013)
15. Leopardi, P.: A generalized FFT for Clifford algebras. Bull. Belg. Math. Soc. **11**, 663–688 (2004)
16. Luo, W., Hu, Y., Yu, Z., Yuan, L., Lü, G.: A hierarchical representation and computation scheme of arbitrary-dimensional geometrical primitives based on CGA. Adv. Appl. Clifford Algebras **27**(3), 1977–1995 (2017). https://doi.org/10.1007/s00006-016-0697-3
17. Papaefthymiou, M., Papagiannakis, G.: Real-time rendering under distant illumination with conformal geometric algebra. Math. Methods Appl. Sci. **41**, 4131–4147 (2017)
18. Parkin, S.T.: A model for quadric surfaces using geometric algebra. Unpublished, October 2012
19. Perwass, C.: Geometric Algebra with Applications in Engineering. Geometry and Computing, vol. 4. Springer, Heidelberg (2009). https://doi.org/10.1007/978-3-540-89068-3
20. Vince, J.: Geometric Algebra for Computer Graphics. Springer, Heidelberg (2008). https://doi.org/10.1007/978-1-84628-997-2
21. Zhu, S., Yuan, S., Li, D., Luo, W., Yuan, L., Yu, Z.: Mvtree for hierarchical network representation based on geometric algebra subspace. Adv. Appl. Clifford Algebras **28**(2), 39 (2018). https://doi.org/10.1007/s00006-018-0855-x

Cubic Curves and Cubic Surfaces from Contact Points in Conformal Geometric Algebra

Eckhard Hitzer[1](✉) and Dietmar Hildenbrand[2]

[1] International Christian University,
Osawa 3-10-2, Mitaka-shi, Tokyo 181-8585, Japan
hitzer@icu.ac.jp
[2] Technical University of Darmstadt, Karolinenpl. 5, 64289 Darmstadt, Germany
Dietmar.hildenbrand@gmail.com

Abstract. This work explains how to extend standard conformal geometric algebra of the Euclidean plane in a novel way to describe cubic curves in the Euclidean plane from nine contact points or from the ten coefficients of their implicit equations. As algebraic framework serves the Clifford algebra $Cl(9,7)$ over the real sixteen dimensional vector space $\mathbb{R}^{9,7}$. These cubic curves can be intersected using the outer product based meet operation of geometric algebra. An analogous approach is explained for the description and operation with cubic surfaces in three Euclidean dimensions, using as framework $Cl(19,16)$.

Keywords: Clifford algebra · Conformal geometric algebra · Cubic curves · Cubic surfaces · Intersections

1 Introduction

Cubic curves in the Euclidean plane have historically already been studied by Isaac Newton. In the context of geometric algebra [6], especially conformal geometric algebra, triple conformal geometric algebra (TCGA) $Cl(9,3)$ of the Euclidean plane provides a frame work for representing cubics and some higher order algebraic curves [7], albeit with the disadvantage of not being able to intersect two cubic curves with each other using the outer product. Yet, TCGA has the advantage of low dimensions, the underlying vector space only has dimension twelve, and modern PCs can easily compute with Clifford algebras over such vector spaces. Another advantage is that the intuitive and efficient quaternion like versor form of geometric transformations is available in TCGA.

Another line of development was the representation of conic curves in the plane by Perwass in Chap. 4.5 of [16] using the extended conformal geometric algebra $Cl(5,3)$, we call conic CGA. Including transformation versors for rotation, translation and scaling, this has been worked out in more detail in [13],

Soli Deo Gloria.

© Springer Nature Switzerland AG 2019
M. Gavrilova et al. (Eds.): CGI 2019, LNCS 11542, pp. 535–545, 2019.
https://doi.org/10.1007/978-3-030-22514-8_53

and with a further simplified set of transformation versors in [11]. Again, nowadays computer algebra systems like Maple [1], Mathematica [2] and Matlab [17], etc., can easily work with $Cl(5,3)$. We now present the algebra of an implementation of cubic curves constructed from nine contact points, or alternatively from the ten coefficients of their implicit equation in the extended conformal geometric algebra $Cl(9,7)$, named *cubic CGA*, over the real vector space $\mathbb{R}^{9,7}$. This is currently at the limit what an implementation like [17] can compute. The expectation is, that optimization will very soon progress, and enable us to apply [17] to this problem, and we even anticipate that other implementations using e.g. the optimization framework GAALOP [8] or even GARAMON [4] or ganja.js [14], may indeed already be able to reasonable compute in the $Cl(9,7)$ framework. The aim of the present paper is not to present a full framework, including a complete software implementation, but rather to outline the algebraic framework, and thus enable other researchers to work with cubic curves in cubic CGA, including the general intersection computation.

The paper is structured as follows. Section 2 outlines the algebraic setup of the extended CGA for cubic curves. Section 3 then proceeds to introduce the notion of cubic points (points in two dimensions, that are extended to include quadratic and cubic coordinate monomials as vector coefficients). This includes explanations on how standard CGA of two dimensional Euclidean space and conic CGA are embedded in cubic CGA. Section 4 explains how to construct cubic curve representing blades either from nine contact points, or from the ten coefficients of the implicit cubic curve equation in two dimensions. Section 5 introduces the way of computing intersections of cubic curves, utilizing the outer product of blades. Furthermore, Sect. 6 extends the approach to the cubic surface CGA $Cl(19,16)$ for describing in an analogous way to the previous sections the construction of cubic surfaces in three Euclidean dimensions, either from 19 surface points, or from the twenty coefficients of the implicit equation of cubic surfaces in three dimensions. The work concludes with Sect. 7, followed by references.

2   Cubic Conformal Geometric Algebra

We use the following notation: Lower-case bold letters denote basis blades and multivectors (vector or multivector **a**). Italic lower-case letters refer to multivector components $(a_1, x, y^2, \cdots)$. For example, a_i is the ith coordinate of the (multi)vector **a**. The superscript star used in $\mathbf{x}^*$ represents the dualization of the multivector **x**. Finally, subscript ϵ on $\mathbf{x}_\epsilon$ refers to the two-dimensional Euclidean vector associated to the vector **x** of cubic CGA.

Note that when used in geometric algebra the inner product, contractions and the outer product have priority over the full geometric product. For instance, $\mathbf{a} \wedge \mathbf{b}\mathbf{I} = (\mathbf{a} \wedge \mathbf{b})\mathbf{I}$.

The inner products between the basis vectors of $Cl(9,7)$ are defined in Table 1.

Table 1. Inner product between cubic CGA basis vectors.

	e_1	e_2	e_{o1}	$e_{\infty 1}$	e_{o2}	$e_{\infty 2}$	e_{o3}	$e_{\infty 3}$	e_{o4}	$e_{\infty 4}$	e_{o5}	$e_{\infty 5}$	e_{o6}	$e_{\infty 6}$	e_{o7}	$e_{\infty 7}$
e_1	1	0	·	·	·	·	·	·	·	·	·	·	·	·	·	·
e_2	0	1	·	·	·	·	·	·	·	·	·	·	·	·	·	·
e_{o1}	·	·	0	-1	·	·	·	·	·	·	·	·	·	·	·	·
$e_{\infty 1}$	·	·	-1	0	·	·	·	·	·	·	·	·	·	·	·	·
e_{o2}	·	·	·	·	0	-1	·	·	·	·	·	·	·	·	·	·
$e_{\infty 2}$	·	·	·	·	-1	0	·	·	·	·	·	·	·	·	·	·
e_{o3}	·	·	·	·	·	·	0	-1	·	·	·	·	·	·	·	·
$e_{\infty 3}$	·	·	·	·	·	·	-1	0	·	·	·	·	·	·	·	·
e_{o4}	·	·	·	·	·	·	·	·	0	-1	·	·	·	·	·	·
$e_{\infty 4}$	·	·	·	·	·	·	·	·	-1	0	·	·	·	·	·	·
e_{o5}	·	·	·	·	·	·	·	·	·	·	0	-1	·	·	·	·
$e_{\infty 5}$	·	·	·	·	·	·	·	·	·	·	-1	0	·	·	·	·
e_{o6}	·	·	·	·	·	·	·	·	·	·	·	·	0	-1	·	·
$e_{\infty 6}$	·	·	·	·	·	·	·	·	·	·	·	·	-1	0	·	·
e_{o7}	·	·	·	·	·	·	·	·	·	·	·	·	·	·	0	-1
$e_{\infty 7}$	·	·	·	·	·	·	·	·	·	·	·	·	·	·	-1	0

The transformation from the common diagonal metric basis to that of Table 1 can be defined as follows: for $1 \leq i, j \leq 7$,

$$\mathbf{e}_{oi} = \frac{1}{\sqrt{2}}(\mathbf{e}_{-i} - \mathbf{e}_{+i}), \qquad \mathbf{e}_{\infty i} = \frac{1}{\sqrt{2}}(\mathbf{e}_{+i} + \mathbf{e}_{-i}). \tag{1}$$

We further define for later use another pair of null vectors

$$\mathbf{e}_\infty = \tfrac{1}{2}(\mathbf{e}_{\infty 1} + \mathbf{e}_{\infty 2}), \qquad \mathbf{e}_o = \mathbf{e}_{o1} + \mathbf{e}_{o2}. \tag{2}$$

Inner products lead to

$$\mathbf{e}_{\infty i} \cdot \mathbf{e}_{oi} = -1, \qquad \mathbf{e}_\infty \cdot \mathbf{e}_o = -1, \qquad \mathbf{e}_o^2 = \mathbf{e}_\infty^2 = 0, \tag{3}$$

$$\mathbf{e}_{\infty k} \cdot \mathbf{e}_o = -1 \quad (k = 1, 2), \quad \mathbf{e}_{\infty l} \cdot \mathbf{e}_o = 0 \quad (l = 3, 4, 5, 6, 7), \quad \mathbf{e}_{\infty i} \cdot \mathbf{e}_\infty = 0, \tag{4}$$

We further define the bivectors E_i, E, as

$$E_i = \mathbf{e}_{\infty i} \wedge \mathbf{e}_{oi} = \mathbf{e}_{+i}\mathbf{e}_{-i}, \qquad E = \mathbf{e}_\infty \wedge \mathbf{e}_o, \tag{5}$$

and obtain the following products

$$E_i^2 = 1, \qquad E_i E_j = E_j E_i, \tag{6}$$

$$\mathbf{e}_{oi} E_i = -E_i \mathbf{e}_{oi} = -\mathbf{e}_{oi}, \qquad \mathbf{e}_{\infty i} E_i = -E_i \mathbf{e}_{\infty i} = \mathbf{e}_{\infty i}, \tag{7}$$

$$\mathbf{e}_{oj} E_i \overset{i \neq j}{=} E_i \mathbf{e}_{oj}, \qquad \mathbf{e}_{\infty j} E_i \overset{i \neq j}{=} E_i \mathbf{e}_{\infty j}, \tag{8}$$

$$E^2 = 1, \quad \mathbf{e}_o E = -E\mathbf{e}_o = -\mathbf{e}_o, \quad \mathbf{e}_\infty E = -E\mathbf{e}_\infty = \mathbf{e}_\infty. \tag{9}$$

We further define the following blades

$$\mathbf{I}_{\infty 12} = \mathbf{e}_{\infty 1}\mathbf{e}_{\infty 2}, \quad \mathbf{I}_{\infty c} = \mathbf{e}_{\infty 4}\mathbf{e}_{\infty 5}\mathbf{e}_{\infty 6}\mathbf{e}_{\infty 7}, \quad \mathbf{I}_{\infty b} = \mathbf{e}_{\infty 3}\mathbf{I}_{\infty c}, \quad \mathbf{I}_{\infty} = \mathbf{I}_{\infty 12}\mathbf{I}_{\infty b}, \tag{10}$$

$$\mathbf{I}_{o12} = \mathbf{e}_{o1}\mathbf{e}_{o2}, \quad \mathbf{I}_{oc} = \mathbf{e}_{o4}\mathbf{e}_{o5}\mathbf{e}_{o6}\mathbf{e}_{o7}, \quad \mathbf{I}_{ob} = \mathbf{e}_{o3}\mathbf{I}_{oc}, \quad \mathbf{I}_{o} = \mathbf{I}_{o12}\mathbf{I}_{ob}, \tag{11}$$

$$\mathbf{I}_{\infty o} = \mathbf{I}_{\infty} \wedge \mathbf{I}_{o} = -E_1 E_2 E_3 E_4 E_5 E_6 E_7, \tag{12}$$

$$\mathbf{e}_{o12}^{\triangleright} = \mathbf{e}_{o1} - \mathbf{e}_{o2}, \quad \mathbf{I}_{o}^{\triangleright} = \mathbf{e}_{o12}^{\triangleright}\mathbf{I}_{ob}, \quad \mathbf{e}_{\infty 12}^{\triangleright} = \mathbf{e}_{\infty 1} - \mathbf{e}_{\infty 2}, \quad \mathbf{I}_{\infty}^{\triangleright} = \mathbf{e}_{\infty 12}^{\triangleright}\mathbf{I}_{\infty b}, \tag{13}$$

Note that we defined the 7-blades $\mathbf{I}_{\infty}$ and $\mathbf{I}_{o}$ as the products of all infinity null vectors, respectively of all origin null vectors. As we will see later in this model, the 6-blades $\mathbf{I}_{\infty}^{\triangleright}$ and $\mathbf{I}_{o}^{\triangleright}$ are frequently used, e.g. to work with the embedding of standard CGA in cubic CGA (Sect. 3), for the dual vector representation of cubics (Sect. 4), and for intersection computations (Sect. 5). The blades $\mathbf{I}_{\infty}$ and $\mathbf{I}_{\infty}^{\triangleright}$ are directly related by (18). A similar relationship exists between $\mathbf{I}_{o}$ and $\mathbf{I}_{o}^{\triangleright}$. As a consequence of the blade definitions we have

$$\mathbf{e}_{\infty 12}^{\triangleright} \cdot \mathbf{e}_{o12}^{\triangleright} = -2, \tag{14}$$

$$\mathbf{I}_{\infty c} \cdot \mathbf{I}_{oc} = \mathbf{I}_{oc} \cdot \mathbf{I}_{\infty c} = \mathbf{I}_{\infty c}\rfloor \mathbf{I}_{oc} = \mathbf{I}_{\infty c}\lfloor \mathbf{I}_{oc} = 1, \tag{15}$$

$$\mathbf{I}_{\infty}^{\triangleright} \cdot \mathbf{I}_{o}^{\triangleright} = \mathbf{I}_{o}^{\triangleright} \cdot \mathbf{I}_{\infty}^{\triangleright} = \mathbf{I}_{\infty}^{\triangleright}\rfloor \mathbf{I}_{o}^{\triangleright} = \mathbf{I}_{\infty}^{\triangleright}\lfloor \mathbf{I}_{o}^{\triangleright} = -2. \tag{16}$$

We have the following outer product relationships

$$\mathbf{I}_{\infty 12} = -\mathbf{e}_{\infty 1} \wedge \mathbf{e}_{\infty 12}^{\triangleright} = -\mathbf{e}_{\infty 2} \wedge \mathbf{e}_{\infty 12}^{\triangleright} = -\mathbf{e}_{\infty} \wedge \mathbf{e}_{\infty 12}^{\triangleright}$$

$$= -\mathbf{e}_{\infty 1}\mathbf{e}_{\infty 12}^{\triangleright} = -\mathbf{e}_{\infty 2}\mathbf{e}_{\infty 12}^{\triangleright} = -\mathbf{e}_{\infty}\mathbf{e}_{\infty 12}^{\triangleright}, \tag{17}$$

which further lead to

$$\mathbf{I}_{\infty} = -\mathbf{e}_{\infty 1} \wedge \mathbf{I}_{\infty}^{\triangleright} = -\mathbf{e}_{\infty 2} \wedge \mathbf{I}_{\infty}^{\triangleright} = -\mathbf{e}_{\infty} \wedge \mathbf{I}_{\infty}^{\triangleright}$$

$$= -\mathbf{e}_{\infty 1}\mathbf{I}_{\infty}^{\triangleright} = -\mathbf{e}_{\infty 2}\mathbf{I}_{\infty}^{\triangleright} = -\mathbf{e}_{\infty}\mathbf{I}_{\infty}^{\triangleright}, \tag{18}$$

Similar to [11] we obtain for products with the simple 6-vector $\mathbf{I}_{\infty}^{\triangleright}$ that

$$\{1, \mathbf{e}_{o}, \mathbf{e}_{\infty}, E\} \wedge \mathbf{I}_{\infty}^{\triangleright} = \{1, \mathbf{e}_{o}, \mathbf{e}_{\infty}, E\}\mathbf{I}_{\infty}^{\triangleright} = \mathbf{I}_{\infty}^{\triangleright}\{1, \mathbf{e}_{o}, \mathbf{e}_{\infty}, E\}, \tag{19}$$

We define the pseudo-scalar $\mathbf{I}_{\epsilon}$ in $\mathbb{R}^2$:

$$\mathbf{I}_{\epsilon} = \mathbf{e}_1\mathbf{e}_2, \quad \mathbf{I}_{\epsilon}^2 = -1, \quad \mathbf{I}_{\epsilon}^{-1} = -\mathbf{I}_{\epsilon}. \tag{20}$$

The full pseudo-scalar $\mathbf{I}$ and its inverse $\mathbf{I}^{-1}$ (used for dualization) are:

$$\mathbf{I} = \mathbf{I}_{\epsilon}\mathbf{I}_{\infty o} = -\mathbf{I}_{\epsilon}E_1 E_2 E_3 E_4 E_5 E_6 E_7, \quad \mathbf{I}^2 = -1, \quad \mathbf{I}^{-1} = -\mathbf{I}. \tag{21}$$

The dual of a multivector indicates division by the pseudo-scalar, e.g., $\mathbf{a}^* = -\mathbf{a}\mathbf{I}$, $\mathbf{a} = \mathbf{a}^*\mathbf{I}$. From Eq. (1.19) in [10], we have the useful duality between outer and inner products of non-scalar blades A, B in geometric algebra:

$$(A \wedge B)^* = A \cdot B^*, \quad A \wedge (B^*) = (A \cdot B)^* \quad \Leftrightarrow \quad A \wedge (B\mathbf{I}) = (A \cdot B)\mathbf{I}, \tag{22}$$

which indicates that

$$A \wedge B = 0 \quad \Leftrightarrow \quad A \cdot B^* = 0, \qquad A \cdot B = 0 \quad \Leftrightarrow \quad A \wedge B^* = 0. \tag{23}$$

3   Point in Cubic CGA

The point $\mathbf{x}$ of cubic CGA corresponding to the Euclidean point $\mathbf{x}_\epsilon = x\mathbf{e}_1 + y\mathbf{e}_2 \in \mathbb{R}^2$, is defined as[1]

$$\mathbf{x} = \mathbf{x}_\epsilon + \tfrac{1}{2}(x^2\mathbf{e}_{\infty 1} + y^2\mathbf{e}_{\infty 2}) + xy\mathbf{e}_{\infty 3} + x^3\mathbf{e}_{\infty 4} + x^2 y\mathbf{e}_{\infty 5} + xy^2\mathbf{e}_{\infty 6} + y^3\mathbf{e}_{\infty 7} + \mathbf{e}_o. \tag{24}$$

Note that basically each quadratic and cubic coordinate monomial is assigned to a different infinity null vector. Standard CGA $Cl(3,1)$ has only one infinity null vector, which means that only objects of constant curvature (flat or round) can be described. Already, the fundamental approach for the description of conics by Perwass [16] in $Cl(5,3)$ needed to assign each of the quadratic monomials x^2, y^2 and xy to individual, linearly independent (mutually orthogonal) null vector dimensions. Our point definition (24) is the consequent continuation of this approach. Note further that the five null vectors $\mathbf{e}_{o3}, \mathbf{e}_{o4}, \mathbf{e}_{o5}, \mathbf{e}_{o6}, \mathbf{e}_{o7}$ are not present in the definition of the point. This is chiefly to keep the convenient properties of the CGA points, namely, the inner product between two points is identical with the squared distance between them. Let $\mathbf{x}_1$ and $\mathbf{x}_2$ be two points, their inner product is

$$\mathbf{x}_1 \cdot \mathbf{x}_2 =$$
$$(\mathbf{x}_{1\epsilon} + \tfrac{1}{2}x_1^2\mathbf{e}_{\infty 1} + \tfrac{1}{2}y_1^2\mathbf{e}_{\infty 2} + x_1 y_1\mathbf{e}_{\infty 3} + x_1^3\mathbf{e}_{\infty 4} + x_1^2 y_1\mathbf{e}_{\infty 5} + x_1 y_1^2\mathbf{e}_{\infty 6} + y_1^3\mathbf{e}_{\infty 7} + \mathbf{e}_o)$$
$$\cdot (\mathbf{x}_{2\epsilon} + \tfrac{1}{2}x_2^2\mathbf{e}_{\infty 1} + \tfrac{1}{2}y_2^2\mathbf{e}_{\infty 2} + x_2 y_2\mathbf{e}_{\infty 3} + + x_2^3\mathbf{e}_{\infty 4} + x_2^2 y_2\mathbf{e}_{\infty 5} + x_2 y_2^2\mathbf{e}_{\infty 6} + y_2^3\mathbf{e}_{\infty 7} + \mathbf{e}_o). \tag{25}$$

from which together with Table 1, it follows that

$$\mathbf{x}_1 \cdot \mathbf{x}_2 = \mathbf{x}_{1\epsilon} \cdot \mathbf{x}_{2\epsilon} - \tfrac{1}{2}(x_1^2 + y_1^2 + x_2^2 + y_2^2) = -\tfrac{1}{2}(\mathbf{x}_{1\epsilon} - \mathbf{x}_{2\epsilon})^2. \tag{26}$$

We see that the inner product is equivalent to the minus half of the squared Euclidean distance between $\mathbf{x}_1$ and $\mathbf{x}_2$.

By wedging a cubic CGA point with the blade $\mathbf{I}_{\infty c}$ we obtain

$$\mathbf{x} \wedge \mathbf{I}_{\infty c} = \left(\mathbf{x}_\epsilon + \tfrac{1}{2}(x^2\mathbf{e}_{\infty 1} + y^2\mathbf{e}_{\infty 2}) + xy\mathbf{e}_{\infty 3} + \mathbf{e}_o\right) \wedge \mathbf{I}_{\infty c} \tag{27}$$
$$= \mathbf{x}_{\text{conic}} \wedge \mathbf{I}_{\infty c} = \mathbf{x}_{\text{conic}}\mathbf{I}_{\infty c}, \tag{28}$$

that is all four third power terms in the coordinates x^3, $x^2 y$, xy^2, y^3 drop out, and what remains is identical to the conic point definition $\mathbf{x}_{\text{conic}}$ in conic CGA $Cl(5,3)$ generated by the basis $\{\mathbf{e}_1, \mathbf{e}_2, \mathbf{e}_{o1}, \mathbf{e}_{\infty 1}, \mathbf{e}_{o2}, \mathbf{e}_{\infty 2}, \mathbf{e}_{o3}, \mathbf{e}_{\infty 3}\}$ in [11]. The conic point can be obtained explicitly by

$$\mathbf{x}_{\text{conic}} = \mathbf{x}_\epsilon + \tfrac{1}{2}(x^2\mathbf{e}_{\infty 1} + y^2\mathbf{e}_{\infty 2}) + xy\mathbf{e}_{\infty 3} + \mathbf{e}_o = (\mathbf{x} \wedge \mathbf{I}_{\infty c})\lfloor \mathbf{I}_{oc}. \tag{29}$$

A consequence of this embedding of conic CGA in cubic CGA is, that all results of conic CGA are perfectly valid in cubic CGA.

---

[1] The use of the factor one half in $\tfrac{1}{2}(x^2\mathbf{e}_{\infty 1} + y^2\mathbf{e}_{\infty 2})$ is taken over from the point definition in standard CGA [6], and has importance in preserving the inner product to distance relationship of CGA in (26).

Furthermore, by wedging a cubic CGA point with the blade $\mathbf{I}_\infty^\triangleright$ we obtain

$$
\begin{aligned}
\mathbf{x} \wedge \mathbf{I}_\infty^\triangleright &= \left(\mathbf{x}_\epsilon + \tfrac{1}{2}(x^2 \mathbf{e}_{\infty 1} + y^2 \mathbf{e}_{\infty 2}) + \mathbf{e}_o\right) \wedge \mathbf{I}_\infty^\triangleright = \left(\mathbf{x}_\epsilon + \tfrac{1}{2}(x^2 + y^2)\mathbf{e}_\infty + \mathbf{e}_o\right) \wedge \mathbf{I}_\infty^\triangleright \\
&= \left(\mathbf{x}_\epsilon + \tfrac{1}{2}\mathbf{x}_\epsilon^2 \mathbf{e}_\infty + \mathbf{e}_o\right) \wedge \mathbf{I}_\infty^\triangleright = \mathbf{x}_C \wedge \mathbf{I}_\infty^\triangleright = \mathbf{x}_C \mathbf{I}_\infty^\triangleright,
\end{aligned} \tag{30}
$$

that is all four third power terms in the coordinates x^3, $x^2 y$, xy^2, y^3 and the mixed second order term xy drop out, and what remains is identical to the standard CGA point definition $\mathbf{x}_C$ in standard CGA $Cl(3,1)$ of the Euclidean plane generated by the basis $\{\mathbf{e}_1, \mathbf{e}_2, \mathbf{e}_o, \mathbf{e}_\infty\}$. The standard CGA point $\mathbf{x}_C$ can be obtained explicitly[2] by

$$
\mathbf{x}_C = \mathbf{x}_\epsilon + \tfrac{1}{2}\mathbf{x}_\epsilon^2 \mathbf{e}_\infty + \mathbf{e}_o = -\tfrac{1}{2}(\mathbf{x} \wedge \mathbf{I}_\infty^\triangleright)\lfloor \mathbf{I}_o^\triangleright. \tag{31}
$$

We thus see, that standard CGA of the Euclidean plane in $Cl(3,1)$ is fully embedded in cubic CGA $Cl(9,7)$. The sequence of embedding is standard CGA in conic CGA in cubic CGA.

4   Cubic Curve

This section describes how cubic CGA handles plane cubic curves. A cubic curve in $\mathbb{R}^2$ is formulated as

$$
F(x,y) = ax^3 + bx^2 y + cxy^2 + dy^3 + ex^2 + fy^2 + gxy + hx + iy + j = 0. \tag{32}
$$

We note, that *the set of cubic curves has a natural structure of a projective space* $\mathbb{P}^9$ [15]. The first way to represent a cubic curve in cubic CGA is constructive by wedging nine contact points together as follows

$$
\mathbf{q} = \mathbf{x}_1 \wedge \mathbf{x}_2 \wedge \cdots \wedge \mathbf{x}_9. \tag{33}
$$

The multivector $\mathbf{q}$ corresponds to the primal form of a cubic curve in cubic CGA, with grade nine and essentially ten components, with ten coefficients a, b, ..., j. If we further wedge[3] the 9-blade $\mathbf{q}$ with the 6-blade $\mathbf{I}_o^\triangleright$, we obtain a 15-blade

$$
\begin{aligned}
\mathbf{q} \wedge \mathbf{I}_0^\triangleright &= \left(-(2e\mathbf{e}_{o1} + 2f\mathbf{e}_{o2} + g\mathbf{e}_{o3} + a\mathbf{e}_{o4} + b\mathbf{e}_{o5} + c\mathbf{e}_{o6} + d\mathbf{e}_{o7}) + h\mathbf{e}_1 + i\mathbf{e}_2 - j\mathbf{e}_\infty\right) \mathbf{I} \\
&= (\mathbf{q} \wedge \mathbf{I}_0^\triangleright)^* \mathbf{I},
\end{aligned} \tag{34}
$$

---

[2] The operation $(\mathbf{x} \wedge \mathbf{I}_\infty^\triangleright)\lfloor \mathbf{I}_o^\triangleright$ combining outer product and contraction is typical for projection operations in geometric algebra. For example, in $Cl(3,0)$ the projection of multivector $\mathbf{a}$ onto a blade $\mathbf{b}$ is given by $(\mathbf{a} \wedge \mathbf{b})\lfloor \mathbf{b}^{-1}$. Since $\mathbf{I}_\infty^\triangleright$ is a product of null vectors and has no inverse, the projection operation is completed by contracting with $\mathbf{I}_o^\triangleright$ from the right, see (16).

[3] This is a strategy similarly employed by Perwass for conics [16] and in [11], and for quadrics in [3,12]. Treating the outer product of contact points (33) as the actual algebraic representation of the geometric object in question, was essential for the formulation of rotations, translations and scaling by means of versors in [12]. We intuitively expect that this may turn out to be similar in the current cubic CGA $Cl(9,7)$.

The expression for the dual 1-vector $(\mathbf{q} \wedge \mathbf{I}_o^{\triangleright})^*$ is therefore simply

$$(\mathbf{q} \wedge \mathbf{I}_o^{\triangleright})^* = -(2e\mathbf{e}_{o1} + 2f\mathbf{e}_{o2} + g\mathbf{e}_{o3} + a\mathbf{e}_{o4} + b\mathbf{e}_{o5} + c\mathbf{e}_{o6} + d\mathbf{e}_{o7}) + h\mathbf{e}_1 + i\mathbf{e}_2 - j\mathbf{e}_{\infty}. \tag{35}$$

Proposition 4.1. *A point* $\mathbf{x}$ *lies on the cubic curve* $\mathbf{q}$ *if and only* $\mathbf{x} \wedge \mathbf{q} \wedge \mathbf{I}_o^{\triangleright} = 0$.

Proof.

$$\begin{aligned}
\mathbf{x} \wedge (\mathbf{q} \wedge \mathbf{I}_o^{\triangleright}) &= \mathbf{x} \wedge ((\mathbf{q} \wedge \mathbf{I}_o^{\triangleright})^* \mathbf{I}) = \mathbf{x} \cdot (\mathbf{q} \wedge \mathbf{I}_o^{\triangleright})^* \mathbf{I} \\
&= \mathbf{x} \cdot \big(-(2e\mathbf{e}_{o1} + 2f\mathbf{e}_{o2} + g\mathbf{e}_{o3} + a\mathbf{e}_{o4} + b\mathbf{e}_{o5} + c\mathbf{e}_{o6} + d\mathbf{e}_{o7}) \\
&\quad + h\mathbf{e}_1 + i\mathbf{e}_2 - j\mathbf{e}_{\infty} \big) \mathbf{I} \\
&= (ax^3 + bx^2y + cxy^2 + dy^3 + ex^2 + fy^2 + gxy + hx + iy + j) \mathbf{I}.
\end{aligned} \tag{36}$$

This corresponds to the formula (32) representing a general cubic curve.

The dualization of the primal cubic $\mathbf{q}$ wedged with $\mathbf{I}_o^{\triangleright}$ leads to the 1-vector dual form $(\mathbf{q} \wedge \mathbf{I}_o^{\triangleright})^*$ of (35).

Corollary 4.2. *A point* $\mathbf{x}$ *lies on the cubic curve defined by* $\mathbf{q}$ *if and only if* $\mathbf{x} \cdot (\mathbf{q} \wedge \mathbf{I}_0^{\triangleright})^* = 0$.

The ten coefficients $\{a, \ldots, j\}$ of the cubic equation (32) can be easily extracted from the cubic curve 9-blade $\mathbf{q}$ of (33) by computing the following scalar products with vector $(\mathbf{q} \wedge \mathbf{I}_o^{\triangleright})^*$ as

$$\begin{aligned}
a &= (\mathbf{q} \wedge \mathbf{I}_o^{\triangleright})^* \cdot \mathbf{e}_{\infty 4}, \quad b = (\mathbf{q} \wedge \mathbf{I}_o^{\triangleright})^* \cdot \mathbf{e}_{\infty 5}, \quad c = (\mathbf{q} \wedge \mathbf{I}_o^{\triangleright})^* \cdot \mathbf{e}_{\infty 6}, \\
d &= (\mathbf{q} \wedge \mathbf{I}_o^{\triangleright})^* \cdot \mathbf{e}_{\infty 7}, \quad e = \tfrac{1}{2}(\mathbf{q} \wedge \mathbf{I}_o^{\triangleright})^* \cdot \mathbf{e}_{\infty 1}, \quad f = \tfrac{1}{2}(\mathbf{q} \wedge \mathbf{I}_o^{\triangleright})^* \cdot \mathbf{e}_{\infty 2}, \\
g &= (\mathbf{q} \wedge \mathbf{I}_o^{\triangleright})^* \cdot \mathbf{e}_{\infty 3}, \quad h = (\mathbf{q} \wedge \mathbf{I}_o^{\triangleright})^* \cdot \mathbf{e}_1, \quad i = (\mathbf{q} \wedge \mathbf{I}_o^{\triangleright})^* \cdot \mathbf{e}_2, \\
j &= (\mathbf{q} \wedge \mathbf{I}_o^{\triangleright})^* \cdot \mathbf{e}_o.
\end{aligned} \tag{37}$$

Remark 4.3. Based on the ten coefficients of the implicit cubic equation (32), the vector $(\mathbf{q} \wedge \mathbf{I}_o^{\triangleright})^*$ of (35), can easily be constructed, providing another valid dual representation of the cubic curve in cubic CGA, that can e.g. be used for intersection computations as described in the next Section.

5   Intersections

Any number of linearly independent embedded standard CGA objects, embedded conics and cubic curves $\{\mathbf{A}, \mathbf{B}, \ldots, \mathbf{Z}\}$, after wedging with the 6-blade $\mathbf{I}_o^{\triangleright}$, can be intersected by computing the dual of the outer product of their duals

$$(\mathbf{M} \wedge \mathbf{I}_o^{\triangleright})^* = (\mathbf{A} \wedge \mathbf{I}_o^{\triangleright})^* \wedge (\mathbf{B} \wedge \mathbf{I}_o^{\triangleright})^* \wedge \ldots \wedge (\mathbf{Z} \wedge \mathbf{I}_o^{\triangleright})^*. \tag{38}$$

The approach is analogous to intersecting two circles in CGA $Cl(3,1)$ of two-dimensional Euclidean space, or two spheres in CGA $Cl(4,1)$ of three-dimensional Euclidean space. But in $Cl(3,1)$ [8] and $Cl(4,1)$ [6,10] there is only one pair of null-vectors $\mathbf{e}_o$, $\mathbf{e}_\infty$, and both are used in the point construction. In cubic CGA $Cl(9,7)$, there are seven pairs of null vectors $\mathbf{e}_{oi}$, $\mathbf{e}_{\infty i}$, $1 \leq i \leq 7$, and only one fixed combination of origin null vectors $\mathbf{e}_o = \mathbf{e}_{o1} + \mathbf{e}_{o2}$ of (2) is actually used for the cubic point construction (24). That is essentially six origin null vector dimensions do not appear in the point construction, and therefore also not in the multivector $\mathbf{q}$ representing a cubic curve (33). To make up for that, and to maintain the computation of intersections from dual 1-vector representations, the outer product with the 6-blade $\mathbf{I}_o^\triangleright$ extends the multivector $\mathbf{q}$ to a 14-blade $\mathbf{q} \wedge \mathbf{I}_o^\triangleright$, which by dualization results in the dual 1-vector representation.

A criterion for a general point $\mathbf{x}$ to be on the intersection $\mathbf{M}$ is

$$\mathbf{x} \cdot (\mathbf{M} \wedge \mathbf{I}_o^\triangleright)^* = 0, \qquad \mathbf{M} = -\tfrac{1}{2}((\mathbf{M} \wedge \mathbf{I}_o^\triangleright)^* \mathbf{I}) \lfloor \mathbf{I}_\infty^\triangleright. \tag{39}$$

The last equation allows to extract the intersection blade $\mathbf{M}$ itself. The product with $\mathbf{I}$ reverses dualization, and the subsequent right contraction with $\mathbf{I}_\infty^\triangleright$ removes the factor $\mathbf{I}_o^\triangleright$, according to (16).

6   Cubic Surfaces

Though it may still be far beyond today's computing power, cubic surfaces are a classical subject in mathematics, and they indeed can be represented in a cubic surface CGA (CSCGA) $Cl(3 + 16, 16) = Cl(19, 16)$ over the real vector space $\mathbb{R}^{19,16}$. We are not able to state all the details here, but will try to outline the algebraic approach.

The vector basis of $\mathbb{R}^{19,16}$ consists of the three Euclidean orthonormal vectors $\{\mathbf{e}_1, \mathbf{e}_2, \mathbf{e}_3\}$, their product forming the Euclidean three dimensional unit pseudoscalar

$$\mathbf{I}_3 = \mathbf{e}_1 \mathbf{e}_2 \mathbf{e}_3, \quad \mathbf{I}_3^2 = -1, \quad \mathbf{I}_3^{-1} = -\mathbf{I}_3; \tag{40}$$

the remaining vectors form 16 pairs of null vectors, $\{\mathbf{e}_{\infty i}, \mathbf{e}_{oi}\}$, $1 \leq i \leq 16$,

$$\mathbf{e}_{\infty i}^2 = \mathbf{e}_{oi}^2 = 0, \quad \mathbf{e}_{\infty i} \cdot \mathbf{e}_{oi} = -1, \quad E_i = \mathbf{e}_{\infty i} \wedge \mathbf{e}_{oi}, \quad E_i^2 = 1. \tag{41}$$

We also define

$$\mathbf{e}_\infty = \tfrac{1}{3}(\mathbf{e}_{\infty 1} + \mathbf{e}_{\infty 2} + \mathbf{e}_{\infty 3}), \qquad \mathbf{e}_o = \mathbf{e}_{o1} + \mathbf{e}_{o2} + \mathbf{e}_{o3}. \tag{42}$$

We further define the following blades

$$\mathbf{I}_{\infty a}^\triangleright = (\mathbf{e}_{\infty 1} - \mathbf{e}_{\infty 2}) \wedge (\mathbf{e}_{\infty 2} - \mathbf{e}_{\infty 3}), \quad \mathbf{I}_{\infty b} = \mathbf{e}_{\infty 4} \mathbf{e}_{\infty 5} \mathbf{e}_{\infty 6}, \tag{43}$$

$$\mathbf{I}_{\infty c} = \mathbf{e}_{\infty 7} \mathbf{e}_{\infty 8} \mathbf{e}_{\infty 9} \mathbf{e}_{\infty 10} \mathbf{e}_{\infty 11} \mathbf{e}_{\infty 12} \mathbf{e}_{\infty 13} \mathbf{e}_{\infty 14} \mathbf{e}_{\infty 15} \mathbf{e}_{\infty 16}, \quad \mathbf{I}_\infty^\triangleright = \mathbf{I}_{\infty a}^\triangleright \mathbf{I}_{\infty b} \mathbf{I}_{\infty c}, \tag{44}$$

$$\mathbf{I}_{oa}^\triangleright = (\mathbf{e}_{o1} - \mathbf{e}_{o2}) \wedge (\mathbf{e}_{o2} - \mathbf{e}_{o3}), \quad \mathbf{I}_{ob} = \mathbf{e}_{o4} \mathbf{e}_{o5} \mathbf{e}_{o6}, \tag{45}$$

$$\mathbf{I}_{oc} = \mathbf{e}_{o7} \mathbf{e}_{o8} \mathbf{e}_{o9} \mathbf{e}_{o10} \mathbf{e}_{o11} \mathbf{e}_{o12} \mathbf{e}_{o13} \mathbf{e}_{o14} \mathbf{e}_{o15} \mathbf{e}_{o16}, \quad \mathbf{I}_o^\triangleright = \mathbf{I}_{oa}^\triangleright \mathbf{I}_{ob} \mathbf{I}_{oc}, \tag{46}$$

Inner products yield

$$\mathbf{I}_{\infty a}^\triangleright \cdot \mathbf{I}_{oa}^\triangleright = -3, \quad \mathbf{I}_\infty^\triangleright \cdot \mathbf{I}_o^\triangleright = +3, \quad \mathbf{I}_{\infty c} \cdot \mathbf{I}_{oc} = -1. \tag{47}$$

In this setting a cubic surface point in three dimensions is defined from its position in three dimensional Euclidean space $\mathbf{x}_\epsilon = x\mathbf{e}_1 + y\mathbf{e}_2 + z\mathbf{e}_3$ as an extension to the CGA point or to the quadric QCGA point [3]

$$
\begin{aligned}
\mathbf{x} =& \mathbf{x}_\epsilon + \tfrac{1}{2}(x^2\mathbf{e}_{\infty 1} + y^2\mathbf{e}_{\infty 2} + z^2\mathbf{e}_{\infty 3}) + xy\mathbf{e}_{\infty 4} + xz\mathbf{e}_{\infty 5} + yz\mathbf{e}_{\infty 6} \\
&+ x^3\mathbf{e}_{\infty 7} + x^2 y\mathbf{e}_{\infty 8} + x^2 z\mathbf{e}_{\infty 9} + xy^2\mathbf{e}_{\infty 10} + xyz\mathbf{e}_{\infty 11} + xz^2\mathbf{e}_{\infty 12} \\
&+ y^3\mathbf{e}_{\infty 13} + y^2 z\mathbf{e}_{\infty 14} + yz^2\mathbf{e}_{\infty 15} + z^3\mathbf{e}_{\infty 16} + \mathbf{e}_o.
\end{aligned} \tag{48}
$$

Note, that the vectors $\{\mathbf{e}_{o4}, \ldots, \mathbf{e}_{o16}\}$ are not used in the above point definition in order to preserve the CGA property that

$$
\mathbf{x}_1 \cdot \mathbf{x}_2 = \tfrac{1}{2}(\mathbf{x}_{1\epsilon} - \mathbf{x}_{2\epsilon})^2. \tag{49}
$$

By wedging a cubic surface point $\mathbf{x}$ with the 10-blade $\mathbf{I}_{\infty c}$, we effectively remove all third power coordinate components

$$
\begin{aligned}
\mathbf{x} \wedge \mathbf{I}_{\infty c} &= \left(\mathbf{x}_\epsilon + \tfrac{1}{2}(x^2\mathbf{e}_{\infty 1} + y^2\mathbf{e}_{\infty 2} + z^2\mathbf{e}_{\infty 3}) + xy\mathbf{e}_{\infty 4} + xz\mathbf{e}_{\infty 5} + yz\mathbf{e}_{\infty 6} + \mathbf{e}_o\right) \wedge \mathbf{I}_{\infty c} \\
&= \mathbf{x}_Q \mathbf{I}_{\infty c},
\end{aligned} \tag{50}
$$

which means to project down to the subalgebra of quadric surfaces $Cl(9,6)$ [3] with

$$
\begin{aligned}
\mathbf{x}_Q &= \mathbf{x}_\epsilon + \tfrac{1}{2}(x^2\mathbf{e}_{\infty 1} + y^2\mathbf{e}_{\infty 2} + z^2\mathbf{e}_{\infty 3}) + xy\mathbf{e}_{\infty 4} + xz\mathbf{e}_{\infty 5} + yz\mathbf{e}_{\infty 6} + \mathbf{e}_o \\
&= -(\mathbf{x} \wedge \mathbf{I}_{\infty c})\lfloor \mathbf{I}_{oc}
\end{aligned} \tag{51}
$$

By alternatively wedging a cubic surface point $\mathbf{x}$ with $\mathbf{I}_\infty^\triangleright$ we effectively project the point to a subalgebra isomorphic to standard CGA [6]

$$
\mathbf{x} \wedge \mathbf{I}_\infty^\triangleright = \left(\mathbf{x}_\epsilon + \tfrac{1}{2}(x^2 + y^2 + z^2)\mathbf{e}_\infty + \mathbf{e}_o\right) \wedge \mathbf{I}_\infty^\triangleright \tag{52}
$$

with standard CGA point

$$
\mathbf{x}_C = \mathbf{x}_\epsilon + \tfrac{1}{2}\mathbf{x}_\epsilon^2 \mathbf{e}_\infty + \mathbf{e}_o = \tfrac{1}{3}(\mathbf{x} \wedge \mathbf{I}_\infty^\triangleright)\lfloor \mathbf{I}_o^\triangleright. \tag{53}
$$

This means that we have standard CGA of three dimensions embedded in quadric CGA embedded in cubic surface CGA. So all the known results of standard CGA, and quadric CGA can be applied in cubic surface CGA.

Cubic surfaces in three dimensions are described by the implicit equation with 20 coefficients $a, b, \ldots t$,

$$
\begin{aligned}
F(x,y,z) =& ax^2 + by^2 + cz^2 + dxy + exz + fyz + gx^3 + hx^2 y + ix^2 z + jxy^2 + kxyz \\
&+ lxz^2 + my^3 + ny^2 z + oyz^2 + pz^3 + qx + ry + sz + t = 0.
\end{aligned} \tag{54}
$$

We note, that *cubic surfaces are parametrized by the points in (projective space)* $\mathbb{P}^{19}$ [5]. We can use 19 cubic surface contact points $\{\mathbf{x}_i, 1 \leq i \leq 19\}$, to form a 19-blade multivector in $Cl(19,16)$, describing a cubic surface $\mathbf{q}$ as

$$
\mathbf{q} = \mathbf{x}_1 \wedge \mathbf{x}_2 \wedge \ldots \mathbf{x}_{19}. \tag{55}
$$

Similar to the case of cubic curves we can identify points on a cubic surface as follows.

Proposition 6.1. *A point* $\mathbf{x}$ *lies on the three dimensional cubic surface* $\mathbf{q}$ *if and only* $\mathbf{x} \wedge \mathbf{q} \wedge \mathbf{I}_o^{\triangleright} = 0$.

The proof is analogous to the case of cubic curves. And we also obtain the corollary.

Corollary 6.2. *A point* $\mathbf{x}$ *lies on the cubic surface defined by* $\mathbf{q}$ *if and only if* $\mathbf{x} \cdot (\mathbf{q} \wedge \mathbf{I}_o^{\triangleright})^* = 0$.

The construction of the dual representation of a cubic surface $(\mathbf{q} \wedge \mathbf{I}_0^{\triangleright})^*$ is similarly possible from the 20 coefficients of the implicit Eq. (54). Finally intersection operations of linearly independent cubic surfaces work analogous to the description of the intersection of cubic curves given in Sect. 5.

7   Conclusion

This work described how to represent cubic curves by multivector blades in cubic conformal geometric algebra $Cl(9,7)$. The construction can either proceed from nine contact points or by using the ten coefficients of the implicit equation of a cubic curve in the plane. The multivector expressions obtained for cubic curves can then e.g. be used for computing the intersection of curves, using the outer product. It is found, that cubic CGA contains an embedding of conic CGA [11] and of standard CGA [6] of the Euclidean plane.

In future work, it is intended to optimize the Clifford Multivector Toolbox for Matlab [17] and GAALOP [8] further, so as to be able to compute with $Cl(9,7)$ on a standard PC. Furthermore, we intend to establish the geometric transformation versors for rotation, translation and scaling, which we expect to be somewhat more intricate than for conics in conic CGA [11,13,16]. We hope, that the current work on cubic curves in CGA will find applications, wherever cubic curves occur in computations and graphics, where they may be used for interpolation, etc.

In the last part, we described the analogous construction for the representation of cubic surfaces in three dimensions and their intersections in cubic surface CGA $Cl(19,16)$. This latter algebra may not yet be attainable to computations with current computer algebra systems, except perhaps with super computers. In this case as well research should be done for constructing versors for rotations, translations and scaling.

We deeply thank the Computer Graphics International 2019 organizers and the ENGAGE 2019 workshop organizers for providing the opportunity to present our latest research results. We gratefully acknowledge the helpful comments of the anonymous reviewers, and a last minute correction by S. De Keninck for Eq. (24). Author E. H. Requests that any application of this research should respect the Creative Peace License [9].

References

1. Abłamowicz, R.: Clifford algebra computations with maple. In: Baylis W.E. (eds), Clifford (Geometric) Algebras. Birkhäuser Boston (1996)
2. Aragon-Camarasa, G., et al.: Clifford algebra with mathematica. In: Proceedings of the 29th International Conference on Applied Mathematics, Budapest (2015). Preprint: arXiv:0810.2412
3. Breuils, S., Nozick, V., Sugimoto, A., Hitzer, E.: Quadric conformal geometric algebra of $\mathbb{R}^{9,6}$. Adv. Appl. Clifford Algebras **28**(35), 1–16 (2018). https://doi.org/10.1007/s00006-018-0851-1
4. Breuils, S., Nozick, V., Fuchs, L.: GARAMON: geometric algebra library generator. In: Xambo-Descamps, S., et al. (eds.) Early Proceedings of the AGACSE 2018 Conference, 23–27 July 2018, Campinas, São Paulo, Brazil, pp. 97–106 (2018)
5. Buckley, A., Košir, T.: Determinantal representations of smooth cubic surfaces. Geom. Dedicata **125**(1), 115–140 (2007). https://doi.org/10.1007/s10711-007-9144-x
6. Dorst, L., Fontijne, D., Mann, S.: Geometric Algebra for Computer Science: An Object-Oriented Approach to Geometry. Morgan Kaufmann, Burlington (2007)
7. Easter, R.B., Hitzer, E.: Triple conformal geometric algebra for cubic plane curves. Math. Methods Appl. Sci. **41**(11), 4088–4105 (2018). https://doi.org/10.1002/mma.4597. Preprint: http://vixra.org/pdf/1807.0091v1.pdf
8. Hildenbrand, D.: Introduction to Geometric Algebra Computing. CRC Press, Taylor & Francis Group, Boca Raton (2018)
9. Hitzer, E.: The Creative Peace License. https://gaupdate.wordpress.com/2011/12/14/the-creative-peace-license-14-dec-2011/. Accessed 5 Apr 2019
10. Hitzer, E., Tachibana, K., Buchholz, S., Yu, I.: Carrier method for the general evaluation and control of pose, molecular conformation, tracking, and the like. Adv. Appl. Clifford Algebras **19**(2), 339–364 (2009). https://doi.org/10.1007/s00006-009-0160-9
11. Hitzer, E., Sangwine, S. J.: Foundations of conic conformal geometric algebra and simplified versors for rotation, translation and scaling, to be published
12. Hitzer, E.: Three-dimensional quadrics in conformal geometric algebras and their versor transformations. Adv. Appl. Clifford Algebras **29**, 46 (2019). https://doi.org/10.1007/s00006-019-0964-1. Preprint: http://vixra.org/pdf/1902.0401v4.pdf
13. Hrdina, J., Navrat, A., Vasik, P.: Geometric algebra for conics. Adv. Appl. Clifford Algebras **28**(66), 21 (2018). https://doi.org/10.1007/s00006-018-0879-2
14. De Keninck, S.: ganja.js - geometric algebra for Javascript. https://github.com/enkimute/ganja.js. Accessed 03 May 2019
15. Newstead, P.E.: Geometric invariant theory. In: Bradlow, S.B., et al. (eds.) Moduli Spaces and Vector Bundles, pp. 99–127. Cambridge University Press, Cambridge (2009). https://doi.org/10.1017/CBO9781139107037.005. https://www.cimat.mx/Eventos/cvectorbundles/newsteadnotes.pdf
16. Perwass, C.: Geometric Algebra with Applications in Engineering. Springer, Heidelberg (2008). https://doi.org/10.1007/978-3-540-89068-3
17. Sangwine, S.J., Hitzer, E.: Clifford multivector toolbox (for MATLAB). Adv. Appl. Clifford Algebras **27**(1), 539–558 (2017). https://doi.org/10.1007/s00006-016-0666-x. Preprint: http://repository.essex.ac.uk/16434/1/authorfinal.pdf

ENGAGE'19 Workshop Short Papers

Non-parametric Realtime Rendering of Subspace Objects in Arbitrary Geometric Algebras

Steven De Keninck[✉]

Matrix Factory, Hingene, Bornem, Belgium
enkimute@gmail.com

Abstract. This paper introduces a novel visualization method for elements of arbitrary Geometric Algebras. The algorithm removes the need for a parametric representation, requires no precomputation, and produces high quality images in realtime. It visualizes the outer product null space (OPNS) of 2-dimensional manifolds directly and uses an isosurface approach to display 1- and 0-dimensional manifolds. A multi-platform browser based implementation is publicly available.

Keywords: Geometric algebra · Implicit visualization · OPNS

1 Introduction

Since its inception, Clifford's Geometric Algebra has become the host of a wide range of algebras, and with it an equally wide range of geometries. They go from the projective $\mathbb{R}^*_{3,0,1}$, (aka PGA [1]), the smallest model with versors covering SE(3), over the popular conformal $\mathbb{R}_{4,1}$ (aka CGA [2,3]), all the way up to $\mathbb{R}_{9,6}$ (aka QCGA [9]), where 9 points in general configuration can be joined into the quadric surface passing through them.

These GA's naturally embed points, lines, planes, spheres, quadrics and much more. Such a wealth of objects comes with its own challenges, one of which is visualization. For a subset of these algebras (notably PGA [1] and CGA [3]), parametric representations of (non degenerate) algebraic elements are well known, and have been the primary method for visualization. (with GAViewer [4] and CLUCalc [5] still being the go-to tools). For higher dimensional algebras the visualization methods used are limited to either raytracing or voxel-based OPNS rendering (see for example [9], 2018). These methods are limited in the items they can render, not realtime, require substantial precomputation, produce low quality images, work only for one algebra, or suffer a combination of these drawbacks.

The algorithm presented in this paper overcomes all of these problems. The quality of its images easily compares to raytracing, without the need for algebra-specific ray-intersection or normal/tangent formulas. Additionally, it can visualize isosurfaces around 1- and 0-dimensional manifolds, as well as non-blade

© Springer Nature Switzerland AG 2019
M. Gavrilova et al. (Eds.): CGI 2019, LNCS 11542, pp. 549–555, 2019.
https://doi.org/10.1007/978-3-030-22514-8_54

and/or mixed multivectors. In Sect. 2 we present the algorithm and review some of the implementation details. In Sect. 3 we present some examples, concluding in Sect. 4 (Fig. 1).

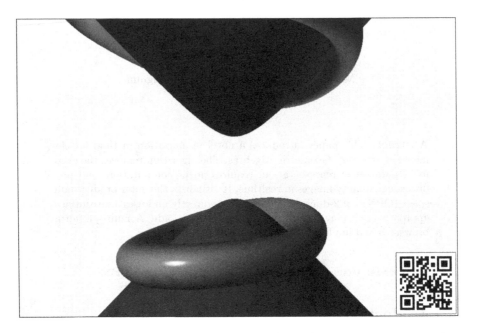

Fig. 1. A quadric (purple) and its intersection (orange) with another quadric (not drawn) in $\mathbb{R}_{9,6}$. (Color figure online)

2 Implicit OPNS Rendering

2.1 OPNS Representation

The graded nature of Clifford's algebras aligns naturally with a geometric interpretation where 0-, 1- and 2-dimensional manifolds embedded in three dimensional Euclidean space are constructed using the outer product. (or depending on the algebra, the regressive ($\vee$) product.)

For these algebras (including PGA [1], CGA [3], MA [10], QCGA [9], ..), a point p lies on the geometric object defined by the multivector $\mathbf{M}$ iff:

$$p \wedge \mathbf{M} = 0 \tag{1}$$

This is the implicit definition of the geometry of $\mathbf{M}$. The collection of all points p for which (1) holds is called the Outer Product Null Space (OPNS). Our algorithm directly visualizes the outer product null space using a ray marching technique to find the roots of the squared norm of the outer product (where the overline denotes the Clifford conjugate):

$$(p \wedge \mathbf{M})\overline{(p \wedge \mathbf{M})} = 0 \tag{2}$$

The result of (2) is a scalar value that is used to modify the ray-marching step size. For 2-dimensional manifolds embedded in Euclidean 3-space, the result of (2) will be signed, and the ray-marching method can easily be used to detect the sign change as each ray intersects the surface. For 1- and 0-dimensional items, curves and (collections of) points, (2) will not always admit a sign-change, and a threshold value (γ) is used to visualize the isosurface belonging to the shape of these subspaces, by finding the locations p that solve:

$$f(p, \mathbf{M}) = ((p \wedge \mathbf{M})\overline{(p \wedge \mathbf{M})}) - \gamma \tag{3}$$

The metric properties of (3) can vary greatly depending on the algebra, its point parametrization, and the grade of the element being rendered. In all cases however (3) is a continuous smooth function along a display ray and its roots can be found using numerical methods. We propose using (3) as a signed distance bound, and introduce a linear scale α and an exponential scale β to guarantee:

$$\left|(\alpha(p \wedge \mathbf{M})\overline{(p \wedge \mathbf{M})})^{\beta} - \gamma\right| \leq \min_{q \in \mathbf{M}} \|q - p\| \tag{4}$$

i.e. that the absolute value of the signed distance bound $f(p, \mathbf{M})$ between the point p and the multivector $\mathbf{M}$ is strictly smaller than the distance from p to any of the points that make up $\mathbf{M}$. In practice, the algorithm is robust even for sub-optimal choices for α and β, only affecting rendering performance.

2.2 Sphere Tracing

Originally introduced by Hart [7] in 1994, sphere tracing is now commonly known as signed distance field rendering. Over the past decade, with increased GPU flexibility, the technique has gained popularity, (e.g. [8]), despite its limited scope (it is not trivially suited to render polygonal meshes). It is however well-suited for our purposes. At heart it is a simple modification of the ray marching algorithm, where the step size is adjusted in each iteration based on the value of the signed distance bound. Starting from the camera position, specified by the Euclidean vector $\mathbf{p}_c$, we aim to find the smallest positive distance d along a ray with unit direction vector $\mathbf{r}$ for which the signed distance bound is zero:

$$f(\mathbf{p}_c + d\mathbf{r}, \mathbf{M}) = 0 \tag{5}$$

Starting from $d = 0$, the algorithm updates d each step with the result from the distance bound until it changes sign or is sufficiently close to zero.

$$d_{n+1} = d_n + |f(\mathbf{p}_c + d_n\mathbf{r}, \mathbf{M})| \tag{6}$$

Given our limited space, we refer the interested reader to [7] for more details and instead focus on the challenges specific to the rendering of GA elements. Notably, we will need to convert Euclidean points along the camera ray to their GA equivalent, and calculate the result of (4) without using the storage it would naively require.

2.3   Point Parametrization

With the exception of PGA, point parametrizations in Geometric Algebras are typically non-linear, and we start by adjusting (5) to reflect this change.

$$d_{n+1} = d_n + f(\text{up}(\mathbf{p}_c + d_n \mathbf{r}), \mathbf{M}) \tag{7}$$

where "up" is a multivector valued function of a vector. It is used to convert the point at location $\mathbf{p}_c + d_n \mathbf{r}$ to its GA representation (typically a 1-vector). To facilitate automatic code generation, point parametrizations have to be specified using only the unit basis vectors. (no n_o or n_∞). Table 1 lists those parametrizations for a selection of modern GA's.

Table 1. Point parametrizations for a selection of GA's.

Algebra		Parametrization
PGA [1]	$\mathbb{R}^*_{3,0,1}$	$[1, x, y, z]$
CGA [3]	$\mathbb{R}_{4,1}$	$[x, y, z, \frac{1}{2}(x^2 + y^2 + z^2) - \frac{1}{2}, \frac{1}{2}(x^2 + y^2 + z^2) + \frac{1}{2}]$
MA [10]	$\mathbb{R}_{4,4}$	$[\frac{1}{2}, \frac{1}{2}x, \frac{1}{2}y, \frac{1}{2}z, \frac{1}{2}, \frac{1}{2}x, \frac{1}{2}y, \frac{1}{2}z]$
CCGA [11]	$\mathbb{R}_{6,3}$	$[x, y, z, \frac{1}{2}x^2 - \frac{1}{2}, \frac{1}{2}y^2 - \frac{1}{2}, \frac{1}{2}z^2 - \frac{1}{2}, \frac{1}{2}x^2 + \frac{1}{2}, \frac{1}{2}y^2 + \frac{1}{2}, \frac{1}{2}z^2 + \frac{1}{2}]$
QCGA [9]	$\mathbb{R}_{9,6}$	$[x, y, z, \frac{1}{2}x^2 - \frac{1}{2}, \frac{1}{2}y^2 - \frac{1}{2}, \frac{1}{2}z^2 - \frac{1}{2}, xy, xz, yz, \frac{1}{2}x^2 + \frac{1}{2}, \frac{1}{2}y^2 + \frac{1}{2}, \frac{1}{2}z^2 + \frac{1}{2}, xy, xz, yz]$

2.4   Code Generation

A straightforward implementation of the formula in (4) requires storing the result of the outer product $p \wedge \mathbf{M}$. While a graded, sparse format provides substantial savings, in an algebra like QCGA this would still require several hundred components to be stored.

With one ray per pixel and hundreds of these evaluations per ray, a realtime implementation seems impossible on today's GPU hardware. We note however that the result of the outer product in (4) is only used to calculate the norm, an operation that can be replaced with squaring each coefficient and multiplying it with its weight (the corresponding element on the diagonal of the Cayley table).

If we calculate the norm in this way, we can also reorder the operations for the outer product so that we reduce the storage requirements to just two floating point variables. One is used to calculate the next component of the outer product while the other accumulates the squared norm. (see listing 1 for an example).

To generate the required GLSL (openGL Shading Language) code, we first added a graded, sparse, numerical GA generator to the ganja.js [6] library. This generator was then extended with a symbolic generator capable of dynamically creating the shader code. The source code for these generators is publicly available and we include a listing (listing 1) of the resulting shader that calculates the signed distance bound between a Euclidean point defined by (x, y, z) and a circle in $\mathbb{R}_{4,1}$ CGA. Using the generated distance bound function, implementation of the ray marching algorithm is trivial, and enables us to find the intersection between a ray and an arbitrary multivector.

```
float bound (in float z, in float y, in float x, in float[10] b, in float A,
in float B) {
  float sum; float res;
  res = x*b[6] - y*b[3] + z*b[1] - (.5*(x*x+y*y+z*z)-.5)*b[0];
  sum = res*res;
  res = x*b[7] - y*b[4] + z*b[2] - (.5*(x*x+y*y+z*z)+.5)*b[0];
  sum -= res*res;
  res = x*b[8] - y*b[5] + (.5*(x*x+y*y+z*z)-.5)*b[2] - (.5*(x*x+y*y+z*z)+.5)*b[1];
  sum -= res*res;
  res = x*b[9] - z*b[5] + (.5*(x*x+y*y+z*z)-.5)*b[4] - (.5*(x*x+y*y+z*z)+.5)*b[3];
  sum -= res*res;
  res = y*b[9] - z*b[8] + (.5*(x*x+y*y+z*z)-.5)*b[7] - (.5*(x*x+y*y+z*z)+.5)*b[6];
  sum -= res*res;
  return pow(A*sum,B);
}
```

listing 1. Reordering the outer product components and interleaving the norm calculations allows for a storage-free evaluation (here between CGA circle (given by b) and Euclidean point at location $[x, y, z]$).

2.5 Normals

Finding the point of intersection is however not sufficient for lighting and shading, for which we need to find or approximate the tangent space to the multivector at the point of intersection. Recognizing that our distance bound function is a smooth function (around the intersection point), we exploit the local isomorphy to $\mathbb{R}^3$, and calculate the local normal using the method known as central differences. (see listing 2, the h value is chosen to produce a sub-pixel offset).

```
vec3 n = normalize(vec3(
      bound(d2[0]+h,d2[1],d2[2],b,alpha,beta)-bound(d2[0]-h,d2[1],d2[2],b,alpha,beta),
      bound(d2[0],d2[1]+h,d2[2],b,alpha,beta)-bound(d2[0],d2[1]-h,d2[2],b,alpha,beta),
      bound(d2[0],d2[1],d2[2]+h,b,alpha,beta)-bound(d2[0],d2[1],d2[2]-h,b,alpha,beta)
      ));
```

listing 2. Using central differences to calculate the normal.

3   Some Examples

3.1   High Dimensional

Using only the parametrizations from Table 1, we produce a number of realtime images in $\mathbb{R}_{4,4}$, $\mathbb{R}_{6,3}$ and $\mathbb{R}_{9,6}$. (4k/60+ fps on nVidia 1080, HD/30+ fps on mobile Adreno 630, for all examples) (Fig. 2).

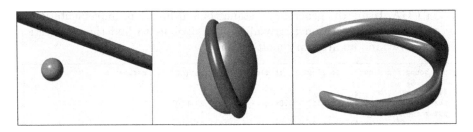

Fig. 2. A line and point in $\mathbb{R}_{4,4}$ (left), an ellipsoid and its intersection with a plane in $\mathbb{R}_{6,3}$ (middle), and a grade-14 element in $\mathbb{R}_{9,6}$ (right).

3.2   Non-Blade Elements

The Algorithm is also capable of rendering the OPNS of non-blade elements. Figure 3 reveals the shape of the subspace of the interpolation between two circles in $\mathbb{R}_{4,1}$ CGA. The author is unaware of any other visualizations of the approximate OPNS of these objects, and we feel this may add the geometric interpretation of these non-object entities. (see e.g. Hadfield and Lasenby [12]).

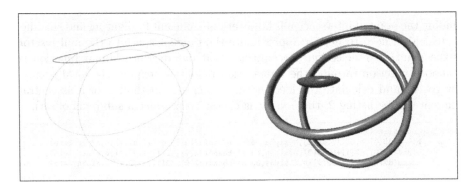

Fig. 3. The interpolation between two circles (gray) produces a non-blade object (red). (left) classic visualization techniques fail to represent the actual shape of the approximate OPNS revealed by our implementation (right) (Color figure online)

4   Conclusion

In this paper we have described a technique that can be used to adapt the Sphere Tracing algorithm to render isosurfaces of elements in arbitrary Geometric Algebras. Avoiding parametrizations or algebra specific ray intersection formulas, the algorithm is readily applicable to even the most challenging algebras, and capable of producing high quality images in real time. It represents a significant increase in flexibility and applicability compared to the visualization methods in use today.

Acknowledgments. The author would like to thank Vincent Nozick for posing the challenge that ultimately led to the implementation presented here, Stephane Breuils for such an exquisite stress test with his QCGA and Leo Dorst for his extensive review of the manuscript. Further thanks go to Charles Gunn and Hugo Hadfield for proofreading.

References

1. Gunn, C.: Geometric algebras for Euclidean geometry. Adv. Appl. Clifford Algebra **27**(1), 185–208 (2017). https://arxiv.org/abs/1411.650
2. Hestenes, D.: New Foundations for Classical Mechanics, 2nd edn. D. Reidel, Dordrecht/Boston (1999)
3. Dorst, L., Fontijne, D., Mann, S.: Geometric Algebra for Computer Science: An Object-Oriented Approach To Geometry. Morgan Kaufmann, Burlington (2007)
4. Dorst, L., Fontijne, D., Mann, S.: GAViewer. http://www.geometricalgebra.net
5. Perwass, C.: CLUCalc/CLUViz. http://www.clucalc.info
6. De Keninck, S.: Ganja.js. Geometric Algebra - Not Just Algebra (2017). https://github.com/enkimute/ganja.js
7. Hart, J.C.: sphere tracing: a geometric method for the antialiased ray tracing of implicit surfaces (1994). https://doi.org/10.1007/s003710050084
8. Inigo Quilez - iq/rgba: Rendering worlds with two triangles. NVSCENE (2008). http://www.iquilezles.org/www/material/nvscene2008/rwwtt.pdf
9. Breuils, S., Nozick, V., Sugimoto, A., Hitzer, E.: Quadric conformal geometric algebra of $\mathbb{R}_{4,4}$. Adv. Appl. Cliord Algebras **28**, 35 (2018). https://doi.org/10.1007/s00006-018-0851-1
10. Juan, D., Goldman, R., Mann, S.: Modeling 3D Geometry in the clifford algebra $\mathbb{R}_{4,4}$ Adv. Appl. Appl. Clifford Algebras **27**(4), 3039–3062 (2017)
11. Zamora-Esquivel, J.: $G_{6,3}$ geometric algebra; description and implementation. Adv. Appl. Clifford Algebras **24**(2), 493–514 (2014)
12. Hadfield, H., Lasenby, J.: Direct linear interpolation of geometric objects in conformal geometric algebra. To be published

Automatic Normal Orientation in Point Clouds of Building Interiors

Sebastian Ochmann$^{(\boxtimes)}$ and Reinhard Klein

Institute of Computer Science II, University of Bonn, Bonn, Germany
{ochmann,rk}@cs.uni-bonn.de

Abstract. Correct and consistent normal orientation is a fundamental problem in geometry processing. Applications such as feature detection and geometry reconstruction often rely on correctly oriented normals. Many existing approaches make severe assumptions on the input data or the topology of the underlying object which are not applicable to measurements of urban scenes. In contrast, our approach is specifically tailored to the challenging case of unstructured indoor point cloud scans of multi-story, multi-room buildings. We evaluate the correctness and speed of our approach on multiple real-world point cloud datasets.

Keywords: Point clouds · Normal orientation

1 Introduction

For many applications, surface normals are an important property of 3D point cloud or mesh data. While normal *directions* can usually be estimated well by local surface properties using e.g. principal component analysis (PCA), correct *orientation* is generally much harder to estimate. There exists a wide variety of approaches for mesh data based on principles such as voting, visibility, and propagation. Since point clouds are increasingly used in fields like architecture, methods working directly on point clouds have also received attention. However, point clouds pose specific challenges since information about connectivity or surfaces for ray casting are not directly available from the data. Urban environments also do not fulfill requirements such as that the object is a closed 2-manifold. Our work targets the challenging case of unstructured 3D point cloud datasets of building interiors. We are specifically interested in floor, ceiling and wall structures as a prerequisite for reconstruction of higher-level 3D models. The proposed method combines different ideas to provide efficient processing of large real-world scans. We first simplify the scene by detecting planes in the point cloud and subsequently working on surface patches instead of individual points. This also enables us to employ a path tracing approach with higher-order visibility using multiple ray bounces to estimate which side of each patch is probably room interior, wall, or outside area. Using this initial estimation, we then vote for a global orientation for each surface. Our approach is evaluated on multiple real-world datasets with known ground truth orientations for comparison.

© Springer Nature Switzerland AG 2019
M. Gavrilova et al. (Eds.): CGI 2019, LNCS 11542, pp. 556–563, 2019.
https://doi.org/10.1007/978-3-030-22514-8_55

2   Related Work

The propagation-based approach by Hoppe et al. [3] derives a consistent orientation of tangent planes for data points by solving an optimization problem on the
Riemannian graph of the points. Based on this approach, König et al. [4] propose
a new unreliability cost for traversing the Riemannian graph based on Hermite
curves. The approach by Schertler et al. [8] generalizes propagation as a graph-
based energy minimization problem. Xie et al. [12] segment an input point cloud
into mono-oriented regions via an active contour method. A consistent in/out
partitioning is achieved by means of voting. Alliez et al. [1] present a variational
framework for combined normal direction and orientation estimation. They compute a tensor field using a Voronoi diagram of the input point set and derive
a best-fitting isosurface by solving a generalized eigenvalue problem. Another
variational approach which finds normal directions and orientations simultaneously is presented by Wang et al. [11]. An approach using stochastic ray voting
is presented by Mullen et al. [5]. An unsigned distance function is first estimated
on a 3D Delaunay triangulation. Initial estimates for the sign of the distance
function are obtained by ray shooting and testing for intersections with an ε-
band of the unsigned function which is then smoothed and propagated. Borodin
et al. [2] combine a proximity- and visibility based approach to orient meshes. A
connectivity graph between patches of the model is constructed in which each
patch has two visibility coefficients which encode visibility from outside. One of
the proposed methods is a ray casting approach similar to ours. However, the
assumption is that most of the object's surface is visible from outside. Takayama
et al. [10] also employ ray casting to orient facets in polygon meshes. They cast
rays in both directions of facets to locate outside space. For inner facets, they
estimate which side of the facet has more free space which is similar to our idea
for inner walls. Since this method may fail in cavities, they also propose a method
based on intersection parity which is prone to modeling errors. In contrast, we
employ path tracing with multiple bounces to deal with cavities in the scene.

3   Method

The input of our approach is a set of points in $\mathbb{R}^3$ representing the interior of
a building, possibly with parts façade and outside area. If (unoriented) normals
are not given, they are estimated by means of local PCA for each point.

Plane Detection and Patch Generation. We first detect planes in the point
cloud data to obtain a simplified representation. We use the CGAL implementation [6] of the random sample consensus (RANSAC) method by Schnabel et
al. [9]. The rationale for using planes is that the main structure of buildings
can usually be represented well in a piecewise planar manner. For each of the
detected planes, a coarse 2D *occupancy bitmap*, i.e. a uniform grid on the surface
on which each cell or pixel may have the value 0 or 1, represents the support of
the plane by points constituting the plane. A pixel of the bitmap has the value
1 iff at least one point is located within the pixel. All pixels with value 1 yield

the set P of patches which will be used in the following steps. Each patch $p \in P$ originates from an original surface (i.e. plane) s_p, has a center position $c_p \in \mathbb{R}^3$ and an initial normal $\tilde{n}_p$ with arbitrary but fixed orientation.

Orientation by Path Tracing. We now estimate initial normal orientations for each patch. Given a patch $p \in P$, there are two possible orientations for its normal, $\tilde{n}_p$ and $-\tilde{n}_p$. For most points, we wish to select the one orientation which points towards the room interior. Conversely, the normal should point away from outside area (in case the patch is part of a surface separating room interior and outside area), and away from the interior of wall, floor or ceiling structures (in case the surface separates neighboring rooms). This classification is formulated as a voting scheme based on path tracing. Intuitively, for each patch, we trace a number of random paths into both hemispheres for the two possible orientations. We then use the number of ray bounces as well as the path lengths to analyze two aspects. First, we classify whether patches belong to interior or exterior walls, or are located completely outside of the building. Second, we use this classification as well as the path lengths to flip the normal of each patch to the more likely correct orientation. Finally, the reoriented patch normals vote for a normal orientation of whole surfaces. We now formalize the approach. All ray intersections are tested against the set of patches P. Let us first consider a patch p with center $c_p \in \mathbb{R}^3$ and one specific orientation $\tilde{n}_p$. We cast k rays r_i, $i \in \{1, \ldots, k\}$, each with origin c_p and a direction randomly sampled within a $120°$ cone directed towards $\tilde{n}_p$. In our experiments, $k = 50$. If a ray r_i with direction d_{r_i} intersects with a patch p', the ray is reflected into a sampled direction within a cone oriented towards the hemisphere of the incoming ray. The direction n_H of the hemisphere is computed as $n_H = \begin{cases} \tilde{n}_{p'}, & \text{if } \langle \tilde{n}_{p'}, d_{r_i} \rangle < 0, \\ -\tilde{n}_{p'}, & \text{otherwise.} \end{cases}$
Note that the normal $\tilde{n}_{p'}$ of the intersected patch p' used for this computation is arbitrary but fixed. In particular, the path tracing is invariant under the initial orientation of the patches. We allow up to $b = 8$ ray bounces for each initial ray r_i. If a ray does not hit any patch, the respective path is terminated. The result are k ray paths, each with up to b bounces for the considered patch p and orientation $\tilde{n}_p$. Let $l_{p,\tilde{n}_p}^{i,j}$ be the length of the jth segment along the ith path traced for patch p and orientation $\tilde{n}_p$ (note that segments after termination of a ray are considered to have zero length). We define the accumulated length $L_{p,\tilde{n}_p}$ as $L_{p,\tilde{n}_p} = \sum_{i=1}^{k} \sum_{j=1}^{b} \log(1 + l_{p,\tilde{n}_p}^{i,j})$. The rationale for taking the logarithm is to decrease the influence of particularly long segments while distinguishing between short and medium-length segments. Furthermore, let b_i be the number of bounces of the ith path. We consider the average number of ray bounces $B_{p,\tilde{n}_p}$ over all k paths $B_{p,\tilde{n}_p} = \frac{1}{k} \sum_{i=1}^{k} b_i$. Note that we analogously have $L_{p,-\tilde{n}_p}$ and $B_{p,-\tilde{n}_p}$ for the opposite direction. We now define a classification function $C(p) : P \to \{in, ex, out\}$ of patch p into interior, exterior, or outside as

$$C(p) = \begin{cases} out & \text{if } (B_{p,\tilde{n}_p} < \tau) \text{ and } (B_{p,-\tilde{n}_p} < \tau) \\ ex & \text{if } (B_{p,\tilde{n}_p} < \tau) \text{ xor } (B_{p,-\tilde{n}_p} < \tau) \\ in & \text{otherwise,} \end{cases}$$

where τ is a threshold which was empirically chosen as 4 in our experiments. A patch p with $C(p) = out$ is considered to be clutter outside of the building and ignored. A patch with $C(p) = ex$ is considered to be part of a surface separating room from outside. Its corrected normal orientation $\hat{n}_p$ is set to point away from the outside area, i.e. $\hat{n}_p = \begin{cases} \tilde{n}_p & \text{if } B_{p,-\tilde{n}_p} < \tau \\ -\tilde{n}_p & \text{if } B_{p,\tilde{n}_p} < \tau. \end{cases}$ A patch with $C(p) = in$ is considered to be part of a surface between neighboring rooms. In this case, we assume that the orientation with the longer total path length points towards the room interior and we thus set the corrected normal orientation to $\hat{n}_p = \begin{cases} \tilde{n}_p & \text{if } L_{p,\tilde{n}_p} > L_{p,-\tilde{n}_p}, \\ -\tilde{n}_p & \text{otherwise.} \end{cases}$ The orientation estimation up to this point was performed separately for each patch. Assuming that all points of each of the originally detected planes share a common normal orientation, we can vote for an orientation using all patches belonging to a plane. Let s be one of the detected planes with arbitrarily oriented normal $\tilde{n}_s$ and let $P_s = \{p \mid s_p = s\}$ be the set of patches originating from surface s. For voting, we determine the value $\theta_s = \sum_{p \in P_s} \text{sgn}\left(\langle \hat{n}_p, \tilde{n}_s \rangle\right)$, where $\text{sgn}(\cdot)$ is the signum function, and determine the corrected surface normal as $n_s = \begin{cases} \tilde{n}_s, & \text{if } \theta_s > 0, \\ -\tilde{n}_s, & \text{otherwise.} \end{cases}$ Then all patch normals are flipped to point in the same direction as n_s. For simplicity, we will still call this corrected normal $\hat{n}_p$.

Correction for façade Parts. Surfaces belonging to exterior façade are sometimes encountered due to scanning through windows. For such patches, the above estimation may erroneously prefer the direction pointing away from the outside area since ray paths towards the outside area are terminated quickly while rays towards the exterior wall of the building generate longer paths. An example for such an error is shown in Fig. 3. To correct this, we perform a second, simpler ray casting pass. For each patch p with center c_p and orientation $\hat{n}_p$ as estimated above, we cast k rays r_i, $i \in \{1, \ldots, k\}$, originating at c_p with directions d_i sampled in a cone oriented towards $\hat{n}_p$ *without* allowing ray bounces. Let p_i' be the patch which is hit by ray r_i. We then consider $\phi_p = \sum_{i=1}^{k} \text{sgn}\left(\langle \hat{n}_{p_i'}, d_i \rangle\right)$. If $\phi_p > 0$, the estimated orientation $\hat{n}_p$ is probably incorrect since it points towards the back side of a surface of a room interior. We thus define the corrected oriented normal $\overline{n}_p$ as $\overline{n}_p = \begin{cases} \hat{n}_p & \text{if } \phi_p < 0, \\ -\hat{n}_p & \text{otherwise.} \end{cases}$ The patch normals are then again used to vote for an orientation within each surface in the same way as described above. Finally, the oriented normals of the patches are used to orient the normals of the original points which lie within the patch.

4   Evaluation

The results of our experiments on multiple real-world datasets are summarized in Table 1. The first part shows general statistics about the datasets. Note that information about scanner positions is only used for generating ground truth normal orientations. It also lists the percentage of the total points which are

Table 1. Evaluation results on real-world datasets. "Statistics": Number of points and scans of the input data, the ratio of points on patches, and on patches that are not discarded as outside. "Plane detection": The number of detected planes and the runtime of the shape detection algorithm. "Correctness": Ratio of correctly oriented points to the total number of points on non-outside patches. The percentage after phase 2B is the final result. "Runtime": The computation time for the individual steps of our approach. The images show cross sections of the upper story of each dataset. For each story, the unlabeled point cloud is shown, the classification into interior/exterior/outside surfaces (green/blue/yellow), and whether the orientation is correct/incorrect (green/red).

Dataset 1	Dataset 2	Dataset 3	Dataset 4
Statistics	**Statistics**	**Statistics**	**Statistics**
5,151,388 pts / 21 scans	7,688,111 pts / 29 scans	12,409,443 pts / 13 scans	34,964,707 pts / 39 scans
points on patches: 73%	points on patches: 71%	points on patches: 73%	points on patches: 83%
points non-outside: 68%	points non-outside: 59%	points non-outside: 67%	points non-outside: 80%
Plane detection	**Plane detection**	**Plane detection**	**Plane detection**
# planes: 228	# planes: 320	# planes: 322	# planes: 556
Runtime: 29,320ms	Runtime: 94,468ms	Runtime: 114,929ms	Runtime: 228,903ms
Correctness	**Correctness**	**Correctness**	**Correctness**
1A: 97.94%, 1B: 98.75%	1A: 96.14%, 1B: 97.11%	1A: 98.08%, 1B: 98.05%	1A: 98.64%, 1B: 98.98%
2A: 98.09%, 2B: **98.82%**	2A: 98.20%, 2B: **98.75%**	2A: 97.53%, 2B: **99.42%**	2A: 98.45%, 2B: **98.68%**
Runtime	**Runtime**	**Runtime**	**Runtime**
1A: 1885ms, 1B: 186ms	1A: 3751ms, 1B: 780ms	1A: 3963ms, 1B: 582ms	1A: 4142ms, 1B: 1462ms
2A: 102ms, 2B: 186ms	2A: 212ms, 2B: 756ms	2A: 163ms, 2B: 581ms	2A: 232ms, 2B: 1461ms

part of detected planes (and thus belong to patches), and the percentage of points which are on patches that are *not* classified as outside area. Note that it is this set of non-outside points for which our algorithm estimates orientations, and that the correctness is measured w.r.t. this set of points.

Correctness. The next part of Table 1 shows the percentage of points on non-outside patches which have been correctly oriented by our method w.r.t. the ground truth. We list the correctness after different phases of our algorithm. Phase 1 is after the initial orientation by path tracing, before (1A) and after (1B) making normals consistent within surfaces. Phase 2 is after the façade correction step, again before (2A) and after (2B) ensuring consistency. For each dataset, the images at the bottom of the table show horizontal cross sections for the upper stories. For each story, the upper image shows the unlabeled input point cloud. The middle image shows the classification into interior surfaces (green), exterior (blue), outside (yellow), and points that are not on patches (gray). The lower image shows the final correctness (after phase 2B) of the normal orientation with correctly (green) and incorrectly oriented points (red), outside (yellow), and not on patches (gray). Figure 1 shows the effect of allowing multiple bounces during path tracing. The images show the correctness after path tracing and before ensuring surface consistency. Increasing the number of bounces helps to correctly orient patches which are strongly occluded by surrounding rooms. An overview of the classification of outside area is shown in Fig. 2(a) which shows large areas scanned through windows or from balconies of the building. Outside area is colored yellow. The detail view in Fig. 2(b) shows a cross section of the same building with the more fine grained classification with the same color scheme as in Table 1. An example for façade patches which are initially oriented incorrectly by the path tracing phase is shown in Fig. 3(a). After applying the correction for Façade parts, the normals are oriented correctly (Fig. 3b). A failure case of the façade correction step is shown in Fig. 4. The surface highlighted red was incorrectly oriented since the opened, almost parallel door next to it was interpreted as a wall surface. Note that this example is taken from Dataset 4 which explains the decreased final correctness as shown in Table 1.

Runtime. Table 1 also lists the runtime of our algorithm. Clearly, the path tracing phase 1 A takes more time than the single-bounce façade correction phase 2A. Also, the surface consistency correction 1B and 2B have similar runtimes since they are the same operation performed after phases 1A and 2A, respectively. Even in case of the largest dataset (Dataset 4), the total runtime of the core normal orientation approach takes well below 10 seconds. We are using the NVIDIA OptiX framework [7] for GPU-accelerated ray tracing against the set of patches which makes the actual ray tracing part a minor part of the total runtime requirements. The largest contributor to the overall runtime is the plane detection for which we use a RANSAC implementation in the CGAL library [6].

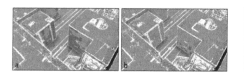

Fig. 1. Orientation correctness (green = correct, red = incorrect) after path tracing, but before applying surface consistency. Note how the region in the center is occluded by surrounding rooms. (a) Using a single bounce leads to uncertainty in occluded regions. (b) Eight bounces, as used in our approach, lead to results which are easily corrected by voting over whole surfaces. (Color figure online)

Fig. 2. Overview of the classification of the point cloud done as part of our orientation algorithm. (a) Classification into outside (yellow) and non-outside (green) parts. Points not on patches are colored gray. (b) Points are furthermore classified as belonging to surfaces between room interior and outside (blue) and between neighboring rooms (green). (Color figure online)

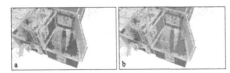

Fig. 3. (a) The path tracing phase may orient points on façade parts incorrectly. (b) The second phase attempts to correct these cases by flipping the respective normals.

Fig. 4. A failure case of the façade correction phase. The surface highlighted red has incorrect orientation since the opened, almost parallel door was interpreted as a wall surface.

5   Conclusion

We have presented a fast and fully automatic approach for orienting normals of the main structures in indoor point clouds without additional knowledge such as scanner positions. Using a path tracing approach, we first classify points as interior, exterior, and outside surfaces, and estimate an initial orientation. In a second phase, we correct the orientation of façade parts which may be incorrectly oriented in the first phase. Additionally, we perform a voting step for consistently orienting normals within surfaces after each phase. We evaluated our approach on multiple, real-world datasets with respect to orientation correctness and runtime. The resulting, automatically estimated orientation information can greatly facilitate or enable tasks such as visualization or reconstruction of building models which rely on correctly oriented surface normals.

Acknowledgments. This work was supported by the DFG projects KL 1142/11-1 (DFG Research Unit FOR 2535 Anticipating Human Behavior) and KL 1142/9-2 (DFG Research Unit FOR 1505 Mapping on Demand).

References

1. Alliez, P., Cohen-Steiner, D., Tong, Y., Desbrun, M.: Voronoi-based variational reconstruction of unoriented point sets. In: Symposium on Geometry Processing, vol. 7, pp. 39–48 (2007)
2. Borodin, P., Zachmann, G., Klein, R.: Consistent normal orientation for polygonal meshes. In: 2004 Computer Graphics International, pp. 18–25. IEEE (2004)
3. Hoppe, H., DeRose, T., Duchamp, T., McDonald, J., Stuetzle, W.: Surface reconstruction from unorganized points, vol. 26. ACM (1992)
4. König, S., Gumhold, S.: Consistent propagation of normal orientations in point clouds. In: VMV, pp. 83–92 (2009)
5. Mullen, P., De Goes, F., Desbrun, M., Cohen-Steiner, D., Alliez, P.: Signing the unsigned: robust surface reconstruction from raw pointsets. Comput. Graph. Forum **29**, 1733–1741 (2010)
6. Oesau, S., Verdie, Y., Jamin, C., Alliez, P., Lafarge, F., Giraudot, S.: Point set shape detection. In: CGAL User and Reference Manual, 4.12 edn. CGAL Editorial Board (2018). https://doc.cgal.org/4.12/Manual/packages.html# PkgPointSetShapeDetection3Summary

7. Parker, S.G., et al.: OptiX: a general purpose ray tracing engine. ACM Trans. Graph. (TOG) **29**(4), 66 (2010)
8. Schertler, N., Savchynskyy, B., Gumhold, S.: Towards globally optimal normal orientations for large point clouds. Comput. Graph. Forum **36**, 197–208 (2017)
9. Schnabel, R., Wahl, R., Klein, R.: Efficient RANSAC for point-cloud shape detection. Comput. Graph. Forum **26**(2), 214–226 (2007)
10. Takayama, K., Jacobson, A., Kavan, L., Sorkine-Hornung, O.: A simple method for correcting facet orientations in polygon meshes based on ray casting. J. Comput. Graph. Tech. **3**(4), 53 (2014)
11. Wang, J., Yang, Z., Chen, F.: A variational model for normal computation of point clouds. Vis. Comput. **28**(2), 163–174 (2012)
12. Xie, H., McDonnell, K.T., Qin, H.: Surface reconstruction of noisy and defective data sets. In: Proceedings of the Conference on Visualization 2004, pp. 259–266. IEEE Computer Society (2004)

Colour Image Segmentation by Region Growing Based on Conformal Geometric Algebra

Jaroslav Hrdina$^{(\boxtimes)}$ [ID], Radek Matoušek[ID], and Radek Tichý[ID]

Faculty of Mechanical Engineering, Brno University of Technology,
Brno, Czech Republic
{hrdina,matousek}@fme.vutbr.cz, Radek.Tichy@vutbr.cz
http://www.fme.vutbr.com

Abstract. We apply conformal geometric algebra (CGA) to classical algorithms for colour image segmentation. Particularly, we modify standard Prewitt quaternionic filter for edge detection and region growing segmentation procedure and use them simultaneously, which is only allowed by common CGA language, more precisely by the notion of flat point in normalised and unnormalised form.

Keywords: Conformal geometric algebra · Image segmentation ·
Region growing · Flat point

1 Introduction to Conformal Geometric Algebra

This section is based on classical books [2–4,12] and papers [5–8]. In general, the elements of Clifford algebra of $Cl(m, n)$ form free, associative, distributive algebra over the set $\{e_1, \ldots, e_m, e_{m+1}, \ldots, e_{m+n}\}$ such that the following identities are satisfied:

$$e_i^2 = 1,\ i \in \{1, \ldots, n\},\quad e_i^2 = -1,\ i \in \{n+1, \ldots, n+m\},$$
$$e_i e_j = -e_j e_i,\ i \neq j,\ i, j \in \{1, \ldots, n+m\}.$$

In this case we get 2^{m+n} dimensional vector space. The elements of conformal geometric algebra (CGA), i.e. Clifford algebra $Cl(4, 1)$ are in this sense generated by $\{e_1, e_2, e_3, e_+, e_-\}$ such that the following identities are satisfied:

$$e_1^2 = e_2^2 = e_3^2 = e_+^2 = 1,\ e_-^2 = -1,$$

$$e_i e_j = -e_j e_i,\ i \neq j,\ i, j \in \{1, 2, 3, +, -\}.$$

The first two authors were supported by a grant of the Czech Science Foundation (GAČR) number 17–21360S, "Advances in Snake-like Robot Control" the last author was supported by Grant No. FSI–S–17–4464.

© Springer Nature Switzerland AG 2019
M. Gavrilova et al. (Eds.): CGI 2019, LNCS 11542, pp. 564–570, 2019.
https://doi.org/10.1007/978-3-030-22514-8_56

In our case we get $2^5 = 32$ dimensional vector space. If we consider the vector space $\mathbb{R}^{4,1} = \{e_1, e_2, e_3, e_+, e_-\}$, i.e. the associated quadratic space, we can define two additional products based on the algebra (geometric) one for any $u, v, \in \mathbb{R}^{m,n}$ we have $u \cdot v = \frac{1}{2}(uv + vu)$, and $u \wedge v = \frac{1}{2}(uv - vu)$, called the dot product and wedge product, respectively. We define a new basis of $\mathbb{R}^{4,1}$ as the set $\{e_1, e_2, e_3, e_0, e_\infty\}$ such that $e_0 = \frac{1}{2}(e_- + e_+)$ and $e_\infty = (e_- - e_+)$. Then the following properties hold:

$$e_0^2 = \frac{1}{4}(e_-^2 - e_-e_+ - e_+e_- + e_+^2) = \frac{1}{4}(-1 + 0 + 1) = 0,$$

$$e_\infty^2 = \frac{1}{4}(e_-^2 + e_-e_+ + e_+e_- + e_+^2) = \frac{1}{4}(-1 + 0 + 1) = 0,$$

$$e_0e_\infty = \frac{1}{2}(e_- + e_+)(e_- - e_+) = -\frac{1}{2} - \frac{1}{2}e_-e_+ + \frac{1}{2}e_+e_- - \frac{1}{2} = -1 - (e_- \wedge e_+),$$

$$e_\infty e_0 = \frac{1}{2}(e_- - e_+)(e_- + e_+) = -\frac{1}{2} + \frac{1}{2}e_-e_+ - \frac{1}{2}e_+e_- - \frac{1}{2} = -1 + (e_- \wedge e_+),$$

i.e. finally $e_\infty e_0 = -e_0 e_\infty - 2$.

In CGA, the fundamental geometric objects are represented as follows. The point x with the coordinates (x_1, x_2, x_3) in $\mathbb{R}^3$ is represented as an element P of $Cl(4,1)$ by $P = x + \frac{1}{2}x^2 e_\infty + e_0$, where by x we understand the Euclidean embedding $x = x_1 e_1 + x_2 e_2 + x_3 e_3$. The sphere S with centre point P and radius r is given by $S = P - \frac{1}{2}r^2 e_\infty$. A new geometric object appears referred to as a point pair P given by the wedge of two points P_1, P_2 as $P = P_1 \wedge P_2$.

object	CGA element (OPNS)
Point	$Q = x + \frac{1}{2}x^2 e_\infty + e_0$
Point pair Q_1, Q_2	$P = Q_1 \wedge Q_2$
Line L	$L = Q_1 \wedge Q_2 \wedge e_\infty$

Each geometric transformation (rotation, translation, dilation, inversion) of a geometric object represented by an algebra element $\mathcal{O}$ is realized by conjugation $\mathcal{O} \mapsto M\mathcal{O}\tilde{M}$, where M is an appropriate multi-vector and $\tilde{M}$ is its reversion, i.e. it is an operation that reverses the order of the basis vectors in the coordinate expression of the elements of M. For instance, the translation in the direction $t = t_1 e_1 + t_2 e_2 + t_3 e_3$ is realized by conjugation by the multi-vector $T = 1 - \frac{1}{2}te_\infty$, which can be written as $e^{-\frac{1}{2}te_\infty}$, and the rotation around the axis L by angle ϕ is realized as conjugation by the multi-vector $R = \cos\frac{\phi}{2} - L\sin\frac{\phi}{2}$. Similarly to the case of a translation, the rotation can be also written as $e^{-\frac{1}{2}\phi L}$. The intersections of geometric objects A and B in CGA are given as the wedge product $A \wedge B$ (or dually by $A^* \cdot B$), where the operations $\wedge$ and $\cdot$ are extended to all elements of CGA. Consequently, the following property for wedge product of a vector P and an arbitrary r-vector Q holds $P \wedge Q = \frac{1}{2}(PQ + (-1)^r QP)$ and similarly for a dot product we have $P \cdot Q = \frac{1}{2}(PQ + (-1)^{r+1}QP)$.

Note that $A^* = -Ae_- e_+ e_3 e_2 e_1$ denotes the dual to A in CGA and the operation $A \mapsto A^*$ is realized by the multiplication of the inverse unit pseudoscalar.

Note that the duality is just an algebraic operation and does not affect the object geometrically, it is indeed just a transformation between the *IPNS representation* and *OPNS representation*, see e.g. [3].

2   Colour Image Segmentation Based on Flat Points

The points in CGA are represented by the vectors in *the null-cone* $P = xe_1 + ye_2 + ze_2 + \frac{1}{2}(x^2 + y^2 + z^3)e_\infty + e_0$ and the linear part of any point can be coded by bivectors called flat points.

$$\hat{P} = P \wedge e_\infty = xe_1e_\infty + ye_2e_\infty + ze_3e_\infty + e_0 \wedge e_\infty.$$

Following classical books [1,10,11], the segmentation of the image denoted I regroups connected pixels with similar colours into N regions R_i, $i = 1, ..., N$. The pixels of each region must respect homogeneity and connectedness conditions. The homogeneity of a region R_i is defined by a uniformity-based predicate, denoted $Pred(R_i)$, which is true if the colours of R_i are homogeneous and false on the opposite. The regions must respect the following conditions:

1. $I = \bigcup_{i=1,...,N} R_i$, $R_i \cap R_j = \emptyset$, $i \neq j$, i.e. each pixel must be assigned to one single region and the set of all the regions must correspond to the image.
2. R_i contains only connected pixels $\forall i \in \{1, ..., N\}$. A region is defined as a subset of connected pixels.
3. $Pred(R_i)$ is true $\forall i \in \{1, ..., N\}$. Each region must respect the uniformity based predicate.
4. $Pred(R_i \cup R_j) = $ false $\forall i \neq j$, R_i and R_j being adjacent in I. Two adjacent regions do not respect the predicate.

We use this idea in our algorithm in order to find one particular region which represents an object in the picture (for some applications see for example [9]). The most common colour Image Segmentation scheme, [14], is based on *edge detection*. In CGA settings, the Prewitt colour filter can be defined by two quaternion-valued bi-convolution masks over a 3×3 neighbourhood as

$$\alpha \begin{pmatrix} 1 & 1 & 1 \\ 0 & 0 & 0 \\ q & q & q \end{pmatrix} [f] \begin{pmatrix} 1 & 1 & 1 \\ 0 & 0 & 0 \\ \bar{q} & \bar{q} & \bar{q} \end{pmatrix}$$

where $q = \exp(\mu\pi/2)$ (μ is equivalent to the gray line) and $\alpha = 1/6$ is a scale factor to account for the addition of the six non-zero pixel values, and f denotes the input image. Figure 1 illustrates the result of Prewitt filter used on colour image. The output is a greyscale image with coloured edges.

In CGA, the use of Prewitt colour filter with the same bi-convolution mask is possible if the image is represented by flat points instead of quaternions and the elements q in the matrix mask are formed by the appropriate CGA motors representing rotation around the grey axis.

The algorithm starts from one chosen pixel and then proceeds iteratively. In each step we check the neighbouring pixels of the region already included. Let

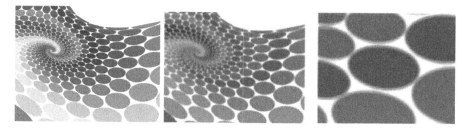

Fig. 1. Quaternion edge detection: (A) input, (B) output, (C) detail. (color figure online)

us describe k-th iteration step. Denote by P the pixel analysed in k-th iteration. Let R be the subset of all already selected pixels, $N(P)$ is the set of neighbouring pixels of P belonging to R and Q is a pixel that lies in the region representing the segmented object and that characterizes the colour of the object and $I(P)$ is the colour of the pixel P. Now, P belongs to R if the three following aggregating conditions are respected:

$$||I(P) - I(Q)|| < T_1 \Rightarrow \quad I(P) \in S_{(I(Q),T_1)} \Rightarrow \quad I(P) \cdot S_{(I(Q),T_1)} > 0$$
$$||I(P) - \mu_{N(P)}|| < T_2 \Rightarrow \quad I(P) \in S_{(\mu_{N(P)},T_2)} \Rightarrow \quad I(P) \cdot S_{(\mu_{N(P)},T_2)} > 0$$
$$||I(P) - \mu_R|| < T_3 \Rightarrow \quad I(P) \in S_{(\mu_{R_i},T_3)} \Rightarrow \quad I(P) \cdot S_{(\mu_{R_i},T_3)} > 0$$

where $S_{(A,T)}$ is a CGA representation of a sphere with the centre A and the radius T, the thresholds T_j are adjusted by the analyst, $|| \cdot ||$ is the Euclidean distance, $\mu_{N(P)}$ represents the mean colour of the pixels that belong to $N(P)$, $||\cdot||$ is the Euclidean distance, μ_R represents the mean colour of the whole region already processed. The result for two particular colour choices is demonstrated in Fig. 2.

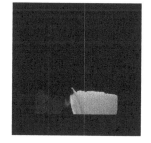

Fig. 2. Colour segmentation

Example 1. As an example of computation, one can see the mask in Fig. 3. We have the pixel P such that $I(P) = (1,3,1)$ and $R = \{Q_1, Q_2, Q_3\}$ such that

$I(Q_1) = (1,1,1)$, $I(Q_2) = (2,2,1)$ and $I(Q_3) = (1,3,1)$, now $N(P) = \{Q_1, Q_2\}$ and

$$\mu_{N(P)} = \frac{1}{2}(1+2, 1+2, 1+1) = (\frac{3}{2}, \frac{3}{2}, 1),$$

$$\mu_R = \frac{1}{3}(1+2+1, 1+2+3, 1+1+1) = (\frac{4}{3}, 2, 1).$$

If $||\cdot||$ is Euclidean norm then we have

Fig. 3. Example of mask

$$||I(P) - I(Q_1)|| = ||(0,2,0)|| = 2 < T_1,$$

$$||I(P) - I(Q_2)|| = ||(-1,1,0)|| = \sqrt{2} < T_1$$

$$||I(P) - \mu_{N(P)}|| = ||(-\frac{1}{2}, \frac{1}{2}, 0)|| = \frac{\sqrt{2}}{2} < T_2,$$

$$||I(P) - \mu_R|| = ||(-\frac{1}{3}, 1, 0)|| = \frac{10}{9} < T_3$$

and finally $P \in R$ for $(T_1, T_2, T_3) = (\sqrt{3}, \sqrt{2}, \sqrt{2})$.

3   Experiments

The key fact for our implementation is that, similarly to Prewitt edge detection filter, the convolution of flat points in CGA is also available. All experiments are realised in Matlab Clifford package [13]. Recall that the discrete equivalent of the convolution, used in image processing, is given by:

$$(f \star h)[n,m] = \sum_{i=0}^{N-1} \sum_{j=0}^{M-1} f[n-i, m-j]h[i,j]$$

where f, g are multi-valued (complex, quaternion etc.) functions defined on the discrete region with M times N elements. For example

$$\begin{pmatrix} 0 & 1 & 0 \\ 1 & 0 & 1 \\ 0 & 1 & 0 \end{pmatrix} \star \begin{pmatrix} 0 & I(P_1) & 0 \\ I(P_2) & Q & I(P_3) \\ 0 & I(P_1) & 0 \end{pmatrix} = \begin{pmatrix} \cdots & \cdots & \cdots \\ \cdots & (I(P_1)+I(P_2)+I(P_3)+I(P_4)) & \cdots \\ \cdots & \cdots & \cdots \end{pmatrix}$$

i.e. if $f[m,n] = I(Q)$ then $(f \star h)[m,n] = \frac{1}{4}\sum_{P \in N(Q)} I(P)$ and we can define the convolution over the projective class of flat points which is of the form

$$
\begin{aligned}
(f \star h)[m,n] = \hat{P}_1 + \hat{P}_2 + \hat{P}_3 + \hat{P}_4 &= (x_1 + x_2 + x_3 + x_4)e_1 e_\infty \\
&+ (x_1 + x_2 + x_3 + x_4)e_2 e_\infty + (x_1 + x_2 + x_3 + x_4)e_3 e_\infty + 4e_0 \wedge e_\infty \\
&\sim \frac{1}{4}((x_1 + x_2 + x_3 + x_4)e_1 e_\infty + (x_1 + x_2 + x_3 + x_4)e_2 e_\infty \\
&+ (x_1 + x_2 + x_3 + x_4)e_3 e_\infty) + e_0 \wedge e_\infty = \mu_{(P_1, P_2, P_3, P_4)}.
\end{aligned}
$$

The above methods may be combined by iterated application of convolution and bi-convolution, respectively, if the weighting of the points within the detected region is used when the Prewitt filter is applied. First the colour respecting segmentation is processed. Particularly, the car colour region in the left image of Fig. 4, is depicted in the middle image. Consequently, we use the flat point in the form $aI(P)$ and the parameter $a = 0.2$ to set lower priority for pixels excluded during the colour segmentation. In our particular example, the picture between colour segmentation and edge detection is in the form $I = aI_{ex} + I_{in}$, where I_{ex} is the image of excluded pixels by colour segmentation and I_{in} is the image of included pixels by colour segmentation. Finally the resulting image is on the right in Fig. 4. We could set the value equal to zero in order to obtain edge detection of the car only, however non-zero values provide us the information of the picture outside of the segmented region during the algorithm which might be useful for some future analysis of the picture.

Fig. 4. Combined algorithm

In Fig. 5, right, we display the result of the flat point edge detection where the border edges around the segmented colours are detected. On the left, classical edge detection without the colour choice is used. As expected with using weights we obtain mainly edges of the previously segmented region, i.e. the car. There are still edges outside of the region detected that is behaviour dependent on the value of the weight.

Fig. 5. Combined algorithm - weighted and non-weighted

Acknowledgment. We would like to thank to Aleš Návrat for helpful discussions. We thank the anonymous reviewers whose comments have greatly improved this manuscript.

References

1. Busin, L., Vandenbroucke, N., Macaire, L.: Color spaces and image segmentation. Adv. Imaging Electron Phys. **151**, 65–168 (2008)
2. Dorst, L., Fontijne, D., Mann, S.: Geometric Algebra for Computer Science: An Object-Oriented Approach to Geometry, 1st edn. Morgan Kaufmann Publishers Inc., San Francisco (2007)
3. Hildenbrand, D.: Foundations of Geometric Algebra Computing, 1st edn. Springer, Hiedelberg (2013). https://doi.org/10.1007/978-3-642-31794-1
4. Hildenbrand, D.: Introduction to Geometric Algebra Computing. CRC Press, Taylor & Francis Group, Boca Raton (2019)
5. Hrdina, J., Návrat, A., Vašík, P., Matoušek, R.: CGA-based robotic snake contol. Adv. Appl. Clifford Algebr. **27**(1), 621–632 (2017). https://doi.org/10.1007/s00006-016-0695-5
6. Hrdina, J., Návrat, A., Vašík, P.: Geometric algebra for conics. Adv. Appl. Clifford Algebr. **28**, 66 (2018). https://doi.org/10.1007/s00006-018-0879-2
7. Hrdina, J., Návrat, A.: Binocular computer vision based on conformal geometric algebra. Adv. Appl. Clifford Algebr. **27**(3), 1945–1959 (2017)
8. Hrdina, J., Vašík, P., Matoušek, R., Návrat, A.: Geometric algebras for uniform colour spaces. Math. Methods Appl. Sci. **41**(11), 4117–4130 (2018). https://doi.org/10.1002/mma.4489
9. Janku, P., Kominkova Oplatkova, Z., Dulik, T., Snopek, P., Liba, J.: Fire detection in video stream by using simple artificial neural network. MENDEL **24**(2), 55–60 (2018)
10. Ohta, N., Robertson, A.R.: Colorimetry: Fundamentals and Applications, 6th edn. Wiley, New York (2005)
11. Oleari, C.: Standard Colorimetry: Definitions, Algorithms, and Software, 1st edn. Wiley, Hoboken (2016)
12. Perwass, C.: Geometric Algebra with Applications in Engineering, 1st edn. Springer, Heidelberg (2009). https://doi.org/10.1007/978-3-540-89068-3
13. Sangwine, S.J., Hitzer, E.: Clifford multivector toolbox (for MATLAB). Adv. Appl. Clifford Algebr. **27**, 539–558 (2017). https://doi.org/10.1007/s00006-016-0666-x
14. Ell, T.A., Le Bihan, N., Sangwine, S.: Quaternion Fourier Transforms for Signal and Image Processing. FOCUS Series Periodical. Wiley-ISTE, Hoboken (2014)

GAC Application to Corner Detection Based on Eccentricity

Jaroslav Hrdina[ID], Aleš Návrat, and Petr Vašík[✉][ID]

Institute of Mathematics, Faculty of Mechanical Engineering,
Brno University of Technology, Brno, Czech Republic
{hrdina,navrat.a,vasik}@fme.vutbr.cz

Abstract. The geometric algebra GAC offers the same efficiency for calculations with arbitrary conic sections as provided by CGA for spheres. We shall exploit these properties in image processing, particularly in corner detection. Indeed, the point cluster will be approximated by a conic section and, consequently, classified as points with ellipse–like or hyperbola–like neighbourhood. Then, by means of eccentricity, we decide whether the points form a corner.

Keywords: Geometric algebras · GAC · Corner detection

1 Introduction

The corresponding theory of geometric algebras based on conics was originally partially elaborated for $\mathbb{G}_{5,3}$ and $\mathbb{G}_6$ by C. Perwass [5], for double conformal geometric algebra (DCGA) by R. B. Easter and E. Hitzer [2], and for quadric geometric algebra (QGA) by J. Zamora-Esquivel [7]. The planar version of QGA is a geometric algebra $\mathbb{G}_{4,2}$ together with an embedding of the Euclidean plane $\mathbb{R}^2$ constructed as two independent stereographic projections for each axis separately and therefore just axes–aligned conics are well defined. Moreover, rotation works neither for conics nor points correctly. The planar concept of DCGA corresponds to the geometric algebra $\mathbb{G}_{6,2}$. It contains two subalgebras isomorphic to the compass ruler algebra $\mathbb{G}_{3,1}$. Unfortunately DCGA lacks the duality between the inner and outer representation.

Note that a conic section can be defined as a second-degree equation in the Cartesian coordinates

$$A_{xx}x^2 + 2A_{xy}xy + A_{yy}y^2 + 2B_x x + 2B_y y + C = 0 \tag{1}$$

The conic sections described by this equation can be classified in terms of the discriminant

$$D = \begin{vmatrix} A_{xx} & A_{xy} \\ A_{xy} & A_{yy} \end{vmatrix} \tag{2}$$

The authors were supported by a grant of the Czech Science Foundation (GAČR) number 17–21360S, "Advances in Snake-like Robot Control".

M. Gavrilova et al. (Eds.): CGI 2019, LNCS 11542, pp. 571–577, 2019.
https://doi.org/10.1007/978-3-030-22514-8_57

This determinant is conventionally called the discriminant of the conic section. If the conic is non-degenerate, then $D < 0$ represents an ellipse; if A = C and B = 0, the equation represents a circle, if $D = 0$, the equation represents a parabola; if $D > 0$, the equation represents a hyperbola; if $A + C = 0$, the equation represents a rectangular hyperbola.

$$\Delta = \begin{vmatrix} A_{xx} & A_{xy} & B_x \\ A_{xy} & A_{yy} & B_y \\ B_x & B_y & C \end{vmatrix} \tag{3}$$

This determinant Δ is also sometimes called the discriminant of the conic section. For example, the major and minor semiaxes a and b of a hyperbola are defined by the equations

$$a^2 = -\frac{\Delta}{\lambda_1 D} = -\frac{\Delta}{\lambda_1^2 \lambda_2} \quad \text{and} \quad b^2 = -\frac{\Delta}{\lambda_2 D} = -\frac{\Delta}{\lambda_1 \lambda_2^2}$$

where λ_1 and λ_2 are roots of the quadratic equation $\lambda^2 - (A_{xx} + A_{yy})\lambda + D = 0$.

2   Geometric Algebra of Conics (GAC)

The inner and outer product null space representations of GAC objects are given by the usual formulas with slight changes, [3]. Let us recall that analogously to CGA we denote the corresponding basis elements as follows

$$\bar{n}_+, \bar{n}_-, \bar{n}_\times, e_1, e_2, n_+, n_-, n_\times.$$

Geometrically, the basis elements e_1, e_2 will play the usual role of standard basis of the Euclidean plane while the null vectors $\bar{n}$, n will represent the origin and infinity, respectively. Namely, a circle C centered in (p_1, p_2) with radius ρ and a line L with unit normal (n_1, n_2) and a shift d from the origin are given by

$$C_I = \bar{n}_+ + p_1 e_1 + p_2 e_2 + \tfrac{1}{2}(p_1^2 + p_2^2)n_+ - \tfrac{1}{2}\rho^2 n_+,$$
$$L_I = n_1 e_1 + n_2 e_2 + dn_+$$

in IPNS representation. In OPNS representation, they are given by the spanning points as follows

$$C_O = P_1 \wedge P_2 \wedge P_3 \wedge n_- \wedge n_\times,$$
$$L_O = P_1 \wedge P_2 \wedge n_+ \wedge n_- \wedge n_\times.$$

An arbitrary conic section is represented by a 1–vector not containing $n_-, n_\times$. For example, an ellipse E with the semi–axes a, b centred in $(u, v) \in \mathbb{R}^2$ rotated by angle θ is in the GAC inner representation given by

$$E_I = \bar{n}_+ - (\alpha \cos 2\theta)\bar{n}_- - (\alpha \sin 2\theta)\bar{n}_\times + (u + u\alpha \cos 2\theta - v\alpha \sin 2\theta)e_1$$
$$+ (v + v\alpha \cos 2\theta - u\alpha \sin 2\theta)e_2$$
$$+ \tfrac{1}{2}\left(u^2 + v^2 - \beta - (u^2 - v^2)\alpha \cos 2\theta - 2uv\alpha \sin 2\theta\right)n_+,$$

where
$$\alpha = \frac{a^2 - b^2}{a^2 + b^2}, \beta = \frac{2a^2b^2}{a^2 + b^2}.$$

- A *hyperbola H* with the semi–axes a, b centred in $(u, v) \in \mathbb{R}^2$ rotated by angle θ is in the GAC inner representation given by the same expression but with

$$\alpha = \frac{a^2 + b^2}{a^2 - b^2}, \beta = \frac{-2a^2b^2}{a^2 - b^2}.$$

- A *parabola P* with the semi–latus rectum p centred in $(u, v) \in \mathbb{R}^2$ rotated by angle θ is in the GAC inner representation given by

$$P_I = \bar{n}_+ + \cos 2\theta \bar{n}_- + \sin 2\theta \bar{n}_\times + (u + u \cos 2\theta + v \sin 2\theta - 2p \sin \theta)e_1 \quad (4)$$
$$+ (v - v \cos 2\theta + u \sin 2\theta + 2p \cos \theta)e_2$$
$$+ \tfrac{1}{2} \left(u^2 + v^2 + (u^2 - v^2) \cos 2\theta + 2uv \sin 2\theta - 4pu \sin \theta + 4pv \cos \theta \right) n_+.$$

Indeed, Geometric Algebra for Conics (GAC) is the Clifford algebra $\mathbb{G}_{5,3}$ together with the embedding $\mathbb{R}^2 \to \mathbb{R}^{5,3}$ given by

$$(x, y) \mapsto \bar{n}_+ + xe_1 + ye_2 + \frac{1}{2}(x^2 + y^2)n_+ + \frac{1}{2}(x^2 - y^2)n_- + xyn_\times.$$

in the basis $\bar{n}_+, \bar{n}_-, \bar{n}_\times, e_1, e_2, n_+, n_-, n_\times$. Intrinsic to GAC are Euclidean transformations and scaling. The generators for rotation, x–translation, y–translation and scaling are

$$r = \tfrac{1}{2}e_1 \wedge e_2 + \bar{n}_\times \wedge n_- + n_\times \wedge \bar{n}_-,$$
$$t_1 = -\tfrac{1}{2}e_1 \wedge n_+ - \tfrac{1}{2}e_1 \wedge n_- - \tfrac{1}{2}e_2 \wedge n_\times,$$
$$t_2 = -\tfrac{1}{2}e_2 \wedge n_+ + \tfrac{1}{2}e_2 \wedge n_- - \tfrac{1}{2}e_1 \wedge n_\times,$$
$$s = \bar{n}_+ \wedge n_+ + \bar{n}_- \wedge n_- + \bar{n}_\times \wedge n_\times.$$

The outer product representation of a conic Q given by five points with GAC representatives $P_1, \ldots, P_5$ is $Q_O = P_1 \wedge P_2 \wedge P_3 \wedge P_4 \wedge P_5$. If the conic is aligned to an axis, it is given by four points as $Q_O = P_1 \wedge P_2 \wedge P_3 \wedge P_4 \wedge n_\times$.

3   The Analysis Based on Eccentricity

First, we apply the edge detecting algorithm (for example based on QFT). Next, the edges are segmented with respect to the scaling period, see e.g. [6]. Now, each point cluster is fitted with a conic and a circle by GAC fitting [4]. Finally, we compare residues and radius (semi-axes) of fitting objects according to the following table.

574 J. Hrdina et al.

	conic semi-axes	circle radius	conic residue	circle residue
edge crossing	small	big	small	big
line edge	big	big	big	small

After edge detecting procedure, we receive 33 clusters of points (with scaling period 30px), see Fig. 1. In the right image, we approximate the point clusters by circles in CGA, too. Their radii then play the role of another parameter.

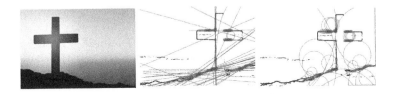

Fig. 1. The residue analysis

We classify the point clusters according to the residues of conic fitting (left image) and circle fitting (right image) in Fig. 1. Consequently, we sort them into the following categories (R = residue) listed in Table 1.

Table 1. The residue analysis

$R \in$	$(-,10^{-10})$	$(10^{-10},10^{-9})$	$(10^{-2}, 10^{-6})$	$(10^{-1},-)$
circle	9	9	8	7
conic	12	2	18	1

For example the cross point in Fig. 2 has the circle residue 14.7 and the conic residue $6 \cdot 10^{-11}$ and thus it is determined uniquely.

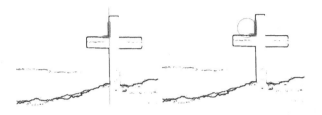

Fig. 2. Cross point

If the resulting approximated object is a hyperbola, the analysis may be refined. For a hyperbola in the above canonical form, the eccentricity is given by

$$e = \sqrt{1 + \frac{b^2}{a^2}}. \tag{5}$$

Two hyperbolas are geometrically similar to each other – meaning that they have the same shape, so that one can be transformed into the other by rigid left and right movements, rotation, taking a mirror image, and scaling (magnification) – if and only if they have the same eccentricity. Generally, the shape of an conics section is represented by its eccentricity, which for an ellipse can be any number from 0 (the limiting case of a circle) to arbitrarily close to but less than 1. The general form of the eccentricity is

$$e = \sqrt{\frac{2\sqrt{(A_{xx} - A_{yy})^2 + A_{xy}^2}}{\pm(A_{xx} - A_{yy}) + \sqrt{(A_{xx} - A_{yy})^2 + A_{xy}^2}}} \tag{6}$$

where $\pm$ corresponds to the choice of hyperbola or ellipse, respectively. In Fig. 3 we show that with the maximum eccentricity choice 0.6 (0.7 in the second image) we are able to detect most corners (left image) and with shifted mask we detect the rest (right image).

Fig. 3. Eccentricity 0.6 (0.7)

The key fact in the considerations above is that the cross is rather perpendicular. If the terrain contour is analysed, Fig. 4, we receive eccentricity close to zero for points approximated by both ellipse and hyperbola and thus these points are not detected.

(a)   (b)

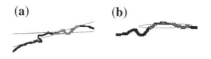

Fig. 4. Terrain: (A) Hyperbola point, (B) Ellipse point

The same holds for points on the straight line, Fig. 5. Indeed, they may be approximated by both ellipse and hyperbola. In case of hyperbola, the eccentricity is high, 10 in our particular example, and therefore these points are not detected.

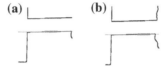

Fig. 5. Straight line: (A) Hyperbola point, (B) Ellipse point

4 Conclusion

The discussion of a particular choice of the detection level should follow. For instance, the points depicted in Fig. 6 are detected as corners with eccentricity 0.3. If the eccentricity maximum is increased, up to e.g. 0.6 and 0.1, we receive the results in Fig. 7.

Fig. 6. Eccentricity 0.3   **Fig. 7.** Increased eccentricity

With different eccentricity level choice we are able to detect most of the corners. Our example worked for almost perpendicular corners, for more complicated image the multi–criteria analysis is appropriate where the eccentricity and residues of conic sections and circles are combined. This will be the topic for further research. Finally, Fig. 8 shows the output for random combinations of evaluation criteria.

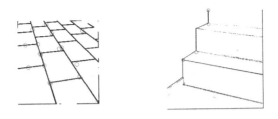

Fig. 8. The other examples

Note that our method is suitable for e.g. feature detection where the procedure ends either if a feature is found or by the predefined number of eccentricity change. On the other hand, because a pair of lines both parallel and intersecting under any angle form a conic section, particularly a hyperbola, we claim that the method is robust w.r.t. different corner angles detection. An algorithm of the parametric eccentricity choice is necessary to design, yet this is the task for further research and tests. Also resistance of the method w.r.t. to the level of noise has to be discussed, yet this is rather the question of good approximation choice and may lead to clustering of groups of geometric objects, see [1].

References

1. Dorst, L., Fontijne, D., Mann, S.: Geometric Algebra for Computer Science: An Object-Oriented Approach to Geometry, 1st edn. Morgan Kaufmann Publishers Inc., Burlington (2007)
2. Easter, R.B., Hitzer E.: Double conformal geometric algebra for quadrics and darboux cyclides. In: Proceedings of the 33rd Computer Graphics International (CGI 2016), pp. 93–96. ACM, New York (2016)
3. Hrdina, J., Návrat, A., Vašík, P.: Geometric algebra for conics. Adv. Appl. Cliord Algebras **28**, 66 (2018). https://doi.org/10.1007/s00006-018-0879-2
4. Hrdina, J., Návrat, A., Vašík, P.: Conic fitting in geometric algebra setting. Adv. Appl. Clifford Algebras (2019, to appear)
5. Perwass, C.: Junction and Corner detection through the extraction and analysis of line segments. In: Klette, R., Žunić, J. (eds.) IWCIA 2004. LNCS, vol. 3322, pp. 568–582. Springer, Heidelberg (2004). https://doi.org/10.1007/978-3-540-30503-3_42
6. Perwass, C.: Geometric Algebra with Applications in Engineering, 1st edn. Springer, Heidelberg (2009). https://doi.org/10.1007/978-3-540-89068-3
7. Zamora-Esquivel, J.: $\mathbb{G}_{6,3}$ Geometric algebra; description and implementation. Adv. Appl. Cliord Algebras **24**, 493 (2014). https://doi.org/10.1007/s00006-014-0442-8

Ray-Tracing Objects and Novel Surface Representations in CGA

Sushant Achawal[1], Joan Lasenby[1], Hugo Hadfield[1(✉)],
and Anthony Lasenby[2]

[1] Department of Engineering, Cambridge University, Cambridge, UK
{ssa43,jl221,hh409}@cam.ac.uk
[2] Department of Physics, Cambridge University, Cambridge, UK
a.n.lasenby@mrao.cam.ac.uk

Abstract. Conformal Geometric Algebra (CGA) provides a unified representation of both geometric primitives and conformal transformations, and as such holds great promise in the field of computer graphics [1–3]. In this paper we implement a simple ray tracer in CGA with a Blinn-Phong lighting model and use it to examine ray intersections with surfaces generated from interpolating between objects [7]. An analytical method for finding the normal line to these interpolated surfaces is described. The expression is closely related to the concept of surface principal curvature from differential geometry and provides a novel way of describing the curvature of evolving surfaces.

Keywords: Conformal Geometric Algebra · Ray-tracing ·
Direct object interpolation · Surface curvature

1 Motivation and Related Work

The development of Conformal Geometric Algebra (CGA) has shown how simple expressions can explain complex geometrical operations [1–3]. This suggests the use of CGA in Computer Graphics, and indeed ray-tracers using CGA have been implemented in the past [3–6]. Recent developments have explored direct-interpolation and its use in generating surfaces and splines [7]. In this paper we investigate some of the properties of these surfaces and their incorporation into an experimental ray tracer.

2 Conformal Geometric Algebra, CGA

The ray-tracer used in this paper is constructed using CGA and all algebraic expressions given will be in terms of elements of this algebra. CGA adds two more basis vectors, e and $\bar{e}$, to the original basis vectors of 3D Euclidean space, giving a complete basis for the 5D space with the following signature: $e_1^2 = e_2^2 = e_3^2 = e^2 = 1$ and $\bar{e}^2 = -1$. These extra basis vectors are used to define two null

© Springer Nature Switzerland AG 2019
M. Gavrilova et al. (Eds.): CGI 2019, LNCS 11542, pp. 578–584, 2019.
https://doi.org/10.1007/978-3-030-22514-8_58

vectors: $n = e + \bar{e} \equiv n_\infty$ and $n_0 = \frac{\bar{n}}{2} = \frac{e - \bar{e}}{2}$. The mapping from a 3D vector, x, to its corresponding CGA vector, X, is given by:

$$X = F(x) = \frac{1}{2}\left(x^2 n + 2x - \bar{n}\right)\frac{1}{2} \equiv \frac{1}{2}x^2 n + x - n_0 \qquad (1)$$

All vectors formed from such a mapping are null. More background on CGA can be found in [1–3].

3   Camera Model and Ray Casting

A pinhole camera model is used with the geometry shown in Fig. 1. It is defined by a rotor R_{MV} incorporating rotation and translation that takes the camera from the origin to its pose in space, a focal length f and two bounds x_{max} and y_{max} on the size of the image plane.

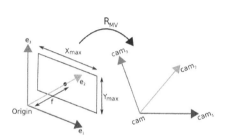

Fig. 1. The camera is defined by a focal length, a transformation from the origin, and bounds on the image plane.

Fig. 2. An image from the ray-tracer containing examples of disks, spheres and planes.

We take $(i, j) = (0, 0)$ to be at the bottom left hand corner of the image. For an image of width w and height h the world coordinates of the point P_{ij} at the centre of pixel (i, j) are given by:

$$P_{ij} = R_{MV}\left[F(fe_2 - \frac{x_{max}}{2}(1 - (2i/w))e_1 - \frac{y_{max}}{2}(1 - (2j/h))e_3)\right]\tilde{R}_{MV} \qquad (2)$$

We then generate the ray from the camera centre, L_{ij}, that passes through P_{ij}, via the expression

$$L_{ij} = cam \wedge P_{ij} \wedge n_\infty$$

4   Ray Tracing Evolved Circles

The intersection and reflection of lines with the other blades of CGA (planes, disks, spheres) has already been investigated in [2,3,5] and we will not repeat those results here. Instead we will turn directly to an interesting class of surface

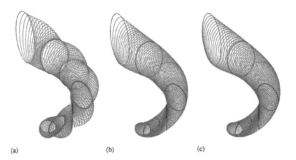

(a)   (b)   (c)

Fig. 3. Interpolation through circular control objects. (a) linear, (b) quadratic, (c) cubic

that arises from the direct interpolation of CGA circles [7], examples of which are shown in Fig. 3. In order to generate such a surface, a direct interpolation is first performed between two boundary circles, C_1 and C_2:

$$X_\alpha = \alpha C_1 + (1 - \alpha)C_2 \tag{3}$$

where we take α moving between 0 and 1, which moves us from C_2 to C_1. The result of this interpolation is not itself a valid circle and needs to be 'projected' onto a blade via multiplication by a *projector*. This projector has *only* scalar and 4-vector parts and its construction is detailed in [7] and outlined in the following. First form

$$K_\alpha = \sqrt{-X_\alpha \tilde{X}_\alpha} \tag{4}$$

where the square root is as defined in [8]. We then form K_α^* by reversing the sign of the 4-vector part, $(K_\alpha^* = \langle K_\alpha \rangle - \langle K_\alpha \rangle_4)$, and use this to produce the following expression for the interpolated circle:

$$C_\alpha = \frac{K_\alpha^*}{K_\alpha^* K_\alpha} X_\alpha \quad \alpha \in [0, 1] \tag{5}$$

Given that these surfaces may find genuine applications in computer graphics and CAD, it is desirable to explore their properties with respect to the ray tracing framework. Specifically, for a given ray and scene object, the geometric constructions of interest for lighting models are the point of intersection between a ray and a surface, and the surface normal at that specific intersection point.

4.1 Intersection Point of Ray and Interpolated Surface

In the intersection of a ray with a circle, the meet produces the 1-vector Σ. If $\Sigma = 0$ there are two intersections and if $\Sigma^2 = 0$ there is one intersection [2]. Therefore, to find the intersection point between our interpolated surface and a ray L, we need to find a value of α for which:

$$(C_\alpha \vee L)^2 = \langle C_\alpha L \rangle_4^2 = 0$$

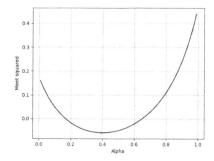

Fig. 4. Left: An image showing an example interpolated surface and a ray passing through it, the circles in blue show the circles which have a meet squared of 0 with the incident ray, the red circle shows where the meet squared is minimised. Right: A plot showing the value of the meet squared as a function of alpha for this case. (color figure online)

Figure 4 provides a simple visual illustration of one example of the shape of this curve as a function of α. While this example shown in the figure is particularly smooth, experiments indicate that in the general case this function is not well approximated by low order polynomials and the roots of this function have to be found by general non-linear root finding techniques such as a bisection search method. These general root finding methods are computationally expensive and an analytical solution would be desirable.

4.2   Analytic Form for Normal

Given the α for which the ray intersects the surface, we have both the interpolated circle, C_α, and the point of intersection X. We now use the result in [2] to extract a tangental line L_C in the plane of the circle at X:

$$L_C = (X \cdot C_\alpha) \wedge n_\infty \tag{6}$$

We would now like an analytic form for the tangent to the surface corresponding to evolving the surface through an increment of α, postulating that this will be orthogonal to L_C and that these two tangent vectors will then be the directions of principal curvature. Clearly $\frac{dC(\alpha)}{d\alpha} \equiv \dot{C}_\alpha$ will be a key quantity in deriving this additional tangent vector. A first observation is that the circle and its derivative will be orthogonal to one another, i.e. $\dot{C} \cdot C = 0$, and that the geometric product is minus itself under reversion, i.e. $\dot{C} C = -C \dot{C}$ (note that here, and in what follows, we will drop the α subscript on C). This follows from the fact that $C^2 = C \cdot C = 1$ (our circles are all normalised), so that:

$$\frac{d}{d\alpha}(C \cdot C) = C \cdot \dot{C} + \dot{C} \cdot C = 0 \quad , \quad \frac{d}{d\alpha}(C C) = C \dot{C} + \dot{C} C = 0 \tag{7}$$

Since $C \cdot \dot{C} = -C \cdot \dot{C}$ and they are both scalars, this tells us $\dot{C} \cdot C = 0$. Since $C \dot{C} = -C \dot{C} = -(C \dot{C})\tilde{}$, this further indicates that the product can only have bivector parts (this is a standard construct in many areas, the most obvious being rigid body dynamics [10]). Let us call this bivector, Ω_C:

$$\Omega_C = C\dot{C} \qquad (8)$$

Using the analogy with rigid body dynamics, we think of this bivector as the *angular velocity bivector* of the circles as they evolve under the parameter α. We note here that a similar construction would be possible for all other main objects that we use in CGA, since they are all normalised to 1 or 0. The null vectors representing points, X, have a constant 'length' due to normalisation, so their 'velocity' can simply be found via the inner product with the angular velocity bivector given in Eq. 8.

$$\dot{X} = X \cdot \Omega_C = X \cdot (C\dot{C}) \qquad (9)$$

It can be shown that this in fact provides the tangential direction required, so the line can be formed by:

$$L_T = \dot{X} \wedge X \wedge n \qquad (10)$$

The fact that lines L_C and L_T are perpendicular can be verified by showing that the quantity $L_T L_C$ has only a bivector part (see [2] for a discussion of when intersecting lines are orthogonal). Given these two tangent lines L_C and L_T, we can construct the plane tangent to the surface at X by computing the join of the two lines. Or, we can bypass the plane entirely and compute the surface normal line directly as:

$$N = \langle L_T L_C I_5 \rangle_3 \qquad (11)$$

5   Blinn-Phong Lighting Model

The ray-tracer employs the Blinn-Phong lighting model, this simple model is well studied in the graphics literature, for more in depth information see [9]. Under this model the intensity value for each pixel is given by the following expression:

$$I_\lambda = c_\lambda k_a + k_r I_{r\lambda} + \sum_i S_i f_{att} I_{pi\lambda} \left(c_\lambda k_d \left(L_i \cdot N \right) + k_s \left(N \cdot H \right)^q \right) \quad \forall \lambda \in \{R, G, B\} \qquad (12)$$

Note that traditionally the terms N, L_i and H are standard 3-vectors. Since the language of our ray-tracer is CGA, these terms in Eq. 12 actually represent the normalised lines which have the same directions as the 3-vectors which pass through the ray-object intersection point. As all these lines are normalised such that $L^2 = 1$ the inner products between them will simply give the cosine of the angles between them as in the traditional 3d vector case [10].

The *normal line* is required across multiple terms and is crucial to the lighting model. This is given in CGA as $N = L' - L$ where L' is the reflected ray and L is the incident ray. Note that L' is necessarily calculated for tracing reflected rays.

The line L_i specifying the direction to the ith light source is given by forming the wedge product between the point of intersection of the incident ray and the object, the point position of the ith light source and n_∞. The half way line H can be found by $H = L_i - V$, where V is the line from the intersection point to the viewer.

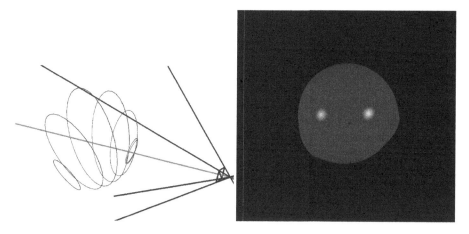

Fig. 5. Left: A scene composed of only an evolved surface in blue and a camera. Right: The rendering of the scene from the camera (color figure online)

6   Examples of Ray Tracing Simple Objects and Evolved Surfaces

Putting together the material from previous sections we can now raytrace both simple objects and evolved surfaces. Figure 2 shows an example of simple objects,

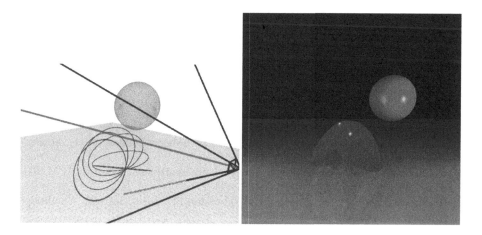

Fig. 6. Left: A scene composed of a ground plane in cyan, an evolved surface in blue and a sphere in red. Right: The rendering of the scene from the camera. (color figure online)

spheres, planes and disks being rendered. Figure 5 shows an example of an evolved surface being rendered on its own. The class of surfaces that are able to be generated with the interpolation of circles is large and Fig. 6 shows a more unusual surface being rendered in a scene with a sphere and a plane.

7   Summary and Conclusions

In this paper we have outlined the basic workings of a CGA ray tracer that can render geometric primitives as well as more advanced interpolated surfaces defined by two circles and an *evolution* parameter, α. We have shown how the ray-surface intersections and surface normals can be determined for these and additionally, the analytic form of the normals for such surfaces promises to provide us with interesting future tools to relate CGA quantities with principal, gaussian and mean curvatures, as well as other important differential geometry concepts.

References

1. Hestenes, D.: Old wine in new bottles: a new algebraic framework for computational geometry. In: Corrochano, E.B., Sobczyk, G. (eds.) Geometric Algebra with Applications in Science and Engineering. Birkhäuser, Boston (2001). https://doi.org/10.1007/978-1-4612-0159-5_1
2. Lasenby, A., Lasenby, J., Wareham, R.: A Covariant Approach to Geometry Using Geometric Algebra., Cambridge University Engineering Department (2004)
3. Dorst, L., Fontijne, D., Mann, S.: Geometric Algebra for Computer Science: An Object-Oriented Approach to Geometry, 1st edn. Elsevier; Morgan Kaufmann, Amsterdam (2007)
4. Breuils, S., Nozick, V., Fuchs, L.: Garamon: geometric algebra library generator. In: AACA: Topical Collection AGACSE 2018, IMECC UNICAM, Campinas, Brazil (2018)
5. Hildenbrand, D.: Geometric computing in computer graphics using conformal geometric algebra. Comput. Graph. **29**(5), 802–810 (2005)
6. Wareham, R.J., Lasenby, J.: Generating fractals using geometric algebra. Adv. Appl. Clifford Algebras **21**(3), 647–659 (2011)
7. Hadfield, H., Lasenby, J.: Direct linear interpolation of conformal geometric objects. In: AACA: Topical Collection AGACSE 2018, IMECC UNICAM, Campinas, Brazil (2018)
8. Dorst, L., Valkenburg, R.: Square root and logarithm of rotors in 3D conformal geometric algebra using polar decomposition. In: Dorst, L., Lasenby, J. (eds.) Guide to Geometric Algebra in Practice, pp. 81–104. Springer, London (2011). https://doi.org/10.1007/978-0-85729-811-9_5
9. Blinn, J.: Models of light reflection for computer synthesized pictures. ACM SIGGRAPH Comput. Graph. **11**(2), 192–198 (1977)
10. Doran, C., Lasenby, A.: Geometric Algebra for Physicists, 1st edn. Cambridge University Press, Cambridge (2003)

Author Index

Printed in the United States
By Bookmasters